Conceptual S[illegible] & Relational Database Design

Conceptual Schema & Relational Database Design

Second Edition

TERRY HALPIN

PRENTICE HALL AUSTRALIA

Acquisitions Editor: Kaylie Smith
Cover design: David Weston

Printed in Australia by Ligare Pty Ltd

1 2 3 4 5 99 98 97 96 95

ISBN 0 13 355702 2

Prentice Hall of Australia Pty Ltd, *Sydney*
Prentice Hall, Inc., Englewood Cliffs, *New Jersey*
Prentice Hall International, Inc., *London*
Prentice Hall Canada, Inc., *Toronto*
Prentice Hall Hispanoamericana, *SA, Mexico*
Prentice Hall of India Private Ltd, *New Delhi*
Prentice Hall of Japan, Inc., *Tokyo*
Prentice Hall Southeast Asia Pty Ltd, *Singapore*
Editora Prentice Hall do Brasil Ltda, *Rio de Janeiro*

PRENTICE HALL

A division of Simon & Schuster

Contents

Foreword

It is a great pleasure to write a Foreword for the second edition of this book. The NIAM method was initiated in the early 1970s by Prof. G. M. Nijssen and his group, at a time when most researchers in the database and information system field still were discussing data modeling on the level of record structures. One of Prof. Nijssen's greatest contributions has been that at a very early stage in the development of the design method, he found that it is not sufficient to provide the designer with a system of metaconcepts and a suitable graphical notation for specifying models. He realized that it is equally important or even more important, to provide the designer with a design procedure, a "cookbook", which tells the designer how to develop a model, step by step, using the metaconcepts and the notation. This way of thinking has proved to be successful in practise, and still is a distinguishing feature of Object-Role Modeling (ORM) methods such as NIAM.

The ORM approach has been growing gradually over the years via extensive feedback from information system development projects, workshops, conferences and the literature on conceptual modeling. In several places around the world, ORM is taught as an effective method to introduce young students to information modeling as a discipline separate from programming. Since the first edition of this book in 1989, which Prof. Nijssen co-authored with Dr. T. A. Halpin, the method has been formalized, refined and improved by Dr Halpin. The results of these improvements are now presented in this book.

We are convinced that semantic data modeling has become an important part of database and information system development. The ORM method, with its simple system of metaconcepts, powerful graphical type-oriented and instance-oriented notation and detailed design algorithms and heuristics, has been a major contribution to the state of the art of semantic data modeling. We trust therefore that this book will be used by many practitioners of requirements analysis, information analysis and database design, as well as by many students in these disciplines.

Prof. R. A. Meersman
University of Brabant
The Netherlands
Member ISO/TC97/SC21 (OSI)
(Open Systems Interconnect)
Chairperson IFIP TC12
(Artificial Intelligence)

Prof. E. D. Falkenberg
University of Nijmegen
The Netherlands
Member IFIP WG 2.6 (Databases)
Member IFIP WG 8.1 (Information Systems)
Chairperson IFIP WG 8.1 TG FRISCO
(Framework of Information Systems Concepts)

Preface to second edition

This book is about information systems, focusing on high level data modeling and relational database systems. It is written primarily for students of computer science or informatics, as well as professional database designers. It should also be useful to anyone wishing to formulate the information structure of applications in a way readily understood by humans yet easily implemented on computers. In addition, it provides a simple, conceptual framework for understanding what relational databases really are.

The major part of this book deals with Object-Role Modeling (ORM), a conceptual modeling approach which views the world in terms of objects and the roles they play. The most well known version of ORM is NIAM (Natural language Information Analysis Method), and the version described in this book is based on extensions to NIAM. Another popular conceptual modeling approach is Entity-Relationship (ER) modeling.

It is our belief that the ORM method has several advantages over the ER approach. For example, ORM diagrams are typically more expressive, and they can be populated with instances allowing validation with the client using natural language. However ER diagrams are good for compact summaries, and this book shows how they can be easily and safely abstracted from ORM diagrams. Hence ER practitioners should also find this book of interest.

In line with the ORM method, this book adopts a "cookbook" approach, uses intuitive diagrams, and provides numerous examples. Each chapter ends with a summary of the major points covered, and a glossary of technical symbols and terms is included at the end of the book. In order to make the text more approachable to the general reader with an interest in databases, the language has been kept simple, and a formalized, mathematical treatment has been deliberately avoided. Where necessary, relevant concepts from elementary logic and set theory are discussed prior to their application.

One of the major features of the book is its large number of carefully graded exercises, which have been thoroughly class-tested. Answers to approximately half of these exercises (typically the odd-numbered questions) appear at the back of the book. Further answers, as well as related pedagogic material, are included in an accompanying Instructor's Guide. This guide is available to the classroom instructor.

Most of the topics have been taught within information systems subjects taken by first year undergraduate students at The University of Queensland. The content has been modularized into a large number of sections, so that instructors wishing to omit some material may make an appropriate selection for their courses.

The first chapter motivates the study of conceptual modeling, and provides a comparison between the ORM and ER approaches. It also includes an historical and structural overview of information systems. Further historical material is presented in Appendix A.

Chapter 2 provides a structural background, introducing a number of key concepts which are dealt with more thoroughly in later chapters. It should be read in full by the reader with little or no database experience.

Chapter 3 is fundamental. Following an overview of the information systems life cycle and the conceptual design procedure (CSDP), it covers the first three steps of the CSDP. The first step (verbalizing familiar examples in terms of elementary facts) may seem trivial, but it should not be rushed, as it provides the foundation for the design. The rest of this chapter covers the basic graphical notation for conceptual schema diagrams, then offers guidance on how to classify objects into types and identify information that can be arithmetically derived.

Chapter 4 begins the task of specifying constraints on the populations of fact types. The most important kind of constraint (the uniqueness constraint) is considered in detail. Then some checks on the elementarity of the fact types are discussed. This chapter also introduces the projection and join operations: these operations are also important in the later work on relational databases.

Chapter 5 covers mandatory role constraints, as well as a check for detecting information that can be logically derived. Reference schemes are then examined in some depth; some of the more complex schemes considered here could be skipped in a short course. The CSDP steps covered so far are then reviewed by applying them in a case study.

Chapter 6 covers value, set comparison (subset, equality and exclusion) and subtyping constraints. Section 6.6 deals with advanced aspects of subtyping: though important in practice, the material in this section could be skimmed over in a first reading. The related topic of subtype matrices is dealt with in Appendix B.

Chapter 7 deals with the final step of the conceptual schema design procedure. Less common constraints are considered (e.g. occurrence frequencies and ring constraints), and final checks are made on the design. Sections 7.3–7.5 are somewhat advanced, and could be skipped in a short course.

Chapter 8 describes how a conceptual model may be implemented in a relational database system. The first three sections are fundamental to understanding how a conceptual schema may be mapped to a relational schema, and should be thoroughly covered. Section 8.4 considers advanced mapping aspects, and could be omitted in an introductory course. Section 8.5 covers relational algebra, and is basic to any course which includes a treatment of relational query languages (e.g. SQL or QBE). To cater for courses with some practical work on SQL, an appendix on this topic is included (Appendix C): this is best studied after the underlying relational algebra has been covered. Section 8.6 provides an overview of how the relational model of data compares with the data models adopted by some relational database management systems.

Chapter 9 discusses the notion of conceptual schema equivalence, and describes various ways in which conceptual schemas may be transformed or reshaped. As one application of this theory, a procedure is specified for optimizing a database design by performing conceptual transformations before mapping. Lower level optimization is also briefly treated. The role of conceptual optimization in database re-engineering is then illustrated. Sections 9.4–9.7 are of an advanced nature and may be skipped in a short course. In a very short course, sections 9.1–9.3 could be also be trimmed.

Chapter 10 examines some other design issues, methods and trends. Section 10.2 provides an overview of normalization by decomposition; though not needed in the design procedure, the notions covered here are fundamental to the mathematical theory of relational databases. Section 10.3 deals with abstraction mechanisms including ER diagrams, and should be read. Section 10.4 outlines some ways of specifying processes and events, to complement the data model, and provides some guidelines for designing the human-computer interface for the external schemas; it is worth reading this section if only to realize that specifying the data model is not the only task in developing an information system. Section 10.5 considers some future trends, with the emphasis on object-oriented databases. Section 10.6 gives an introduction to metamodeling; though fascinating, this could be skipped in a short course.

A final appendix provides a brief overview of the use of CASE tools in developing a database application. Following the selected answers, a bibliography lists the references cited, and a technical glossary and index are provided.

For readers familiar with the previous edition of this book, the major differences from that edition are now summarized. The book has been essentially rewritten from scratch, so the changes are significant. The conceptual schema design procedure has been revised: the basic CSDP now has seven steps instead of nine, and includes a logical derivation check (in the new step 5). Some new graphic constraints have been added (e.g. join constraints) and the FORML language is used to specify textual constraints and rules. Subtyping has been extended to allow context-dependent reference. Some notational changes have been made for conceptual schemas (e.g. frames for nesting) and relational schemas (e.g. square brackets around optional attributes). The relational mapping procedure has been vastly extended, as has the treatment of conceptual schema transformation and optimization.

In the first edition, the final four chapters were written by Prof. Nijssen. Since his return to The Netherlands, Prof. Nijssen has had many work commitments and decided not to co-author this edition. The old chapters 12–15 have now been replaced by the new chapter 10.

Some material in the first edition has been dropped, or de-emphasized by moving it to appendices. Much new material has been added (e.g. relational algebra, SQL, schema abstraction). Many of the original exercises have been improved, and many new exercises have been added. To cater for all these changes and additions, this edition (over 500 pages) is longer than the previous edition (342 pages).

Acknowledgments

The version of Object-Role Modeling discussed in this book is based on revisions and extensions I have made to the NIAM method, which was largely developed in its original form by Prof. Eckhard Falkenberg and Prof. Shir Nijssen, with other contributions from several researchers including Prof. Robert Meersman, Prof. Dirk Vermeir, Mr Frans van Assche and Dr Olga de Troyer. Many other researchers in the seventies made significant contributions to the semantic data modeling movement (e.g. Mr William Kent and Dr Michael Senko) which gave birth to the fact-based, object-role modeling approach.

It is a pleasure to acknowledge my debt to these people for their pioneering work, and for the fruitful discussions I have had with many of them. In particular I would like to express my gratitude to Shir Nijssen not only for his work on the first edition of this book, but also for demonstrating the communicative power of examples and intuitive diagrams.

In writing this edition I have been highly motivated by the continuous support and encouragement received from Jim Harding, Bruce Linn and their team at Asymetrix Corporation, who have now released an exciting CASE tool called InfoModeler to support the ORM method discussed in this book.

A number of passages in the book have been improved by the valuable feedback I have had from my academic colleagues. In particular, Dr Erik Proper reviewed the whole book, and the normalization section was reviewed by Prof. Maria Orlowska, Prof. Bernhard Thalheim and Dr Millist Vincent. In addition I am grateful to the anonymous reviewers arranged by Prentice Hall. Any remaining mistakes are of course my own.

Some of the ideas expressed in this book were developed jointly between myself and two of my PhD students: Linda Campbell worked with me on schema abstraction, and Peter Ritson worked with me on disjunctive reference, relative closure and extensions to the relational mapping procedure. It has been a pleasure working with these students, as well as with the many hundreds of students on which earlier versions of the material in this book were trialed. I also gratefully acknowledge permission by the Computer Science Department at The University of Queensland to include a selection of past assessment questions of mine within the exercises.

Kaylie Smith at Prentice Hall has my appreciation for the competent and friendly way in which she managed the editorial tasks for this book. Finally I would like to thank my wife Norma not only for the excellent job she did in producing most of the figures for this book, but also for being so understanding and supportive while I was busily occupied in the writing task.

Terry Halpin
University of Queensland
1994 July

1 Introduction

1.1 Why study database design?

This book provides a modern introduction to database systems, with the emphasis on information modeling. A *database* is basically a collection of related facts (e.g. a company's personnel records, or a bus timetable). Discovering the essential kinds of facts that underlie an application, and the conditions that apply to them, is both interesting and illuminating. The quality of the database *design* used for these facts and conditions is important. Just as a house built from a good architectural plan is more likely to be safe and convenient for living, a well-designed database simplifies the task of ensuring that its facts are correct and easy to get at. This section motivates the study of data-base design methods by indicating the nature and importance of database systems, and then showing how things can go wrong if the database design is poor.

Each database is used to model some application, typically a part of the real world. Consider a library database. As changes occur in the library (e.g. a book is borrowed, or a new book is purchased) the database is updated to reflect these changes. This task could be performed manually (e.g. using a card-catalog) or be automated (e.g. an on-line catalog), or both. We focus our attention on automated databases. Sometimes these are implemented by means of special-purpose computer programs, coded in a general-purpose programming language (e.g. C). More often, database applications are developed using a *database management system (DBMS)*: this is a software system for maintaining databases and answering queries about them (e.g. Access, DB2, dBase, Ingres, Oracle, Paradox, Sybase). The same DBMS may handle many different data-bases. Although the design methods we discuss are relevant to special-purpose database programs, our implementation focus is on DBMSs.

If an application requires maintenance and retrieval of large amounts of data, a DBMS offers many advantages over manual record-keeping systems. Operations on data may often be performed faster. Data may be stored compactly on disk, and redundancy may be reduced by data sharing. Many data errors can be avoided by automatic integrity checking. With multi-user systems, access rights to data can be enforced by the system. People can spend more time on creative design rather than on routine tasks more suited to computers. A variety of display formats is typically supported (e.g. form-based data entry and graphical output). Finally, the development of the application software and its documentation can be facilitated by use of *computer assisted software engineering (CASE)* tool support.

In developed countries, a study of database systems is desirable for most careers. In terms of the dominant employment group, the Agricultural Age was supplanted late in the nineteenth century by the Industrial Age, which has now been replaced by the Information Age. The ongoing information explosion and mechanization of industrial processes indicate that the proportion of information workers will steadily rise in the foreseeable future. If an information-oriented business does not computerize, its production costs in terms of both money and time may far exceed those of competing companies that do use information technology. Imagine how long a newspaper firm would last if it returned to the methods used before word-processing and computerized typesetting. Apart from direct employment opportunities, the ability to interact efficiently with information systems empowers one to exploit the knowledge residing in accessible commercial, public and personal databases.

Although most employees will need to be familiar with information technology, there are vast differences in the amount and complexity of information management tasks required of these workers. Until recently, most technical computer work was performed by computer specialists such as programmers and systems analysts. However, the advent of user-friendly software and powerful, cheap personal computers (PCs) has led to a redistribution of computing power. End-users now commonly perform many information management tasks, such as spreadsheeting, with minimal reliance on professional computer experts.

This trend toward more users "driving" their own computer systems rather than relying on expert "chauffeurs" does not eliminate the need for computer specialists. There is still a lot of programming going on in languages like C and COBOL. However, there is an increasing demand for higher level skills such as designing complex information systems that can interact productively with end-users. The general area of *information systems engineering* includes many sub-disciplines such as requirements analysis, database design, prototyping, forms development and report writing. Underpinning all of these sub-areas is the notion of information, since all deal with it in one way or another. Since the database design phase selects the structures for representing the relevant information, it is of central importance.

To illustrate this last point, consider Table 1.1, which shows some movie details (some data are fictitious). The *header* of this table is shaded, to help distinguish it from the *rows of data*. Even if the header is not shaded, we do not count it as a table row. We interpret the data in terms of facts. For example, the movie "Awakenings" was released in 1991, was directed by Penny Marshall, and starred Robert De Niro and Robin Williams. The movie "Cosmology" had no stars (it might be a documentary). The table is an example of an *output report*. It provides one convenient way of viewing the information. How the information is actually stored in a database depends on the kind of database used.

Table 1.1 An output report about some motion pictures

Movie	*Year*	*Director*	*Stars*
Awakenings	1991	Penny Marshall	Robert De Niro Robin Williams
Backdraft	1991	Ron Howard	William Baldwin Robert De Niro Kurt Russell
Cosmology	1994	Terry Harding	
Dances with wolves	1990	Kevin Kostner	Kevin Kostner Mary McDonnell

In Table 1.1 each "cell" (row-column slot) may contain many values. For example, Awakenings has two stars recorded in the row 1, column 4 cell. Some database systems allow a cell to contain many values like this, but in a *relational* database each table cell may hold at most one value. Hence the data cannot be stored like this in a relational database. Since relational database systems are now dominant in the industry, this book focuses its implementation discussion on relational systems. How should we design a relational database to store these facts?

Suppose we use the structure shown in Table 1.2. This has only one entry in each cell. The "?" denotes a "null value" (no actual star is recorded for Cosmology). From now on, this book usually saves space in table layout by omitting lines between rows. Each relational table must be named–here we called the table "Movie". Can you see some problems with this design?

Notice that the table contains redundant information. For example, the facts that Backdraft was released in 1991 and directed by Ron Howard are shown three times (once for each star of that movie). We might try to fix this by deleting the extra copies in the ReleaseYr and Director columns; but this artificially makes some rows special and also introduces problems with null values.

Table 1.2 A badly-designed relational database table

Movie:

moviename	*releaseyr*	*director*	*star*
Awakenings	1991	Penny Marshall	Robert De Niro
Awakenings	1991	Penny Marshall	Robin Williams
Backdraft	1991	Ron Howard	William Baldwin
Backdraft	1991	Ron Howard	Robert De Niro
Backdraft	1991	Ron Howard	Kurt Russell
Cosmology	1994	Terry Harding	?
Dances with wolves	1990	Kevin Kostner	Kevin Kostner
Dances with wolves	1990	Kevin Kostner	Mary McDonnell

Cosmology	1994	Terry Harding	?
Dances with wolves	1990	Kevin Kostner	Kevin Kostner
Dances with wolves	1990	Kevin Kostner	Mary McDonnell

Movie (moviename, releaseyr, director)

Starred (moviename, star)

Movie:

moviename	*releaseyr*	*director*
Awakenings	1991	Penny Marshall
Backdraft	1991	Ron Howard
Cosmology	1994	Terry Harding
Dances with wolves	1990	Kevin Kostner

Starred:

moviename	*star*
Awakenings	Robert De Niro
Awakenings	Robin Williams
Backdraft	William Baldwin
Backdraft	Robert De Niro
Backdraft	Kurt Russell
Dances with wolves	Kevin Kostner
Dances with wolves	Mary McDonnell

Figure 1.1 A relational database representation of Table 1.1

Besides wasting space, the Table 1.2 design can lead to errors. For example, there is nothing to stop us adding a row for Backdraft with a different release year (1994, say) and a different director (Peter Weir, say). Our database would then be inconsistent with the real world, where a movie can have only one release year and director.

To correct the design, we use two relational tables named "Movie" and "Starred" (Figure 1.1). The design of these tables is shown in schematic form above the populated tables. The constraints that each movie has only one release year and director are enforced by checking that each movie occurs only once in the Movie table (shown by underlining the moviename column). The constraints that each movie must have a release year and director are enforced by checking that all movies occur in the Movie table and that null values are excluded from the ReleaseYr and Director columns. In the schema this is captured by the dotted arrow (indicating that if a movie is listed in the Starred table it must be listed in the Movie table) and by not marking any columns as optional. These concepts and notations are fully explained later in the book.

Even with this simple example, care is needed for database design. With complex cases, the design problem is much more challenging. The rest of this book is largely concerned with helping you to meet such challenges, using a design method known as object-role modeling. Designing databases is both a science and an art. When supported by a good method, this design process is a stimulating and intellectually satisfying activity, with tangible benefits gained from the quality of the database applications produced. The next section explains why object-role modeling has been chosen as our main design method, and the following section

1.2 Why study object-role modeling?

When we design a database for a particular application, we create a model of it. Technically, the application area that we are modeling is called the **universe of discourse** (**UoD**), since it is the world (or universe) that we are interested in talking (or discoursing) about. Typically the UoD is a "part" of the "real world". To build a good model requires a good understanding of the world we are modeling, and hence is a task ideally suited to people rather than machines. The main challenge is to describe the UoD clearly and precisely. Great care is required here, since errors introduced at this stage filter through to later stages in software development, and the later the errors are detected the more expensive they are to remove.

If we are familiar with thc application, we may proceed with the design ourself. If not, we should consult with other people who, at least collectively, are familiar with the application. Since people naturally communicate (to themselves or others) with words, pictures and examples, the best way to arrive at a clear description of the UoD is to make extensive use of *natural language*, *intuitive diagrams* and *examples*. And as a safety measure, it makes sense to simplify the modeling task by examining the information in the smallest units possible: one *fact* at a time.

These principles entail that the model should first be expressed at the *conceptual* level, in concepts which people find easy to work with. Figure 1.1 gave an example of a model expressed in terms of relational database structures. This is too far away from natural language for us to call it conceptual. Instead, we refer to the relational database approach as conforming to a *logical* data model. Other logical data models exist (e.g. network, hierarchic, nested relational, and various object-oriented proposals), and each DBMS is aligned with one of these logical models. However in specifying a draft conceptual design, the designer should be free of implementation concerns. It is a hard enough job already to develop an accurate model of the UoD, without having to worry at the same time about what kind of DBMS will ultimately be used to implement the model.

Implementation concerns are of course important, but should be ignored in the early stages of modeling. Once an initial conceptual design has been constructed, it can be mapped down to a logical design in any data model we like. This added flexibility also makes it easier to implement and maintain the same application on more than one kind of DBMS.

Although most applications involve processes and events as well as data, we focus on the data, because this perspective is more stable, and all processes and events are contingent on the underlying data. Our decision to do the original data design at the conceptual level excludes some widely practised techniques, such as normalization, for this purpose. For most practical applications, we feel there are two conceptual data modeling methods which stand out: entity-relationship modeling and object-role modeling.

Entity-Relationship (ER) modeling was introduced by Peter Chen in 1976, and is the most widely used approach. It pictures the world in terms of entities that have attributes and participate in relationships. A simple example of an ER diagram is shown in Figure 1.2. This might be used as an information model about movies and their export sales. Symbols used in the diagram are explained in the next paragraph.

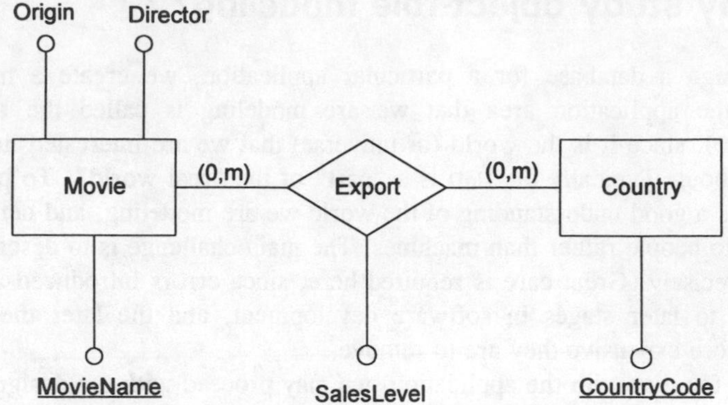

Figure 1.2 An ER diagram about movies and their export sales

Since Chen's original ER notation was too inexpressive to capture detailed features of an information model, many extensions were added independently by various people. So today, dozens of different notations are used in various versions of ER modeling for the same concept. In the absence of a standard ER notation, we use one of the enhanced notations for our current example.

In Figure 1.2 the entity types Movie and Country are shown as named rectangles. The relationship type of exporting a movie to a country is shown as a named diamond. MovieName, Origin and Director are depicted as *attributes* of Movie. The underlining of MovieName indicates that it is used to identify Movie. Similarly, CountryCode is shown as an identifying attribute of Country.

SalesLevel is shown as an attribute of the Export relationship. In some versions of ER, a relationship cannot have an attribute, and SalesLevel might then be depicted as an entity type. In this case, if 3-part relationships are not allowed, an artificial entity type might be used instead. The "(0,m)" next to Movie means that a movie may be exported to zero or many countries; "(0,m)" next to Country means that a country may export zero or many movies.

Object-Role Modeling (ORM) began in the early 1970s as a semantic modeling approach which views the world as objects playing roles. It has appeared in a variety of forms such as Natural-language Information Analysis Method (NIAM) and Binary-Relationship Modeling (BRM). The specific ORM version discussed in this text is called "*Formal* Object-Role Modeling" (FORM). Many of its features are derived from NIAM.

Object-role modeling has so many advantages over ER that the book is based on this method. However ER diagrams provide one useful way of summarizing an application model, so later in the book a simple procedure for generating an ER diagram from an ORM diagram is discussed. Hence as a by-product of learning ORM, one also learns a sound technique for producing an ER model if it is required.

To help you appreciate some of the main ideas behind ORM, and how it differs from ER, we outline how the movie example of Figure 1.2 might be developed in ORM. It is not important that you understand details of the different approaches at this stage, because the concepts are fully explained in later chapters.

Table 1.3 Details about some movies (sales figures are hypothetical)

Movie	*Origin*	*Director*	*Export performance*	
			Country	*Sales level*
Backdraft	USA	Ron Howard	Aus NZ UK	high low medium
Crocodile Dundee	Aus	Peter Faiman	NZ USA	low high
Terminator 2	USA	James Cameron	?	?

Any method consists of both a procedure and a notation. Unlike ER modeling, ORM includes a step-by-step design procedure which is based on *verbalization in natural language*. Specific examples of information related to the application are used as input to this procedure. Such examples may already exist as manual records. Sometimes the application is brand new, or at least an improved solution or adaptation is required. In such cases the modeler constructs examples by discussing the application with the client.

Suppose Table 1.3 provides an example of the information required for our application. The sales figures here are invented for the example, and are not claimed to be accurate. The "?" marks in the row for Terminator 2 denote "missing values" or "null values". Export performance details are not yet available for that movie.

With object-role modeling, we express the information examples in terms of simple *facts*. These are stated in simple sentences, noting what kinds of objects are present, how they are identified, and what roles they play. For example, someone familiar with the application might express the information on the first row thus:

The *Movie* \`Backdraft' **originated in** the *Country* \`USA'.
The *Person* \`Ron Howard' **directed** the *Movie* \`Backdraft'.
The export of the *Movie* \`Backdraft' **to** the *Country* \`Aus' **achieved** the *Sales-Level* \`high'.

The kinds of object are shown in italics, and the kinds of relationship in bold. This verbalization step is critical. By considering the information in simple units like this, expressed in natural language, we minimize the chance of mis-interpretation. The facts could have been worded otherwise (e.g. "The Movie \`Backdraft' was directed by the Person \`Ron Howard'"). Strictly, the reference schemes should be made explicit (e.g. "The Movie named \`Backdraft'", "the Country with code \`USA'").

We now abstract from these examples to see that there are basically three *types* (or kinds) of fact or sentence here. These "fact types" are then diagrammed as shown in Figure 1.3. Here object types (e.g. Movie) are shown as named ellipses with the manner in which they are referenced (e.g. name or code) in brackets, and relationships are depicted as named box-sequences, with one box for each role in the relationship. The relationship name starts inside or beside the first role of the relationship. The three fact types are: ***Movie* originated in *Country*; *Person* directed *Movie*; the export of *Movie* to *Country* achieved *Sales_level*.**

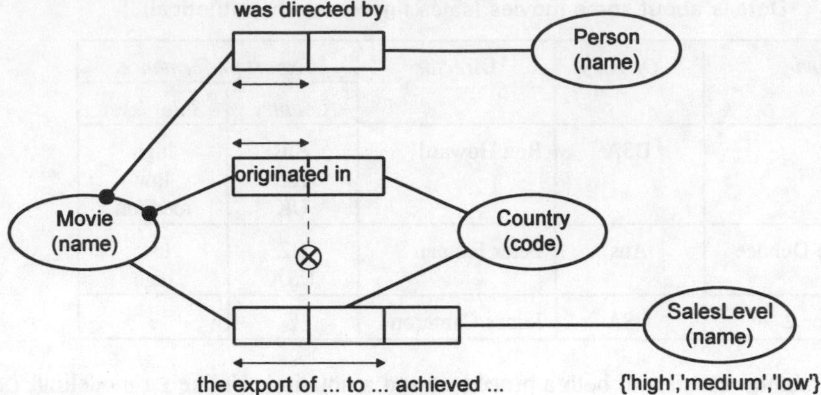

Figure 1.3 An ORM diagram for Table 1.3

Once the fact types are determined, *constraints* are added. In Figure 1.3, the short arrow-tipped bars indicate that each movie had at most one director and originated in at most one country. The dots on Movie indicate that each movie had a director and came from a country. The arrow-tipped bar across two roles on the bottom fact type indicates that for each export of a movie to a country there is just one sales level. The possible sales levels are shown in braces. Finally the "⊗" denotes an exclusion constraint between the role-pairs it connects (i.e. a movie cannot be exported to the country in which it originated).

Compare Figures 1.2 and 1.3. Though useful for overviews, ER diagrams suffer a number of defects in comparison with object-role diagrams. To begin with, they are *further removed from natural language*, and hence more open to mis-interpretation. For example, the relationship type in Figure 1.2 might be misconstrued as Country exporting Movie. While some versions of ER do clarify the direction in which relationships are to be read, the use of attributes can lead to unnatural verbalization (e.g. "Person has DeathDate" instead of "Person died on Date").

By including the *unnecessary attribute construct* in the early stages of design, ER complicates the modeling in a number of ways. The designer often has to agonize over whether to represent some feature as an attribute, an entity type or a relationship type; and such decisions may need to be revised later in the design process. For example, experienced ER modelers would probably replace the Origin attribute by a relationship type (as in our object-role approach). Director might be left as an attribute, but if later we decide to record some other information about directors (e.g. their nationality) the Director attribute must be replaced by a relationship type (as in ORM).

As another example, should the fact type *Employee* heads *Department* be depicted as a relationship type, or by Head as an attribute of Department, or by DeptHeaded as an attribute of Employee? While attributes can be useful later in compact summaries, they should be avoided in the original building of the model.

ER diagrams *cannot be conveniently populated* with instances of the facts. This is a major drawback, since communication at the fact-instance level is the safest way to check that fact types make sense, and that their constraints are correct.

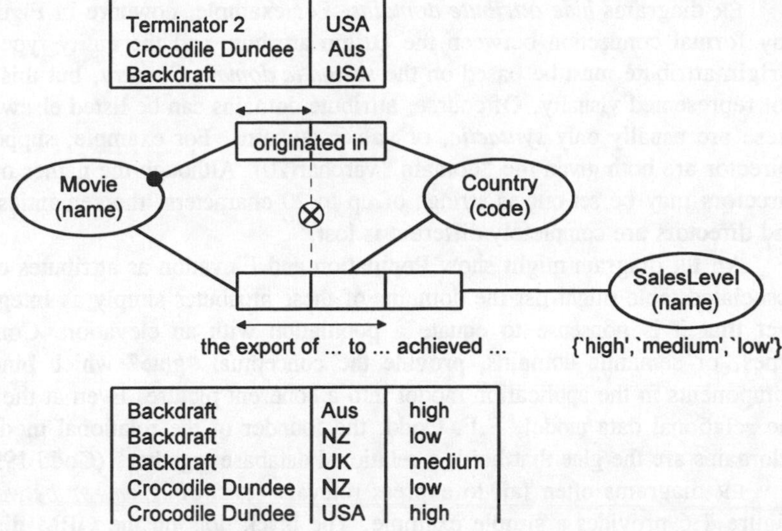

Figure 1.4 Two fact types of an ORM diagram populated with data from Table 1.3

For example, Figure 1.4 populates two fact types with data from Table 1.3, by associating a fact table with each fact type. This also helps one to understand what the constraints mean. For example, the arrow-tipped bar over the top-left role indicates no duplicates in its fact column, and the "⊗" indicates no ⟨Movie, Country⟩ pair can occur in both the fact tables.

In comparison with ORM diagrams, ER diagrams are typically *less expressive with respect to constraints*. This situation has been alleviated somewhat in recent years, as more constraint notations have been added by various proponents of enhanced ER. However, the notations used vary from dialect to dialect. Moreover, because a uniform object-role approach has been avoided, there is no convenient way of displaying constraints like the ⊗ pair-exclusion constraint shown in our ORM example. As another example, consider the constraint that an employee may head a department only if he/she works in that department. On an object-role diagram this is expressed as a pair-subset constraint, shown as a dotted arrow from the fact type *Employee* heads *Department* to the fact type *Employee* works in *Department* (see Figure 1.5). However such a constraint typically cannot be shown on an ER diagram.

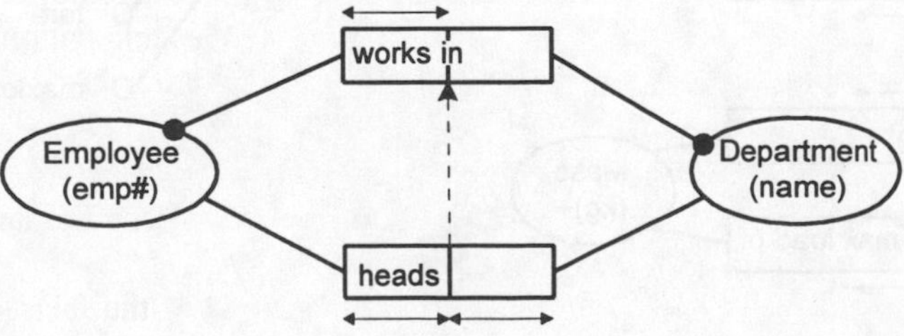

Figure 1.5 An employee can head a department only if s/he works in it

ER diagrams *hide attribute domains*. For example, nowhere in Figure 1.2 is there any formal connection between the Origin attribute and the entity type Country. The Origin attribute must be based on the *semantic domain* Country, but this information is not represented visually. Of course, attribute domains can be listed elsewhere, but in ER these are usually only *syntactic*, or value, domains. For example, suppose Origin and Director are both given the "domain" varchar(20). Although the names of countries and directors may be set out as strings of up to 20 characters, the semantics that countries and directors are completely different is lost.

An ER diagram might show Population and Elevation as attributes of City, and an associated table might list the domains of these attributes simply as Integer, despite the fact that it is nonsense to equate a population with an elevation. Conceptual object types, or semantic domains, provide the conceptual "glue" which binds the various components in the application model into a coherent picture. Even at the lower level of the relational data model, E.F. Codd, the founder of the relational model, argues that "domains are the glue that holds a relational database together" (Codd 1990, p. 45).

ER diagrams often fail to express relevant *constraints on, or between, attributes*. Figure 1.6 provides a simple example. The black dots on the ORM diagram indicate information that *must* be recorded for trucks. In this case, the length and weight must be recorded, and either a purchase date or a lease date must be recorded. It is optional to record the maximum load. The ⊗ mark indicates the same truck cannot be both purchased and leased. None of these constraints are captured on the ER diagram. Only the ORM diagram reveals the semantic domains. For instance, weight may be meaningfully compared with maximum load (both are masses) but not with length. At various stages in the modeling process it is important for the designer to see all the relevant information in the one place.

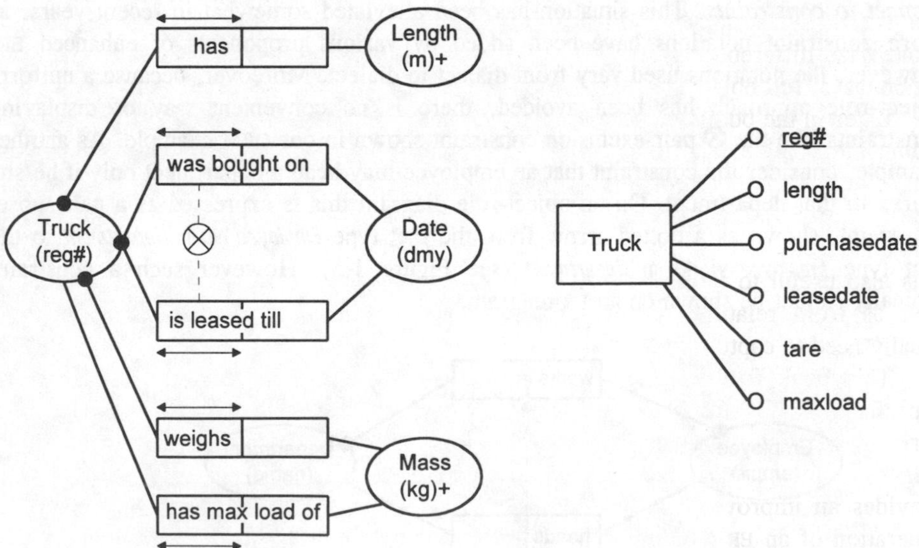

Figure 1.6 The ORM diagram (left) reveals semantic domains and extra constraints

Another feature of ORM diagrams is the flexible way in which *subtyping*, including multiple inheritance, is supported. For example, ClientEmployee might be declared a subtype of both Client and Employee. Those versions of ER which allow subtyping typically offer only limited support in this regard.

Since in principle there are infinitely many kinds of constraints, a textual notation in some formal language is often required for completeness to supplement the diagram. This is true with both ORM and ER modeling. However, the failure of ER diagrams to visually support certain important constraints makes it difficult for the designer to develop a comprehensive model or to perform *transformations* on the model.

For example, suppose that in any movie an actor may have a starring role or a supporting role but not both. This might be modeled by two fact types: *Actor* has starring role in *Movie*; *Actor* has supporting role in *Movie*. The "but not both" condition is expressed as a pair-exclusion constraint between the fact types. Alternatively, these fact types may be replaced by a single longer fact type: *Actor* in *Movie* has role of *RoleKind* {star, support}.

Transformations are rigorously controlled to ensure that constraints in one picture are captured in the alternative. For instance, the pair-exclusion constraint is transformed into the constraint that each ⟨Actor, Movie⟩ pair has only one RoleKind. The formal theory behind such transformations is much easier to apply when the relevant constraints can be visualized.

Besides having solid formal foundations, object-role modeling is suitable for use by all members of a development group, from end-users who can read facts in natural language to systems analysts who require both rigor and clarity in specifying or transforming an information model. Once the model has been developed it can be automatically mapped to fully normalized database structures.

For reasons such as those outlined, we recommend the use of object-role modeling when developing or transforming information models of applications. Once the model has been developed, it is important (especially with large models) to be able to summarize different aspects of the model in a number of ways. For some communication tasks, full object-role diagrams, even of sub-models, can be too expressive.

Later in the book we discuss various ways of summarizing object-role diagrams by hiding information, and of providing attribute views if desired. In this connection, ER diagrams have a role to play. For example, the ER diagram in Figure 1.6 is better than the ORM diagram for the purpose of providing a compact overview of the main features. It is thus useful to develop summary ER pictures from object-role diagrams. In practice it is also useful to be able to reverse-engineer object-role models from ER models as well as from relational database models. To perform this reverse engineering we usually need to capture additional semantics from others familiar with the application.

This book focuses on object-role modeling, then shows how the ORM and ER approaches can "talk to one another" if the need arises. Since the method avoids attribute decisions until the design is finished, and reveals what is lost when an ER diagram is constructed, performing object-role modeling prior to taking an ER view provides an improved method for those who wish to make use of ER modeling. The generation of an ER diagram from an ORM diagram is a simple process, which can be automated. Hence, as a by-product, ORM also provides an ideal way of developing an ER model. As a final point, the ORM approach also provides a conceptual basis for developing "object-oriented" data models.

1.3 Some historical background

This section provides a brief overview of the evolution of computing languages, with particular reference to information systems. A more detailed and general discussion of the history of computer hardware and software is provided in Appendix 1.

Table 1.4 summarizes how *five generations of computing languages* might be used to request a computer to list the names and sizes of the moons of Saturn in order of size, assuming the information is stored in an astronomical database. The higher the generation, the closer one gets to natural language. Nowadays most database applications are coded using third generation languages (3GLs), fourth generation languages (4GLs) or a combination of the two. The widespread use of fifth generation languages is still in the future.

Third generation languages, such as C and COBOL, are *procedural*, emphasizing the procedures used to carry out the task. Fourth generation languages, such as SQL and QBE, are primarily *declarative* in nature: the programmer essentially declares *what* has to be done rather than *how* to do it. With 3GLs we need to specify how to access information in a database one record at a time. With a 4GL, a single statement can be used to perform operations on whole tables (i.e. sets of rows) at once. Hence 4GLs are *set-oriented* rather than record-oriented.

The first database management systems were developed in the early 1960s. From that time, various *logical data models* have been proposed as a basis for specifying the structure of databases. The *network data model* was developed by the Conference on Data Systems and Languages (CODASYL) Database Task Group. This model is fairly complex. Most of the data is stored in records, a single field of which may contain a single value, a set of values, or even a set of value-groups. Record-types are related by owner-member links, and the graph of these connections may take the form of a network: a record-type may have many owners as well as owning many record-types.

Table 1.4 Five generations of computing languages

Generation	*Language example*	*Sample code for same task*
5	Formal English	List the name and size of the moons of the planet `Saturn' in order of size
4	SQL	**select** name, size **from** Moon **where** planet = 'Saturn' **order by** size
3	Pascal	Two pages of instructions like: **for** i := 1 **to** n **do** writeln (names[i], size[i])
2	8086 Assembler	Many pages of instructions like: ADDI AX, 1
1	8086 Machine code	Many pages of instructions like: 00000101 00000001 00000000

In the network model, facts are stored either in records or as record-links. For example, a person's name, sex and birthdate might be stored in a single record, but the fact that a person works for a department might be represented by having that person's record "owned" by a department record. In this case, if we want to query about who works for what department we have to rely upon this access path being predefined between the person record type and the department record type.

This encoding of fact types in access paths complicates the management of the application and makes it less flexible. For example, some new queries will have to wait until access paths have been added for them, and internal optimization efforts can be easily undone as the application structure evolves.

The *hierarchic data model*, which was developed at IBM, is simpler. Record fields can hold only single values. Record types are related by parent-child links, but each child has only one parent. This model is specifically designed to handle an application with a hierarchic structure (e.g. a computer's file directory system). As with the network model, facts are stored either in records or as record-links. While facilitating good performance for hierarchical applications, this model is less suited to other applications, and still relies on predefined access paths for some queries.

In 1970, E. F. Codd, then an IBM research fellow, introduced an even simpler model: the *relational data model*. Here all the facts are stored in tables, which are treated as mathematical relations. Access paths between tables are not used to specify facts. To specify queries and constraints, table columns may be associated by name. This allows ad hoc queries to be specified at will, and simplifies management of the application. Note that constraints specified between tables are not the same as access paths. For example, in Figure 1.1 an arrow is shown "linking" the Starred table to the Movie table. However this expresses a constraint, not a fact.

The relational model is logically cleaner than the network and hierarchic models, but it initially suffered from performance problems, which led to its slow acceptance. However by the late 1980s efficient relational systems had become commonplace. Although many network and hierarchic database systems are in use today, relational DBMSs are now the preferred choice for developing most new database applications.

A DBMS should ideally provide an integrated data dictionary, dynamic optimization, data security, automatic recovery and a user-friendly interface. The two main query languages used with relational databases are SQL (loosely known as "Structured Query Language") and QBE (Query By Example). Many systems support both of these. SQL has been accepted as a standard at the international level, and is becoming the common language for communication between different database systems.

Newer approaches have been proposed, such as *object-oriented databases* and *deductive databases*, but these have a long way to go in terms of standardization and maturity before they have a chance of widespread acceptance. Although relational systems give adequate performance for most applications, they are inefficient for some applications involving complex data structures (e.g. VLSI design). To overcome such difficulties, many relational systems are being enhanced with other features, and these *extended relational systems* will probably compete with object-oriented databases for dominance in the near future. Substantial efforts are under way to support *distributed databases*, where the data may be distributed over several communicating sites. A discussion of object-oriented databases and future trends is included in the final chapter.

1.4 The relevant skills

Since relational database systems are already available we henceforth ignore the less productive database systems based on 3GLs. Although fifth generation systems might not be available, we should develop our designs at this higher level in order to avoid wasting our time acquiring knowledge and skills that will rapidly become obsolete. Recall the impact of the electronic calculator on school mathematics curricula (e.g. the removal of the general square root algorithm).

Fundamentally, there are two skills that will always be relevant to interacting with an information system. Both of these skills relate to *communicating* with the system about our particular application area. Recall that this area is technically known as our *universe of discourse* (UoD). The two requirements are to:

- **describe** the universe of discourse;
- **query** the system about the universe of discourse.

The first skill entails describing the structure or *design* of the UoD, and describing the content or *population* of the UoD: the design aspect is the only challenging part of this. Obviously, the ability to clearly describe the UoD is critical if one wishes to add a UoD description to the system. Complex UoD designs should normally be prepared by experts in the modelling task. The main aim of this text is to introduce you to the fundamentals of information modelling: if you master the methods discussed you will be well on your way to becoming an expert in the design of information systems.

Issuing queries is often easy using a 4GL, but the formulation of complex queries can still be difficult. Occasionally, the ability to understand some answers given by the system requires knowledge about how the system works, especially its limitations. This book provides a conceptual basis for understanding relational structures and queries, explains the relational algebra behind relational query languages, and includes a simple introduction to SQL.

No matter how sophisticated the information system, if we give it the wrong picture of our UoD to start with, we can't expect to get much sense out of it. This is one aspect of the GIGO (Garbage In Garbage Out) principle. Most of the problems with many database applications can be traced to bad database design. This text shows how to specify the design of a UoD at a very high level using natural concepts. For immediate use, these designs can be mapped onto the lower level structures used by today's database systems. This mapping can be performed automatically using an appropriate CASE tool, or manually using an appropriate procedure, as discussed later.

1.5 Summary

This chapter provided a motivation for studying conceptual modeling techniques, and presented an historical and structural overview of information systems.

Database management systems (DBMSs) are gaining widespread use, and are a major productivity tool for businesses that are information-oriented. However, for a database to be used effectively its data should be correct and easy to access. This requires that the database is well-designed. Designing a database involves building a formal model of the application area or universe of discourse (UoD). To do this properly requires a good understanding of the UoD and a means of specifying this understanding in a clear, unambiguous way.

Object-Role Modeling (ORM) simplifies the design process by using natural language, intuitive diagrams and examples, and by examining the information in terms of simple or *elementary facts*. By expressing the model in terms of natural concepts, like *objects* and *roles*, it provides a *conceptual* approach to modeling. Another conceptual approach is provided by Entity-Relationship (ER) modeling.

Although ER models can be of use once the design process is finished, they are less suitable than ORM models for the tasks of formulating, transforming or evolving a design. ER diagrams are further removed from natural language, cannot be populated with fact instances, require complex design choices about attributes, lack the expressibility and simplicity of a role-based notation for constraints, hide information about the semantic domains which glue the model together, and lack adequate support for formal transformations.

Many different ER notations exist which differ not only in the concepts they can express but also in how they express them. For such reasons we use ORM as our basic modeling method. ER diagrams can be useful for providing compact summaries, and are best developed as views of ORM diagrams.

Computer hardware and software have evolved through at least four generations. Fourth generation languages are declarative in nature, enabling the user to declare what has to be done without the fine detail of how to do it. No matter how "intelligent" software systems become, people are needed to describe the universe of discourse and to ask the relevant questions about it.

Chapter notes

Further background on the topics discussed in this chapter may be found in the following references. To obtain the full bibliographic entries for these references, please consult the Bibliography at the back of this book.

Date (1990) provides a clear, standard introduction to most aspects of database systems. Codd (1970) introduces the relational model of data. Codd (1990) suggests future directions for the relational model. The classic paper which introduced Entity-Relationship modeling is Chen (1976). Kent (1978) provides a clear and insightful analysis of the nature of information and data models. A concise introduction to object-role modeling is given in Halpin & Orlowska (1992). This omits some refinements discussed later. For a more rigorous analysis which includes examples of the formal theory for transformations on fact-oriented schemas, see Halpin (1991b) or Halpin (1992).

For a clear discussion on the evolution and future impact of computing technology, Evans (1980) is still relevant and perceptive. Kennedy (1993, esp. Ch. 5) provides a thoughtful analysis of the repercussions of robotics, automation and the new industrial revolution on humankind, within the context of the main challenges facing society as it prepares for the next century.

2 Information levels

2.1 External, conceptual, logical and internal levels

Advanced information systems are sometimes described as "intelligent". Just what intelligence is, and whether machines will ever be intelligent, are debatable questions. In the classic "Turing Test" of intelligence, an opaque screen is placed between a typical human and the object being tested for intelligence. The human can communicate with the object only by means of computer (with keyboard for input and screen for output). The human may communicate in natural language about any desired topic. According to Turing, if the human can't tell from the object's responses whether it is an intelligent human or a machine, then the object should be classified as intelligent. To date, no machine has passed the Turing Test.

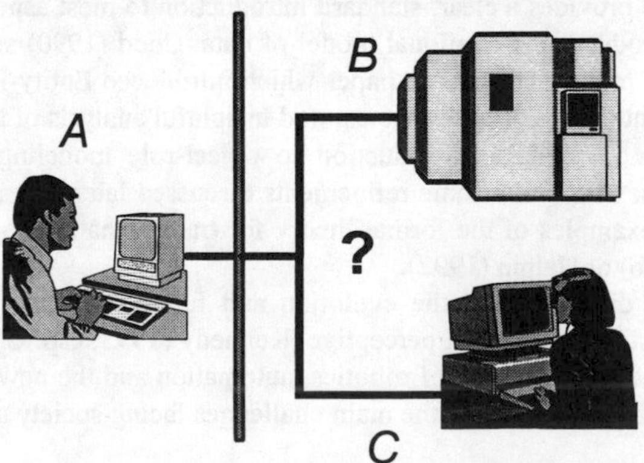

Figure 2.1 **The Turing test: can *A* distinguish between *B* and *C*?**

Notice that two of the key conditions in the test are that natural language be used and that there be no restrictions on the topics chosen for discussion. Once we place restrictions on the language and confine the discussion to a predefined topic, we can find examples where a computer has performed at the level of a human expert (e.g. chess, diagnosis of blood diseases, mineral exploration). Such systems are called "expert systems" since they perform as well as a human expert in some specific domain of application. Expert systems have passed "restricted Turing Tests" specific to particular universes of discourse.

Expert systems use sophisticated programs, often in conjunction with large but highly specific databases. A fifth generation information system (5GIS) is like a "user-definable" expert system in that it allows the user to enter a description of the universe of discourse and then conduct a conversation about this, all in natural language. Just how well the system handles its end of the conversation depends on how powerful its user interface, database management and inference capabilities are.

Although desirable, it is not necessary that a 5GIS always be able to operate at expert level when we communicate with it. It must however allow us to communicate with it in a natural, human way. Natural languages such as English and Japanese are complex and subtle. It will be many years before an information system will be able to converse freely in unrestricted natural language. We will be content in the meantime if a 5GIS supports dialogue in a formalized subset of natural language. We refer to such a language as a Formal Natural Language. There will be many of these, one for English, one for Japanese, and so on. A 5GIS should be able to respond in the same language used by the human. For example, suppose we posed the following query:

What is the age of Selena?

and we received the reply:

jūhachisai.

This would not help much unless we knew that this is Japanese for "18 years old". Even if we can translate from Japanese to English we might still misinterpret the reply, because unlike the usual convention of giving people an age of zero years when born, the Japanese give them an age of one year. So an age of eighteen years in the Japanese system corresponds to an age of seventeen years in the Western system. Besides the requirement for a *common language*, effective communication between two speakers requires that each gives the *same meaning* to the words being used. This is achieved by ensuring that both speakers (a) share the same context or universe of discourse, and (b) speak in sentences that are unambiguous with respect to this UoD.

With our example, the confusion over whether Selena's age is seventeen or eighteen years results from two different UoD frameworks being used, one relating to Western age conventions and the other to Japanese conventions. Natural speech abounds with examples that can be disambiguated only by context. Consider the following example: Pluto is owned by Mickey. This is fine if we treat the UoD to be the world of Walt Disney's cartoon characters. But suppose someone unfamiliar with Mickey Mouse and his dog Pluto interpreted this within an astronomical context, taking "Pluto" to refer to the planet Pluto: a more drastic communication failure! It is clearly essential then, that we have a clear way of describing the UoD to the information system.

An information system may be viewed from *four levels*: *external*, *conceptual*, *logical* and *internal*. Since the conceptual level is the most fundamental, portraying the UoD in a way that is natural and unambiguous, we discuss this level first. At this level, the framework of the UoD is called the **conceptual schema**: this describes the *structure* or *grammar* of the specific UoD (e.g. what types of object populate the UoD, what roles these play, and what constraints are in effect). In other words the conceptual schema is a general design plan of the UoD.

While the conceptual schema indicates the structure of the UoD, the **conceptual database** at any given time indicates the *content* or instances populating a specific *state* of the UoD. Although the term "information base" is more appropriate (ISO, 1982), we use the briefer and more popular term "database". Conceptually, the database is a set of sentences expressing propositions asserted to be true of the UoD. Since sentences may be added to or deleted from the database, the database may undergo transitions from one state to another. However, at any particular time, the sentences populating the database must individually and collectively conform to the application specific grammar or design plan which is the conceptual schema. To summarize:

- The conceptual schema completely specifies all the permitted states and transitions of the conceptual database.

To enforce this law we now introduce a third system component known as the **conceptual information processor**. This component is responsible for supervising updates to the database by the user and for answering user queries. The basic conceptual architecture of an information system is set out in Figure 2.2. This diagram assumes the conceptual schema is already stored within the system. For each application area of choice, a different conceptual schema is entered.

Although the diagram may seem to suggest that the user is interacting directly with the conceptual information processor, the user's interaction with the system is external rather than conceptual. The conceptual schema is not concerned with providing convenient interfaces for various users, or with the physical details of how the database can be efficiently maintained. These concerns may be catered for by including external and internal components within the overall architecture.

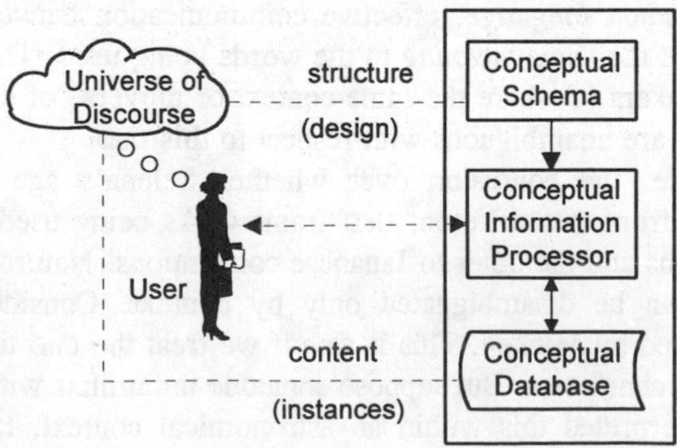

Figure 2.2 Information system: Conceptual level

An **external schema** specifies the UoD design perceived by a particular user or group of users, and how it relates to the conceptual schema. At the external level we specify *what* kind of information may be viewed by users and *how* it is displayed. Often a user has access to only part of the information. This may be for *user convenience*. For example, it is simpler to issue queries if selecting only from the information relevant to one's needs. Sometimes, *security* reasons may require that only certain authorized users have access to sensitive information stored in the system. Basically, the idea is that different user groups may access different subschemas of the global conceptual schema.

Moreover, different users may wish to see the same information displayed in different ways (e.g. in forms, tables or graphs); and users with different expertise levels may prefer different ways of operating on and navigating through the information. Different user interfaces may be designed to support these alternatives.

Conceptual schemas are designed for communication. While they give a clear picture of the UoD, they must usually be converted to some lower level structure to achieve an efficient implementation. For a given application, an appropriate logical data model (e.g. relational, hierarchic, network) is chosen, and the conceptual schema is mapped to a **logical schema** expressed in terms of the abstract structures for data and operations supported in that data model. For example, in a relational schema facts are stored into tables, and constraints are expressed using primary keys and so on.

The logical schema may now be realized as an **internal schema** in a specific DBMS. For example a relational schema might be implemented in Access or DB2. The internal schema includes all the details about the physical storage and access structures used in that system (e.g. indexes, file clustering etc.). Different physical choices can be made for the same DBMS, and different DBMSs often differ in what choices are possible. Hence many different internal schemas might be chosen for the same logical schema.

One advantage of the conceptual level is that it is the most *stable* of all the levels. It is unaffected by changes in user-interfaces or physical storage and access techniques. Suppose a conceptual schema has been implemented in a hierarchic DBMS, and later we wish to use a relational DBMS instead. Unless the UoD has changed, the conceptual schema can remain the same. We need only apply a different mapping procedure, and then convert the data to the new model.

If a language is the object of study it is said to be the *object language*. The language used to study it is then called the *metalanguage*. For example, you might use English as a metalanguage to study Japanese as an object language. An object language may be its own metalanguage, for example, English may be used to learn about English. Note that any conceptual schema may be expressed as a set of sentences and hence may be viewed as a database in its own right. This enables us to construct a **metaschema** for talking about conceptual schemas. This meta conceptual schema specifies the design rules which must be obeyed by any conceptual schema (e.g. each role is played by exactly one object type). CASE tools used to assist in designing conceptual schemas make use of such a metaschema to ensure that schemas entered by the designer are well formed or "grammatical".

While on the subject of grammar, let us agree to accept both "schemas" and "schemata" as plural of "schema". Although "data" is the plural of "datum", we adopt the common practice of allowing "data" to be used in both singular and plural senses.

Exercise 2.1

1. Classify each of the following as: A (external); B (conceptual); or C (internal).
   (a) This level is concerned with the physical details of how data may be efficiently stored and accessed.
   (b) This level is concerned with providing a convenient and authorized view of the database for an individual user.
   (c) This level is concerned with representing information in a fundamental way.

2.2 The conceptual level

At the conceptual level, all communication between people and the information system is handled by the *conceptual information processor* (CIP). This communication may be divided into three main stages:

1. If the conceptual schema for the relevant UoD is not already stored, the designer enters it. The CIP accepts the conceptual schema if and only if it is consistent with the meta conceptual schema.
2. The user updates the database by adding or deleting specific facts. The CIP accepts an update operation if and only if it is consistent with the conceptual schema.
3. The user queries the system about the UoD and is answered by the CIP. The CIP can supply information about the conceptual schema or the database, provided it has stored the information or can derive it.

In executing its task at these three stages the CIP is performing its roles as a *design filter*, *data filter* and *information supplier* respectively. In a more detailed analysis, the design filter could be treated as a separate unit involving a conceptual schema processor with read access to the conceptual metaschema.

When interpreted by people, the conceptual schema and database both provide knowledge about the UoD. Hence the combination of conceptual schema and (conceptual) database may be described as the **knowledge base**. Thus the information system comprises a knowledge base and CIP. The knowledge base is a formal description of the UoD, and the CIP controls the flow of information between the knowledge base and humans. Some authors use the term "knowledge base" in a more restricted sense.

In the overall construction of practical information systems, at least three categories of people are involved. The *UoD expert* or domain expert is familiar with the application area, and can clarify any doubtful aspects of the UoD. For example, if a computerized accountancy system is required for a company, the company's accountant would probably be the UoD expert.

With complex applications, no single person might have expertise in all the relevant areas; in this case the UoD expert is a group of people who are collectively familiar with the application. The *designer* or modeler provides the formal specification of the conceptual schema: this person (or team) is trained in schema design and regularly consults with the UoD expert in developing the conceptual schema.

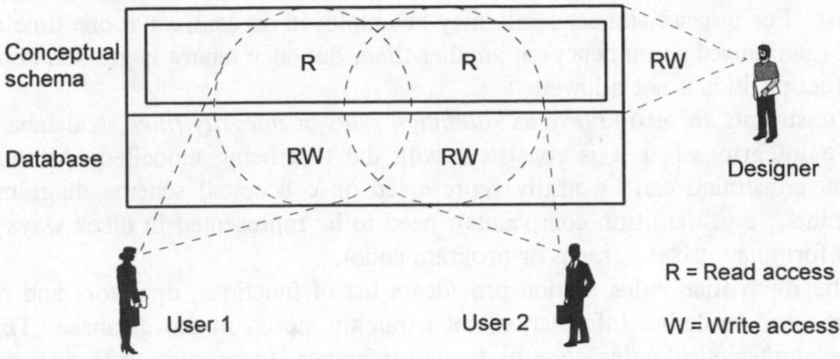

Figure 2.3 Access to the knowledge base

The *end user* makes use of the system once it has been developed (e.g. data entry operators, clerks and executives of the company). For a small system, the UoD expert, designer and user might be the same person. For a large system there might be several partial UoD experts, a team of analysts and designers, and thousands of end users.

For simplicity let us agree that there is one designer but possibly several users. The designer inputs the conceptual schema to the system and has read/write access to the conceptual schema. A user who merely works with an already existing schema has read-only capability for the schema, but typically has read/write access to the database. Some users may have read-only access to the database. Different external schemas might be created for different users so that some users have access to only part of the knowledge base. This situation is summarized in Figure 2.3.

To understand how the CIP deals with updates and queries, we now provide an informal overview of the conceptual schema. We consider it to be comprised of three m main sections, as shown in Figure 2.4.

Basically, the section on **stored fact types** lists the kinds of sentence or *fact* which may be stored in the database. Here we indicate what types of *object* are permitted in the UoD (e.g. Person, Subject), how these are *referenced* by values in the database (e.g. surname, subjectcode), and the various *relationships* they engage in (e.g. studies, passes).

The **constraints** section lists various constraints or restrictions that apply to populations of the fact types. These may be either static or dynamic. *Static constraints* apply to every state of the database. For example, suppose a geographical database stores information about countries and their capital cities. Although a country may move its capital to another city, at any given time it has at most one city recorded as its current capital.

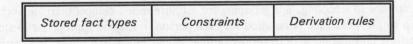

Stored fact types	*Constraints*	*Derivation rules*

Figure 2.4 The three main sections of the conceptual schema

Dynamic constraints exclude or enforce certain transitions between states of the database. For instance, an academic may be employed on contract at one time and have tenure (guaranteed permanency) at another time, but once tenure is granted demotion to a contract position is not allowed.

Constraints are also known as *validation rules* or *integrity rules*. A database is said to have integrity when it is consistent with the UoD being modelled. Although most relevant constraints can be neatly represented on conceptual schema diagrams, some constraints, (e.g. transition constraints), need to be represented in other ways (e.g. by logical formulae, tables, graphs or program code).

The **derivation rules** section provides a list of functions, operators and rules that may be used to derive information not explicitly stored in the database. These may involve *mathematical calculation* or *logical inference*. In practice, many operators and functions may be thought of as generic to particular data types: this permits a large variety of possible queries without the need to document each related derivation. Typical mathematical facilities provided include arithmetic operators, for example +, -, * (multiply), and / (divide), set operators such as ∪ (union), as well as functions for counting, summing, and computing averages, maxima and minima.

In addition to such generic derivation facilities, specific *derived fact types* that are known to be required may be individually listed in the schema by means of rules. Some mathematically computed fact types and almost all logically inferred fact types fit into this category. Fact types derived by use of logical inference typically involve rules which make use of logical operators such as **if**.

Although derivable facts could be stored in the database it is usually better to avoid this. The reason for this is not so much to save storage space, but rather to avoid anomalies when updating the database. For instance, suppose we wanted to regularly obtain individual ages (in years) of students in a class, and, on occasion, the average age for the class. If we stored the average age in the database we would have to arrange for this to be recomputed every time a student was added to or deleted from the class, as well as every time the age of any individual in the class increased.

As an improvement, we might store the number of students as well as their individual ages and have the average age derived only upon request. But this is still clumsy. Can you think of a better design?

As you probably realized, there is no need to store the number of students in a class since this can be derived using a count function. This avoids having to update the class size every time someone joins or leaves the class. Moreover, there is no need to store even the individual ages of students. Computer systems have a built-in clock which enables the current date to be accessed. If we store the birthdate of the students then we can have the system derive the age of any student upon request by using an appropriate date subtraction algorithm. With this arrangement we don't have to worry about updating ages of students as they become a year older.

Sometimes, what is required is not the current age but the age on a certain date (e.g. entrance to schooling, age grouping for a future sports competition). In such cases where a single, stable age is required for each person, it may be appropriate to store it.

Before considering a derivation example using logical inference, we distinguish *propositions* from *sentences*. Propositions are asserted by declarative sentences, and are always true or false (but not both). The same proposition may be asserted by different sentences, for example, "Paris is the capital of France" and "The French capital is Paris". While humans can deal with underlying meanings in a very sophisticated way, computers are completely literally minded: they deal in sentences rather than their meanings. If we want the computer to make what to us are obvious connections, we have to explicitly provide it with the background or rules for making such connections.

Suppose that facts about brotherhood and parenthood are stored in the database. For simplicity we assume that the only objects we want to talk about are people who are identified by their first names. We might now set out facts as follows:

Alan is brother of Betty.
Charles is brother of Betty.
Betty is parent of Fred.

As humans we can look at these facts and readily see that both Alan and Charles are uncles of Fred. In doing so we are using our understanding of the term "uncle". If we want a computer system to be able to make similar deductions we need to provide it with a rule which expresses this understanding. For example:

Given any X, Z:
    X is uncle of Z **if** there is a Y such that
        X is brother of Y **and** Y is parent of Z

This may be abbreviated to:

X is uncle of Z **if** X is brother of Y **and** Y is parent of Z.

This rule is an example of a *Horn clause*. The head of the clause is derivable from the conditions stated on the right hand side of the **if**. Horn clauses are used in languages like Prolog, and enable many derivation rules to be set out briefly.

To appreciate how the CIP works, let's look at an example. The notation is based on a textual version of an ORM language called FORML. A more convenient graphical version is explained in later chapters. For simplicity, some constraints have been omitted. The structure of the UoD is set out by means of the conceptual schema shown.

Reference schemes:
Person (firstname); City (name); Year (AD)+

Stored Fact types:
F1 Person lives in City
F2 Person was born in Year
F3 Person is brother of Person
F4 Person is parent of Person

Constraints:
C1 **each** Person lives in **some** City
C2 **each** Person lives in **at most one** City
C3 **each** Person was born in **at most one** Year
C4 **no** Person is brother of **itself**
C5 **no** Person is parent of **itself**

Derivation rules:
D1 Person *x* is uncle of Person *y* **if** *x* is brother of z **and** *z* is parent of *y*
D2 NrChildren(Person *x*) ::= **count**(*x* is parent of **some** Person)

The Reference Schemes section declares the kinds of *entity* we are interested in, and how they are referenced. Entities are real or abstract things we want to talk about, that are referenced by relating *values* (e.g. character strings or numbers) to them in some way. Entities and values are examples of *objects*. Here we have three kinds of entity: Person, City and Year. In this simple UoD, people are identified by their firstname, and cities are identified by their name. Years are identified by their AD values (e.g. Einstein died in the year 1955 AD); the "+" sign in the Year declaration indicates these values are numeric, and hence can be operated on arithmetically. You may find it strange to treat years as entities, but each year is a segment of time.

The Fact Types section declares the kinds of fact we are interested in. Basically this indicates how relationships are participated in by object types. The names of object types are usually highlighted by starting them with a capital letter. If you are used to working with database tables, where columns have attribute names like "birthyear", you may feel it is better to reword the fact type "Person was born in Year" as "Person has BirthYear". However suppose we added another fact type "Person has DeathYear": the formal connection between BirthYear and DeathYear is now hidden; instead we express the new fact type as "Person died in Year", revealing the semantic connections to "Person was born in Year", and making comparisons between years of birth and death meaningful. Attribute names are often used in ER and relational schemas to express facts. But this way of expressing facts is often very unnatural (compare "Person has DeathYear" with "Person died in Year"); and it is incomplete, since domain names such as "Year" are still required.

The Constraints section declares constraints on the fact types. The examples here are all static constraints (i.e. each is true for each state of the database). Reserved words in the conceptual schema language are shown in bold. Constraint C1 means that for each person referenced in the database, we know at least one city where they live. C2 says nobody can live in more than one city (at the same time). C3 says nobody was born in more than one year; note that we mightn't know their year of birth. Constraint C4 says that nobody is his/her own brother, and C5 says that nobody is his/her own parent: the brother and parent fact types are said to be "irreflexive".

The Derivation Rules section declares a logical rule for determining uncles and a function for computing the number of children of any person. Given any person, the NrChildren function returns a count of the number of fact instances where that person appears as the parent. Instead of the notations used here, an SQL-style notation might be used: in this case, a relational-version of the conceptual fact table is used. Table and attribute names for such relational-versions may be derived from the names of the conceptual fact type and object types, numbering object types which appear more than once. For example, the parenthood fact table is viewed as the relational table IsParentOf (<u>person1, person2</u>) and the NrChildren rule becomes: NrChildren(*x*) ::= select count(*) from IsParentOf where person1 = *x*). The reader unfamiliar with SQL may ignore these details.

At the conceptual level each fact in the database is a simple or *elementary fact*: basically this means it can't be split up into two or more simpler facts without loss of information. We may *add* or insert a fact into the database, and we may *delete* a fact from it. However we may not modify or change just a part of a fact. By "fact" we mean "fact *instance*" not "fact type". The operation of adding or deleting a single fact is an *elementary update* or *simple transaction*. In our example conceptual query language, add and delete requests start with "**add**:" and "**del**:", and queries end with "?". The CIP either accepts updates or rejects them with an indication of the violation. The CIP answers legal queries and rejects illegal ones.

To explain the conceptual notions underlying database transactions, we now discuss some examples of CIP interactions. If this seems tedious, remember that we are talking about the conceptual level, not the *external level where the user actually interacts with the system*. At the external level, the user would typically enter, delete or change values in a screen version of a form or table. Conceptually however, we may think of such an operation being translated into the appropriate delete and add operations on elementary facts before being passed on to the CIP. Suppose now that we start populating our conceptual database as follows:

User:	*CIP:*
add: Person 'Terry' lives in City 'Seattle'. →	accepted

The CIP recognizes the type of this sentence and sees that no constraints are violated; so it adds it to the database and issues the reply "accepted". If an update is inconsistent with the conceptual schema, the CIP rejects it, indicating the reason for rejection. You should now be able to follow the following dialogue:

```
add: Person 'Norma' was born in Year 1950.      →  rejected. C1 violated.
add: Person 'Norma' lives in City 'Brisbane'    →  accepted.
add: Person 'Norma' was born in Year 1950.      →  accepted.
add: Person 'Terry' is brother of Person 'Paul'. →  rejected. C1 violated.
add: Person 'Paul' lives in City 'Brisbane'.    →  accepted.
add: Person 'Terry' is brother of Person 'Paul'. →  accepted.
add: Person 'Paul' is brother of Person 'Paul'.  →  rejected. C4 violated.
add: Person 'Terry' plays Sport 'Judo'.         →  rejected. Unknown fact type
```

For brevity, constraint numbers indicate the constraints violated. In practice of course, since the CIP response is intended to be meaningful to humans, the full text description of the constraint would be displayed. Now suppose that Terry moves from Seattle to Brisbane. How would we record this change? Here are two incorrect attempts:

```
add: Person 'Terry' lives in City 'Brisbane'.   →  rejected. C2 violated.
del: Person 'Terry' lives in City 'Seattle'.    →  rejected. C1 violated.
```

Is there any way of changing Terry's city from Seattle to Brisbane? Yes. Sometimes it is convenient, or even necessary, to submit a whole bundle of elementary updates as a single group. This is referred to as a *compound transaction*. To indicate a compound transaction we use "**begin**" and "**end**" as brackets to open and close the transaction. With compound transactions the CIP considers only the total or *collective effect* of the transaction on the database. It is quite possible that the CIP will accept a compound transaction even if, taken individually, some of its component simple updates would be rejected. To change Terry's location we proceed thus:

```
begin
  del: Person 'Terry' lives in City 'Seattle'.
  add: Person 'Terry' lives in City 'Brisbane'.
end                                             →  accepted.
```

The CIP accepts a transaction if and only if its overall effect is consistent with the conceptual schema. The user entered this compound transaction as a sequence of two elementary updates. It is more natural here to specify the delete before the add operation. However the CIP treats any compound transaction as a set of updates, disregarding the order of the components, and looks only at the total effect. So even if the add operation had been specified before the delete, this would have been accepted with the same result. Note that the CIP cannot accept just part of a compound transaction: it is case of "all or nothing". Here are a few more simple interactions:

add: Person 'Linda' lives in City 'Brisbane'.	→	accepted.
add: Person 'Selena' lives in City 'Brisbane'.	→	accepted.
add: Person 'Terry' is parent of Person 'Linda'.	→	accepted.
add: Person 'Terry' is parent of Person 'Selena'.	→	accepted.
NrChildren(Person 'Terry')?	→	2.
what Person is brother of Person 'Paul'?	→	Terry.
what Person lives in City 'Brisbane'?	→	Norma Linda Selena Terry.
what Person is uncle of Person 'Selena'?	→	No Person.
add: Person 'Paul' is brother of Person 'Terry'.	→	accepted.
what Person is uncle of Person 'Selena'?	→	Paul.
what Person is aunt of Person 'Selena'?	→	rejected. Unknown fact type or rule.

Now suppose the UoD is changed by adding the following constraint:

C6 **each** Person was born in **some** Year

Our current database fails to meet this constraint. Suppose we start over with an empty database, and try to add the following fact. How would the CIP respond?

add: Person 'Bernard' is brother of Person 'John'.

This update request is rejected. It actually violates two constraints (C1 and C6), since all people mentioned in the database must have both their city and birth year recorded. Later on we use the terminology "mandatory roles" or "total roles" to describe such constraints. In general, the order in which constraints are listed in the conceptual schema does not matter. However if an update request violates more than one constraint, this order may determine which constraint is reported as violated. Usually, if a CIP finds a constraint violation then it reports this and doesn't bother looking for any more violations. In this case, the CIP would respond thus to the previous request:

rejected. C1 violated.

Of course, it is possible to program the CIP to report all constraint violations (e.g. "rejected. C1, C6 violated"), but this tends to be less efficient. As an exercise, convince yourself that with C6 added, the following update requests are processed as shown:

add: Person 'Jim' lives in City 'Seattle'. → rejected. C6 violated.

```
begin
  add: Person 'Jim' lives in City 'Seattle'.
  add: Person 'Jim' was born in Year 1960.
end                                            →  accepted.
add: Person 'Jim' was born in Year 1959.       →  rejected. C3 violated.
begin
  del: Person 'Jim' was born in Year 1960.
  add: Person 'Jim' was born in Year 1959.
  add: Person 'Bob' lives in City 'London'.
  add: Person 'Bob' was born in Year 1970.
  add: Person 'Jim' is brother of Person 'Bob'.
end                                            →  accepted.
```

The CIP uses the conceptual schema to supervise updates of the database and to supply information in response to a question. We may think of the designer of the conceptual schema as the *"law giver"*, and the schema itself as the *"law book"* since it contains the laws or ground rules for the UoD. The CIP is the *"law enforcer"*, since it ensures these laws are adhered to whenever the user tries to update the database. Like any friendly policeperson, the CIP is also there to provide information on request.

Whenever we communicate to a person or an information system we have in mind a particular universe of discourse. Typically, this is concerned with some small part of the real universe, such as a particular business environment. In rare cases, we might choose a fictional UoD (e.g. one populated by comic book characters), or perhaps a fantasy world we have invented for a novel that we are writing. Such fictional worlds may or may not be (logically) possible.

You can often rely on your own intuitions as to what is logically possible. For instance a world in which the Moon is coloured green is possible, but a world in which the Moon is simultaneously green all over and red all over is not. A possible world is said to be *consistent* and an impossible world is *inconsistent*.

As humans we carry prodigious amounts of information around in our minds. It is highly likely that somewhere in our personal web of beliefs some logical contradictions are lurking. In most cases it does not matter if our belief web is globally inconsistent, so long as the local portions of the web that we use to communicate about are internally consistent. When reasoning about a particular UoD however, consistency is essential. It can be easily shown that once you accept a logical inconsistency, it is possible to deduce anything (including loads of rubbish) from it. Recall the GIGO (Garbage In Garbage Out) principle discussed earlier.

There are basically two types of garbage: logical and factual. Inconsistent designs contain logical garbage. For example, we might declare two constraints which contradict one another. A good design method supported by a CASE tool which enforces meta-rules can help to avoid such problems. Many factual errors can be prevented by the enforcement of constraints on the database. For example, a declared constraint that each country has only one capital stops us from giving a country two capitals.

However, even if the schema is consistent, and the CIP checks that the database is consistent with this world design, it is still possible to add false data into the knowledge base. For example, if we tell the CIP that Rome is the capital of France it might accept this even though in the actual world Paris is France's capital. If we want our knowledge base to remain factually correct, it is still our responsibility to ensure that all the sentences we enter into the database express propositions that are true of the actual world.

The following exercise gives you an opportunity to check your understanding of the concepts discussed in this section. It also introduces some further constraint types that will be treated more formally later.

Exercise 2.2

1. (a) Assuming the conceptual schema is already stored, what are the two main functions of the conceptual information processor?
   (b) What are the three main components of the conceptual schema?
   (c) "The CIP will reject a compound transaction if any of its component update operations is inconsistent with the conceptual schema.". True or False?

2. Assume the following conceptual schema is stored. The notation "(nr)+" indicates that fitness ratings are identified by numbers. Constraints apply to each database state. C1 means that each person referred to in the database must have his/her fitness rating recorded there. C3 says the possible fitness values are whole numbers from 1 to 10. C4 means no person can be recorded as expert at more than one sport, and C5 says a person can be recorded as being an expert at a sport only if (the same) person is also recorded as playing (the same) sport.

   Reference schemes:

   Person (firstname); Sport (name); FitnessRating (nr)+

   Stored fact types:

   F1 Person has FitnessRating
   F2 Person plays Sport
   F3 Person is expert at Sport

   Constraints:

   C1 **each** Person has **some** FitnessRating
   C2 **each** Person has **at most one** FitnessRating
   C3 FitnessRating **values** 1..10
   C4 **each** Person is expert at **at most one** Sport
   C5 Person *p* is expert at Sport *s* **only if** *p* plays *s*

   Derivation rules:

   D1 Person *p* is martial artist **if** *p* plays Sport 'judo'
   or *p* plays Sport 'karatedo'
   D2 NrPlayers(Sport *x*) :: = **count(some** Person plays *x*)

   The database is initially empty. The user now attempts the following sequence of updates and queries. For each update, circle the letter if the update is accepted; in cases of rejection supply a reason (e.g. state which part of the conceptual schema is violated). For queries supply an appropriate response from the CIP.

   (a) **add**: Person 'Ann' has FitnessRating 9.
   (b) **add**: Person 'Fred' plays Sport 'tennis'.
   (c) **add**: Person 'Bob' has FitnessRating 7.
   (d) **add**: Person 'Ann' has FitnessRating 8.
   (e) **add**: Person 'Chris' has FitnessRating 7.

(f) **add:** Person 'Fred' has FitnessRating 15.
(g) **add:** Person 'Ann' plays Sport 'judo'.
(h) **add:** Person 'Bob' is expert at Sport 'soccer'.
(i) **add:** Person 'Ann' is expert at Sport 'judo'.
(j) **add:** Person 'Ann' programs in Language 'SQL'.
(k) **add:** Person 'Ann' plays Sport 'soccer'.
(l) **add:** Person 'Chris' plays Sport 'karatedo'.
(m) **del:** Person 'Chris' has FitnessRating 7.
(n) **begin**
    add: Person 'Bob' has FitnessRating 8.
    del: Person 'Bob' has FitnessRating 7.
  end
(o) **add:** Person 'Ann' is expert at Sport 'soccer'.
(p) **add:** Person 'Bob' plays Sport 'soccer'.
(q) Person 'Ann' plays Sport 'judo'?
(r) **what** Person plays Sport 'karatedo'?
(s) NrPlayers(Sport 'soccer')?
(t) **what** Person is martial artist?
(u) FitnessRating **values**?
(v) **what** is the meaning of life?

3. The UoD design is given by the following conceptual schema. Constraints apply to the database, not necessarily to the real world being modelled. Although each student in the real world may in fact have a marital status, for this application it is optional as to whether a student's marital status is recorded. There may be good reasons for this, for example, to respect the wishes of particular students to keep their marital status private. Constraint C1 is a shorthand way of entering two weaker constraints, since "exactly one" means "at least one (i.e. some), and at most one".

Reference schemes:
Student (firstname); Degree (code); MaritalStatus (name)

Stored fact types:
F1 Student is enrolled in Degree
F2 Student has MaritalStatus

Constraints:
C1 **each** Student is enrolled in **exactly one** Degree
C2 **each** Student has **at most one** MaritalStatus
C3 MaritalStatus **values** 'single', 'married', 'widowed', 'divorced'
C4 MaritalStatus **transitions:** ("1" = "allowed")

From \ To	*single*	*married*	*widowed*	*divorced*
single	0	1	0	0
married	0	0	1	1
widowed	0	1	0	0
divorced	0	1	0	0

The database is initially empty. The user now attempts the following sequence of updates and queries. For each update, circle the letter if the update is accepted; in cases of rejection supply a reason. Assume questions are legal, and supply an appropriate response.

(a) **add**: Student 'Fred' is enrolled in Degree 'BSc'.
(b) **add**: Student 'Sue' has MaritalStatus 'single'.
(c) **begin**
  add: Student 'Sue' has MaritalStatus 'single'.
  add: Student 'Sue' is enrolled in Degree 'MA'.
end
(d) **add**: Student 'Fred' is enrolled in Degree 'BA'.
(e) **add**: Student 'Fred' is studying Subject 'CS112'.
(f) MaritalStatus **values**?
(g) **add**: Student 'Bob' is enrolled in Degree 'BSc'.
(h) **add**: Student 'Sue' has MaritalStatus 'married'.
(i) **begin**
  del: Student 'Sue' has MaritalStatus 'single'.
  add: Student 'Sue' has MaritalStatus 'married'.
end
(j) **add**: Student 'Bob' has MaritalStatus 'single'.
(k) **begin**
  del: Student 'Bob' has MaritalStatus 'single'.
  add: Student 'Bob' has MaritalStatus 'divorced'.
end
(l) Student 'Sue' is enrolled in Degree 'BSc'?
(m) **what** Student is enrolled in Degree 'BSc'?
(n) **what** Student is enrolled in Degree 'MA'?
(o) **add**: 3 students are enrolled in Degree 'BE'.

What is the final state of the database?

4. Assume the following conceptual schema.

Reference schemes:
  Person (firstname)

Stored fact types:
  F1 Person is male
  F2 Person is female
  F3 Person is parent of Person

Constraints:
  C1 **each** Person is male **or** is female
  C2 **no** Person is male **and** is female
  C3 { each person has at most 2 parents }
  each Person *p* **in** (Person is parent of *p*) **occurs there at most** 2 **times**
  C4 **no** Person is parent of **itself**

Derivation rules:
  D1 Person *x* is grandparent of Person *y* **if**
    x is parent of *z* **and** *z* is parent of *y*

Assume the database is populated with the following data. The user now attempts the following sequence of updates and queries. Indicate the CIP's response in each case.

Males: David, Paul, Terry
Females: Alice, Chris, Linda, Norma, Selena

(a) **add**: Person 'Jim' is male.
(b) **add**: Person 'Bernie' is parent of Person 'Terry'.
(c) **begin**
Person 'Terry' is parent of Person 'Selena'.
Person 'Norma' is parent of Person 'Selena'.
end
(d) **add**: Person 'David' is parent of Person 'David'.
(e) **begin**
Person 'Norma' is parent of Person 'Paul'.
Person 'Alice' is parent of Person 'Terry'.
end
(f) **add**: Person 'Chris' is male.
(g) **add**: Person 'Chris' is parent of Person 'Selena'.
(h) **what** Person is grandparent of Person 'Selena'?

Formulate your own derivation rules for the following:

(i) X is father of Y
(j) X is daughter of Y
(k) X is grand-daughter of Y

5. Consider the following conceptual schema:

Reference schemes:
Employee (surname); Department (name); Language (name)

Stored fact types:
F1 Employee works for Department
F2 Employee speaks Language

Constraints:
C1 **each** Employee works for **some** Department
C2 **each** Employee works for **at most one** Department
C3 **each** Employee speaks **some** Language

(a) Provide an update sequence to add the facts that Adams and Brown, who both speak English, work for the Health department.
(b) Invent some database populations which are inconsistent with the schema.

2.3 Relational database schemas

This section provides an overview of how conceptual schemas may be implemented in relational database systems. An example is used to help illustrate the main ideas. The topic is developed in detail in chapter 8. Consider a company which sells and services products. Some of its employees can speak languages other than English, which can be useful when dealing with foreign customers. Examples of some personnel record forms kept by the company are shown in Figure 2.5.

Employee: Adams
Dept: Sales
Gender: F
Foreign languages: Spanish

Employee: Bond
Dept: Sales
Gender: M
Foreign languages:

Employee: Cooper
Dept: Service
Gender: F
Foreign languages: French
Japanese
Spanish

Figure 2.5 Personnel forms for three employees

For simplicity, we assume employees may be identified by their surname, and we store only a few details about them. Typically employees are identified by employee numbers, and many details about them are recorded.

The company wishes to move from a manual to an automated personnel record system. After verbalizing the information on these forms in English, the information modeller specifies the following conceptual schema (you might like to specify the schema yourself before looking at the answer). We model the male gender (♂) and the female gender (♀) as abstract entities, which are referenced by the gender codes "M" and "F" respectively. The phrase "exactly one" is shorthand for "at least one and at most one".

Reference schemes:

Employee (surname); Department (name); Gender (code); ForeignLanguage (name)

Stored Fact types:

F1 Employee works for Department
F2 Employee has Gender
F3 Employee speaks ForeignLanguage

Constraints:

C1 **each** Employee works for **exactly one** Department
C2 **each** Employee has **exactly one** Gender
C3 Gender **values** 'M', 'F'

Employee:

empname	*dept*	*gender*
Adams	Sales	F
Bond	Sales	M
Cooper	Service	F

Speaks:

empname	*foreignLanguage*
Adams	Spanish
Cooper	French
Cooper	Japanese
Cooper	Spanish

Figure 2.6 Relational database tables for Figure 2.5

The constraints section does not restrict the fact type Employee speaks ForeignLanguage. So some employees may speak no foreign language (e.g. Bond), some may speak many (e.g. Cooper), and many may speak the same foreign language (e.g. Spanish). The conceptual database for this schema contains three tables, one for each elementary fact type. Some important consequences of this approach are that the schema is easy to understand, it is automatically free of redundancy, and constraints are easy to specify.

Once a conceptual schema has been designed, it may be mapped to a *logical schema* which is described in terms of the generic logical data model (e.g. relational, network or hierarchic) chosen for implementation purposes. The physical schema is then constructed by adapting the logical schema to the specific DBMS and improving performance by adding indexes etc. In this book our implementation discussion focuses on relational DBMSs. We refer to a schema specified in terms of the relational data model as a *relational database schema*, or **relational schema** for short.

The remainder of this section briefly considers the the main concepts underlying relational databases. These concepts will be discussed in greater depth in Chapter 8.

A relational database is made up of *named tables*, which may be divided *horizontally* into *unnamed rows*, and *vertically* into *named columns*. A particular row-column location is a *cell*. Each cell contains only one data *value*. Figure 2.6 shows how the information from Figure 2.5 would be stored in a relational database. The Employee table has three rows and three columns. The Speaks table has four rows and two columns. The number of rows of a table increases or decreases as data are added or deleted, but the number of columns stays the same.

In contrast to a conceptual database, a relational database allows facts of different types to be grouped into the same table. For example, Figure 2.6 groups the three elementary fact types into two tables. The Employee table caters for fact types F1 and F2, while the Speaks table caters for fact type F3.

The first row of the Employee table expresses two facts: the Employee with surname "Adams" works for the Department with name "Sales"; the Employee with surname "Adams" has the Gender with code "F". In general, *each row of a table in a relational database contains one or more elementary facts*.

With relational databases, care is needed in grouping fact types into tables. A later chapter provides a simple procedure for mapping a conceptual schema onto a relational schema. This procedure shows that the choice of tables in Figure 2.6 is correct. Suppose however, that we tried to group all three fact types into just one table. This would cause problems similar to those discussed earlier with the movie star example (Table 1.2).

Relational databases are based on the relational model of data developed by E. F. Codd. In this model, the table is the only data structure used. Within a table, duplicate rows are not allowed, and the order of the rows doesn't matter. We may treat a table as a set of rows, and each row as a sequence or *tuple* of data values (actually columns are "ordered" by their names rather than by position). So a table is a set of tuples. Since a relation may be defined mathematically as a set of tuples, each table is a *relation*: hence the name "relational database".

All tables must have different names. Within the same table, all columns must have different names. Columns are often called "fields", though this term is sometimes used for cells. Column names are also called *attribute* names. Each attribute is based on some *domain*, or pool of values from which the column values are drawn. For example, if we added a column for HeadOfDept this would have the same domain as EmpName. The relational concept of domain is connected to our conceptual notion of object type, but in practice most relational DBMSs offer little or no support for semantic domains.

We have seen how conceptual fact types map to table types in a relational schema. What about *constraints*? Relational systems typically supply only a few built-in constraint types. Columns may be specified as *mandatory* or optional for their table. In our example all the columns of the Employee table are mandatory (each entry must be an actual value, not a "null" value). This goes part of the way towards capturing the constraints that each employee is identified by name, works for at least one department and has at least one gender. To complete these constraints we demand that each employee referenced in the Speaks table is also mentioned in the Employee table (this is a *subset* or *referential integrity* constraint).

To restrict each employee to at most one department and at most one gender we demand that the EmpName column in the Employee table is *unique* (i.e. has no duplicates). This would typically be enforced by declaring EmpName a *primary key* for the Employee table (a key is a minimal combination of columns where no duplicates are allowed). In the relational model each table has a primary key which provides the primary way of accessing its rows. Finally, the constraint on Gender values may be enforced by a simple *check clause*.

The relational schema may be set out in diagram form as shown in Figure 2.7. Column names are placed in parentheses (round brackets) after the table name, and keys are underlined. By default, columns are assumed mandatory for their table. The dotted arrow expresses the subset constraint mentioned earlier. The possible values for gender codes are placed in braces (curly brackets). For simplicity, domains are omitted. The diagram shown is generic. Precisely how the tables are defined and the constraints are declared depends on the relational database language used (typically a dialect of SQL or QBE). We provide examples of this in a later chapter.

```
                                      {M,F}
Employee ( empname, dept, gender )
               ⇡
Speaks   ( empname, foreignLanguage )
```

Figure 2.7 The relational schema for Figure 2.5

The process of declaring or defining a schema is often called *data definition*, and the language component specially designed for this task is called a data definition language (DDL). Our example was simple enough for the relational schema to be fully specified within the DDL component of standard SQL. Often however, some constraints have to be coded separately.

In general, a relational schema may contain table definitions, constraints and derivation rules. Most derivation rules declared at the conceptual level may be specified in a relational DBMS by defining virtual tables (or "views") or by coding parametized routines. If a query type is commonly used and requires derivation, it is explicitly included in the derivation rules section of the conceptual schema. In contrast, *ad hoc* queries are catered for by including derivation functions and operators in the query language itself, so that the user may express the required derivation rule within the query formulation itself.

In a relational database language like SQL it is fairly easy to express many mathematical and logical derivation rules (e.g. averages, or grandparenthood derived from parenthood). Some derivation rules cannot be expressed in SQL, but can be easily expressed in other languages. For example, the following Prolog rules recursively define ancestry in terms of parenthood:

```
X is ancestor of Y if X is parent of Y.
X is ancestor of Y if X is parent of Z and Z is ancestor of Y.
```

Although recursive queries like these are unusual in a business application, if the need for them arises one solution is to provide an interface between the database language (e.g. SQL) and the other language (e.g. C or Prolog), so that the languages can "call" one another to do the tasks which they are best at. Languages like Prolog are often used in artificial intelligence (AI) applications. In the past, AI systems tended to work with small populations of a large number of complex fact types, and database systems worked with large populations of fewer and simpler fact types. One of the aims of next generation technology is to combine powerful inference capabilities with efficient database management.

Once the schema is defined, the *data manipulation* phase may begin. The tables, which are initially empty, may be populated with data (i.e. rows are *inserted*). After that, rows may be *deleted* or *modified*. A row is modified if one or more of its values is changed: this is sometimes called "update", but we use the term "update" to include insert, delete and modify operations. Collectively, these three operations are called *data maintenance*. If the constraints have been properly specified, the DBMS will automatically enforce them whenever a maintenance operation occurs.

Note that the row modify operation of a relational DBMS can be expressed conceptually in terms of adding, deleting or replacing elementary facts. For example, changing "Service" to "Sales" on the third row of the Employee table of Figure 2.6 corresponds to deleting the fact that Cooper works for the service department and adding the fact that Cooper works for the sales department. Of course, at the external level, the user would simply modify values in a screen version of a form (as in Figure 2.5) or a table row (as in Figure 2.6).

The other aspect of data manipulation is *data retrieval*. This typically involves three steps: the user requests information; the system searches the database and/or the schema to locate the relevant information, and uses this to obtain the required result; the system then outputs this result. The second stage may involve sorting data and/or deriving results (e.g. an average value). Unlike maintenance, retrieval operations leave the database unaltered.

Data presentation refers to special techniques for displaying information on the screen (screen display) or for producing formatted printed output (report writing). We use the term *"output report"* generically to include screen and hard copy reports. Typically, users of a relational database application do not interact directly with the relational tables in which the data is stored. Usually they enter and access the data via a *forms interface*. Issues such as design and management of screen forms, and *security* enforcement, usually constitute a major part of the application development.

For reasons such as correctness, clarity, completeness and portability, database designs should be first specified as conceptual schemas, before mapping them to relational schemas. The rest of the book is largely devoted to showing how to do this in detail.

2.4 Summary

An information system for a given application may be looked at from at least three levels: conceptual; external; and internal. At each level the formal model or knowledge base comprises a *schema* which describes the structure or design of the UoD, and a database which is populated with the fact instances. Each schema specifies what states and transitions are permitted for its database. The *conceptual schema* does this in terms of simple, human-oriented concepts. For the same global conceptual schema, different *external* schemas can be constructed for different user groups depending on what information is to be accessible and how the information is to be displayed. The *internal* schema specifies the physical storage and efficient access structures (e.g. indexes) for the specific DBMS being used to implement the application.

A conceptual schema comprises three main sections: *stored fact types*; *constraints*; and *derivation rules*. In specifying fact types we indicate what kinds of *object* there are, how these are *referenced* and what *roles* they play. Each role in a *relationship* is played by only one object type. The simplest kind of object is a *value* (character string or number). *Entities* are real or abstract objects which are identified by their relationship to values. For example, a country might be identified by its name. Constraints restrict the populations and transitions of fact types. For example, each city is the capital of at most one country. Derivation rules enable further facts to be derived from the facts that are stored.

Each fact in a conceptual database is elementary. The addition or deletion of a fact is a simple update. In a *compound transaction*, several simple updates may be included: in this case, constraints apply only to the net effect of the complete update sequence, not to each individual update. Updates and queries on a conceptual database or conceptual schema are responded to by the conceptual information processor (CIP).

Each DBMS conforms to a *logical* data model (e.g. network, hierarchic or relational). If a relational DBMS is chosen for the implementation, the conceptual schema is mapped to a *relational schema*, or relational database schema. Here all the stored facts are placed in named *tables*, with named columns and unnamed rows. Each row of a relational table corresponds to one or more elementary facts. Each cell (row-column position) contains only one value. Within a table, no row may be duplicated. The population of a relational table may be changed by inserting, deleting, or modifying a row. Most conceptual constraints and derivation rules can be expressed either within the relational DBMS language or by interfacing to another language.

Chapter notes

The classic discussion of the three architectural levels of an information system is given in Van Griethuysen (ed. 1982). Along with several other authors, we consider the relational model of data to be a *logical* model rather than a conceptual model, mainly because the former is too distant from natural language. With this viewpoint, a relational schema represents the logical portion of an internal schema (omitting details specific to the chosen DBMS, and storage and access details such as indexes). Codd (1990, pp. 33-4) proposes an alternative interpretation of the three-level architecture, in which the base relations of a relational databasc provide the conceptual schema, and views provide an external schema.

In this book many constraints and rules are set out textually in FORML (Formal Object-Role Modeling Language). This language is supported in both graphical and textual form in the InfoModeler CASE tool released by Asymetrix Corporation.

3 Developing an information system

3.1 Information systems life cycle

This section provides an overview of the life cycle of information systems, and the next section outlines the overall conceptual schema design procedure. The rest of the chapter discusses the first few steps in designing a conceptual schema: here we examine how to identify the fact types relevant to the universe of discourse, and display them clearly on a diagram. Later chapters show how to specify constraints on the fact types.

Developing an information system for a particular application is essentially a *problem solving* process. This general process may be broken down into four main stages: define the problem; devise a plan; execute the plan; evaluate what happened. Two of the most generally useful problem solving strategies are: divide the problem into a number of *subproblems* and deal with these individually; try a *simpler* version of the problem first.

When the problem solving process involves the development of computer software, it may be refined into the simple 5-stage *software life cycle* shown in Figure 3.1: *specify* (say what we need the software to do); *design* (decide how to do it); *implement* (code it); *test* (check that it works); *maintain* (keep it working). The arrows indicate the cyclic nature of the process. If a need for change is detected at a later stage of the cycle it is often necessary to return to one of the earlier stages.

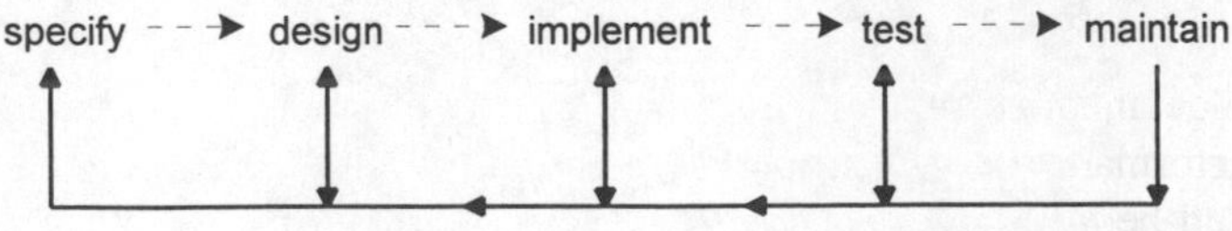

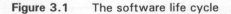

Figure 3.1 The software life cycle

Table 3.1 Typical phases of the information systems life cycle

- Feasibility study
- Requirements analysis
- Conceptual design
  - data
  - operations
- Logical design
  - data
  - operations
- External design
  - data
  - operations
- Prototyping
- Completion of internal design
  - data
  - operations
- Implementation of production version
- Testing and validation
- Maintenance

When the software to be developed is an information system, this cycle may be refined further, as shown in Table 3.1. In practice, the phases listed in Table 3.1 often overlap, feedback cycles are common, and some phases might be omitted. A **feasibility study** identifies the main objectives of the proposed information system and determines which components may be implemented with known resources (e.g. budget allocations). It examines the cost-effectiveness of alternative proposals and assigns priorities to the various system components. The cost/benefit analysis might reveal that some objectives are unrealistic, or that some of the objectives can be best achieved by improved manual procedures rather than by use of computers.

Assuming the go-ahead for the project is given, a detailed **requirements analysis** is undertaken to determine just what the system is required to do. Various components of the system are delineated, and people familiar with the relevant application areas are interviewed, including application experts, intended users and policy makers. Interviews may be supplemented by questionnaires. Relevant documentation (e.g. forms, reports, charts, policy manuals) is examined. Where no such documentation is available, the UoD experts are requested to invent examples of the kind of information which has to be maintained. Simple diagrams are often used to clarify how the information system is to interact with the business environment. The main operations or transactions to be supported are identified and prioritized, and estimates are made of their expected data volumes, frequencies and required response times.

The output of this requirements collection and analysis phase is a *requirements specifications* document, which details functional requirements, non-functional requirements (e.g. performance) and maintenance information (e.g. anticipated changes). This document should be *unambiguous*, *complete*, *verifiable* (there is some way of checking whether the requirements are satisfied), *consistent* (requirements do not contradict one another), *modifiable* (changes can be made easily and safely), *traceable* (requirements can be tracked to their origins, and are identifiable across different versions of the document), and *usable* (by current and future users of the document).

Various textual and graphical notations are used for different aspects of the requirements specification, and CASE tools are beginning to provide support for this phase. We look at some of the notations in use (e.g. context diagrams, data flow diagrams) later in the book. For large, complex projects the requirements analysis stage might take several months. As fact-oriented modeling uses verbalization of familiar examples to clarify the UoD, its conceptual design method is useful for requirements analysis as well as design.

With the understanding that phases may overlap, the next stage in the information systems life cycle is **conceptual design**. With large applications, subproblems of a more manageable size might be selected and a conceptual *subschema* designed for each. The various subschemas may then be *integrated* within a *global* conceptual schema. In this text, the problems we discuss are typically small enough to enable us to design the whole conceptual schema without the need to first design subschemas. We will however break the design process up into various stages. For example, we identify the fact types before adding constraints.

Experienced modelers often notice similarities between new applications and previous ones they have designed. In this case, significant savings in the design effort may result from judicious **reuse** of design strategies adopted in their earlier models. For example, if we have already modeled a university library system, and now have to model a videotape rental business, there are many features of the earlier model which may be reused. We might choose to identify an object type Loan in a similar way, and either adopt or adapt several fact types from the earlier application. By abstracting similar, specific concepts (e.g. "book", "videotape") to more general concepts (e.g. "rentable item"), it is easier to recognize a new application as related to earlier ones.

A comparative survey of information systems design methods (Olle et al., 1991) identifies three design perspectives. The *data-oriented perspective* focuses on what kinds of data are stored in the database, what constraints apply to these data, and what kinds of data are derivable. Because of its fundamental and more stable nature, this is the perspective given emphasis in this text.

The *process-oriented perspective* is concerned with the processes or activities performed in the application area. This perspective may help humans to understand the way a particular business operates. Processes are described, and the direction in which information flows between processes and other components is made clear. Often, a complex process is refined into several subprocesses.

The *behavior-oriented perspective* is concerned with how *events* in the outside world or the information system trigger actions in the information system, and in general with what temporal or "causal" constraints apply between events. The distinction between "process" and "event" is somewhat fuzzy, and in some cases an activity analysis may be rephrased in terms of an event analysis, or vice versa.

The most important thing is to specify the information needed and conditions sufficient for a process to execute or "fire". For example, the process of retrieving an account balance might be triggered by the event of a client requesting an account balance, and require input of information from the client (e.g. client number and account type) as well as from the relevant database tables.

In Table 3.1 the term "*operations*" includes both processes and behavior. Further discussion of these two perspectives is postponed until much later in the text. For the next several chapters we concentrate on the data perspective.

If correctly designed, the conceptual schema provides a formal model of the structure of the UoD. Once this semantic modeling is completed, we select the class of DBMS to be used, and perform a *mapping* of the conceptual design to a **logical design** expressed in terms of the generic data model of the DBMS. For example, we might map a conceptual schema to a relational schema or a network schema. Some CASE tools can perform this mapping automatically.

The **external design** of an information system involves determining which kinds of data and operations will be accessible to which user-groups, and designing the appropriate human-computer interfaces for these groups. Typically, access-rights tables are constructed for different user types, decisions are made about what functions to support on different screen forms, and the layout of screen forms and menus is decided.

Except for trivial applications, the next stage of the life cycle usually involves **prototyping**. A prototype is a simplified version of the intended product, which is used to gain early feedback from the users on the quality of the design. It aims to cover the major functions in the requirements specification, but usually omits most of the error-checking and finer details required for the final version, and it uses only a small set of sample data. Early feedback is more important than efficiency at this stage, so the prototype might be coded in a higher level language than the one(s) ultimately used for the product. The prototype is coded and demonstrated to the clients, and their feedback is used to revise the requirements and designs where necessary.

Once a prototype is accepted, the **internal design** of the full product can be completed. The logical design is adapted to the specific DBMS being used, and various strategies (e.g. indexes or clustering) are specified to improve the efficiency of the physical design.

The **implementation** of the internal design is now completed by writing the actual code for the full production version. The product is now subjected to extensive **testing and validation**. The software is run using carefully chosen databases to check that it functions as expected. Selected users might then be issued with pre-release versions to help find other errors. With certain types of software (e.g. military security systems), correctness proofs may be developed to ensure the program meets its specifications.

We use the term "software **maintenance**" to mean the modification of software after it has been initially released. This maintenance may be of three main types: *corrective* (eliminate bugs); *adaptive* (alter software to cater for changes in the environment or UoD); and *perfective* (add improvements).

In developing information systems, various factors are considered generally important. These include practicality (is use of a computer the best way to solve the problem?), correctness, clarity (designs and code should be readable and well documented), efficiency (memory requirements, speed, production costs), portability, maintainability, adaptability, user-proofing and support.

For large commercial software projects using third generation languages, maintenance typically involves over half of the total cost. The use of higher level languages is associated with a shift of emphasis towards the first two stages of the software life cycle. If the specification and design are done properly, there is comparatively little programming, testing and maintenance required. Hence the use of conceptual modeling techniques and fourth generation software can dramatically reduce the total costs.

3.2 The conceptual schema design procedure

When developing an information system, we first specify what is required and produce a design to meet these requirements. For reasons outlined earlier, we first develop this design at the conceptual level using Object-Role Modeling (ORM). That is, we attempt to formally describe the structure of the UoD in terms of an ORM conceptual schema. In this book we often abbreviate "ORM conceptual schema" to just "conceptual schema".

Object-role modeling is so called because it views the application world in terms of objects playing roles. It is also called "fact-oriented modeling" since it expresses the information in terms of simple facts. Following work on semantic modeling in the early 1970s, various versions of the approach were developed, including BRM (Binary Relationship Modeling), NIAM (Natural language Information Analysis Method), MOON (Normalized Object-Oriented Method), NORM (Natural Object Relationship Model) and PSM (Predicator Set Model). The FORM (Formal ORM) method described in this book is based on extensions to NIAM .

Two main developers of NIAM were E. D. Falkenberg and G. M. Nijssen, currently professors at Dutch universities. Among other things, Falkenberg provided an object-role framework based on use of natural language, while Nijssen saw the need for a design procedure which started with specific examples, using intuitive diagrams that could be easily populated for validation purposes. The term "Object-Role Modeling" originally used by Falkenberg for his modeling framework, is now used generically to cover the various versions of the modeling approach.

Subtyping was added by Prof. R. A. Meersman. Later, T. A. Halpin (the author) provided a rigorous formalization, and added several extensions and refinements. Other contributors to the general fact-oriented approach include J. Abrial, O. De Troyer, H. Habrias, A. ter Hofstede, W. Kent, L. Mark, H. Proper, M. Senko, P. Shoval, F. van Assche, T. van der Weide and D. Vermeir. Besides the extensive research at universities in Australia, Europe, Israel and the USA, various commercial firms such as Asymetrix, CapGemini-Pandata, Control Data, ITS and TopSystems have engaged in research and development to provide CASE tool support for the method.

We refer to the procedure for designing a conceptual schema which is small enough to manage as a single unit as the **Conceptual Schema Design Procedure (CSDP)**. With large applications, the universe of discourse is divided into sub-sections (which may overlap), and a conceptual *subschema* is designed for each. Finally the subschemas are *integrated* or merged into a global conceptual schema which covers the whole UoD. Table 3.2 summarizes this top-down design approach.

Table 3.2 Top-down approach for designing large conceptual schemas

- Divide the universe of discourse into manageable sub-sections
- Apply the CSDP to each sub-section
- Integrate the subschemas into a global conceptual schema

Table 3.3 The conceptual schema design procedure (CSDP)

Step	
1.	Transform familiar information examples into elementary facts, and apply quality checks.
2.	Draw the fact types, and apply a population check.
3.	Check for entity types that should be combined, and note any arithmetic derivations.
4.	Add uniqueness constraints, and check arity of fact types.
5.	Add mandatory role constraints, and check for logical derivations.
6.	Add value, set comparison and subtyping constraints.
7.	Add other constraints and perform final checks.

For each manageably sized application we typically develop the conceptual schema design in **seven steps**, as set out in Table 3.3. The procedure begins with the analysis of examples of information to be output by, or input to, the information system. Basically, the first three steps are concerned with identifying the fact types. In later steps we add constraints to the fact types. Throughout the procedure, checks are performed to detect derived facts and to ensure that no mistakes have been made. In the rest of this chapter we consider the first three steps in detail.

With large applications, the preliminary segmentation and final integration add two further stages, resulting in nine steps overall. Although the CSDP is best learnt in the sequence of steps shown, in practice one might apply the steps somewhat differently. For example, one might add constraints as soon as the fact types are entered, rather than waiting for all the fact types to be entered before adding any constraints.

In the commercial world there are many existing applications which have been implemented using lower level approaches, resulting in database designs that may be inconsistent, incomplete, inefficient or difficult to maintain. Such systems are often poorly documented. These problems can be overcome by **re-engineering** the existing applications using conceptual modeling techniques. For example, sample populations from existing database tables can be used as input to the CSDP.

Even without sample populations, an existing database schema can be *reverse-engineered* to an incomplete, tentative conceptual schema by using information about constraints and domains, and making simplifying assumptions about use of names; the conceptual design can then be validated and completed by communicating with a UoD expert. Designs that have been formulated in terms of ER diagrams can also be reverse-engineered. Once the conceptual schema is determined, it can be *forward-engineered* by applying a conceptual optimization procedure and then mapping to the target database system to provide an improved and maintainable implementation. This re-engineering approach is discussed in section 9.7.

3.3 CSDP step 1: From examples to elementary facts

To specify what is required of an information system, we need to answer the question: *What sort of information do we want from the system?* Clearly, any information to be output from the system must be either stored in the system, or be derivable by the system. To get a detailed and clear picture of how this should be done, we use a conceptual schema design procedure.

Our first step is to begin with *familiar examples* of relevant information, and *express these in terms of elementary facts*. As a check on the quality of our work, we ask the following questions. *Are the entities well identified? Can the facts be split into smaller ones without losing information?*

CSDP step 1: Transform familiar examples into elementary facts, and apply quality checks

If we are designing a conceptual schema for an application that was previously handled either manually or by computer, information examples will be readily available. If not, we work with the UoD expert to provide some examples. Two important types of examples are output reports and input forms. These might appear as tables, forms, diagrams or text. If we are to verbalize such examples in terms of elementary facts, we should understand what an **elementary fact** is.

To begin with, an elementary fact is a simple assertion about the UoD. The word "fact" indicates that the system is to treat the assertion as being true of the UoD (whether this is actually the case is of no concern to the system). Although in everyday speech, unless something is true of the real world it cannot be a fact, in computing terminology we resign ourselves to the fact(!) that it is possible to have "false facts" in the database (just as we agree to use the word "statement" for things that aren't really statements in languages like Pascal). We may think of the UoD as a set of *objects playing roles*. Elementary facts are assertions that particular objects play particular roles. The simplest kind of elementary fact asserts that a single object plays a given role. For example:

1. Ann smokes

Here we have one object (Ann) playing a role (smokes). We later demand a more rigorous scheme for identifying objects (e.g. "Ann" is expanded to "the person with firstname 'Ann'"). With sentences like (1) the role played by the object is sometimes called a *property* of the object. Here an elementary fact asserts that a certain object has a certain property. This is also called a *unary relationship*, since only one role is involved. Usually however, a relationship involves at least two roles. For example:

2. Ann employs Bob.
3. Ann employs Ann.

In (2) Ann plays the role of employer and Bob plays the role of employee. In (3) Ann is self-employed, and plays both roles. In general, *an elementary fact asserts that a particular object has a property, or that one or more particular objects participate together in a relationship*.

The adjective "elementary" indicates that the fact *cannot be "split" into smaller units of information* which collectively provide the same information as the original. Elementary facts do not use logical connectives (e.g. **not**, **and**, **or**, **if**) or logical quantifiers (e.g. **all**, **some**). For example, sentences (4)—(9) are not elementary facts.

4. Ann smokes **and** Bob smokes.

5. Ann smokes **or** Bob smokes.
6. Ann does **not** smoke.
7. **If** Bob smokes **then** Bob is cancer prone.
8. **All** people who smoke are cancer prone.
9. **If any** person smokes **then that** person is cancer prone.

All of these sentences express information. Proposition (4) is a logical conjunction: it should be split into two elementary facts: Ann smokes; Bob smokes. Proposition (5) is a disjunction, (6) is a negation, and (7) is a conditional fact: most database systems do not allow such information to be stored conveniently, and are incapable of making relevant inferences (e.g. deducing that Bob smokes from (5) and (6)). For most commercial applications, there is no need to store such information.

Negative information might be irrelevant and infeasibly large to store. Often the absence of positive information (e.g. Ann smokes) is taken to imply the negative (Ann does not smoke); such "closed world" assumptions are discussed in a later chapter. If required, negative information can be explicitly stored by negative predicates (e.g. is a non-smoker) connected by an exclusion constraint to the positive predicate (e.g. smokes), or by a functional fact type with a value-restricted object type (e.g. Person has SmokingStatus {'S', 'NS'}). We discuss these approaches later.

Universally quantified conditionals like (8) and (9) may be catered for either in terms of a subset constraint (see later) or by a derivation rule. Such rules can be specified readily in SQL by means of a view, and are also easily coded in Prolog. For example: cancer_prone(X) **if** person(X) **and** smokes(X).

Elementary facts assert that objects play roles. How are these objects and roles specified? For now we consider only basic objects: these are either *values or entities*. For our work it is sufficient to recognize two kinds of **value**: *character string* and *number*. These are identified by constants. Character strings are shown inside quotes (e.g. 'USA'). Numbers are denoted without quotes, using the usual Hindu-Arabic decimal notation (e.g. 37 or 5.2). Numbers are abstract objects denoted by character strings called numerals. For example, the number 37 is denoted by the numeral '37'. We assume that any information system supports strings and numbers as built-in data types. Values are displayed textually, but are internally represented by bit-strings.

Conceptually, an **entity** (e.g. a particular person or car) is referenced in an information system by means of a *definite description*. For example, kangaroos hop about on an entity identified as "the Country with name 'Australia'". Entities may also be called "described objects". Unlike values, some entities can change with time. An entity may be a tangible object (e.g. the City with name 'Paris') or an abstract object (e.g. the Subject with code 'CS114'). We consider both entities and values to be objects that exist in the UoD. Usually we want to talk about just the entities, but to reference them we make use of values. Sometimes we want to talk about the values themselves. Consider the following sentences:

10. Australia has six states.
11. "Australia" has nine letters.

Here we have an illustration of what logicians call the use/mention distinction. In (10) the word "Australia" is being used as a label to reference some entity. In (11) the word

"Australia" is being mentioned, and refers to itself. In natural language, quotes are used to resolve this distinction. In everyday talk, entities are often referred to by a *proper name* (e.g. "Bill Clinton") or by some definite description (e.g. "the president of the USA", or "the president with name 'Bill Clinton'"). Proper names work if we can decide what the name refers to from the context of the sentence. For example, in (10) you probably took "Australia" to refer to the country named "Australia". However, the sentence itself does not tell you this. Perhaps (10) was talking about a dog named "Australia" who has six moods (sleepy, playful, hungry etc.).

Since humans may misinterpret, and information systems lack any creativity to add context, we play it safe by demanding that entities be clearly identified by special kinds of definite descriptions. To begin with, the description must specify the kind of entity being referred to: the **entity type**. A *type* is the set of all possible *instances*. Each entity is an instance of a particular entity type (e.g. Person, Subject). For a given UoD, the entity type Person is the set of all people we might possibly want to talk about during the lifetime of the information system. Note that some authors use the word "entity" for "entity type". We sometimes expand "entity" to "entity instance" to avoid any confusion. Consider the sentence:

12. Lee is located in 10B.

This could be talking about a horse located in a stable, or a computer in a room, etc. By stating the entity types involved, (13) avoids this kind of referential ambiguity. Names of object types are highlighted by starting them with a Capital letter.

13. The Patient 'Lee' is located in the Ward '10B'.

This brings to mind the old joke: "*Question:* Did you hear about the man with the wooden leg named 'Smith'? *Answer:* No—What was the name of his other leg?". Here the responder mistakenly took the label "Smith" to refer to an entity of type WoodenLeg rather than of type Man. Sometimes, even stating the entity type fails to fully clarify the situation. Consider the following sentence:

14. The Patient 'Lee' has a Temperature of 37.

Now imagine that the UoD contains two patients named "Lee Jones" and "Mary Lee". There is more than one person to which the label "Lee" might apply. Worse still, there may be some confusion about the units being used to state the temperature: 37 degrees Celsius is normal bodily temperature but 37 degrees Fahrenheit is close to freezing! We resolve this ambiguity by including the **reference mode** (i.e. the manner in which the value refers to the entity). Compare the following two sentences:

15. The Patient with surname 'Lee' has a Temperature of 37 Celsius.
16. The Patient with firstname 'Lee' has a Temperature of 37 Fahrenheit.

A more common way around the potential confusion caused by overlap of firstnames and surnames would be to demand that a longer name be used instead (e.g. "Lee Jones", "Mary Lee"). In some cases however, even these names may not be unique, and another naming convention must be employed (e.g. PatientNr). To avoid confusing "No." with the word "No", we use "Nr" or "#" to abbreviate "Number".

From now on, we usually demand that each entity designator involve three components:

entity type	e.g.	Patient	Temperature
reference mode		surname	Celsius
value		'Lee'	37

This is the simplest kind of entity designation scheme; and we restrict ourselves to it for quite some time. Composite identification schemes are considered later.

Now that we know how to specify objects, how do we specify the roles they play? The approach we adopt is to use logical **predicates**. In logic, a predicate is basically a *sentence with object-holes in it*. To complete the sentence, the object-holes or place-holders are filled in by *object-terms*. Each object-term refers to a single object in the UoD. Object-terms are also called singular terms, or object-designators. For us, values are designated by constants (sometimes preceded by the value-type name), and entities are designated by definite descriptions which relate values to entities. Consider the following sentence:

17. The Person with firstname 'Ann' **smokes**.

Here the object-term is "The Person with firstname 'Ann'", and the predicate identifier is shown in **bold**. The predicate may be shown by itself as:

... smokes

This is a *unary predicate*, or *sentence with one object-hole* in it. It may also be called a property, or a unary relationship type. A *binary predicate* is a *sentence with two object-holes*. Consider the example:

18. The Person with firstname 'Ann' **employs** the Person with firstname 'Bob'.

Here the predicate may be shown as:

... employs ...

Notice that the *order* in which the objects are placed here is important. For example, even though Ann employs Bob, it may be false that Bob employs Ann. A *ternary predicate* is a *sentence with three object-holes*. For instance, the fact that Terry has worked in the Computer Science Department for seven years involves the predicate:

... has worked in ... for ...

In general, an *n-ary predicate* is a sentence with *n* object-holes. Since the order is significant, a filled-in *n*-ary predicate is associated with a *sequence* of *n* object-terms, not necessarily distinct. The value of *n* is said to be the **arity**, or degree, of the predicate. Predicates of arity ≥ 2 are said to be polyadic. An elementary fact may now be thought of as asserting a proposition of the form:

$Ro_1 \ldots o_n$

where *R* is a predicate of arity *n*, and $o_1 \ldots o_n$ are *n* object-terms, not necessarily distinct; moreover, with respect to the UoD the proposition must not be splittable into a conjunction of simpler propositions. This definition ties in with the notation of *predicate logic*.

Table 3.4 Some languages and their designers

Designer	*Language*
Wirth	Pascal
Kay	Smalltalk
Wirth	Modula-2

For naturalness, we write predicates in *mixfix* (or distfix) form, where the terms may be mixed in with the predicate. For example, the following ternary fact uses the predicate "... moved to ... during ... ".

19. The Scientist with surname 'Einstein' **moved to** the Country with code 'USA' **during** the Year 1933 AD.

Step 1 of the CSDP involves translating relevant information examples into sentences like this. As a simple example, consider the output report of Table 3.4. Try now to express the information in the first row in the form of elementary facts. To help with this, use the *telephone heuristic*. Imagine you have to convey the information over the telephone to someone. In performing this visual to auditory transformation, make sure you fully specify each entity in terms of its entity type, reference mode and value, and that you include the predicate name.

In reports like this, the column headings and table names or captions often give a clue as to the object types and predicates. The column entries provide the values. Here is one way of translating row 1 as an elementary fact:

20. The Person with surname 'Wirth' **designed** the Language with name 'Pascal'.

Notice that the entity types and reference modes appear as nouns, and the predicate as a verb phrase. This is fairly typical. In translating row 1 into the elementary fact (20), we read the row from left to right. If instead we read it from right to left, we would come up with something like this:

21. The Language with name 'Pascal' **was designed by** the Person with surname 'Wirth'.

In reversing the order of the terms, we also reversed the predicate. We speak of "was designed by" as the *inverse* of the predicate "designed". Although semantically we might regard sentences (20) and (21) as expressing the same fact, syntactically they are different. Most logicians would describe this as a case of two different sentences expressing the same proposition. Linguists like to describe this situation by saying the two sentences have different *surface structures* but the same deep structure.

For example, one linguistic analysis might portray the *deep structure* sentence as comprising a verb phrase (Design), various noun phrases (the object-terms) each of which relates to the verb in a different case (e.g. agentive for Wirth, and objective for Pascal), together with a modality (past tense). Different viewpoints exist as to the "correct" way to portray deep structures (e.g. what primitives to select), and the task of translation to deep structures is often complex. In practice, most information systems can be designed without delving further into such issues.

Table 3.5 An output report about marriages

Married couples	
Adam	Eve
Jim	Mary

It is important not to treat sentences like (20) and (21) as different, unrelated facts. Our approach with binary fact types is to choose one standard way of stating the predicate, but optionally allow the inverse reading to be shown as well. For example:

22. The Person with surname 'Wirth' **designed / was designed by** the Language with name 'Pascal'.

Here the predicate on the left of the slash "/" is used for the standard (left-to-right) reading (20). The predicate on the right of the slash is used for the inverse reading (21). The slash visually suggests jumping over the other predicate when reading left-to-right, and jumping under the other predicate when reading right-to-left. Having two ways to talk about a binary fact type can help communication, and can simplify constraint specification. For example, the specification "each Language was designed by some Person" is preferable to the equivalent "for each Language, some Person designed that Language)". For non-binary fact types there are many possible orderings, and a different scheme is used for providing alternative readings (not discussed in this book).

As another example, consider Table 3.5. This is a bit harder to verbalize since the columns don't have separate names. You may assume that Adam and Jim are males and that Eve and Mary are females. As an exercise, express the information on the top row in terms of elementary facts before reading on. Perhaps you verbalized this as shown in (23). For completeness we have included the inverse.

23. The Person with firstname 'Adam' **is married to / is married to** the Person with firstname 'Eve'.

Notice that the standard predicate is the same as the inverse. This is an example of a *symmetric* relationship. Such relationships create special problems (as discussed in a later chapter). To help avoid such problems, at the conceptual level *no predicate should be the same as its inverse*. You can always rephrase the fact to ensure this. For example, (24) does this by highlighting the different roles played by each partner.

24. The Person with firstname 'Adam' **is husband of / is wife of** the Person with firstname 'Eve'.

As another example, consider Table 3.6. This is like our earlier Table 3.4 but with an extra column added. Try to express the information on the first row in terms of elementary facts, before reading on. We might at first consider expressing this information as sentence (25), using the ternary predicate "... designed ... in ...". Do you see any problems with this?

25. The Person with surname 'Wirth' **designed** the Language with name 'Pascal' **in** the Year 1971 AD.

Table 3.6

Designer	*Language*	*Year*
Wirth	Pascal	1971
Kay	Smalltalk	1972
Wirth	Modula-2	1979

Recall that an elementary fact must be simple or irreducible. It cannot be split into two or more simpler facts in the context of the UoD. The appearance of the word "and" in a sentence usually indicates that the sentence may be split into simpler facts. Here there is no "and", but "common sense" tells us that the fact can be split into the following two elementary facts with no information loss:

26. The Person with surname 'Wirth' designed the Language with name 'Pascal'.
27. The Language with name 'Pascal' was designed in the Year 1971 AD.

Here "no information loss" means that if we know (26) and (27) then we also know (25). The phrase "common sense" hides some formal ideas. In order to split (25) into (26) and (27) we need to know that each language was designed in only one year (or that each language had only one designer). In Step 4 of the CSDP we add a formal check to reveal this dependency. So if our "common sense" fails us here, we will pick up this error at a later stage. For now though, let's work with our intuitions. Suppose we split the ternary into the two binaries: Person designed Language; Person carried out design in Year. Would this be acceptable? As an exercise, use the table's population to show that this kind of split would actually lose information.

After you have had plenty of practice at Step 1, you may wish to write the elementary facts down in abbreviated form. To start with, we drop words such as "the" and "with" where they introduce object types and reference modes. Reference modes are placed in parentheses after the object types. A "+" indicates the referencing value is numeric, and hence may appear in addition (+) and other numeric operations.

In some cases we might shorten some identifiers used for object types, reference modes and predicates so long as the shorter names are still meaningful to us. Don't forget to start the name of object types with a capital letter. We usually start the name of reference modes with a small letter, unless capitals have significance (e.g. "AD"). For example, facts (26) and (27) may be set out more concisely as (26′) and (27′).

26′. Person (surname) 'Wirth' designed Language (name) 'Pascal'.
27′. Language (name) 'Pascal' was designed in Year (AD) 1971.

To save more writing still, the reference schemes for entity types are declared once only up-front. Then the reference modes may be omitted in setting out the facts. For example, (26) and (27) may be specified as:

Reference schemes:	Person (surname); Language (name); Year (AD) +
Facts:	Person 'Wirth' designed Language 'Pascal'. Language 'Pascal' was designed in Year 1971.

Even more conveniently, a fact type may be displayed in diagram form (see next section), and facts may be entered into its associated fact table simply by entering the values. The InfoModeler CASE tool for FORML can automatically translate between any of these representations, and is very flexible in the way it allows facts to be expressed.

The task of defining a formal grammar sufficient to capture any sentence expressed in natural language is daunting, partly because of the many ways in which objects may be referenced. For example, consider the sentence: "The next person to step on my toe will cop it". Some artificial intelligence research is directed towards sorting out the semantics in sentences like this.

Fortunately for us, such sentences don't appear in database tables, where simple value-based schemes are used to reference objects. Our approach is capable of formally capturing the relevant semantics of any fact that can be represented in a database table. Structured object-terms and predicates provide the logical deep structure, independent of the natural language (English, Japanese etc.) used to express the fact. By supporting ordered, mixfix predicates FORML enables this deep structure to be expressed in a surface structure in harmony with the ordered, mixfix nature of natural language.

Consider Figure 3.2. Here the two tables convey the same fact in different languages. The fact may be expressed in English as (28) and in Japanese as (29). The reference modes are italicized and the predicates are in bold.

28. The Employee with *employee#* '37' **works in** the Department with *name* 'Sales'.
29. Jugyo in *jugyo in bango* '37' **wa** 'Eigyo' to iu *namae* no Ka **ni shozoku suru**.

These are parsed into the structures shown in 28′ and 29′. They have the same deep structure. Object terms are enclosed in square brackets. The infix predicate "... works in ..." corresponds to the mixfix predicate "... wa ... ni shozoku suru".

28′. [Employee (*employee#*) '37'] **works in** [Department (*name*) 'Sales'].
29′. [Jugyo in (*jugyo in bango*) '37'] **wa** [Ka (*namae*) 'Eigyo'] **ni shozoku suru**.

Although we prefer to use ordered, mixfix predicates for naturalness, another approach is to treat a fact as a named set of (object, role) pairs: $F\{(o_1,r_1),\ldots,(o_n,r_n)\}$. Here each object o_i is paired with the role r_i that it plays in the fact F. For example, (22) might be specified as: Design{ (The Person with surname 'Wirth', agentive), (The Language with name 'Pascal', objective) }. Instead of the case-adjectives "agentive" and "objective", other role names could be used (e.g. "designer" and "language", or "designing" and "being designed by"). By pairing objects with their roles, the order in which the pairs are listed is irrelevant. This approach is used in RIDL (Reference and Idea Language). An example of a RIDL formulation is given in section 8.1.

Now consider the output report of Table 3.7, and try to express the information contained in its top row in terms of one or more elementary facts. Here the table itself has a name ("Result"), which can help us with the interpretation.

Employee#	*Department*
37	Sales

Jugyo in	*Ka*
37	Eigyo

Figure 3.2 The same fact in English and Japanese

Table 3.7

Result:	*student*	*subject*	*rating*
	Bright S	CS112	7
	Bright S	CS100	6
	Collins T	CS112	4
	Jones E	CS100	7
	Jones E	CS112	4
	Jones E	MP104	4

To save writing later, let us declare the reference schemes: Student (name); Subject (code); and Rating (nr)+. Because this table looks similar to Table 3.6, you might have been tempted to try to split the information into two facts. For example:

30. The Student 'Bright S' **studied** the Subject 'CS112'.
31. The Student 'Bright S' **scored** the Rating 7.

This approach is incorrect because it results in loss of information. Since Bright studies more than one subject, we don't know for sure from these two facts that Bright's 7 rating is for CS112. In some cases a ternary which is not splittable into two facts may be split into three facts. Here we might try to split the information into the above two facts as well as:

32. The Rating 7 **was obtained for** the Subject 'CS112'.

However even these three facts don't guarantee that Bright got a 7 for CS112. For example, Jones studied CS112, Jones scored a 7, and a 7 was obtained for CS112, but Jones did not score a 7 in CS112. So the whole of the first row should be expressed as one elementary fact. For example, using the predicate "... for ... scored ..." we obtain:

33. The Student 'Bright S' **for** the Subject 'CS112' **scored** the Rating 7.

Notice that we chose to think of a rating not as a number, but as an entity which is referenced by a number. This has two advantages. Suppose that students are rated numerically on their exam performance and are also rated numerically on their popularity. In this case we have the object types ExamRating and PopularityRating. Is an exam rating of 7 the same thing as a popularity rating of 7? We feel it is natural to answer "No—Only the numbers are the same".

If we treated ratings as numbers we would have to answer "Yes" to the previous question. We prefer to think of ratings as entities rather than as numbers. Another advantage of this approach is that decisions about preferred reference schemes can be delayed until the conceptual schema is to be mapped to a logical schema. For example, exam ratings are often given in both numbers and codes. A 7 might correspond to "HD" (high distinction). With our approach, the same rating is involved no matter which way we reference it.

As another example, consider the report shown in Table 3.8. Try step 1 yourself on this table before reading on. One of the tricky features of this table is the final column. Entries in this column are sets of degrees, not single degrees.

Table 3.8

Lecturer:	*name*	*birthyear*	*age*	*degrees*
	Adams JB	1946	46	BSc, PhD
	Leung X	1960	32	BE, MSc
	O'Reilly TA	1946	46	BA, BSc, PhD

You should phrase your sentences to include only one degree at a time. When applied to the first row, step 1 results in four facts which may be set out as follows.

34. The Lecturer with name 'Adams JB' **was born in** the Year 1946 AD.
35. The Lecturer with name 'Adams JB' **has** the Age 42 years.
36. The Lecturer with name 'Adams JB' **holds** the Degree with code 'BSc'.
37. The Lecturer with name 'Adams JB' **holds** the Degree with code 'PhD'

Here the entity types and reference modes are: Lecturer (name); Year (AD)+; Age (years)+; and Degree (code). There are three fact types: Lecturer **was born in** Year; Lecturer **has** Age; Lecturer **holds** Degree. The entity types Year and Age are semantically different. For example, Year involves a starting point in time, whereas Age is a merely a duration of time.

A harder example is shown in Table 3.9. This is a an extract of a report listing details of tutorial groups. Perform step 1 yourself before reading on.

Since verbalization of an example involves interpretation, it is important that the kind of example is *familiar* to us or another person (e.g. the UoD expert) who is assisting us with step 1. One way to verbalize the top row of this report is as follows:

38. The TuteGroup with code 'A' **meets at** the Time with dayhrcode 'Mon 3 p.m.'.
39. The TuteGroup with code 'A' **meets in** the Room with room# 'CS-718'.
40. The Student with student# 302156 **belongs to** the TuteGroup with code 'A'.
41. The Student with student# 302156 **has** the StudentName 'Bloggs FB'.

Table 3.9 An output report indicating tutorial allocations

Tute group	*Time*	*Room*	*Student#*	*Student name*
A	Mon. 3 p.m.	CS-718	302156	Bloggs FB
			180064	Fletcher JB
			278155	Jackson M
			334067	Jones EP
			200140	Kawamoto T
B1	Tue. 2 p.m.	E-B18	266010	Anderson AB
			348112	Bloggs FB
...	...	...	...	...

There are many features in this example that rely on interpretation. For instance, we assumed that Student# and StudentName refer to students, and that if a student number and student name occur on the same row then they refer to the same student. We also filled in the associations "meets at", "meets in", "belongs to", "has". The report itself does not tell us this: we use our background familiarity with the situation to make these assumptions.

We also made decisions about entity types and their reference schemes. For example, we chose to think of Time as an entity type referenced by a day-hour-code rather than introducing Day and Hour as separate entity types. A similar comment applies to Room and StudentName. We selected Student# rather than StudentName to identify Student: the report helps here since Student# appears first (on the left) and "Bloggs FB" appears with two different student numbers; but we are still making assumptions (e.g. we assumed that students have only one student number, or that students belong to only one group). Another major assumption is that each tutorial group meets only once a week. We need to know this to justify using separate facts for the time and room (rather than verbalizing this as: TuteGroup meets at Time in Room). Of course the fact that group *A* is not repeated in the report helps us with this decision; but we have assumed the sample is representative in this regard.

Since interpretation is always involved in the initial step, if we are not familiar with the kind of example we should resolve any doubts by contacting a person who is familiar with the UoD. We stress that communication with the UoD expert and end-users should make use of examples familiar to these people. Although we as schema designers might be expert in expressing ourselves at a formal, type level the same cannot be said of the average user for which the application is being designed. By working with examples familiar to the user we can tap that user's implicit understanding of the UoD without forcing the user to abstract and express, perhaps incorrectly, the structure we are seeking.

Notice that sentence (41) expresses a relationship between an entity (a student) and a value (a student name). When verbalizing facts in this way, the **value type** is stated just before the value (e.g. StudentName 'Bloggs FB'). Unlike entity-terms, value-terms do not include a reference mode. In the next section we discuss the connection between value-types and reference modes.

With many kinds of reports it is sometimes useful to draw a connection between the relevant fields as we verbalize the corresponding fact. For example, we might add links between the columns of Table 3.9 as shown in Figure 3.3. This informal summary of the fact types may help us to see if some connections have been missed (each field is normally involved in at least one connection).

Besides tables, *forms* are a common source of information examples. These are more often used for input than output, but may be used for both (e.g. the personnel forms considered in the previous chapter).

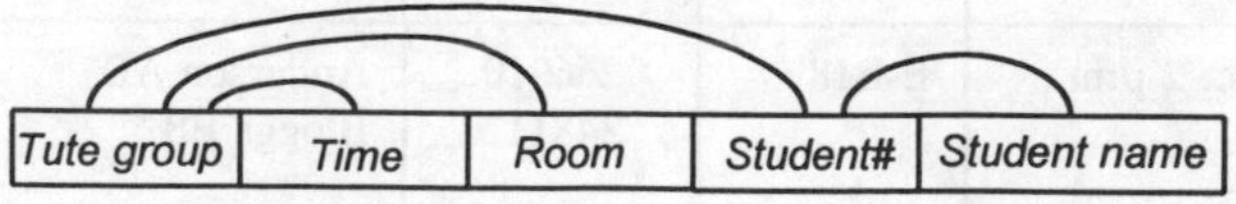

Figure 3.3 Drawing connections for the verbalized relationships

CS114 Tutorial preferences form

Please complete the form below to assist in tutorial allocation.
Tutorials are of 1 hour duration, and are available at these times:

Monday	Tuesday	Thursday
		10 a.m.
		11 a.m.
		12 noon
	2 p.m.	2 p.m.
3 p.m.		3 p.m.

Student number: . . . .

Student surname: . . . .

Student initials: . . . .

Tutorial preference 1: . . . .

Tutorial preference 2: . . . .

Tutorial preference 3: . . . .

Figure 3.4 An input form for collecting tutorial preferences

As another example, consider the input form shown in Figure 3.4. Suppose students indicate their first, second and third preferences regarding which tutorial time is suitable for them: if this information is to be taken into account in determining tutorial allocations it must be stored in the system. To perform step 1 here, you should fill out the form with some examples first. If "302156" and "Mon 3 p.m." are entered in the first and fifth slots, this says that the Student with student# 302156 chooses as second preference the Time with dayhrcode "Mon 3 p.m.".

Notice that this input form lacks some of the information needed for the output report (Table 3.9). For example, it does not show how groups are assigned to rooms and times. This helps to prevent students from entering wrong data (they enter the times they prefer directly rather than indirectly through associated group codes), and allows flexibility in offering many tutorials at the same time.

Taken individually, the output report and the input form reveal only partially the kinds of information needed for the system. In combination however, they might be enough for us to arrive at the structure of the UoD. In this case the pair of examples is said to be significant. In general, a set of examples is **significant** or adequate with respect to a specific UoD only if it illustrates all the relevant sorts of information and constraints required for that application.

With complex UoDs, significant example sets are rare. With our current application, if a student can be allocated to only one group then Table 3.9 is significant in this respect. However, if more than one group can be held at the same time, Table 3.9 is not significant in this other respect. A further row is needed to show this possibility (e.g. a row indicating that group B2 meets at Tue 2 p.m.).

It is seen later that no set of examples can be significant with respect to derivation rules or subtype definitions. In such cases the use of a UoD expert is essential. With the current application, we made no mention of the rules used to arrive at the tutorial allocations. If in addition to storing information about preferences and allocations, the information system has to compute the allocations in a nearly optimal way, respecting preferences and other practical constraints (e.g. size of groups), the design of the derivation rules becomes the challenging aspect of the schema. While this can be automated, an alternative is to divide the task between the human expert and the system; use of high level languages facilitates such cooperative solutions.

A comprehensive set of output reports (which includes intermediate stages) may include all the information on input forms. Output reports tend to be easier to interpret, especially if the input forms have been poorly designed. Care is needed in the design of the input forms to make them clear and simple for users.

Sometimes information examples appear in *diagram* form. For example, Figure 3.5 might be used to display information about what flight connections are provided by a particular airline, with the arrowheads indicating the direction of the flights. As an exercise, perform step 1 for this graph before reading on.

How did you go? There is only one entity type: City (name). There is also only one fact type: City has a flight to City. The "to" in the predicate is important, since it conveys direction and avoids the symmetry problem that we mentioned with the marriage example. In this UoD, not all the connections are two-way. As an extra exercise, consider the change in the model if flight numbers are introduced to identify a flight from one city to another.

By now you may have some sense of the power of verbalizing examples in terms of elementary facts. No matter what kind of example you start with, if you or an assistant understands the example then you should be able to express the information in simple facts. Actually this does require practice at the technique, but this is fun anyway—isn't it? If you can't do step 1, there is little point in proceeding with the design—you either don't understand the UoD or you can't communicate it clearly.

Although it might sound hard to believe, if you have performed step 1 properly, you have completed most of the "hard part" of the conceptual schema design procedure. The remaining steps may seem difficult at first, but, apart from the problem of detecting unusual constraints and derivation rules, once you learn the techniques you can carry out those steps almost automatically. With step 1, however you will always need to draw upon your interpretation skills.

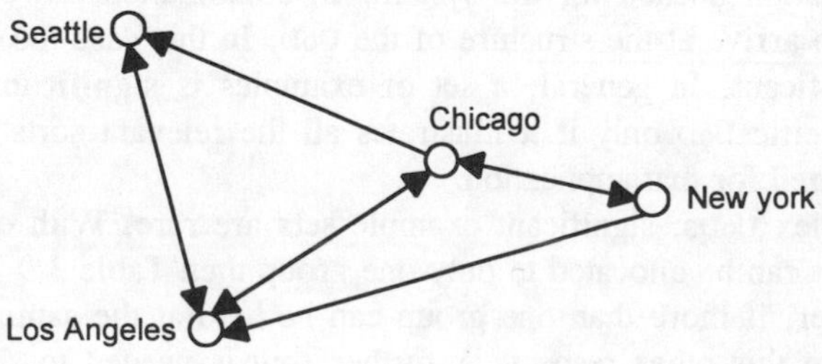

Figure 3.5 A graph showing flight connections between cities

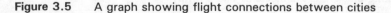

Exercise 3.3

1. Assuming suitable entity types and reference modes are understood, which of the following sentences express exactly one elementary fact?

   (a) Adam likes Eve.
   (b) Bob does not like John.
   (c) Tom visited Los Angeles and New York.
   (d) Tom visited Los Angeles or New York.
   (e) If Tom visited Los Angeles then he visited New York.
   (f) Sue is funny.
   (g) All people are funny.
   (h) Some people in New York have toured Australia.
   (i) Brisbane and Sydney are in Australia.
   (j) Brisbane and Sydney are in the same country.
   (k) Who does Adam like?

2. Indicate at least two different meanings for each of the following sentences, by including names for object types and reference modes.

   (a) Pluto is owned by Mickey.
   (b) Dallas is smaller than Sydney.
   (c) Arnold can lift 300.

Perform Step 1 of the CSDP (Conceptual Schema Design Procedure) for the following output reports. In writing down the elementary facts, you may restrict yourself to the top row of the table unless you feel that another row reveals a different kind of fact.

3.

Athlete	*Height (cm)*
Jones EM	166
Pie QT	166
Smith JA	175

4.

Athlete	*Height (cm)*
Jones EM	400
Pie QT	450
Smith JA	550

5.

Person	*Height (cm)*	*Birth year*
Jones EM	166	1955
Pie QT	160	1970
Smith JA	175	1955

6.

Person	*Height (cm)*	*Year*
Jones EM	160	1970
	166	1980
	166	1990

7.

Advisory panel	*Internal member*	*External member*
Databases	Codd	Ienshtein
	Kowalski	Spock
Logic programming	Colmerauer	Robinson
	Kowalski	
	Spock	

8.

Parents	*Children*
Ann, Bill	Colin, David, Eve
David, Fiona	Gus

9.

Country	*Friends*	*Enemies*
Disland	Oz	
Hades		Oz
		Wundrland
Wundrland	Oz	Hades
Oz	Disland	Hades
	Wundrland	

10.

apple	Australia	June, July, August
	America	Oct, Dec, Jan
	Ireland	Oct, Dec
mango	Australia	Nov, Dec, Jan, Feb
pineapple	America	June, July
	Australia	Oct, Nov, Dec, Jan

3.4 CSDP step 2: Draw fact types, and populate

Once we have translated the information examples into elementary facts, and performed quality checks, we are ready for the next step in the conceptual schema design procedure. Here we *draw* a conceptual schema diagram which shows all the *fact types*. This illustrates the relevant object types, predicates and reference schemes.
Once the diagram is drawn, we check it with a *sample population*.

> *CSDP step 2: Draw the fact types, and apply a population check*

Consider the sample output report of Table 3.10. Let us agree that the information in this report can be expressed by the following three elementary facts, using "reg#" to abbreviate "registration number":

The Person with name 'Adams B' **drives** the Car with reg# '235PZN'.
The Person with name 'Jones E' **drives** the Car with reg# '235PZN'.
The Person with name 'Jones E' **drives** the Car with reg# '108AAQ'.

Before looking at the conceptual schema diagram for this situation we present an *instance diagram* (Figure 3.6). Such diagrams illustrate particular instances of facts. Taking advantage of the concrete nature of the entities in this example, we use cartoon drawings to denote the actual people and cars. The values are shown as character strings. A particular fact or Drives relationship between a person and a car is shown as a solid line. A particular reference between a value and an entity is shown as a broken line. Throughout this book, we use the term "line" informally to mean "line segment" or "edge" (in geometry, lines have no beginning or end).

A *conceptual schema diagram* for the same example is shown in Figure 3.7. On both instance diagrams and conceptual schema diagrams, an *entity type* is depicted as a *named, solid ellipse*: this may be a circle (the simplest form of an ellipse). We represent a *value type* as a *named, broken ellipse*. The name of the object type is written either inside the ellipse or just beside it. On an instance diagram, individual objects of a given population are explicitly portrayed (by cartoon figures or other symbols). However on a conceptual schema diagram, individual objects are never shown: recalling that a type is the set of permitted instances, we may imagine that objects of a particular type are represented as points inside the ellipse.

Table 3.10

Drives:

person	*car*
Adams B	235PZN
Jones E	235PZN
Jones E	108AAQ

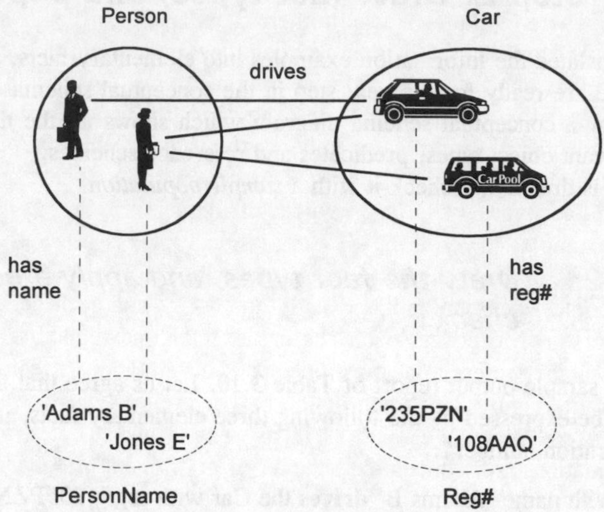

Figure 3.6 An instance diagram

On a conceptual schema diagram, the *roles* played by objects are explicitly shown as *boxes*. Each *n-ary predicate* is depicted as a *named, contiguous sequence of n role boxes* ("contiguous" means the boxes adjoin one another, with no gaps in between). Predicates are ordered from one end to the other, with their name starting inside or beside their first role box (which must be an end role). Each role is connected to exactly one object type by a *line*, indicating that the role is played only by objects of that type. A complete conceptual schema diagram includes the relevant constraints; we show how to add these later.

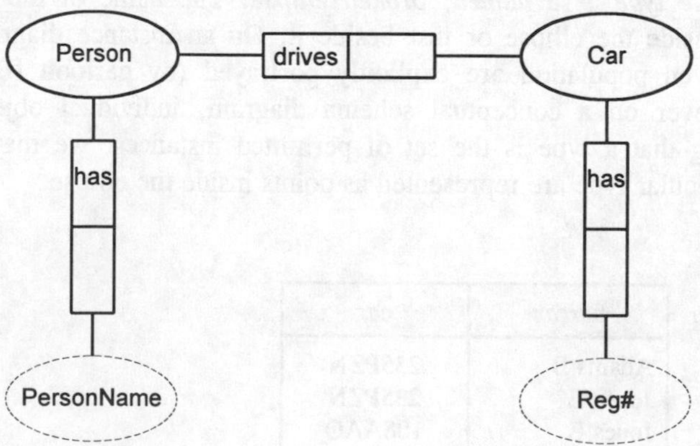

Figure 3.7 A conceptual schema diagram (constraints omitted)

A relationship between entities is an example of a *fact*. A relationship between an entity and a value where the latter is used to help identify the former is an example of a *reference*. References provide the bridge between the world of entities and the world of values. Figure 3.7 has one fact type and two reference types. Although both reference predicates are displayed with the name "has", they are different predicates. Internally a CASE tool would identify the predicates either by expanded names (e.g. "has_name", "has_reg#") or surrogates (e.g. "R2", "R3"). Although the predicate name "has" may also be used with fact types, it is best avoided if there is a more descriptive, natural alternative. For example, "Person drives Car", if accurate, is better than "Person has Car", which could mean many things (e.g. Person owns Car).

For this example, each person has exactly one name, and each person name refers to at most one person. Moreover, each car has exactly one registration number, and each registration number refers to at most one car. This situation is seen most clearly in the instance diagram, Figure 3.6. Each of the two reference types is said to provide a *simple 1:1 reference scheme*. We read "1:1" as "one-to-one". Later we learn how to specify this information on a conceptual schema diagram using uniqueness and mandatory role constraints.

When a simple 1:1 naming convention exists we may indicate the *reference mode* simply by placing its name in *parentheses* next to the name of the entity type. Assuming appropriate constraints have been added, the conceptual schema depicted in Figure 3.7 may be displayed more concisely by Figure 3.8. Unless we want to illustrate the reference schemes explicitly, this concise form is to be preferred because it is closer to the way we verbalize facts and it simplifies the diagram. Until we introduce composite identification schemes, you may assume that all reference schemes in our examples and exercises are simple 1:1 schemes.

Using reference modes, we rarely need to display value types explicitly on a schema diagram. However to understand the abbreviation scheme, we need to know how to translate between reference modes and value types. Different versions of ORM have different approaches to this. Our method for doing this is now outlined. Let the notation "*E (r)* → *V*" mean "Entity type *E* with reference mode *r* generates the Value type *V*". Reference modes are partitioned into three classes: popular; unit-based; and general. The *popular reference modes* are: *name*; *code*; *title*; *nr*; # and *id*. To obtain the value type name, a popular reference mode has its first letter shifted to upper case, and is then appended to the name of entity type. For example: Person (name) → PersonName; Item (code) → ItemCode; Song (title) → SongTitle; Rating (nr) → RatingNr; Room (#) → Room#; Member (id) → MemberId.

The *unit-based reference modes* include a built-in list of physical units (e.g. cm, kg, Celsius, mile), monetary units (e.g. $, yen) and abnormal units (e.g. AD), as well as user-defined units. Value type names are generated from unit-based reference modes by appending the word "Value". For example: kg → kgvalue; $ → $Value.

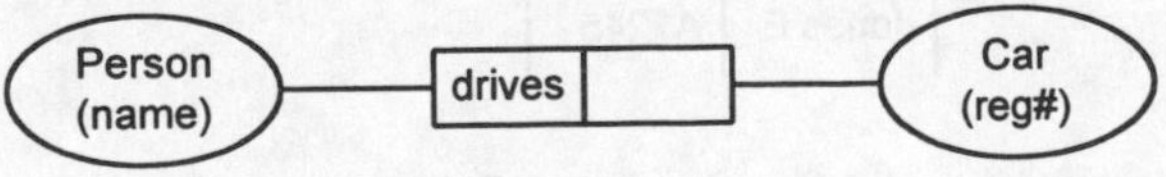

Figure 3.8 Reference modes in parentheses depict simple 1:1 reference schemes

Table 3.11

Person	*License#*	*Cars driven*
Adams B Jones E	A3050 A2245	235PZN 235PZN, 108AAQ

All other reference modes are called *general reference modes*. These generate value type names simply by shifting their first letter to upper case. For example: surname → Surname; reg# → Reg#.

As a check that we have drawn the diagram correctly, we should populate each fact type on the diagram with some of the original fact instances. We do this by adding a **fact table** for each fact type, and entering the values in the relevant columns of this table. The resulting diagram is called a *knowledge base diagram*, since it shows both the schema and a sample database. To illustrate this, consider the output report of Table 3.11.

Let us assume "License#" refers to the person's driver's license. Performing step 1 reveals that there are two binary fact types involved (check this for yourself). We can now draw the conceptual schema diagram. As a check, we populate it with the original data to produce the knowledge base diagram shown in Figure 3.9. If desired, the inverse predicate may be included, as shown in this figure. At this stage the diagram is incomplete because constraints are not shown.

At least one fact from each fact-table should be verbalized to ensure the diagram makes sense. Populating the schema diagram is useful not only for detecting schema diagrams that are nonsensical, but also for clarifying constraints (as we see later).

Nowadays most non-smokers prefer a smoke-free environment in which to work, travel, eat and so on. So for some applications, a report like Table 3.12 is relevant. Please perform step 1 on this table before reading on.

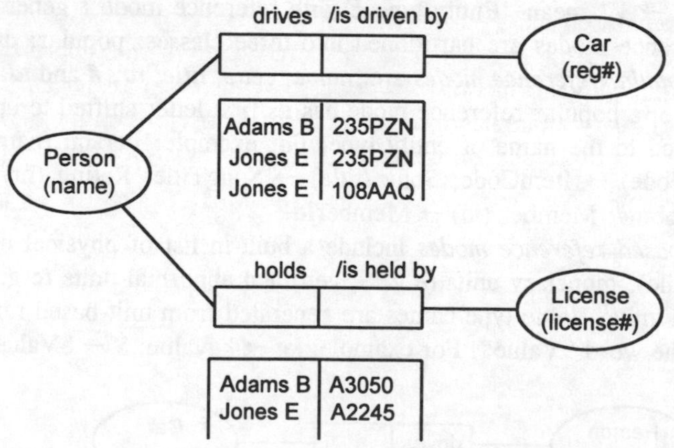

Figure 3.9 A knowledge base diagram for Table 3.11 (constraints omitted)

Table 3.12

Smokers	*Nonsmokers*
Pat Lee	Norma Shir Terry

One way of expressing the facts on row 1 is: Person (firstname) 'Pat' smokes; Person (firstname) 'Norma' is a nonsmoker. Each of these facts is an instance of a different *unary fact type*. With a unary fact type, there is only one role. The knowledge base diagram is shown in Figure 3.10.

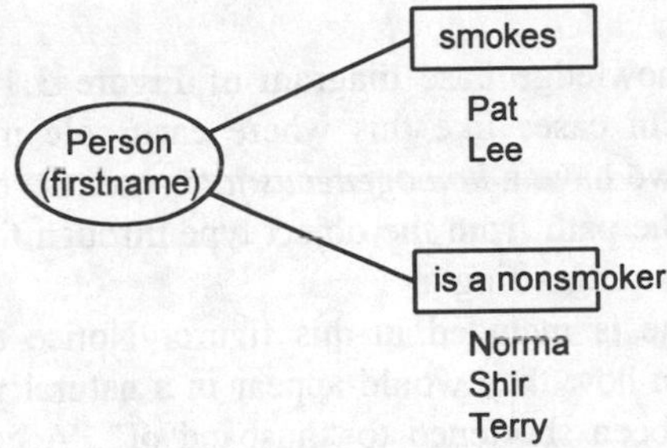

Figure 3.10 Knowledge base diagram for Table 3.12 (unary version)

Here we have two roles, but they belong to different fact types. This is shown visually by separating the role boxes. If desired, this schema may be transformed into an alternative portrayal using a binary. For example, the two unaries here may be replaced by a single binary fact type by introducing SmokingStatus as another entity type, with codes "S" for smoker and "N" for non-smoker. So the first row of Table 3.12 could be rephrased as: Person (firstname) 'Pat' has SmokingStatus (code) 'S'; Person (firstname) 'Norma' has SmokingStatus (code) 'N'. This approach is shown in Figure 3.11. Schema transformations are discussed in depth in a later chapter.

Each of the binary examples discussed had two different entity types. Fact types involving different entity types are said to be *heterogeneous fact types*. Most fact types are of this kind.

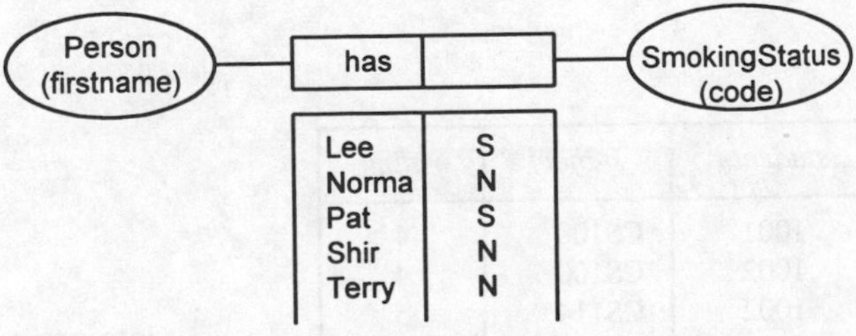

Figure 3.11 Knowledge base diagram for Table 3.12 (binary version)

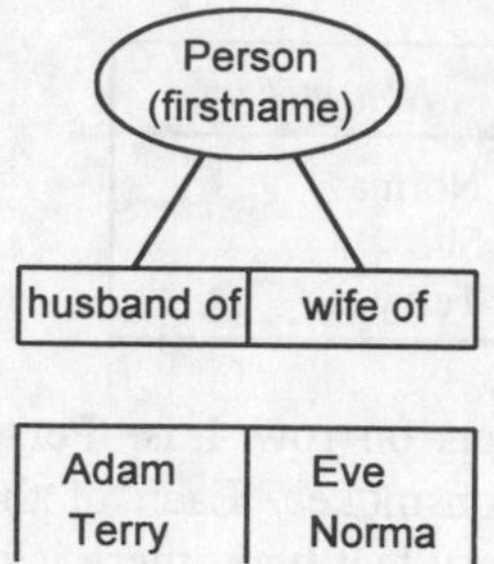

Figure 3.12 A ring fact type with sample population

Consider however the knowledge base diagram of Figure 3.12. Here we have only one entity type—Person. In cases like this where each role in the fact type is played by the same object type we have a *homogeneous fact type*; the binary case of this is called a *ring fact type* since the path from the object type through the predicate loops back to the same object type, forming a ring.

The inverse predicate name is included in this figure. Notice that the predicate names have been shortened from how they would appear in a natural verbalization. For example, "is husband of" has been shortened to "husband of". A conceptual schema diagram serves two purposes. Firstly, it provides a clear, simple picture of the UoD for humans. It is best to use full predicate names wherever practical, since this provides a natural verbalization. So with the present example we recommend that "is" be included. However, we may abbreviate names for predicates, object types and reference modes if their expanded versions are obvious to other people; abbreviations can help keep diagrams compact.

The second purpose of a schema diagram is to provide a formal specification of the structure of the UoD, so that the model may be processed by a computer system. For this reason the diagrams we draw must conform to the formation rules for legal schema diagrams. They are not just cartoons.

Now consider the output report of Table 3.13. This is similar to an example discussed previously. To be more realistic, we identify students by their student number. Here we have a *ternary fact type*. The object types and reference schemes are: Student (student#); Subject (code); Rating (nr)+. Given this, we may express the fact on the first row as: Student '1001' **for** Subject 'CS100' **scored** Rating 4.

Table 3.13

Result:

student#	*subject*	*rating*
1001	CS100	4
1002	CS100	4
1002	CS114	5

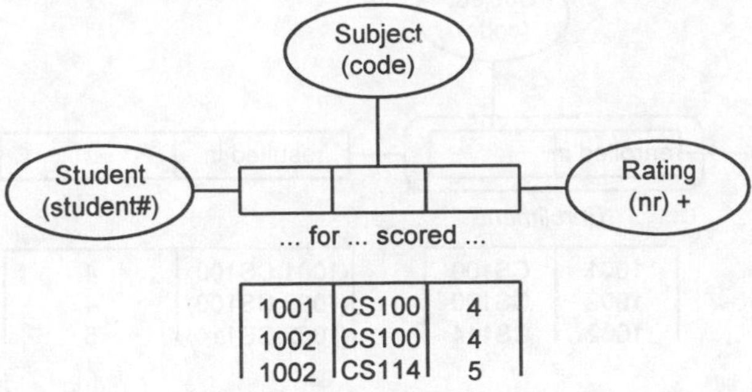

Figure 3.13 A populated ternary fact type for Table 3.13

On a conceptual schema diagram, a ternary fact type appears as a sequence of three role boxes, each of which is attached to an object type, as shown in Figure 3.13. When names for ternary and longer predicates are written on a diagram, the placeholders are included, each being depicted by an ellipsis "...". Figure 3.13 includes a sample population. No matter how high the *arity* (number of roles) of the fact type, we can easily populate it for checking purposes. Each column in the fact table is associated with one role in the predicate.

Earlier we gave an example of transforming unaries into a binary. We now introduce another kind of transformation known as **nesting**. This basically amounts to *treating a relationship between objects as an object itself*. Consider once more the top row of Table 3.13. Instead of expressing this as a single sentence, we might convey the information in the following two sentences:

Student '1001' enrolled in Subject 'CS100'.
This Enrollment resulted in Rating 4.

Here "This Enrollment" refers back to the enrollment relationship between the specific person and the specific subject mentioned in the first sentence. Any such enrollment may be treated as an object in its own right. We call this a *nested object* or an *objectified relationship*. We indicate a **nested object type** or *objectified predicate* on a schema diagram by drawing a **frame** around the predicate being objectified (see Figure 3.14). A frame or fillet is a rectangle with rounded corners. The objectified predicate usually has two roles, but may have more: ⊏⊐. An alternative notation uses an ellipse instead of a frame. Some versions of ORM allow objectified unaries.

Optionally an explicit name for the nested object type may be added beside it, in double quotes. In some versions, names must always be supplied and quotes are omitted. However in practice we may want to nest without having any natural name for the nested object type. Moreover, it is sometimes more natural to think of a nested object as an ordered *pair* (or triple etc.) of objects in the particular relationship type. With our example, we might think of a rating being scored by a ⟨Person, Subject⟩ pair which was involved in an enrollment, rather than a rating resulting from an enrollment. For such reasons we leave it optional whether nested object types are explicitly named on diagrams.

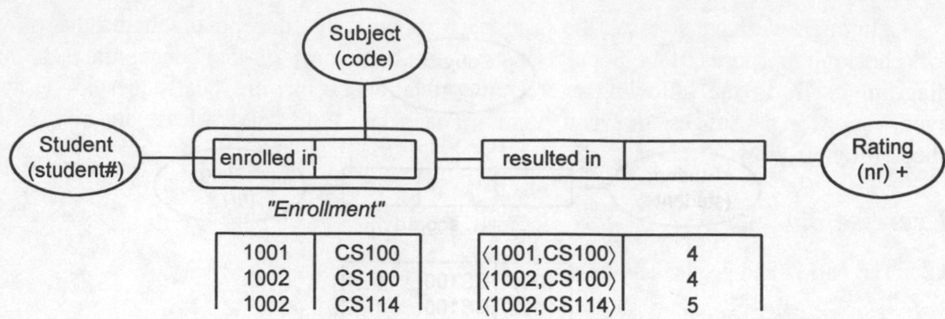

Figure 3.14 Knowledge base for Table 3.13 (nested version)

Entries in fact columns for nested objects may be shown as pairs (triples etc.) of values, separated by commas and flanked by angle-brackets. For example, the enrollment of student 1001 in CS100 appears as "⟨1001, CS100⟩" in the fact table for the resulted in predicate. Note that *nesting is not to be regarded as splitting*. Figure 3.14 does not show two independent binaries; the resulted in predicate cannot be shown without including the enrolled in predicate. So the ternary in Figure 3.13 is still elementary. Figure 3.13 is said to be the *flattened*, or *unnested*, version.

Chapter 9 deals with the notion of schema equivalence in detail. The nested and flattened versions are not equivalent unless the role played by the nested object type is mandatory. With our current example, this means that a rating must be known for each enrollment. In this case we prefer the flattened version, since it is simpler to diagram and populate. As discussed later, nesting is often preferred if the nested object type has an optional role, or more than one role to play.

We conclude this section with a review of some terminology. Three terms for objects have now been introduced. Entities are the objects in the UoD which we reference by means of descriptions. Values (characters strings or numbers) are depicted as entries in database tables and are used to refer to entities. Finally, we allow relationships between objects to be treated as objects themselves: these are nested objects (or objectified relationships).

There are two commonly used notations used for describing the arity or "length" of a predicate. We have set these out for the first four cases. Our preference is shown as the main descriptor.

Table 2.14 Classification of predicates according to number of roles

Nr roles	*Main descriptor*	*Alternate descriptor*
1	unary	monadic
2	binary	dyadic
3	ternary	triadic
4	quaternary	tetradic
...	...	...

Although we have stressed the practice of populating conceptual schema diagrams for checking purposes, fact populations do not form part of the conceptual schema diagram itself. In the following exercise, population checks are not requested. However, we strongly suggest that you populate each fact type with at least one row as a check on your work.

Exercise 3.4

1. The names and gender of various people are indicated below:

   Male: Fred, Tom
   Female: Ann, Mary, Sue

   (a) Express the information about Fred and Ann in unary facts.
   (b) Draw a conceptual schema diagram based on this choice.
   (c) Express the same information in terms of binary elementary facts.
   (d) Draw a conceptual schema diagram based on this choice.

Note: For the rest of this exercise, avoid using unary facts.

2. Draw a conceptual schema diagram for the fact types in the following questions of Exercise 3.3:

   (a) Q. 3; (b) Q. 4; (c) Q. 5; (d) Q. 6; (e) Q. 7; (f) Q. 8; (g) Q. 9; (h) Q. 10.

Perform steps 1,2 of the CSDP for the following output reports.

3.

Retailer	*Item*	*Quantity sold*
CompuWare	SQL+	330
	Zappo Pascal	330
	WordLight	200
SoftwareLand	SQL+	330
	Zappo Pascal	251

4.

Item	*Retailer*	*Quantity sold*
SQL+	CompuWare	330
	SoftwareLand	330
Zappo Pascal	CompuWare	330
	SoftwareLand	251
WordLight	CompuWare	200

5.

Tute group	*Day*	*Hour*	*Room*
A	Mon	3 p.m.	69-718
B	Tue	2 p.m.	42-B18
C1	Thu	10 a.m.	69-718
C2	Thu	10 a.m.	67-103

6. (*Hint:* Make use of nesting)

Subject	*CreditPts*	*Semester*	*Enrollment*	*Lecturer*
CS100	8	1	500	DBJ
CS102	8	2	500	EJS
CS114	8	1	300	TAH
CS115	8	2	270	TAH
CS383	16	1	50	RMC
CS383	16	2	45	PNC

7. Assuming appropriate names are supplied for entity types, reference modes and predicates, and that appropriate constraints are added, which of the following conceptual schema diagrams are legal? Where illegal, briefly explain the error.

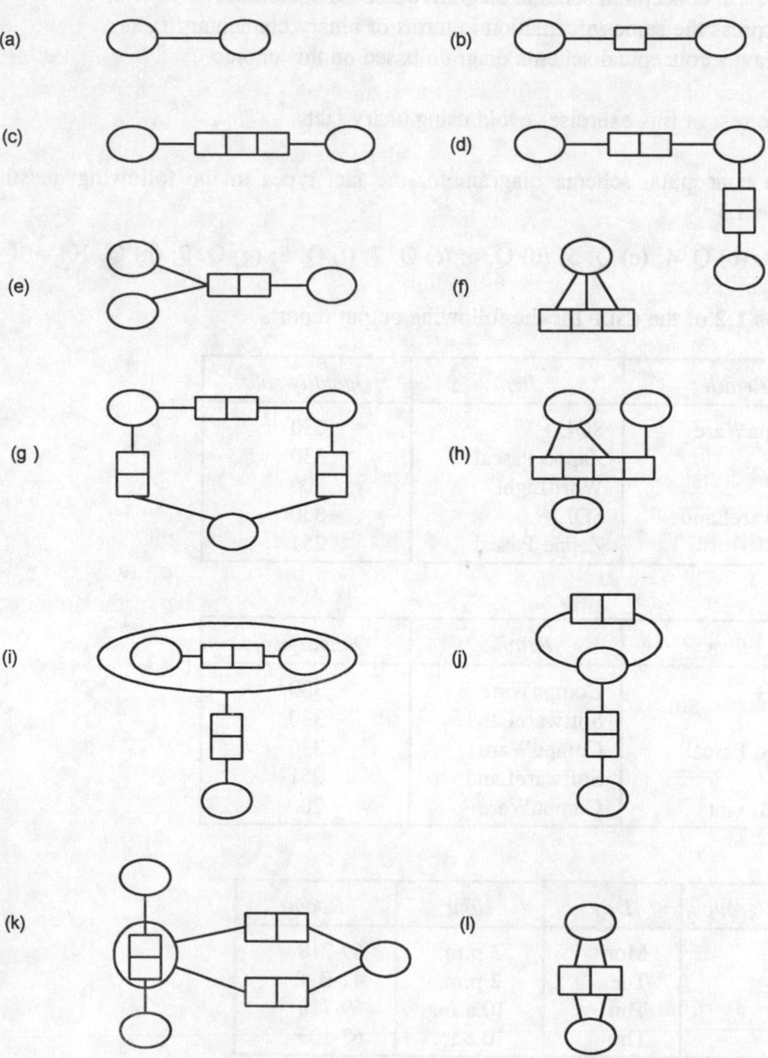

3.5 CSDP step 3: Trim schema; note basic derivations

Having drawn the fact types, and performed a population check, we now move on to step 3 of our design procedure. Here we check to see if there are some entity types which should be combined. We also check to see if some fact types can be derived from the others by arithmetic computation.

> *CSDP step 3: Check for entity types which should be combined; note any arithmetic derivations*

To understand the first part of this step, we need to know how the objects in the UoD are classified into types. Figure 3.15 (a) shows our basic division of objects into entities (non-lexical objects) and values (lexical objects). Entities are identified by definite descriptions, whereas values are identified by constants. *Atomic entities* are treated as individual entitites in their own right (e.g. persons, cars, engines). For modeling purposes, an atomic entity is treated as having no internal structure—any portrayal of structure must be depicted externally in terms of roles played by the entity. For example: Car (reg#) contains Engine (engine#).

Nested entitites are those relationships which we wish to think of as objects (i.e. objectified relationships, e.g. enrollments). Unlike atomic entitites, nested entities are portayed as having an internal structure (composed of the roles in the relationship). In our version of ORM, relationships are not objects unless we think of them that way, and want to talk about them.

Values are character strings or numbers. The notion of value could be extended to include other objects directly representable on a medium (e.g. sounds). However we ignore such possibilities in this text.

These subdivisions are **mutually exclusive** (i.e. they have no instance in common). For example, no string can be an entity. The division of a whole into exclusive parts is called a **partition**. You may think of it as cutting a pie up into slices. The slices are *exclusive* (they don't overlap) *and exhaustive* (together they make up the whole pie).

Figure 3.15 (b) gives an example of how the entities might be further divided into entity types for a particular UoD. Only a few entity types are listed. Which kinds of entities exist depends on the UoD. Basically, entities are grouped into the same type if we want to record similar information about them.

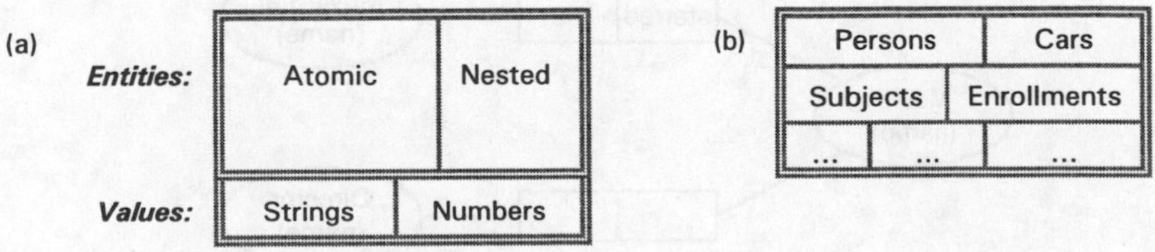

Figure 3.15 Partitioning into types of (a) objects and (b) primitive entities

Table 3.15 Some motion pictures

Movie	*Stars*	*Director*
Awakenings	Robert De Niro, Robin Williams	Penny Marshall
Backdraft	Kurt Russell, Robert De Niro, William Baldwin	Ron Howard
Dances with wolves	Kevin Kostner, Mary McDonnell	Kevin Kostner
...	...	...

For any UoD, there will always be a top-level partitioning of its entities into exclusive types: these are called **primitive entity types**. Later we may introduce *subtypes* of these primitive types, if they have some specific roles to play. It is possible that subtypes of a given entity type may overlap (e.g. Manager and FulltimeEmployee might be subtypes of Employee). However, *primitive entity types never overlap*. For example, no person can be a car. On a conceptual schema diagram, this exclusive nature is shown by depicting the primitive entity types as *separate* ellipses or frames. Subtypes are discussed in detail in chapter 6.

Value types often overlap. For example, Surname and StateName may have a common instance (e.g. "Washington"). Overlapping value types may appear separately on a schema diagram since they are assumed to be either equal to, or a subtype of, String or Number. Later we show how value types may be constrained to be a specific subtype of String or Number. For example, both Surname and StateName might be restricted to strings of at most 20 characters, and RatingNr to integers in the range 1..7.

Step 3 of the design procedure begins with a check to see if some entity types should be combined. At this stage we are concerned only with primitive entity types, not entity subtypes. So if you spot some entity types which do overlap, you should combine them into a single entity type. For example consider Table 3.15, which concerns the movie application discussed in Chapter 1. Suppose as a result of applying steps 1 and 2 we arrived at the diagram shown in Figure 3.16. Do you see what's wrong with this diagram?

MovieStar and Director are displayed as separate, primitive entity types. This implies that these types are mutually exclusive (i.e. no movie star can be a director). But is this the case? Our sample population lists the value "Kevin Kostner" in both the Stars column and the Director column. Does this refer to the same person?

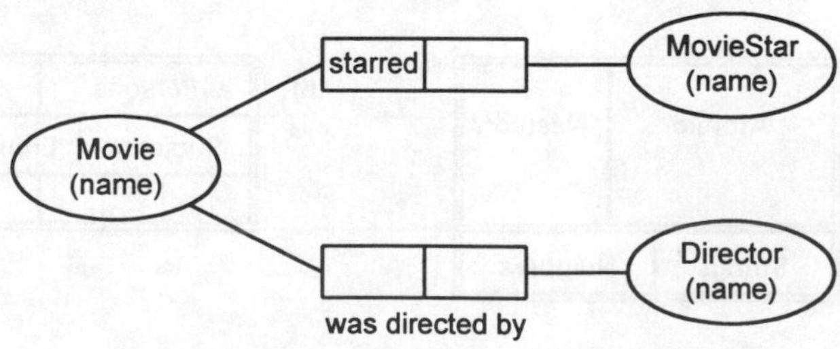

Figure 3.16 A faulty conceptual schema

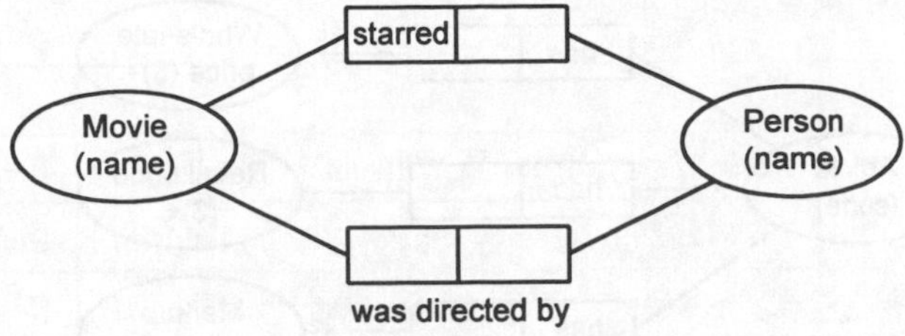

Figure 3.17 The result of applying step 3 to Figure 3.16

If in doubt you can ask a UoD expert. In actual fact, it is the same person. So we must combine the Movie Star and Director entity types into a single entity type as shown in Figure 3.17. This shows it is possible to be both a star and a director. Of course, it does not imply that every movie star is a director. In chapter 6 we discuss how to add subtypes later if necessary. For example, if some other facts to be recorded only for directors, we form a Director subtype of Person for those additional facts.

One reason for suspecting that two entity types should be combined is if they both have the *same unit-based reference mode*. Here the entity is typically envisaged as a quantity of so many units (e.g. kilograms or years). Let's look at a few examples. Consider the output report of Table 3.16. At first glance, we might consider representing the design of this UoD by the diagram shown in Figure 3.18. Note however that the three entity types Wholesale price, Retail price and Markup all have the same unit-based reference mode ($).

Moreover, looking at the instances in the table we note that $50 appears as both a wholesale price and a mark-up. In both cases the $50 denotes the same amount of money. So these entity types overlap and hence should be combined. If the table population is significant, the set of retail prices does not overlap the set of mark-ups; nevertheless, it is *meaningful to compare* retail prices and mark-ups since they have the same unit (dollars). For instance, article A1 has a retail price which is three times its mark-up. These considerations lead us to collapse the three entity types into one, as shown in Figure 3.19. The combined entity type is naturally verbalized as "Amount of Money"; however we commonly abbreviate this to "MoneyAmt" or "Money".

There is one other point to be noted with this example. If you look at the output report you will notice that the following mathematical relationship holds between the values in the last three columns: mark-up = retail price - wholesale price.

Table 3.16

Article	*Wholesale price ($)*	*Retail price ($)*	*Markup ($)*
A1	50	75	25
A2	80	130	50
A3	50	70	20
A4	100	130	30

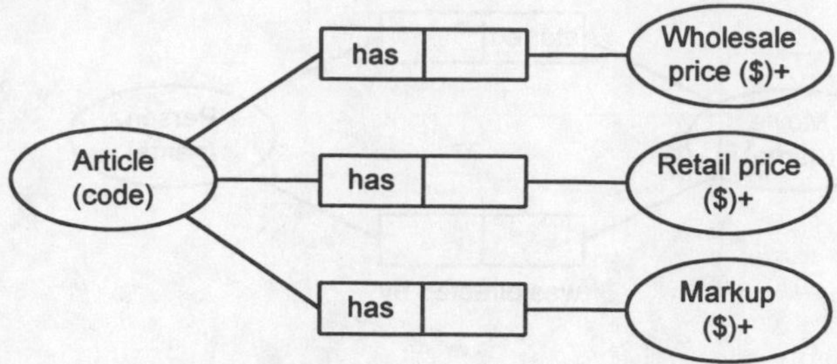

Figure 3.18 Another faulty conceptual schema

Hence the mark-up value may be **derived** from the wholesale and retail values by means of this rule. To minimize the chance of human error it is usually best to have the system derive this value rather than have humans compute and store it. This also saves on storage. *Derivation rules may be written as text below the schema diagram.* An informal version of the rule may be written as a comment in braces. See Figure 3.19.

What about a formal version of the rule? Notice the "+" after "($)" in the reference mode for Money. This indicates that Money is a numerically-referenced entity type. This permits us to add or subtract amounts of money by adding or subtracting their corresponding numeric values. The derivation rule may be stated formally as shown in Figure 3.19. Here object type variables are shown in lower-case italics. Notice the use of "**iff**": this abbreviates "*if and only if*", indicating the conditional rule works in both directions. Other formalisms may be used instead to specify the rules. With the rule for deriving mark-ups noted, there is *no need to include the derived fact type on the diagram.*

Notice that the mark-up formula allows any one of the three values to be derived from knowledge of the other two. So there is in principle a degree of choice as to which value is selected as the derived one. For instance, we might have chosen the retail price to be derived from the wholesale price and the mark-up. Our choice of mark-up as the derived value is a pragmatic one based on the assumption that it will probably be required less frequently than the other two values in retrieval requests.

Let's consider now a somewhat similar example. Look at the output report of Table 3.17, and try to schematize it before reading on.

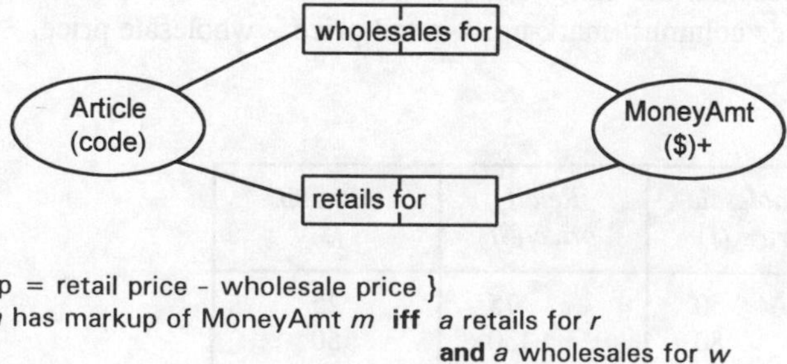

{ markup = retail price - wholesale price }
Article *a* has markup of MoneyAmt *m* **iff** *a* retails for *r*
and *a* wholesales for *w*
and *m* = *r* - *w*

Figure 3.19 The result of applying step 3 to Figure 3.18

Table 3.17

Poster	*Height (cm)*	*Width (cm)*	*Area (cm²)*
P1	40	30	1200
P2	200	60	12000
P3	80	40	3200
P4	20	10	200

As you probably guessed, we can get by with fewer than four entity types here. Seeing that the values shown in the last three columns are all numbers, you may have been tempted to combine Height, Width and Area into one entity type. You might argue that Height and Width overlap since the value 40 is common, and that Height and Area overlap since each has a value 200. But notice that Area is measured in square centimeters, which is quite a different unit from centimeters.

Heights and widths may be meaningfully compared with each other since both are lengths: a length of 40 cm may be an instance of a height or a width. But a length of 200 cm is not the same entity as an area of 200 cm^2. If our final column was Perimeter, we could collapse three headings into one entity type as for the previous example. But since Area is fundamentally a different type of quantity, we must keep it separate, as shown in Figure 3.20.

Derived fact types are usually specified only as rules, to avoid cluttering up the diagram. However, it is sometimes instructive to show a derived fact type on the diagram; in this case it must be marked as being derived, to distinguish it from the stored fact types. Our convention is to ***place an asterisk beside any derived fact type that is included on the diagram***, as shown in Figure 3.20.

Now consider Figure 3.21. This might describe part of a UoD concerning practitioners in a medical clinic. Here the entity types Doctor, Dentist and Chemist have a similar reference mode (name) but this is not unit-based; so this is no reason to combine the types. If somebody could hold more than one of these three jobs then the overlap of the entity types would normally force a combination.

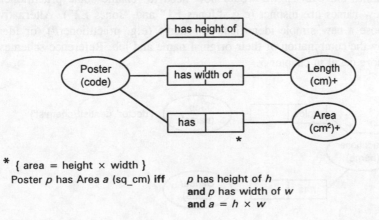

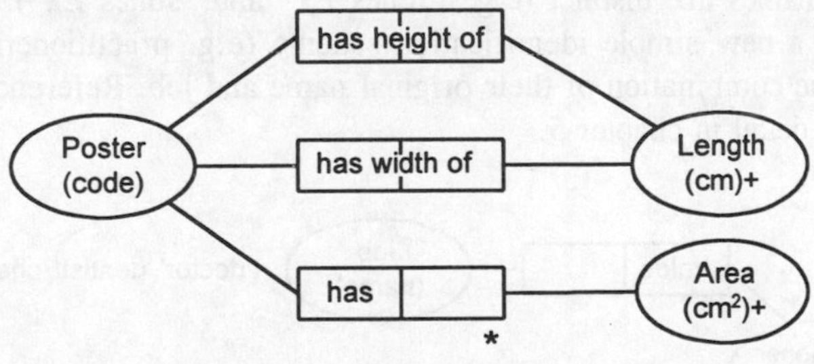

* { area = height × width }
Poster *p* has Area *a* (sq_cm) **iff** *p* has height of *h*
and *p* has width of *w*
and *a* = *h* × *w*

Figure 3.20 Schema diagram for Table 3.17

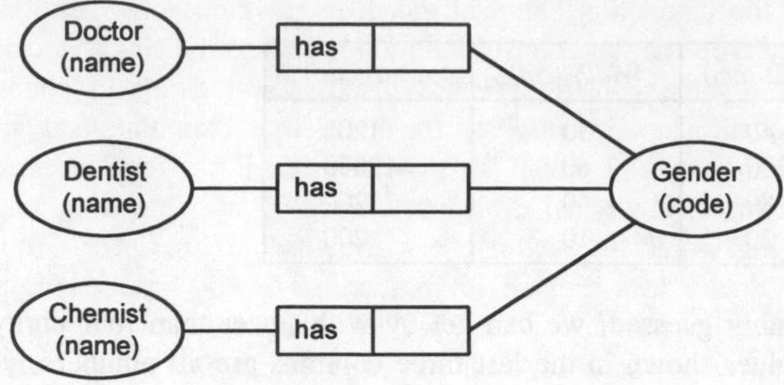

Figure 3.21 Should Doctor, Dentist and Chemist be combined?

However, suppose that the entity types are mutually exclusive (i.e. nobody can hold more than one of these jobs). In this case we still need to consider whether the entity types should be combined, since the *same kind of information* (having a gender) is recorded for each.

In such we ask ourselves the following question. *Do we ever want to list the same kind of information for the different entity types in the same query?* For example, do we want to make the request "List all the practitioners and their gender"? If we do, then we should normally combine the entity types as shown in Figure 3.22. If we don't then there may be grounds for leaving the schema unchanged. Later when we discuss subtyping, this issue will be examined in more detail.

Even if no doctor can be a dentist, the schema of Figure 3.21 permits a doctor and a dentist to have the same name (e.g. "Jones E"). In Figure 3.22, the use of "(name)" with Practitioner implies that each instance of PractitionerName refers to only one Practitioner.

Suppose we add the constraint: **each Practitioner holds at most one Job**. A graphical notation for this kind of constraint is discussed in the next chapter. With this constraint added, Figure 3.22 would forbid any doctor from having the same name as a dentist. If the original names did overlap we would now need to rename some practitioners to ensure their new names are distinct (e.g. "Jones E1" and "Jones E2"). Alternatively, we might choose a new simple identification scheme (e.g. practitioner#), or identify practitioners by the combination of their original name and job. Reference schemes are discussed in more detail in chapter 5.

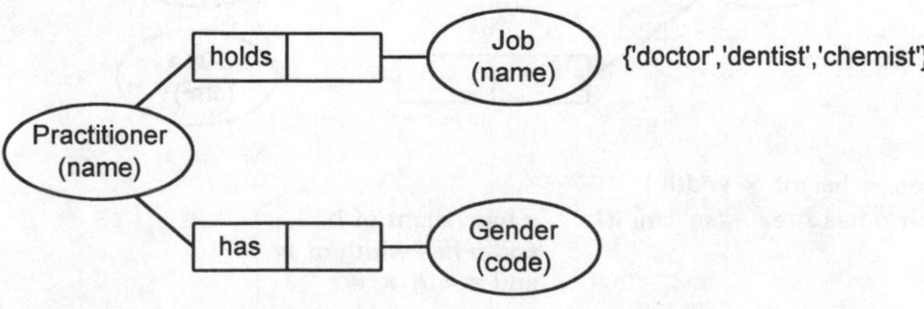

Figure 3.22 An alternative schema for the UoD of Figure 3.21

To preserve the distinction between the different kinds of practitioner, we introduced a new entity type Job, and constrained job names to the set {"doctor", "dentist", "chemist"}. Such "value constraints" are discussed in detail in chapter 6. As an exercise, please invent a small population for this UoD and populate both schemas.

The new schema is simpler than the old one since it has replaced three binary fact types with two binaries. If we had even more kinds of practitioner (e.g. acupuncturist, herbalist) the saving would be even more worthwhile. If we have only two kinds of practitioner (e.g. doctor and chemist) both schemas would have the same number of fact types: but even in this case we generally favor the new version. If additional information is required for specific kinds of practitioners, this complicates the issue, as explained later when we discuss subtyping.

In rare cases, entity types might overlap but we are not interested in knowing this, and collapsing the types is awkward. We may then leave the types separate so long as we declare that our model differs from the real world in this respect.

In performing step 3 of the CSDP, the relevant questions to ask ourselves may be summarized thus:

1. Can the same entity be a member of two entity types?
   If so, combine the entity types into one (unless such identities are not of interest).

2. Can entities of two different types be meaningfully compared (e.g. to compute ratios)? Do they have the same unit or dimension?
   If so, combine the entity types into one.

3. Is the same kind of information recorded for different entity types, and will you sometimes need to list the entities together for this information?
   If so, combine the entity types into one, and if necessary add another fact type to preserve the original distinction.

4. Is a fact type arithmetically derivable from others?
   If so, provide a derivation rule. If you leave the fact type on the diagram, mark it with "*".

At this step the derivation rules which concern us are of an arithmetic nature. These are usually fairly obvious. Logical derivations can be harder to spot, and are considered in a later step.

Exercise 3.5

Perform steps 1 - 3 of the CSDP for the following output reports. In setting out derivation rules, you may use any convenient notation.

1.

Software	*Distributor*	*Retailer*
Blossom 1234	CompuWare	PCland SoftKing
SQL++	TechSource	PCland
WordLight	TechSource	CompuWare SoftKing

2.

Project	*Manager*	*Budget*	*Salary*	*Birth year*
P1	Smith J	38000	50000	1946
P2	Jones	42000	55000	1935
P3	Brown	20000	38000	1946
P4	Smith T	36000	42000	1950
P5	Collins	36000	38000	1956

3.

Dept	*Budget*	*NrStaff*	*Emp#*	*Salary*	*Salary total*
Admin	80000	2	E01	40000	
			E02	25000	65000
Sales	90000	3	E03	30000	
			E04	25000	
			E05	30000	85000
Service	90000	2	E06	45000	
			E07	25000	70000

4.

Employee	*Project*	*Hours*	*Expenses*
E4	P8	24	200
E4	P9	26	150
E5	P8	14	100
E5	P9	16	110
E6	P8	16	120
E6	P9	14	110

5.

Female staff		**Male staff**	
name	*dept*	*name*	*dept*
Sue Bright	Admin	John Jones	Sales
Eve Jones	Admin	Bob Smith	Admin
Ann Smith	Sales		

3.6 Summary

The *information systems life cycle* typically involves the following stages: feasibility study; requirements analysis; conceptual design of data and operations; logical design of data and operations; external design of data and operations; prototyping; internal design of data and operations; implementation of production version; testing and validation; and maintenance. Feedback from a later stage may indicate a need to modify the work of earlier stages. Careful attention to the earlier stages reduces the overall effort involved, as does reuse of design strategies used previously on similar applications.

With large scale applications, the UoD is divided into convenient modules, the *conceptual schema design procedure* (CSDP) is applied to each, and the resulting subschemas are integrated into the global conceptual schema. The CSDP itself has seven steps, of which the first three were discussed in this chapter.

Step
1. Transform familiar information examples into elementary facts, and apply quality checks.
2. Draw the fact types, and apply a population check.
3. Check for entity types that should be combined, and note any arithmetic derivations.

Step 1 is the most important. Relevant information *examples* (e.g. tables, forms, diagrams), which are familiar to the UoD expert, are *verbalized in terms of elementary facts*. An elementary fact is a simple assertion that an object has some property, or that one or more objects participate together in some relationship. With respect to the UoD, an elementary fact cannot be split into smaller facts without information loss.

Elementary facts are expressed as instantiated logical predicates. A logical *predicate* is a sentence with object-holes in it. To complete the sentence, the holes are filled in by object-terms. With simple reference schemes, an entity-term is a definite description which includes the name of the *entity-type*, *reference mode* and *value* (e.g. "the Scientist with surname 'Einstein'"). A value-term comprises the name of the value-type and the value (e.g. "the Surname 'Einstein'").

Each object-hole corresponds to a *role*. A predicate with 1 role is *unary*, with 2 roles is *binary*, with 3 roles is *ternary*, with 4 roles is *quaternary*, and with *n* roles is *n*-ary. The value *n* is the *arity* of the predicate.

In CSDP *step 2* we draw the fact types, and apply a population check. Entity types are depicted as named, solid ellipses and value types as named, broken ellipses. An *n*-ary predicate is shown as a named, contiguous sequence of *n* role-boxes. Predicates are ordered; the predicate name is placed in or beside the first role of the predicate. Each role is played by exactly one object type, as shown by a connecting line.

A *simple 1:1 reference scheme* involves a reference predicate between an entity type and a value type, where each entity is associated with exactly one value, and each value is associated with only one entity; this kind of scheme may be abbreviated by enclosing the *reference mode in parentheses* next to the entity type name. If the value type is *numeric*, this is indicated by adding a *"+" sign*.

Once a fact type is drawn, it should be checked by *populating* it with at least one fact and reading it back in natural language. Each column in the associated *fact table* corresponds to a specific role.

A given relationship, or the sequence of objects which instantiate the relationship, may be thought of as an object itself. *Nested object types* or *objectified predicates* are depicted by a *frame*. The main graphic notations met so far are summarized in Figure 3.23. Objects may be classified into three main divisions: atomic entities; nested entities (objectified relationships); and values (strings or numbers).

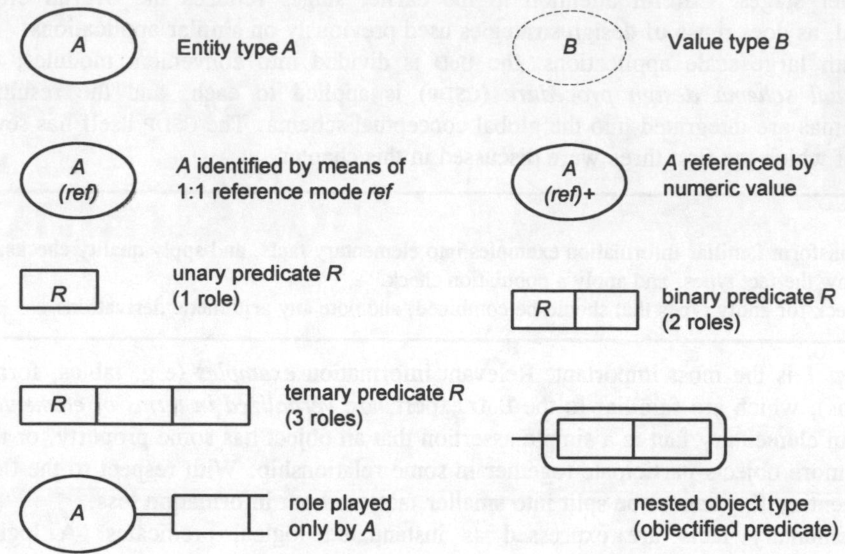

Figure 3.23 Some basic symbols used in conceptual schema diagrams

In *step 3* of the CSDP, we check for entity types which should be combined, and note any arithmetic derivations. For any given UoD, each entity belongs to exactly one of the *primitive entity types* which have been selected (e.g. Person, Car). Hence, if we have drawn two entity types which may have a common instance, we should combine them. Even if they don't overlap, entity types which can be meaningfully compared should normally be combined; these typically have the same unit-bearing reference mode (e.g. $). If the same kind of information is to be recorded for different entity types, these should often be combined, and if needed a fact type should be added to preserve the original distinction.

If a fact type is arithmetically derivable from others, an appropriate derivation rule should be provided below the diagram. Usually the derived fact type is omitted from the diagram, but if included it should be marked with an asterisk.

Chapter notes

A standard reference on requirements analysis is the ANSI/IEEE Standard 830-1984. For a comparison of different design methods, including a treatment of the data, process and behavior perspectives, see Olle et al. (1991). A classic paper on linguistics which influenced the early development of a number of modeling methods is Fillmore (1968). For a clear overview of logicians' approaches to proper names and descriptions, see Chapter 5 of Haack (1978). Some heuristics to help with step 1 in interpreting common forms used in business are discussed in Choobineh et al. (1992).

4 Uniqueness constraints

4.1 CSDP step 4: Uniqueness constraints; arity check

So far, the conceptual schema design procedure has focused on specifying the elementary fact types, both stored and derived. The rest of the CSDP is concerned mostly with specifying **constraints**. Constraints apply to the database, and are either static or dynamic. Most static constraints may be readily indicated on a conceptual schema diagram. Dynamic constraints are expressed in other formalisms (e.g. transition diagrams). In this text our treatment of constraints focuses on static constraints.

In this chapter we look at **uniqueness constraints**. These play a pivotal role when the conceptual schema is later mapped onto a relational schema. Once uniqueness constraints have been added to a fact type, some further checks are made to see whether the fact type is of the right arity or length. In particular, there is a simple check based on uniqueness which shows that certain kinds of fact types are not elementary and hence should be split.

CSDP step 4: Add uniqueness constraints, and check the arity of fact types

We often describe static constraints as being "constraints on the fact types". More accurately, *static constraints apply to every possible state of the database*. Here "every state" means "each and every state, taken one at a time". Hence, static constraints apply to all possible *populations* of the fact types. Consider the schema:

Employee (surname); Department (name)

F1: Employee works for Department
C1: **each** Employee works for **at most one** Department

During the lifetime of the information system, the database goes through a sequence of states. In one of these states, the employee Jones might be recorded as working for the Sales department. At another time, Jones might be recorded as working for the Production department. However, in no state of the database may Jones be recorded as working for both of these departments. This is how a constraint like C1 should be interpreted.

In this chapter we learn how to specify uniqueness constraints on the conceptual schema diagram. As we soon see, each stored fact type must be assigned at least one uniqueness constraint. Typically, we may ignore derived fact types in our discussion of constraints since, given the constraints on the stored fact types, such "derived constraints" are typically implied by the derivation rules. For example, with regard to the derived mark-up fact type considered in an earlier chapter, if each article has only one wholesale price and only one retail price, the derivation rule (mark-up = retail price - wholesale price) implies that each article has only one mark-up price. We will have more to say about this issue later in the book.

The rest of the chapter discusses CSDP step 4 in the following order. First we learn how to mark uniqueness constraints on unary and binary predicates. Then we consider uniqueness constraints on longer predicates. After that we examine external uniqueness constraints (these apply between different predicates). Finally we discuss ways of checking that our fact types are of the right arity.

4.2 Uniqueness constraints on unaries and binaries

Unary fact types are the easiest, so let's look at them first. Suppose as part of a fitness application we record which people are joggers. This can be handled with a unary fact type, as shown in Figure 4.1. A sample population is included. From the conceptual viewpoint, the fact population is the set containing the following facts:

The Person with surname 'Adams' jogs.
The Person with surname 'Brown' jogs.
The Person with surname 'Collins' jogs.

Given that these facts are stored, what would happen if we tried the following update?

add: The Person with surname 'Adams' jogs.

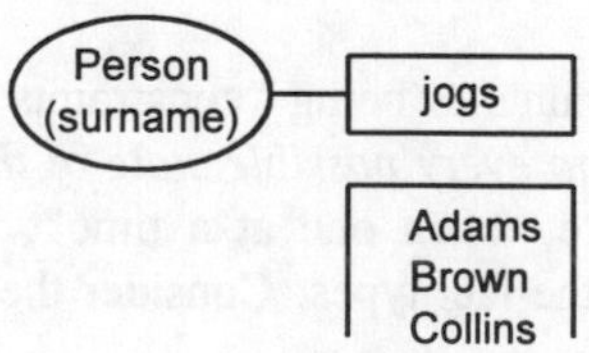

Figure 4.1 A unary fact type with same population

Figure 4.2 Identical sets but different bags

The database is a variable whose population at any state is a set of elementary facts. Since the fact that Adams jogs is already present in the database, if this fact was now added the population would remain unaltered (sets are insensitive to repetition). So the two fact tables shown in Figure 4.2 are equivalent if we look at each as a set of instances. From this viewpoint, there is no problem with accepting the update.

From the internal viewpoint however, when an elementary fact is added to a database it is typically stored in a previously unallocated space. So accepting this update would mean that the fact that Adams jogs is actually stored twice, in two physically separate locations. This is an example of **redundancy**. If redundancy occurs we need to view the database as a *bag* of facts rather than a *set* of facts. Informally, a bag or multiset is just like a set except repetition of its members is made significant. For example, although the sets {1} and {1,1} are equal, the bags [1] and [1,1] are different.

Let us review our reasons for wanting to avoid redundancy in a database. The most important reason is to maintain the integrity of the database by simplifying the correct handling of update operations. For instance, suppose the fact that Adams jogs was stored twice in the database. If we later wanted to delete this fact then we would have to make sure we deleted both the recorded instances of this fact. Managing updates can become difficult if we allow redundancy in the database. A second reason for avoiding redundancy is to save space (computers have finite storage capabilities).

On the other hand, redundancy can be useful in making retrieval of information more efficient. Sometimes to make information systems work fast enough it may be necessary to allow certain kinds of controlled redundancy at the logical schema level. However, for our conceptual schema design we demand that *no redundancy may occur in the conceptual database*. Redundancy is simply the repetition of an elementary fact. Since each row of a conceptual fact table corresponds to one elementary fact, this means that *no row of a fact table may be repeated*. In our example, this means that the right-hand fact table is illegal, since the Adams row is repeated (Figure 4.3).

Here, for any particular state of the database, each person can be recorded as being a jogger at most once. In other words, each entry in the column is unique. We represent this *uniqueness constraint* by placing an **arrow-tipped bar** above the fact table as shown in Figure 4.4.

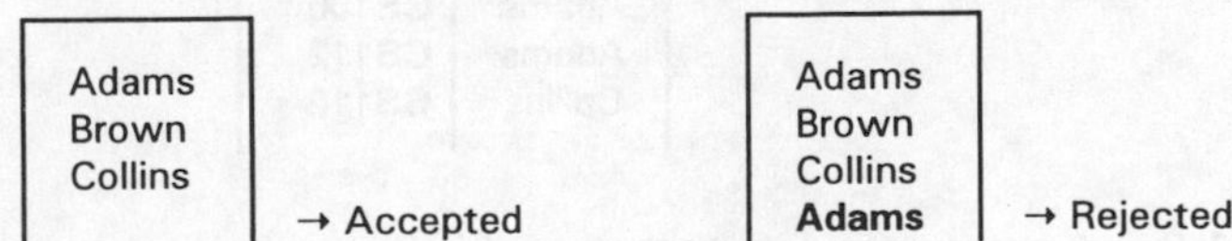

Figure 4.3 Duplicate rows are not allowed

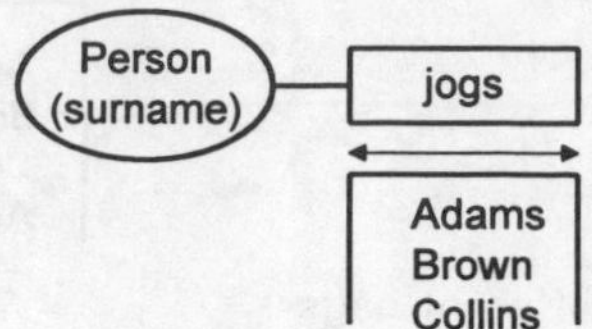

Figure 4.4 Arrow-tipped bar notation for uniqueness constraint

Notice that the uniqueness constraint also appears next to the role. We can show the constraint on the conceptual schema diagram alone by placing the symbol next to the role (see Figure 4.5). It doesn't matter on what side (top or bottom) of the role we place the constraint symbol.

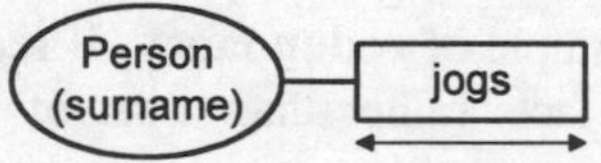

Figure 4.5 Uniqueness constraint shown next to the role

For unary and binary predicates, a *plain bar* may be used instead of an arrow-tipped bar. In this text we usually include the arrow-tips. Since elementary facts are unique to the database, all unary fact types automatically have a uniqueness constraint. If desired, the constraint marker may be omitted on unaries since it is implied.

So much for unaries. Now let's consider *binary* predicates, starting with the populated binary fact type shown in Figure 4.6. First note that no whole row of the fact table is repeated. This must be the case, since each row corresponds to an elementary fact, and we have agreed not to repeat facts in our database.

Although each row is unique, we cannot say the same for each student. For example, the student Adams appears twice in the first column. Nor is the subject unique. For example, CS112 occurs twice in the second column. This is an example of a *many to many* (or *m:n*) relation. A student may study many (i.e. at least two) subjects, and a subject may be studied by many students. This feature is shown more clearly in the instance diagram of Figure 4.7, where the objects are denoted by dots.

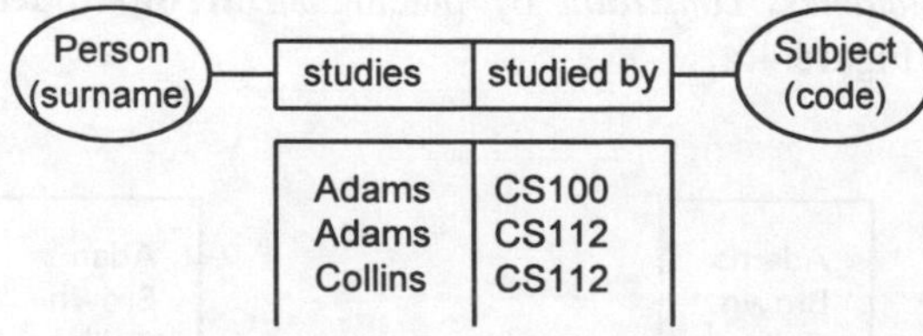

Figure 4.6 A person may study many subjects, and vice versa

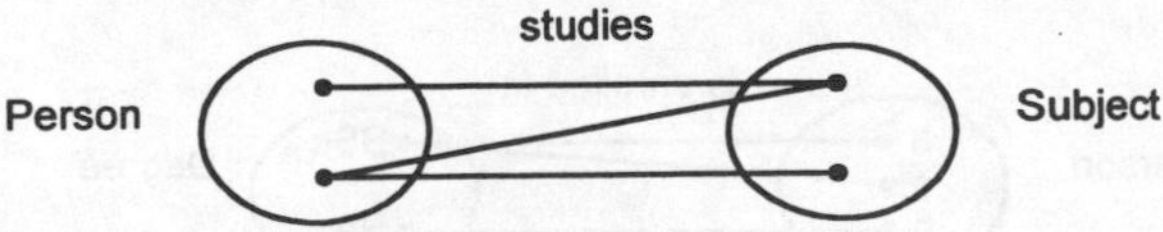

Figure 4.7 A many to many relation

For this fact type then, the only uniqueness constraint which applies to every one of its possible populations is that the *combination* of student and subject is unique. We depict this uniqueness constraint by means of an arrow-tipped bar which spans both columns of the fact table (see Figure 4.8).

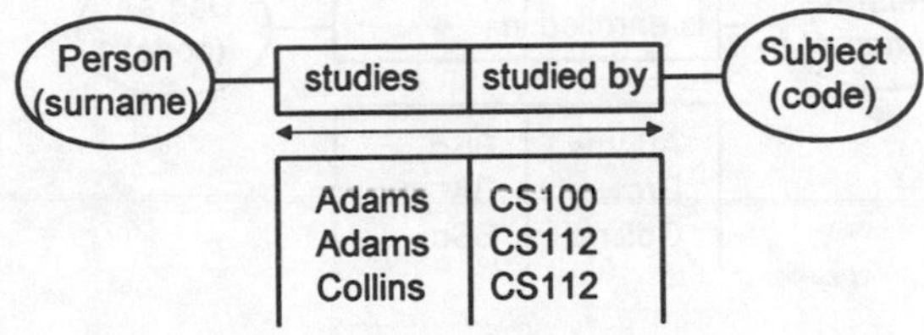

Figure 4.8 Uniqueness constraint across whole row only

We may show the uniqueness constraint on the conceptual schema diagram alone by placing the bar next to the roles (just remove the fact table from Figure 4.8). Now consider the example shown in Figure 4.9.

For this UoD, although many students may enroll in the same degree, no student may be enrolled in many degrees. This situation may be depicted as shown in Figure 4.10. Many people may enroll in the one degree, but many degrees may not be enrolled in (simultaneously) by the one person. We say that the predicate "... is enrolled in ..." is *many to one* (or *n:1*). The inverse predicate "... is enrolled in by ..." is said to be *one to many* (or *1:n*).

If you look at the fact table you will see that the constraint that each person may enroll in at most one degree amounts to saying that each entry in the Person column must be unique: no surname can be duplicated in that column. We indicate this uniqueness constraint by placing a bar over that column, as shown in Figure 4.11.

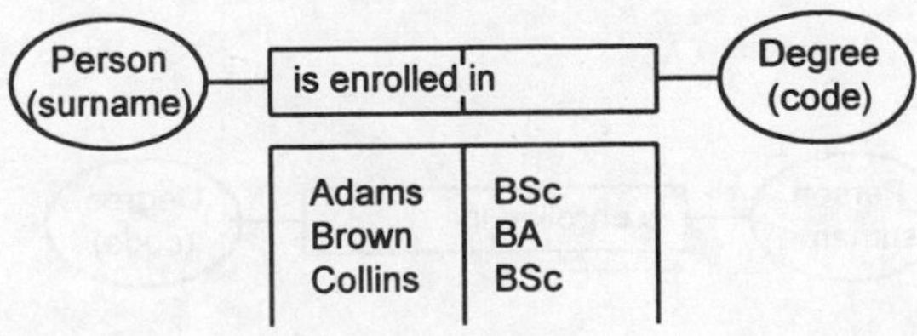

Figure 4.9 Many students may be enrolled in the same degree

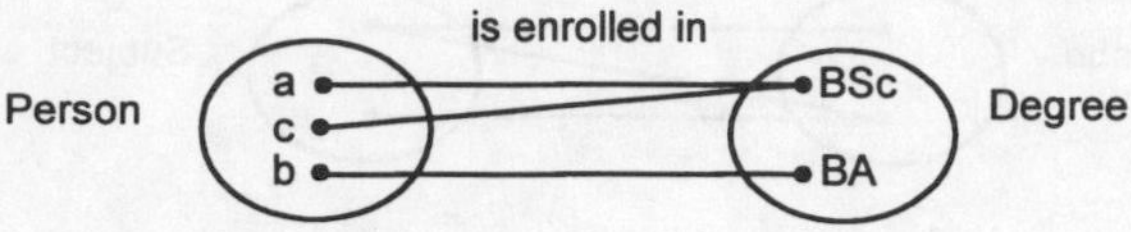

Figure 4.10 A many to one relation

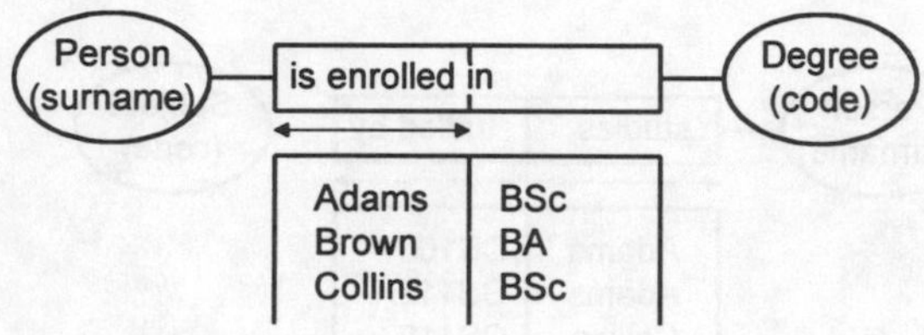

Figure 4.11 Entries in the marked column must be unique

Notice that some instances in the Degree column are repeated (here "BSc"). So we do not place a uniqueness marker over this column. As usual, we show the constraint on a conceptual schema diagram by omitting the fact table from this result (see Figure 4.12).

Although the terms "many to one" and "one to many" are often used in describing uniqueness constraints on binaries, this terminology is confusing to many people. A common error is to interpret the "many" side as the "one" side and vice versa. The ORM convention of showing both roles, and marking the constraint beside the relevant role clearly indicates the column where entries must be unique.

Now consider Figure 4.13, which concerns heads of government (e.g. Presidents or Prime Ministers). At any point in time, a politician can head the government of at most one country, and each country can have at most one head of government. For a little variety, we have shown the entity types connected to the top of the role boxes instead of the sides.

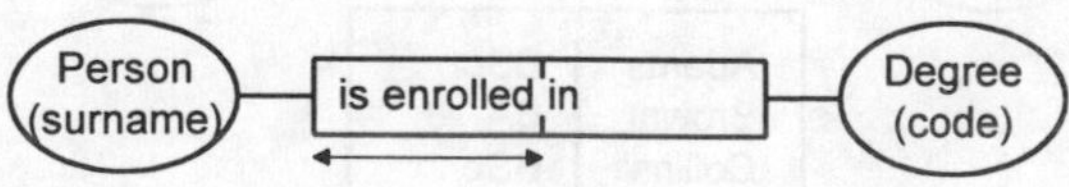

Figure 4.12 Each person is enrolled in at most one degree

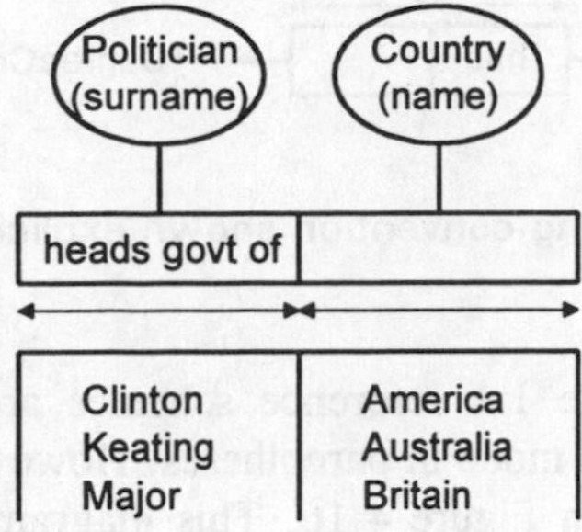

Figure 4.13 What are the uniqueness constraints?

For any state of the database, any one politician can be recorded as government head of only one country, and vice versa. Hence each population of this fact type is said to be a *one to one* (or *1:1*) relation. The instance diagram of Figure 4.14 illustrates the idea.

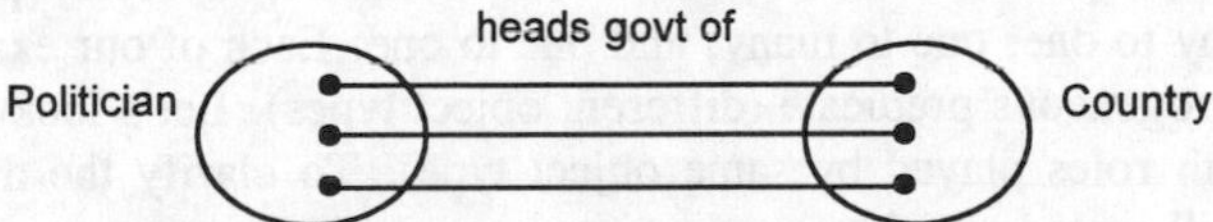

Figure 4.14 A one to one relation

With 1:1 relations, no repetition is allowed in either column of the fact table. Here each politician is referenced only once in the first column, and each country is referenced only once in the second column. So we mark uniqueness constraints above each of these columns (see Figure 4.15). The conceptual schema diagram for this fact type is obtained by removing the fact table.

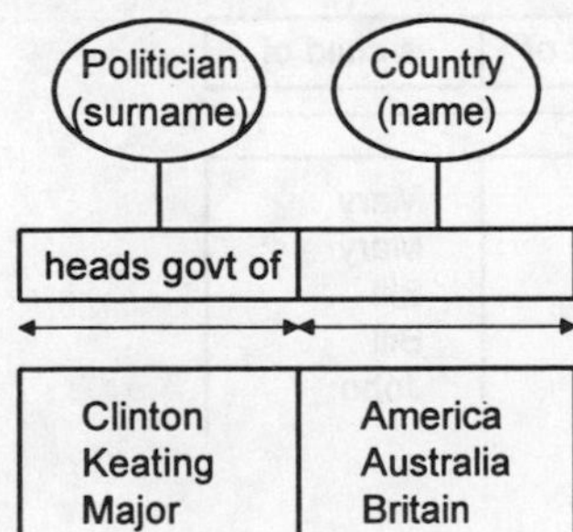

Figure 4.15 Entries in each column must be unique

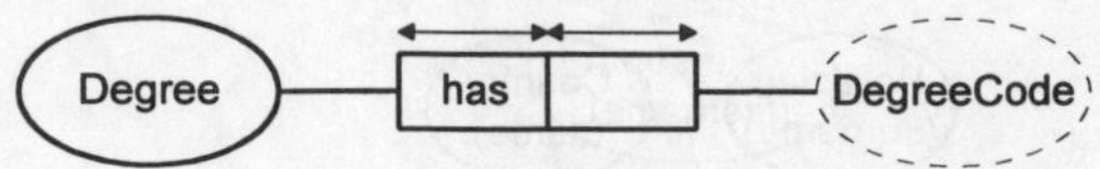

Figure 4.16 A simple 1:1 naming convention shown explicitly

As discussed earlier, simple 1:1 reference schemes are usually abbreviated by placing the name of the reference mode in parentheses. However, if desired we may set them out more fully as shown in Figure 4.16. This diagram is still incomplete; in a later section we show how to add the constraint that each degree has a degreecode.

Note that here we have a reference type rather than a fact type. When there is only one means of referring to an entity type, the uniqueness constraints on the reference type are the responsibility of the user rather than the system to enforce.

For example, we had better ensure that there really is only one degree with the degreecode "BA". If two 1:1 naming conventions are used (e.g. code or title) we choose one for our primary reference type for identification, and treat the other like any other fact type. Such cases are discussed further in a later chapter.

The four possible patterns of uniqueness constraints for a binary predicate are: many to many; many to one; one to many; and one to one. Each of our examples so far has involved a heterogeneous predicate (different object types). Let's look now at some ring predicates (both roles played by same object type). To clarify the different roles being played, we will include the inverse predicate names.

Our first example concerns parenthood (see Figure 4.17). As the sample fact table reveals, a person may have many children. Moreover a person may have many parents. The column entries need not be unique but the whole row must be. So the uniqueness constraint spans the whole row.

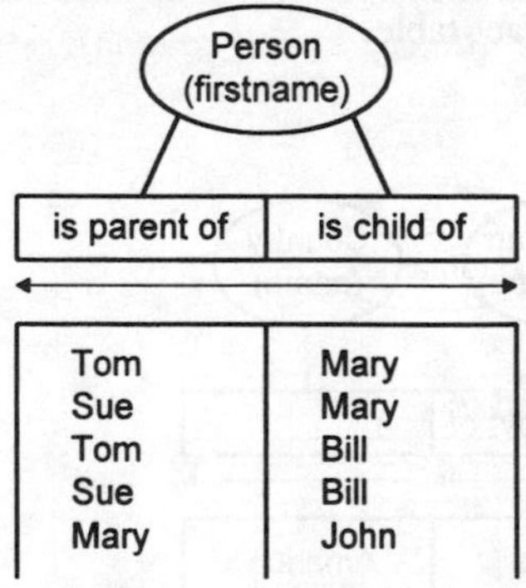

Figure 4.17 Parenthood is many to many

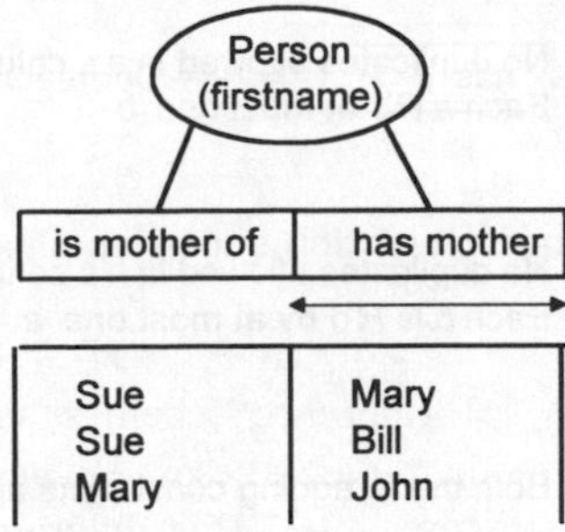

Figure 4.18 Each person has only one mother

Contrast this with motherhood (see Figure 4.18). Although a mother may have many children, each person has only one mother. So we mark the constraint as shown. Entries in the second column of the fact table must be unique to that column (not necessarily unique to the table, e.g. Mary).

The example shown in Figure 4.19 is consistent with monogamy: at any time each man has at most one wife, and each woman has at most one husband. So entries in each column must be unique. As an exercise, draw a knowledge base for the following marriage conventions: polyandry (a woman may have many husbands but not vice versa); polygyny (a man may have many wives but not vice versa); and polygamy (a man may have many wives, and a woman may have many husbands).

Uniqueness constraints are best understood in the context of a populated schema diagram, in the way we have introduced them in this section. With this understanding, for any given fact type **each role is associated with a corresponding column of the fact table.**

In terms of logical predicates, the role boxes are the "object-holes". For a set of relationship instances of this type the holes expand to columns. Marking a *single role with a uniqueness bar* means that entries in the associated column must be unique to that column (i.e. *no duplicates are allowed in that column*).

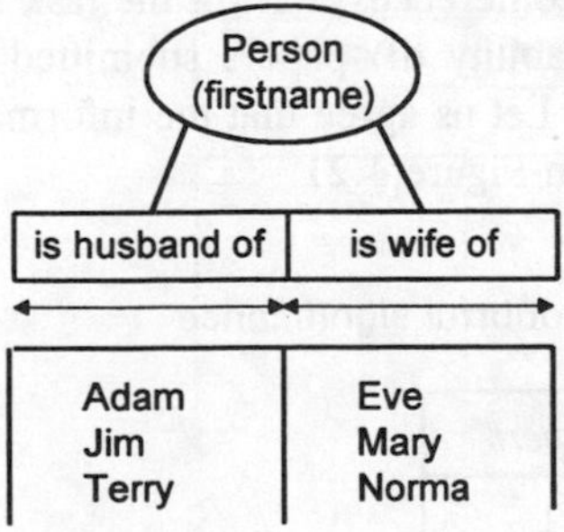

Figure 4.19 Monogamy is one to one

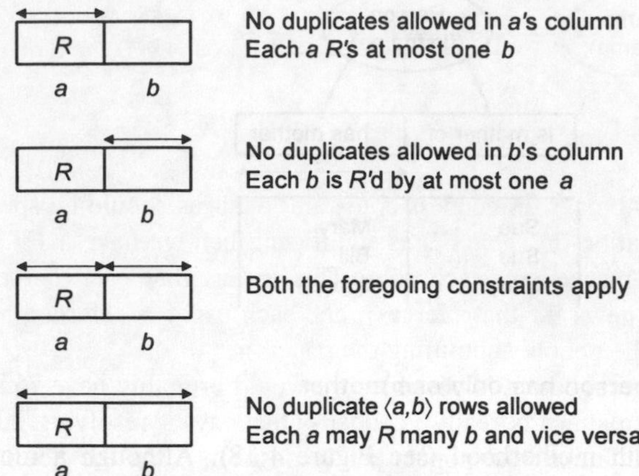

Figure 4.20 The four uniqueness constraint patterns for a binary

A uniqueness bar that spans the whole predicate means that each whole row is unique to the table. Since we never allow whole rows to be repeated, this whole row constraint applies to any fact type that we consider. If we have a stronger uniqueness constraint, then the whole row constraint is implied by this and hence is redundant. For this reason, we never mark the whole row constraint across a fact type unless that is the only uniqueness constraint that applies.

With this understanding, we must choose exactly one of the four constraint patterns shown in Figure 4.20 for any binary predicate. For brevity we use *a* and *b* as object variables, and *"a R*'s *b"* to mean *"a* bears the relation *R* to *b"*.

Provided a significant example is supplied, the uniqueness constraints on a predicate can be determined simply by looking for duplicates in its fact table. If we are not familiar with the application, we may be unsure as to whether the population is significant. Consider for example the output report of Table 4.1.

Suppose this is presented as one of the sample reports to be provided by an information system for managing conferences. Part of the task involves getting qualified people to referee (assess the suitability of) papers submitted by people who hope to present a paper at the conference. Let us agree that the information in the table may be dealt with by the fact type shown in Figure 4.21.

Table 4.1 An output report of doubtful significance

Referee	*Paper#*
Jones E	1
Smith JB	2

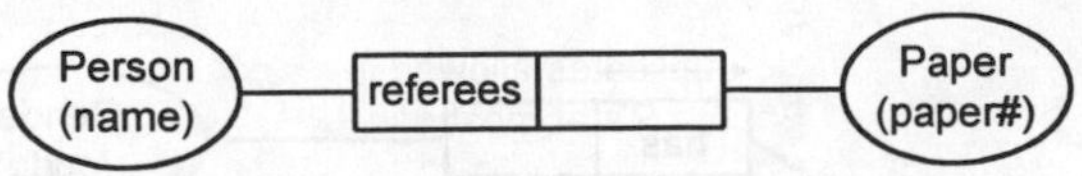

Figure 4.21 The fact type for Table 4.1

Which of the four binary uniqueness constraint patterns should be specified for this fact type? If the population of Table 4.1 is significant then we have a 1:1 situation, and constraints should be marked on each role. This means that each person referees at most one paper (good news for the referees), and each paper is refereed by at most one person (bad news for the people submitting the papers).

Now while this arrangement is possible, we would probably have some doubt as to whether this constraint pattern is really intended. One way of resolving our doubts is to add another fact which makes the population inconsistent with the doubtful constraint pattern, and ask the UoD expert whether the new population is permitted. For example, suppose we suspect that the fact type is really many:many. To test our hypothesis we add a carefully chosen row to the fact table, as shown in Figure 4.22.

If this change is accepted, we know that the many to many constraint pattern should be specified. If not, there are still three possibilities left (one to one, one to many, many to one): we leave it to you as an exercise to provide further rows to test these three hypotheses.

Another way to check the significance of a sample population is to put the relevant constraint questions to the UoD expert: "Can a person referee more than one paper?"; "Can a paper be refereed by more than one person?".

Remember that all constraints on fact types are to be interpreted as applying to what is recorded in the database, not necessarily to the real world. An information system can only enforce constraints on its formal model of the application. The constraint schema for the "real world" need not be the same as for the "recorded world". For example, consider the conceptual schema of Figure 4.23.

What do the uniqueness constraints in Figure 4.23 actually say? For any particular state of the database, each patient is recorded as having at most one gender and at most one phone. Now it may be the case in the real world that some patients have more than one phone (e.g. a home phone and a business phone). We might display this "real world schema" as in Figure 4.24.

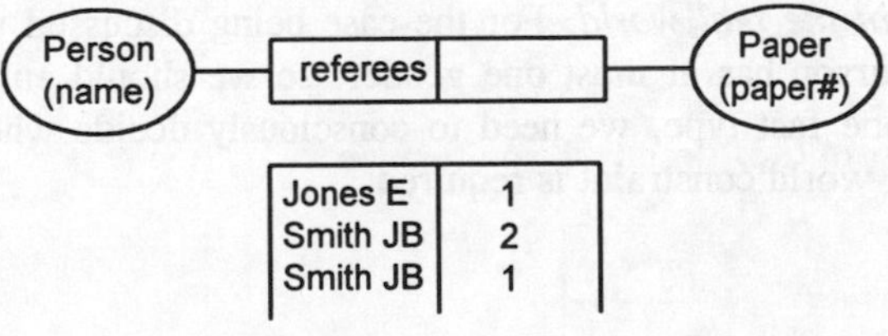

Figure 4.22 A population to test the many-to-many hypothesis

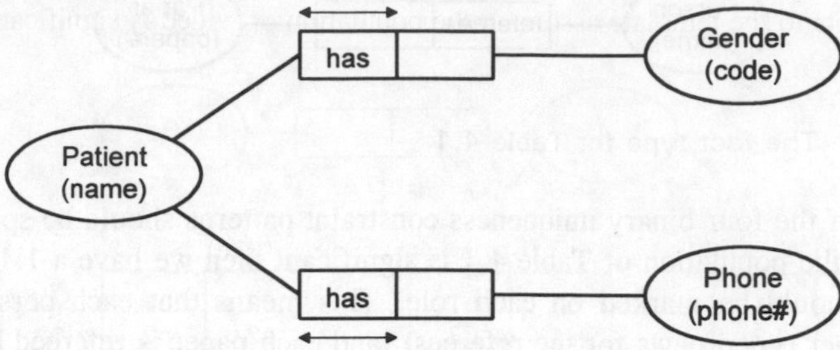

Figure 4.23 The conceptual schema actually used

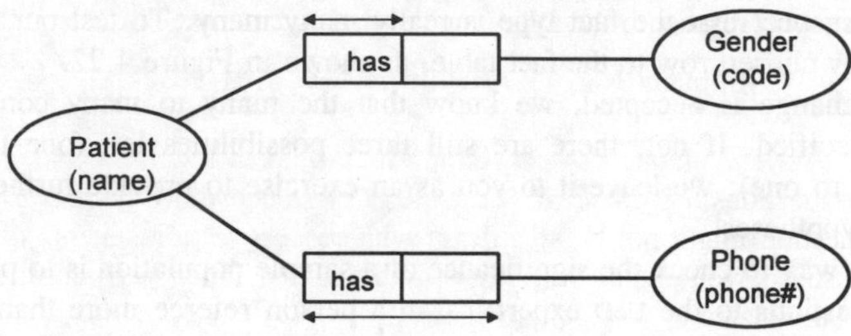

Figure 4.24 A different "real world schema"

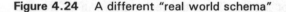

For some reason, the designer of the information system has decided that no patient will be recorded to have more than one phone. So the constraints in the first schema (Figure 4.23) fit the intended model which is to be implemented in the information system. Unless otherwise indicated, *when we speak of a conceptual schema we mean the recorded world schema*.

Nevertheless, we often use our background knowledge of the "real world schema" when designing the conceptual schema. With respect to uniqueness constraints we observe the following principle: *the uniqueness constraints should be at least as strong as those which apply in the real world*. For the case being discussed we know that in the real world each person has at most one gender: so we should enforce this in our schema. With the phone fact type, we need to consciously decide whether a stronger constraint than the real world constraint is required.

Exercise 4.2

1. For a given fact type, a sample population is significant with respect to uniqueness constraints if all the relevant uniqueness constraints can be deduced from the sample. A template is shown for a binary fact type. The names of the predicate and the reference

modes are omitted for simplicity. For each of the fact tables shown, add the uniqueness constraints to the template assuming the population provided is significant.

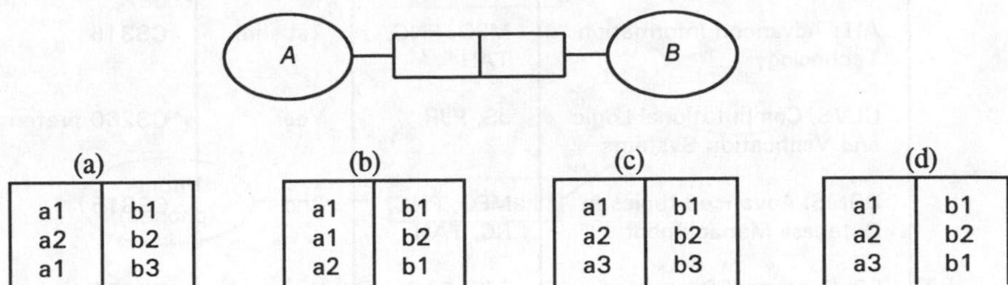

2. In a given department, employees are identified by employee numbers "e1", "e2" etc., and projects are identified by project numbers "p1", "p2" etc. Draw a schema diagram for the fact type Employee works on Project, and provide populations which are significant with respect to the following constraint patterns:

   (a) 1:many (b) many:1 (c) many:many (d) 1:1

3. Add the relevant uniqueness constraints to the conceptual schema diagrams for the Exercise questions listed below. For some of these questions the output report provided in the question might not be significant with respect to uniqueness constraints. Using common sense, you should be able to avoid adding uniqueness constraints which are likely to be violated by a larger population.

   (a) Exercise 3.4 Question 1b (b) Exercise 3.4 Question 1d
   (c) Exercise 3.4 Question 2 (d) Exercise 3.4 Question 5
   (e) Exercise 3.5 Question 2 (f) Exercise 3.5 Question 3

4. By now you must be feeling like a challenge. Here is a question based on a real-life application. We extend this question in later exercises. The following report is an extract from an actual Computer Science Department Handbook. Verbalize this report in terms of *binaries*, draw the fact types and add uniqueness constraints.

   The first column headed "Subject title" actually lists the codes and titles of postgraduate topics (don't expect all the names in real-life examples to be well chosen!). A topic is not the same kind of thing as a subject. A postgraduate student first enrolls in a subject (identified by subject code, e.g. CS451) then later chooses a topic to study for this subject. Subject enrollments are not part of this question. A topic may be offered in semester 1 only, in semester 2 only, or over the whole year (at half the pace).

   The fact that different students might be enrolled in the same subject (as identified by subject code) and yet be studying different topics is a source of possible confusion. As information modelers, one of the most signficant contributions we can make is to suggest improvements to the UoD itself. In this example, we might argue it would simplify things if topics were treated as subjects. The department involved eventually accepted this change. For this exercise however, you are to model things as they were.

Postgraduate coursework topics in Computer Science

Subject title	*Staff*	*When*	*Prerequisites*
AIT: Advanced Information Technology	MEO, PNC, TAH	1st sem	CS315
CLVS: Computational Logic and Verification Systems	JS, PJR	Year	CS260 preferred
DBMS: Advanced topics in Database Management	MEO, PNC, RC, TAH	2nd	CS315
FP: Functional Programming	EJS, PAB	Year	CS225 CS220 preferred
GA: Geometric Algorithms	PDE	1st	CS340

N.B. Topics are offered subject to the availability of staff and to there being sufficient demand for a topic. In each case the first-mentioned member of staff is lecturer-in-charge of the subject. Preferred prerequisites may become mandatory in later years.

4.3 Uniqueness constraints on longer fact types

This section shows how to specify uniqueness constraints on fact types of arity 3 and beyond, including nested versions. Let's begin with an example. Figure 4.25 shows a populated ternary fact type of the form: **Person scored Rating for Subject**. Even if we are not familiar with the example, sample populations supplied by the UoD expert can reveal that certain constraints don't apply.

Looking at the fact table, we first consider each column individually. Here, with each column there is at least one value that is repeated. So no column by itself has a uniqueness constraint. We see later that this must be true of any ternary fact type that is elementary.

Now let's look at pairs of columns. For ease of reference here, we number the columns 1,2,3 in the order shown in the diagram. Beginning with columns 1 and 2 we note that the pair ⟨Adams, 7⟩ is repeated. With columns 1 and 3, each pair is unique. That is, each ⟨Person, Subject⟩ combination occurs on only one row of the table. With columns 2 and 3 the pair ⟨7, PD102⟩ is repeated.

There are only three ways of pairing the columns in a ternary. So if the population of the fact table is significant, the only pair-unique constraint is that each ⟨Person, Subject⟩ pair must be unique to the table. If we are familiar with the application, we can usually decide whether the population is significant in this regard simply by using common sense. With the present example, this constraint means that for each ⟨Person, Subject⟩ combination, at most one rating may be obtained. This agrees with our background knowledge about the UoD and so the uniqueness constraint suggested by the table is accepted.

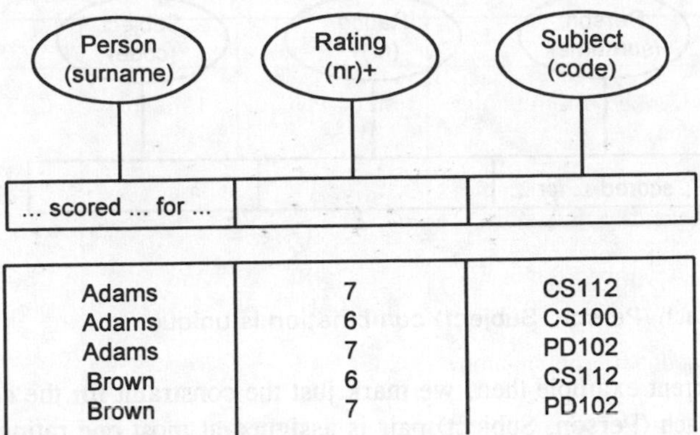

Adams	7	CS112
Adams	6	CS100
Adams	7	PD102
Brown	6	CS112
Brown	7	PD102

Figure 4.25 What are the uniqueness constraints?

Sample fact tables may be obtained from output reports (which often represent a combination of separate fact tables) or from simple factual knowledge about the UoD. Unless the population is large, or well chosen, it is unlikely to be completely significant with respect to all uniqueness constraints. For instance, suppose row 3 was deleted from the table in Figure 4.25. For the smaller sample, both the column 1,2 pair and the column 2,3 pair would then show no duplicates. The table would then suggest a uniqueness constraint for all three column pairs.

So we need to be wary of relying on just a sample fact table to determine uniqueness constraints. We should *ask ourselves whether any suggested constraint really makes sense*. A uniqueness constraint on the column 1,2 pair would mean that a ⟨Person, Rating⟩ combination could occur for at most one subject: this would forbid somebody obtaining the same rating for two subjects—an unrealistic restriction! Similarly, the suggested constraint on the column 2,3 pair must be rejected as unrealistic (it would prevent two people from scoring the same rating for a particular subject).

Uniqueness constraints may often be determined simply by background knowledge about how the UoD works. As we saw in the previous section, real world uniqueness constraints usually determine the weakest uniqueness constraints that may be considered for the actual database. If we know the fact table is significant then we can always generate the constraints from it.

Usually however, we won't know in advance that the table is significant, and we will have to use some of our background knowledge. If we lack such knowledge we should consult the UoD expert about any doubtful constraints. As discussed, one effective way of questioning the UoD expert is by adding further facts to the population and asking whether these should be accepted or rejected. Alternatively, the relevant questions may be posed directly.

With a ternary fact type, the constraint spanning all three columns is always implied, since no whole row may be repeated. We mark this constraint if and only if no other uniqueness constraint holds.

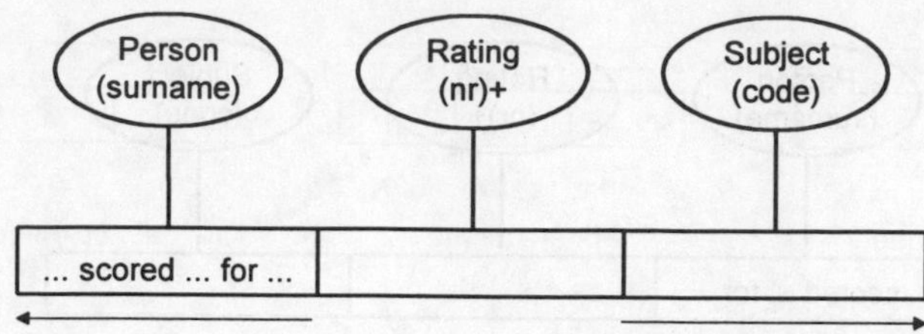

Figure 4.26 Each ⟨Person, Subject⟩ combination is unique

For our current example then, we mark just the constraint for the column 1,3 pair, indicating that each ⟨Person, Subject⟩ pair is assigned at most one rating. Since the two role boxes involved are not adjacent, we use a *divided constraint bar* as shown in Figure 4.26. Notice that this time *we must include the arrow heads*. If we omitted them we would interpret the bars as two separate constraints, one for each of the two columns.

To avoid confusion, let us agree to always include arrow heads on constraint bars for any fact type longer than a binary. Suppose we had worded the fact type instead as: Person for Subject scored Rating. In this case there would be two contiguous roles spanned by an undivided constraint bar.

We use the term *n-role constraint* for a constraint that spans *n* roles. A uniqueness constraint that spans just one role is a **simple** uniqueness constraint. The constraint in Figure 4.26 is a 2-role constraint since it spans two of the three roles involved in the fact type. With a binary fact type we had three basic constraints (two 1-role and one 2-role) which gave rise to four possible cases. In section 4.5 it will be demonstrated that *no (elementary) ternary fact type can have a simple uniqueness constraint*. So with a ternary fact type there are four basic uniqueness constraints to be considered: three 2-role constraints and one 3-role constraint (see Figure 4.27).

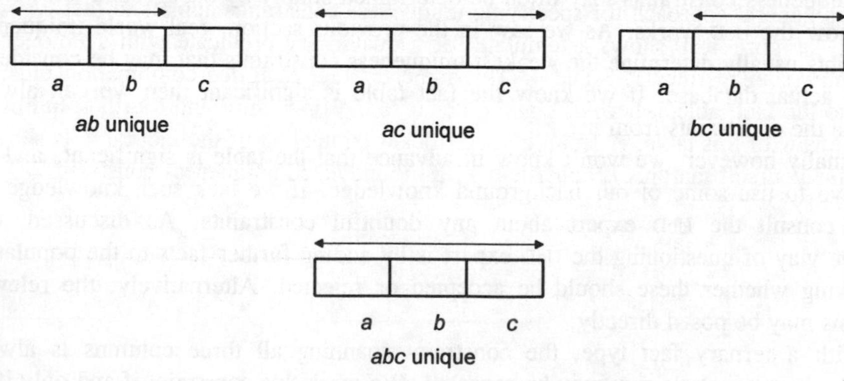

Figure 4.27 Allowed basic uniqueness constraints for a ternary

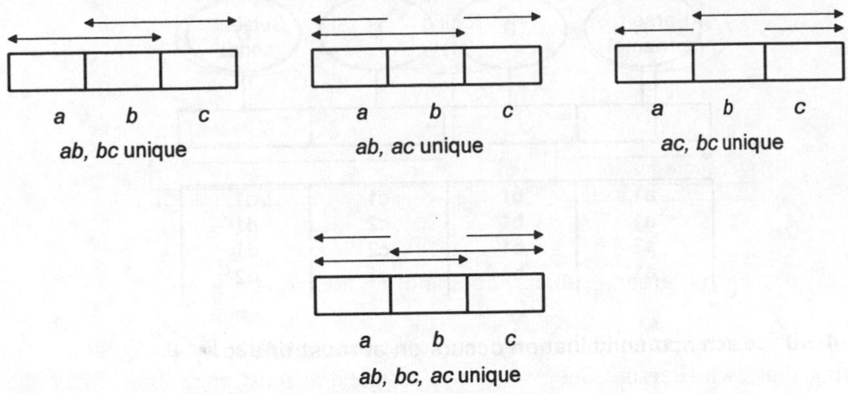

Figure 4.28 Allowed uniqueness constraint combinations for a ternary

With a ternary fact type, we should systematically test each of the three 2-role constraints to see which ones hold. Only if none of these hold should the 3-role constraint be specified. There is only one way of having a 3-role uniqueness constraint. There are three ways of having precisely one 2-role constraint, and three ways of having exactly two 2-role constraints. Finally there is one way of having three 2-role constraints.

Thus there are eight different uniqueness constraint patterns that may arise with a ternary fact type. Four of these involve just one constraint (Figure 4.27) and four involve combinations (see Figure 4.28).

All other constraint patterns for a ternary are illegal (i.e. disallowed). Some examples of these are shown in Figure 4.29. The first two of these are fundamentally wrong, since a ternary fact type with a simple uniqueness constraint cannot be elementary. The third example is wrong because the 3-role constraint is implied by the 2-role constraint and hence should not be displayed.

This general approach for specifying uniqueness constraints applies to fact types of any arity. Figure 4.30 shows a template for a quaternary predicate with a uniqueness constraint spanning roles 1, 3 and 4. This indicates that each *acd* combination must be unique to the fact table, where *a*, *c* and *d* occur in the first, third and fourth columns on the same row of this table. A small but significant population of the fact table is shown. Verify for yourself that this is consistent with the indicated uniqueness constraint.

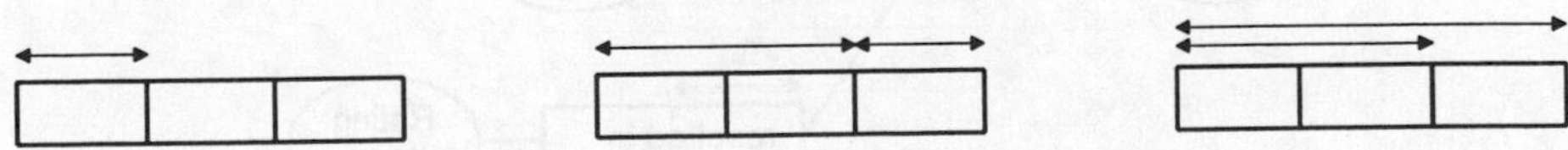

Figure 4.29 Some illegal constraint patterns

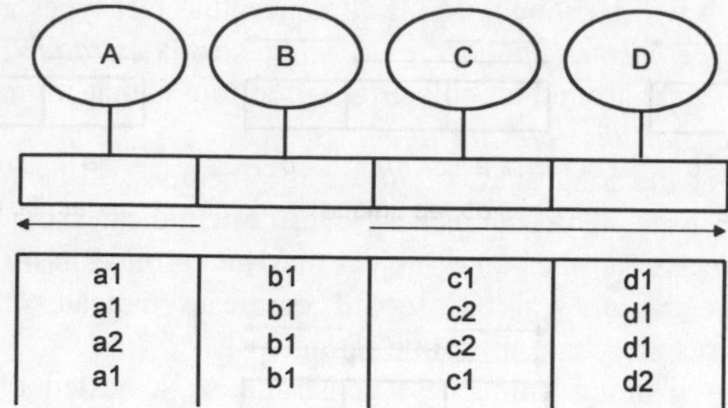

Figure 4.30 Each *acd* combination occurs on at most one row

It is shown later that any uniqueness constraints on a quaternary must span at least three roles. As an exercise, you might like to explore all the possible cases. Since elementary fact types are almost never longer than quaternaries, we do not illustrate any such examples here.

To visualize the connection between roles and columns of the fact table, think of the role boxes as the holes in which the objects get placed to complete the fact. No matter what the arity of the fact type, a uniqueness constraint across a combination of role boxes means that any instance of that column combination which does appear in the table must occur on one row only, and hence can be used to identify that row.

Since a role combination governed by a uniqueness constraint thus provides a "key to unlock" any row of the fact table, this combination is sometimes referred to as a *key* for that table. In later work when we consider the (often non-elementary) tables used in relational databases we will have more to say about this notion.

Now let's consider nesting. In Figure 4.26 the subject ratings example was set out in flattened form. Suppose that instead we used a nested approach as shown in Figure 4.31. Here each ⟨Person, Subject⟩ enrollment is treated as an object which may result in a rating. For example, the enrollment ⟨Adams, CS112⟩ results in a 7.

Figures 4.26 and 4.31 are not actually equivalent unless we add a further constraint that a rating must be known for each enrollment (see next chapter). However, at this stage we are interested only in how to specify the uniqueness constraints.

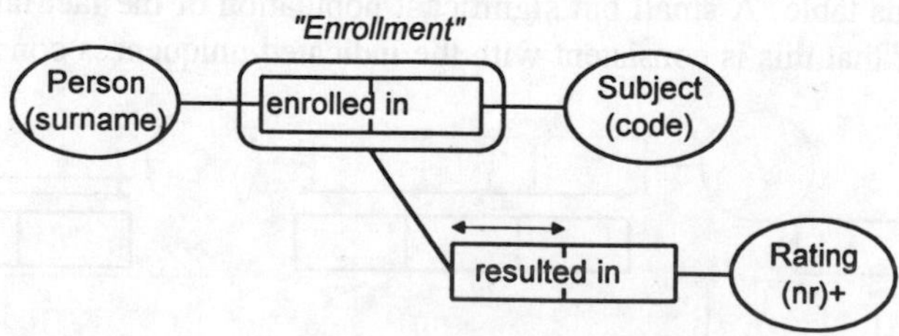

Figure 4.31 A uniqueness constraint implicitly spans the nested object type

In section 4.5, it will be shown that if all conceptual fact types are elementary then *each nested object type must be spanned by a uniqueness constraint*. In this case, part of the meaning of the *frame* around an objectified predicate is that it *includes a uniqueness constraint which spans all the roles inside*.

Visually, one of the long sides of the frame includes a line (or uniqueness bar) spanning the roles inside. This uniqueness constraint indicates that each person may enroll in many subjects, and the same subject may be enrolled in by many people. The simple uniqueness constraint on the scored predicate indicates that each ⟨Person, Subject⟩ enrollment resulted in at most one rating.

If desired, the spanning uniqueness constraint on a nested object type may be shown explicitly. Alternatively, an ellipse may be used instead of a frame: in this case the uniqueness constraint must be explicitly marked. Figure 4.32 shows the three notations for nesting. For our purposes, these may be considered equivalent.

We will generally use notation (a) since it is more compact, it stops incorrect uniqueness constraints on the inside roles, and it simplifies the visual application of the mapping algorithm to be considered later. Notation (b) is best if it is desired to highlight the uniqueness constraint, and is also the best choice if the ORM version allows nested objects without a spanning uniqueness constraint. Section 8.4 discusses such a case (nesting a 1:1 marriage object); however such cases violate elementarity and in this book we will generally assume this is not allowed.

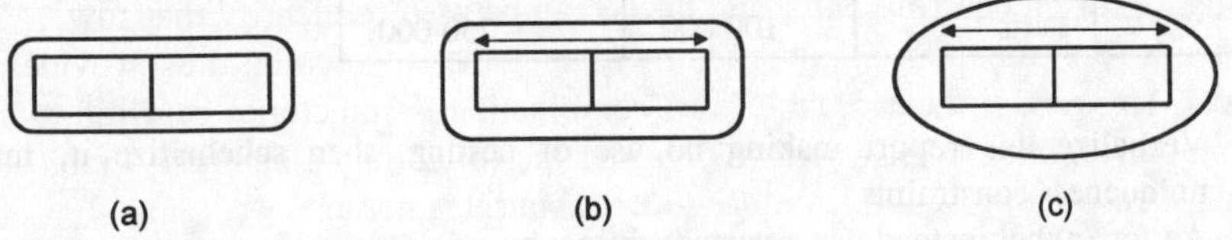

Figure 4.32 Alternative notations for nesting

Exercise 4.3

1. A template for a ternary fact type is shown. For each of the fact tables provided, add the uniqueness constraints, assuming that the population is significant in this regard.

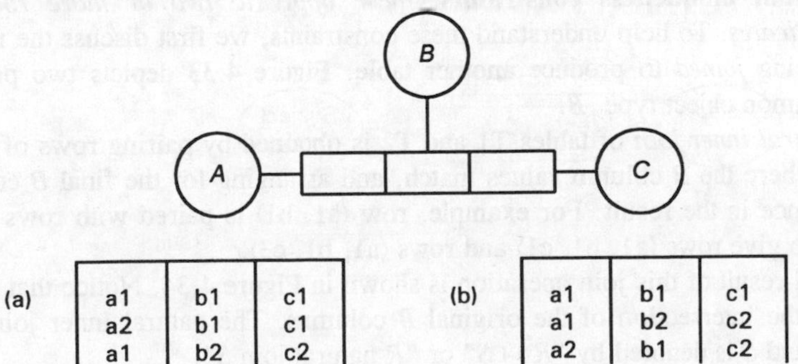

(a)

a1	b1	c1
a2	b1	c1
a1	b2	c2

(b)

a1	b1	c1
a1	b2	c2
a2	b1	c2

(c)

a1	b1	c1
a2	b2	c1
a1	b1	c2
a1	b2	c1

(d)

a1	b1	c1
a2	b2	c2
a1	b2	c2
a2	b2	c1

2. Verbalize then schematize the following report, marking uniqueness constraints.

Department	*Staff category*	*Number*
CS	Professor	3
CS	Senior Lecturer	6
CS	Lecturer	10
EE	Professor	3
EE	Senior Lecturer	7
EE	Lecturer	7

3.

Year	*Branch*	*Profit ($)*	*Total profit ($)*
1987	New York Paris	100 000 50 000	150 000
1988	New York Paris	150 000 100 000	250 000

(a) Verbalize this report making no use of nesting, then schematize it, marking uniqueness constraints.

(b) As for (a) but instead use a nested approach.

4.4 External uniqueness constraints

The uniqueness constraints discussed so far are called *internal* uniqueness constraints, since each applies to one or more roles inside a single predicate. In this section we discuss **external uniqueness constraints**: these *apply to two or more roles from different predicates*. To help understand these constraints, we first discuss the notion of two tables being *joined* to produce another table. Figure 4.33 depicts two predicates sharing a common object type, *B*.

The *natural inner join* of tables T1 and T2 is obtained by pairing rows of T1 with rows of T2 where the *B* column values match, and arranging for the final *B* column to appear just once in the result. For example, row ⟨a1, b1⟩ is paired with rows ⟨b1, c1⟩ and ⟨b1, c3⟩ to give rows ⟨a1, b1, c1⟩ and rows ⟨a1, b1, c3⟩.

The final result of this join operation is shown in Figure 4.34. Notice that the final *B* column is the intersection of the original *B* columns. The natural inner join of any two tables *R* and *S* is denoted by "*R* ⋈ *S*" or "*R* natural join *S*".

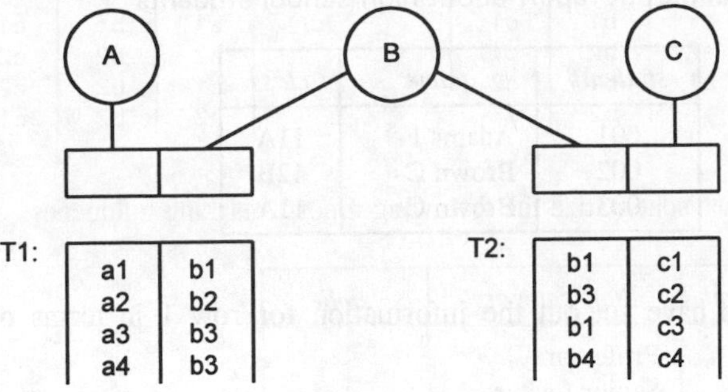

Figure 4.33 Tables T1 and T2 share a common object type

The term "natural join" or even "join" is often used without qualification for the natural inner join. Other kinds of joins are sometimes discussed (e.g. joins based on operators other than equality, and outer joins). A left (right, full) *outer join* is obtained by adding to the inner join those rows, if any, where the join column value occurs in just the left (just the right, just one of) the tables, and padding the missing entries of such rows with null values.

For example, the full outer join of T1 and T2 includes the rows ⟨a2, b2, ?⟩ and ⟨?, b4, c4⟩ where "?" denotes a null value. Since conceptual fact tables cannot have null values, we have little use for outer joins at the conceptual level. However, outer joins are often used at the relational database level.

With this background, let's consider an example with an external uniqueness constraint. An output report concerning high school students is shown in Table 4.2. As an exercise, perform step 1 for the top row of this report before reading on.

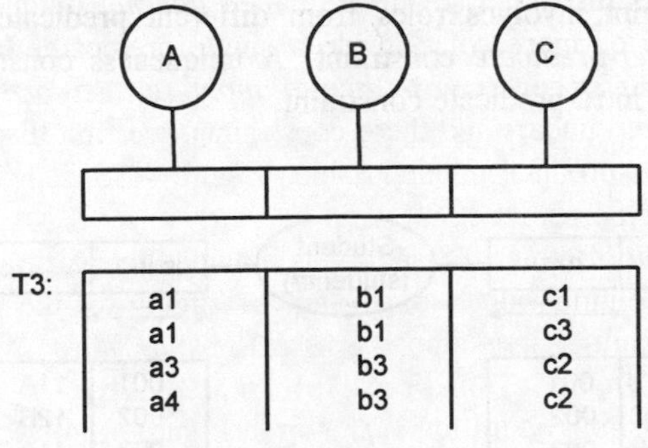

Figure 4.34 Table T3 is the (natural inner) join of T1 and T2

Table 4.2 An output report about high school students

Student:

student#	*name*	*class*
001	Adams J	11A
002	Brown C	12B
003	Brown C	11A

You should have set out the information for row 1 in terms of two elementary facts:

> The Student with student# '001' **has** the StudentName 'Adams J'.
> The Student with student# '001' **is in** the Class with code '11A'.

The first of these facts is a relationship between an entity and a value. The second fact is a relationship between two entities. Note that in this UoD, students are identified by their student numbers. As rows 2 and 3 show, it is possible for two different students to have the same student name ("Brown C"). We might now set out a populated schema diagram as shown in Figure 4.35 (a).

Let us agree that the population supplied is significant. It follows that each student has at most one name, and each student is in at most one class. These uniqueness constraints have been captured on the schema diagram. However, there is another uniqueness constraint that we have missed. What is it?

The output report is reproduced in Table 4.3, with uniqueness constraints marked above the relevant columns. Notice that the combination of name and class is unique. Although a student's name need not be unique to the UoD it is unique to the student's class. While there are two students named "Brown C" there can be only one student with this name in class 12B, and only one student with this name in class 11A.

Each row of the output report splits into two elementary facts, one for the name and one for the class. So to specify the name-class uniqueness constraint on the schema diagram we need to involve two fact types. The relevant role boxes to which the constraint applies are joined by dotted lines to a *circled "u"* symbol "ⓤ" as shown in Figure 4.35 (b). The "u" stands for "unique".

Because this constraint involves roles from different predicates it is called an *external* constraint or *inter-predicate* constraint. A uniqueness constraint on a single predicate is an internal or intra-predicate constraint.

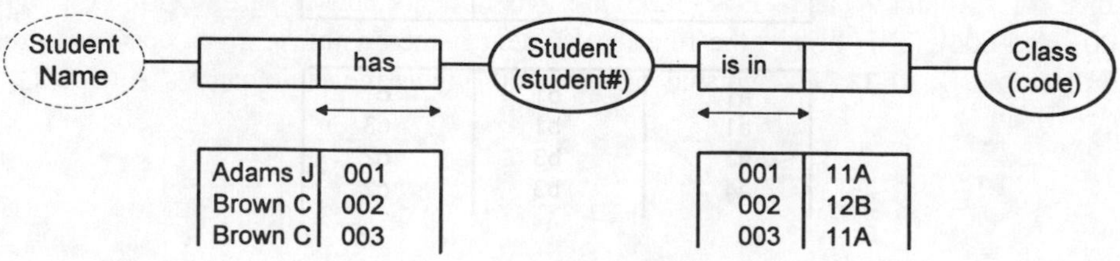

Figure 4.35 (a) A populated schema diagram for Table 4.2 (draft version)

Table 4.3

Student:

student#	*name*	*class*
001	Adams J	11A
002	Brown C	12B
003	Brown C	11A

In this example, the external uniqueness constraint indicates that for each student the *combination* of student name and class is unique: given any student name and class code from the tables, there is *at most one* student who is paired with both. For instance, given "Adams J" and "11A" there is only one student# sharing rows with both ("001"). Given "Adams J" and "12B" there is no student# paired with both.

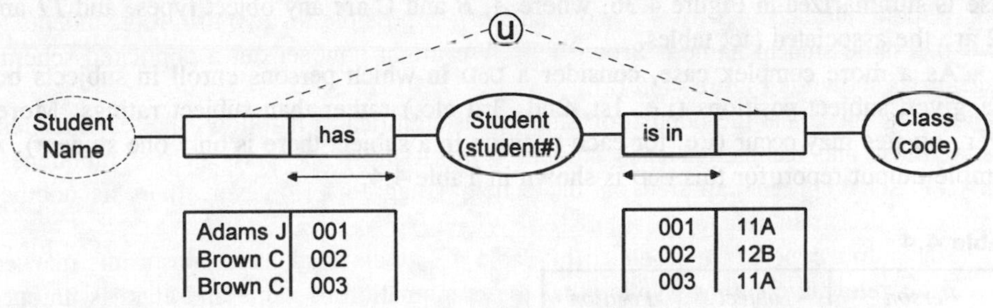

Figure 4.35 (b) The external uniqueness constraint has been added

Perhaps the easiest way to understand this constraint is to say that if we perform the natural *join* operation on the two fact tables, then the resulting table has a uniqueness constraint across the ⟨name, class⟩ column pair. Note that when we join the two fact tables we obtain the table in the report (Table 4.3).

The join operation provides a simple way of relating this schema constraint to the corresponding constraint on the report. To ensure you understand this kind of constraint, see if you can explain why the population shown in Figure 4.35 (c) is not valid for this schema.

The extra row added to each table provides a counterexample to the constraint, since for "Adams J" and "11A" there are two student# entries paired with these entries (001 and 004). This breaks the rule that student names within a given class are unique to that class. In class 11A two students (001, 004) have the same name ("Adams J").

Adams J	001
Brown C	002
Brown C	003
Adams J	004

001	11A
002	12B
003	11A
004	11A

Figure 4.35 (c) A population inconsistent with the schema

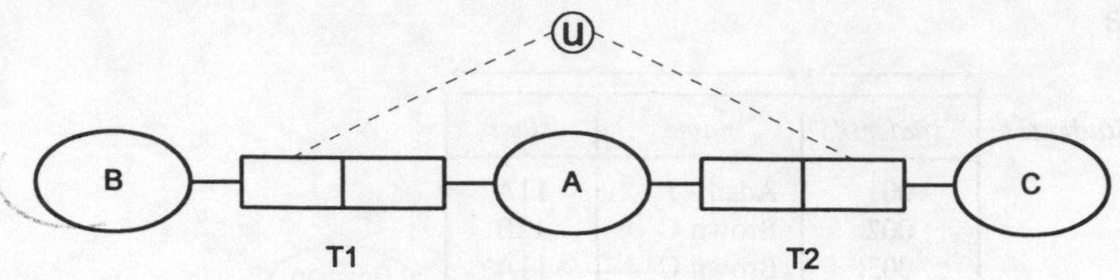

Each *b, c* combination is paired with at most one *a*.
For each population, T1 **natural join** T2 has *bc* unique.

Figure 4.36 An external, or inter-predicate, uniqueness constraint

More simply, if we join the two tables in Figure 4.35 (c) the combination ⟨"Adams J", "11A"⟩ occurs on two rows, thus violating the uniqueness constraint. The general case is summarized in Figure 4.36, where *A*, *B* and *C* are any object types, and *T1* and *T2* are the associated fact tables.

As a more complex case, consider a UoD in which persons enroll in subjects but are given subject positions (i.e. 1st, 2nd, 3rd etc.) rather than subject ratings. Moreover, no ties may occur (i.e. for each position in a subject there is only one student). A sample output report for this UoD is shown in Table 4.4.

Table 4.4

Person	*Subject*	*Position*
Adams J	CS114	3
Adams J	CS100	10
Adams J	PD102	3
Brown C	CS114	10
Brown C	PD102	5

Performing step 1 on the first row, we might express the information as the following ternary: Person (name) "Adams J" is placed in Subject (code) "CS114" at Position (nr) 3. This leads to the schema of Figure 4.37. Notice the overlapping uniqueness constraints. Check these with the population and make sure you understand them.

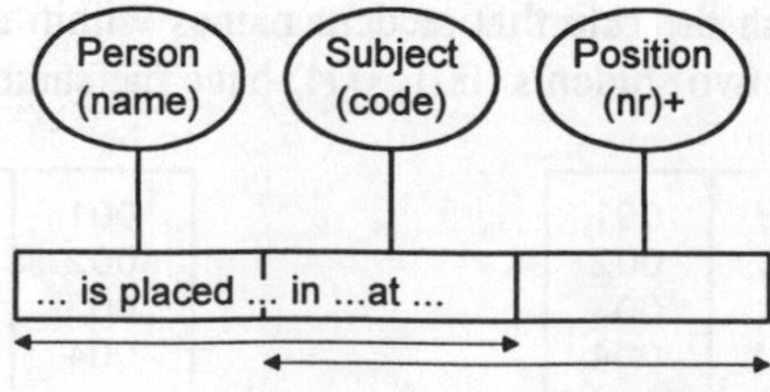

Figure 4.37 A schema diagram for Table 4.4

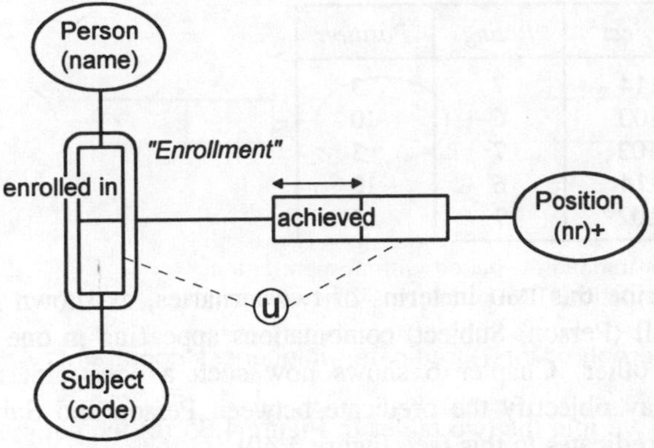

Figure 4.38 Another schema diagram for Table 4.4 (nested version)

Now suppose we adopted a nested approach instead. For example we might have expressed the information on row 1 as follows: Person (name) "Adams J" enrolled in Subject (code) "CS114"; this Enrollment achieved Position (nr) 3. This leads to the nested version shown in Figure 4.38. Actually, for this to be equivalent to the ternary, the role played by the nested object type must be mandatory (see next chapter).

The frame indicates that the Enrollment predicate is many:many. With this in mind, the simple uniqueness constraint on the other predicate captures the uniqueness constraint spanning the first two roles in the flattened version (Figure 4.37). The inter-predicate uniqueness constraint corresponds to the constraint spanning the last two roles in the flattened version—each ⟨Subject, Position⟩ combination is unique.

In other words, if we *flatten* the nested version into a ternary then any ⟨Subject, Position⟩ pair occurs on at most one row of the ternary table. To help understand this we suggest you add the fact tables to the diagram. The fact table for the outer predicate effectively matches the output report.

External uniqueness constraints sometimes connect more than two roles. In all cases however, the underlying predicates can involve at most one object type that doesn't play or include one of these roles. Otherwise the complete fact type under discussion is not elementary. Basically this means that when the fact tables are combined to produce a single table (by joining or flattening) there is at most one column not spanned by the uniqueness constraint. We justify this rule later in the chapter.

As you may have gathered from these examples, nesting tends to produce a more complex constraint picture. For this example, the flattened version is preferred. However, if the Position information is optional (e.g. to be added later) then we would choose the nested approach.

Another reason for nesting is to avoid embedding the same relationship type within more than one fact type. For example, suppose we have to record both a rating and a unique subject position for each student taking any given subject. A sample output report for this situation is shown in Table 4.5.

Table 4.5

Person	*Subject*	*Rating*	*Position*
Adams J	CS114	7	3
Adams J	CS100	6	10
Adams J	PD102	7	3
Brown C	CS114	6	10
Brown C	PD102	7	5

We might describe this UoD in terms of two ternaries, as shown in Figure 4.39. Note however that all ⟨Person, Subject⟩ combinations appearing in one fact table must also appear in the other. Chapter 6 shows how such a constraint may be added. Alternatively, we may objectify the predicate between Person and Subject and attach rating and position predicates to this (see Figure 4.40).

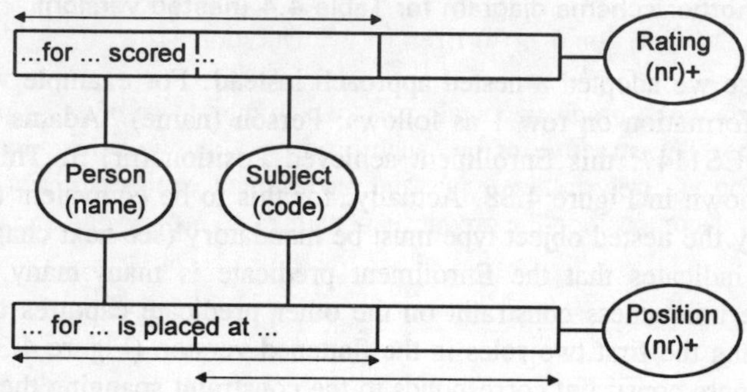

Figure 4.39 A schema diagram for table 4.5 (flattened version)

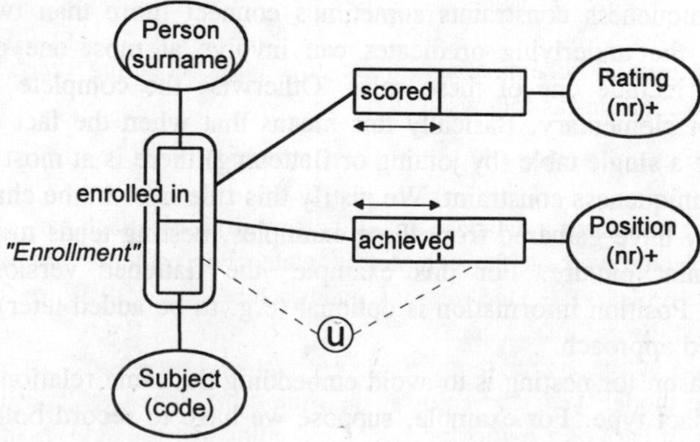

Figure 4.40 Another schema diagram for Table 4.5 (nested version)

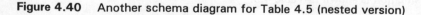

The nested approach corresponds to reading the information on row 1 of the table as: Person (name) "Adams J" enrolled in Subject (code) "CS114"; this Enrollment scored Rating (nr) 7; this Enrollment achieved Position (nr) 3. To indicate that rating and position must be recorded, additional constraints are needed (see next chapter).

Note that if a role has a simple, internal uniqueness constraint then it should not also be included in an external uniqueness constraint. Even if a join path exists to enable an external uniqueness constraint to be declared, the external constraint would be implied by the stronger, simple uniqueness constraint; and our preference is to omit implied constraints.

As an exercise to illustrate this point, modify Figure 4.35 (b) so that student names are actually unique, then show that the external constraint is implied.

Exercise 4.4

1. Add the uniqueness constraints to the conceptual schema diagrams for:

   (a) Exercise 3.4 Question 6 (b) Exercise 3.5 Question 4

2. Many manufactured products contain parts which may themselves be products of even smaller parts. The structure of one such product is shown below, by two equivalent representations (a tree or hierarchy, and an indented explosion). For instance, at its first level of decomposition the product *A* contains two *B* parts and one *C* part.

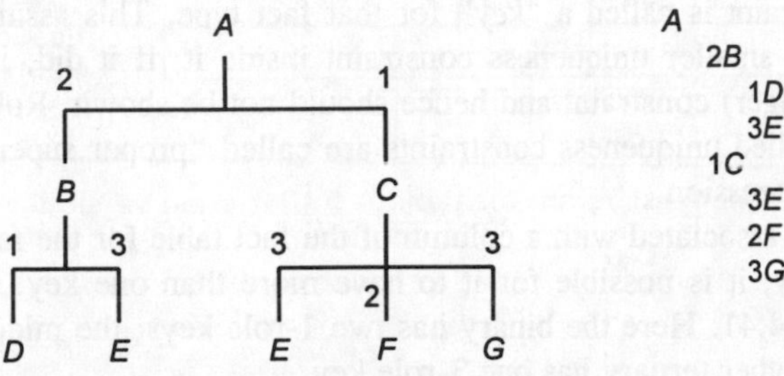

   Draw a conceptual schema diagram for this UoD, including uniqueness constraints. Provide two solutions as follows:

   (a) Make no use of nesting (b) Use nesting

3. A car dealer maintains a database on all the cars in stock. Each car is designated by the car number engraved on the compliance plate. For each car the dealer records the model (e.g. Pulsar XT), the year of manufacture (e.g. 1987), the retail price (e.g. $15,000) and the color (e.g. blue).

   Because of space limitations the dealer will never have in stock more than one car of the same model, year and color at the same time. The dealer also keeps figures on the number of cars of a particular model and color that are sold in any given year. For example, in 1986, five blue Pulsar XTs were sold. Draw the conceptual schema diagram, including all uniqueness constraints.

4.5 Key length check

In step 1 of the CSDP we tried to express information examples in terms of elementary facts. At that stage we relied on familiarity with the UoD to determine whether a fact type was simple or compound (splittable). Once uniqueness constraints have been added, we conduct a more thorough and formal check in this regard. This section discusses a check based on uniqueness constraints, and the next section discusses a projection-join check.

Until we are very experienced at conceptual schema design, we might include some fact types that are too long or too short. By "too long" we mean that the arity of the fact type is higher than it should be—the predicate has too many roles. In this case we must split the compound fact type up into two or more simple fact types. For example, the fact type **Scientist was born in Country during Year** should be split into two fact types: **Scientist was born in Country; Scientist was born during Year**.

By "too short" we mean that the arity of some fact types is too small, resulting in loss of information. We have wrongly split an elementary fact type. In this case we need to combine the relevant fact types into one of higher arity.

For example, given that scientists may lecture in many countries in the same year, it is wrong to split the fact type **Scientist lectured in Country during Year** into the fact types: **Scientist lectured in Country; Scientist lectured during Year**. This kind of error is rare, but serious nevertheless.

Earlier we saw that, for a given fact type, a combination of roles spanned by a uniqueness constraint is called a "*key*" for that fact type. This assumes the uniqueness constraint has no smaller uniqueness constraint inside it; if it did, it is implied by the smaller (but stronger) constraint and hence should not be shown. Role combinations for such longer, implied uniqueness constraints are called "proper superkeys"; we exclude these from our discussion.

Each role is associated with a column of the fact table for the fact type. Unless the fact type is unary, it is possible for it to have more than one key. Consider the cases shown in Figure 4.41. Here the binary has two 1-role keys, the middle ternary has two 2-role keys, and other ternary has one 3-role key.

The first two predicates also have implied uniqueness constraints across their whole length, but these are not counted as keys for these predicates. The *length* of a role sequence is the number of roles it contains. A key of length 1 is a *simple key*. All other keys are *composite*.

One can imagine unaries or binaries that should be split, but in practice not even a novice designer is likely to verbalize one (e.g. "The Barrister with surname 'Rumpole' smokes and drinks"). So the question of splittability is really an issue only with ternaries and longer fact types.

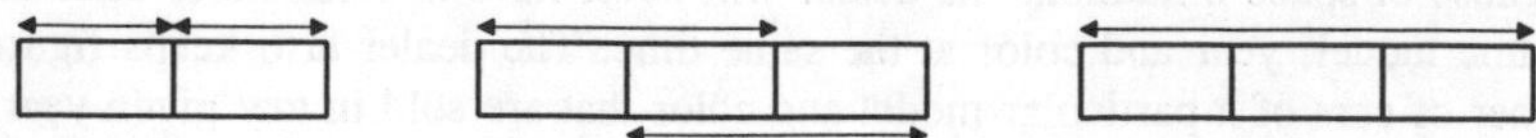

Figure 4.41 A fact type may have one or more keys

Table 4.6 Key length check for ternaries and longer fact types

Arity of fact type	*Minimum key length*	*Illegal key lengths*
3	2	1
4	3	1, 2
5	4	1, 2, 3
⋮	⋮	⋮
n	*n*−1	1, ..., *n*−2

To help us decide when to split in such cases, we now consider a rule, whose proof is sketched later in the section. **An *n*-ary fact type has a key length of at least *n*-1**. If this rule is violated, the fact type is not elementary, and hence should be split. See Table 4.6.

If a fact type is elementary, all its keys must be of the same length. Either there is exactly one key and this spans the whole fact type, or there are one or more keys and each is one role shorter than the fact type. To start with the simplest case, ***a ternary fact type can be split if it has a simple key***. Consider Table 4.7.

Table 4.7

Person	*Degree*	*Gender*
Adams	BSc	M
Brown	BA	F
Collins	BSc	M

We interpret the first row thus: the Person with surname "Adams" seeks the Degree with code "BSc" and has Gender with code "M". The presence of "and" suggests that the fact is splittable. Suppose however that we foolishly ignore this linguistic clue, and schematize the report as a ternary (see Figure 4.42).

Our familiarity with the UoD tells us that, for any state of the database, each person seeks at most one degree and has at most one gender. So there is a uniqueness constraint on the Person column of the fact table. The population of Table 4.7 shows that there is no such constraint on Degree or Person, either singly or in combination. So we mark the constraint on the diagram as shown.

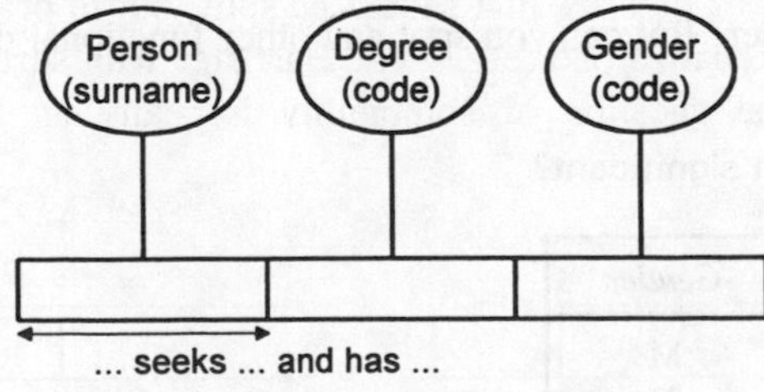

Figure 4.42 A splittable fact type

Figure 4.43 Two elementary fact types

Now let's apply the rule mentioned earlier. Here the key has length 1, which is 2 less than the length of the fact type. So the fact type is not elementary, and must be split. But *how do we split it?* Examining our verbalization of row 1, we find a conjunction of two facts about the same person. Assuming our interpretation of the output report is correct, we must split the fact type into two as shown in Figure 4.43.

Here the common entity type is Person, and we say we have "split *on* Person". If we have correctly captured the semantics of the output report in step 1 then it would be wrong to split this fact type in any other way. Before considering this point further, let us try to see why the splittability rule works in this case.

Look back at Table 4.7. A uniqueness constraint on the Person column means that, given any state of the database, no person can be referenced more than once in this column. Each person seeks at most one degree and each person has at most one gender. So for any given person, if we are given as separate pieces of information that person's degree and that person's gender we can reconstruct that person's row in the output report. Since the ternary fact type of the output report can be split and recombined without information loss it is not elementary.

Before considering other ways of splitting, we note some terminology commonly used in the normalization approach to database design. For a given fact table, let *X* denote a single column or combinations of columns, and let *Y* denote a single column. Then we say that *Y* is ***functionally dependent on*** *X* if and only if, for each value of *X* there is at most one value of *Y*. In other words, *Y* is a *function of X*.

A function is just a many:1 relation (including 1:1 as a special case). If *Y* is a function of *X*, then *X* is said to (functionally) determine *Y*. We abbreviate "**functional dependency**" to "**FD**".

Now let us return to the output report of our example. For your convenience, this has been reproduced in Table 4.8. If this population is significant, then any functional dependencies should be exposed here.

Note that Degree is functionally dependent on Person, since for any given person there is only one degree. Moreover, Gender is a function of Person since for any given person there is only one gender. But can you spot any other functional dependencies?

Table 4.8 Is the population significant?

Person	*Degree*	*Gender*
Adams	BSc	M
Brown	BA	F
Collins	BSc	M

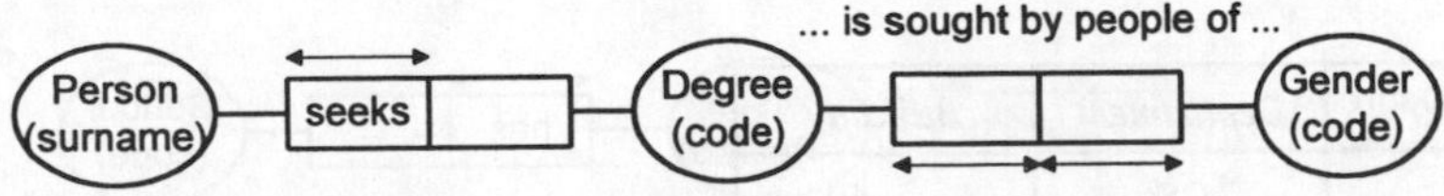

Figure 4.44 A weird UoD where Degree and Gender are functions of each other

If the population is significant, then Gender is a function of Degree, and Degree is a function of Gender! Does this make sense? To answer this question we need to know more about the semantics of the UoD. Spotting a functional dependency within a population is a formal game. Knowing whether this dependency reflects an actual constraint in the UoD is not. To assume the population is significant begs the question. Only someone familiar with the UoD can resolve the issue.

If one column functionally determines another column, this reflects a many:1 relationship type (or 1:many depending on the direction of reading) which can be given a meaningful name by the UoD expert. For example, suppose the UoD expert informs us that row 1 of the output report should actually be read as: the Person with surname "Adams" seeks the Degree with code "BSc", and the Degree with code "BSc" is sought by people of Gender with code "M". Here we have two facts about the same degree, and so we split on Degree rather than Person (see Figure 4.44).

If Gender really is a function of Degree, then any given degree is restricted to one gender (e.g. only males can seek a BSc). If Degree really is a function of Gender then all people of a given gender seek the same degree (e.g. all females seek just a BA). These two FDs are captured in Figure 4.44 by the two uniqueness constraints on the relationship type between Degree and Gender.

While such a UoD is possible, our knowledge about degree awarding institutions makes this interpretation highly unlikely. One way to resolve our doubts is to add test rows to the population. For example, if the UoD expert accepts the population of Table 4.9 as being consistent with the UoD, then no FDs occur between Degree and Gender.

This by itself does not guarantee that our earlier schema (Figure 4.43) is now correct. For example, the schema of Figure 4.44 with the 1:1 constraint changed to a many:many constraint is still a remote possibility; but it would be silly to have a report with so much redundancy (e.g. the fact that the BSc is sought by males would be shown twice already). Of course, if we simply checked our interpretation at step 1 with the UoD expert, we could have avoided all this hassle.

While the notion of FD is sometimes useful, it is impractical to treat fact tables in a purely formal way, hunting for FDs etc. The number of dependencies to check increases very rapidly as the length of the fact type grows.

Table 4.9 A counterexample to any FD between degree and gender

Person	*Degree*	*Gender*
Adams	BSc	M
Brown	BA	F
Collins	BSc	M
Davis	BSc	F

Table 4.10

Lecturer	*Department*	*Building*
Halpin	CS	69
Okimura	JA	1
Orlowska	CS	69
Wang	CN	1

Although our conceptual focus on elementary fact types constrains this length, the search for such dependencies can still be laborious. While an automated FD checker can be of use in a CASE tool, this kind of exhaustive checking is not fit for humans. We can short-circuit this work by taking advantage of human knowledge of the UoD.

As another simple example consider the output report of Table 4.10. Suppose that, with the help of the UoD expert, we express row 1 thus: the Lecturer with surname "Halpin" works for the Department with code "CS" which is located in the Building with nr "69". Is this fact splittable, and if so, how?

Here the pronoun "which" introduces a non-restrictive clause about the department that may be stated separately. So we have two facts about the department (Halpin works for the CS department; and the CS department is located in building 69). We split on Department to get two fact types as shown in Figure 4.45.

As a challenge question, would it also be acceptable to split on Lecturer (e.g. Lecturer works for Department; Lecturer works in Building)? The logical derivation theory discussed in the next chapter shows it is unwise to split on Lecturer. If the population is significant then each lecturer works for only one department, and each department is located in only one building. If these constraints are confirmed by the UoD expert we add them to the schema as shown.

We now sketch an outline proof of the splittability rule. An *n*-ary fact type with a key of length less than *n*-1 has at least two columns in its fact table that are functionally dependent on this key. Split the table by pairing the key with exactly one of these columns in turn. Recombining by join on this key must generate the original table since only one combined row is possible (otherwise the common key portion would not be a key). Although the *n*-ary fact table thus formally splits in this way, in practice the splitting might need to be made on part of the key or even a nonkey column if an FD applies there (consider the previous examples).

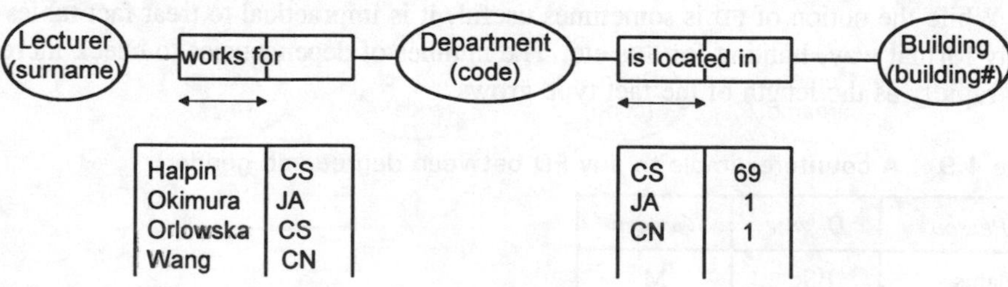

Figure 4.45 Knowledge base for Table 4.10

Table 4.11

Person	*Degree*	*Subject*	*Rating*
Adams	BSc	CS112 CS110 PD102	7 6 7
Brown	BA	CS112 PD102	6 7
Collins	BSc	CS112	7

As an example of a *quaternary* case, consider the report shown in Table 4.11. Suppose we did a bad job at step 1 and schematized this situation as in Figure 4.46. Notice the uniqueness constraint. Here we have a fact type of length 4, and a key of length 2. *Since two roles are excluded from this key, we must split the fact type*. How do we split it? Each person seeks at most one degree, but this constraint is not captured by the 2-role uniqueness constraint, so we split on Person. In terms of FD theory, the Person role functionally determines the Degree role (shown in Figure 4.46 as a solid arrow).

If an FD like this is involved, splitting takes place on its source. So the quaternary splits on Person into a binary (Person seeks Degree) and a ternary (Person for Subject scored Rating). As an exercise, draw these, being sure to include all constraints. Once the schema is correct, all FDs should be captured by uniqueness constraints. So we make no use of FD arrows on correct conceptual schema diagrams. Any quaternary splits if it has a key of length 1 or 2.

Now consider Figure 4.47. Suppose our interpretation of the UoD is correct. For example, suppose the first row of the output report behind this schema really does express the information: the Person with surname "Adams" seeking the Degree with code "BSc" studies the Subject with code "CS112". Should the ternary be split?

This ternary has no simple key. We said that a ternary can be split **if** it has a simple key. However, we did *not* say "a ternary can be split **only if** it has a simple key". The ternary in this example does actually split. One way to see this is to *try to rephrase the information in terms of a conjunction*.

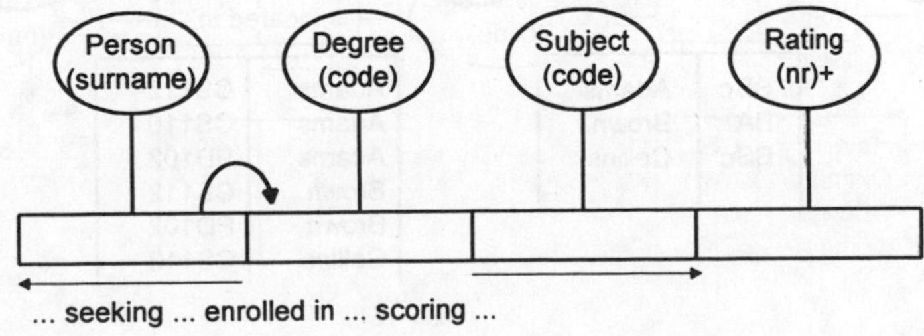

Figure 4.46 A quaternary fact type that is splittable (FD added)

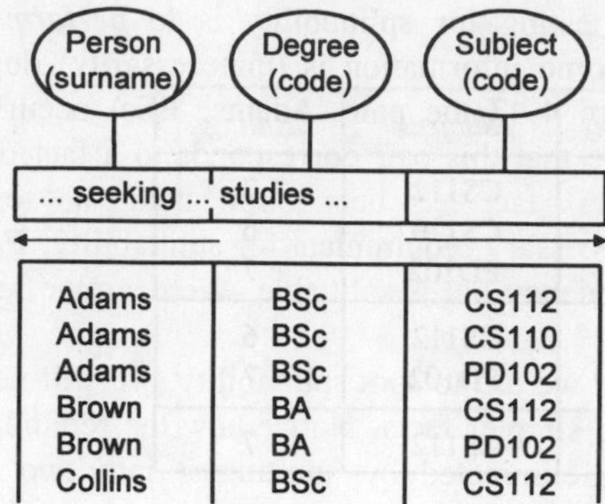

Figure 4.47 Is this ternary splittable?

Initially we expressed the information on the first row using the present participle "seeking". But this information may be rephrased as:

> The Person with surname 'Adams' seeks the Degree with code 'BSc' **and** studies the Subject with code 'CS112'.

which is equivalent to:

> The Person with surname 'Adams' seeks the Degree with code 'BSc'
> **and**
> the Person with surname 'Adams' studies the Subject with code 'CS112'.

This is obviously a conjunction with Person common to each conjunct. So the ternary should be split on Person into two binaries (see Figure 4.48).

In general, given a significant fact table, the fact type is splittable if a column is functionally dependent on only some of the other columns. By "only some" we mean "some but not all". This result corresponds to a basic rule in normalization theory (see section 10.2). With our present example, the Degree column is functionally dependent on the Person column only; so it should not be combined in a fact type with Subject information.

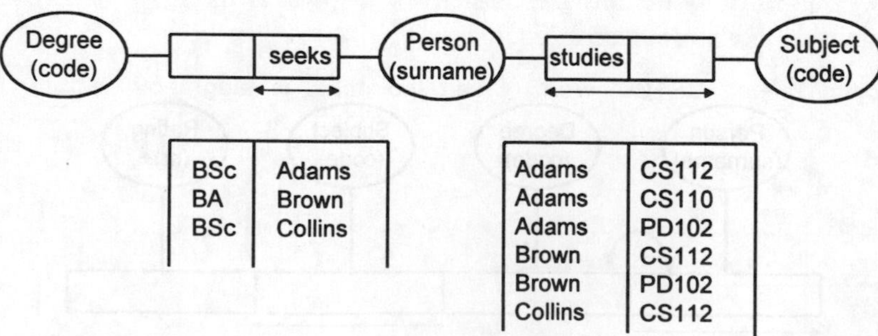

Figure 4.48 The ternary in Figure 4.47 should be split like this

Another way of testing for splittability is to *perform a redundancy check* by determining whether some information is (unnecessarily) duplicated in the fact table. For example, in Figure 4.47 the pair ⟨Adams, BSc⟩ occurs three times. Using our semantic insight we see that this pair corresponds to a fact of interest (Adams seeks a BSc degree). Since this fact has been duplicated, the ternary is not elementary. Redundancy is not a necessary requirement for splittability. For example, the ternary in Table 4.9 has no redundancy but is splittable. We examine redundancy checks in more detail in a later chapter.

Whichever method we use to spot splittability, we still need to phrase the information as a conjunction of simpler facts. Notice how the redundancy within the ternary of Figure 4.47 has been eliminated by splitting it into two binaries in Figure 4.48. Although we may allow redundancy in output reports, we should avoid redundancy in the actual tables stored in the database.

Our examples so far have avoided nested fact types. Recall that nesting is not the same as splitting. If nesting is used, the following rule can be used to avoid splittable fact types: **the uniqueness constraint on a nested object type must span the whole of this predicate.**

This simply adapts our earlier results to the nested case. Suppose the objectified predicate has a uniqueness constraint over only some of its roles. If an attached, outside role has a uniqueness constraint on it, when the outer predicate is flattened we have at least two roles not spanned by a uniqueness constraint. If an attached role does not have a uniqueness constraint on it, then flattening generates a predicate with an embedded FD not expressed as a uniqueness constraint (consider the cases of Figures 4.46 and 4.47).

In either case, the flattened version must split because it is not elementary. Hence the nested version must obey the rule stated. Some other modelling methods allow this rule to be violated because they do not demand that facts be elementary. Our method simplifies the modeling as well as the later mapping algorithm.

Consider the output report of Table 4.11. Here the credit for a given subject is measured in points. The "?" on the second row is a null value, indicating that a real value is not recorded (e.g. a lecturer for CS109 might not yet have been assigned). Although null values are forbidden in conceptual fact tables, they often appear in output reports.

Now let's play the part of an inexperienced, and not very clever, schema designer, so that we can learn by the mistakes made. Looking just at the first row, we might be tempted to treat the information as a ternary:

Subject (code) 'CS100' worth Credit (points) 8 is taught by Lecturer (initials) 'DBJ'.

Table 4.11

Subject	*Credit*	*Lecturer*
CS100	8	DBJ
CS109	5	?
CS112	8	TAH
CS113	8	TAH

If we drew the schema diagram now and populated it we would discover an error, since the information on the second row doesn't fit this pattern (remember we don't allow null values in our fact tables). On looking at the second row we see that we need to be able to record the credit points for a subject without indicating the lecturer. So we then rephrase the first row as follows:

> Subject (code) 'CS100' is worth Credit (points) 8.
> This SubjectCreditOffering is taught by Lecturer (initials) 'DBJ'.

This overcomes the problem with the second row, since we can now express the information there simply as: Subject (code) "CS109" is worth Credit (points) 5. Using this approach, we now develop the schema shown in Figure 4.49.

Assuming the population of the output report is significant, we mark the uniqueness constraints as shown. Note that a 1-role uniqueness constraint has been added to the nested object type. This breaks our new rule: an objectified relationship type can't have a key shorter than itself. So we know something must be wrong. Since the schema diagram follows from our handling of step 1, this means that we must have made a mistake at step 1.

Have another look at the way we set out the information for row 1. The second sentence here is the problem. In this UoD each subject has exactly one credit point value, so this is independent of who teaches the subject. So there is no need to mention the credit point value of a subject when we indicate the lecturer. In FD terminology, the Credit column is functionally dependent on the Subject column alone. The information on the first row can be set out in terms of two simple binaries:

> Subject (code) 'CS100' is worth Credit (points) 8.
> Subject (code) 'CS100' is taught by Lecturer (initials) 'DBJ'.

leading to the correct schema shown in Figure 4.50. Note that Lecturer depends only on Subject, not Credit. With the nested schema we incorrectly suggested that Lecturer was dependent on both, by relating Lecturer to the objectified relationship type.

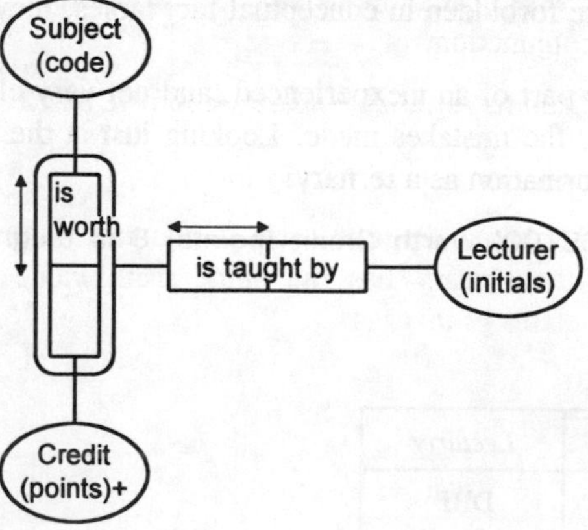

Figure 4.49 A faulty schema diagram

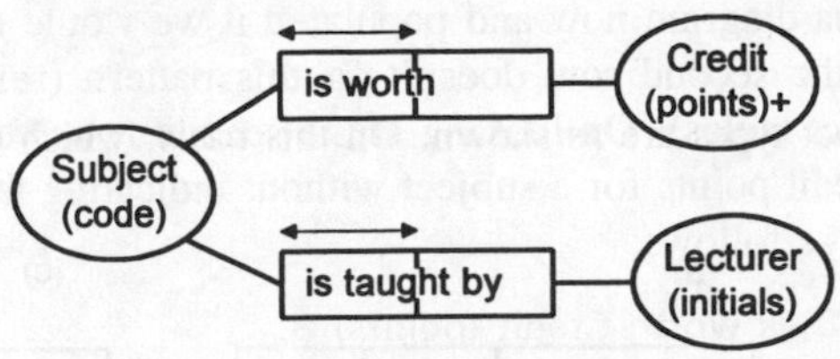

Figure 4.50 The corrected schema diagram for Figure 4.49

With this example, Lecturer is a function of Subject, but this has no bearing on the splittability. We should use two binaries even if the same subject can have many lecturers. It is the functional dependency of Credit on Subject which disqualifies the nested approach.

One lesson to be learned from this section is that it pays to look out for uniqueness constraints even when performing step 1. Consider the output report of Table 4.12. If you are told the population is significant, how would you schematize this?

If you used either a ternary or a nested fact type you have made a mistake! Although similar to a UoD discussed earlier, the UoD being described by this table is more restricted. Given that the population is significant, the lack of duplicates in the Person column indicates that, at any given time, each person can be enrolled in only one subject. For example, these people might be your employees, and you are funding their studies and want to ensure they don't take on so much study that it interferes with their work performance.

Since we store information only about the current enrollments, and each person is enrolled in only one subject it follows that each person can get only one rating. So if we know the subject in which a person is enrolled and we know the rating obtained by the person, we do know the subject in which this rating is obtained by that person. To begin with, we might express the information on the first row of the table in terms of the ternary: Person (surname) "Adams" scores Rating (nr) 7 for Subject (code) "CS112". However, because of the uniqueness constraint on Person we should rephrase this information as the conjunction:

Person (surname) 'Adams' studies Subject (code) 'CS112'
and
Person (surname) 'Adams' scores Rating (nr) 7.

leading to a conceptual schema diagram with two binary fact types. Because of this uniqueness constraint, the ternary has the same truth value as the conjunction of binaries for all possible states of this UoD.

Table 4.12

Person	*Subject*	*Rating*
Adams	CS112	7
Brown	CS112	5
Collins	PD102	5

Exercise 4.5

1. The keys for certain fact types are as shown. On this basis, which of these fact types are definitely splittable?

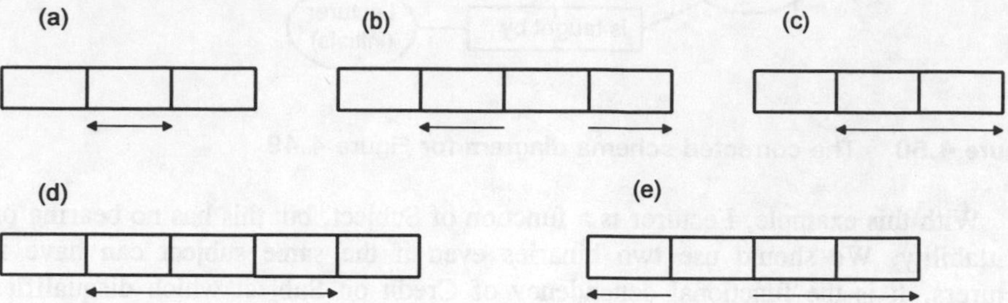

2. The following output report provides information on aeroplane flights between cities. The population of this table is significant with respect to uniqueness constraints. A novice information designer expresses the information on the first row in terms of the following ternary:

   Flight (#) 'T74' **goes from** City (name) 'Paris' **to** City (name) 'London'.

   Discuss the correctness or otherwise of this approach, and draw a correct conceptual schema diagram, including uniqueness constraints.

FlightNr	*Origin*	*Destination*
T74	Paris	London
A52	Paris	London
B80	Sydney	New York
T23	London	Paris
B45	New York	Sydney

3. Executives may be contacted at work on one or more phone numbers and at home on one phone number. The following output report provides a sample population for this UoD. A novice information designer notes that this ternary table lacks a simple key, and on this basis decides to schematize in terms of a single ternary fact type. Evaluate this approach, and draw a correct conceptual schema diagram.

Executive	*Work phone*	*Home phone*
Adams A	235402	837900
Adams A	235444	
Adams S	235444	837900
Brown T	235300	578051

4. Refer back to Table 1.3 but omit the Director column. Suppose we model this using the quaternary: **Movie exported from Country to Country achieved SalesLevel**. Draw the schema diagram for this approach. Is this acceptable? If not, explain clearly why.

4.6 Projection-join check

In the previous section we discussed two *sufficient* conditions for splitting a fact type: a fact type splits if it has more than one role excluded from a key; a nested object type splits if it has a shorter key. Since these are not *necessary* conditions for splitting, in some cases further analysis is required to make a definite decision. At the heart of such an analysis is the question: *can the fact type be rephrased as a conjunction of smaller fact types?*

With a bit of experience behind us, we can usually answer this question fairly quickly. In this section we discuss a formal procedure for addressing this question in a systematic way. The procedure makes use of two operations known as "projection" and "joining", which are of considerable importance in relational database work. The *join* operation has already been discussed, and involves combining two tables by matching values referencing the same object to form a new table (review Section 4.4).

The **projection** operation also produces a table, but it is performed on a single table. To project on one or more columns of a table, we *choose just the columns of interest* (removing all other columns) and then *ensure each row in the result appears just once* (removing any duplicates).

Notationally, we list the columns on which a projection is made in *italic square brackets* after the table name, separated by commas. For example, *R [a, b]* is a projection on columns *a* and *b* of table *R*. This may also be written as $\pi_{a,b}(R)$. See Figure 4.51 for some examples.

Scores:

person	*subject*	*rating*
Adams	CS112	7
Adams	CS110	6
Adams	PD102	7
Brown	CS112	6
Brown	PD102	7
Collins	CS112	7

Scores *[person]* =

person
Adams
Brown
Collins

Scores *[rating]* =

rating
7
6

Scores *[person, subject]*:

person	*subject*
Adams	CS112
Adams	CS110
Adams	PD102
Brown	CS112
Brown	PD102
Collins	CS112

Scores *[person, rating]*:

person	*rating*
Adams	7
Adams	6
Brown	6
Brown	7
Collins	7

Figure 4.51 Some projection examples

Table 4.13

Person	*Degree*	*Subject*
Adams	BSc	CS112
Adams	BSc	CS110
Adams	BSc	PD102
Brown	BA	CS112
Brown	BA	PD102
Collins	BSc	CS112

Notice that Scores *[person,subject]* is a projection on the key, and hence must have the same number of rows as the original table (Why?). Now that we know about joins and projections, the following method for checking whether a doubtful fact type is splittable may be discussed:

Provide a significant fact table for the fact type.
Split this table into two or more projections.
Recombine by natural (inner) join.
The fact type is splittable in this way **iff** the result is the same as the original.

Here "iff" abbreviates "if and only if". An inner join is acceptable since the conceptual fact table (and hence its projections) cannot have null values. Let's see how this algorithm works by considering some examples for which the key length rule doesn't apply. Consider first an earlier example which is reproduced in Table 4.13.

Recall that we first tried to represent this information in terms of the ternary: Person seeking Degree studies Subject. Using our understanding of the UoD, we saw that this could be rephrased as the conjunction: Person seeks Degree **and** Person studies Subject. Suppose however that we only suspect that the ternary can be split into two binaries in this way, and we want some way of testing our intuition.

The best way is simply to ask the UoD expert (who was needed anyway to confirm that the fact table is significant). If the UoD expert is not currently available we can use the projection-join test. To start, we split on Person by projecting on two columns, with Person being common to both projections (see Figure 4.52).

We then recombine into a 3-column table by performing the natural join on these two projections. As an exercise, perform this join. The result is the same as the original table. So no information loss is caused by the splitting. So, assuming the population was significant, the fact type splits in this way. The correct schema involves two binary fact types, one for each projection. Refer to the previous section for the schema diagram.

Person	*Degree*
Adams	BSc
Brown	BA
Collins	BSc

Person	*Subject*
Adams	CS112
Adams	CS110
Adams	PD102
Brown	CS112
Brown	PD102
Collins	CS112

Figure 4.52 Two projections obtained by splitting Table 4.13 on Person

While the application of this technique is purely mechanical, a brief explanation of why it works is in order. With the current example, the technique was used to test the following equivalence.

In this UoD, given any Person *p*, Degree *d* and Subject *s*:

p seeking *d* studies *s* **iff** *p* seeks *d*
and
p studies *s*

Assuming predicate names are supplied, the projection corresponds to the conditional: *if* the ternary is true *then* the conjunction is true. The join corresponds to the conditional: *if* the conjunction is true *then* the ternary is true.

Now consider our familiar ternary example about people scoring ratings for subjects. Look back at the fact table at the top of Figure 4.51. Suppose we suspect that this ternary is splittable on Person. For example, we might feel that in this UoD the following equivalence holds:

Person *p* scores Rating *r* for Subject *s* **iff** *p* studies *s*
and
p scores *r*

To test this way to split, we form the two binary projections shown in Figure 4.51, and then recombine by joining on Person. The result is shown in Table 4.14 (as an exercise, confirm this result). In forming the join, several new rows (marked "×", in bold italics) appeared which were not in the original table. Any one of these new rows is enough to prove that the fact type cannot be split this way (i.e. on Person).

Consider for instance the information on the first row of our original table: Adams scores a 7 in CS112. We have attempted to split this fact into the two separate facts: Adams studies CS112; Adams scores 7 (see first rows of the two projections). If this splitting is legitimate the two separate facts must, in combination, be equivalent to the original fact. However they are not. Knowing that Adams scores a 7 does not tell us the subject in which this rating is scored. It could be any of Adams's subjects (CS112, CS110 or PD102). Joining the projections causes all such possibilities to be listed.

Table 4.14 The join of the binary projections in Figure 4.51

	Person	*Subject*	*Rating*
	Adams	CS112	7
×	***Adams***	***CS112***	***6***
×	***Adams***	***CS110***	***7***
	Adams	CS110	6
	Adams	PD102	7
×	***Adams***	***PD102***	***6***
	Brown	CS112	6
×	***Brown***	***CS112***	***7***
×	***Brown***	***PD102***	***6***
	Brown	PD102	7
	Collins	CS112	7

Some of these rows were not present in the original, and the join does not tell us which are the correct ones. Since this information has been lost, the ternary fact type cannot be split in this way.

The forward conditional of the equivalence does hold (*if* ternary *then* conjunction). However, the backward conditional fails (it is not generally true that: *if* conjunction *then* ternary). If you use a bit of insight it should be clear that trying to split on Subject or Rating or all three would be pointless. In this case we could conclude that the fact type is unsplittable, and leave it as a ternary. If this is not clear then you can use the algorithm to test all possible ways of splitting. You would find that none of them work and then conclude that the fact type is unsplittable.

In general, for a ternary A-B-C there are four ways in which it might split: A-B, A-C; B-A, B-C; C-A, C-B; A-B, A-C, B-C. In the fourth case the schema diagram is triangular in shape: this is referred to as 3-way splitting. As an exercise, draw these four possibilities. With 3-way splitting the join should be done in two stages. For example, first join A-B and A-C (with A common); then join the A-B-C result of this join with B-C (with B and C common).

A classic example of testing for 3-way splitting involves the fact type: Agent sells Cartype for Company. Even if the key spans the whole fact type, the fact type can be split into three binaries if a derivation rule allows the ternary to be deduced from the binaries (see section 10.2). Such examples are very rare in practice. For an *n*-ary fact type, if the *n*-way split fails (by generating new rows in the final join) then all other ways of splitting can be ruled out too: the fact type is unsplittable.

Though useful for understanding the notion of splittability, the projection-join test should only be used as a last resort. Since it is tedious, it is best automated (this can easily be done). This test works only with a significant population. But the problem of determining whether the population is significant is at least as hard as determining whether the fact type splits. If you have access to the UoD expert, then you should instead work directly with this expert, using meaningful names for the fact types, and asking the relevant questions.

Exercise 4.6

1. A template for a ternary fact type is outlined below. The population shown in the fact table is significant.

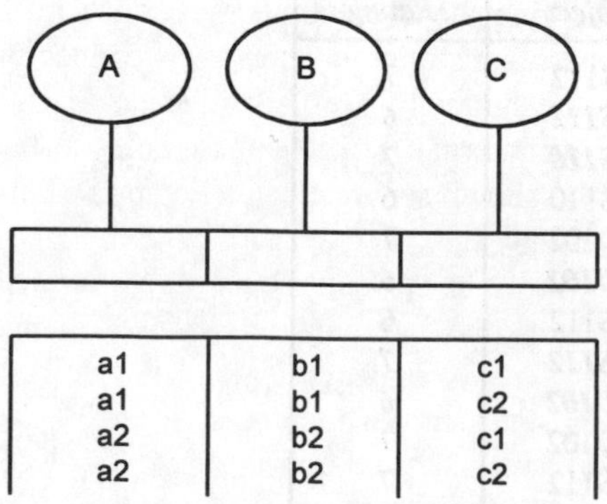

(a) Add the uniqueness constraints for this fact type.
(b) Use the projection-join test to show that this fact type cannot be split into two binaries with C as the common node.
(c) Use the projection-join test to show that this fact type can be split into two binaries with B as the common node.
(d) Draw a schema outline for this result.

4.7 Summary

This chapter discussed Step 4 of the conceptual schema design procedure: *add uniqueness constraints, and check the arity of fact types*. Uniqueness constraints (UCs) come in two varieties: internal and external. An *internal* (or intra-predicate) uniqueness constraint applies to one or more roles of a single predicate. It is marked as a bar across the role(s) it constrains. Arrow-tips may be added to the ends of the bar. If the roles are non-contiguous, the bar is divided, and arrow-tips at the outer ends must be included.

Redundancy is repetition of an elementary fact. Since redundancy is not permitted in a conceptual fact table, each row must be unique. This is shown as a UC across the whole predicate, unless a stronger UC exists. If an internal UC spans just some of the roles spanned by another internal UC, the former UC implies the latter UC, and the implied UC should not be displayed.

Each unary predicate has a UC across its role. For binary predicates there are four possibilities: UC on role 1 only; UC on role 2 only; UC on role 1, and another UC on role 2; one UC spanning both roles. These cases are respectively described as many to one, one to many, one to one, and many to many. For example, if each Employee works for at most one Department, but each department may employ many employees, the predicate "works for" is many to one, and has a UC across its first role.

Each role in a predicate is associated with a column of the predicate-table. A UC across just one role means no duplicates are allowed in its column. A UC spanning *n* roles means each sequence of *n* entries taken from the associated columns can occur in that column-sequence on only one row.

Let *R* and *S* be tables of two predicates with one or more common object types *B*. The natural inner *join* of *R* and *S* is obtained by pairing rows of *R* with rows of *S* where the *B* values match, and showing the *B* column(s) just once in the result. An *external* (or inter-predicate) uniqueness constraint is shown by connecting two or more roles from different predicates to the symbol "ⓤ". This indicates that when the join operation is applied to the predicates, an internal UC spans these roles in the result. For example, Surname and Initials might be shown separately for Person, where each combination of surname and initials refers to only one person.

Uniqueness constraints apply to the recorded information, and must be at least as strong as those in the real world. A combination of roles spanned by an internal UC, with no smaller UC inside it, is a *key* of its predicate. A 1-role key is a *simple key*.

Because conceptual predicates are elementary, a ternary fact type cannot have a simple key. It either has a 3-role UC, or one or more 2-role UCs. For binaries and beyond, *an n-ary predicate has a minimum key length of n-1*. This rule may be applied as a *key-length check*. This rule also implies that *a nested object type must be spanned by a UC*: the frame notation is understood to include a UC which spans all the roles inside. Violation of this rule is a sufficient but not necessary condition for splittability.

For a given predicate, let *X* denote a combination of one or more roles (or columns) and *Y* denote a single role (or column). We say *X functionally determines Y*, written $X \rightarrow Y$, if and only if for each value of *X* there is at most one value of *Y*; in this case *Y* is said to be *functionally dependent* on *X*. The term "*FD*" abbreviates "functional dependency". If the conceptual schema is correct, all FDs are implied by UCs. If a non-implied FD $X \rightarrow Y$ exists, the predicate should be split on the source *X*.

With experience, one can usually determine whether a fact type splits by using background knowledge of the UoD to answer the question: "Is information lost by splitting the fact type?". The shortest key rule and the detection of a non-implied FD provide simple ways of checking that our intuitions are correct here.

If we are ever fortunate enough to have a significant population for the fact type, the *projection-join check* can be used. To *project* on one or more columns of a table, we remove the other columns, then remove any duplicate rows that might appear in the result. If we suspect that a predicate might split in a certain way, we split its significant table in this way by projection, then recombine by natural join: if new instances appear in the result then the fact type cannot be split in this way.

Chapter notes

By depicting each role as a box associated with a table column, object-role modeling enables uniqueness constraints to be portrayed in a very natural way. Entity-relationship modeling depicts internal uniqueness constraints using a variety of notations for "cardinality constraints"; typically only some kinds of external uniqueness constraints are supported, and for these cases additional object types may have to be introduced to talk about the combination. Object-role modeling makes minimal use of the notion of functional dependency, but this notion is central to many other methods. For a clear treatment of an ER approach as well as functional dependency theory, see Elmasri & Navathe (1989).

Although it is generally wise to objectify a predicate only if it has a spanning uniqueness constraint, rare cases may arise where it may be useful to remove this restriction (see the marriage example in section 8.4). For further discussion on this point, see Halpin (1993c).

5 Mandatory roles

5.1 Introduction to CSDP step 5

So far we have learned how to proceed from familiar information examples to a conceptual schema diagram in which the elementary fact types are clearly set out, with the relevant uniqueness constraints marked on each. We also learnt to perform some checks on the quality of our schemas. In practice, other kinds of constraints and checks need to be considered also. Next in importance to uniqueness constraints are mandatory role constraints. Basically these indicatc which roles must be played by the population of an object type, and which are optional. Once mandatory role constraints have been specified, a check is made to see if some fact types may be logically derived from others. This constitutes the next step in the design procedure.

CSDP step 5: Add mandatory role constraints, and check for logical derivations

The next two sections cover this step in detail. The rest of this section discusses some basic concepts used in our treatment of mandatory roles and later constraints. Once mandatory roles are understood we are in a good position to examine reference schemes in depth, especially composite reference—we do this later in the chapter.

We now introduce a shorthand notation for talking about *populations*. For a *given state* of the database and a given fact type *F*, we define *pop(F)*, the population of *F*, to be *the set of facts which are instances of F in that state*. For a given schema, types are fixed or unchanging. However, as the database is updated, the population of a given type may change. For example, suppose the ternary shown in Figure 5.1 is used to store information about medals won by countries in the next Olympic Games. The fact type and roles are numbered for easy reference.

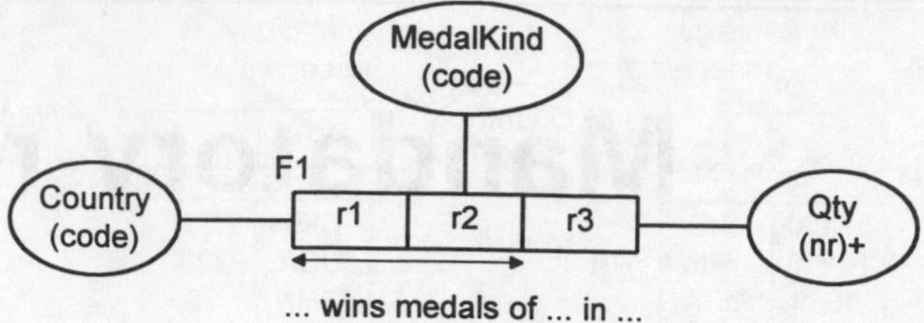

Figure 5.1 A fact type for Olympic Games results

Initially the fact table for F1 is empty, since so far no sporting results are known. Let us use "{ }" to denote the *empty set* (or *null set*), i.e. the set with no members. To begin with, pop(F1) = { }. Now suppose the database is to be updated after each sporting event, and in the first event the gold and bronze medals are won by the USA and the silver medal by Japan. The new state of the fact table is shown in Figure 5.2, using "G", "S", "B" for gold, silver and bronze. Now the population of the fact type contains three facts. The population grows each time the results of an event are entered.

It is convenient to speak of the *population of a role*. Each role of a fact type is associated with a column in its fact table. Values entered in the column refer to instances of the object type which plays that role. Given any role *r* and any state of the database:

pop(r) = population of role *r*
= set of objects referenced in the column for *r*

Typically the objects referenced are entities, not values. For example, in Figure 5.2, pop(r1) = {the Country with code 'USA', the Country with code 'JPN'}. The *valuation* of a role *r*, written *val(r)*, is the set of values entered in its column. For example, in Figure 5.2, val(r1) = {'USA', 'JPN'}. When there is no chance of confusion, we often abbreviate object terms to constants in listing populations. With this understanding, in Figure 5.2, pop(r1) = {USA,JPN}, pop(r2) = {G,S,B} and pop(r3) = {1}.

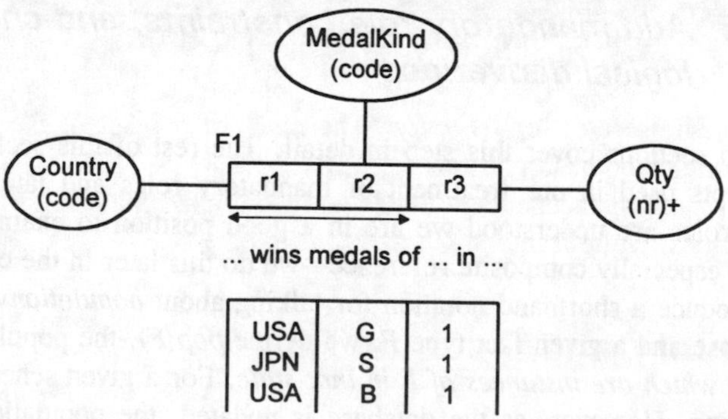

Figure 5.2 The fact type populated with results of the first event

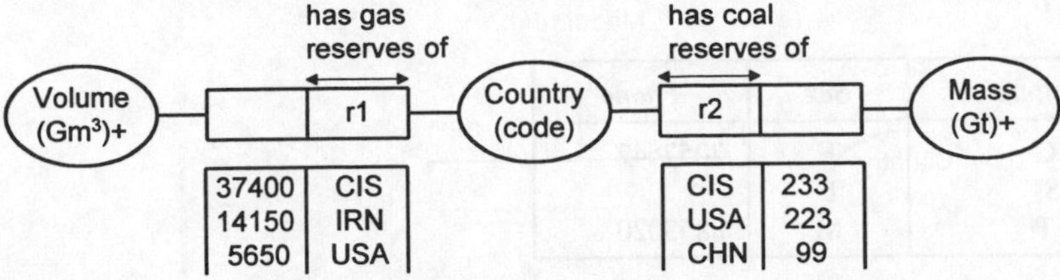

Figure 5.3 pop(Country) = pop(r1) ∪ pop(r2)

Role populations are used to determine *object type populations*. With our current example, if each country referenced in the database must play r1, then after the first event pop(Country) changes from { } to {USA,JPN}, and pop(CountryCode) changes from { } to {'USA','JPN'}. Assuming the application is just about the Olympics, the entity type Country is the set of all countries which might possibly compete in the Games: this set contains a large number of countries.

A predicate may be a fact type or reference type. Reference types are usually abbreviated as a parenthesized reference mode. Roles in a reference type are called *referential roles*. Roles in a fact type are called "*fact roles*" or "*non-referential roles*". Each entity type in a conceptual schema plays at least one referential role and at least one fact role. In general, the *population of an entity type equals the union of the population of its roles*. Unless the entity type is lazy (see later) its population is the union of the populations of its fact roles.

For example, consider the UoD schematized in Figure 5.3. Here we are interested in the countries with the largest natural gas and coal reserves (1982 figures are shown). The unit symbols "Gt" and "Gm³" stand for gigatonnes and giga cubic metres (giga = 10^9, i.e. 1,000,000,000).

For this state of the database, only the top three countries in each category have been recorded. Here each instance of the entity type Country plays the role r1 or r2, or both. So its population is the set of all the instances referenced in either the r1 column or the r2 column. We could set this out as:

$$\begin{aligned} \text{pop(Country)} &= \text{pop(r1)} \cup \text{pop(r2)} \\ &= \{\text{CIS, IRN, USA}\} \cup \{\text{CIS, USA, CHN}\} \\ &= \{\text{CIS, IRN, USA, CHN}\} \end{aligned}$$

We use "∪" as an operator for *set union*. The union of two sets is the set of all the elements in either one or both. For instance {1,2} ∪ {2,3,4} = {1,2,3,4}. In the above case, the Commonwealth of Independent States and the United States of America occur in both role populations, while Iran and China occur in only one.

5.2 Mandatory and Optional Roles

Consider the output report of Table 5.1. The question mark "?" denotes a null value, indicating that an actual value is not stored. For instance the patient with name "Brown S" may actually have a phone but this information is not recorded, or she may simply have no phone.

Table 5.1

Patient	*Sex*	*Phone*
Adams C	F	2057642
Brown S	F	?
Collins T	M	8853020

A knowledge base diagram for this situation is shown in Figure 5.4. Here we have two binary fact types. If this population is significant, we must record the sex of each patient but it is optional whether we record a phone number for a patient.

In Step 5 of the design procedure we indicate, for each role on the diagram, whether it is mandatory or optional. A **role is mandatory** if and only if, for all states of the knowledge base, the role must be played by every member of the population of the attached object type; otherwise the role is **optional**. A mandatory role is sometimes called a *total role*, since it is played by the total population of its object type. Which of the four roles in Figure 5.4 are mandatory and which are optional?

If the diagram includes all the fact types for the application, and its sample population is significant, we can easily determine which roles are mandatory. In practice however, we work most of the time with subschemas rather thanthe complete, or global schema; and sample populations are rarely significant. In such cases we check with the client whether the relevant information must be recorded for all instances of the object type (e.g. must we record sex for each patient?).

Consider the two roles played by the entity type Patient. For the database state shown, the population of the top role = {Adams C, Brown S, Collins T} and the population of the bottom role = (Adams C, Collins T}. If these are the only roles played by Patient, then pop(Patient) = {Adams C, Brown S, Collins T}. The first role is played by all recorded patients, and the second role is played by only some. Assuming the population is significant in this regard, the first role is mandatory and the second is optional.

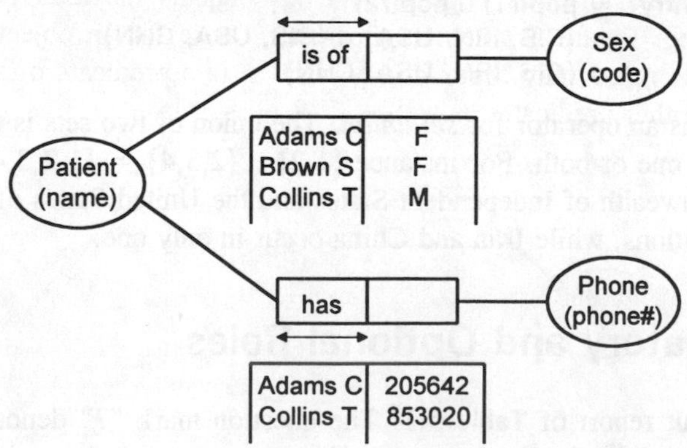

Figure 5.4 A knowledge base diagram for Table 5.1

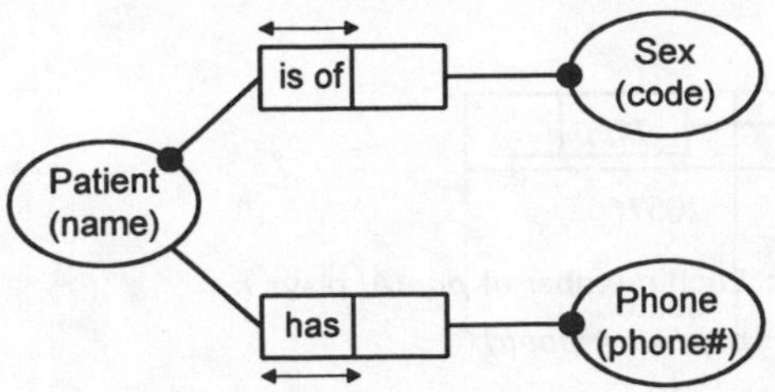

Figure 5.5 All mandatory role constraints specified explicitly

Trivially, the roles played by Sex and Phone are mandatory if each is the only role played by that entity type. To indicate explicitly that a role is mandatory we add a **mandatory role dot** to its attached object type, at the point where the line from the role meets the entity type: ○•–. If we do this for each mandatory role, the absence of a dot then indicates that the role is *optional*. Thus the mandatory role constraints for the UoD under discussion may be specified explicitly as shown in Figure 5.5.

Unless lazy (see next chapter), each primitive entity must play in some fact. *By default, if a primitive atomic entity type plays only one fact role* (in the global schema), *this role is mandatory*. In this case the mandatory role dot is usually omitted because it is implied (see Figure 5.6).

This implicit specification is usually preferable. It highlights the mandatory role constraints that are really important, i.e. the ones we need to enforce. Moreover, the diagram is easier to draw (e.g. fewer dots to be added), and if the schema is later merged with another there are usually fewer changes to make. This convention also simplifies the specification of theorems which have local as well as global application. However, the explicit specification may be preferred if we wish to draw the attention of a human reader to the implied constraints.

This rule for implicit mandatory roles does not apply to objectified predicates and subtypes: these are not primitive atomic types, and if they play just one fact role this may be optional. Examples are considered later in the book.

If a role is mandatory, its population always equals the total population of its attached object type. Figure 5.7 depicts the general case for an object type *A* and an attached role *r*. The role *r* may occur in any position in a predicate of any arity, and *A* may participate in other predicates as well.

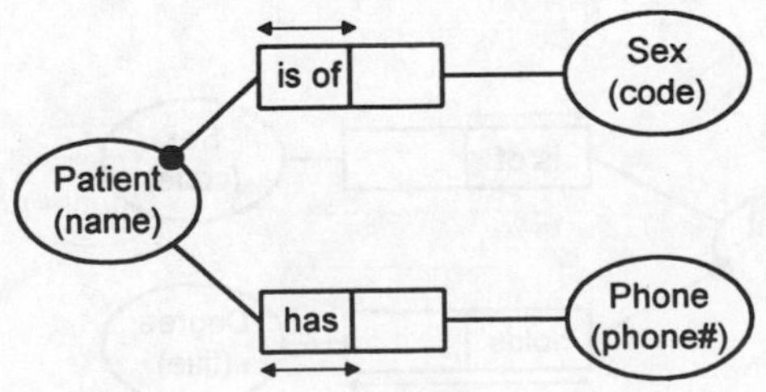

Figure 5.6 Implicitly, right hand roles are mandatory (no other fact roles)

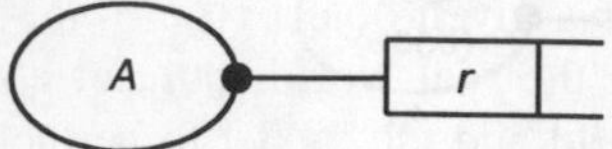

For each state: Each member of *pop(A)* plays *r*

pop(A) = *pop(r)*

Figure 5.7 The role *r* is mandatory

In Figure 5.7 it is not required that all members of the object type *A* are recorded as playing *r*. Mandatory role constraints are enforced on populations rather than types. For example, suppose the only fact stored in the database is that the person named "Adams C" is female. The role played by Sex is still mandatory, even though no instance of the male sex is recorded.

In Figure 5.6 the first role of the top predicate is both mandatory and unique. The mandatory role constraint says that each (recorded) patient has *at least one* sex recorded. The uniqueness constraint tells us that each patient has *at most one* sex. In combination these constraints state that each recorded patient has *exactly one* sex recorded. In general, *at least one* + *at most one* = *exactly one*.

In discussing uniqueness constraints we contrasted the UoD (real world portion of interest) with the knowledge base (the formal model of the UoD). As with other schema constraints, mandatory role constraints are assertions about our model, and do not necessarily apply to the real world. With our current example, it is optional whether a patient has a phone. This simply means that we do not need to record a phone number for every patient. Maybe this is because in the real world not every patient has a phone; or perhaps each patient does in fact have a phone but not all patients wish to give us their phone number.

As a more striking example, the schema of Figure 5.8 could be used to model a situation in which applicants for a position are given the choice whether to have their sex recorded or not, but must provide details about their degrees. In this case it is optional whether sex is recorded. This contrasts sharply with the real world where of course all applicants are of a particular sex.

With respect to mandatory roles, the relationship between the real world and the knowledge base may be stated as follows. *For a given object type, if a role is optional in the real world, then it is optional in the knowledge base, but the converse need not apply.*

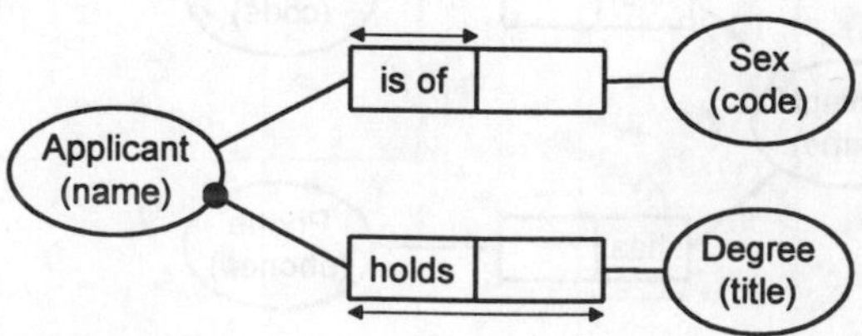

Figure 5.8 Recording the sex of an applicant is optional

Equivalently, if a role is mandatory for a given object type in the knowledge base then it is mandatory for that object type in the real world, but not conversely. These rules require the object types in the real world and the model to be the same, and need not hold if one is merely a subtype of the other.

Do *not* read a mandatory role constraint as saying "if an object plays that role in real life then we must record it". The information system can work only with the model we give it of the real world—it cannot enforce real world constraints not expressed in this model.

To help ensure that we have correctly specified the mandatory role constraints, we can apply the following checking procedure. For each mandatory role: is it mandatory in the real world? If not, make it optional. For each optional role: is it optional in the real world? If not, what reasons are there for making it optional? We will have more to say about this in the section on subtypes.

You may recall from Section 2.2 that when an object type plays more than one role, special care needs to be taken in updating the database to take account of mandatory roles. Suppose we wanted to add some facts from Table 5.1 into a database constrained by the conceptual schema of Figure 5.6 (recall that it is mandatory to record sex but optional to record a phone). Assuming the database is initially empty, an untutored user might proceed as follows:

User		*CIP*
add: Patient 'Adams C' is of Sex 'F'.	→	accepted.
add: Patient 'Adams C' has Phone '2057642'.	→	accepted.
add: Patient 'Collins T' has Phone '8853020'	→	rejected. Violates constraint: **each** Patient is of **some** Sex.

To add the third fact into the database we must either first record the fact that Collins is a male, or at least include this fact with the phone fact in a compound transaction.

Now consider the two report extracts shown in Figure 5.9. These list sample details maintained by a sporting club. Membership of this club is restricted to players and coaches. The term "D.O.B." means date of birth. As an exercise, try to specify the conceptual schema before looking at the solution.

Member	*D.O.B.*	*Joined*
Adams F	02/15/46	01/01/72
Anderson A	12/25/60	10/20/90
Brown C	01/01/72	11/14/92
Collins T	02/15/46	05/05/80
Crystal B	03/15/73	11/14/90
Downes S	11/02/50	06/17/85
...	...	...

Team	*Coach*	*Players*
A	Downes S	Adams F Brown C Collins T ...
B	Collins T	Anderson A Crystal B ...

Figure 5.9 Extracts of two reports from a sporting club

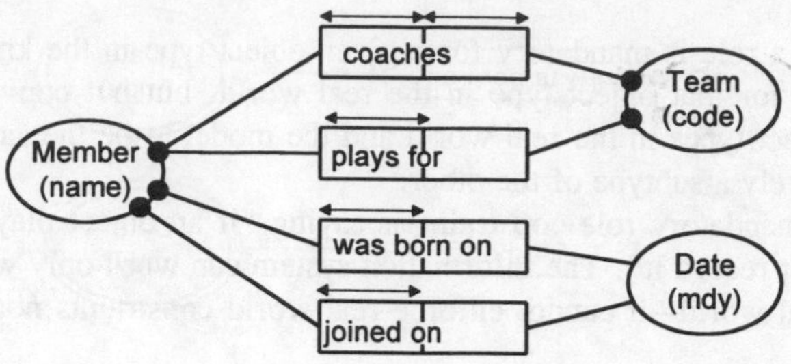

Figure 5.10 Each member either coaches or plays

Now check your solution against Figure 5.10. The uniqueness constraints assert that each person coaches at most one team, plays for at most one team, was born on at most one date, joined the club on at most one date, and each team has at most one coach. The reference mode "mdy" for Date indicates that date instances are in mm/dd/yy format (month/day/year)—of course, this conceptual choice does not exclude other formats being specified for external schemas.

The mandatory role dots on Team assert that each team has a coach and a player. The lower mandatory role dots on Member indicate that for each member we must record their birth date as well as the date they joined the club. The upper mandatory role dot on Member is linked to two roles: this is a **disjunctive mandatory role** constraint, indicating that the disjunction of these two roles is mandatory for Member. That is, each member *either* coaches *or* plays (*or both*). For example, Adams is a player only, Downes is a coach only, and Collins is both a player and a coach. We also allow that a coach of one team may play for the same team.

If Figure 5.10 includes all the roles played by Date in the global schema, then the disjunction of Date's roles is also mandatory (each date is a birth date or a join date): this could be shown explicitly by linking these roles to a disjunctive mandatory role dot; however this constraint is implicitly understood, and it is better to leave the figure as is.

This Date example illustrates the following generalization of the rule mentioned earlier for single mandatory roles: *by default, the disjunction of fact-roles played by a primitive atomic entity type is mandatory* (this default can be over-ridden by declaring the entity type lazy—see next chapter). Apart from highlighting the important cases where disjunctive mandatory roles need to be enforced (e.g. the coach-player disjunction), and simplifying schema merging and theorem specification, this rule facilitates the drawing of schemas. For example, object types like Date, Quantity, and MoneyAmt often have several roles which are disjunctively mandatory, and it may be awkward to have the role lines connect to a single point.

With large, complex schemas an object type may play so many roles that it becomes very awkward to connect a single ellipse for the object type to all its roles. To solve this problem, *object types may be duplicated* on a schema as often as desired. In this case, the rule for implicit mandatory disjunctive roles applies to the union of all the duplicate ellipses for the object type. Large schemas are typically divided into pages, and the same object type might appear on many pages. In addition, an object type might be duplicated on a single page.

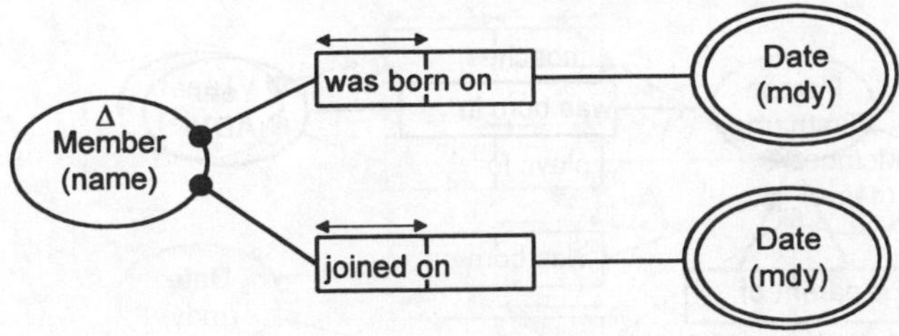

Figure 5.11 Date is duplicated on this page; Member appears on another page

We use a *double-ellipse notation* to indicate duplication on the same schema page. For example, the two fact types for Date in Figure 5.10 could be shown instead as in Figure 5.11. However, this duplicate notation is best reserved for cases where it is needed to avoid cluttered diagrams. To indicate that an object type is duplicated on another schema page, we use the *delta* symbol "Δ" (think of this here as a pointer to another page). In a CASE environment, we might click on this symbol to jump to an occurrence of the object type on another page; display of this symbol could be toggled. Different versions of ORM might use other notations for duplication.

To avoid confusion, a mandatory role, or disjunctive mandatory role should be shown *explicitly* if the object type it constrains has an explicit identification scheme or a subtype. For example, consider a global schema comprising just the coach and play fact types from Figure 5.10. If the identification scheme for Member is left implicit (i.e. the reference mode is parenthesized, as in Figure 5.10) then the disjunctive mandatory role constraint may be left implicit. However, if the reference type for Member is shown explicity (Member has MemberName) the mandatory disjunction of coaches and plays should be shown explicitly. Similarly, the explicit notation should be used if a Member subtype (e.g. Coach) is introduced (subtypes are discussed later).

Figure 5.12 indicates in general how to explicitly specify that a disjunction of roles r_1, r_2, ..., r_n is mandatory by linking the n roles to a dot on the object type: O<. The roles may occur at any position in a predicate, and the predicates need not be distinct.

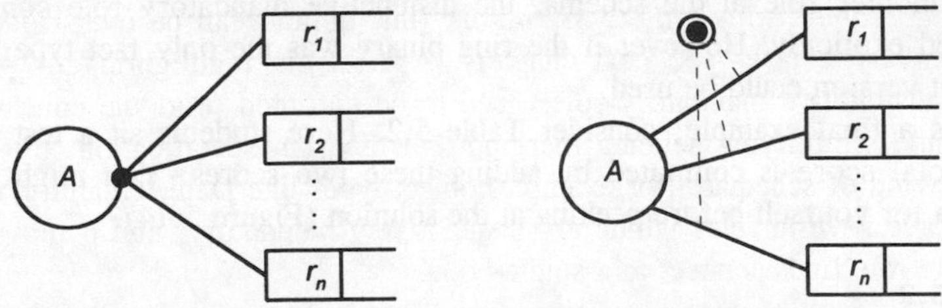

For each state:

Each member of *pop(A)* plays r_1 or r_2 or ... or r_n

$pop(A) = pop(r_1) \cup pop(r_2) \cup ... \cup pop(r_n)$

Figure 5.12 The role disjunction is mandatory (two equivalent notations)

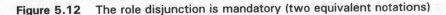

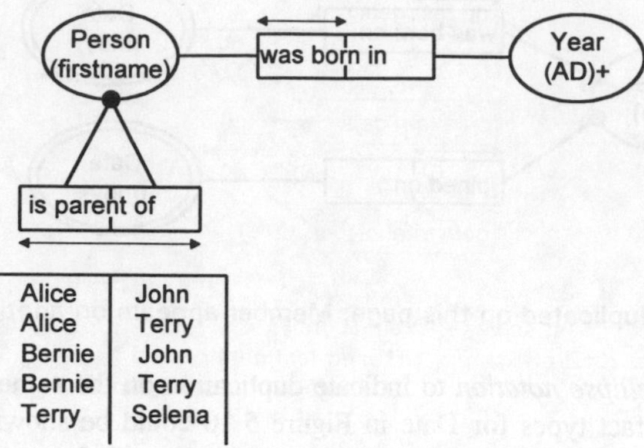

Figure 5.13 Each person is a parent or has a parent

In Figure 5.12 we use *"or"* in the *inclusive* sense; so we accept the possibility of some member of pop(*A*) being recorded as playing all the roles r_1 .. r_n. If we did want to assert the stronger constraint that all *n* roles played by *A* are mandatory, we would instead have the *n* roles meeting *A* at separate points, with a mandatory role dot on each. The right-hand side of Figure 5.12 shows an alternative notation for disjunctive mandatory roles. Here a circled dot is connected by dotted lines to the line segments which link the roles to the object type.

Because of its tidiness we generally prefer the left-hand notation. However, in rare cases the right hand-notation might have to be used. For example, suppose the disjunction of r_1 and r_2 is mandatory, and the disjunction of r_2 and r_3 is mandatory. We can express this using two constraints using the right-hand notation. We cannot express it at all with the left-hand notation.

Disjunctive mandatory role constraints sometimes apply to roles in the same predicate. Consider Figure 5.13. A sample population is shown for the ring binary: here each person plays either (or both) of the two roles. For instance, Terry is recorded as being a child of Alice and Bernie, and as being a parent of Selena. Since Person plays another role in the schema, the disjunctive mandatory role constraint must be depicted explicitly. However if the ring binary was the only fact type for Person, the implicit version could be used.

As a final example, consider Table 5.2. Here students sit a test and exam, and their total score is computed by adding these two scores. You might like to try the schema for yourself before peeking at the solution (Figure 5.14).

Table 5.2

student	*test*	*exam*	*total*
Adams	15	60	75
Brown	10	65	75
Einstein	20	80	100

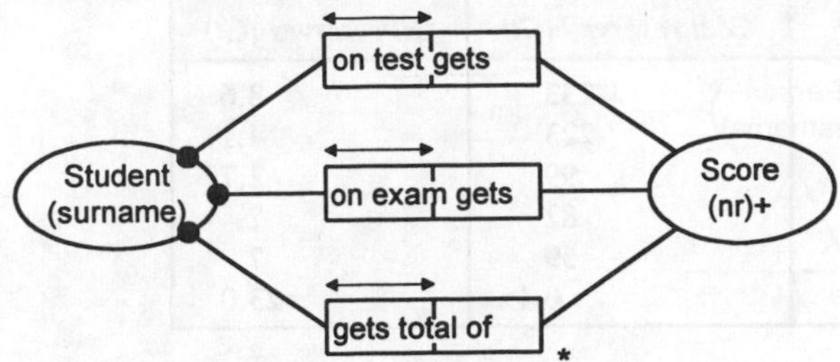

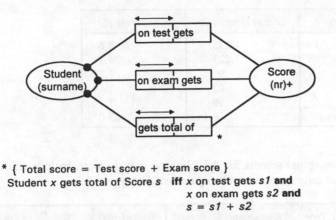

* { Total score = Test score + Exam score }
Student x gets total of Score s **iff** x on test gets $s1$ **and** x on exam gets $s2$ **and** $s = s1 + s2$

Figure 5.14 Constraints on the derived fact type are derivable

The new aspect of this example is the inclusion of a derived fact type. We usually prefer to omit derived predicates from the diagram, and show just the derivation rule. If included on the diagram, a derived fact type must be marked with an asterisk, and we also recommend that all its constraints be shown explicitly (in spite of the fact that these constraints are typically derived).

The uniqueness constraint on the total score fact type is derivable from the derivation rule and the uniqueness constraints on the other fact types (each student has only one test score and only one exam score and the total score is the sum of these). The mandatory role on the total score fact type is derivable from the derivation rule and the other mandatory roles (each student has a test score and an exam score, and the rule then provides the total score). *By default, all constraints shown on a derived fact type are derivable*. We discuss this default rule in more detail later. In very rare cases we may want to draw a derived fact type with a non-derivable constraint—in this case the fact type is marked with an "®" to indicate an extra rule exists for this predicate.

In principle, a derived fact type may be drawn with no constraints if these can be derived. Typically however, a derived fact type is only included on the diagram for discussion purposes, and in such cases it is illuminating to show the constraints explicitly.

Note that we use the term "mandatory role" in the sense of "must be *known*" rather than "must be stored", and allow ourselves to talk about the population of derived fact types as well as stored fact types. For a given object type *A*, the population of *A*, pop(*A*) includes all members of *A* that play either stored or derived roles. Derived roles may be optional. For example, if either the test or the exam role in Figure 5.14 is optional, the total score role is also optional (though it is still unique).

Exercise 5.2

1. Draw a conceptual schema diagram for the UoD described by the following sample output report. Include uniqueness and mandatory role constraints.

Country	*Coal reserves (Gt)*	*Oil reserves (Gt)*
CIS	233	8.6
USA	223	4.1
China	99	2.7
Germany	82	?
Australia	59	?
Saudi-Arabia	0.1	23.0

2. Set out the conceptual schema for the following output report. Include uniqueness and mandatory role constraints. Identify any derived fact type(s).

Subject	*Year*	*Enrollment*	*Rating*	*NrStudents*	*%*	*Lecturer*
CS121	1982	200	7	5	2.50	P.L.Cook
			6	10	5.00	
			5	75	37.50	
			4	80	40.00	
			3	10	5.00	
			2	5	2.50	
CS123	1982	150	7	4	2.67	R.V.Green
			6	8	5.33	
			5	60	40.00	
			4	70	46.67	
			1	6	4.00	
CS121	1983	250	7	10	4.00	A.B. White
			6	30	12.00	
			5	100	40.00	
			4	80	32.00	
			3	15	6.00	

3. A cricket fan maintains a record of boundaries scored by Australia, India and New Zealand in their competition matches. In the game of cricket a *six* is scored if the ball is hit over the field boundary on the full. If the ball reaches the boundary after landing on the ground a *four* is scored. In either case, a *boundary*" is said to have been scored.

	Australia			*India*			*New Zealand*		
Year	*4s*	*6s*	*total*	*4s*	*6s*	*total*	*4s*	*6s*	*total*
1984	120	30	150	135	23	158	115	35	150
1985	112	33	145	110	30	140	120	25	145
1986	140	29	169	135	30	165	123	35	158

Although it is possible to score a 4 or 6 by running between the wickets, such cases do not count as a boundaries and are not included in the database. A sample output report from this information system is shown. Here "4s" means "number of fours" and "6s" means "number of sixes". Schematize this UoD, including uniqueness constraints, mandatory roles and derived fact types. Use nesting.

4. Report extracts are shown from an information system used for the 1990 Australian federal election for the House of Representatives (the main body of political government in Australia). The table lists codes and titles of political parties that fielded candidates in this election or the previous election (some parties competed in only one of these elections). For this exercise we *treat Independent as a party*.

PartyCode	*Title*
ALP	Australian Labor Party
AD	Australian Democrats
GRN	Greens
GRY	Grey Power
IND	Independent
LIB	Liberal Party of Australia
NDP	Nuclear Disarmament Party
NP	National Party of Australia
...	...

A snapshot of voting details is shown about two seats (i.e voting regions) in the 1990 election. This snapshot was taken during the later stage of the vote counting. The number of votes for each politician, as well as the informal vote, is initially set to 0. During the election the voting figures are continually updated. The percentage of votes counted is calculated assuming all those on roll actually vote. For simplicity, *assume each politician and each seat has a unique name*. Figures are maintained for all seats in all states.

QLD:

FADDEN (On roll: 69110)	
CROSS (AD)	7555
FRECKLETON (NP)	2001
JULL (LIB)	24817
HEYMANN (IND)	641
WILKINSON (ALP)	21368
Informal	1404
% counted: 84	
Previous election: AD 4065; ALP 24481; LIB 21258; NP 9581	

NSW:

HUME (On roll: 70093)	
JONES (IND)	9007
* FIFE (LIB)	29553
KIRKWOOD (IND)	507
MARTIN (ALP)	20554
ROBERTS (AD)	3889
Informal	1309
% counted: 92	
Previous election: AD 2498; ALP 24516; IND (total): 2086; LIB 33687; NDP 1105	

An asterisk (*) preceding a politician's name indicates a sitting member (e.g. Fife is the sitting member for the seat of Hume): express this as a binary. Sitting members are recorded only if they seek re-election. Some seats may be new (these have no results for the previous election). States are identified by codes (e.g. "QLD" denotes Queensland). Each state has many seats (not shown here).

Draw a conceptual schema diagram for this UoD. Include uniqueness constraints and mandatory roles. If a fact type is derived, omit it from the diagram but include a derivation rule for it (you may specify this rule informally). Do not attempt any nesting.

5.3 Logical derivation check

Step 3 of the design procedure included a check for basic arithmetic derivations—these are usually obvious (e.g. totals). Now that we have specified uniqueness constraints and mandatory roles we are in a good position to *check for logical derivations*—these can be harder to spot, especially if some important facts were missed at Step 1. As a simple example, consider the report extract shown in Table 5.3.

You may recall that this table was considered in the previous chapter, where we showed it was wrong to schematize this as a ternary. We now deliberately make another kind of error, to illustrate our logical derivation check. Suppose we verbalized the first row as the two facts: Lecturer (surname) "Halpin" works for Department (code) "CS"; Lecturer (surname) "Halpin" works in Building (nr) "69". Assuming the table is significant with respect to uniqueness constraints and mandatory roles, this leads to the schema shown in Figure 5.15.

To begin our logical derivation check we now ask ourselves: *are there any other relationships of interest between the object types, especially functional relationships?* A binary relationship type is *functional* if at least one of its roles is a simple key: ○═; each column entry for this role functionally determines the entry for the other role. A simple key, or role with a simple uniqueness constraint, is said to be a *functional role*.

Looking at Figure 5.15, we now notice that the following fact type is also of interest: Department is located in Building. Suppose we interpret Table 5.3 as also giving us this information. For example, the first row of the table also tells us that the computer science department is located in building 69. Is the new fact type functional? From rows 2 and 3 we see that the same building may house more than one department. However the population suggests that each department is located in only one building. Suppose our client (the UoD expert) verifies that this is the case.

Table 5.3

Lecturer	*Department*	*Building*
Halpin	CS	69
Okimura	JA	1
Orlowska	CS	69
Wang	CN	1

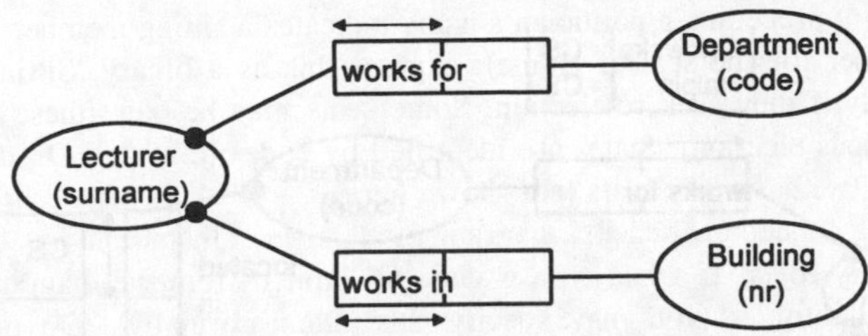

Figure 5.15 A first draft schema for Table 5.3

We might now add this fact type to our schema, to obtain Figure 5.16. The optional roles on Department and Building allow for other possibilities in the global schema (departments without lecturers, or buildings without departments) not covered by Table 5.3.

We now ask ourselves the question: *can any fact type be derived from the others?* Looking at the three binaries in Figure 5.16, you would probably suspect that one can be derived from the other two. Is this suspicion justified? If so, which binary should be derived? Is there a choice? What do you think?

Suppose we decide to make the new fact type about department location derivable, adding the following logical rule to our derivation rule section:

Department is located in Building iff some Lecturer works for Department and that Lecturer works in Building

Suppose our client agrees that this rule does apply. Is it now OK to make the department location derived? No! Why not? Recall our discussion from the previous section where we specified the following design guideline: *by default, all constraints on a derived fact type are derivable*. Is this true with our choice of derived fact type?

With our example, the uniqueness constraint on the fact type **Department is located in Building** is not derivable. How can we know this? One way of seeing this is to provide a *counterexample*—in this case, a sample population which satisfies all constraints except the uniqueness constraint that each department is located in at most one building.

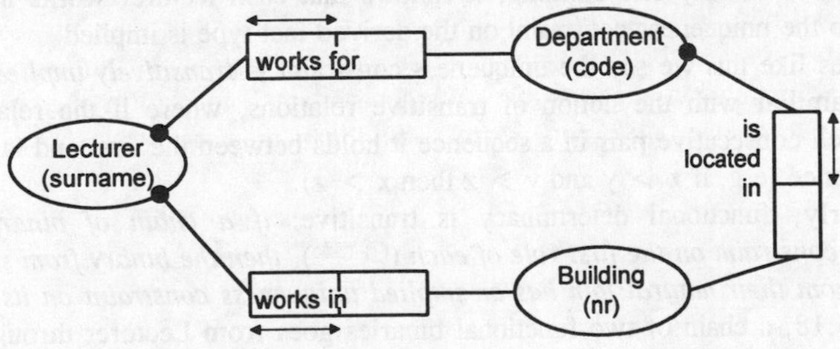

Figure 5.16 A second draft schema for Table 5.3

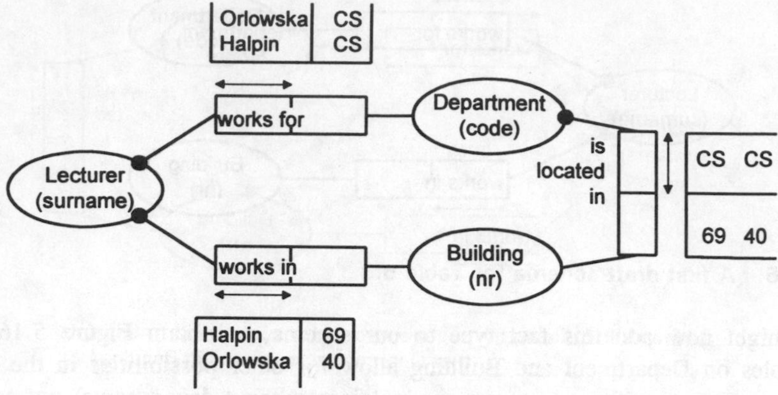

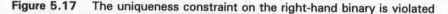

Figure 5.17 The uniqueness constraint on the right-hand binary is violated

One such population is shown in Figure 5.17. If we populated the horizontal binaries as shown, the derivation rule proposed earlier generates a population for the vertical binary which locates the CS department in two buildings. Another problem with the proposed rule is that it requires both roles of Department to be mandatory, but perhaps some departments have no lecturers.

If we choose to store the horizontal binaries, leaving the vertical binary derived, we must specify the uniqueness on the derived fact type as an additional non-derived constraint which needs to be enforced separately—i.e. when the database is updated we need to check that all lecturers working for the same department work in the same building. Sometimes a design decision like this is made in order to speed up queries, even though updates become more expensive. However, our default design guideline is the one we usually follow, since this simplifies updates.

To satisfy this guideline, the choice of derived fact type must be: Lecturer works in Building (see Figure 5.18). The derived fact type is included on the diagram for discussion purposes, but would usually be omitted, with just the rule being stated. In the context of this rule, if each lecturer works for only one department, and each department is located in only one building, it follows that each lecturer works in only one building. So the uniqueness constraint on the derived fact type is implied.

In cases like this we say the uniqueness constraint is *transitively implied*. You are probably familiar with the notion of transitive relations, where if the relation holds between each consecutive pair in a sequence it holds between the first and last member of the sequence (e.g. if $x > y$ and $y > z$ then $x > z$).

Similarly, functional determinacy is transitive: *if a chain of binaries has a uniqueness constraint on the first role of each (○–▭▭), then the binary from start to end projected from their natural join has an implied uniqueness constraint on its first role.* In Figure 5.18, a chain of two functional binaries goes from Lecturer through Department to Building, and the derivation rule defines the *[Lecturer, Building]* projection on the natural join of these two binaries. Hence in such cases we may use the uniqueness constraint pattern as an easy way to choose the candidate derived fact type.

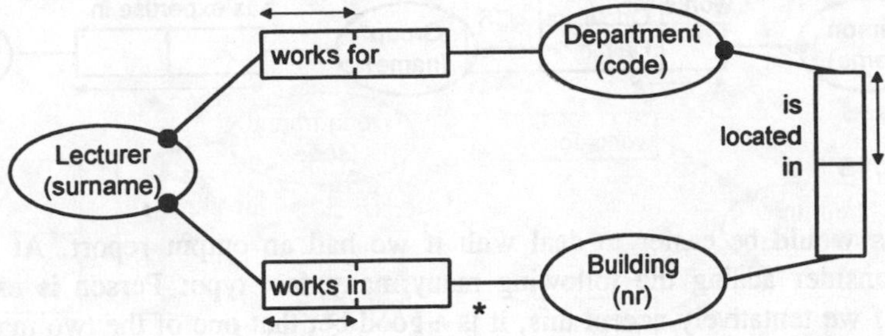

Figure 5.18 The constraints on the derived fact type are implied

We still need to check with the client whether our derivation rule is semantically correct. The mere existence of a such a constraint pattern doesn't guarantee that one of the fact types is derived. For example, the same constraint pattern may occur if we replace the derived fact type in Figure 5.18 by: Lecturer has lunch in Building. If even some lecturers have their lunch in a building different from their work building then the lunch fact type is *not* derivable since the following derivation rule does not apply: Lecturer has lunch in Building iff Lecturer works for some Department and that Department is located in Building.

As an aside, the derivation rule in Figure 5.18 may also be expressed by means of a "pair-equality" constraint between the works_in predicate and the join-path formed by connecting the outer roles of Department's predicates. Such "join constraints" are discussed in section 7.4.

Now consider the mandatory role on the derived fact type in Figure 5.18. How do we know that this constraint is implied? In the context of the rule, this follows from the other mandatory roles: each Lecturer works for some Department; and each Department is located in some Building. Actually, all we need is for the first role in the chain to be mandatory and for each co-role to subset the next role (subset constraints are discussed in the next chapter).

For this example, this means that each department which has a lecturer must be included in the departments which have buildings. If this were not the case, then there are two approaches we may take. The first approach is to use the schema as is, except the first role of WorksIn is declared optional.

The other alternative is fairly messy. We make the WorksIn fact type *partly derived* and partly stored. The main operator of the derivation rule is weakened to "if" instead of "iff". The first role of WorksIn may be kept as mandatory by agreeing to supply and store those fact instances missed by the derivation rule. While this approach is often used in logic programming examples (e.g. grandparent_of may be partly derived from parent_of, and partly stored directly) it is usually best avoided in business applications.

In some cases, non-functional relationships arise in the context of logical derivation. Consider the schema shown in Figure 5.19. Can you see any logical derivation possibilities?

Figure 5.19

This would be easier to deal with if we had an output report. At any rate, we might consider adding the following many:many fact type: Person is expert in Language. If we tentatively accept this, it is a good bet that one of the two many:many fact types (HasExpertiseIn and IsExpertIn) can be derived. Which would you pick?

Clearly, knowledge about each member of a group is more precise than knowledge about the group as a whole. So if we were interested in knowing the language expertise of each person we should store this, and derive the group expertise from the rule: **Group has expertise in Language iff Person works for Group and Person is expert in Language.** Obviously we cannot derive the expertise of a person from that of his/her group. But what if we are *not interested* in knowing each person's expertise? In this case the schema of Figure 5.19 may be left unchanged!

Exercise 5.3

1. In a certain computer company, workers are standardly identified by their initials, but they also have a unique name. Each worker has access to exactly one PC (Personal Computer), and each PC is accessed by at least one worker. For each PC a record is kept of the room in which it is located, the worker(s) who access it, and the computer language(s), if any, installed on it, e.g.

PC	*Room*	*Workers with access*		*Languages installed*
pc01	507	EFC TAH	(Ed Codfish) (Terry Halpin)	Pascal, Prolog, SQL
pc02	507	NW	(Nancy Wirth)	Pascal, Modula-2
pc03	618	PAB JM	(Paul Bailes) (Joan McCarthy)	Hope, Miranda
pc04	508	IN	(Ima Newie)	
pc05	508	PNC	(Peter Creasy)	COBOL, SQL
...	...	...	...	...

Each computer language is one of three types (declarative, functional or procedural), and *either* is installed on a PC *or* has an expert (or both). The PC a worker accesses must be in the room in which he/she works. The next table provides a full record of the languages, their types, who are expert at each, and each expert's room. The missing value symbol "•" indicates no expert currently exists for that language.

A workshop on computer languages is to be delivered by some of the workers. The full workshop program is shown in the final table, indicating how many hours (h) speakers talk about each language, and the total hours for each language type.

Draw a conceptual schema for this UoD. Include uniqueness and mandatory role constraints. If a fact type is derived, specify a derivation rule for it below the diagram.

Language	*Type*	*Experts (rooms)*
COBOL	procedural	PNC (508), REK (611)
Hope	functional	•
LISP	functional	JM (618)
Modula-2	procedural	NW (507)
Miranda	functional	PAB (618), DC (708)
Pascal	procedural	NW (507), TAH (507)
Prolog	declarative	JS (407)
SQL	declarative	EFC (507), PNC (508), TAH (507)

Declarative (6 h)		*Functional (4 h)*		*Procedural (6 h)*	
Prolog:	JS (3 h)	Hope:	PAB (1 h)	Modula-2:	NW (3 h)
SQL:	PNC (1 h)	Miranda:	PAB (3 h)	Pascal:	NW (2 h)
	TAH (2 h)				TAH (1 h)

5.4 Reference schemes

Now that we have a good grasp of uniqueness constraints and mandatory roles, it is time to consider reference schemes in more depth. Up to now we have considered only simple identification schemes. In practice, more complex reference schemes are often encountered, and we need to deal with them even as early as Step 1 of the CSDP, when we verbalize facts. Before examining these harder cases, we refine our treatment of simple reference schemes with the aid of an example.

Consider Table 5.4. You might like to draw the conceptual schema for this yourself before looking at the solution (Figure 5.20). Here we have abbreviated the reference schemes in the usual way, using parentheses.

The schema is repeated in Figure 5.21, this time with the reference schemes depicted explicitly—each appears as a *mandatory, 1:1 reference type*. For example, each person has exactly one surname, and each surname refers to at most one person. Technically, this is called an *injection* (or *1:1 into* mapping). The has_surname predicate maps each person to exactly one surname, and the inverse predicate (is_surname_of) maps each surname to at most one person. In this explicit version of the schema, each of the value types Surname, Cityname, IQNr, kgValue and cmValue play just one role; so it is better not to mark this role as mandatory.

Table 5.4

Person	*City*	*Height (cm)*	*Chest (cm)*	*Mass (kg)*	*IQ*
Adams	Brisbane	175	100	77	100
Brisbane	Sydney	182	91	80	120
Collins	Sydney	173	80	67	100
Darwin	Darwin	175	95	90	90

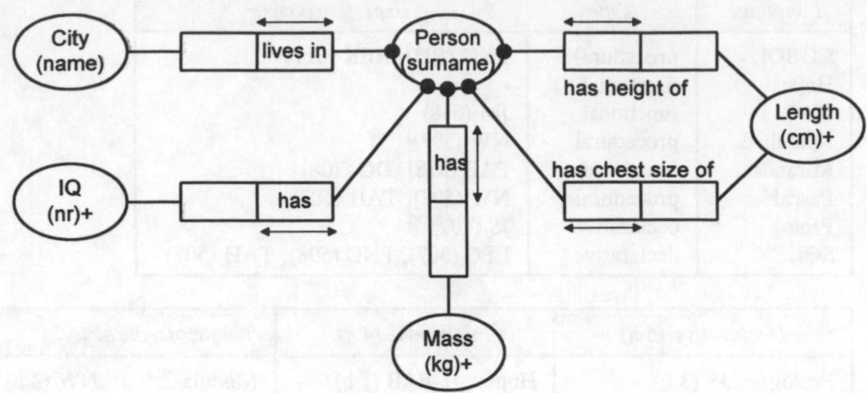

Figure 5.20 Conceptual schema for Table 5.4 (reference schemes abbreviated)

Implicitly, each value type is considered to be either identical to, or a subtype of, a primitive value type (e.g. String or Number). To help avoid cluttered diagrams, the primitive value types and their subtype graphs are not displayed. It should be remembered however that string value types often overlap with one another, as do numeric value types. For example, Surname and CityName are both subtypes of String; their populations do overlap here since both include the string "Brisbane".

Figure 5.21 also illustrates our earlier decision to indicate mandatory roles explicitly when the reference scheme is made explicit. For example, the fact roles played by City, IQ and Mass are marked mandatory, as is the disjunction of fact roles played by Length. Clearly, the abbreviated version shown in Figure 5.20 is usually preferable. However, the explicit version is useful if one needs to clarify the distinction between entities and the labels which refer to them. For example, assuming the population shown in Table 5.4, and an appropriate query language, consider the following dialogue between a user and the CIP.

User: Who lives in a city with the same name as his/her surname?
CIP: Darwin.
User: Which person is a city?
CIP: None: Entity types Person and City are mutually exclusive.

It is meaningful to compare the names for Person and City, since they are both character strings. But it is not sensible to compare persons and cities—they are different types of entity.

Notice that the value types for IQ, mass and length are all numeric (as indicated by the "+" mark). However mass and length have different units, while IQ is dimensionless (i.e. it has no units). Conceptually, two numerically referenced entities may be compared or added only if they have the same unit (or both have no unit). Hence the following queries do not make sense:

List persons whose mass equals their IQ.
List persons whose height is more than twice their mass.
List height + mass for each person.

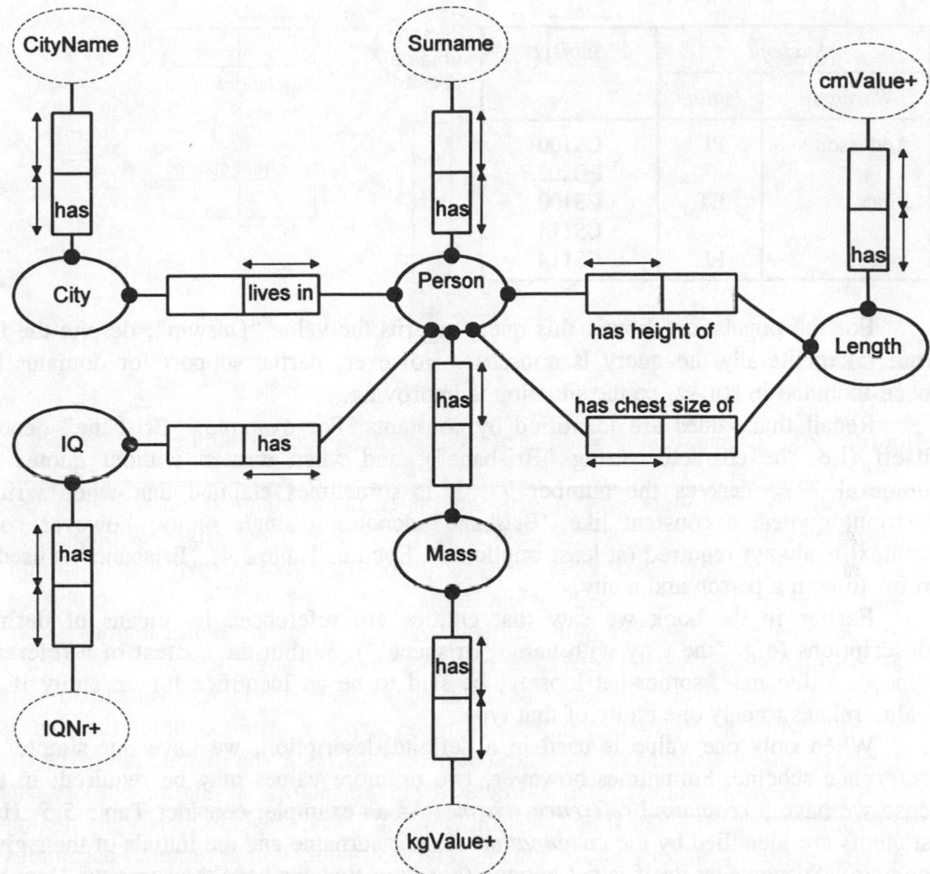

Figure 5.21 Conceptual schema for Table 5.4 (reference schemes explicated)

Of course, the numbers themselves may always be compared. Also, height and chest size are both based on the same domain and unit, so they are compatible. So the following queries are acceptable.

List persons whose mass number equals their IQ number.
List persons whose height number is more than twice their mass number.
List height + chest size for each person.

Most current database systems provide little or no support for the distinction between entities and their values. Operations specified in queries are always interpreted as applying directly to the values. For example, assuming Table 5.4 is stored in a relational database as the table *Athlete* (person, city, height, chest, mass, iq) the following SQL query is quite legal:

```
select person from Athlete
where person = city
  and mass = iq   and chest + mass > height
```

Table 5.5

Student		*Subject*
Surname	*Initials*	
Anderson	PJ	CS100 PD102
Jones	ET	CS100 CS114
Jones	PJ	CS114

For the population shown, this query returns the value "Darwin", despite the fact that taken literally the query is nonsense. However, partial support for domains has been included in SQL-92, so the situation is improving.

Recall that values are identified by constants. For example, "Brisbane" denotes itself (i.e. the character string "Brisbane"), and when written without quotes the numeral "77" denotes the number 77. It is sometimes claimed that when written without quotes, a constant like "Brisbane" denotes a single entity; however some context is always required (at least implicitly). Even in Table 5.4, "Brisbane" is used to refer to both a person and a city.

Earlier in the book we saw that entities are referenced by means of definite descriptions (e.g. "the City with name 'Brisbane'"). Within the context of a reference type, a value may, somewhat loosely, be said to be an identifier for an entity if the value relates to only one entity of that type.

When only one value is used in a definite description, we have our simple 1:1 reference scheme. Sometimes however, two or more values may be required: in this case we have a *compound reference scheme*. As an example, consider Table 5.5. Here students are identified by the *combination* of their surname and the initials of their given name(s). Surname by itself is not enough (e.g. two students have the surname "Jones"). If this table was an input form rather than an output report, we might still decide to concatenate the surname and initials into a single student name in our model. This choice results in the simple 1:1 reference scheme: Student (name).

Suppose however that the table is a sample output report, or that we wish to formulate queries such as: List all students with the surname "Jones". In this case, we need to be able to access surname, and possibly initials, separately. Hence somewhere in our model we need to have Surname as a value type, and Initials as another value type. There are two main ways of doing this: store the two components separately; or derive the components from a single, combined name. The first alternative is schematized in Figure 5.22.

The mandatory roles and internal uniqueness constraints declare that each student has exactly one surname and exactly one sequence of given name initials. The external uniqueness constraint declares each combination of surname and initials refers to at most one student. Each student maps to one ⟨surname, initials⟩ pair, and each ⟨surname, initials⟩ pair refers to at most one student. In general, compound reference schemes involve a mandatory 1:1 map of objects to a tuple of two or more values. Here "tuple" is used in the relational sense of "ordered *n*-tuple".

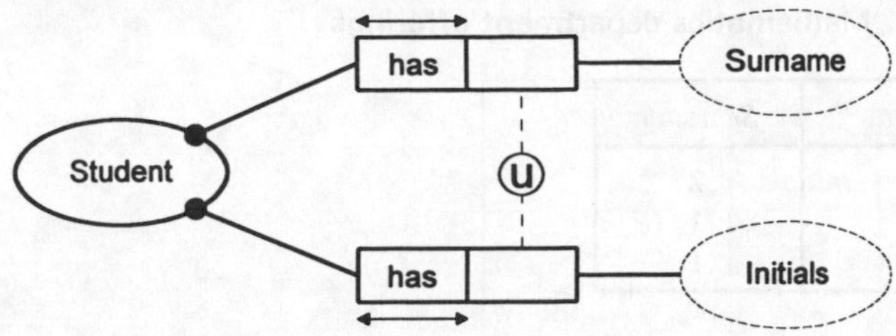

Figure 5.22 A compound reference scheme

The values of the tuple are ordered to agree with the order in which the reference predicates are used in verbalizing the reference scheme. No positional order is implied by the schema diagram, so any order may be chosen, e.g. ⟨initials, surname⟩ or ⟨surname, initials⟩.

As an alternative to storing surname and initials as separate components, we could store full student names as character strings and provide derivation rules for extracting the surnames and initials. This would be appropriate if in most output reports the student names were left intact, and only rarely was there a need for information about surnames and initials. For example, students with the surname "Jones" could be listed by issuing the SQL command: **select** name **from** Student **where** name **like** 'Jones %'.

The example just considered illustrates the simplest kind of compound reference scheme. The reference predicates are given the short name "has", and connect directly to a value type. In such cases, facts may be verbalized using reference modes. For example, the fact on row 1 of Table 5.5 may be stated as:

> The Student with surname 'Anderson' and initials 'PJ' enrolled in the Subject with code 'CS100'.

Alternatively, the reference schemes may be declared first, then the fact stated in shortened form:

Reference schemes: Student (surname, initials); Subject (code)
Fact: Student ⟨'Anderson', 'PJ'⟩ enrolled in Subject 'CS100'.

Identification schemes are *relative* to the particular UoD. Often, a simple scheme which works in a local context fails to work in a UoD of wider scope. This is important to bear in mind when merging subschemas into a larger schema. For example, suppose that within a given University department each subject offered by that department can be identified by its title. For instance, consider the output report in Table 5.6, which indicates for the Physics Department which subjects it offers in which semesters.

Table 5.6 Physics department offerings

Subject	*Semester*
Electronics	1
Mechanics	1
Optics	2

Table 5.7 Mathematics department offerings

Subject	*Semester*
Algebra	2
Calculus	1
Mechanics	1

In designing a schema for the Physics Department we have a 1:1 correspondence between subjects and their titles. So this table may be schematized as the fact type: Subject (title) is offered in Semester (nr). A similar schematization could be used for the Mathematics Department, a sample output report for which is shown in Table 5.7.

But now suppose we need to integrate departmental schemas into an overall schema for the whole university. Our simple identification scheme for subjects will no longer work because, in this wider UoD, different subjects may have the same title. For example, the subject Mechanics offered by the Physics Department is different from the subject Mechanics offered by the Mathematics Department. A combined output report would look like Table 5.8.

The first row may be verbalized using a compound reference scheme as follows. Note the use of "that" and "and". For persons, "who" is best used instead of "that".

The Subject that is offered by the Department with name 'Physics' and has SubjectTitle 'Electronics' is offered in the Semester with nr 1.

Alternatively, the reference schemes may be stated first:

Reference schemes: Department (name); Semester (nr);
Subject (is offered by Department, has SubjectTitle)
Fact: Subject ('Physics', 'Electronics') is offered in Semester 1.

This approach is schematized in Figure 5.23.

Though conceptually this picture is illuminating, in practice its implementation is somewhat awkward, with two labels (one for the department and one for the title) needed to identify a subject. In such cases, a new identification scheme is often introduced to provide simple 1:1 reference. For example, each subject may be assigned a unique subject code, as shown in Table 5.9.

Table 5.8 University subject offerings

Department	*Subject title*	*Semester*
Physics	Electronics	1
	Mechanics	1
	Optics	2
Mathematics	Algebra	2
	Calculus	1
	Mechanics	1
...	...	...

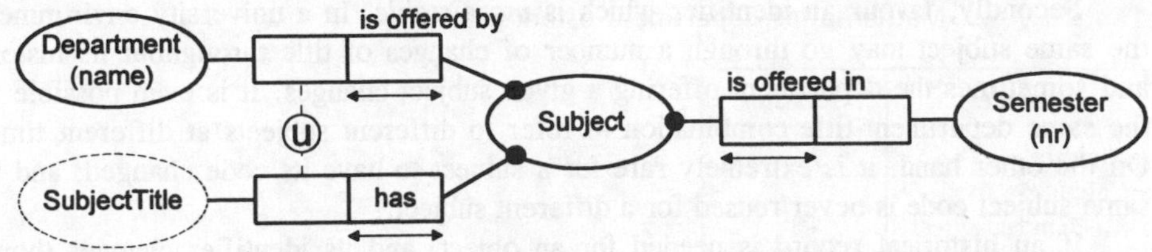

Figure 5.23 A schema for Table 5.8 using a compound reference scheme

Table 5.9 Subject codes provide a simple reference scheme

Subject	*Title*	*Department*	*Semester*
PH101	Electronics	Physics	1
PH102	Mechanics	Physics	1
PH200	Optics	Physics	2
MP104	Algebra	Mathematics	2
MP210	Calculus	Mathematics	1
MA109	Mechanics	Mathematics	1

In this output report there are two *candidate identifiers* for Subject. We could identify a subject by its code (e.g. "PH102") or by combining its department and title (e.g. ⟨"Physics, Mechanics"⟩). We choose one of these as the *primary identifier* (i.e. the standard means of referring to the entity). In this case, we would usually pick the subjectcode as the primary identifier. To indicate this choice on the schema diagram we parenthesize the primary reference mode (see Figure 5.24).

The Department and SubjectTitle predicates are treated just like any other fact types; they are no longer considered to be reference types; of course, the external uniqueness constraint between them must still be declared.

When two or more candidate identification schemes exist, we may use the following *guidelines for selecting the primary identifier*. First, *minimize the number of labels* needed. A single subject code is easier to enter than two labels for department and title; moreover, a compound identifier adds extra overhead in the later database implementation (joins, indexes and integrity checks over composite columns require more effort).

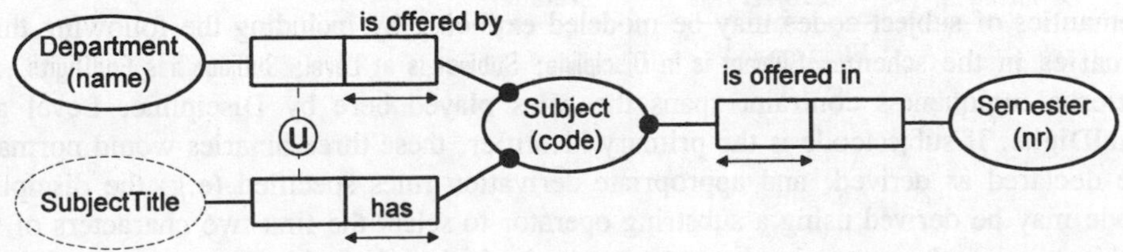

Figure 5.24 A schema for Table 5.9, using subject code as the primary identifier

Secondly, favour an identifier which is *more stable*. In a university environment, the same subject may go through a number of changes of title throughout its history; and sometimes the department offering a given subject changes. It is even possible for the same department-title combination to refer to different subjects at different times. On the other hand, it is extremely rare for a subject to have its code changed; and the same subject code is never reused for a different subject.

If an historical record is needed for an object, and its identifier changes though time, extra work is required to keep track of these changes so that we know when we are talking about the same object. This extra effort can be minimized by making the identifier as stable as possible. Ideally, the object has the same identifier throughout the lifetime of the application: this is known as a *rigid identifier*. Most organizations choose rigid identifiers such as employee#, client#, serial# for their employees, clients, equipment and so on.

To explain some basic concepts in a friendly way, we have used identifiers such as PersonName, Surname or even Firstname in some examples. However except for trivial applications this kind of identification is unrealistic. Often, two people may have the same name. Moreoever, people may change their name—women usually change their surname when they marry, and anyone may change one's name by deed-poll. A philosophy lecturer of mine once changed his surname to "What" and his wife changed her surname to "Who"!

A third criterion sometimes used for selecting an identifier is that it be easy for users to recognize. This criterion is mainly used to mimimize errors when users enter or access artificial identifiers such as subject or stockitem codes. This effectively endows codes with semantics, at least implicitly. For example, the subject code "CS114" is used in my university for a particular first year subject in information systems. The first two characters "CS" indicate the discipline area (Computer Science), the first digit indicates the level (first), and the last two digits merely distinguish it from other computer science subjects at the same level. Certainly such a code is less likely to be misread than a purely arbitary code (e.g. "09714").

Such "information-bearing" codes should be avoided if the semantic relationships involved are unstable, since the codes would then often need changing. In the current example however, the semantics are fairly stable—the subject discipline is unlikely ever to change, and the subject level would normally be stable too. The linking of the two letters to discipline (e.g. "MP" for pure maths and "MA" for applied maths) rather than department is better, since disciplines are more stable than departments.

If information-bearing codes are used, we need to decide whether their semantics are to be modeled in the system, or simply assumed to be understood by users. The semantics of subject codes may be modeled explicitly by including the following three binaries in the schema: Subject is in Discipline; Subject is at Level; Subject has EndDigits. An external uniqueness contraint spans the roles played here by Discipline, Level and EndDigits. If subjectcode is the primary identifier, these three binaries would normally be declared as derived, and appropriate derivation rules specified (e.g. the discipline code may be derived using a substring operator to select the first two characters of the subject code); the external uniqueness constraint is then derivable.

Selecting a primary identifier from two or more candidate identifiers might be regarded as an implementation decision rather than as a conceptual issue. At any rate, such a decision is needed before the conceptual schema can be mapped to a relational schema. To avoid certain problems, we demand that *an entity type's primary identification scheme 1:1 maps each entity to a tuple of one or more values*.

In everyday life, weaker kinds of identification scheme are used in some contexts. For example, some people have identifying nicknames (e.g. "Tricky Dicky" denotes president Nixon, and "the great white shark" denotes the golfer Greg Norman). However in a typical application not everybody will have a nickname, so nicknames are not used for primary reference (they are not mandatory).

Sometimes a 1:many reference scheme is used. For example, a plant or animal type may have more than one identifying, common name. For instance, the bird kind with the scientific name of *dacelo gigas* may also be identified by any of the following common names: "laughing kookaburra"; "great brown kingfisher"; "laughing jackass"; "bushman's clock". As a botanical example, "gorse" and "furze" refer to the same plant. We reject common name as a primary reference since it is not 1:1. For primary reference we must choose a mandatory 1:1 scheme. Such a scheme may already exist (e.g. scientific name). If not, we create one. This might be partly artificial (e.g. standard common name), or completely artificial (e.g. birdkind#).

Simple 1:1 naming schemes relate entities directly to values (e.g. subjects to subject codes). In life we sometimes identify entities by 1:1 relating them to other entities (e.g. "the Olympics that was held in the Year 1992", "the Warehouse that is located in the City 'Brisbane'", "the Director who heads the Department 'Sales'"). In principle such identification schemes may be chosen for primary reference, and depicted as mandatory 1:1 binaries (e.g. Olympics was held in Year (AD)). These binaries are then regarded as reference types, not fact types.

However this is rarely done. The binaries may be retained as facts, and other primary reference schemes used (e.g. Olympics (sequence#), Warehouse (wh#), Director (employee#)). Alternatively, the relevant entity types may be removed by using suitably descriptive predicates. For example, the assertion "The olympics of Year 1992 was located in City 'Barcelona'" may be portrayed as a binary between the entity types Year and City. If the original referential semantics are not needed, another alternative is to use simple value reference (e.g. "Warehouse (name) 'Brisbane'" loses the semantics that this warehouse is located in the city Brisbane).

Earlier we considered examples of compound reference schemes. Typically each reference predicate is mandatory. In such cases, each entity of that type ends up being identified by the same number of values. However, in life we sometimes run across identification schemes where some of the reference roles are optional—however their disjunction is still mandatory. We call this *disjunctive reference*. In these cases, different entities of the same type may be referenced by different numbers of values. For example, consider the botanical identification scheme depicted in Figure 5.25.

Some kinds of plants are identified simply by a genus name (e.g. agrostis). Many other plant varieties are referenced by a combination of genus and species (e.g. acacia interior). Still others are identified by a genus, species and infraspecies, where the infraspecies itself is identified by a rank and infraname (e.g. eucalyptus fibrosa ssp. nubila). So depending on which kind of plant it is, there may be two, three or four values required to identify it. Because such cases require special treatment when implemented, we use a special notation for the relevant external uniqueness constraint.

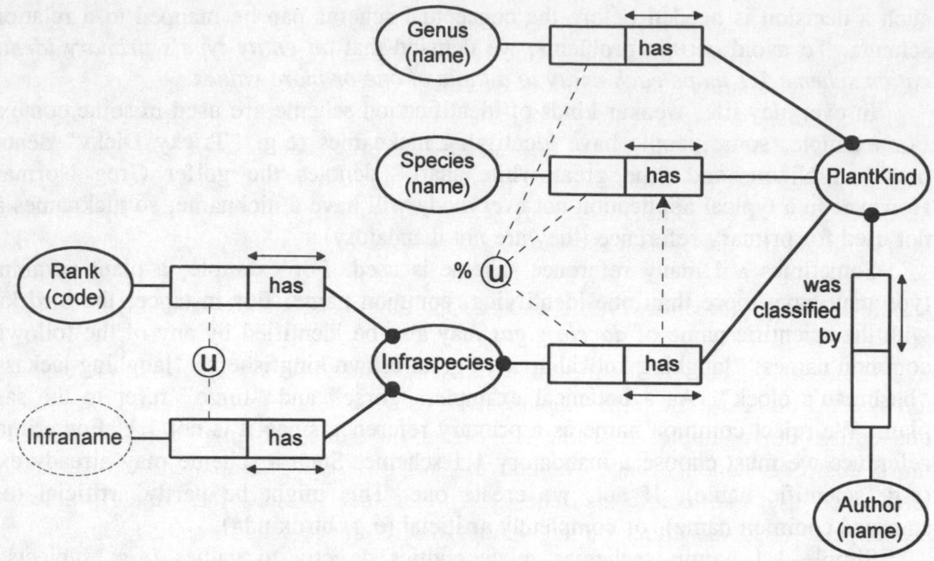

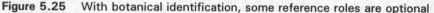

Figure 5.25 With botanical identification, some reference roles are optional

For disjunctive reference, a percentage sign is added to the usual external uniqueness marker: "ⓤ%". Here this indicates that each tuple or subtuple of (genus, species, infraspecies) refers to at most one plant kind. The "%" intuitively suggests that "partial" sequences are allowed. Just which parts of the sequence are optional is determined by which roles are optional in the reference scheme. With our present example, only the genus is mandatory. Moreover, for each genus there is at most one plantkind with only a genus name. And for each genus-species combination there is at most one plantkind with no infraspecies.

The other "ⓤ" symbol at the left in Figure 5.25 depicts an ordinary external uniqueness constraint (each rank and infraname combination determines at most one infraspecies). You may have noticed the dotted arrow running from the first role of has_Infraspecies to that of has_Species: this denotes the subset constraint that infraspecies is recorded only if species is. We discuss subset constraints in detail in the next chapter.

Believe it or not, the reference scheme of Figure 5.25 is a simplified version of the actual identification scheme used in botany, where complications such as hybrids and cultivars also need to be catered for. Life can be messy! Even if we decide to introduce a simpler primary reference scheme (e.g. plantkind#), we still need to model the disjunctive reference scheme as a disjunctive fact scheme. Like other uniqueness constraints the use of "ⓤ%" is not confined to primary reference schemes.

With disjunctive reference, there is a disjunction of mapping functions: genus or genus-species or genus-species-infraspecies. Each entity 1:1 maps to a tuple of one or more values via one of these functions.

Sometimes reference chains can get lengthy. A value is identified by a constant. Each entity or nested object is referenced directly by a sequence of objects, which in turn may be values, entities or nested objects; in the latter cases the reference chain continues, recursively, until finally the referencing objects are all values. In this way, each object ultimately gets referenced by one or more values which appear as entries in named columns of output reports or database tables.

Now that we have discussed the various reference schemes, we summarize how to *indicate the choice of primary reference* when more than one candidate identification scheme exists. If a simple 1:1 naming scheme is chosen, abbreviate its reference mode in parenthesis. If the chosen scheme is a composite or disjunctive reference, and other schemes exist, replace the "ⓤ" by a circled "P" (for "Primary"), i.e. Ⓟ or Ⓟ%. If a simple 1:1 link to an entity type is chosen, and other schemes exist, mark the reference predicate with "Ⓟ".

Candidate identifiers for the same entity are said to be *synonyms*. In the information systems literature the term *"homonym"* is used for a label which refers to more than one entity. For example, in Table 5.5 earlier the same surname "Jones" referred to more than one student. Since "homonym" has different grammatical senses, another term such as "non-identifying label" is preferable. At any rate, the "problem of homonyms" is solved either by augmenting the reference scheme until identification is achieved (e.g. combining surname and initials, as discussed earlier) or by using a completely different primary identification scheme.

Up to now we have assumed that an object's reference scheme is the same throughout the whole schema. The next chapter examines some cases involving subtypes where this assumption is removed: we then have *context dependent reference*. We end this section by considering a different case of such variable reference schemes—an application which uses *different units for the same physical quantity*.

For example, in Australia pieces of lumber have their longest length specified in meters but their breadth and depth are measured in millimeters. Because this is a standard in the building industry, an output report on lumber sizes might look like Table 5.10.

One might propose a schema like Figure 5.26 to deal with this. This schema is versatile enough to allow comparisons of breadth and depth (e.g. to determine lumber with square cross sections) and perform some arithmetic operations (e.g. computation of average lengths or cross sectional perimeters though derivation functions).

However suppose we want to compare a length with a width (e.g. Which sizes of lumber are 20 times as long as their breadth?) or compute volumes in standard units (e.g. What is the volume of lumber size C7 in cubic meters?). How would you handle this situation?

Table 5.10

Lumber size	*Length (m)*	*Breadth (mm)*	*Depth (mm)*
A4	3	100	100
B7	2	100	75
C7	5	200	100

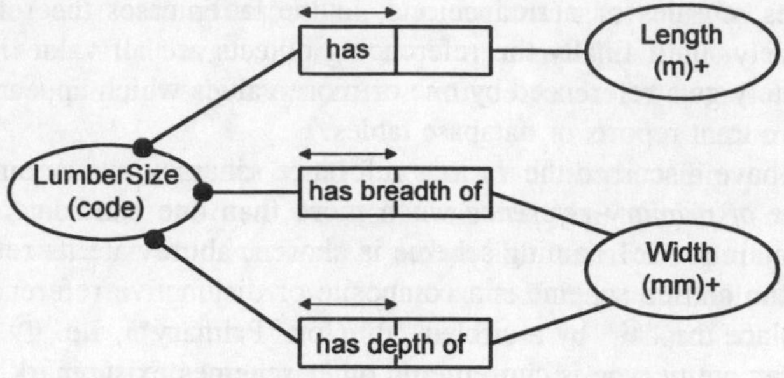

Figure 5.26 A tentative conceptual schema for Table 5.10

Such queries require three things. Firstly we need to know that Length and Width are meaningful to compare. So we collapse them into the same entity type, say "Length" used in the more general sense. Secondly we need to retain the knowledge of which units are used in which contexts. These first two objectives are met by duplicating the object type Length on the schema (using the double-ellipse notation) but indicating the different units by means of different reference modes (see Figure 5.27).

The third thing we need to do is specify *conversion rules* between the units. Since several units might be used for the same physical quantity, we can reduce the number of conversion rules by choosing a *standard unit* and just supplying rules to convert to this standard (rather than separate conversions between each unit pair). The reference mode of the standard unit is set out in the normal way (in parentheses, with a "+"). However in the case of a *derived unit*, an asterisk is appended. Being a kind of derivation rule, any conversion rule is written below the schema diagram. A derived unit is always placed on the left of the equals sign. See Figure 5.27.

Different approaches are sometimes used for dealing with the problem of different units. If we are not interested in modeling the connections between different units, then we could avoid collapsing physical quantities to the same dimension. For example, an astronomy application might have an entity type StellarDistance measured in parsecs, and TelescopeDiameter measured in centimeters. What should we do here?

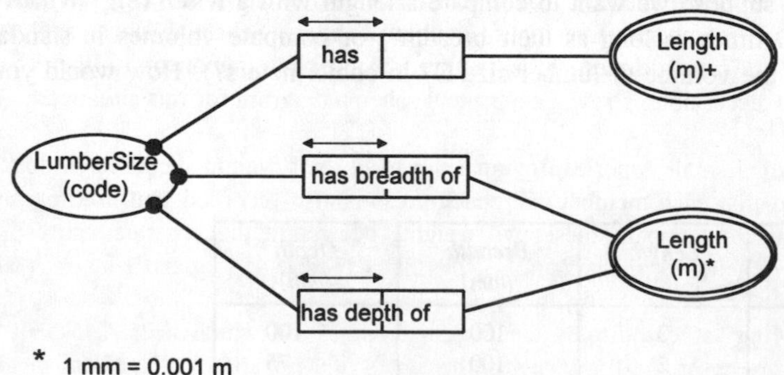

Figure 5.27 This schema captures the semantic connections between the units

The populations of the StellarDistance and TelescopeDiameter types would never overlap. If we never wanted to compare them we could leave them just like this—the semantic connection between these lengths which exists in the real world is then excluded from our model.

In principle, one might argue that each unit-based quantity should have just one unit for the conceptual schema and the internal schema, with other units provided at the external level as required. However, this makes it very unnatural for users to work with table populations in validating the conceptual schema.

In some cases the capacity to work in completely different unit systems is required. For example, we may need both metric and imperial measures to be displayed as users gradually move from one unit system to a newer one. In such a case the cleanest way out is to store the values in the new system and provide derivation rules to convert these into the older units as required (e.g. cm to inches).

Exercise 5.4

1. It is desired to identify a warehouse by its physical location. Design an appropriate identification scheme for the each of the following contexts:

   (a) UoD restricted to one suburb. The street in which the warehouse is located is identified by its name.
   (b) UoD restricted to one city. Each suburb is identified by its name.
   (c) UoD restricted to one country. Cities are identified by name.
   (d) UoD restricted to planet Earth. Countries are identified by name.
   (e) UoD restricted to Milky Way galaxy. Planets are identified by name.

2. The UoD is restricted to Earth, and we wish to store facts of the form: Warehouse contains Item in Quantity. Is the identification scheme discussed in Question 1(d) practical from the implementation point of view? If not, suggest a better scheme and support your scheme by comparing a sample population for the two approaches.

3. Members of a small social club are identified by the combination of their given names and surname. Each member has at least one and at most three given names. For example, one member is Eve Jones, another is Johann Sebastian Bach, and another is Eve Mary Elizabeth Jones. It is required that each component of their names be individually accessible. Draw a conceptual schema diagram for this situation.

4. Members of a small American gymnasium have their weight recorded in pounds (lb). The weight that each member can bench press is also recorded, but in kilograms (kg). It is desired to compare these two weights but retain the separate units. Specify a conceptual schema for this situation. Note that 1 lb = 0.454 kg and 1 kg = 2.205 lb.

5. The following table indicates the common names by which beer drinks of various volumes may be ordered in hotels in the States of Australia. Volumes are measured in fluid ounces (oz). The population of the table is significant. A double hyphen "--" indicates that beer drinks of that volume are not on sale in that State. For instance, in

Queensland exactly three different beer drinks may be ordered. Draw the conceptual schema diagram for this UoD.

	4 oz	5 oz	6 oz	7 oz	8 oz	10 oz	15 oz	20 oz
Qld	--	Small beer	--	--	Glass	Pot	--	--
NSW	--	Pony	--	Seven	--	Middy	Schooner	Pint
Vic	--	Pony	Small	Glass	--	Pot	Schooner	--
SA	--	Pony	--	Butcher	--	Schooner	Pint	--
WA	Shetland Pony	Pony	--	Glass	--	Middy	Schooner	Pot
Tas	Small beer	--	Beer or Six	--	Eight	Pot or Ten	--	--
NT	--	--	--	Seven	--	Handle	Schooner	--

5.5 Case study: a compact disk retailer

To consolidate the main ideas we have learnt so far, we consider a small case study. To derive maximum benefit from this section, you should attempt to solve the problem yourself before looking at the solution. A description of the application is now given.

A retailer of compact disks maintains an information system to help with account and stock control, as well as to provide a specialized service to customers seeking information about specific musical compositions and artists. Figure 5.28 illustrates the kind of musical information required for compact disks (some of the data is fictitious). Only four disks are mentioned here. Each disk contains several individual musical items, referred to as "tracks". Although compact disks usually have about 20 tracks, for this example only a few tracks are listed.

Before reading the next two paragraphs, try to verbalize information from Figure 5.28 as elementary facts. Pay particular attention to the reference schemes involved.

Each compact disk has a cd# as its primary identifier (although not shown here, different disks may have the same name). An artist may be a person or a group of persons. The artist is recorded if and only if most of the tracks on the disk have the same artist (this constraint is enforced by the data entry operator, not by the system). The record company which releases the disk must be recorded. A track is identified by its position on a given compact disk. Although each track has exactly one title, the same title may refer to different tracks (e.g. there are two tracks titled "Sultans of Swing"), possibly even on the same disk.

The duration of a track is the time it takes to play. Each track has exactly one duration, measured in seconds. Most tracks have one or more singers. Some tracks may have no singers (these are instrumental rather than vocal tracks, although this dichotomy is left implicit).

Table 5.11 lists the quantity in stock and recommended retail price (in dollars) of each compact disk. This table is updated when required, on a daily basis. The stock quantity of a disk may drop to zero.

Sales records are kept only for the current year of operation. For each month that has passed, figures are kept of the quantity of copies sold and the revenue (profit) accruing from sales of the compact disks in that month (see Table 5.12).

cd#: 654321-2 **name:** Special Oldies

artist: **record company:** EMI

track#	*title*	*duration*	*singers*
1	Maya's Dance	225	Donovan
2	Wonderful Land	200	
3	King of the Trees	340	Cat Stevens
4	Sultans of Swing	240	Mark Knopfler
...	...	...	...

cd#: 792542-2 **name:** The Other Side of the Mirror

artist: Stevie Nicks **record company:** EMI

track#	*title*	*duration*	*singers*
1	Rooms on Fire	300	Stevie Nicks
2	Two Kinds of Love	250	Bruce Hornsby, Stevie Nicks
...	...	...	...

cd#: 836419-2 **name:** Money for Nothing

artist: Dire Straits **record company:** Phonogram

track#	*title*	*duration*	*singers*
1	Sultans of Swing	346	Mark Knopfler
2	Walk of Life	247	Mark Knopfler
...	...	...	...

cd#: 925838-2 **name:** Fleetwood Mac Greatest Hits

artist: Fleetwood Mac **record company:** Warner Bros

track#	*title*	*duration*	*singers*
1	Say You Love Me	200	Chris McVie, Stevie Nicks
2	Seven Wonders	300	Stevie Nicks
...	...	...	...

Figure 5.28 Musical details about four compact disks

Table 5.11 Stock quantity and recommended retail price of compact disks

cd#	*cd name*	*stock qty*	*rrp*
654321-2	Special Oldies	5	17.95
792542-2	The Other Side of the Mirror	100	25.00
836419-2	Money for Nothing	10	20.00
925838-2	Fleetwood Mac Greatest Hits	50	23.95
...	...	...	...

For simplicity we have restricted these figures to the four compact disks of Figure 5.28—in reality this table would have thousands of rows and much larger totals. This table is updated on a monthly basis. Daily sales figures are kept manually but are not part of the application. For each month, if a disk was on the stock list and had no sales for that month then a figure of zero is recorded for it. If a disk is a new stock item in the month then it has no sales figures recorded for previous months (e.g. disk 792542-2 was not in stock in January).

Before peeking at the solution, try to schematize this application for yourself. Include all uniqueness and mandatory role constraints, and derivation rules.

There are two challenging aspects of this problem: the identification scheme for tracks; and the modeling of monthly sales. Let's consider these in order. To understand the terms used in the application, and clarify what is possible, you often need to talk things over with the client or UoD expert. The term "track" is commonly used in two senses: the *physical track* on a compact disk; and the musical composition, or *work*, recorded on this track.

How do we identify a physical track? It sometimes helps to sketch the object we are describing. A track on a compact disk occupies an annular (or ring-shaped) region as shown in Figure 5.29.

Here we have shaded track 1 of disk 654321-2. Note that we use both "disk" and "track" in a general sense—we don't mean a particular copy (there may be thousands of copies of the same disk).

Table 5.12 Monthly sales figures (small sample only)

month	*cd#*	*cd name*	*qty sold*	*revenue*
Jan	654321-2	Special Oldies	0	0.00
	836419-2	Money for Nothing	30	180.00
	925838-2	Fleetwood Mac Greatest Hits	50	400.00
			------	----------
			80	580.00
Feb	654321-2	Special Oldies	5	33.50
	792542-2	The Other Side of the Mirror	70	630.00
	836419-2	Money for Nothing	15	90.00
	925838-2	Fleetwood Mac Greatest Hits	50	350.00
			------	----------
			140	1103.50

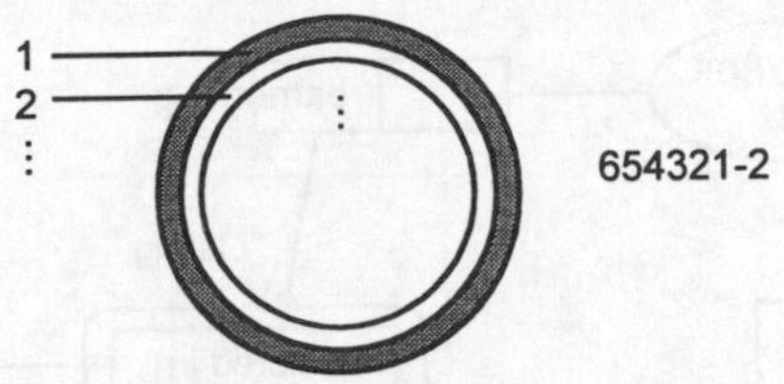

Figure 5.29 Track 1 of disk 654321-2 is shaded

Since there are many disks in the application, we need both the track# and the cd# to identify the track. According to the data of Figure 5.28, this track has a composition titled "Maya's Dance" recorded on it. Using "track" in the physical sense, we may verbalize this fact as follows:

> The Track that has track# 1 and is on the CompactDisk with cd# '654321-2' stores a work with the Title 'Maya's Dance'.

Notice that we said "*a*" work of that title, not "*the*". Different musical works may have the same title. Moreover, the same work may appear on many disks. Although the physical track identifies a work, this reference scheme is not 1:1. In the previous verbalization we did not include Work as an entity type. Should we do this? Do we need to know whether a work on one disk is exactly the same as a work on another disk? Only the client can tell us whether he/she wants to know this.

For our solution we assume the answer to our question is "No". However if the answer were "Yes" we would need to come up with a 1:1 identification scheme for Work: a natural scheme is hard to find (even the combination of title, artist and duration might not be enough); we might introduce some artificial identifier (e.g. work#).

Our solution is depicted in Figure 5.30. Here "Track" means "physical track", not "musical work" (this point should be included in the system documentation). The compound identification involves a 1:1 map between tracks and (track#, cd#) pairs.

Now let's consider the monthly sales (Table 5.12). The reference schemes here are obvious: Month (code); CompactDisk (cd#); Quantity (nr)+; MoneyAmt ($)+. The totals for quantity sold and revenue are obviously derived. You may have schematized the stored fact types thus: CompactDisk has CDname; CompactDisk in Month sold in Quantity; CompactDisk in Month earned MoneyAmt. This is acceptable (although as we see later, an equality constraint then needs to be added).

However it is better to nest the common part of the two ternaries, as shown in Figure 5.30. Here we have used the name "Listing" for the objectified fact type which records which compact disks were listed for sale in what months. For each individual listing (of a given compact disk in a given month) the number sold (possibly zero) and money earned (also possibly zero) are recorded. Apart from a more compact schema, the nested solution leads to a more efficient relational schema (as discussed later).

Other aspects of the schema are straightforward, and are not discussed here. Two main points arising from this case study are that care is often required in choosing and identifying object types, and sample populations are not always significant.

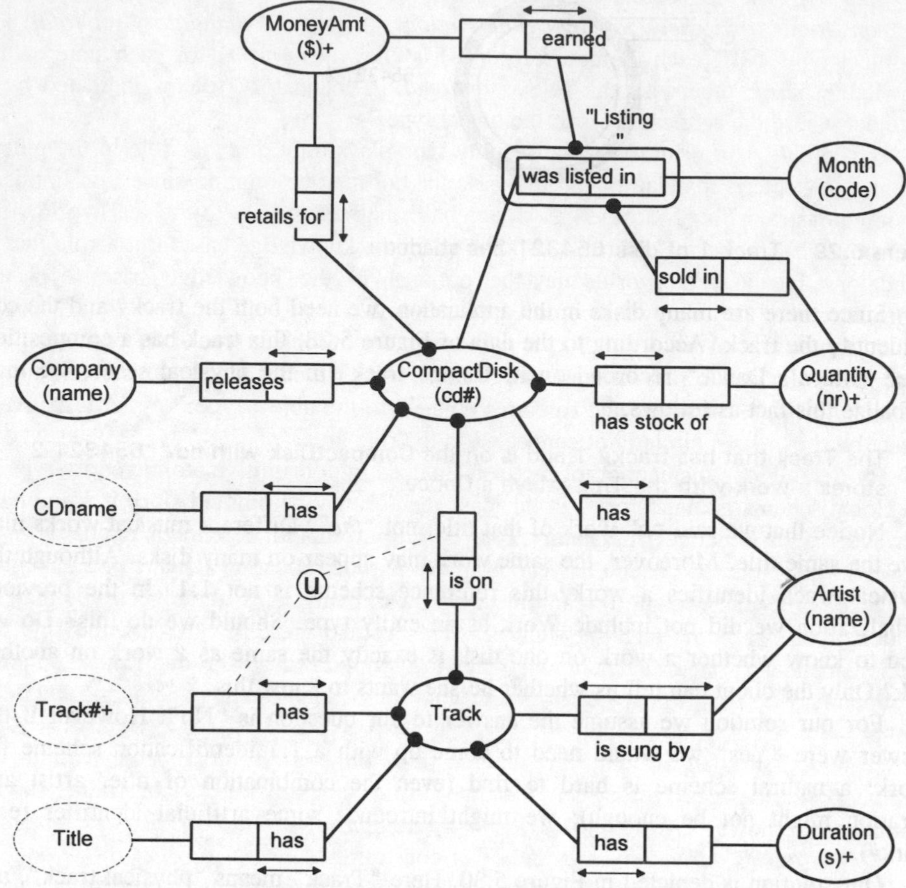

* TotalQtySold (Month *m*) ::= **sum**(Quantity) **from** (Listing(CompactDisk, *m*) sold in Quantity)
* TotalRevenue (Month *m*) ::= **sum**(MoneyAmt) **from** (Listing(CompactDisk, *m*) earned MoneyAmt)

Figure 5.30 One way of schematizing the application

5.6 Summary

For a given state of the knowledge base, the *population* of a role *r*, *pop(r)*, is the set of objects referenced as playing that role in that state. $A \cup B$, the *union* of sets *A* and *B*, is the set of all elements in *A* or *B* or both. The *null set* or empty set, { }, has no members. The population of an entity type *A*, *pop(A)*, is the union of the populations of its roles. Roles of a fact type are called *fact roles*. A relationship type used purely to identify or reference some object is a reference type: its roles are called *reference roles*. For a given state, the population of a fact type (stored or derived) is its set of fact instances.

Step 5 of the conceptual schema design procedure requires us to *add mandatory role constraints, and check for logical derivations*. A role *r* is *mandatory* (or *total*) for an object type *A* **iff**, each member of pop(*A*) is known to play *r* (for each state of the knowledge base); otherwise the role is *optional*. A mandatory role is indicated by a large dot where the role connects to the object type: .

By default, if a primitive atomic entity type plays only one fact role in the global schema, this role is mandatory—in this case the dot may be omitted since it is implied. Schema constraints apply to the knowledge base, not necessarily to the real world. If a role is optional in the real world, it is optional in the knowledge base. But a role that is mandatory in the real world may be optional in the knowledge base (e.g. the information may be unknown or omitted for privacy).

A *disjunction* of roles r_1, ..., r_n is *mandatory* for an object type *A* **iff** each member of pop(*A*) is known to play at least one of these roles (in each state). This constraint is shown by a large dot where the role arcs connect to the object type: . Alternatively it may be shown as a circled dot connected to the role arcs.

By default, the disjunction of fact-roles played by a primitive atomic entity type in the global schema is mandatory—in this case the dot may be omitted since it is implied. However, a [disjunctive] mandatory role constraint should be shown explicitly if it applies to an object type which has either an explicit identification scheme or a subtype.

To simplify the depiction of an object type with many roles, the object type may be duplicated on a schema page as well as over several pages. In this case the rule for implicit mandatory role disjunctions applies to the union of all the duplicates. Suitable notations may be used to depict such duplication (e.g. double-ellipse notation, and delta button).

Derived fact types are normally omitted from the diagram—just the derivation rule is shown. If a derived fact type is included on the diagram, all its constraints should normally be shown. *By default, all constraints shown on a derived fact type are derivable* (from its derivation rule, and other constraints).

Once mandatory role constraints are added, we perform a *logical derivation check*, to see if some fact types are derivable using logical rather than arithmetic operations. First we check for missing fact types by asking: *are there any other relationships of interest* between the object types, especially functional relationships? A binary relationship type is *functional* if at least one of its roles is functional (i.e. the role is a simple key): . Each column entry for a functional role functionally determines the entry for the other role.

We now ask: *can any fact type be derived* from the others? To help us decide this, remember that constraints on a derived fact type should normally be derivable. If we have a chain of two or more functional fact types with uniqueness constraints on all the first roles, then a functional binary from the start to the end of this chain is derivable if it is defined by projecting on the join of these fact types—its uniqueness constraint is said to be *transitively implied*. In this case, the first role of the derived fact type is mandatory iff the first role of the chain is mandatory and the second role of each binary subsets the first role of the next binary in the chain (e.g. if the first role of each binary in the chain is mandatory).

Derivation rules should normally be biconditionals (i.e. their main operator is "**iff**"); if their main operator is "**if**", the fact type is only *partly derived*. Derived fact types do not have to have simple keys. Whether derived or not, a fact type should be excluded from the schema unless it is of interest for the application.

Each entity type must have one or more candidate reference schemes. One of these is picked as the *primary identification* scheme, and the others are treated as fact types. Ideally, primary reference schemes should be as simple and stable as possible. A *rigid identifier* identifies the same object throughout the application's lifetime. The primary identification must provide a mandatory 1:1 map of each entity to a tuple of one or more values.

A *simple reference* scheme maps each entity to a single value (e.g. Subject to SubjectCode). A *compound reference* scheme maps each entity to two or more values (e.g. Person to Surname and Initials). Apart from nested cases, the identification aspect of compound reference is denoted by an external uniqueness constraint: ⓤ. With *disjunctive reference*, the number of values may vary for different entities of the same type (e.g. Person to Surname and Firstname and optionally Middlename). The identification aspect of disjunctive reference is marked by a ⓤ% symbol.

Candidate identifiers for the same entity are called *synonyms*. When more than one candidate identification scheme exists, the primary reference scheme is indicated on the schema as follows: if simple, parenthesize it; if compound or disjunctive use Ⓟ or Ⓟ% respectively; if a 1:1 link to an entity type mark it Ⓟ.

If *different units* are used for the same quantity and the semantic connection between these units must be modeled, the quantity may be duplicated on the schema using the double ellipse notation with the relevant unit shown. One unit is picked as the standard unit; the other derived units are marked with an asterisk and conversion rules to the standard unit are supplied.

Chapter notes

Some versions of ORM use a universal quantifier (∀) instead of the mandatory role dot, and place this along the role connector instead of at the start (e.g. DeTroyer et al. 1988). Most versions of ER provide at least limited support for the notion of mandatory role. Some use a solid line for mandatory and a broken one for optional (e.g. Barker 1990), some use double lines for mandatory (e.g. Elmasri & Navathe 1989), some use cardinality markers such as 0 for optional and 1 for mandatory (e.g. Batini et al. 1992), and many other notations are used. Most versions of ER do not distinguish between optional and mandatory when the attribute construct is used to express a fact type.

The botanical example used in the discussion of disjunctive reference schemes came from Peter Ritson, who worked with me to develop a method for modeling such schemes. For a technical discussion of this topic see Halpin & Ritson (1992).

6 Value, set comparison and subtype constraints

6.1 CSDP step 6: value, set and subtype constraints

So far we have learnt how to verbalize familiar examples in terms of elementary facts, draw the fact types on a diagram, mark uniqueness constraints and mandatory roles, and specify rules for derived fact types. We have also examined a variety of reference schemes used to identify entities in carrying out these steps.

In the next step of the conceptual schema design procedure we specify three kinds of constraints: value; set comparison; and subtype. Set comparison constraints are themselves of three kinds: subset; equality; and exclusion.

> *CSDP step 6: Add value, subset, equality, exclusion and subtype constraints*

This chapter covers step 6 in detail. The next section deals with value constraints (i.e. restrictions on value types). For example, in an application about color monitors the values of ColorCode might be restricted to "R", "G" and "B" (for Red, Green and Blue). This section also deals with the related notion of lazy entities. We then review some basic set theory before discussing the three set comparison constraints—here we learn how to declare whether the population of one role sequence must be included in, be equal to, or be exclusive with the population of another.

Once we have dealt with subset, equality and exclusion constraints we examine the notion of subtyping in some depth. Subtyping is one of the key features of the object-oriented approach to modeling. It refines our ability to declare precisely what kinds of objects play various roles, and enables us to declare the same entity to be a member of various types (e.g. each manager is also an employee). Our treatment of subtyping proceeds from basics through to some reasonably advanced aspects.

6.2 Value constraints and lazy entities

You may recall an example from the previous chapter where a ternary fact type was used to model medal results of an Olympic Games. A modified version of this is depicted in Figure 6.1, together with a sample population from the final results of the 24th summer Olympics held in Seoul, Korea in 1988 (ordered alphabetically by Country).

For this application, only three kinds of medal are allowed: gold, silver and bronze, denoted by the codes "G", "S" and "B". This constraint is specified on the schema by *listing the set of possible values* {'G','S','B'} beside the entity type MedalKind. We call this a *value constraint* since it specifies all values of a value type (in this case, MedalKindCode). If the value type were shown explicitly the set would be listed next to this.

The members of a set are collectively known as the *extension* of the set. When a set has few members, it is practical to define the set by listing all its members individually. With larger extensions this may be impractical. For example, in the 1988 Olympics there were 237 events, with one gold, silver and bronze medal to be awarded for each event (assume there are no ties). It is logically possible (although highly unlikely) that the same country wins all medals of a given kind. So if we use this fact type for these Games, the largest value for Quantity is 237. What is the smallest value?

If we want to store facts indicating that a country wins 0 medals of a given kind, the lowest quantity is 0. However, if we want to minimize the size of the database we would store only facts about actual wins: this approach is suggested by our sample population. In this case Quantity has a lower limit of 1. Taking the closed world assumption, the fact that a country has won 0 gold medals could then be derived from the absence of a stored fact about that country winning some gold medals. In principle, we could specify this restriction on Quantity by listing the numbers 1, 2, 3 and so on up to 237. However this would be a lengthy listing!

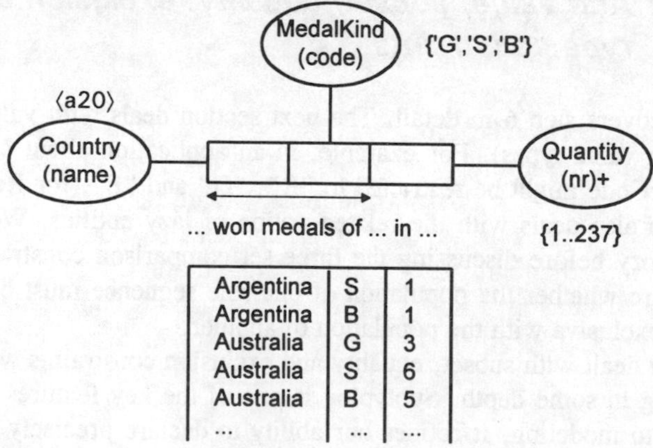

Figure 6.1 Value constraints are declared

Happily there are two aspects of this case which allow a convenient shorthand notation. First, because the values are integers, they have a clearly defined *order* (e.g. 1 is less than 2, which is less than 3, and so on). Secondly we are talking about a *continuous* range of integers—we wish to include all the integers in the range from 1 to 237, without leaving any gaps that can be filled by other integers. So we may safely indicate the integers from 1 to 237 simply as {1..237}, where ".." abbreviates the integers in between. This is like a *subrange definition* in a language like Pascal. This value constraint is marked besides the relevant object type (see Figure 6.1).

We have declared value constraints for MedalKind and Quantity. What about Country? We can specify a *format pattern* for country names. In Figure 6.1, the notation "⟨a20⟩" beside Country declares that each country name is a character string of at most 20 alpha characters (i.e. letters). This is a weak kind of value constraint. For example, a string like "ZZZZZZ" is still allowed as a country name, even if we think this is silly. However there is no short, systematic way to list all possible country names. So a pattern indicator is acceptable for this situation.

Patterns may be specified for numeric as well as character data. Many different format conventions are in use. In our system, "c" denotes a character, "a" a letter, and "d" a digit (i.e. 0..9). A number *n* before/after one of these indicates "exactly/at-most *n* occurrences". Symbols may be concatenated. For example, the format of subject codes such as "CS114" might be specified as ⟨aaddd⟩ or ⟨2a3d⟩. The symbol "–" means a + or - sign, and "." is a decimal point. Optional components are placed in square brackets "[ ]". Here are some examples:

⟨c20⟩	a string of at most 20 characters
⟨20c⟩	a string of exactly 20 characters
⟨a15⟩	a string of at most 15 letters
⟨d6.2d⟩	at most 6 digits, followed by a decimal point and 2 digits
⟨dddaaa⟩	3 digits followed by three letters
⟨3d.3a⟩	same as above
⟨[–]d3⟩	optionally a + or - sign, followed by at most 3 digits

Some of these patterns map directly to an implementation data type (e.g. c20 corresponds to varchar(20) in SQL), others are directly supported in some application languages, and others require separate checking code to be written. Note that our use of "pattern" refers to the value type, not just a display choice for an external schema.

We often omit pattern indicators from conceptual schema diagrams, or at least toggle their display off, because they tend to make the diagrams cluttered, and we may not want to concern ourselves with such detail until we are ready to map the schema to a database system (when data types at least need to be decided).

Consider once more the entity type Country in Figure 6.1. Here "Country" might denote the set of all nations on Earth, or perhaps just nations competing in the Olympics. In principle we could specify a full list of country names as a value constraint, but this would be impractical, mainly because the list is so long. For example, 161 nations competed in the 1988 summer Olympics. Also, the list of countries changes over the years (e.g. in 1991 the former Soviet Union fragmented into 15 nations). So if the schema is to be reused for different games this value constraint would need to be continually updated. Although schemas often do evolve, we usually try to design them to be as stable as possible. A classic strategy used is to model the feature so that the changes occur in the database population rather than the schema itself. How can we do this for the current example?

Suppose that the schema is to be reused each time an Olympics is held, and that users want to know answers to the following questions. *Which countries competed? Which countries didn't compete?* The first question could be addressed by adding the unary predicate "competed" to Country; the competing countries would then all be entered in the single-column table for this unary fact type. Alternatively we could explicitly record zero for each competing country not winning a given medalkind.

But what about the second question? This effectively asks: Which countries exist but didn't compete? This list is usually very small, but sometimes it may be large (e.g. because of a boycott). You might be tempted to add a unary predicate "exists" to Country. But such a predicate would apply to all object types in the schema. Moreover, there are formal problems with treating "exists" (an existential quantifier) as a predicate. In principle one could address the problem by adding another unary predicate "did not compete" for Country, and storing non-competitors here. But such an approach is awkward—Country might play several roles (birthplace, location etc.) and it may be arbitrary which role is negated to cater for the rest of the countries.

A cleaner approach is to allow all existing countries to be entered in a *reference table* for Country. A particular country may appear in this table without playing any fact roles in the schema. Such a country is said to be *lazy*, since it exists in our model but doesn't really do anything. We define a *lazy entity type* to be a *primitive entity type whose disjunction of fact roles is optional*. The term is not used for subtypes or value types. A lazy type may have non-lazy instances. Nested entity types are often lazy, but it is rare for atomic entity types to be lazy. We indicate that an atomic entity type is lazy by appending " !" to its name on the diagram. Figure 6.2 depicts Country as lazy. Its reference table lists all existing nations. The first row of this table may be verbalized as "The Country with name 'Afghanistan' exists": we call this a reference, not a fact.

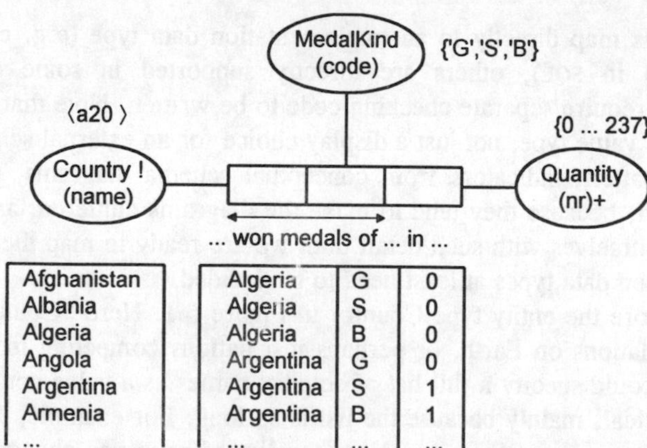

Figure 6.2 In this schema, Country is a lazy object type

Figure 6.2 records wins of zero. So all competing nations play the first role of the ternary. This role is optional, since some nations don't compete (the data here is fictitious). If wins of zero were excluded (as in Figure 6.1) and the unary "competed" were added, the disjunction of this role and the wins role would be optional (and a subset constraint would run from the wins to the competed role—subset constraints are treated later). So the implied mandatory role rule does not apply to lazy entity types.

As with any object type, the reference scheme of a lazy object type is mandatory. So no country may be recorded to compete or win unless it is recorded in the reference population of Country. To fully populate Country with a list of all nations is a tedious task; but once done it can be imported into various applications as required. In practice, most lazy object types have fewer instances. As a minor point, the value constraint on Quantity may need to be updated or weakened to allow for more events.

If we did not want to know about non-competing countries, then as an alternative to adding the unary "competed", we could restrict the meaning of Country to "Competing nation", mark it as lazy, and record only non-zero wins. Note that if an object type has two candidate reference schemes it cannot be lazy. For example, if all nations had codes as well as names and we chose code for primary reference, then Country has CountryName would become a mandatory fact type.

Use of a lazy entity type or unary predicates instead of a value-list constraint adds flexibility since the data can be changed without recompiling the schema (and relevant forms etc.). Note however that the responsibility for this feature is now in the hands of the person entering the relevant data rather than the schema designer.

Exercise 6.2

1. Schematize the following sample report about elementary particles. Include uniqueness, mandatory role and value constraints. Set an upper limit of 2000 amu for mass.

Family	*Particle*	*Charge*	*Mass (amu)*
lepton	neutrino	0	0
	electron	–	1
	positron	+	1
meson	eta	0	1074
baryon	proton	+	1836
	neutron	0	1839

2. It is desired to record a list of all sports, and for each sport which Olympic games (if any) included it. Some sports (e.g. running) have been included in each Olympics, some (e.g. jūdō) only in some, and others (e.g. surfing) never. Schematize this application. You may identify Olympics by its year or by an olympiad#.

3. A software retailer, SoftMart, maintains an information system to help with invoice and stock control. It has recently opened for business, and has made only a few sales so far. The details of the software items it has in stock are shown. The software items are standardly identified by itemcodes, but also have unique titles. There are exactly three software categories, identified by codes (SS = spreadsheet, DB = database, WP = wordprocesssor); the fullnames of these categories are not recorded.

Itemcode	*Title*	*Category*	*Stock qty*	*Listprice*
B123	Blossom 123	SS	8	799.50
DL	DataLight	DB	10	700.00
DB3	Database 3	DB	5	1999.99
Q	Quinquo	SS	6	400.00
SQL+	SQL plus	DB	4	1890.50
TS	TextStar	WP	5	500.00
WL	WordLight	WP	10	700.00

The list price of an item is the normal price at which the item is currently sold. However, SoftMart may sell an item at less than the current list price (e.g. SoftMart may give a discount for bulk orders or to favoured clients, and the list price itself may change with time). There is no rule to enable the unit price (i.e. the actual price charged for a copy of an item) to be derived from the current list price.

A customer is an entity to which an invoice may be issued. Customers are identified by a customer number, but the combination of their name and address is also unique. For simplicity, customer name is treated as a single character string, and so is address. Customers have at most one phone number recorded. The next table shows customer details.

Customer#	*Name*	*Address*	*Phone*
001	Starcorp	5 Sun St, St Lucia 4067	3765000
002	Eastpac	30 Beach Rd, Sandgate 4017	2691111
003	Dr I.N. Stein	7 Sesame St, St Lucia 4067	?

Customer details may be recorded before the customer places an order. Once an order is placed, the items are issued to the customer together with an invoice. At the time the database snapshot was taken for the output reports, only four invoices had been issued (see later Figure). When a customer pays for the items listed in an invoice, the date of payment is recorded. The following table lists the payments so far. Each invoice is identified by its invoice number. For this simple exercise, you may assume that an invoice is paid in full or not at all.

Invoice#	*Date paid*
0501	10/07/88
0502	20/07/88
0503	unpaid
0504	unpaid

The four actual invoices are shown. The invoice header giving the address of SoftMart is not stored. An invoice include a table of one or rows, called "invoice lines". Each invoice line lists details about the order of one or more units (copies) of a software item. For simplicity, assume that on a given invoice the same item can appear on only one invoice line. For each invoice line, the itemcode, title, quantity of units ordered, and unit price are listed. The total charge for invoice line is displayed as a subtotal. The total charge for the whole invoice is displayed as the amount due.

SoftMart, 46 Gallium Street, Brisbane 4001

invoice#: 0501 **date:** 03/07/88
customer#: 001 **customer name:** Starcorp
address: 5 Sun St, St Lucia 4067

Item code	*Title*	*Qty ordered*	*Unit price*	*subtotal*
WL	WordLight	5	650.00	3250.00
Q	Quinquo	1	400.00	400.00
SQL+	SQL plus	5	1701.45	8507.25
B123	Blossom 123	1	799.50	799.50
			☛ **total amount due:**	$12956.75

SoftMart, 46 Gallium Street, Brisbane 4001

invoice#: 0502 **date:** 03/07/88
customer#: 002 **customer name:** Eastpac
address: 30 Beach Rd, Sandgate, 4017

Item code	*Title*	*Qty ordered*	*Unit price*	*subtotal*
Q	Quinquo	4	400.00	1600.00
TS	TextStar	4	500.00	2000.00
			☛ **total amount due:**	$3600.00

SoftMart, 46 Gallium Street, Brisbane 4001

invoice#: 0503 **date:** 10/07/88
customer#: 001 **customer name:** Starcorp
address: 5 Sun St, St Lucia 4067

Item code	*Title*	*Qty ordered*	*Unit price*	*subtotal*
Q	Quinquo	4	350.00	1400.00
			☛ **total amount due:**	$1400.00

SoftMart, 46 Gallium Street, Brisbane 4001

invoice#: 0504 **date:** 20/07/88
customer#: 003 **customer name:** Dr I.N. Stein
address: 7 Sesame St, St Lucia 4067

Item code	*Title*	*Qty ordered*	*Unit price*	*subtotal*
B123	Blossom 123	1	799.50	799.50
DL	DataLight	1	700.00	700.00
			☛ **total amount due:**	$1499.50

Schematize this UoD, including uniqueness, mandatory role and value constraints. Identify an invoice line or the sale recorded on it by using the invoice# and the itemcode. If a fact type is derived, omit it from the diagram but include a derivation rule for it.

4. Consider the previous question, but suppose that the same item may appear on more than one line of the same invoice. Devise an alternative identification scheme to deal with this situation. (*Hint:* Compare this with the compact disk example. Sometimes you need to identify things in terms of their position).

5. Now suppose that a cumulative record of purchases from suppliers is also to be recorded, an extract of which is shown in the following table. Only a cumulative record is kept (individual deliveries from suppliers are not recorded in the information system). No supplier can be a customer.

Itemcode	*Suppier*	*Quantity*
B123	Macrosoft	7
	TechAtlantic	3
DL	Macrosoft	11
DB3	PacificTech	5
etc.		

(a) Draw a conceptual schema for this table.

(b) Assume this subschema is integrated with your solution to 3, and that your fact type for stock quantity is now declared to be derivable.

(i) Specify a derivation rule for this approach.

(ii) In a real business, how practical would it be to use such a rule to avoid storing stock quantity? Discuss.

6.3 Basic set theory

Readers well versed in set theory may skip this section. Since the next section examines set comparison constraints in detail, we take time out here to cover some basic theory about sets. In the interests of providing a comprehensive summary of the required background, some ideas met earlier are included.

Intuitively, a *set* is a well defined collection of items. The items may be concrete (e.g. people, computers) or abstract (e.g. numbers, points), and are called *elements* or *members* of the set. Sets themselves are abstract. They are numerically definite in the sense that each has a definite number of elements. A *type* is a set of possible items. Each item of a particular type is an instance or element of that particular set.

The members of a set collectively constitute the *extension* of the set. While a set may *contain* members it does not *consist* of those members. For example, the set of Martian moons is an abstraction over and above its members (Phobos and Deimos) and consequently has no physical properties such as mass or volume. Although sets (unlike heaps) are not to be equated with their members, they are determined by their members, since two sets are *identical* or **equal** just in case they have the same extension. Using "iff" for "if and only if", the *Law of Extensionality* may be stated thus:

Given any sets A and B, $A = B$ iff A and B have the same members.

Since sets are determined by their members, one simple way of *defining* a set is to enumerate the elements of the set. In so doing we often use braces as delimiters and commas as item separators (e.g. $A = \{3,6\}$). Here A is defined as the set containing just the elements 3 and 6. One consequence of the Law of Extensionality is that a set is not changed by *repeating* any of its members. For instance, if $B = \{3,6,6\}$ it follows that $A = B$ since both sets contain precisely the same members (3 and 6).

When enumerating sets it is usual not to repeat the members; however it is sometimes useful to permit this. For example, when stating general results about the set variable $\{x,y\}$ it may be handy to include the case $x = y$. Sometimes repetition of members occurs undetected. For instance, some people do not realize that the entity set {Morning Star, Evening Star} contains just one member (the planet Venus). Of course, the label set {"Morning Star", "Evening Star"} contains two members.

If repetition is made significant, we have a *bag* or *multiset*. To help distinguish between bags and sets it is advisable to use different delimiters (e.g. square brackets for bags and braces for sets). For instance the bag [3,6,6] has a count of 3, and is not equal to [3,6] which has a count of 2. One use of bags is in collecting values for statistical work. For example, the set {3,6,6} has an average of 4.5 but the bag [3,6,6] has an average of 5. Bags are frequently used with languages like SQL.

Another consequence of the Law of Extensionality is that the *order* in which elements are listed is irrelevant. For example, if $A = \{3,6\}$ and $B = \{6,3\}$ then we have $A = B$, since each set contains the same members. Bags are also insensitive to order, as in [3,6] = [6,3]. If order is made significant we have an "ordinal set".

Usually, when order is made significant, so is repetition: in this case we have a *sequence* or list or permutation. Thus a sequence is an ordered bag. Sequences are often delimited either by angle brackets (e.g. $\langle 1,2 \rangle$) or parentheses (e.g. (1,2)). The sequence $\langle 6,3,6 \rangle$ has three members and is different from the sequence $\langle 3,6,6 \rangle$. In practice several different delimiting notations are used. For example, square brackets are used as set delimiters in Pascal and list delimiters in Prolog.

Although when a set is enumerated in full the ordering does not matter, often a natural ordering provides an obvious pattern: in such cases a partial enumeration will serve to define the set. For example, the set of decimal digits may be shown as {0..9}, where the ".." indicates the missing digits. Infinite sets may be represented with ".." at one end (e.g. the set of natural numbers may be shown as {1,2,3..}).

The preceding set definitions enumerate, wholly or partially, the extension of the set and are thus examples of an *extensional definition*. A set may also be defined by an *intensional definition*. Here an identifying description is provided which is held by just those members of the set. That is, a description is given which constitutes both a necessary and sufficient condition (an "iff condition") for an item to belong to the set. For example, the set A, defined extensionally as {1,2,3}, may be defined intensionally as: A = the set of natural numbers less than 4. This definition may be recast in set builder notation as $\{x$: x is a natural number less then 4 $\}$ or more briefly as $\{x: x \in \mathbf{N} \; \& \; x < 4\}$ where "$\in$" abbreviates "is a member of", and **N** is the set of natural numbers.

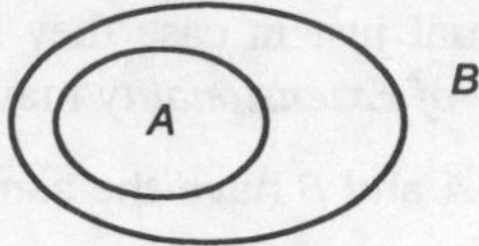

Figure 6.3 Standard Euler diagram for: A is a proper subset of B

In set builder notation a stroke "|" may be used instead of a colon, e.g. $\{x|x<4\}$. The number of elements in a set is called the *cardinality* of the set (e.g. the set {2,4,6} has a cardinality of 3).

Some set operations result in propositions while others result in sets. We note the following *proposition-forming operators*: $=$, $\neq$, $\subseteq$, $\subset$, $\supseteq$, and $\supset$. These are read respectively as "equals", "is not equal to", "is a subset of", "is a proper subset of", "is a superset of" and "is a proper superset of".

Given any sets A and B, we say that A is a **subset** of B iff every member of A is also a member of B. For example, $\{1,3\} \subseteq \{1,2,3\}$. An equivalent definition is: A is a subset of B iff A has no members that are not in B. This second definition makes it easy to see that the *null set* is a subset of every set. The null or empty set has no members and may be represented as { } or $\emptyset$.

Note also that every set is a subset of itself. For example, $\{1,3\} \subseteq \{1,3\}$. We say that A is a *proper subset* of B iff A is a subset of B but is not equal to B. For instance, $\{1,3\} \subset \{1,2,3\}$. We say that A is a **superset** of B iff B is a subset of A, and that A is a *proper superset* of B iff B is a proper subset of A. For example, {1,2,3} is both a superset and a proper superset of {1,3}.

Such relationships between two sets are sometimes depicted by *standard Euler diagrams*. As developed by the Swiss mathematician Leonhard Euler, these were *spatial* and *existential*. Each set is pictured as a set of points inside an ellipse. This enables the relationship between the sets to be "seen" by the spatial arrangement of the ellipses. For example, placing ellipse A inside ellipse B shows that A is a proper subset of B (see Figure 6.3).

Here we see that every element of A is also an element of B (so A is a subset of B). Moreover, the existential viewpoint implies that each of the regions in the Euler diagram are assumed to contain some elements. So B has some elements not in A. So A is a proper subset of B. To show that A is a subset of B on standard Euler diagrams we need to use a disjunction of two diagrams, as shown in Figure 6.4. The right hand diagram caters for the possibility that $A = B$. The notion of subsethood is a actually more useful than proper subsethood. Partly to enable such relationships to be shown on a single diagram, we introduce a notation which we call *Hypothetical Euler Diagrams* (HEDs).

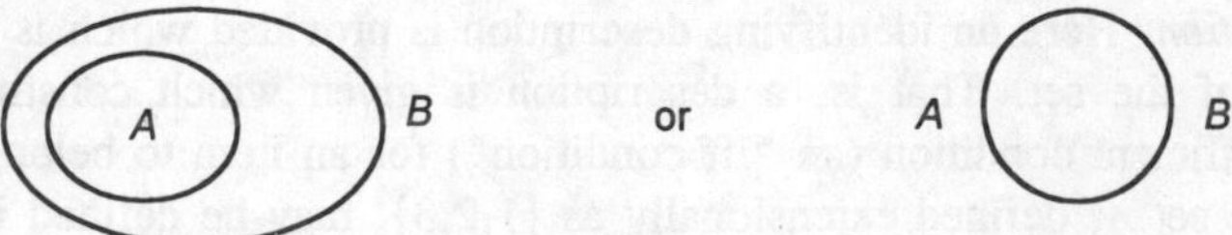

Figure 6.4 Standard Euler diagram disjunction for: A is a subset of B

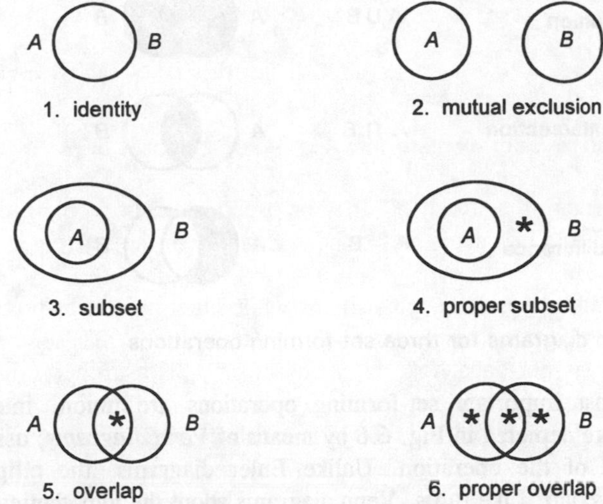

Figure 6.5 Hypothetical Euler Diagrams for set comparisons

In a HED, an asterisk is placed in a region to show something exists there, while shading the region indicates that it is empty. If a region is unmarked the question of whether any elements exist there is left open or hypothetical. Figure 6.5 sets out the HEDs for the six most important relationships or comparisons between two sets.

Case 1 is that of *equality* or identity (e.g. $A = B = \{1,2\}$). In case 2, A and B are *disjoint* or *mutually exclusive*, that is they have no members in common (e.g. $A = \{1\}$, $B = \{2\}$). In case 3, A is a *subset* of B (equivalently, B is a superset of A). In case 4, A is a *proper subset* of B (equivalently, B is a proper superset of A). For example both $A = \{1\}$, $B = \{1,2\}$ and $A = \{1\}$, $B = \{1\}$ are instances of case 3, but only the former is an instance of case 4.

Case 5 is that of *overlap*: the sets have some members in common. Case 6 is that of *proper overlap*: the sets have common as well as extra members. For example, both $A = \{1,2\}$, $B = \{2,3\}$ and $A = \{1\}$, $B = \{1,2\}$ are instances of overlap but only the former is a case of proper overlap.

We now turn to *set-forming operations*, where the result is a set rather than a proposition. Given any sets A and B, and reading "or" in the inclusive sense, we define $A \cup B$ (i.e. *A union B*) to be the set of all elements in A or B. We define $A \cap B$ (i.e. *A intersect B*) to be the set of all elements common to both A and B. Each of these operations is commutative, so the order of the operands doesn't matter. That is, $A \cup B = B \cup A$, and $A \cap B = B \cap A$.

The *set difference* (or relative complement) operation is defined thus: $A - B$ (i.e. A minus B) is the set of all elements that are in A but not in B. This operation does not commute (i.e. cases may arise where $A - B \neq B - A$). If we let U = the *universal set* (i.e. the set of all elements under consideration) we may define the *complement* of A as $A' = \mathrm{U} - A$. The symmetric difference between A and B is the set of elements in just one of A or B (i.e. the union minus the intersection).

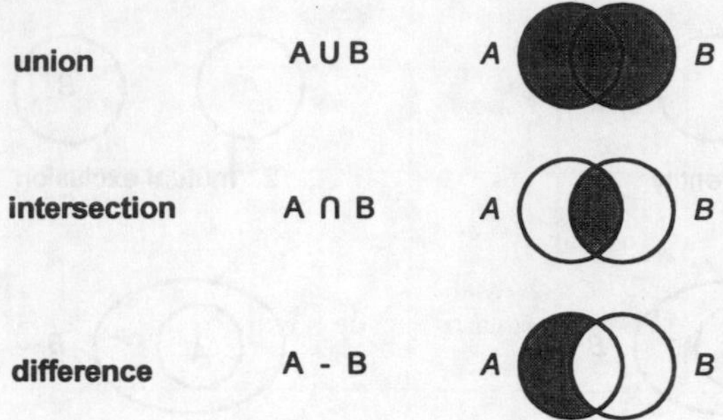

Figure 6.6 Venn diagrams for three set-forming operations

The three most important set-forming operations are union, intersection and difference. These are depicted in Fig. 6.6 by means of *Venn diagrams*, using shading to indicate the result of the operation. Unlike Euler diagrams, the ellipses in Venn diagrams always overlap. Like HEDs, Venn diagrams adopt the hypothetical viewpoint.

As examples of these operations, if $A = \{1,2,3\}$ and $B = \{2,4\}$ then $A \cup B = \{1,2,3,4\}$, $A \cap B = \{2\}$, $A - B = \{1,3\}$ and $B - A = \{4\}$. There are dozens of different diagram methods for working with sets. However, most of these methods become extremely unwieldy as soon as the number of sets exceeds 3. For instance, a Venn diagram for 4 sets is shown in Fig. 6.7.

We have used Hypothetical Euler Diagrams to explain various relationships between sets, and Venn diagrams to explain various set-forming operations on sets. So long as few sets are involved, these diagrams are well suited for these purposes. Later in the chapter we introduce another diagram notation for subtype connections which enables many compatible object types to be related without incurring the jumble of line crossings which Euler and Venn diagrams would produce for such cases.

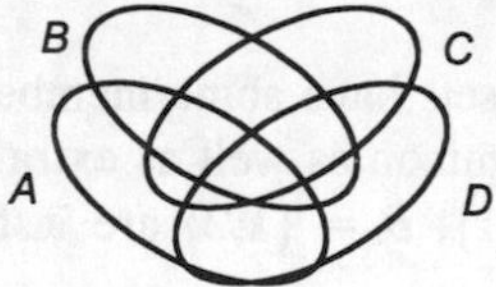

Figure 6.7 A Venn diagram for four sets

6.4 Subset, equality and exclusion constraints

Set comparison constraints restrict the way the population of one role, or role sequence, relates to the population of another. In the previous section we considered six ways in which two sets might be related: subset, equality, exclusion, proper subset, overlap and proper overlap. The last three of these require some objects to exist in at least one of the sets being compared. However static constraints must apply to every state of the database, including the empty state. So the only set comparison constraints of interest are subset, equality and exclusion. We now turn to their study.

Table 6.1 Details about members of a fitness club

Member	*Sex*	*Birth Year*	*Sport*	*Booking*	*Reaction time (ms)*	*Heart Rate (beats/min)*
Anderson PE	M	1940	tennis	Mon 5 p.m.	250	80
Bloggs F	M	1940				
Fit IM	F	1975	squash		250	70
Hume D	F	1946	squash	Tue 9 a.m.		
Jones T	M	1965			300	93

Suppose a local fitness club maintains an information system concerning its members, and that Table 6.1 is an extract of an output report from this system. Membership includes access to the club's normal fitness equipment (e.g. a weights gym). However the club also has a few squash and tennis courts. To help ensure fair access to these courts, the club has a policy that members may play only one of these two racquet sports.

Members pay an extra fee for this right, and optionally may book one regular weekly hour to use a court. For simplicity we exclude the handling of casual bookings and court allocations from our example. As a service to its members, the club arranges a fitness test to measure the resting heart rate and reaction time of any member who requests it. For simplicity we assume only the latest results are kept for each memeber.

The determination of fact types, uniqueness constraints, mandatory roles and value constraints for this example is straight-forward (see Figure 6.8). For simplicity we assume that hours may be simply identified, without needing to separate out their day and time components.

However there are two more constraints which apply to this example. To begin with, only those members who have opted to play a sport may book a court. In terms of the schema diagram, each object in the population of the booking role must also appear in the population of the playing role.

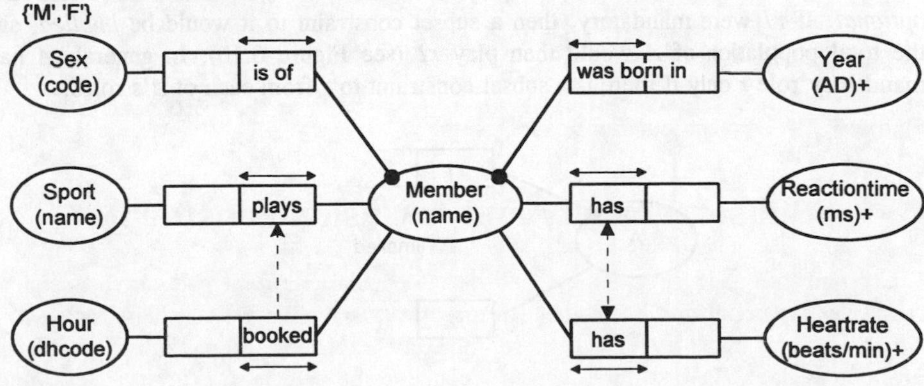

Figure 6.8 A conceptual schema for Table 6.1

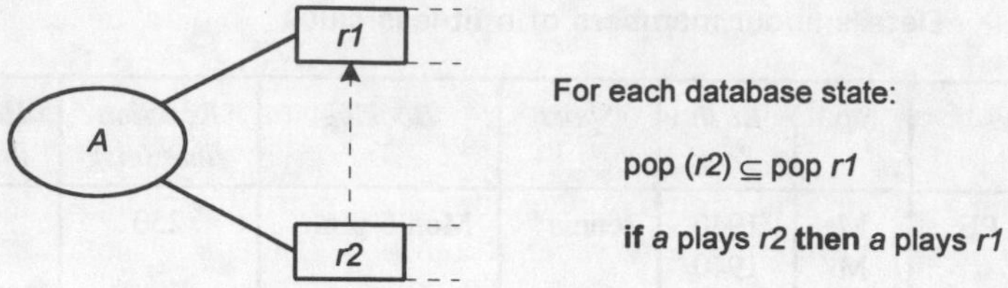

Figure 6.9 A subset constraint between two roles

In other words, the set of members who book an hour must be a subset of the set of members who play a sport. As shown in Figure 6.8, we mark this **subset constraint** by a *dotted arrow* "----▸" running from the subset role to the superset role. Our sample data agrees with this constraint since {'Anderson PE', 'Hume D'} ⊆ {'Anderson PE', 'Fit IM', 'Hume D'}. If we tried to add a booking for Jones without also adding a sport for him we would violate this constraint. In words, the constraint may be expressed in either of the following ways:

if Member *m* booked **some** Hour **then** Member *m* plays **some** Sport

or

Member *m* booked **some** Hour **only if** Member *m* plays **some** Sport

One reason for choosing the arrow notation for subset constraints is that the logical connective "**if** ... **then** ..." is often symbolized as an arrow "→". Figure 6.9 summarizes the general case where a subset constraint runs from one role to another. For this comparison to make sense, both roles must be played by the same object type (or a supertype—see later). It is not necessary that the roles belong to different predicates.

In Figure 6.9, *a* is any member of *A*. The reference to database states reminds us that the constraint applies to our application model (not necessarily to the real world); so "*a* plays *r*" means *a* plays *r* in our model. In terms of fact tables, the set of values in the column for *r2* is always a subset of the set of values in the column for *r1*. It doesn't matter if any of these columns has duplicate values: we are comparing sets, not bags.

In Figure 6.9, we assume that *A* plays some other role, and that both *r1* and *r2* are *optional*. If *r1* were mandatory, then a subset constraint to it would be *implied*, since the total population of *A* would then play *r1* (see Figure 6.10). In general, *A* has a mandatory role *r* only if there is a subset constraint to *r* from each of *A*'s roles.

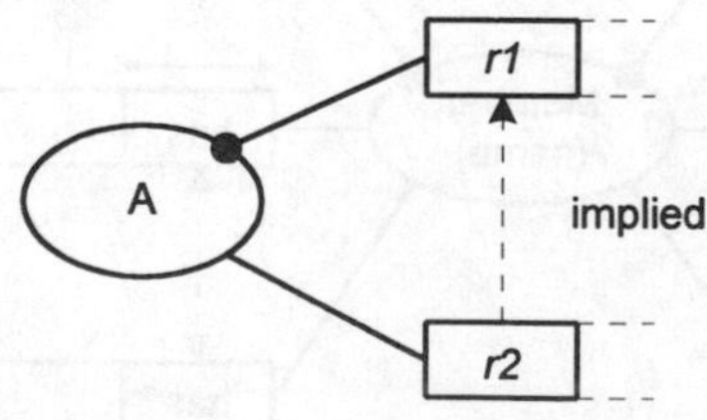

Figure 6.10 The implied subset constraint should not be shown

To reduce clutter, such implied subset constraints should be omitted from our schemas. Thus a subset constraint between two roles may be marked only if both of these roles are optional (this rule does not extend to composite subset constraints, as we see later).

Returning to our fitness club application, there is one more constraint to consider. Reaction time is recorded for a member if and only if his/her heart rate is too. Either the member has both fitness measures taken or neither. This constraint might be motivated by the club's desire to provide a balanced estimate of fitness, rather than risk reliance on a single figure. When the test data are entered, a compound transaction is used to enter both measures.

Such a constraint is called an **equality constraint**, since for any state of the database the set of people whose reaction time is recorded equals the set of people whose heart rate is recorded. We depict this constraint by means of a *dotted arrow with two heads*, "◄----►", connecting the relevant roles (see Figure 6.8). It asserts that the populations of these two roles must always be equal. Clearly an equality constraint is equivalent to two subset constraints, running in opposite directions.

One reason for using a double headed arrow to mark an equality constraint is because a double arrow symbol "↔" is often used in logic for "if and only if". In words, the equality constraint in Figure 6.8 may be expressed as:

Member *m* has **some** ReactionTime **iff** Member *m* has **some** HeartRate

Figure 6.11 summarizes the notion of an equality constraint between two optional roles. If both roles are mandatory, an equality constraint is implied since each of pop(*r1*) and pop(*r2*) equals pop(*A*).

Implied equality constraints should not be shown (see Figure 6.12). If one role is mandatory and the other is optional, then an equality constraint cannot exist between them since it is possible to have a state in which only some of *A*'s population plays the optional role. If neither role is mandatory but their disjunction is, then we do not have an equality constraint because if we did both the roles would then be mandatory (Why?).

In principle, all mandatory roles and equality constraints on a conceptual schema could be replaced by groups of subset constraints. In practice however, this would lead to untidy schema diagrams, with subset constraint lines running all over them. Hence, the notions of mandatory role and equality constraint are very convenient.

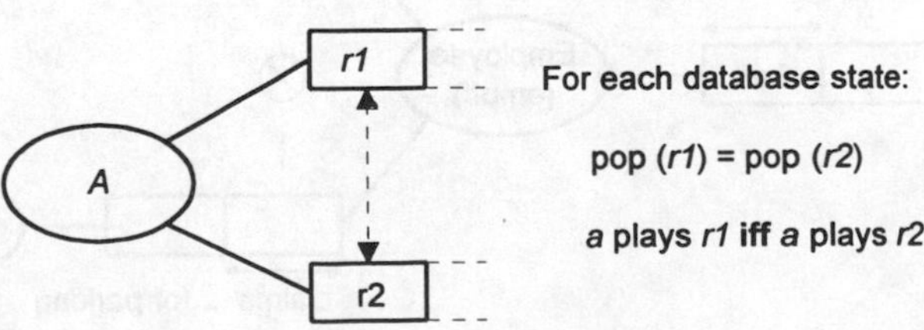

Figure 6.11 An equality constraint between two roles

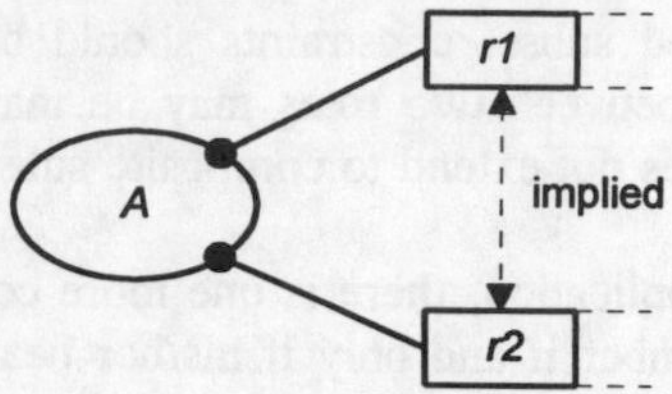

Figure 6.12 The implied equality constraint should not be shown

Now consider the report extract shown in Table 6.2. In this UoD employees may request a company parking bay or a refund of their parking expenses but not both. Employees may make neither request (e.g. they might not have a car, or they might simply want more time to decide). For this report different kinds of null value are displayed differently. The "–" value indicates "*not to be recorded*" (because the other option is chosen). The "?" value simply indicates "not recorded": an actual value might still be recorded for employee 005 later (e.g. after this employee buys a car); once such a value is recorded however, the system must disallow the other option.

Table 6.2

Emp#	*Employee name*	*Parking bay*	*Parking claim ($)*
001	Adams B	C01	–
002	Bloggs F	–	200
003	Collins T	B05	–
004	Dancer F	–	250
005	Eisai Z	?	?

Figure 6.13 shows a schema for this example. An "⊗" indicates an **exclusion constraint** between the roles it connects. This asserts that for each state of the data-base no employee can be recorded as playing both these roles; that is, the populations of these roles are *mutually exclusive*. A textual version of this constraint is: no Employee is allocated some ParkingBay and also claims some MoneyAmt for parking.

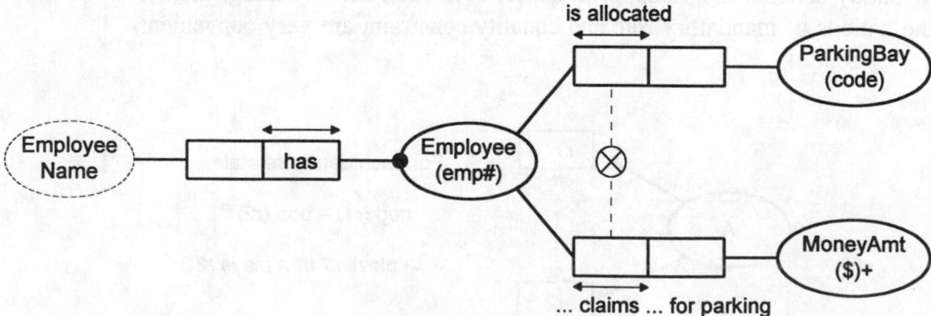

Figure 6.13 Conceptual schema for Table 6.2

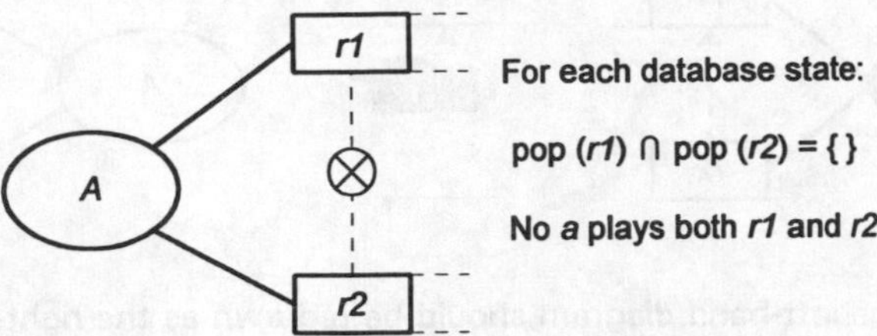

Figure 6.14 An exclusion constraint between two roles

Figure 6.14 formalizes this notion of an exclusion constraint between two roles: their populations are exclusive just in case their intersection is the null set (i.e. they have no element in common). If two roles are played by different, primitive entity types then an implied exclusion constraint exists between them (since the entity types are mutually exclusive): such implied exclusion constraints are always omitted.

An exclusion constraint may be asserted between two roles only if these roles are optional and are played by the same object type (or possibly a supertype—see later). If one of the roles were mandatory, any object playing the other role would also have to play the mandatory one; so an exclusion constraint could not apply. It is possible however that the disjunction of these two roles is mandatory.

As an example of an exclusive, mandatory disjunction consider Figure 6.15. In this simple application, married partners are identified by their firstnames. For the ring predicate "is husband of", the inverse predicate name "is wife of" is also shown. Taken together, the disjunctive mandatory role and exclusion constraints assert that each partner is either a husband or a wife (of some one) but not both.

This is a case of *exclusive or*. No entry can appear in both columns of this fact table. Contrast this with the parenthood binary considered earlier (Figure 5.13), where each person is a parent or child or both—a case of *inclusive or*. As an alternative to marking separate mandatory role and exclusion constraints, both may be asserted by connecting the role arcs to the partition symbol: "⊗".

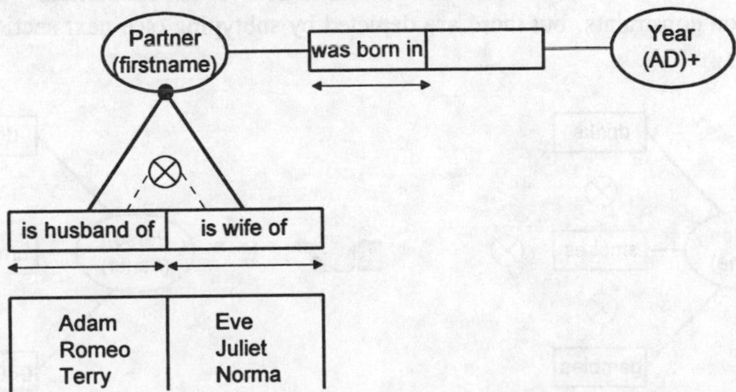

Figure 6.15 *Exclusive or:* each partner is a husband or wife but not both

Figure 6.16 The left-hand diagram should be redrawn as the right-hand diagram

Note that subset or equality constraints should not be displayed with disjunctive mandatory roles. For example, if the two constraints in the left diagram of Figure 6.16 apply, then it follows that role r_1 is mandatory (as an exercise, prove this). For clarity, the mandatory role should be shown explicitly; the subset constraint is now implied by this, and hence should be omitted (see right diagram of Figure 6.16).

Similarly, an equality constraint between disjunctive mandatory roles should be redrawn as two mandatory roles. Such redrawing rules are pragmatic. Formally the left-hand diagram is equivalent to the right-hand one; however the right-hand version is preferred because it is simpler for people to work with. As another case of redrawing, an exclusion constraint among three or more roles may be depicted by a single "⊗" connecting the roles, in preference to exhaustively marking exclusion constraints between each pair of roles. A simple example of this is shown in Figure 6.17. In this UoD each person is limited to at most one of three vices.

In the left-hand diagram of Figure 6.17, three exclusion constraints are needed to cover all the ways in which the three roles may be paired. Four roles may be paired in six ways. In general, a single exclusion constraint across n roles replaces $n(n-1)/2$ separate exclusion constraints between two roles. An equality constraint across n-roles could be specified using "⊜" instead of "⊗"; however because its application would be rare we avoid this. No notation for a subset constraint over n roles is used, since direction is involved and actual cases are rare.

Although exclusion constraints between roles are not uncommon, in practice simple subset and equality constraints are seldom used on conceptual schemas (though they are often used on relational schemas). One often encounters "qualified" set comparison constraints, but these are depicted by subtyping (see next section).

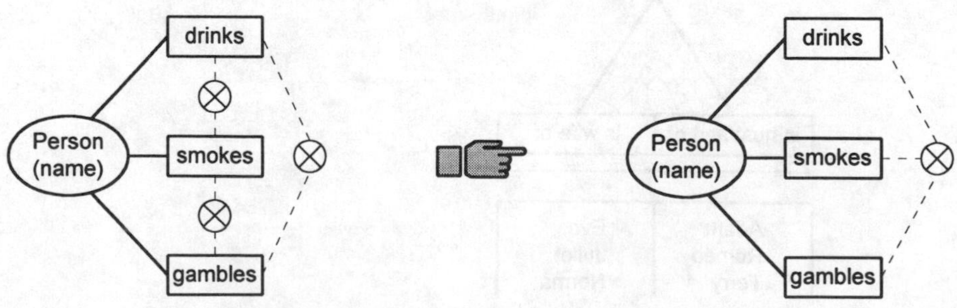

Figure 6.17 In this UoD, each person has at most one of three vices

Table 6.3

Person	*Gender*	*Cars owned*	*Cars driven*
Fred	M	272NCP, 123BOM	272NCP, 123BOM
Sue	F	272NCP, 123BOM	272NCP
Tina	F	105ABC	
Tom	M		

However, applications commonly involve ***set comparison constraints between role-sequences*** (not just between single roles), which we cannot handle by subtyping. We now turn to their study.

Consider Table 6.3, which provides details about people and the cars they own or drive. For simplicity we assume that people are identified by their first name, and that each car is identified by a registration number stamped on its license plate. If we allowed a car to change its license plate we would need to pick some other identifier (e.g. its compliance plate number).

Figure 6.18 shows the populated conceptual schema. The ownership fact type is many:many. A person may own many cars and the same car may be owned by many people. For example, Fred and Sue are co-owners of two cars (e.g. they might be married). The driver fact type is also many:many.

Note that although Fred and Sue both own car 123BOM, only Fred drives it. For example, it might be Fred's "pride and joy" and he won't let Sue drive it; or perhaps it is a "bomb" of a car and Sue refuses to drive it! Tina owns a car but doesn't drive it (maybe she has a chauffeur). Tom neither owns nor drives a car.

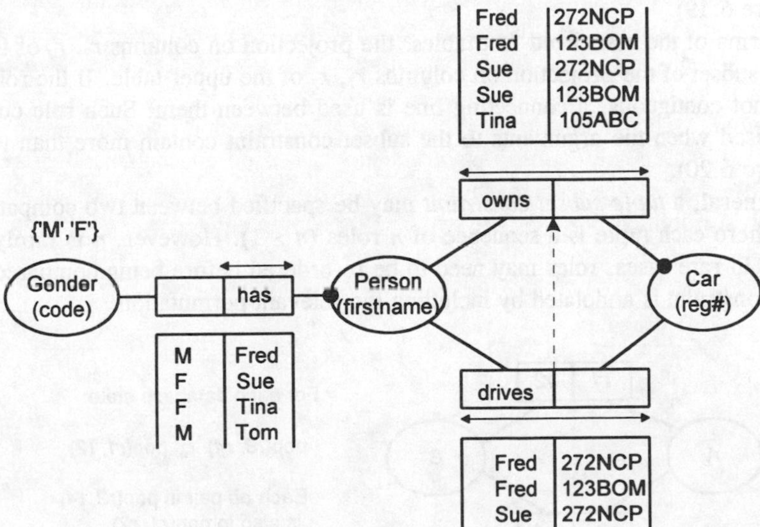

Figure 6.18 A knowledge base diagram for Table 6.3

For the population shown, people own every car that they drive. This might be considered unusual, but for discussion purposes let us assume the sample database is significant in this respect. In other words, in this restricted UoD nobody may drive a car unless they own it. We need to indicate this constraint in some way. We do this in Figure 6.18 by the *pair-subset constraint* running from the middle of the Drives predicate to the middle of the Owns predicate. This asserts that, for each state of the database, the set of ⟨Person, Car⟩ pairs referenced in the Drives fact-table is a subset of the set of pairs listed in the Owns table. We may think of each pair as a tuple of values from a row of a fact table.

For the database state shown, the Drives table has three pairs: ⟨Fred, 272NCP⟩; ⟨Fred, 123BOM⟩; and ⟨Sue, 272NCP⟩. The Owns table has five pairs. Each pair in the Drives table is also in the Owns table: the subset constraint indicates that this is true for each state of the database. This constraint may be expressed textually either as:

if Person *p* drives Car *c* **then** Person *p* owns Car *c*

or as:

Person *p* drives Car *c* **only if** Person *p* owns Car *c*

As usual, the direction of the subset constraint is quite important. With our present example, if the arrow pointed instead to the Drives fact type this would signify that each person who owns a car also drives that car, which is quite a different constraint (false for this UoD, but as an exercise invent a population consistent with this new constraint).

To indicate that the subset constraint applies between role pairs rather than single roles, each end of the arrow is positioned at the division between the two roles involved in the pair. This notation may be used whenever the roles in the pair are contiguous (see Figure 6.19).

In terms of the associated fact tables, the projection on columns r_3, r_4 of the lower table is a subset of the projection on columns r_1, r_2 of the upper table. If the roles in the pair are not contiguous, a connecting line is used between them. Such role connectors are also used when the arguments to the subset constraint contain more than two roles (see Figure 6.20).

In general, a *tuple-subset constraint* may be specified between two compatible role tuples, where each tuple is a sequence of *n* roles ($n \geq 1$). However, *n* is rarely greater than two. In rare cases, roles may need to be re-ordered before being compared; in this case the constraint is annotated by including the relevant permutation.

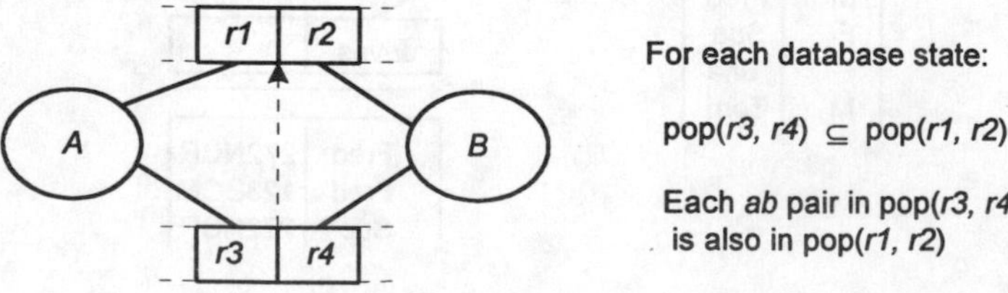

Figure 6.19 A pair-subset constraint

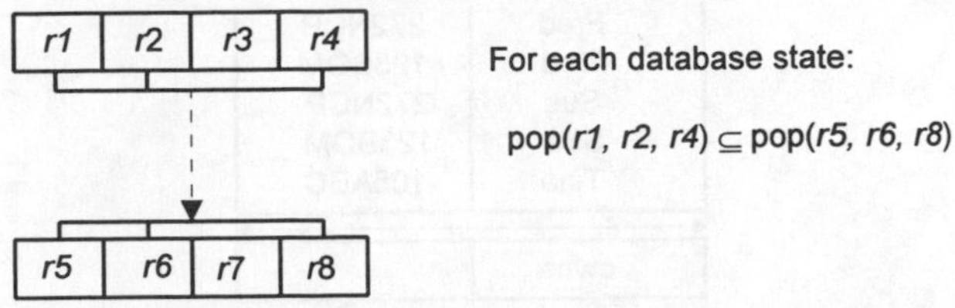

Figure 6.20 An example of a tuple-subset constraint between sequences of 3 roles

Now consider the case where people own a car if and only if they drive that car. Here we have subset constraints in both directions: this is a *pair-equality* constraint. In cases like this, where the role-pairs form a whole predicate, we usually store only one fact type. For example, we might store Drives and derive Owns, or collapse both to IsOwnerDriverOf. However if a role-pair is embedded in a longer predicate, an equality constraint is not equivalent to a derivation rule (Why not?). Figure 6.21 summarizes the case of pair-equality for contiguous roles.

Exclusion constraints may be specified between two or more role sequences. As a simple example, suppose we want to record information about cars that people own and cars that they want to buy. Clearly, nobody would want to buy a car that they already own: we can indicate this by the *pair-exclusion constraint* shown in Figure 6.22.

Notice that this constraint is weaker than an exclusion constraint between the just the first roles of these predicates (which would instead say that no car owner wants to buy any car, and hence would disallow Fred's appearance in both the fact tables shown). For simplicity, the gender predicate (included in Figure 6.18) is omitted from the left of the Figure 6.22. However since this is the only mandatory fact type for Person, we allow that some people (e.g. Linda) might have their gender recorded but neither own nor want to buy a car.

In this section, set-comparison constraints have been considered between pairs of role-sequences, where each role sequence comes from a single predicate. More generally, set-comparison constraints may be defined between compatible role-paths formed by joining different predicates (join-constraints are discussed in section 7.4).

We conclude this section by discussing some general results, or theorems, about set-comparison constraints. Suppose we declare a tuple-subset constraint from role sequence *rs1* to role sequence *rs2*, where each sequence has *n* roles ($n \geq 1$). Is it now possible for these role sequences to be exclusive?

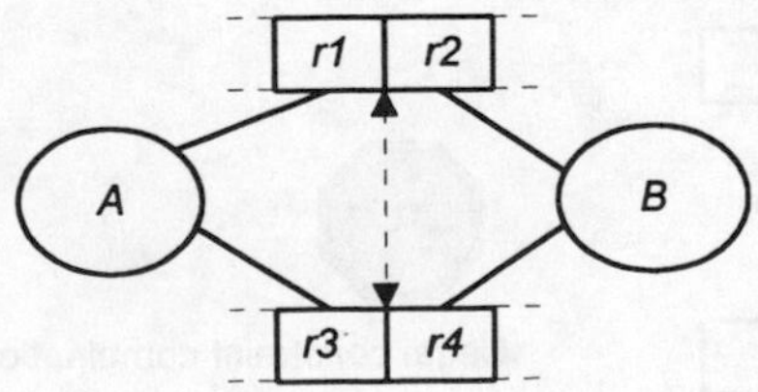

Figure 6.21 A pair-equality constraint

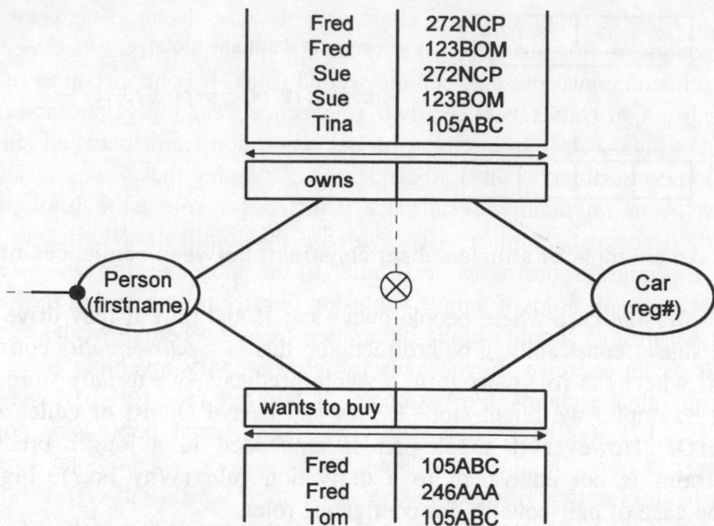

Figure 6.22 A pair-exclusion constraint: nobody wants to buy a car that they own

If both role sequences are unpopulated then both the subset and exclusion constraints are trivially satisfied. But for practical reasons we demand that every conceptual schema must be *strongly satisfiable* (or *population consistent*); that is, each role sequence used as a predicate or as a constraint argument can be populated in some state. We don't require that all role sequences can be populated together in the same state.

Let's populate *rs1* with some sequence *a*: given the subset constraint, *a* now populates *rs2* as well, thus violating the exclusion constraint. Swapping *rs1* with *rs2* in this reasoning shows a subset constraint in the other direction cannot hold either, if an exclusion constraint does.

This proves theorem *NXS* (*N*o e*X*clusion with a *S*ubset constraint), which is depicted in Figure 6.23. Here a long box depicts a sequence of one or more roles, and the constraints apply between the *whole* sequences (not different parts of them). Recall that an equality constraint is equivalent to, and used in preference to, two subset constraints. Hence at most one set-comparison constraint may be declared between two (whole) role sequences.

Figure 6.23 Theorem *NXS*: *N*o e*X*clusion with a *S*ubset constraint

However, different set-comparison constraints may be declared between different parts of role sequences. For instance, we may have a subset constraint between the first roles and an exclusion constraint between the second roles. It is important to realize that subset or equality constraints between two role sequences imply similar constraints between the individual roles. In contrast, an exclusion constraint between single roles implies exclusion constraints between all sequences containing these roles.

These *constraint implication* results are depicted for role pairs in Figure 6.24, using "⇨" for "necessarily implies". In each case the implication is in one direction only. Results for equality constraints are similar to the subset results. In the exclusion example, a similar result holds if simple exclusion constraint is between the right-hand roles. Implied constraints should usually be omitted from a schema. We leave the proof of these results as an exercise. If you have trouble here, try inventing some counter-examples to equivalence claims. For example, if pop(r_1,r_2) = {⟨a1,b1⟩, ⟨a2,b2⟩} and pop(r_3,r_4) = {⟨a1,b2⟩, ⟨a2,b1⟩}, then pop(r_1) = pop(r_3) and pop(r_2) = pop(r_4) but pop(r_1,r_2) ≠ pop(r_3,r_4).

Other constraint implication theorems exist, some of which will be mentioned later in the book. One of the most important results deals with the case where the target of a pair-subset constraint includes a functional role. For example, consider the top-left pattern in Figure 6.24. Here we have a pair-subset constraint from the lower role-pair to the top role-pair. Suppose we add a simple uniqueness constraint over the left-hand role of the top role-pair. What does this imply about the left-hand role of the lower role-pair? If the lower predicate is just a binary, this role must also be unique! As an exercise, prove this. An important corollary of this result is that if the lower predicate is longer than a binary then it must split in this case, since there will be an implied FD from the first role to the second role. This result is illustrated later in our treatment of normalization (section 10.2).

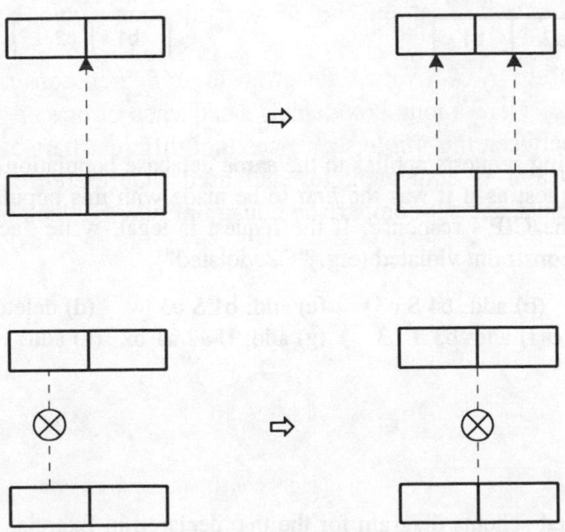

Figure 6.24 The implied constraints should not be shown

Exercise 6.4

1. A company allows some of its employees to use one or more of its company cars. The rest of its employees are given a travel allowance instead. The following report is an extract from the company's records in this regard. Schematize it.

Emp. Nr	*Emp. name*	*Cars used*	*Driver's license*	*Travel allowance ($)*
001	Harding J	123ABC	A74000	–
002	Oh C	111KOR, 123ABC	A51120	–
003	Halpin T			200

2. The diagram below indicates the conceptual schema and current population for a particular UoD. Reference schemes are omitted for simplicity. Fact tables are shown below their fact types. Predicates are identified as **R**..**U**, and constraints as *C1*..*C9*.

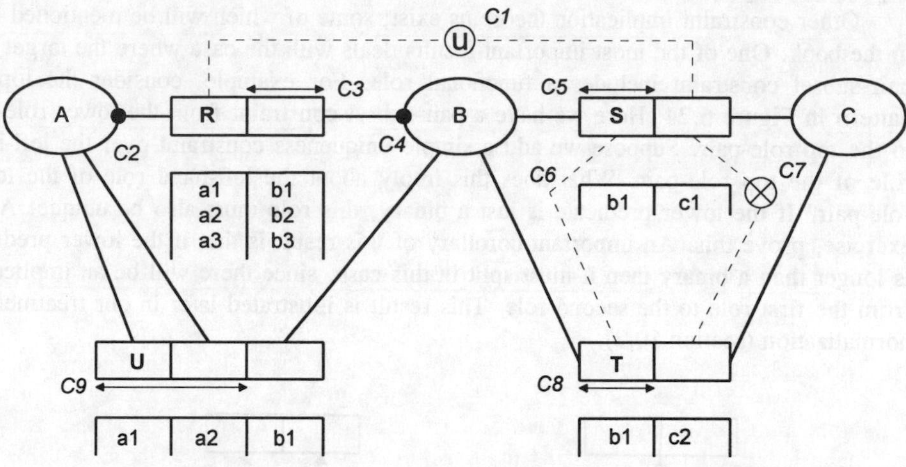

Each of the following requests applies to the **same** database population as shown above (i.e. treat each request as if it was the *first* to be made with this population). For each request, indicate the CIP's response. If the request is legal, write "accepted". Otherwise, indicate the constraint violated (e.g. "C2 violated").

(a) add: a1 R b2 (b) add: b4 S c3 (c) add: b1 S c3 (d) delete: b1 S c1
(e) add: b2 S c2 (f) add: b3 T c3 (g) add: U a2 a1 b2 (h) add: U a1 a2 b2
(i) begin
add: a1 R b4
add: b4 S c1
end

3. Draw the conceptual schema diagram for the UoD declared in Exercise 2.2 Question 2, adding constraint labels C1..C5 to the relevant constraints marked on the diagram.

4. The following table records details about various (fictitious) movies. Schematize this UoD. The population is not fully significant, so make some educated guesses.

Movie	*Director*	*Stars*	*Supporting cast*
Earth Song	Ima Beatle	Bing Crosby Elvis Presley	Neil Diamond Tina Turner
Me and my echo	Hugh Who	Hugh Who	
Kangaroos	Doc U. Mentary		

5. A software company has a large number of shops located in the state of Queensland, and requires detailed knowledge of their distribution. The table shows some of their locations. City shops are located in suburbs, but country shops are located in towns. City and town names are unique (other states are not of interest). Schematize this UoD, revealing the reference scheme of the entity type Location in full detail. Model street addresses as labels but towns, suburbs and cities as entities.

Shop#	*Location*			
	Suburb	*City*	*Town*	*St address*
1	St Lucia	Brisbane		Suite 5, 77 Sylvan Rd
2			Strathpine	Unit 3, 1000 Gympie Rd
3	Sandgate	Brisbane		7 Sun St
4	Clontarf	Redcliffe		25 Beach Rd
5	Sandgate	Cairns		25 Beach Rd

6. The application described here is partly based on a real life banking system, but simplifications and changes have been made. To help you appreciate the privacy implications of a universal identification scheme, all clients and staff of the bank are identified throughout the application by their tax file number (tax#). Thus, all bank customers and personnel are taxpayers.

An information system is required to manage accounts and staff records for Oz Bank, which has branches at various locations. Each branch is standardly identified by its branch number but also has a unique name. The first table is an extract from staff records of Oz Bank.

Branch#	*Branch name*	*Emp. tax#*	*Emp. name*	*Emp. phone*
1	Uni. of Qld	200 390 ...	Jones E Presley E ...	3770000 ? ...
2	Toowong Central	377 ...	Jones E ...	? ...
3	Strathpine	222 ...	Wong M ...	2051111 ...

Each employee works at exactly one branch and has at most one phone listed. The mark "?" denotes a null value. The mark "..." indicates "etc." (other instances exist but are not shown here).

Within the one branch, each account has a unique serial#, but different accounts in different branches may have the same serial#. Account users are identified by their tax#, but also have a name and possibly a phone number (see the second table).

Account		*User*		
Branch#	***Serial#***	***Tax#***	***Name***	***Phone***
1	55	200	Jones E	3770000
		311	Jones T	3770000
1	66	199	Megasoft	3771234
2	55	199	Megasoft	3771234
2	77	377	Jones E	?
3	44	300	Wong S	2051111

Each account is a passbook account. Five sample passbook entries are shown. For each account, transactions are numbered sequentially 1, 2, 3 .... Here dates are set out in day/month/year format. For simplicity, assume each transaction is either a deposit (DEP) or withdrawal (WDL). In practice of course, other types of transaction are possible (e.g. interest and fees). The balance column shows the account balance after the transaction has been executed.

Although the balance is derivable, for efficiency purposes *the balance is stored as soon as it is derived*. For example, this speeds up production of monthly statements for the bank's customers (Oz bank has a few million customers who average several transactions each month). This *derive on update* decision contrasts with our normal *derive on query* policy.

branch#	**serial#**
1	55

OZ BANK

branch name: Uni. of Qld
users: Jones E; Jones T

Tran#	*Date*	*Deposit*	*Withdrawal*	*Balance*
1	3/1/90	1000		1000
2	5/1/90		200	800
3	5/1/90		100	700

branch#	**serial#**
1	66

OZ BANK

branch name: Uni. of Qld
users: Megasoft

Tran#	*Date*	*Deposit*	*Withdrawal*	*Balance*
1	10/2/90	2000		2000
2	10/2/90		500	1500

branch#	serial#	OZ BANK
2	55	**branch name:** Toowong central **users:** Megasoft

Tran#	*Date*	*Deposit*	*Withdrawal*	*Balance*
1	23/1/90	9000		9000
2	7/2/90	5000		14000
3	10/2/90		2000	12000
4	2/3/90		5000	7000

branch#	serial#	OZ BANK
2	77	**branch name:** Toowong Central **users:** Jones E

Tran#	*Date*	*Deposit*	*Withdrawal*	*Balance*
1	3/1/90	500		500

branch#	serial#	OZ BANK
3	44	**branch name:** Strathpine **users:** Wong S

Tran#	*Date*	*Deposit*	*Withdrawal*	*Balance*
1	5/1/90	100		100
2	12/1/90			700

(a) Draw a conceptual schema diagram for this UoD. Make use of an entity type indicating the type of transaction: Trantype (code) {'DEP', 'WDL'}. Include the account balance fact type on the diagram; mark it with "*S" since it is derivable but it is required to be stored. Express the derivation rule as clearly and simply as you can.

(b) Consider the fragment of your conceptual schema which captures the kind of information required for deposits and withdrawals (only two fact types are involved). Transform this subschema into an equivalent subschema which uses two different fact types, removing the entity type Trantype altogether. Include all relevant constraints.

(c) In a realistic banking application there are several kinds of transaction besides deposits and withdrawals. In such a situation is it better to include Trantype as an object type, or to extend the alternative approach you proposed in (b)?

6.5 Subtyping

Earlier in the chapter we used Euler diagrams to depict one set as a subset of another. In designing a conceptual schema we often need to introduce subtypes, and in so doing spell out clearly what is a subtype of what. Euler diagrams may be used to do this for simple cases. In practice however, an object type may have many subtypes, which might overlap, and a subtype may have many supertypes. For such cases Euler diagrams become hopelessly complicated. Moreover, in schema diagrams we also want to display the specific roles played by each subtype. Many different diagram notations based on Euler diagrams are in current use, which work fine for simple cases but become too cluttered, or simply fail, for various complex cases.

What we need is a simple notation which can be used to display subtypehood and subtype roles no matter how large or complex the situation is. This is achieved by displaying subtypes *outside* their supertype(s) and depicting the subtype-supertype connections by means of an *arrow*. To distinguish it from a subset constraint, the arrow line is thicker and unbroken. The basic idea is shown in Fig. 6.25.

Here A and B are object types. Suppose A = Employee and B = Manager. The type Employee is the set of all employees about which facts might possibly be recorded. The subtype Manager is the set of all managers about which facts might be recorded. At any given database state, pop(Employee) and pop(Manager) are respectively the set of employees and set of managers actually referenced in the database.

In general, B is a **proper subtype** of A if and only if, pop(B) is always a subset of pop(A), and $A \neq B$. In this case, A is a *proper supertype* of B. If $A = B$ we do not specify any subtype connection. With this understanding, we usually omit "proper" when speaking about subtypes and supertypes. The adjective "proper" applies to the type relationship, but not necessarily to the *population* relationship. There may be a database state in which pop(A) = pop(B). For example, if no facts about A have yet been entered, both pop(A) and pop(B) equal { }; and with our example, we may choose to enter information about managers before the other employees.

Now consider the subtype graph shown in Figure 6.26. Here we might have A = Person, B = Woman, C = AsianPerson, D = JapaneseWoman. We say that A is a *common supertype* of B and C, and D is a *common subtype* of B and C. In general, a common supertype is at least the union of its subtypes; if it is the union of its subtypes then its subtypes are said to *exhaust* it. In our example, B and C do not exhaust A.

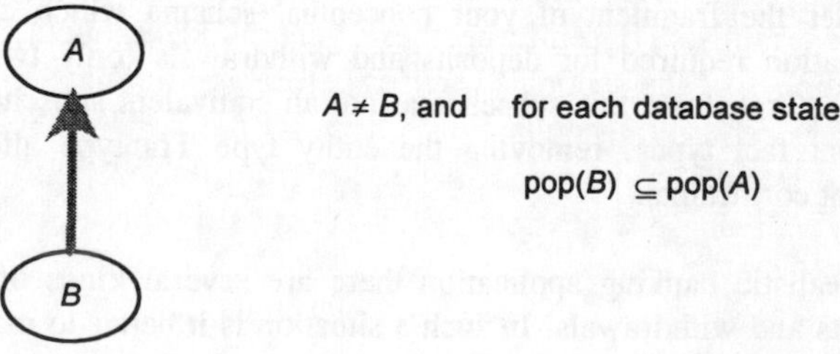

Figure 6.25 *B* is a proper subtype of *A*

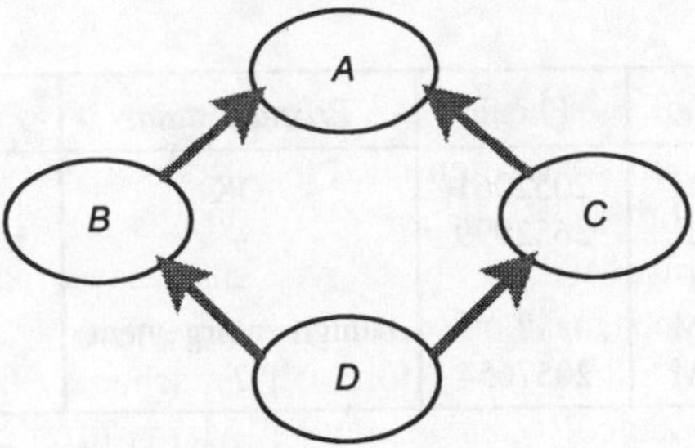

Figure 6.26 *D* is a subtype of *B* and *C*, which are subtypes of *A*

In general a common subtype is at most the intersection of its supertypes. In our example, $B \cap C$ = AsianWoman, and *D* is a proper subset of this. Since *B* is attached directly to its supertype *A*, we say that *B* is a *direct subtype* of *A*. Since *D* is a subtype of *B*, and *B* is a subtype of *A* it follows that every member of *D* is also a member of *A*: we say that *D* is an *indirect subtype* of *A*.

In general, the relation of subtypehood is *transitive*: if *X* is a subtype of *Y*, and *Y* is a subtype of *Z* then *X* is a subtype of *Z*. Indirect subtype links should be omitted from diagrams since they are transitively implied.

A supertype may have many direct subtypes, and a subtype may have many direct supertypes: so in general we have a *subtype graph* rather than a tree. The supertype and subtypes are referred to as the *nodes* of the graph. Since the arrowheads provide direction we have a directed graph. Since no type can be a proper subtype of itself it follows that no cycles or loops are permitted. Thus any pattern of type-subtype relationships forms a *directed acyclic graph*.

An entity type which is not a proper subtype of any other entity type in the schema is said to be a *primitive entity type* for the schema. The JapaneseWoman subtype might occur in a schema whose primitive entity types include Person, Sex, and Country. A single conceptual schema may have many subtype graphs. Each subtype graph must stem from exactly one primitive entity type (possibly nested), which is the common supertype, or *root* node (or *top*) of that graph.

Subtype graphs have only one top since primitive entity types are mutually exclusive. In contrast, subtypes in a graph necessarily overlap with their supertype(s), and may even overlap with one another (e.g. Woman and AsianPerson). Since root types are mutually exclusive, there is no overlap between subtypes that belong to different subtype graphs. To reinforce these general ideas about subtypes, you may wish to try Question 1 of the section exercises before continuing.

Now consider a hospital application where all the patients are adults, and hence may be classified as men or women. An extract from the hospital records is shown in Table 6.4. Only males have a prostate gland. In later life this gland may suffer various medical problems. Only women can become pregnant. In this table, a *minus sign* "–" indicates that an actual value is *not to be recorded* in that spot. We met something like this when we considered subset and exclusion constraints. But there is a difference. Here the "–" means that an actual value is inapplicable *because of the specific value of some other entry* (or entries) for the entity involved.

Table 6.4

Patient#	*Name*	*Sex*	Phone	*Prostate status*	*Pregnancies*
101	Adams A	M	2052061	OK	–
102	Blossom F	F	3652999	–	5
103	Jones E	F	?	–	0
104	King P	M	?	benign enlargement	–
105	Smith J	M	2057654	?	–

On the first row, pregnancies must not be recorded for patient 101, because that patient is male (as shown by the "M" entry for sex). Similarly, prostate status must not be recorded for women. The number of pregnancies must be recorded for women, even if this number is zero. In contrast to "–", the "?" mark merely indicates that the information is missing. For example, patients 103 and 104 might have no phone, and patient 105 might not have had his prostate checked. Suppose we now schematize this UoD as in Figure 6.27.

Notice the optional roles. Although correct as far as it goes, this schema fails to express the constraints that prostate status is recorded *only for* men, and the number of pregnancies is recorded *just for* the women. The phrase "just for" means "for and only for" (i.e. "for all and only"). To capture these constraints we introduce subtypes, and attach their specific roles, as shown in Figure 6.28. The subtypes Man and Woman are formally defined beneath the diagram. By default, subtypes inherit the identification scheme of their supertype, so there is no need to repeat it.

Recall that a role is played only by the object type to which it is attached. Hence the subtyping reveals that prostate status is recorded **only if** the patient is male, and pregnancy count is recorded **only if** the patient is female. The role attached to Man is optional. Not all men need to have their prostate status recorded. However the role attached to Woman is mandatory. So pregnancy count is recorded **if** the patient is female. The combination of the subtype constraint and mandatory role on Woman means that pregnancy count is recorded **if and only if** the patient is female.

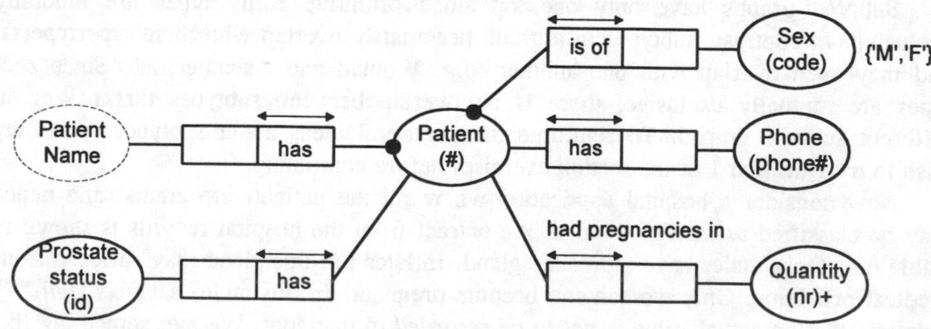

Figure 6.27 An incomplete conceptual schema for Table 6.4

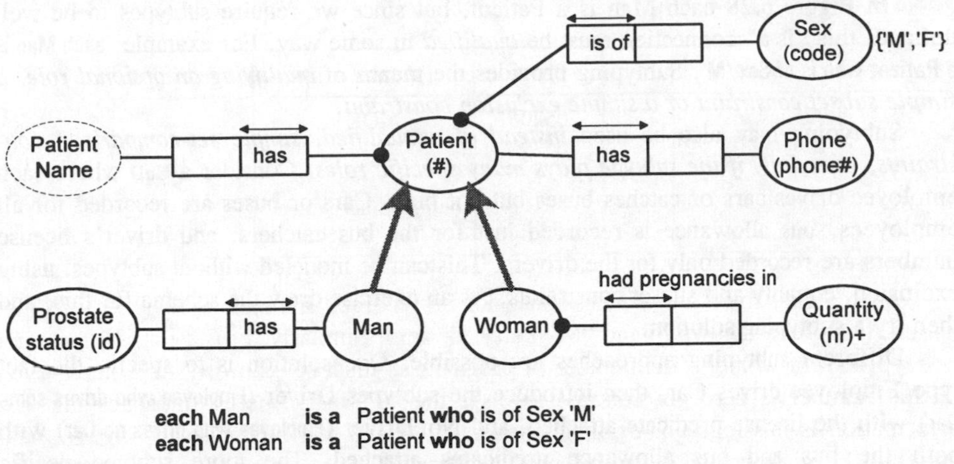

each Man is a Patient who is of Sex 'M'
each Woman is a Patient who is of Sex 'F'

Figure 6.28 Subtyping completes the conceptual schema for table 6.4

In this case the Man subtype plays only one role, and this is optional. Unlike primitive atomic entity types, there is no default assumption of mandatory if only one role is attached. *With subtypes, and objectified predicates, any mandatory role constraints must be explicitly shown* (including disjunctive cases).

We do not introduce a subtype unless there is at least one specific role recorded only for that subtype. As with primitive entity types, we demand that *each subtype must have an attached role*. Some other modeling methods allow role-less subtypes. For example, Man and Woman subtypes might be introduced merely to display that patients can be classified in this way. We prefer to display such a taxonomy, or classification scheme, as a binary fact type with a value constraint (e.g. Figure 6.28 uses: Patient is of Sex {'M','F'}) or as unaries (e.g. isMan and isWoman may be attached to Patient as exclusive, disjunctively mandatory unaries). The binary form is much neater when the classification scheme involves several subtypes.

While specific fact types are attached to the relevant subtype, common fact types are attached to the supertype. In this example, name, sex and phone may be recorded for any patient, so we attach these directly to Patient. In general, each subtype inherits all the roles of its supertype(s). Although drawn outside its supertype, the subtype is totally contained inside the supertype. In Figure 6.28 all instances of Man or Woman have their name, sex and possibly phone recorded. Attaching a common fact type to the supertype avoids duplicating it on all the subtypes.

To determine membership of subtypes, we demand that *each subtype must be defined in terms of at least one role played by its supertype(s)*. With the present example, the sex fact type is used to determine membership in Man and Woman. The subtype definitions are shown below the diagram. These definitions are formal—they are not just comments. In FORML, "**is a**", "**is an**" or "::=" is used for "is defined as", and the reserved word "**who**", "**that**" or "**which**" is used after the supertype name. For persons, "who" sounds more natural. Optionally, "**each**" may be used before the name of the subtype being defined, as shown in Figure 6.28 .

In Figure 6.28 each Man is a Patient, but since we require subtypes to be well defined, this "is a" connection must be *qualified* in some way. For example: **each Man is a Patient who is of Sex 'M'**. Subtyping provides the means of *qualifying an optional role, a simple subset constraint or a simple exclusion constraint*.

Subtyping may also be used *instead of unqualified, simple set-comparison constraints, especially if the subtype plays many specific roles*. Consider a UoD where each employee drives cars or catches buses but not both. Cars or buses are recorded for all employees, bus allowance is recorded just for the bus catchers, and driver's license numbers are recorded only for the drivers. This can be modeled without subtypes, using exclusion, equality and subset constraints. As an exercise draw the schema for this, and then try a subtyping solution.

Different subtyping approaches are possible. One solution is to specify the fact type Employee drives Car, then introduce the subtypes Driver (**Employee who drives some Car**) with the license predicate attached, and NonDriver (**Employee who drives no Car**) with both the bus and bus allowance predicates attached. The more subtype-specific information required (e.g. total distance traveled by bus, driving violations) the more tidy the subtyping portrayal becomes in comparison to the non-subtyping alternative. Note however that subtyping cannot replace composite set-comparison constraints (between sequences of two or more roles).

Be careful to avoid circular definitions—don't try to define a subtype in terms of itself. For example, suppose we defined BusCatcher as **Employee who catches some Bus**, and then attached the bus predicate to this subtype (i.e. BusCatcher catches Bus). This specifies that the role of catching a bus is played only by those who play the role of catching a bus. Such circular reasoning is not very informative! In very rare cases, a role used to define a subtype may be a reference role. For example, we might record some fact only for people whose surname begins with the letter "Z".

A subtype graph may arise in a top-down way, by specializing an object type into different types, or in a bottom-up way, by generalizing different types into a common supertype. The *specialization* (subtype introduction) procedure may be summarized as follows. Here "well-defined" means a precise subtype can be defined in terms of roles played by its supertype(s). A subtype definition is stronger than a set-comparison constraint if it adds a restriction to the defining predicate (e.g. Sex 'M', Rating >3). The procedure is recursive: since a subtype may itself have optional roles we apply the procedure to it to see if we need to form subtypes of it.

Specialization Procedure (SP):

Specify all mandatory roles;
For each optional role:
if this role is to be recorded only for a well-defined proper subtype of its attached object type
and (the subtype definition is not just a set-comparison constraint
or another role is recorded only for this subtype)
then introduce the subtype;
attach its specific roles;
add the subtype definition;
apply SP to the subtype

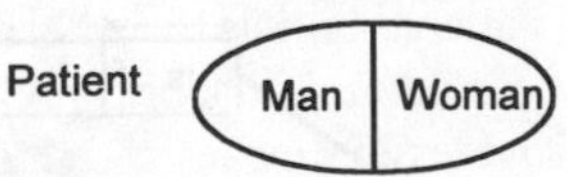

Figure 6.29 A partition of Patient

For the schema of Figure 6.28, the subtypes form a **partition** of their supertype: Man and Woman are *mutually exclusive and collectively exhaustive*. We may display this situation on a hypothetical Euler diagram as shown in Figure 6.29. The subtype names "Man" and "Woman" are meaningful to us, and our background understanding of these terms helps us to see this partition. But such names are only character strings to the computer system, so how is the partition formally captured in the model?

Look back at Figure 6.28. The mutual exclusion between Man and Woman is implied by their definitions together with the uniqueness constraint on the sex predicate (each Patient is of at most one Sex). The constraint that Man and Woman exhaust Patient is implied by the subtype definitions, the {'M','F'} constraint, and the mandatory role on the sex predicate (each Patient is of at least one Sex). Because we demand that subtypes be well-defined and all relevant constraints on defining predicates be declared (graphically or textually), *any subtype exclusion or exhaustion constraints that do exist are always implied*.

As humans, we can use our background understanding of meaningful subtype names to immediately "see" whether subtypes are exclusive or exhaustive. This short cut for us depends on a judicious choice of subtype names. For example, if it is not clear that the terms "Man" and "Woman" cover all patients (e.g. we might want to include children) then the exhaustion constraint is more clearly "seen" by using the subtype names "Male patient" and "Female patient" instead of "Man" and "Woman".

In rare cases we may wish to highlight subtype exclusion and exhaustion constraints by showing them explicitly on the schema diagram. Mutual exclusion among subtypes may be shown by connecting "⊗" with dotted lines to their subtype arrows. The symbol "⦿" is used for exhaustion or totality of subtypes. For a partition these two symbols are overlayed: "⊗". In Figure 6.30 the partition constraint is portrayed explicitly. With complex subtype graphs, the explicit display of such implied constraints makes the diagram appear cluttered. Ideally a CASE tool would enable display of such constraints to be toggled on or off by the user.

Since Man and Woman are exclusive, and we demand that any object type can be populated, it would be illegal to introduce an object type that is a subtype of both, since such a type would always be empty (nobody is simultaneously both a man and a woman). In general, *exclusive object types cannot have a common subtype*.

In some other modeling methods a classification predicate or attribute (e.g. sex) may be specified, then subtypes introduced but not formally defined, and relevant exclusion and exhaustion constraints added. This alternative approach suffers two problems. Firstly, exclusion and exhaustion constraints are weaker than subtype definitions. For example, if the subtype definitions are removed from Figure 6.30 we may still record prostate status for women or pregnancies for men so long as no person has both recorded.

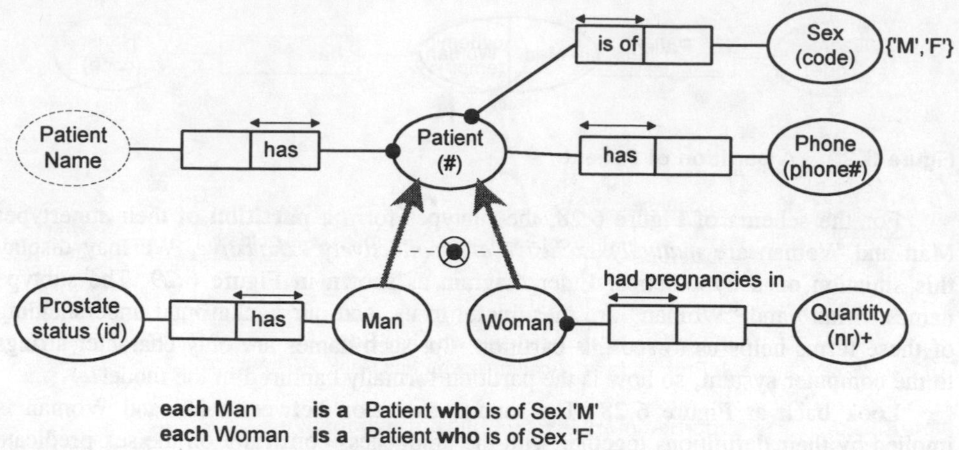

Figure 6.30 The implied subtype exclusion and exhaustion shown explicitly

Secondly, an inconsistent constraint picture might arise. For example, the exclusion constraint between Man and Woman might be missed or an exhaustion constraint applied wrongly (e.g. between SeniorLecturer and Professor when ordinary lecturers also exist). Hence if a classification predicate is used in addition to subtyping, these should be related by formal subtype definitions.

If subtyping is used without an additional classification predicate then the problems above can be avoided if the exclusion and exhaustion constraints themselves provide the relevant classification constraints. However sometimes a classification predicate is required. For example, we may need to record the salary of employees, then use this predicate to subtype employees. Employees with a salary ≥ $50000 might be classified as HighlyPaidEmployee, for instance. Here exclusion and exhaustion constraints cannot convey the full semantics of the subtyping. For such reasons as well as uniformity, our approach always requires formal subtype definitions based on predicates attached to the supertype(s).

When subtypes collectively exhaust their supertype, this is sometimes called a "total union" constraint, since the union of the subtypes equals the total supertype. This holds for the type populations too, since a subtype population is determined by applying the subtype definition to the supertype population. However unless each subtype has a specific mandatory role, the union of the populations of the subtype-specific roles need not equal the population of the supertype. For example, in Figure 6.30 the population of Man is the set of male patients but some of these might not have their prostate status recorded.

Please note that exclusion and exhaustion constraints among subtypes are to be interpreted in a *static* sense. For example, since the subtypes Man and Woman are exclusive, in any given database state their populations cannot overlap. However this does not rule out an object migrating from one type to another between database states. This is unlikely for our present example! However our next example includes the subtypes SeniorLecturer and Professor (Figure 6.31).

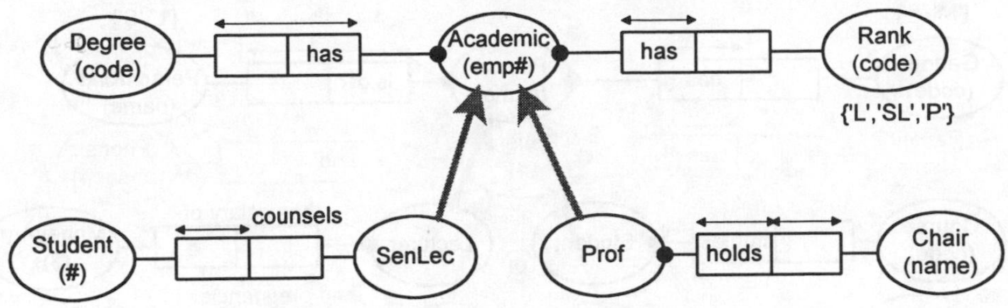

Figure 6.31 The subtypes are exclusive but not exhaustive

SeniorLecturer and Professor are exclusive in the sense that no academic can be a member of both types simultaneously. However a senior lecturer in one state can be promoted to professor in a later state.

In this application, academics have exactly one rank (lecturer, senior lecturer or professor) and have been awarded one or more degrees. Each professor holds a unique "chair" (e.g. information systems), indicating the research area that he or she manages. Each student has exactly one counsellor, and this must be a senior lecturer. Nothing special is recorded for lecturers so we don't bother introducing a subtype for them. The subtype definitions and the constraints on the rank predicate imply that the SenLec (Senior Lecturer) and Prof (Professor) subtypes are exclusive but not exhaustive. To avoid clutter, the implied exclusion constraint is omitted from the diagram.

In our schema diagrams, subtypes are drawn outside their supertypes. Don't forget however that every member of a subtype is also a member of its supertype(s). To clarify this point, Figure 6.32 depicts the subtyping of Figure 6.31 by means of a hypothetical Euler diagram (HED); the shaded region is empty. For simplicity, reference schemes and subtype definitions are omitted. Although such diagrams may be used in simple cases for explanatory purposes, they are too awkward for complex cases, and should not be regarded as a replacement for our subtyping notation.

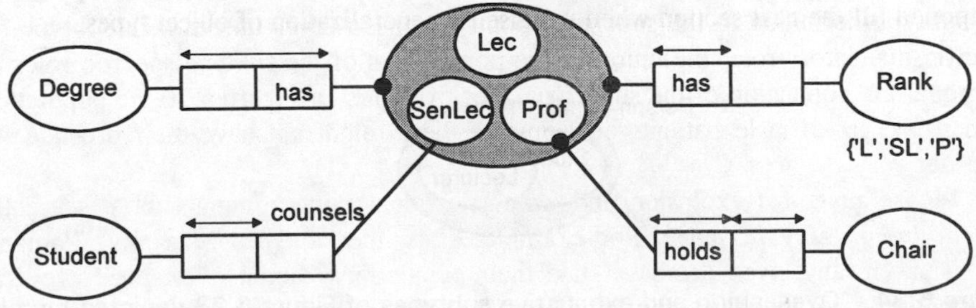

Figure 6.32 The subtyping of Figure 6.31 shown with a hypothetical Euler diagram

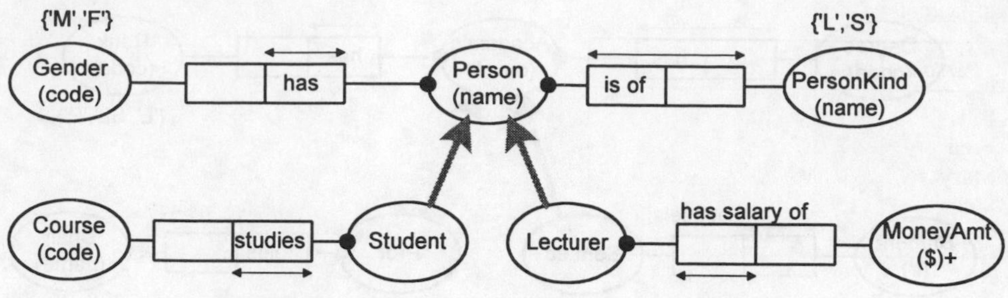

Figure 6.33 In this UoD a student may be a lecturer

Consider now a UoD peopled just by lecturers and students who may be identified by name. Gender and PersonKind (L = Lecturer; S = Student) are recorded for all persons, salary is recorded just for lecturers, and course of study is recorded just for students (see Figure 6.33).

In this UoD it is possible for a person to be both a lecturer and student, as indicated by the many:many constraint. So the Student and Lecturer subtypes overlap. Although not exclusive, they are exhaustive, given the mandatory role and {'L','S'} constraint on the personkind fact type. Figure 6.34 displays the subtyping on a HED. Since these subtypes overlap, they may have a common subtype. For example, if some further information was required only for those lecturers studying a course we could introduce a subtype StudentLecturer (both Student and Lecturer).

Suppose we expanded the UoD to include administrative staff, who may be students but not lecturers. This classification scheme may be depicted by three unaries (is_student, lectures, administrates) with an exclusion constraint between the last two. If specific details were required for administrators we would introduce a third subtype for this. As an exercise, draw a schema diagram and a HED to depict this situation.

For discussion purposes we have identified people by name in this example. But this is clearly unrealistic. In practice we would normally identify students by student numbers, and lecturers and administrators by employee numbers. But then a student employee would have two identification schemes. A treatment of this problem is postponed till the next section when we discuss generalization of object types.

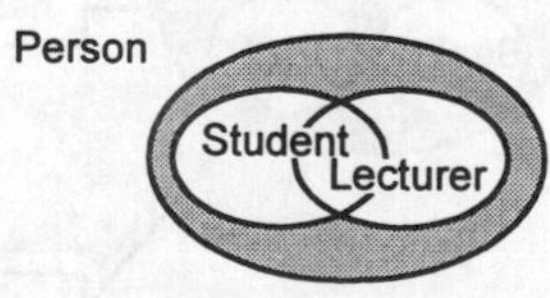

Figure 6.34 Overlapping and exhaustive subtypes of Figure 6.33 depicted by a HED

Table 6.5

Person	*Age*	*Favorite group*
Bill	17	Abba
Fred	12	–
Mary	20	–
Sue	13	Dire Straits
Tom	19	Beatles

In the rest of this section we work through a couple of examples, focusing on the problem of providing a correct definition for the subtypes. Sometimes it is not obvious from an output report what criteria have been used to decide whether some fact is to be recorded. As a simple example, consider Table 6.5. What rule determines when to record a person's favorite group?

One pattern that fits the sample data is that a person's choice of favorite group is recorded if and only if that person is aged between 13 and 19 inclusive (i.e. the person is a teenager). This is not the only pattern which fits however. Maybe favorite group is recorded just for people with odd ages (13, 17 and 19 are odd numbers). While these might be argued to be the two most "obvious" patterns, there are very many patterns that are consistent with the data. Just based on age we could specify any set of natural numbers minus the set {12,20} and within the age range of the UoD.

A database population is ***significant with respect to a constraint class*** if and only if it satisfies just one constraint from this class (excluding weaker constraints implied by this choice): in this case the constraint may be deduced from the population. We saw earlier that obtaining a sample population which is significant with respect to uniqueness constraints can be tedious; but at least it can be done in a modest amount of time. Unfortunately, no decision procedure exists to automatically churn out the correct subtype definitions.

If we remove the restriction that a computer system has finite memory then we open ourselves out to the problem that for any finite set of data there will always remain an infinite number of possible patterns which fit the data. This is the basis of the philosophical "problem of induction".

Rather than get bogged down in philosophical speculation at this point we adopt the following pragmatic approach to finalizing subtype definitions: look carefully at the data, use "common sense" to spot what we feel is the simplest pattern, then check with the UoD expert whether this pattern is the one intended. Since the subtyping constraints reflect the decision of the UoD expert on what should be recorded for what, the UoD expert will always be able to resolve the matter.

Although output reports cannot be significant with respect to subtype definitions, *input forms* such as tax returns or application forms often do provide a significant set of *conditional instructions* from which the subtyping can be deduced. Typically such forms include a number of fields which are to be filled in only by certain kinds of people. To let users know which questions they must answer, instructions are included which reveal the conditions under which the specific details are to be recorded. From these instructions it is usually fairly easy to determine the subtyping. As a simple example, consider the media survey form shown in Figure 6.35.

Form#: 5001

1. Age (years): ....

2. Nr hours spent per week watching TV: ....

If you answered 0 then go to Question 4

3. What is your favorite TV channel? ....

4. Nr hours spent per week reading newspapers: ....

If you answered 0 then Stop (no more answers are required).

5. What is your favorite newspaper? ....

If you are younger than 18, or answered 0 to question 2 or 4 then Stop (no more answers are required)

6. Which do you prefer as a news source? ❑ Television
(Tick the box of your choice)

❑ Newspaper

Figure 6.35 A sample media survey form

Each copy of the form has a unique form#. Each form is filled out by a different person, and each person fills out only one form. The enforcement of this 1:1 correspondence between people and forms is the responsibility of the firm conducting the survey rather than the information system itself. In our model we choose to leave this fact type implicit, identifying the people directly by form#.

The conditional instructions on this form are shown in italics. Everybody must answer questions 1, 2 and 4. Anybody who answers 0 to question 2 is told to skip question 3. Hence favorite TV channel is recorded just for those who indicate they do watch some TV; let's call this subtype Viewer. People who answered 0 for question 4 are told to skip all later questions. Hence favorite newspaper (question 5) is recorded just for those who read newspapers; let's call this subtype Reader.

People who are younger than 18 or who are not viewers or newspaper readers are to skip question 6. Hence preferred news source is recorded just for adult viewers or adult readers; let's call this subtype MediaAdult. This analysis leads to the schema of Figure 6.36.

Alternatively, an output report from the application might be used to help with the modeling (see Table 6.6). As an exercise, try using this table to arrive at the schema.The sample data in Table 6.6 have been carefully chosen to be significant with respect to the subtype graph.

Given this, and recalling that the "–" signs mean "not to be recorded", we may reason as follows. Age, viewing and reading figures are recorded for everybody. The set of people for which favorite channel is recorded properly overlaps with the set of people for which favorite paper is recorded, so these correspond to overlapping subtypes. The set of people for which preferred news source is recorded is a proper subset of the previous two sets, so this corresponds to a common subtype.

Table 6.6 An output report from the media survey

Person	*Age (y)*	*Television (h/week)*	*Newspaper (h/week)*	*Favorite channel*	*Favorite paper*	*Preferred news*
5001	41	0	10	–	The Times	–
5002	60	0	25	–	The Times	–
5003	16	20	2	9	The Times	–
5004	18	20	5	2	Daily Mail	TV
5005	13	35	0	7	–	–
5006	17	14	4	9	Daily Sun	–
5007	50	8	10	2	Daily Sun	NP
5008	33	0	0	–	–	–
5009	13	50	0	10	–	–

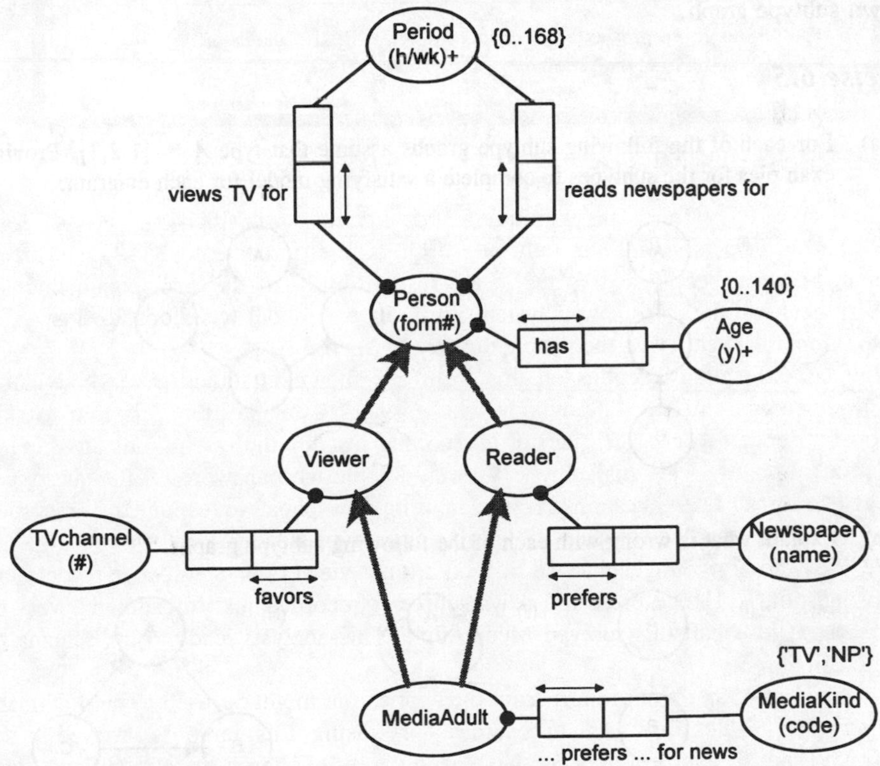

Figure 6.36 The conceptual schema for the media survey example

This analysis yields the "diamond shaped" subtype graph of Figure 6.35, as well as the information recorded for each node in the graph. However we can only make educated guesses as to the actual subtype definitions—these should be checked with a UoD expert if one is available.

To help you do the section exercises without a UoD expert, the populations provided are significant with respect to the subtype graph. However this is an artificial situation. In designing real world applications you would rarely be handed a population guaranteed to be significant in this way. Only the UoD expert could provide this guarantee, and to do this he or she must know the subtyping constraints anyway. It is better to get these constraints directly from the UoD expert simply by asking.

Apart from the methods discussed here, Appendix B discusses two matrix algorithms for deducing the configuration of a subtype graph from a population significant in this regard. Although it is not safe to assume populations are significant, such procedures can be used to check whether a population is significant with respect to a known subtype graph.

Exercise 6.5

1. (a) For each of the following subtype graphs assume that type $A = \{1,2,3\}$. Provide examples for the subtypes to complete a satisfying model for each diagram.

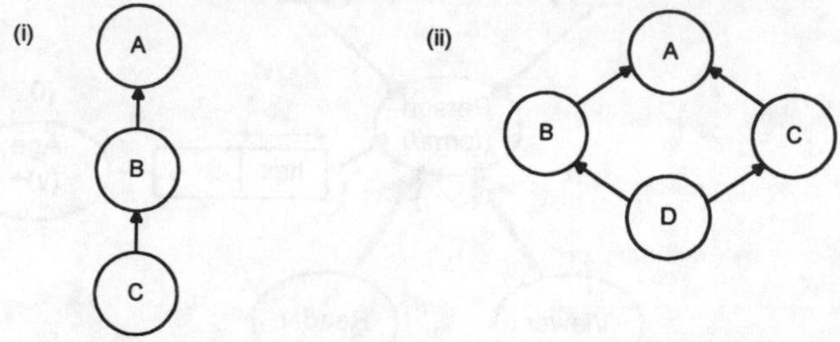

(b) Explain what is wrong with each of the following subtype graphs.

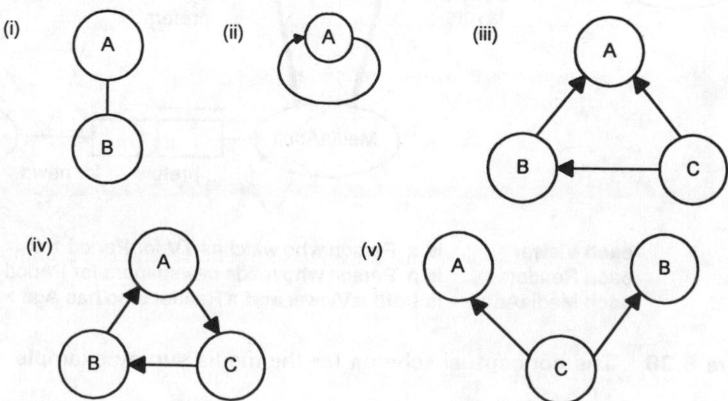

Note: ***In the following questions, populations are significant with respect to the subtype graph, and "–" means "not to be recorded".***

2. **The following table is a sample weekly report about animals in a certain household. Provide a conceptual schema for this UoD, including uniqueness constraints, mandatory roles, value constraints, and subtype constraints. Include a definition for each subtype.**

Animal	*Animal kind*	*Sex*	*Nr cars chased*	*Nr mice caught*
Fido	dog	M	12	–
Felix	cat	M	–	1
Fluffy	dog	F	0	–
Tweetie	bird	F	–	–

3. **A simplified fragment of an income tax return form is shown.**

1. Your Tax File Number: ....
2. Your full name: ....
3. Indicate the kind(s) of income you received from an employer by ticking the relevant box(es). If you had no employer income, leave this blank and go to question 7.

   ❑ salary ❑ benefit (employment related)

4. Your main employment occupation: ....
5. If you earned a salary, complete the following income details:

Employer	*Tax paid*	*Gross salary*

6. If you earned employment related benefits indicate total benefit: ....
7. etc.

(a) **Schematize this UoD, assuming that in section 5 the same employer can appear on only one line.**

(b) **Modify your solution to part (a) to handle these changes. The same employer may appear on more than one line of section 5. For each of these lines, the taxpayer attaches a group certificate from his/her employer which includes the employer's name as well as the employee's tax file number, gross salary and tax instalments deducted (i.e. tax paid). Group certificates are identified by serial numbers.**

4. Schematize the following table. Here a supervisor supervises one or more persons. You may find it helpful to draw a tree showing who supervises whom. As usual, the missing value "–" means "inapplicable because of some other information". The missing value "•" means "does not exist".

Emp#	*Emp name*	*Supervisor*	*Smoker?*	*Home phone*	*Health bonus ($)*	*Company car*
101	Brown CA	102	N	–	300	–
102	Jones E	103	Y	2053771	–	–
103	White TA	•	N	2062050	500	597VTP
104	Mifune K	103	N	3651000	500	123KYO
105	Nelson HF	102	N	–	300	–
106	Adams PC	102	N	3719872	400	321ABC
107	Wong S	104	N	–	300	–
108	Collins T	104	Y	–	–	–
109	Smith JB	106	Y	–	–	–

5. A loan agency records information about clients borrowing money. The following report is extracted from this information system. Clients are identified by client#. Marital codes are: "D" (divorced); "M" (married); "S" (single); "W" (widowed). Residential codes are: "B" (home buyer); "O" (home owner); "R" (home renter).

Client#	*Marital status*	*Residential status*	*Number of dependants*	*Home value ($)*	*Spouse's income ($)*	*Spouse's share of home (%)*
103	M	O	3	100000	40000	50
220	M	R	3	–	0	–
345	S	O	–	150000	–	–
444	W	B	2	90000	–	–
502	D	R	0	–	–	–
600	S	R	–	–	–	–
777	M	B	0	100000	0	40
803	D	B	1	60000	–	–
905	W	O	0	90000	–	–

Each client has borrowed one or more loans. For this agency, any given loan can be borrowed by only one client. The following report from the same information system provides details on some of the loans. Schematize this UoD.

Client#	*Loans borrowed*		
	Loan#	*Amount ($)*	*Term (years)*
103	00508	25000	7
220	00651	25000	7
	00652	3000	1
etc.			

6. The following three reports come from an information system which maintains data about the following bodies in our solar system: the Sun, the naked eye planets and their moons. Planets travel in roughly circular orbits about the Sun. A planet is in inferior conjunction if it is directly lined up between the earth and the Sun. A planet is in opposition if the Earth is directly lined up between it and the Sun. The missing value "•" means "does not exist". The symbol "M_E" denotes one Earth mass. One astronomical unit (a.u.) equals 150 000 000 km. Schematize this UoD.

Sun:

Name	*Mass (M_E)*	*Radius (km)*
Sun	34 000	69 000

Planets:

Name	*Nr of moons*	*Mean distance from Sun (a.u.)*	*Mass (M_E)*	*Radius (km)*	*Orbital period (y d)*	*Next inf. conj.*	*Next oppos.*	*Atmosphere (main gases)*
Mercury	0	0.39	0.06	2 440	0y 88d	Dec	–	•
Venus	0	0.72	0.81	6 050	0y 224d	Jan	–	CO_2
Earth	1	1	1	6 378	1y 0d	–	–	N_2,O_2
Mars	2	1.5	0.11	3 095	1y 322d	–	Feb	CO_2
Jupiter	16	5.2	318	71 400	11y 315d	–	Sep	H_2,He
Saturn	17	9.5	95	60 000	29y 167d	–	Sep	H_2,He

Moons:

Name	*Planet orbited*	*Radius (km)*	*Orbital period (y d)*	*Mean apparent magnitude*
Luna	Earth	1737	0y 27.3d	-13.0
Phobos	Mars	6	0y 0.3d	11.5
Deimos	Mars	4	0y 30.0d	12.0
Io	Jupiter	1867	0y 1.7d	5.5
etc.				

6.6 Generalization of object types

In the previous section we discussed a specialization procedure, in which subtypes of a more general object type are introduced to declare that specific roles are recorded only for these subtypes. Apart from this top-down procedure, a subtype graph may also arise in a bottom-up way, when we need to introduce a supertype of object types that already occur in the model. The process of introducing a supertype for object types that already exist is known as object type *generalization*. Hence generalization is the reverse of specialization. A supertype is a more general form of its subtypes, and a subtype is a special form of its supertype(s).

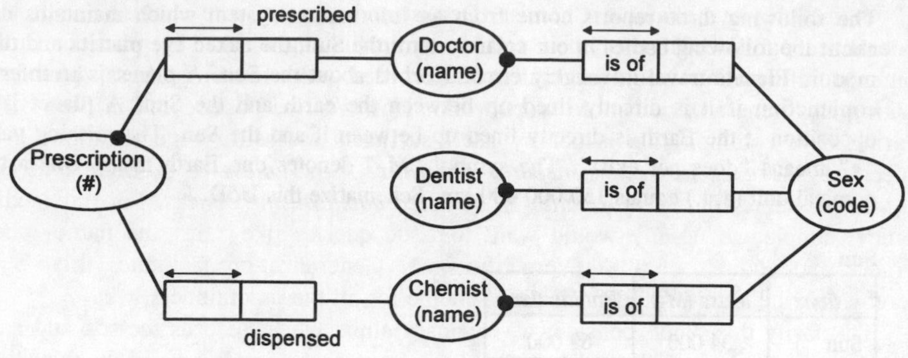

Figure 6.37 A schema before generalization has been applied

Step 3 of the CSDP outlined the main criteria for deciding when to generalize existing object types (e.g. Doctor, Dentist, Chemist) into a more general type (e.g. Practitioner), but at that stage we ignored any need to retain one or more of the original object types as subtypes of the new general type. This need arises when the original object types have specific roles. As a simple example, consider Figure 6.37. Here sex is recorded for each kind of practitioner. If we want to list all the practitioners together in some query then we should introduce a practitioner supertype, attach the common role to it, and add a fact type to retain the classification scheme (see Figure 6.38). We have assumed that all practitioners can be identified simply by their name, and that chemists, dentists and doctors are mutually exclusive.

The original schema shows that prescriptions may be prescribed only by doctors, and dispensed only by chemists (i.e. pharmacists). These constraints are retained in the new schema by using Doctor and Chemist subtypes for the prescription predicate. For this simple example, no specific role is recorded only for dentists, so there is no need to display a dentist subtype.

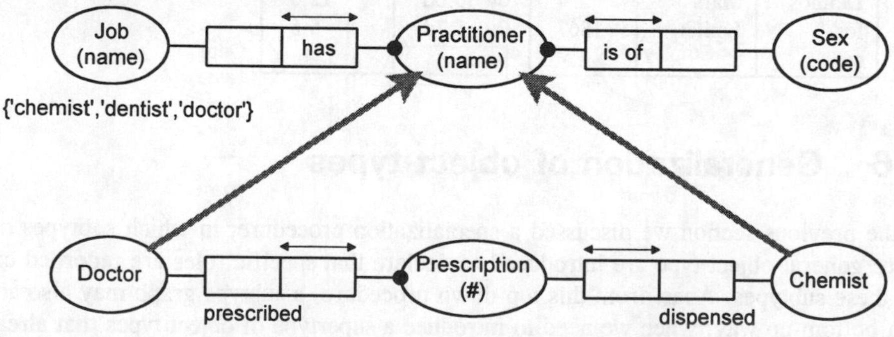

Figure 6.38 The schema after generalization has been applied

In the previous example Chemist, Dentist and Doctor were exclusive, but were generalized partly because of their common role (having a sex). In practice, further common information would normally be recorded (e.g. name, address, birthdate), making this generalization more worthwhile. However, as pointed out in Step 3, the sharing of a common role is not by itself sufficient to justify generalization. *If the object types are exclusive, we needn't generalize them unless in a single query we require the same kind of information to be listed about all the objects.* For our medical clinic example we usually would want to issue queries like "List the name, phone number and address of all the practitioners". Generalization facilitates this, if we thereby provide a uniform identification scheme for all the practitioners.

To clarify this point, consider a veterinary clinic which records the sex and name of its employees, as well as the sex and name of the animals treated in the clinic. Employees are identified by employee numbers, but animals are identified by some other scheme (e.g. combining their name with the client# of their owner). It would be highly unlikely that we would ever want to list the same information about the staff and the animals together in the same query. So Employee and Animal may be left as primitive object types, without generalizing them to EmployeeOrAnimal.

As a related example, consider the schema of Figure 6.39. Here an organization records the cars owned by its employees (e.g. to help the car park attendant to check whether a car is legally parked). It also records equipment (e.g. computers, photocopiers) owned by its departments. Cars are identified by their registration number and equipment items by an item number. Here the ownership predicate appears twice in the schema. Employee and Department are exclusive, but both play the role of owning. Car and Equipment are exclusive, but both play the role of being owned.

Suppose we generalize Employee and Department to Owner, and Car and Equipment to Asset. As an exercise, try to draw the resulting schema for yourself. The ownership predicate now appears just once, in the fact type Owner owns Asset. But the rest of the schema is less tidy. New identifiers are required for the general types, and classification predicates must be added. For example: Owner(owner#) is of OwnerKind (code) {'Emp','Dep'}; Asset (asset#) has AssetKind (code) {'Car','Equip'}.

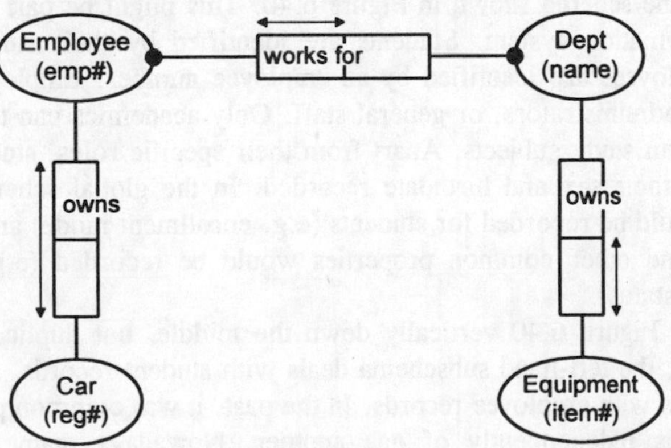

Figure 6.39 Should the object types be generalized?

It would be wrong to model the working predicate as Owner works for Owner. Because of their specific roles (working, employing), Employee and Department are retained as subtypes, so we still have the fact type Employee works for Department. Subtype definitions need to be added. Assuming the subtypes inherit the identifiers of their supertype, the employee number and department name predicates must now be explicitly depicted as fact types. Moreover, additional textual constraints need to be specified to declare that each Equipment item is owned by at most one Department (note the different constraints on the original ownership predicates), that only employees own cars, and that only departments own equipment.

Should we generalize exclusive object types in such a case? Not unless we want to ask a common question for all members of the general type (e.g. List all owners and their assets). If the objects are not to be listed together in the same column of an output report, then there is no need to generalize them. The more common properties there are, the more likely it is that such queries would be formulated.

If we don't generalize object types that share common roles, we allow the same predicate name to be repeated on the schema. For example, in Figure 6.39 there are two predicates called "owns". On a diagram, we can distinguish between these predicates simply by their position (e.g. by pointing to them). In a CASE tool environment, two predicates with the same external name may be distinguished internally by different names or surrogate codes (e.g. "owns1", "owns2" or "P65", "P66"). Apart from such obvious cases as "has" and "is of" however, if we find ourselves duplicating a predicate name on a schema we should ask ourselves whether we ought to generalize. CASE tools can assist here by prompting the designer appropriately.

The examples so far have considered exclusive types. What about overlapping types? Recall that the primitive entity types on a conceptual schema are taken to be mutually exclusive. The only way we can allow different entity types on a schema to overlap is to make them subtypes of something else. So generally speaking, if we find we have two primitive entity types on our schema which do overlap then we should introduce a supertype for them. In rare cases however, we might portray entity types that overlap in reality, to be mutually exclusive in our model, because we are not interested in knowing about any overlap for our application.

Consider the schema shown in Figure 6.40. This might be part of a schema for a university information system. Students are identified by their student number, and university employees are identified by an employee number. Employees are classified as academics, administrators, or general staff. Only academics can teach subjects, and only students can study subjects. Apart from their specific roles, students and employees both have their sex and birthdate recorded. In the global schema, other specific information would be recorded for students (e.g. enrollment mode) and employees (e.g. department); and other common properties would be recorded (e.g. name, address, phone, marital status).

If you cut Figure 6.40 vertically down the middle, but duplicate Sex, Date and Subject in both, the left-hand subschema deals with student records, and the right-hand subschema deals with employee records. In the past, it was common practice to develop such subsystems independently of one another. Nowadays many organizations are integrating their subsystems into a general system to provide access to more information and to enforce constraints between the formally separate schemas.

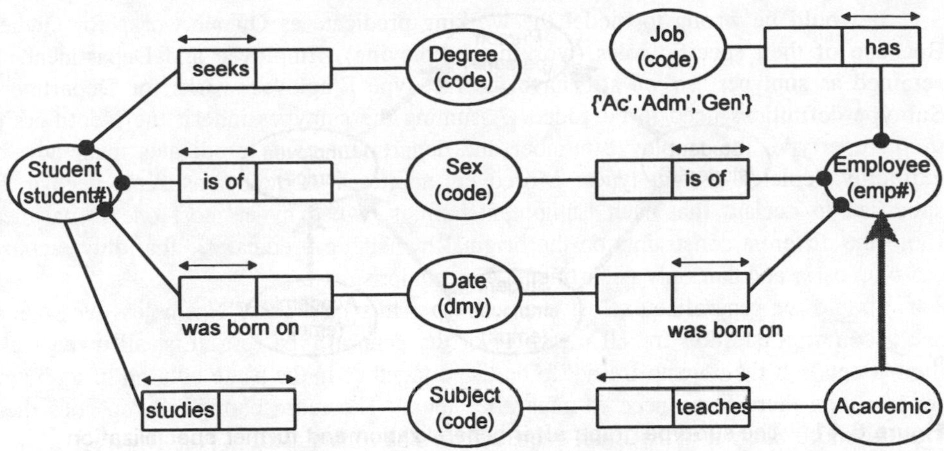

Figure 6.40

Suppose Student and Employee are mutually exclusive. In spite of their common roles, it is unlikely that we want to list such information for both students and employees in the same query. In this case we may leave the schema as it is.

Now suppose that in the real world Student and Employee overlap (i.e. a student may be an employee at the same time). If we want to model this possibility we must introduce a supertype (e.g. Person). Suppose however that we are not interested in knowing whether a student is an employee. If we are sure about this, and we have no common question for the two types, then we may leave the schema as is. However, our model now differs in this respect from the real world.

By presenting Student and Employee as primitive, our model declares that these types are exclusive, whereas in reality they overlap. To avoid misunderstanding, any such disagreement between the model and reality must be clearly documented in the technical and user manuals for the application, so that people are adequately warned of this decision.

Such decisions should not be taken lightly, as there will often be good reasons for wanting to know whether some instance is a member of both types. For example, suppose we want to enforce the constraint that no academic can be enrolled in a subject he or she is teaching. If we want the information system to enforce this constraint for us, we have to provide it with a way of detecting whether some student is an employee. To do this we must introduce a supertype (e.g. Person) preferably with a global identification scheme (e.g. person#).

Moreover, we might want to record specific data for student employees (e.g. study leave): in this case we also need to introduce StudentEmployee as a subtype of both Student and Employee. Figure 6.41 depicts the subtype graph for this situation. As an exercise, expand this graph to the full schema by adding fact types and subtype definitions. The sex and birthdate fact types attach to Person. If included, the constraint about teachers should be specified textually.

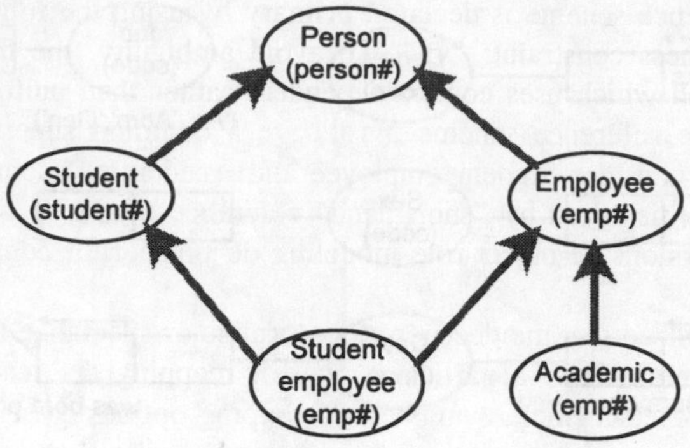

Figure 6.41 The subtype graph after generalization and further specialization

Note that one or more predicates should be attached to Person to classify people into students and employees. We could use the unary predicates IsStudent and IsEmployee if we made their disjunction mandatory. The procedure for generalizing object types may now be summarized as follows. Here *A* and *B* are entity types which are initially depicted separately, with no common supertype.

Generalization Procedure (GP):

if *A* and *B* overlap, or can be compared (e.g. to compute ratios)
and we are interested in modeling this
or
A and *B* are mutually exclusive
and common information is recorded for both
and we wish to list *A* and *B* entities together for this information

then introduce their supertype $A \cup B$ with its own identification scheme;
add predicate(s) to the supertype to classify members into *A*, *B*;
attach common roles to the supertype;
if *A* (or *B*) plays some specific roles
then define it as a subtype and attach these roles

Another feature of Figure 6.41 needs discussion. Up to now we have assumed that subtypes always inherit the identification scheme of the root supertype, and hence have omitted reference display from the subtype nodes. In practice however, we sometimes use a primary identification scheme for a subtype which is different from that of its supertype. In this case we have a *context-dependent reference scheme*, since the primary identifier of an object depends on the context in which it is being considered.

Suppose that within the context of student records, we want to identify students by student#, and in the context of employee records we want to identify employees by emp#. We indicate this choice on the subtype graph by *specifying the primary reference scheme for each node in the subtype graph* (see Figure 6.41). Note that StudentEmployee still inherits student# but now as a fact type not a reference type.

A composite reference scheme is declared primary by using the following symbol for the external uniqueness constraint: "Ⓟ". To avoid ambiguity, the following rules apply to a subtype graph which uses context-dependent rather than uniform reference. Subtypes with the same reference scheme must have a common supertype with this reference scheme (e.g. consider Student_employee and Academic). Context-dependent reference should not be displayed by "short-hand" reference modes (e.g. name, code, nr). Note that some versions of object-role modeling do not permit context-dependent reference at all.

It should be emphasized that the decision to generalize or specialize is a conceptual one. This does not commit us to a particular way of mapping the resulting subtype graph to a logical database schema. A number of mapping options exist (e.g. subtypes may be absorbed into the same table as their supertype, or mapped to separate tables). In a later chapter we discuss these mapping options in detail.

Exercise 6.6

1. A taxi company records these details about its employees: employee#; name; address; sex; phone; salary; and weight. It records these details about its cars: reg#; model; year manufactured; cost; and weight. It also records who drives what cars (optional *m:n*).
   (a) Schematize this UoD without subtyping. Use two predicates with the external name "weighs".
   (b) Generalize Employee and Car, so that "weighs" appears only once.
   (c) Which of these solutions is preferable? Discuss.

2. A hospital maintains an information system about its employees and patients. The following report is an extract from its **employee records**. Employees are standardly identified by their employee number (emp#). Each employee has exactly one job: administrator (admin); doctor (doc); or pharmacist (pharm). A pager is a portable electronic device which beeps when its number is rung. Some employees are assigned unique initials, which may be used as a secondary identifier. The mark "–" means "inapplicable because of other data".

emp#	*name*	*job*	*office*	*pager#*	*initials*
e10	Adams A	admin	G17	–	–
e20	Watson M	doc	302	5333	MW1
e30	Jones E	pharm	–	–	EJ
e40	Kent C	admin	G17	–	–
e50	Kildare J	doc	315	5400	JK
e60	Brown C	pharm	–	–	CB
e70	Collins T	pharm	–	–	TC
e80	Watson M	doc	315	5511	MW2

In the following extract from the **patient records**, patients are standardly identified by their patient number (pat#), and are typed as in-patients (in) or out-patients (out), but not both. Some patients are placed in wards. Patients may be allergic to various drugs. Prescriptions are identified by their script#. Each dispensed prescription has been prescribed by a doctor, dispensed by a pharmacist, and issued to a patient. Each prescription specifies exactly one drug. Since initials are easier for humans to remember, they are used in this report; however, the system uses emp# as the primary identifier for employees. Unlike "–", a blank simply means "not recorded".

				Prescriptions dispensed to patients			
pat#	*type*	*ward*	*allergies*	*script#*	*prescriber*	*dispenser*	*drug*
p511	in	5B	aspirin doxepin	7001	MW1	EJ	warfarin
p632	out	–		7132 7250	JK MW1	CB EJ	aspirin paracetamol
p760	in	4C	warfarin	8055	JK	EJ	aspirin
p874	in	5B					

The population is significant with respect to mandatory roles, and the subtype graph. Note however that any patient may be dispensed a prescription, any doctor may prescribe one, and any pharmacist may dispense one.

(a) In the real world, *no patient can be an employee*. Schematize this UoD.

(b) In reality, a patient may be an employee. However we are not interested in knowing facts of this kind. What changes, if any, should you make to the model or the system documentation.

(c) In reality, a patient may be an employee. Moreover, the hospital has recently decided that facts of this kind should be known. For example, we may want to ensure that no doctor prescribes a drug for himself/herself. The hospital is willing to replace its old identification schemes for employees and patients by a new one. Modify your schema to deal with this situation.

(d) In reality, a patient may be an employee, and we want to know this. However the hospital demands that emp# and pat# be retained as primary identifiers within their context. Modify your schema to deal with this situation.

6.7 Summary

In CSDP *step 6* we add any value, set comparison (subset, equality, exclusion), and subtype constraints. A *value constraint* specifies the members of a value type. It may provide a *full listing* or *enumeration* of all the values (e.g. {'M','F'}). It may specify a *subrange definition* (e.g. {1..7}, {'A'..'E'}). Or it may indicate a *format pattern* (e.g. ⟨c20⟩ allows any string of up to 20 characters, and ⟨aaddd⟩ or ⟨2a3d⟩ requires two letters followed by three digits). If "a" or "c" is used, the value type is a subtype of String; otherwise the host type may be String or Number (as indicated by "+" after the type name or reference mode).

A *lazy entity type* is a primitive entity type whose disjunction of fact roles is optional. Lazy atomic entity types have " !" appended to their name. For example, we may populate a reference table for "Country !" with the names of all existing countries, even if some of these countries do not play in any facts. In principle, the values which reference members of a lazy object type could instead be declared in a value constraint; however this is awkward if there are many values or the values may change.

A *set* is determined by its members, so order and repetition don't matter (e.g. $\{3,6\} = \{6,3,6\}$). A *bag* or *multiset* makes repetition significant (e.g. $[3,6] = [6,3]$ but $[3,6] \neq [3,6,6]$). A *sequence* is an ordered bag (e.g. $\langle 3,6 \rangle \neq \langle 6,3 \rangle$). A set A is a *subset* of B (written $A \subseteq B$) iff each member of A belongs to B; in this case B is a *superset* of A. A is a *proper subset* of B iff $A \subseteq B$ and $A \neq B$. A and B are *mutually exclusive* or disjoint iff they have no common members (i.e. their *intersection*, $A \cap B = \{\ \}$). If sets have common members they *overlap*; if each also has extra members, we have a case of *proper overlap*.

Set comparison constraints restrict the way the population of a role, or role sequence, relates to the population of another. Let *rs1* and *rs2* be role sequences (of one or more roles) played by compatible object types. A *subset constraint* from *rs1* to *rs2* is denoted by a dotted arrow "□---->□", indicating pop(*rs1*) ⊆ pop(*rs2*). An *equality constraint* is equivalent to subset constraints in both directions, and is shown by a dotted arrow with two heads "□<---->□", demanding that pop(*rs1*) = pop(*rs2*). An *exclusion constraint* among two or more role sequences is shown by connecting them to "⊗" with dotted lines: this means their populations must be disjoint.

If each role sequence contains two roles, we talk of *pair*-subset, pair-equality and pair-exclusion. A tuple-subset constraint implies simple subset constraints. A simple exclusion constraint implies tuple exclusion. Role sequences may not simultaneously be whole arguments to both subset and exclusion constraints.

An object type A is a (proper) subtype of B iff ($A \neq B$ and) for each database state, pop(A) ⊆ pop(B). We show this by a *solid arrow* from A to B: ○——>○. If A is a subtype of B, and B is a subtype of C then it is transitively implied that A is a subtype of C; such indirect subtype links should not be displayed.

An object type may have many subtypes and many supertypes. Subtype connections among a family of compatible object types are displayed in a directed, acyclic *subtype graph*. This graph has exactly one root node (or top), which must be a primitive entity type (or, in rare cases, a nested object type).

With our approach, subtypes are introduced to declare that one or more roles are played only by that subtype. This is known as *specialization*. Subtypes inherit all the roles of their supertype(s), as well as having at least one specific role. By default, a subtype inherits the primary reference scheme of the root supertype; in this case the reference scheme is not displayed on the subtype. With subtypes (and objectified predicates), any mandatory roles must be explicitly shown. Each subtype must be formally defined using one or more roles of its supertype(s). For example, each Woman is a Person who is of Sex 'F'. With our approach, subtypes must be well-defined and all relevant constraints on defining predicates must be declared; this ensures that any subtype exclusion "⊗" or totality "⊙" constraints that do exist are implied. Note that exclusive object types (e.g. Man, Woman) cannot have a common subtype.

Output reports often have missing values or null values. Subtyping is indicated if a missing value means *"not to be recorded"* (i.e. inapplicable because of other recorded data). In this book we use a minus sign "–" for this purpose. If an output report is significant with respect to the subtype graph we can determine the graph by examining the pattern of "–" marks. However, background knowledge is required to determine the subtype definitions, and hence meaningful subtype names. Input forms often provide a set of conditional instructions which indicate the conditions under which particular entries on the form are needed. Such instructions can be used to deduce the subtyping constraints.

If we don't have a full set of output reports, we may wrongly declare object types to be primitive. There is then a need to introduce supertypes: this is called object type *generalization*. This process is the reverse of specialization. We introduce a supertype if object types overlap, and we want to know about this. A supertype is also introduced if the object types are exclusive, have common roles and we want to list them together for this common information. If the original object types have specific roles as well, they must be retained as subtypes. In this way a subtype graph is developed in a bottom-up fashion. The usual rules about subtype graphs still apply.

In some cases there is a need for subtypes to have a primary reference scheme different from that of their supertype. Such *context-dependent reference* is indicated by displaying the primary reference scheme for each node in the subtype graph.

Chapter notes

Not all versions of ORM allow lazy entity types. Some use other notations for subset constraints (e.g. a circled "<"), and equality constraints (circled "="). Some demand role connectors for a pair of contiguous roles. Most versions of ER do not allow subset, equality and exclusion constraints between role-sequences to be included on the schema diagram. A few do (e.g. Rochfeld et al. 1991), but the notation is comparatively awkward, especially for tuple cases, and can't be populated for validation purposes. Moreoever when attributes are used instead of fact types, ER typically fails to cater for these constraints.

Some versions of ORM allow subtypes with no specific roles, do not require formal subtype definitions, but do require subtype exclusion and exhaustion constraints to be shown explicitly (e.g. see De Troyer 1991). Context-dependent reference is not supported in some versions. The PSM variant adopts a different approach to generalization in which the supertype uses a disjunction of the identification schemes of its subtypes (e.g. see ter Hofstede et al. 1993); although this raises additional implementation problems when a common query is executed on overlapping subtypes, this does provide another solution to the problem.

Some versions of ER do not support subtyping at all. Many newer versions do, but these are often simplistic, using an Euler-based notation and ignoring various cases. A popular commercial implementation is discussed in Barker (1990).

7 Other constraints and final checks

7.1 CSDP step 7: other constraints; final checks

In previous steps of the CSDP, we verbalized familiar examples in terms of elementary facts, sketched the fact types on a diagram, then added various constraints and derivation rules. Most applications include uniqueness, mandatory role, value, set comparison and subtyping constraints. Though less common, other kinds of constraint may also apply. We provide graphic notations for some of these; the rest are specified textually rather than on the diagram. Once all the constraints have been specified, some final checks can be made to help ensure our information model is consistent and free of redundancy. This concludes the basic conceptual schema design procedure.

CSDP step 7: Add other constraints, and perform final checks

This chapter deals with step 7 in detail. The next two sections discuss some important graphic constraints (occurrence frequencies, and ring constraints). Then some other graphic constraints are briefly introduced (e.g. join constraints, relative closure). After that, we consider some constraints that must be declared textually. Finally we examine some ways of checking that the schema is consistent and redundancy-free.

7.2 Occurrence frequencies

To indicate that each entry in a fact column must appear there *exactly n times*, we write "*n*" beside the role (see Figure 7.1). This is called an **occurrence frequency constraint** since it restricts the frequency with which any given entry occurs in a given fact column, in any given state of the database.

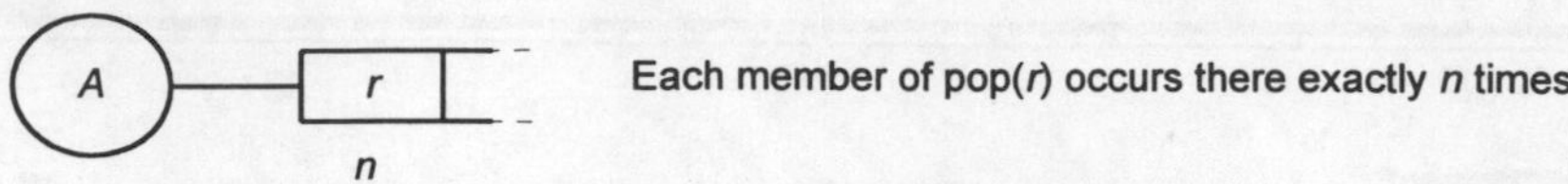

Figure 7.1 A simple occurrence frequency constraint on role *r*

If $n = 1$, this is equivalent to a uniqueness constraint—in this case the usual arrow-tipped bar notation for uniqueness should be used instead of a "1" mark. One use of occurrence frequencies is to ensure that details are recorded for all instances of an enumerated object type. For example, suppose a company stocks and sells three kinds of computer drives (F = Floppy disk drive, H = Hard disk drive, T = tape drive), and operates in just two cities (Los Angeles and Tokyo). Now consider the populated conceptual schema shown in Figure 7.2.

The frequency constraint of 3 on the first role requires each city that occurs in the first column to do so three times. The uniqueness constraint across the first two roles ensures that each ⟨City, DriveKind⟩ pair appears on only one row. Hence if any stock figures are recorded for a city, then figures for all three kinds of drive must be recorded. Similarly, the frequency constraint of 2 on the second role ensures that each drive kind in the second column must appear there twice. Because of the uniqueness constraint, this means that if stock is recorded for a drive kind then figures for both cities must be included.

Here the combination of occurrence frequency, uniqueness and value constraints ensures that any stock figures that are kept are *complete* with respect to both cities and drive kinds. A compound transaction is needed to initially populate this fact type, requiring at least six facts to be added.

Sometimes, an occurrence frequency constraint spans two or more roles of a fact type. In this case, we link the relevant roles by a line and write the number beside this line. This is called a *compound occurrence frequency*.

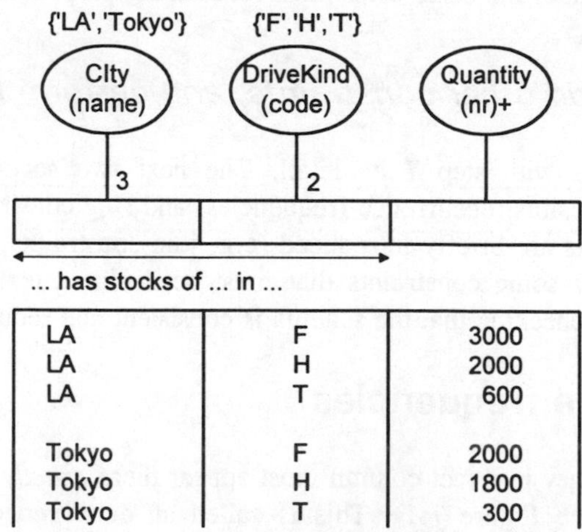

Figure 7.2 Stock figures are recorded for each city and each kind of drive

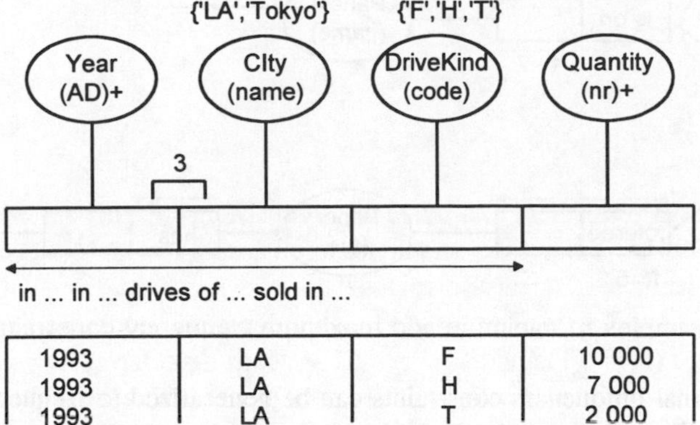

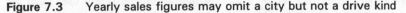

Figure 7.3 Yearly sales figures may omit a city but not a drive kind

For example, in Figure 7.3 each ⟨Year, City⟩ pair in the fact table must occur there three times. Given the uniqueness constraint across the first three roles, sales must be recorded for all three drives for each ⟨Year, City⟩ pair in the table. Note however that this schema does not require that yearly sales be recorded for both cities. The population shown includes only one city, yet it satisfies all the constraints.

Figure 7.4 strengthens the constraints by requiring yearly sales figures for both cities as well as the three kinds of drive. Given the uniqueness and value constraints, this is achieved by the simple occurrence frequency of 6 on the first role—as an easy exercise, prove this. The compound frequency of 3 across ⟨Year, City⟩ is omitted since it is implied. A compound frequency of 2 across ⟨Year, DriveKind⟩ is also implied, and hence omitted.

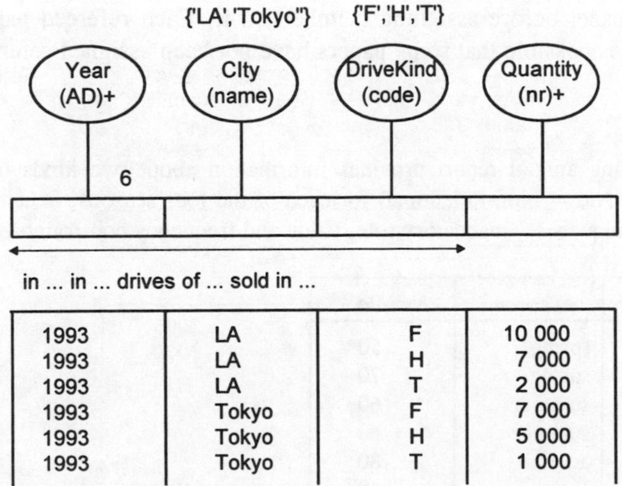

Figure 7.4 Yearly sales figures must cover both cities and all three drive kinds

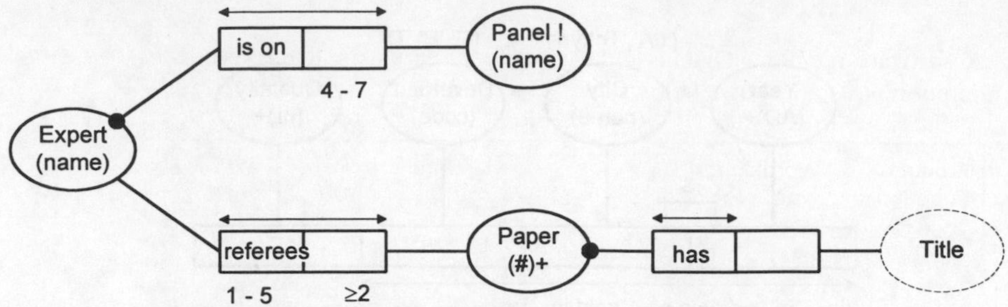

Figure 7.5 Examples of minimum and maximum frequency constraints

Just as internal uniqueness constraints can be generalized to frequency constraints, we could generalize external uniqueness constraints and mark these as a circled *n* (*n* > 1) instead of a circled "u". However such a constraint would be rarely used, and we make no use of this notation in this book.

In place of an exact occurrence frequency, we may need to declare a frequency constraint of *at most n* where *n* > 1. This may be marked either as 1–*n* or as ≤*n*. A frequency constraint of *at least n* is shown as ≥*n*. Finally, a frequency constraint of *at least n and at most m* is shown as *n–m*. Since occurrence frequencies apply to entries in columns, a lower frequency of 1 is the smallest frequency allowed (since each entry in a column is already there once). Because the constraint applies to the population of the role(s), not the population of the object type(s), it doesn't make sense to declare an occurrence frequency of zero. An optional role indicates that members of an object type population might not play the role at all.

As an example, consider Figure 7.5. This is part of a schema for a conference application. Each expert is on at least one panel (as shown by the mandatory role) and referees at most 5 papers (possibly none, since the role is optional). Each panel with members has at least 4 and at most 7 members. Since Panel is lazy, we may record the existence of a panel before assigning members to it. Each refereed paper has at least two referees. It is possible that some papers have not been assigned referees yet.

Exercise 7.2

1. The following annual report provides information about two kinds of DBMS (R = Relational, NR = Non-Relational) for each of the four seasons. Schematize this UoD, including uniqueness, mandatory role, value and frequency constraints.

Database	*Season*	*Nr sold*
R	spring	50
NR	spring	70
R	summer	60
NR	summer	60
R	autumn	80
NR	autumn	40
R	winter	120
NR	winter	15

2. A software retailer maintains a database about various software products. two sample output reports are shown below.

Product: WordLight 4.0 **List price:** *ex tax* $500 *with tax* $600
Functions: word processor

	Poor	*OK*	*Good*	*Excellent*
Performance			✓	
Documentation				✓
Ease of learning			✓	
Ease of use			✓	
Error handling				✓
Support			✓	
Value				✓

Release date: 1993 Feb
Next upgrade: ?

Product: PCjobs 1.0 **List price:** *ex tax* $1000 *with tax* $1200
Functions: word processor
spreadsheet
database

	Poor	*OK*	*Good*	*Excellent*
Performance			✓	
Documentation	✓			
Ease of learning		✓		
Ease of use	✓			
Error handling		✓		
Support			✓	
Value		✓		

Release date: 1992 Oct
Next upgrade: 1993 Jun

There is a sales tax of 20 percent on all software. The *ex tax* price excludes this tax; the *with tax* price includes it. The functions of a software product are the tasks it can perform. A "✓" indicates the rating of the product for the criterion listed on that row (e.g. both products shown have a good performance). A "?" denotes missing information.

Schematize this UoD, including uniqueness, mandatory role, value and occurrence frequency constraints. Specify a rule for any derived fact types. Do not attempt to nest or subtype. Try to capture the information about product evaluation (ratings for performance etc.) in terms of a single fact type.

3. The Megasoft corporation has a number of salespeople. At the start of each year, each salesperson is assigned at most three different software products to sell during that year (not necessarily the same each year). At the end of each year, each salesperson reports how many of each product he/she sold in each month of that year. The corporation maintains an historical information system on who is assigned what to sell in each year, and the monthly sales figures for that person (when the figures are available). No month may be omitted in these annual sales figures. The system retains information from previous years. Schematize this UoD, including relevant value constraints and occurrence frequencies. Make use of nesting.

4. (Acknowledgment: This question is based on an exercise devised by Prof. E. D. Falkenberg, and is used by permission).

The following tables are sample reports from a system which maintains information about communities and roads. A "–" mark means "inapplicable because of other data" (see the explanatory notes). Mayors are identified by the combination of their first name and surname. A person can be mayor of only one city, and each city has exactly one mayor. Each road connects *exactly two* communities.

Schematize this UoD, including uniqueness, mandatory role, value, subtype and frequency constraints.

Community	*Population*	*Longitude* *	*Latitude* *	*Size (sq. km)* **	*Mayor* ***	
					Firstname	*Surname*
Astraluna	900 000	–	–	145	Fred	Bloggs
Bradman	90 000	+120°50′	+48°45′	12	–	–
Cupidville	9 000	+120°50′	+48°40′	–	–	–

Notes:

* Recorded only for villages and towns (at most 100 000 inhabitants).

** Recorded only for towns and cities (more than 10 000 inhabitants).

*** Recorded only for cities (more than 100 000 inhabitants).

Road number	*Kind of road* *	*Connection* **		*Length (km)*	*Average travel time* ***	*Maximum slope (%)* ****
		Community	*Community*			
11000	f	Astraluna	Bradman	25	0 h 20 m	–
11500	h	Astraluna	Bradman	22	0 h 25 m	2
11561	p	Bradman	Cupidville	17	0 h 20 m	2
11562	d	Bradman	Cupidville	15	–	15

Notes:

* f = freeway; h = highway; p = paved minor road; d = dirt road.

** All connections are two-way (so the order of the connection is irrelevant).

*** Recorded only for freeways, highways and paved minor roads.

**** Recorded only for dirt roads, paved minor roads and highways.

7.3 Ring constraints

When two roles in a predicate are played by the same object type, the path from the object type through the role pair and back to the object type forms a "ring". If the roles are played by subtypes with a common supertype, the path from and back to the supertype also forms a ring. The role pair may form a binary predicate, or be part of a longer predicate (see the shaded role pairs in Figure 7.6). A *ring constraint* may apply only to a pair of roles like this.

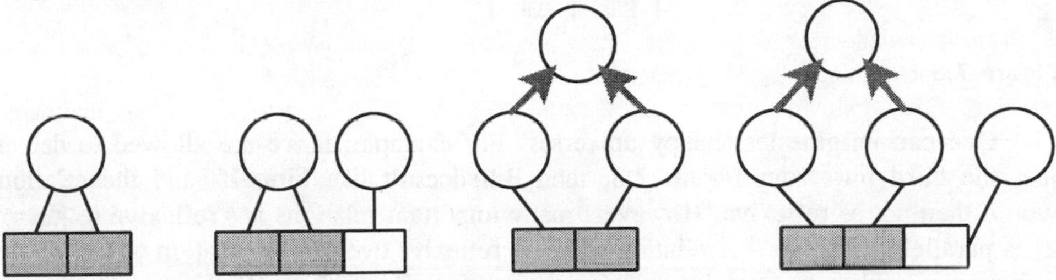

Figure 7.6 Ring constraints may apply to the shaded role pairs

Before discussing the various kinds of ring constraint, some standard definitions from the logic of relations are noted. We use Figure 7.7 as a template to discuss any ring binary (the predicate *R* might be obtained from a longer predicate by projecting on roles *r1* and *r2*, and *A* might be a supertype of the object types playing *r1* and *r2*). For each state of the database, pop(*r1*,*r2*) is a set of ordered pairs, and hence a relation, of type *R*. We allow derived as well as stored relations.

The infix notation "*xRy*" (read "*x Rs y*") is convenient for defining various properties of relations such as reflexivity, symmetry and transitivity. We discuss such notions by way of example. Consider the populated fact type shown in Figure 7.8. The fact table or relation contains three facts. Note that, for this population, each person likes himself/herself. Suppose that in our UoD, this is true for all possible populations—each person who plays the role of liking or of being liked, must like himself/herself. In this case, the Likes predicate is said to be ***reflexive over its population***. For the general case shown in Figure 7.7, we have:

R **is reflexive over its population** iff, for all *x* in pop(r1) ∪ pop(r2), *xRx*

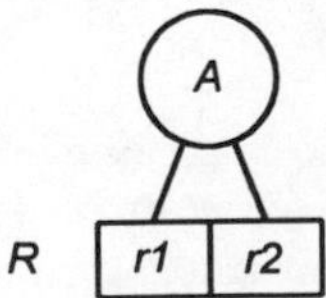

Figure 7.7 A ring binary (possibly embedded in a longer fact type)

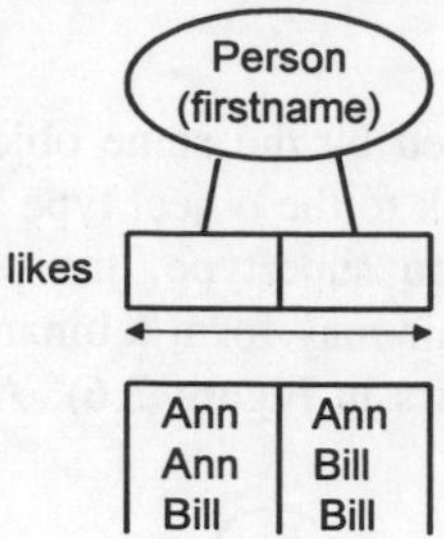

Figure 7.8

One can imagine less happy universes. For example, if we are allowed to delete just the third row from Figure 7.8, then Bill doesn't like himself, and the relation would then not be reflexive. However, many important relations are reflexive (e.g. =, ≤, is parallel to, implies). A relation which is reflexive over the population of the whole universe is said to be "totally reflexive" (i.e. for all x, xRx). Of the four examples cited, only "=" is totally reflexive. For example, "implies" is defined for propositions but not for people (people do not imply people). When we say a relation is reflexive we usually mean reflexive over its population (not necessarily over everything in the universe).

Now suppose that in our UoD, anybody who likes a person is liked by that person. One satisfying population comprises the three facts: Ann likes Bill; Bill likes Bill; Bill likes Ann. Here given any persons x and y, not necessarily distinct, if x likes y then y likes x. If this is always the case, we say that Likes is *symmetric*. Using "→" for "implies", we may define this notion for any predicate R as follows:

R is **symmetric** iff for all x, y $\quad xRy \rightarrow yRx$

Now suppose that for our UoD if one person likes a second, and the second person likes a third, then the first person must like the third. In this case we say that likes is *transitive*. The definition includes the case where the persons are the same.

Table 7.1 illustrates this property. In general, transitivity may be defined as follows. Here we use "&" for "and", and give "&" precedence over "→" (so that the & operation is evaluated first). Note that x, y and z need not be distinct.

R is **transitive** iff for all x, y, z $\quad xRy \;\&\; yRz \rightarrow xRz$

Table 7.1 For this population, the Likes relation is transitive

Likes:

liker	*likee*
Ann	Bill
Bill	Colin
Ann	Colin
David	Ann
David	Bill
David	Colin

Table 7.2 Extract from a poorly constructed table of synonyms

Word	*Synonym*
abandon	leave, forsake, relinquish
abate	diminish, lessen, reduce, decline
abbreviate	shorten, reduce, condense
:	:
condense	compress, consolidate, abridge
:	:
reduce	shorten, weaken, abate
:	:

We leave it as an exercise to prove that a relation which is both symmetric and transitive must also be reflexive over its population. A relation which is reflexive, symmetric and transitive is called an "RST relation" or "equivalence relation". The classic example of this is the identity relation "=".

Relational properties such as reflexivity, symmetry and transitivity might be thought of as constraints, since they limit the allowable relations. However, we describe such properties as *positive* since they may often be used to *derive* additional facts. For example, suppose we need to maintain information about synonyms. Recall that a synonym for a word has roughly the same meaning as that word. A sample taken from a book of synonyms is shown in Table 7.2.

Suppose we decide to store this information in the has_synonym binary shown in Figure 7.9 (a). Is this reflexive? Although one might argue that each word is a synonym of itself, this is a trivial result that humans are not usually interested in seeing. So, as far as this relation goes, let us agree that no word is its own synonym (this actually makes the relation irreflexive—we discuss this notion later).

If one word is a synonym of another, then the other is a synonym for it. So has_synonym is symmetric. But Table 7.2, which was extracted from a book of synonyms, violates this condition. For example, the pair ("abbreviate", "reduce") appears in this order only. If we look up the word "reduce" we won't see "abbreviate" as one of its synonyms. This is a defective feature of the synonym book which we should avoid in a computerized synonym system. How can we avoid this problem?

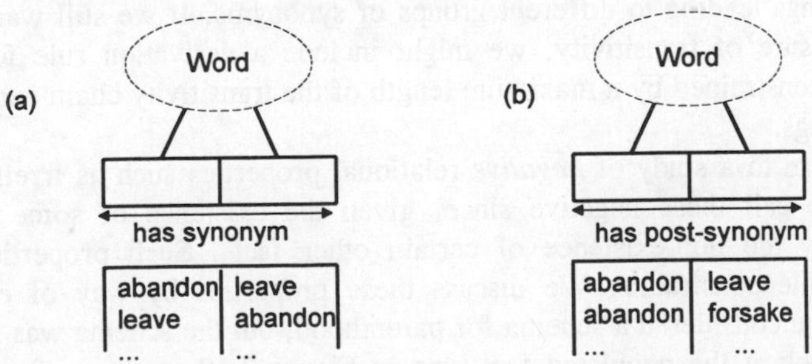

Figure 7.9 Examples of (a) symmetric and (b) asymmetric fact types

In principle, we could add the textual constraint: sym (has_synonym). The notations "reflex(*R*)", "sym(*R*)", and "trans(*R*)" mean that *R* is reflexive, symmetric and transitive respectively. Suppose the symmetric constraint is declared, the table is currently empty, and the following update is attempted:

add: 'abbreviate' has synonym 'shorten'

A naive CIP would simply reject this as violating the symmetry constraint. A more sophisticated CIP might accept the fact and automatically add its converse: "shorten" has synonym "abbreviate". A consistent scheme would be adopted for the delete operation. Although this approach works, it has the disadvantage of doubling the size of the table, since each pair of synonyms is stored twice, once for each ordering.

To save space, we could store each pair in one order only. For example, the post-synonym binary shown in Figure 7.9 (b) has the second member of the pair alphabetically after the first. The pair ⟨"abandon", "leave"⟩ is stored in this order only. The relation is then asymmetric—we discuss this notion later. The larger synonym relation can now be derived, using a derivation rule such as:

Word1 has synonym Word2 **iff** Word1 has post-synonym Word2
or
Word2 has post-synonym Word1

In an SQL system, the derived relation could be defined as a view on the stored relation by making use of the **union** operator (the reader familiar with SQL may wish to do this as an exercise; to speed up queries, both columns can be indexed). In a simple setup, users might perform updates through the stored relation, but issue queries through the derived relation.

Thus, one sometimes has a choice as to whether to capture an aspect of the UoD in terms of a database constraint or as a derivation rule. Here we distinguished the stored and derived fact types by name. Later we consider the possibility of having the same fact type partly stored and partly derived.

Now what about transitivity of synonymy? This issue is complex. You may be familiar with the "bald-hairy paradox" based on the premise: in all cases, if we add one hair to the head of a bald man he is still bald (where is the paradox?). A similar acervus argument can be proposed to argue against synonym transitivity (sequences of approximations finally lead to non-approximations). Moreover the same word may have different meanings leading to different groups of synonyms. If we still want to pursue with some measure of transitivity, we might include a derivation rule for synonym transitivity but constrained by a maximum length of the transitivity chain and relativized to group meanings.

We now turn to a study of *negative* relational properties such as irreflexivity and asymmetry. We call these negative since, given the existence of some facts, such properties imply the non-existence of certain other facts. Such properties are best handled as simple constraints. We discuss these properties by way of example. In previous work we considered a schema for parenthood, but the schema was incomplete. Have a close look at the populated fact type in Figure 7.10, and see if you can spot anything that seems wrong.

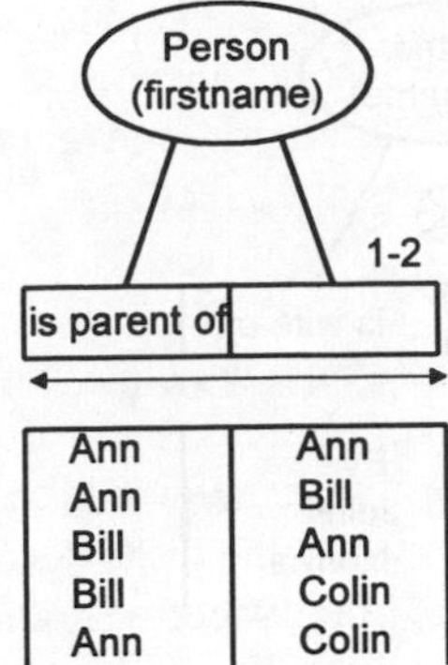

Figure 7.10 What is wrong here?

The population shown is consistent with the constraints specified. But as you no doubt noticed, some of the facts in the table are inconsistent with the real world concept of parenthood. We need to add more constraints so that the information system is able to reject such erroneous populations.

To begin with, the first fact (Ann is parent of Ann) has to be rejected since nobody can be his/her own parent. We say that the parenthood relation is *irreflexive*. We define this notion for any relation type *R* as follows. Here tilde " ~ " denotes the logical "**not**" (i.e. "it is not the case that").

R is **irreflexive** iff for all *x* $\sim xRx$

To indicate that parenthood is irreflexive, we write "°*ir*" beside this predicate on the diagram. The inclusion of the ring-shaped "∘" in this symbol reminds us that this is a ring-constraint. The textual version of this constraint is: "no Person is parent of itself". Figure 7.11 adds this constraint and reduces the population accordingly. A ring constraint may be written beside either role of the role-pair.

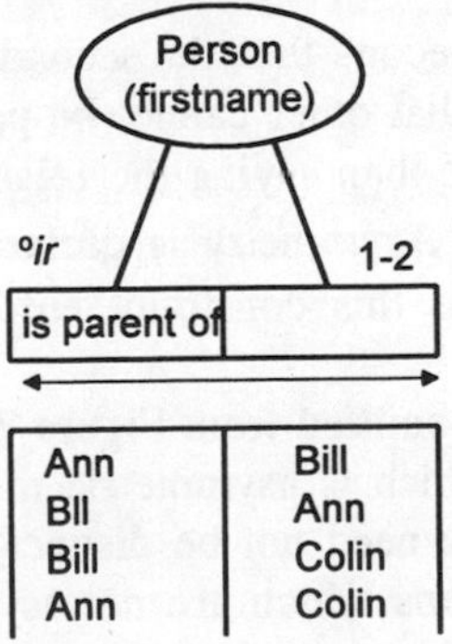

Figure 7.11 The relation is now irreflexive, but something is still wrong

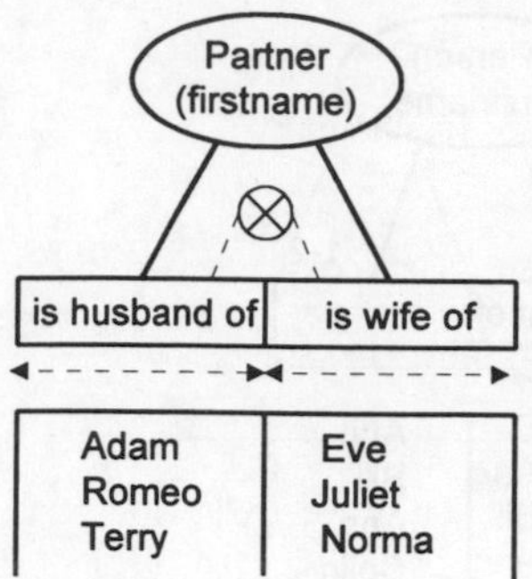

Figure 7.12 The exclusion constraint implies irreflexivity and asymmetry

If the role-pair is embedded in a longer predicate, the roles should be linked by a line " ┌┐ " and the constraint written beside this (as for compound occurrence frequencies).

Note that "irreflexive" is stronger than "not reflexive". For example, if Likes is irreflexive then nobody likes themselves; if some but not all people like themselves then Likes is neither reflexive nor irreflexive. Irreflexivity is an intra-row constraint (i.e. violation of the constraint by a row can be determined by examining that row only). It specifies that no entry may occur in both columns of the same row.

In contrast, an exclusion constraint is much stronger, since it applies between columns. Recall the marriage example (Figure 7.12): here no entry may occur in both columns. Since an exclusion constraint implies irreflexivity we do not display the latter.

Note that the parenthood relation is irreflexive but not exclusive. For example, Bill may appear both as a parent of Colin and as a child of Ann. There are still some problems with Figure 7.11. If we accept the first row we should reject the second. If Ann is a parent of Bill, then it cannot be true that Bill is a parent of Ann. The parenthood relation is *asymmetric*. In general, for any relation type *R*:

R is **asymmetric** iff for all *x, y* $xRy \rightarrow \sim yRx$

That is, if the first object *R*s the second then the second cannot *R* the first. Here, if one person is parent of another then that other cannot be parent of the first. To say that a relation as asymmetric is stronger than saying the relation is not symmetric (we leave the proof of this as an exercise). Asymmetry is declared by writing "°*as*" beside the role-pair (see Figure 7.13). With this constraint enforced, the population has been reduced as shown.

The irreflexive constraint is omitted from Figure 7.13. Is this a mistake? No. It is easy to prove that any relation which is asymmetric must be irreflexive. The proof is left as an exercise (Hint: *x* and *y* need not be distinct). The converse does not hold. There are some irreflexive relations which are not asymmetric (e.g. is sister of). To avoid showing implied constraints, we should omit "°*ir*" if "°*as*" applies. Note that an exclusion constraint implies asymmetry as well as irreflexivity (consider Figure 7.12). We leave the proof of this as an exercise.

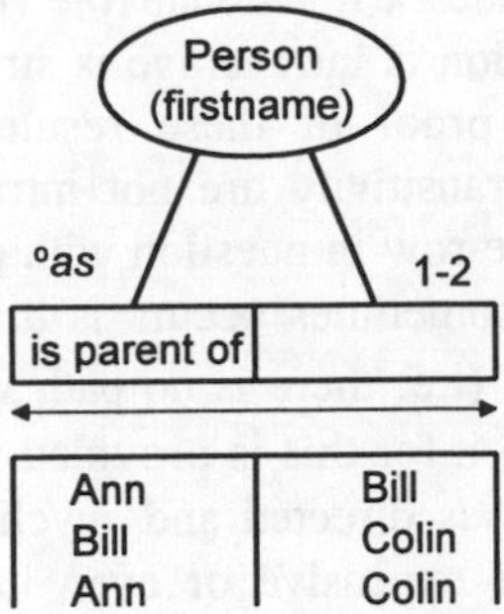

Figure 7.13 The relation is now asymmetric, but something is still wrong

If we remove the requirement for irreflexivity we obtain the weaker property of antisymmetry. For example, ≤ and ⊆ are *antisymmetric* (°*ans*) but not asymmetric. It should be clear that °*as* is just the combination °*ans* and °*ir*.

R is **antisymmetric** iff for all *x, y* $x \neq y \;\&\; xRy \rightarrow \sim yRx$

There is still a problem with Figure 7.13. Can you spot it? Let us agree that incest cannot occur in our UoD. If Ann is parent of Bill and Bill is parent of Colin, then Ann cannot be parent of Colin. The parenthood relation is *intransitive*. In general, for any relation type *R*:

R is **intransitive** iff for all *x, y, z* $xRy \;\&\; yRz \rightarrow \sim xRz$

Here, if one person is a parent of a second and the second person is parent of a third, then the first person cannot be parent of the third. To signify that the parenthood is intransitive we write "°*it*" besides the fact type. Since we already have an asymmetry constraint, we may list the two ring constraints together as shown in Figure 7.14. The population has been reduced to satisfy the constraints.

We leave it as an exercise to prove that intransitivity implies irreflexivity (Hint: *x*, *y* and *z* need not be distinct). The term "atransitive" is sometimes used instead of "intransitive".

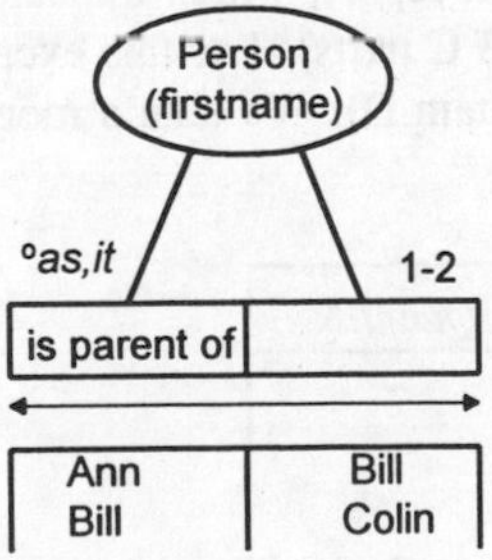

Figure 7.14 The relation is now asymmetric and intransitive

If an irreflexive relation includes a functional role (rather than being *m:n*) it must also be intransitive. Saying a relation is intransitive is stronger than saying the relation is not transitive. We leave the proof of these results as an exercise. Note that antisymmetry, asymmetry and intransitivity are not intra-row constraints, since their enforcement requires comparing the row in question with other existing rows.

Another ring constraint that sometimes occurs is *acyclicity*. A relation is **acyclic** (denoted "°*ac*") if it has no cycles (i.e. there is no path via the relation from an object back to itself). A recursive definition for this is provided in the section exercise. Recall that the graph of a subtype family is directed and acyclic. Because of their recursive nature, acyclic constraints may be expensive or even impossible to enforce in some database systems—in this case the task of checking these constraints may be given to humans rather than the system.

Other properties of ring relations might apply (e.g. connectivity) but we do not discuss them here. A classic example of an embedded ring relation is the "Bill of Materials" or "Parts Explosion" problem, which was included in an earlier Exercise. This involved the ternary: Part contains Part in Quantity. You are invited to provide a more complete solution to this problem in the exercise that follows.

Exercise 7.3

1. For each predicate shown state which, if any, of the following properties hold:

   reflexive, irreflexive
   symmetric, asymmetric
   transitive, intransitive

   (a) has the same age as
   (b) is brother of
   (c) is sibling of
   (d) is shorter than
   (e) is an ancestor of
   (f) is at least as clever as
   (g) lives next to

2. Schematize the following output report, which indicates the composition of items (e.g. Item A contains 2 B parts and 3 C parts). For this exercise read "contains" as "directly contains" (e.g. A does not contain D). We take a more general reading for "contains" in a later exercise.

Item	*Part*	*Quantity*
A	B	2
A	C	1
B	D	1
B	E	3
C	E	3
C	F	2
C	G	3

3. If you are familiar with predicate logic, prove the following theorems.

(a) irreflex(*R*) & trans(*R*) → asym(*R*)

(b) *R* is reflexive over its population iff ∀*xy*(*xRy* ∨ *yRx* → *xRx*). Show this is implied by sym(*R*) & trans(*R*).

4. The diagram shows the conceptual schema and current population for a given UoD. Reference schemes are omitted for simplicity. Fact tables appear next to their fact types. Predicates are identified as **R**..**W**. Constraints are identified as *C1*..*C15*.

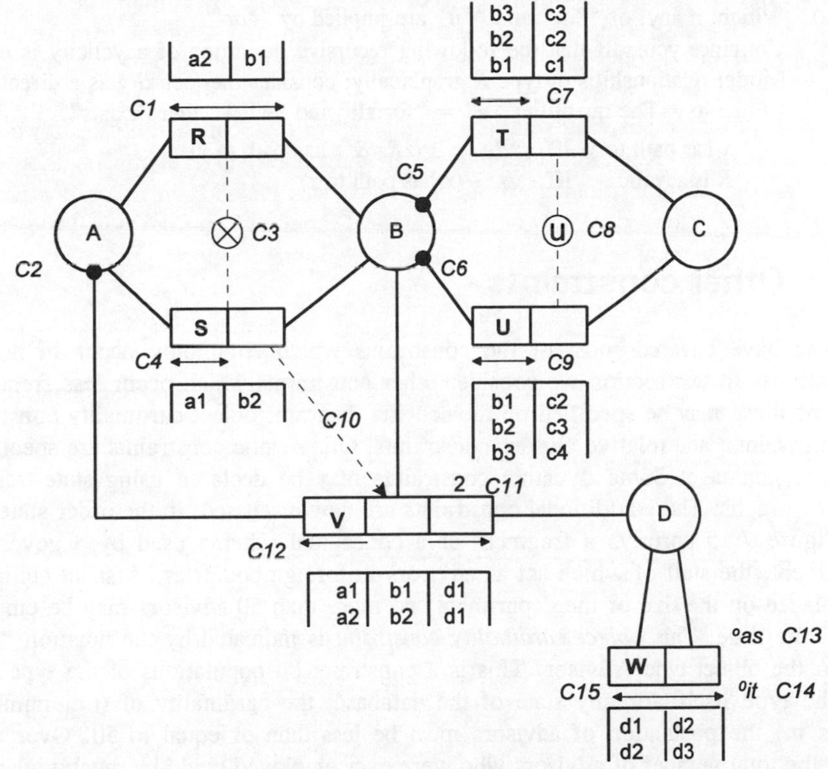

Each of the following requests applies to the **same** database population as shown (i.e. treat each request as if it was the *first* to be made on this population). For each request, indicate the CIP's response. If the request is legal, write "accepted". Otherwise, indicate a constraint violated (e.g. "C2 violated").

(a) add: a1 S b1 (b) add: a3 R b3 (c) add: V a1 b1 d2 (d) add: a1 R b2

(e) add: a1 R b3 (f) add: a2 S b3 (g) delete: b3 T c3

(h) begin
 add: b4 T c1
 add: b4 U c2
end

(i) begin
 add: b4 T c3
 add: b4 U c2
end

(j) begin
 add: V a1 b2 d2
 add: V a1 b3 d2
end

(k) add: d1 W d3 (l) add: d1 W d1

5. Schematize the following output report. Here "bordering" means sharing a land border. In this sense, countries like Australia have no bordering nations.

Nation	*Bordering nations*
Australia	
Belgium	France, Germany, Luxembourg, Netherlands
France	Belgium, Germany, Italy, Luxembourg, Spain, Switzerland
...	...

6. (a) Which, if any, of "°*as*" and "°*it*" are implied by "°*ac*"?
   (b) Convince yourself that the following recursive definition of acyclicity is correct. Model relationships of type *R* graphically: consider the fact *xRy* as a directed line from *x* to *y*. The quantifier "∀" = "for all" and "∃" = "there exists".

   x has path to *y* **iff** *xRy* **or** ∃*z*(*xRz* & *z* has path to *y*)
   R is acyclic **iff** ∀x ~(*x* has path to *x*)

7.4 Other constraints

We now have covered most of the constraints which commonly occur in practical applications. In this section we consider other constraints which occur less frequently. Three of these may be specified on the schema diagram: object cardinality constraints; join constraints; and relative closure constraints. Other static constraints are specified in a textual language. Some dynamic constraints may be declared using state-transition tables or graphs. These additional constraints are now discussed, in the order stated.

Figure 7.15 portrays a fragment of a conceptual schema used by a government department, the staff of which act as advisors in foreign countries. A strict ceiling has been placed on the size of the department: no more than 50 advisors may be employed at any one time. This *object cardinality constraint* is indicated by the notation "#≤50" next to the object type Advisor. This is a constraint on populations of the type rather than the type itself: for any state of the database, the cardinality of (i.e. number of objects in) the population of advisors must be less than or equal to 50. Over a long period the total number of advisors who were ever employed could be much higher.

Object cardinality constraints are rarely included on diagrams, since they are often implied by existing value constraints or occurrence frequency constraints. For example, an {'m','f'} constraint on Sex (code) implies #≤2 on Sex.

The pair-subset constraint in Figure 7.15 declares that if an advisor serves in a country then he or she must speak at least one language used in that country. For example, an advisor serving in Belgium would need to speak Dutch or French since these are the official languages used there. This is an example of a *join constraint* since the ⟨Advisor, Country⟩ pair in the superset position of this constraint is formed by projecting on a natural join of the Speaks and Uses predicates. The roles in this pair are connected by a line; this role-pair is then targeted by the subset constraint. To clarify this, you may wish to populate the fact types with a few lines of data.

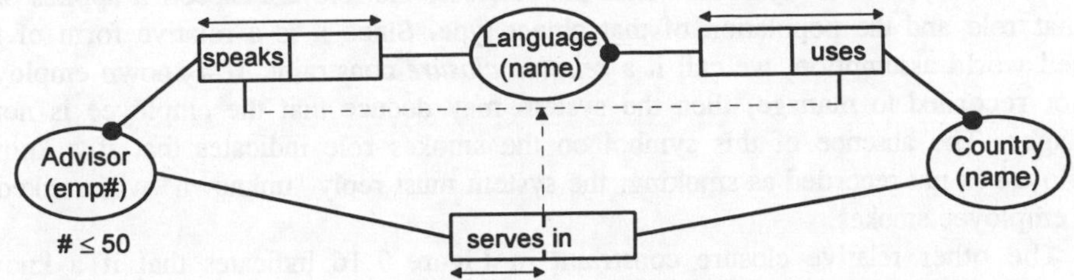

Figure 7.15 An object cardinality constraint and a join subset constraint

In general, if the population of a sequence of roles connected by a line is determined by natural joins or unnesting of the predicates involved, the role sequence may be used in the declaration of compatible set comparison (subset, equality or exclusion), external uniqueness or frequency constraints. In those rare cases where an object type plays more than one role in the join, extra marks are needed to indicate which role(s) is/are used for the join.

Now consider Figure 7.16. Suppose we populate this schema with just the single fact: Employee 501 is of Sex 'M'. In our knowledge base, this employee is not recorded as smoking. Does this mean the employee doesn't smoke in the real world? With a *closed world* approach, the knowledge base has complete information about the UoD; in this case we may deduce that employee 501 does not smoke. With an *open world* approach, the knowledge base may have only incomplete information about the UoD; in this case, employee 501 might actually smoke but we don't know it. This is the approach we take.

Although we adopt an underlying open world semantics, we allow aspects of a schema to be closed by adding constraints. For example, mandatory role and frequency constraints ensure various kinds of completeness in our knowledge. We can also demand completeness of optional information by marking optional roles accordingly. In Figure 7.16 the "□" on the optional manages role indicates that if an employee recorded in the database is a manager, this information is known (to the system).

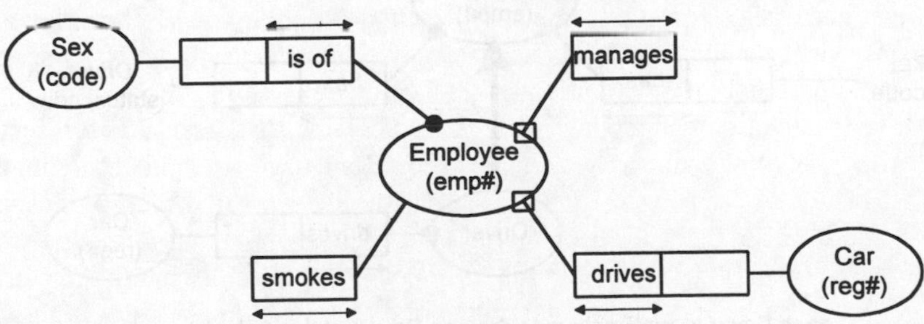

Figure 7.16 If a recorded employee manages or drives a car, these facts are known

Intuitively, the "□" symbol "boxes in" or closes the relevant aspect: it applies only to that role and the population of that object type. Since it is a relative form of the closed world assumption, we call it a *relative closure* constraint. If a known employee is not recorded to manage, then the system may deduce that the employee is not a manager. The absence of this symbol on the smokes role indicates that if a known employee is not recorded as smoking, the system must reply "unknown" when asked if that employee smokes.

The other relative closure constraint in Figure 7.16 indicates that if a known employee drives a car, this is known to the system. Relative closure is defined in such a way that the schema in Figure 7.16 is treated as an abbreviation of the schema in Figure 7.17. Notice the different value constraints in the binary version of the unaries. The schema is implicitly transformed into this unabbreviated version before being mapped to an actual database implementation.

While relative closure constraints provide a safe, convenient way of clarifying how complete our knowledge of optional information is, some modelers may prefer to assume that users fully understand the semantics of optionality and null values that occur in the database implementation.

Like the mandatory role dot, the relative closure box marks a constraint on the population of the object type. Recall that a functional role has a simple uniqueness constraint. For mandatory functional roles the closure constraint is implied and hence omitted. For disjunctive mandatory roles that are exclusive, we will assume closure by default. For disjunctive mandatory roles that are not exclusive, the closure box is positioned half-way towards the relevant role box(es).

There are degrees of information completeness. A stronger form of completeness is closure relative to the actual population of the object type in the universe of discourse (e.g. this would also demand that all employees must be known). A weaker form is closure relative to the role population.

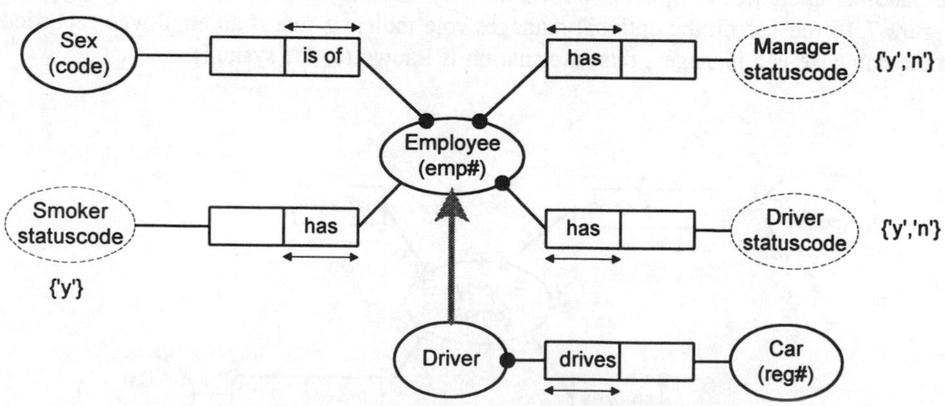

Figure 7.17 An equivalent version of the schema in Figure 7.16

When the role is non-functional, relative closure is not implied by a mandatory role constraint. For example, if each employee must drive a car and may drive several cars, we might want complete information about this.
Such cases are not covered in this book.

We have now met essentially all the graphical notations used on our conceptual schema diagrams. Although we could invent new graphic notations for further constraints, this could make the graphical language hard to learn, and lead to cluttered diagrams. A conceptual schema diagram provides a human-oriented, unambiguous but typically incomplete specification of the UoD structure. Static constraints which cannot be expressed on the diagram may be specified as *textual constraints*, preferably in a high level formal language. Predicates affected by these constraints may be marked with a circled "R" to remind us that extra rules apply. The constraints themselves may be written below the diagram (along with any subtype definitions and derivation rules).

Figure 7.18 includes three textual constraints, labelled TC1-TC3. The first of these indicates that employees joined the firm after their birth year. A pair-exclusion constraint also exists between the birth and appointment predicates, but this is omitted since it is implied by TC1. Constraint TC2 says that non-executives use at most one company car. This is a *restricted uniqueness constraint*, since it strengthens the uniqueness constraint on Employee uses CompanyCar, but restricts this to a subtype of Employee.

Constraint TC3 says that each executive must have use of a company car. This is a *restricted mandatory role constraint*, since it makes a role mandatory for a subtype of Employee. Some other versions of ORM declare restricted constraints by repeating the predicate on the subtype, with the stronger constraint shown there. However, to avoid clutter, we feel the stronger constraints should be graphically displayed only in views which restrict the supertype to the subtype.

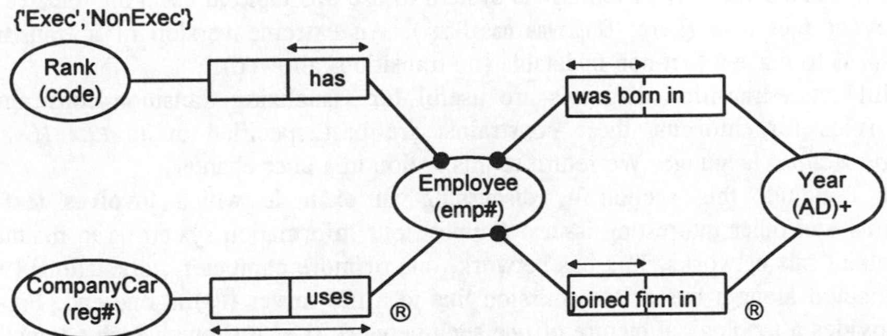

TC1 **If** Employee was born in Year *y1* **and** Employee joined firm in Year *y2* **then** *y1* < *y2*
TC2 **each** Employee **who** has Rank 'Non-Exec' uses **at most one** CompanyCar
TC3 **each** Employee **who** has Rank 'Exec' uses **some** CompanyCar

Figure 7.18 Three examples of textual constraints

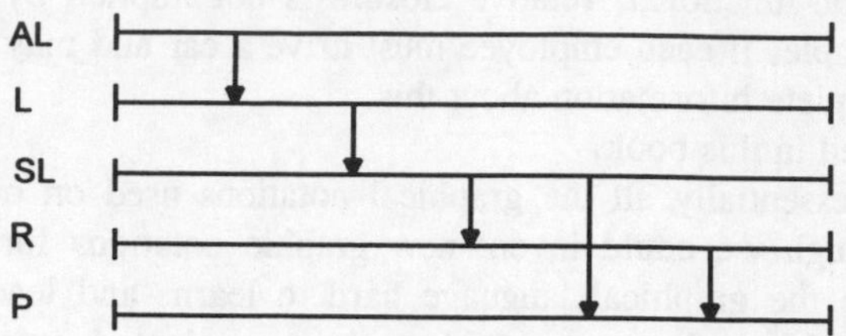

Figure 7.19 A state-transition diagram indicating possible promotions

So far our constraints have been static: they apply to database states, taken one at a time. *Dynamic constraints* restrict changes between database states, typically by specifying what transitions are allowed from one state to the next state. These are often visualized using ***state-transition diagrams***. For example, suppose that the possible ranks of an academic are associate-lecturer (AL), lecturer (L), senior lecturer (SL), reader (R) and professor (P). Here the term "reader" denotes a high ranking position with similar research expectations to "professor".

On a conceptual schema we include the object type Rank (code) {'AL','L','SL','R','P'}. Now suppose that no academic may be demoted, and promotions must comprise a single step to the next rank on the list, except that senior lecturers may be promoted to either reader or professor. Figure 7.19 sets out these restrictions on promotion in a state-transition diagram. Here each state is shown as a named, horizontal bar and allowed transitions are depicted as vertical arrows.

Transition constraints may also be declared in a transition matrix (recall the marital state example from an earlier chapter). We could store the allowed transitions in a fact table (e.g. consider the ring binary: Rank may be promoted to Rank); however we would still need some way of telling the system to use this table in checking updates on the relevant fact type (here: Employee has Rank). An extreme version of a transition constraint is to make a fact non-updatable (no transitions allowed).

While state-transition diagrams are useful for visualizing transition constraints, formal rules for enforcing these constraints are best specified in an *ECA* (*Event-Condition-Action*) language. We return to this notion in a later chapter.

We conclude this section by discussing an example which involves textual constraints and other interesting issues. Suppose our information system is to maintain details about bus networks. In a bus network, one or more computer workstations (WS) are connected along a bus or transmission line to a file-server (FS) at one end. Figure 7.20 provides a topological picture of one such network (i.e. it shows which computers are connected to which but not their distance apart or directional pattern).

To simplify our discussion, the computers are identified by a single letter. The main memory of each node, and the hard disk capacity of the file server are recorded. This diagram actually packs in a lot of information. Our task is to design an information system to record this information, and similar details about other bus networks, so that users can extract as much information from this system as they could extract from the actual network diagrams. Try this yourself before reading on. There are many different, correct solutions.

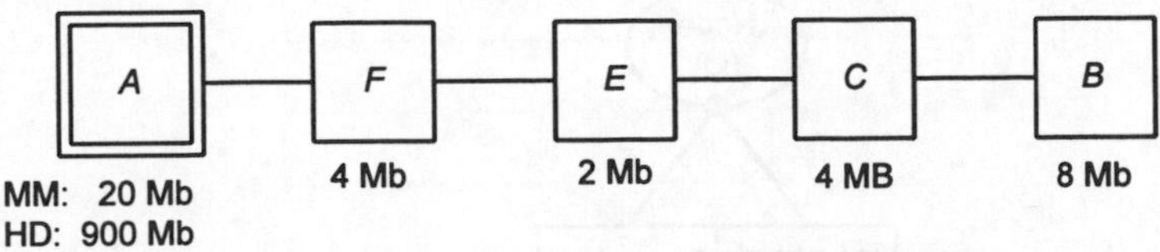

Figure 7.20 Topology of network 1

By verbalizing the diagram in terms of elementary facts you should have found several fact types. For example: **Node belongs to Network; Node is of NodeKind {'FS,'WS'}; Node has main memory of Capacity; FileServer has disk of Capacity.** The reference schemes are obvious. For a subtype definition, we may use: **each FileServer is a Node that is of NodeKind 'FS'**. Now comes the hard part: how do we describe how the nodes are linked together?

Depending on what we choose to be our primitive predicates, there are a number of choices. We might find it hard initially to express the information in terms of elementary sentences. To get the ball rolling we might just jot down samples of whatever comes to mind. For example:

1. Node 'A' is directly connected to Node 'F'.
2. Node 'F' is directly connected to Node 'A'.
3. Node 'A' is indirectly connected to Node 'E'.
4. Node 'A' is an end node.
5. There is at most one link between each pair of nodes.
6. No link connects a node to itself.
7. Each node is directly connected to at most 2 nodes.

Let's stand back from the problem for a minute. There are two basic aspects about the topology that need to be captured. Firstly, the nodes in a given network all lie along the same *continuous line segment* (in contrast to other shapes such as star networks, ring networks, fancy loop structures, separate segments etc.). Secondly, the nodes are *positioned in some order* on this line.

If we consider the linearity of the structure to be a constraint, then how do we express the order of the nodes? Given that the nodes are positioned on a line, and that the file server is at one end of this line, let's first establish a *direction* for the line by saying the line starts at the file server. This avoids potential redundancy problems associated with an undirected, symmetric predicate (e.g. is directly connected to).

The ordering may be specified in terms of relative ordering or absolute ordering. With the first approach, we use a predicate for *directed linkage* (e.g. is just before). With the second approach we assign each node an absolute position (e.g. 0, 1, 2, 3, 4 numbered from the file-server end).

The first approach leads to the ring fact type shown in Figure 7.21. This is populated with data from the sample network. The disjunctive mandatory role constraint should be displayed explicitly, since Node plays other roles in the complete schema. You are invited to add the relevant ring constraints, as well as the other fact types. If only complete networks are considered, the kind of node can now be derived (e.g. a node is a file server if and only if it has no nodes before it).

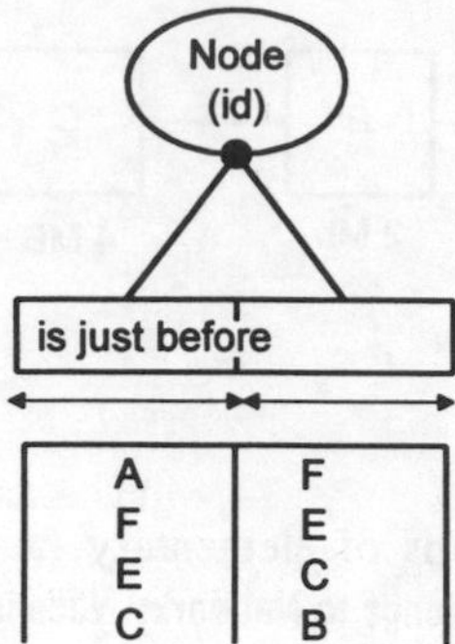

Figure 7.21 A fact type for direct, directed links (some constraints missing)

By storing linkage information only for direct, directed links, we reduce the size of our database as well as avoiding the problems of symmetry and transitivity. If desired information about indirect links can be derived by using a recursive rule such as:

X is before Y **iff** X is just before Y **or**
X is just before Z **and** Z is before Y

There are still some constraints left to specify. For example, each network has exactly one file server. If we are using the fact type Node belongs to Network, this must be specified textually. We can specify it graphically if we instead use separate fact types: Node is file server for Network; Node is workstation for Network. However some constraints have to be specified textually no matter how we choose our fact types. For example: directly linked nodes belong to the same network. The reader is invited to express this constraint (and any others) formally.

As an exercise, try to model the linkage information using node positions numbers instead, and notice the impact on constraints and derivation rules. Note that this absolute position approach makes it more awkward to add, delete or swap nodes in the network since global changes to positional information would be required. For instance if we add a node, say D, between F and E then not only will D be assigned the position 2 but nodes E, C and B will all need to have their position numbers increased by 1. With our previous approach, only a local change would be needed. Swapping nodes is simple with both approaches. As an exercise, set out the compound transactions involved for some sample updates.

We end this section by noting that in practice we often run into *soft constraints*. These specify conditions that are generally desirable, but for which violations may at times be permitted. When something occurs to violate a soft constraint, a warning is normally issued rather than the update being rejected. For example, we might specify a desirable upper limit of 30 on the size of tutorial groups. If a student attempts to join a group of size 30, we might have the system issue a warning message so that the lecturer in charge may see if the student can be re-allocated, and if not, let the student join the group. Another classic example is monogamy. If we specify that there is a soft (rather than hard) 1:1 constraint on the husband/wife fact type, this allows recording of violations to monogamy that might sometimes occur in the real world.

Exercise 7.4

1. An information system maintains details about politicians, the party they belong to, and the bills they vote for. A politician may vote for a bill only if his/her party supports it. Politicians have the option of not voting. Some bills may be supported by many parties. There are positions in government for at most 200 politicians. Schematize this UoD.

2. Job applications are submitted by various people. These applications are recorded, and later will receive a status of accepted or rejected. Model this UoD: (a) making use of relative closure; (b) without using relative closure.

3. A television survey on soap operas is conducted. Participants in this survey are identified by a number, but their sex is recorded as well as what soap operas they watch. Women may nominate all the soap operas they watch, if any, but to be included in the survey each man must specify exactly one soap opera. Model this UoD.

4. An information system keeps track of changes in the seasons over the years, as they cycle through spring, summer, autumn and winter. Specify the dynamic constraint using: (a) a state-transition diagram; (b) a transition matrix or table.

5. A *star network* has a centrally located file server directly linked to zero or more work-stations. A sample star network is shown. For each node the kind of computer is recorded (XT, AT or PS/2). Only for the file server is the processor type recorded. The maximum number of computers in any network is 20. The cable distance (in meters) of each node from the file server is shown beside each link. Schematize.

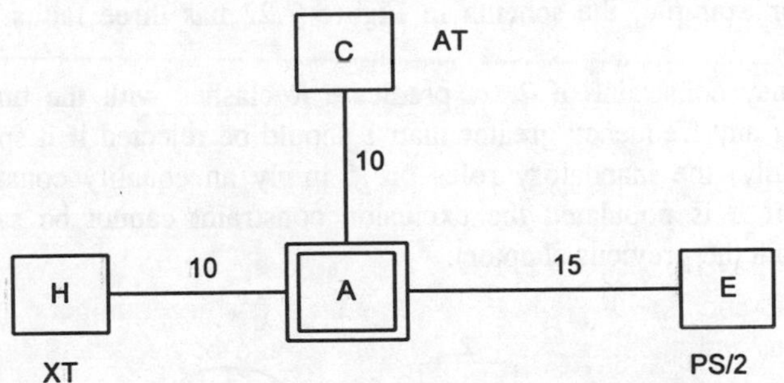

6. With reference to the Community-Roads UoD of Exercise 7.2, assume that roads are continuous, but may connect more than two communities. Discuss whether or not it is appropriate to use the ternary fact type: Road connects Community to Community.

7. With reference to the Bill of Materials question in Exercise 7.3, an output report is required which displays parts contained at all levels (e.g. the fact that A contains part D is to be shown). Design a conceptual schema for this UoD.

8. A *ring network* has a central file server with work-stations arranged in a ring. A sample network is shown. Details are as for question 5, except no metric information is required. Specify the conceptual schema for this UoD.

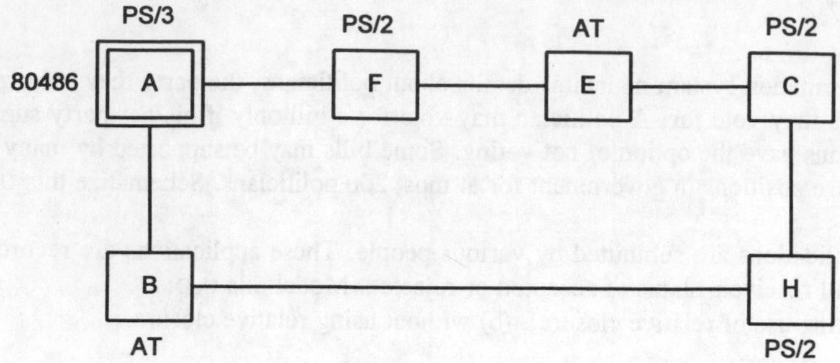

7.5 Final checks

The conceptual schema design procedure facilitates early detection of errors by various checks, including communication with the user by way of examples. We now perform four final checks, to help pick up any errors that might have slipped through. These are designed to ensure: internal consistency; external consistency; lack of redundancy; and completeness. We now consider these in order.

A conceptual schema is ***internally consistent*** if and only if each role sequence used as a predicate or constraint argument can be populated in some state. This topic was discussed in the previous chapter, where it was called "*population consistency*" or "strong satisfiability". Basically it means that the constraints specified do not contradict one another. For example, the schema in Figure 7.22 has three faults. can you spot them?

The frequency constraint of 2 on predicate *R* clashes with the uniqueness constraint; moreover any frequency greater than 1 should be rejected if it spans the whole predicate. Secondly, the mandatory roles on *A* imply an equality constraint between these roles; so if *A* is populated the exclusion constraint cannot be satisfied (recall theorem NXS from the previous chapter).

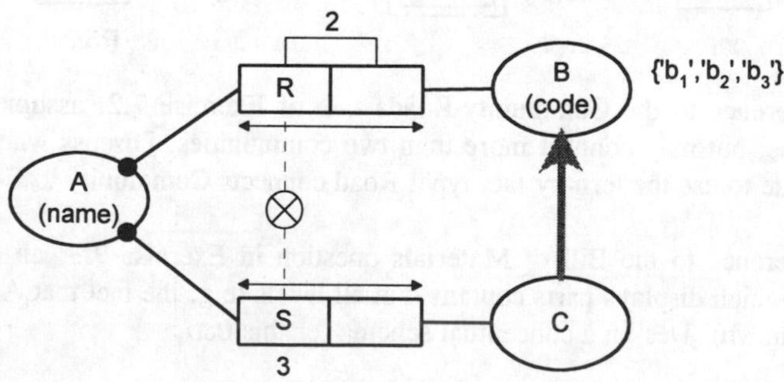

Figure 7.22 This schema is population-inconsistent on three counts

Table 7.3

Person	*Subject*	*Degree*
Ann	CS112	BSc
Ann	CS100	BSc
Bob	?	BA
Sue	CS112	BA
Tom	CS213	BSc

Finally, the frequency constraint of 3 on the first role of *S* cannot be satisfied once *A* is populated. If it were satisfied then *C* would include at least 3 instances (since each row of *S* is unique); but this is impossible since *C* is a proper subtype of *B* and hence has a maximum cardinality below 3 (the value constraint indicates *B* has only three possible values).

With practice it is usually easy to spot contradictory constraint patterns. CASE tools can be of assistance here. For example, InfoModeler prevents most inconsistencies from even being entered, as well as performing a detailed consistency check before the conceptual schema is mapped to an implementation.

A conceptual schema is *externally consistent* if agrees with the original examples and requirements used to develop the schema. If not done earlier, we populate the schema with some of the sample data, and look to see if some constraints have been violated by the population. If they have, then the constraints are *too strong* in this respect, since they reject legal examples. We should then modify the schema, typically by removing or softening some constraints, until the population is permitted.

As a simple illustration, consider Table 7.3. To simplify the discussion we assume people may be identified by their first name. The null value indicates that Bob seeks a BA degree but we do not know any of Bob's subjects.

Now suppose that we come up with the schema shown in Figure 7.23. Assuming our fact types are correct, we might still get the constraints wrong. Apart from asking the client directly about the constraints, we can run a check by populating the fact tables with the sample data, as shown in the Figure. Consider first the uniqueness constraint on studies. This asserts that each entry in this column is unique (i.e. each person studies at most one subject).

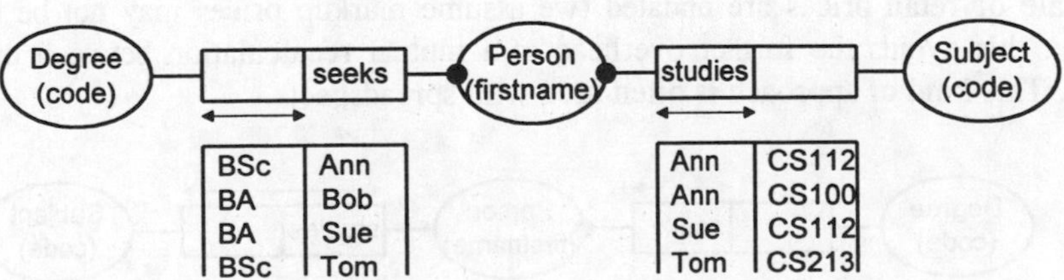

Figure 7.23 The constraints are inconsistent with the data

However, "Ann" appears twice here. So this constraint is wrong. The population of the fact table makes it clear that the uniqueness constraint should span both columns. Now consider the uniqueness constraint on Person seeks Degree: this asserts that each entry in the degree column is unique. But the entry "BSc" appears twice there, and so does the entry "BA". The presence of either of these cases proves that this constraint is wrong. This does not imply that the correct uniqueness constraint should span both columns: although the population is consistent with this weaker constraint, it is also consistent with a uniqueness constraint over the Person column.

To decide between the two possibilities, it is best to ask the client an appropriate question (e.g. Can a person seek more than one degree at the same time?). If the answer to this is No, then we should replace the old uniqueness constraint with one across the Person column for this fact type.

Finally, note that the mandatory role constraint on studies is violated by the sample data, since Bob is referenced elsewhere in the database but does not play this role. So this role should be made optional. Figure 7.24 shows the fully corrected schema. While populating the schema with original examples may detect constraints that shouldn't be there, this will not automatically reveal missing constraints. In other words, while this check can pick up aspects of the constraint section that are too strong, we require significant examples or background knowledge to determine whether the constraint section is *too weak* in other respects.

We now check that the schema is free of *redundancy*, by ensuring that no elementary fact can appear twice. Stored redundancy was covered in Step 4, in the context of arity checking. We now turn to the notion of *derived redundancy*. The most common case of this is when a recorded fact can be derived from other facts by means of specified derivation rules. The task of identifying derived fact types was considered in earlier steps. For example, the markup of an article was derived by subtracting its wholesale price from its retail price; here it would be redundant to store the markup values. If markup values are not stored then they need to be computed upon request: this has the disadvantage of adding slightly to the response time for markup queries.

If markup values are stored this takes up extra storage space. Moreover, if either the wholesale price or the retail price of an article is changed, then failure to update markup accordingly leads to an inconsistent database. If such an update anomaly can occur then the redundancy is "*unsafe*".

One can arrange for "*safe redundancy*" or "*controlled redundancy*" in derived cases by having the derivation rule triggered by relevant updates. For example, the system can be configured to automatically "recalculate" the markup prices whenever wholesale or retail prices are updated (we assume markup prices may not be updated directly: this avoids the further overhead of a mutual recalculation between the three prices). This kind of approach is often used with spreadsheets.

Figure 7.24 The corrected conceptual schema for Table 7.3

Another derived case of safe redundancy occurs when the relevant facts are made non-updatable. For example, a bank account balance may be computed at the end of each transaction, and then stored immediately. This is a case of "derive on update" rather than "derive on query". This "eager evaluation" of derived information can improve the performance of an application considerably. For example, if a bank with millions of customers produces monthly statements of account for each customer, accessing stored balances can save lots of recomputation. This is safe if the bank has a policy of never over-writing any balances. If an accounting error is found, it is left there but compensated for by a later correcting transaction. This practice can also facilitate the task of auditing.

One sometimes runs into cases where a stored fact type is *partially derivable*. Recall the owner-driver example from the previous chapter (reproduced in Figure 7.25). In this UoD if a person drives a car then that person also owns that car. This feature is captured by the pair-subset constraint shown. From a logical point of view, this same feature may be specified as a derivation rule: **Person *p* owns Car *c* if Person *p* drives Car *c***. However, unlike our usual derivation rules, which have "iff" as their main operator, this is just an "if" rule. Some people might own a car but not drive it. So the ownership fact type must be at least partly stored.

From an implementation viewpoint, it is usually better to store the whole of the ownership relation, under the control of the subset constraint. This may take up a bit more storage, but access to ownership facts is fast. Moreover this approach is safe, and easy to understand.

If storage space is a problem, one could reduce storage of owner facts about owner-drivers by using the derivation rule. In the extreme case, a pair-exclusion constraint could even be enforced between owner and driver facts.

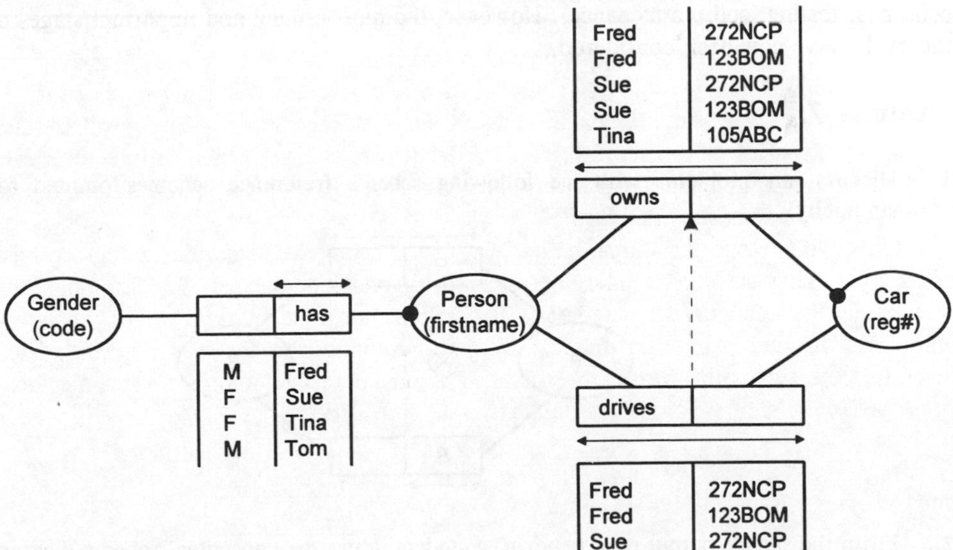

Figure 7.25 Some owner facts are both stored and derivable

However this exclusion constraint approach should be taken with caution, as it requires great care in managing updates. For example, consider deleting a driver fact for a person who remains an owner. Unless memory is tight, the subset constraint approach has much to recommend it. From the *external* rather than the conceptual viewpoint, a user interface may be constructed to automatically add the required owner fact when a drives fact was added, and to delete the required driver fact when its owner fact was deleted. Such an interface would typically inform the user of its intended action and provide the option of cancelling the transaction if this was not desired.

Apart from stored and derived redundancy, redundancy can occur within the set of derivation rules. For instance, it might be possible to derive a fact in more than one way, using different rules. Moreover, some rules might be derivable from more primitive rules. This situation is fairly common in formal inference systems (e.g. computer aided reasoning systems).

In a wider context, redundancy can sometimes be very useful from the point of view of information retrieval, understanding (e.g. human communication), and coping with partial system failure (e.g. backup systems). This book itself exhibits a great deal of redundancy (e.g. by repeating important points). Although this makes the book longer, it hopefully makes it easier to follow.

The last check in the conceptual schema design procedure is to see if it is *complete* with respect to the original requirements specified for the application. This can be done systematically by going through each of the requirement, one at a time, and identifying which aspects of the conceptual design cater for it. If some requirements are found to be unfulfilled, the design should be extended to cater for them.

This completes the conceptual schema design procedure. In terms of the application development life cycle there are still several things to be done (e.g. mapping the conceptual design to a database schema; implementing the internal and external schemas; testing; and maintenance). However, the most crucial and important stages of the cycle have now been considered.

Exercise 7.5

1. Discuss any problems with the following schema (reference schemes omitted for simplicity).

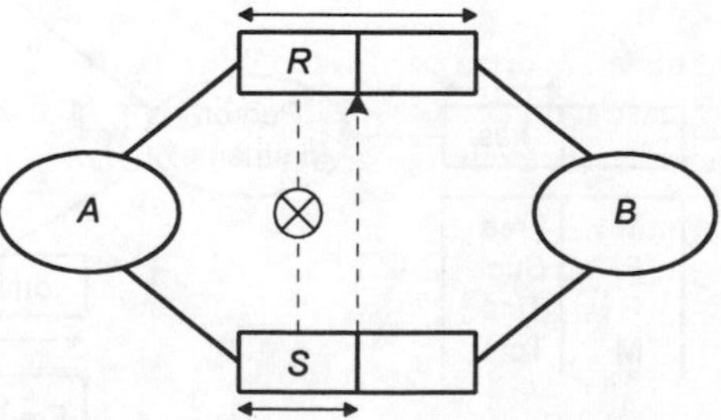

2. From the sample output report shown, a student draws the conceptual schema diagram shown. Check to see if the data in the original report can be a legal population of this schema. If not, modify the schema accordingly.

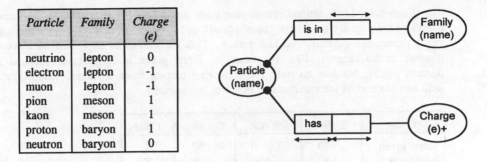

Particle	*Family*	*Charge (e)*
neutrino	lepton	0
electron	lepton	-1
muon	lepton	-1
pion	meson	1
kaon	meson	1
proton	baryon	1
neutron	baryon	0

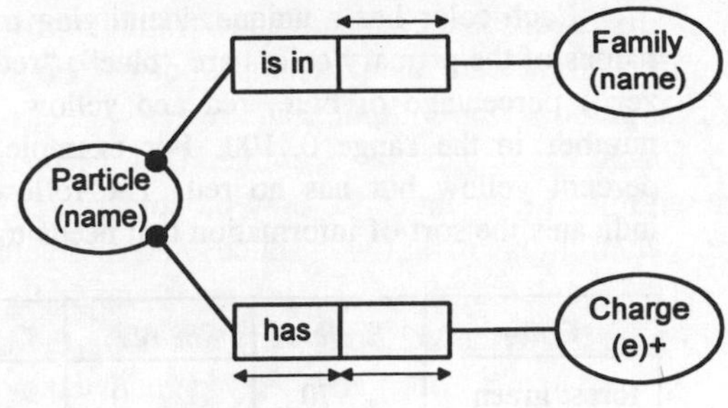

3. Is the following schema guilty of redundancy? If so, correct it.

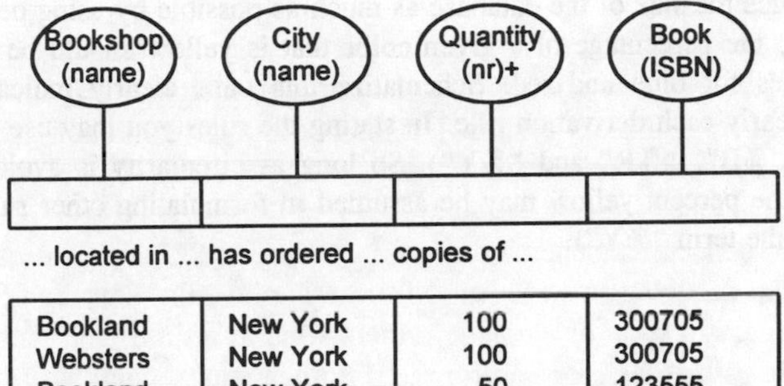

Bookland	New York	100	300705
Websters	New York	100	300705
Bookland	New York	50	123555
OKBooks	London	200	123555

4. With respect to the previous question, suppose it is now possible that bookshops in different cities have the same name. For example, the following population is legal. Draw the correct conceptual schema diagram for this UoD.

Bookland	New York	100	300705
Websters	New York	100	300705
Bookland	New York	50	123555
Bookland	London	200	123555

5. In Prolog, relations are often partly stored and partly derived. For example, at one state the knowledge base might consist of the following facts and rules. Discuss this situation making reference to the notion of derived redundancy.

```
parent_of(ann,bob).
parent_of(bob,chris).
grandparent_of (david,chris).
grandparent_of (X,Y) if parent_of(X,Z) and parent_of(Z,Y).
```

6. An information system is to deal with various colors which are classified as primary (P), secondary (S) or tertiary (T). There are three primary colors: blue; red; and yellow. A secondary color is comprised of a mixture of exactly two primary colors. A tertiary color is comprised of exactly three primary colors.

Each color has a unique, identifying trade name (e.g. "forest green"). The trade names of the primary colors are "blue", "red" and "yellow". Each color has a (perhaps zero) percentage of blue, red and yellow. This percentage is expressed as a whole number in the range 0..100. For example, forest green is 70 percent blue and 30 percent yellow but has no red. The following extract from a sample output report indicates the sort of information that needs to be accessed.

Color	*% blue*	*% red*	*% yellow*	*Class*
forest green	70	0	30	S
mud brown	30	30	40	T
red	0	100	0	P

It is required to reduce the size of the database as much as possible by using derivation rules. For example, the percentage of a given color that is yellow should be derived from the percentages for blue and red. Schematize this UoD, clearly indicating all constraints. State clearly each derivation rule. In stating the rules you may use obvious abbreviations (e.g. "%B", "%R" and "%Y"). So long as circularity is avoided, the rule for computing the percent yellow may be assumed in formulating other rules (i.e. other rules may use the term "%Y").

7.6 Summary

In *CSDP step 7* we add other constraints and perform final checks. An *occurrence frequency constraint* indicates that an entry in a column (or column combination) must occur there exactly *n* times (*n*), at most *n* times (1–*n*), at least *n* times (≥*n*), or at least *n* and at most *m* times (*n*–*m*). A simple occurrence frequency appears next to the role. A compound occurrence frequency appears next to the role connector (┌┐).

A *ring constraint* may apply only to a pair of roles played by the same (or a compatible) object type. The role pair may form a binary predicate or be embedded in a longer predicate. Let *R* be the relation type comprising the role pair. *R* is *reflexive* (over its population) iff for all *x* playing either role, *xRx*. *R* is *symmetric* iff for all *x*, *y*, *xRy* → *yRx*. *R* is *transitive* iff for all *x*, *y*, *z*, *xRy* & *yRz* → *xRz*. These positive properties tend to be used for derivation rather than as constraints.

The following negative properties may be marked as ring constraints next to the role pair (or role connector in embedded cases). *R* is *irreflexive* (°*ir*) iff for all *x*, ~*xRx*. *R* is *asymmetric* (°*as*) iff for all *x*, *y*, *xRy* → ~*yRx*. *R* is *antisymmetric* (°*ans*) iff for all *x*, *y*, *x* ≠ *y* & *xRy* → ~*yRx*. *R* is *intransitive* (°*it*) iff for all *x*, *y*, *z*, *xRy* & *yRz* → ~*xRz*. Asymmetry and intransitivity each imply irreflexivity. Exclusion implies asymmetry (and irreflexivity). A recursive ring constraint which may be difficult to enforce is: *acyclicity* (°*ac*).

An *object cardinality constraint* sets a limit on the cardinality of any population of any object type. An upper limit of *n* is set by marking "#≤*n*" next to the object type. If the population of a role sequence linked by a connector is determined by natural joins or unnesting of the predicates involved, the role sequence may be used in declaring compatible set comparison, external uniqueness or frequency constraints. These constraints may then be called *join constraints*.

A *relative closure constraint* marked as "□" on an optional functional role indicates that if an object in the population of the object type plays that role in the real world it also plays that role in the knowledge base. These constraints are converted to equivalent open world constructs before mapping.

Constraints for which no graphic symbol exists may be specified as *textual constraints*. The relevant predicates are marked "®" to indicate an extra rule is involved. A restricted uniqueness constraint declares stronger uniqueness for a given subtype. A restricted mandatory role constraint indicates an optional role is mandatory for a given subtype.

Dynamic constraints restrict changes between database states. Allowed transitions from one database state to the next may be specified in a *state-transition diagram*, matrix or table.

All constraints discussed so far have been "hard constraints": updates which violate a hard constraint are rejected. *Soft constraints* may also be needed: updates which violate a soft constraint generate a warning rather than being rejected.

When modelling connections between nodes, choose directed, immediate links for the stored relation. Indirect links may then be derived recursively.

At the end of the *CSDP*, final checks are made to ensure the conceptual schema is internally consistent (its constraint pattern can be populated without contradiction), is externally consistent (agrees with original data and conditions), is redundancy free (elementary facts can't be repeated) and is complete (covers all the requirements). Various cases of derived redundancy can be safely managed.

Chapter notes

In contrast to our usage, occurrence frequencies are sometimes defined as the number of times members of an object type population must play a role—frequencies of 0 are then allowed and mean optional. Ring constraints are often discussed in logic books, within the context of the theory of dyadic relations, but do not appear to be used in ER or other versions of ORM. Some extended versions of intransitivity have been introduced by Peter Ritson, who also collaborated with me in developing the notion of relative closure. For some further discussion of this topic, see Halpin & Ritson (1992).

Join constraints were formalized in Halpin (1989). The "®" notation was introduced by Jim Harding for the InfoModeler tool. State-transition diagrams are ancient but still useful, and are discussed in standard textbooks on systems analysis. Automation of checking the internal consistency of a conceptual schema is discussed in Halpin & McCormack (1992).

8 Relational implementation

8.1 Implementing a conceptual schema

Now that we know how to design a conceptual schema, we consider how to implement this on a given software/hardware configuration. Current CASE tools often enable entry of an ORM or ER conceptual schema, but typically require this to be mapped down to a logical schema (e.g. relational) in order for the database to be populated and queried. So updates and queries tend to be carried out either in a logical query language (e.g. SQL or QBE) or via an external forms interface defined on top of the logical schema.

Research has been conducted on *conceptual query languages* which, besides allowing the conceptual schema to be specified, enable database updates and queries to be formulated directly in terms of the conceptual schema constructs. Such query languages have tended to be textual, but some graphical versions have recently appeared. Suppose a military conceptual schema includes the fact types: Officer has Rank; Officer was born in Year. To find which sergeants were born before 1950 we might issue the following query in FORML: which Officer has Rank 'sergeant' and was born in Year < 1950. Alternatively, we might use a mouse to enter the query on the schema diagram by marking the query path and entering conditions.

Much of this research was pioneered by the development of RIDL (Reference and IDea Language), a powerful conceptual query language for ORM, with both procedural and declarative constructs. For example, the following RIDL query will list pairs of officers of the same rank who are born before 1950:

```
for each o1, o2 in Officer born-in Year < 1950 do
    if Rank of o1 = Rank of o2
       then list o1, o2
    end-if
end-for
```

While conceptual query languages offer advantages, they are not yet widely available in industry. Until the next century, most database applications are likely to be implemented in a relational DBMS. For this reason, we focus our implementation discussion on the relational model of data. The most important relational query language is SQL (originally, Structured Query Language): this is standard on most larger relational systems (e.g. DB2, Ingres, Oracle). Next in importance is QBE (Query By Example): this is often used on smaller systems (e.g. Access, Paradox).

International standards for SQL were approved in 1987 (based on the ANSI 1986 standard), 1989 and 1992, and a further revision (code-named "SQL3") is likely to be approved in 1996. All the major relational DBMSs either support SQL directly, or provide translation facilities to and/or from SQL. For this reason, we include some examples from SQL in our discussion. However, to clarify the underlying concepts and to assist the reader who uses another language such as QBE, we make use of generic notations that can readily be converted to the syntax of any given relational language.

Basic ideas about relational databases were introduced earlier. The next section summarizes these points, and expands briefly on them. We then discuss a procedure for mapping a conceptual schema onto a relational schema. The main query operations on a relational database are then explained, using relational algebra. Finally, some points are noted about relational database systems, in principle and in practice.

8.2 Relational schemas

A *relational schema* (or relational database schema) is a set of relational table definitions, constraints and perhaps derivation rules. You may wish to review section 2.3, where the basic ideas were discussed. Recall that each row of a relational table expresses one or more elementary facts. The structure of a single relational table is called a *table scheme*. This is basically a named set of *attributes* (columns) which draw their values from *domains*. For example, the conceptual schema of Figure 8.1 maps to the following table scheme:

Employee (emp#: Emp#, salary: Money, tax: Money)

Here the table name is "Employee", the attribute emp# is based on the domain Emp#, and the attributes salary and tax are both based on the domain Money. We adopt the convention of starting table and domain names with a capital letter, and attribute names with a lower-case letter.

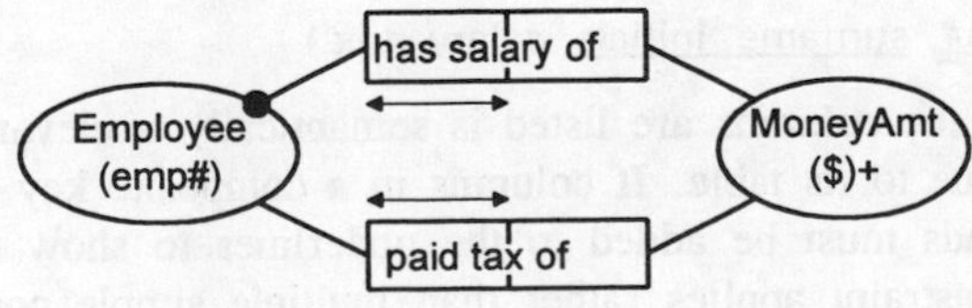

Figure 8.1

For compactness, it is usual to omit the domain names in setting out table schemes. For example:

Employee (emp#, salary, tax)

In theory, the relational model supports semantic domains, which basically correspond to our conceptual object types. In practice however, most relational systems at best provide only weak support for domains. Prior to 1992, the SQL standard required that each attribute be defined directly over a numeric or character string data type. For example, adding our shorthand notation for data patterns underneath, the first two columns in the following table scheme accept strings of up to 20 characters, and the last two columns accept numbers of up to three digits.

Person (surname, city, height, weight)
c20 c20 d3 d3

This failure to model reference schemes can lead to semantic nonsense. For example, people and cities may be compared, as may height and weight. The SQL-92 standard now allows attributes to be defined over user-defined domains, which specify the underlying data type and optionally a value list and/or default value. The underlying data types in SQL-92 now support date, time and bit-strings but not Money, which is instead defined in terms of a numeric data type (e.g. decimal(9,2), or ±d7.2d in our notation). Even with SQL-92, support for domains is still weak. In our examples from now on, we will typically omit domain (and data pattern) details.

We now consider the main notations used for specifying constraints in a relational schema. Later sections discuss how to group fact types into table schemes and how to map constraints and rules in more detail. **Uniqueness constraints** on relational columns are shown by underlining. Each unique column, or unique column combination, provides a *candidate key* for identifying rows in the table.

A key is a *minimal* set of uniquely constrained attributes (i.e. if an attribute is removed from a compound key, the remaining attributes are not spanned by a uniqueness constraint). If there is only one candidate key, this is automatically the *primary key*. For example, we indicate that emp# is the primary key of the Employee table thus:

Employee (emp#, salary, tax)

If more than one candidate key exists, one of these must be selected as the primary key; the others are then called "alternate keys" or "secondary keys". Primary keys are doubly underlined if alternate keys exist. For example, suppose we also record the surname and initials of each employee, and the combination of surname and initials is different for each. The primary and secondary keys may be shown thus:

Employee (emp#, surname, initials, salary, tax)

The order in which the columns are listed is semantically irrelevant, since each column has a name unique to its table. If columns in a composite key are not listed consecutively, arrow heads must be added to the underlines to show that a single, composite uniqueness constraint applies rather than multiple simple constraints. For example, the previous Employee table scheme may also be displayed thus:

Employee (emp#, surname, salary, initials, tax)

A column that does not allow null values is said to be **mandatory** *(for its table)*. A column that does allow null values is said to be *optional*. We adopt the following conventions: optional columns are enclosed in *square brackets*; a column is mandatory in its table unless it is marked optional. This practice is consistent with the well-known BNF (Backus-Naur Form) notation. For example, since paying tax is optional, Figure 8.1 maps as shown, with the tax column optional (null values allowed):

Employee (emp#, salary, [tax])

If all roles played by an object type map to the same table, its mandatory roles can be specified simply as mandatory columns. However, the relational model often requires different facts about the same object to be stored in different tables. In general, *mandatory role constraints are captured by making their columns mandatory in their table, and running a subset constraint from other tables (if any) which contain facts about that object type*. Consider Figure 8.2, which adds two fact types to Figure 8.1. Each employee's sex is now recorded. Optionally, up to three cars may also be recorded for each employee (e.g. details for a parking permit).

As discussed in the next section, the *m:n* nature of the drives fact type requires it to be mapped to a different relational table from the other three fact types. So information about Employee is spread over two relational tables as shown below. Clearly, some constraints have been lost in this mapping. To begin with, the mandatory role constraints have only been partly captured—there is nothing to stop us entering employee numbers in the Drives table that do not occur in the Employee table.

Employee (emp#, sex, salary, [tax])

Drives (emp#, car)

How then do we map the conceptual mandatory role constraints? Recall that a role *r* is mandatory for an object type *O* if and only if the population of each other role played by *O* must be a subset of the population of *r*. Hence if Figure 8.2 includes all the roles of Employee, the mandatory role constraints may in principle be replaced by the subset (and equality) constraints shown in Figure 8.3.

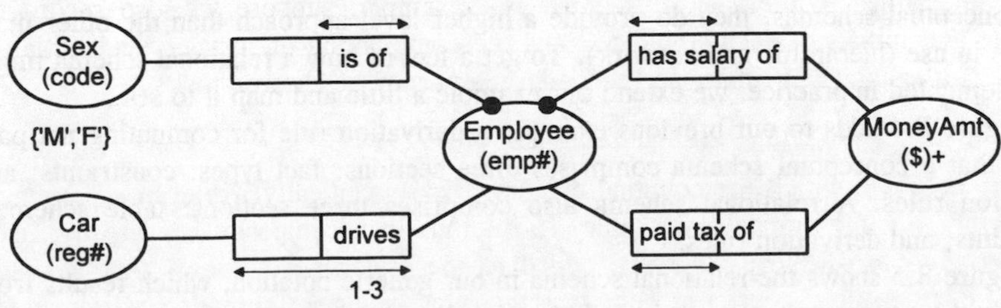

Figure 8.2 The drives fact type will map to a separate table

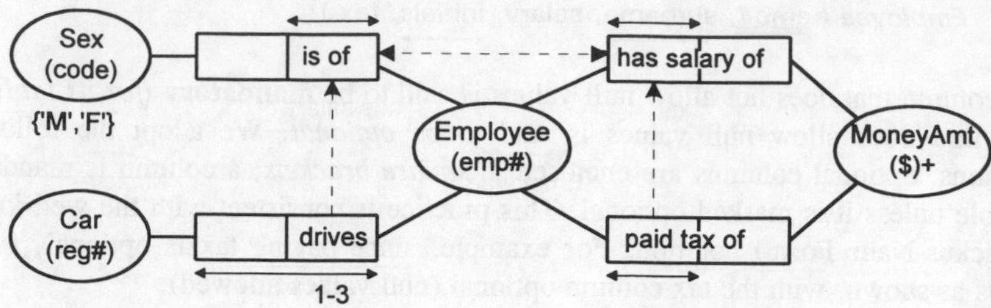

Figure 8.3 Mandatory role constraints of Fig. 8.2 replaced by subset constraints

The subset (and equality) constraints on the sex, salary and tax predicates are captured by having tax as the only optional column in the Employee table. But to capture the subset constraint from the drives to the sex predicate we need to add to the relational schema a corresponding subset constraint from the emp# column of the Drives table to the emp# column of the Employee table (see below). This ensures that any employee listed as driving a car is also referenced in the Employee table, where sex and salary are mandatorily recorded.

Employee (<u>emp#</u>, sex, salary, [tax])
↑
Drives (<u>emp#, car</u>)

In relational jargon, this subset constraint is said to be a *referential integrity constraint*, and the emp# attribute of the Drives table is a *foreign key* which references the emp# attribute of the Employee table. In the relational model, there are two basic integrity rules. The *entity integrity rule* demands that primary keys contain no null values (i.e. each column in a primary key is a mandatory column for its table).

The *referential integrity rule* basically says that each non-null value of a foreign key must match the value of some primary key. Recent proposals for the relational model include many other integrity rules, as well as different kinds of "missing value" in place of the null value. There are problems with the original as well as the new proposals, but we will ignore such problems here.

While relational schemas are unnatural and semantically deficient in comparison with conceptual schemas, they do provide a higher level approach than the other main systems in use (hierarchic and network). To get a feel of how a relational schema might be implemented in practice, we extend our example a little and map it to SQL.

Figure 8.4 adds to our previous example a derivation rule for computing net pay. Recall that a conceptual schema comprises three sections: fact types: constraints; and derivation rules. A relational schema also comprises three sections: table schemes; constraints; and derivation rules.

Figure 8.5 shows the relational schema in our generic notation, which results from mapping the conceptual schema, including value list and frequency constraints and the derivation rule.

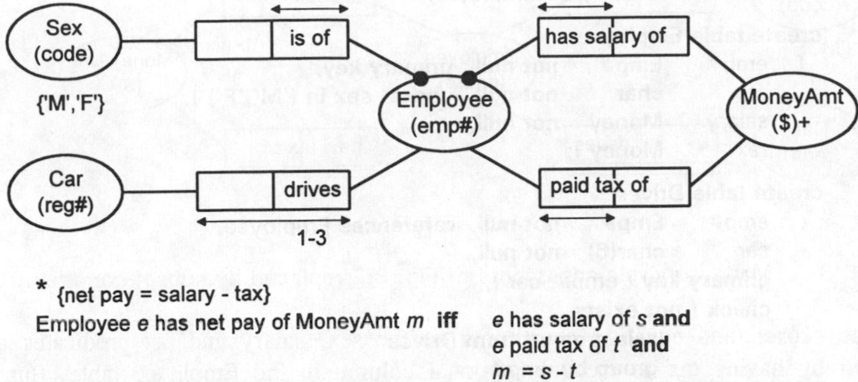

Figure 8.4 Conceptual fact types, constraints and derivation rule

Most ORM conceptual constraint notations may be used in a similar way in setting out relational schemas. Sometimes we adapt these notations or introduce new ones (see later sections). While our semi-graphical notation is compact and fairly intuitive, practical systems usually require relational schemas to be entered in textual form.

For example, the same relational schema may be specified in SQL-92 as set out in Figure 8.6. To save some writing, domains on which more than one column are defined have been declared initially (Emp# and Money). The create-table statements declare the schemes for the Employee and Drives tables. A not-null clause indicates a column is mandatory for its table. Primary keys are declared with primary-key clauses. The inter-table subset constraint is declared with a references-clause. Check-clauses are used to declare the value and frequency constraints. A derived table for the net salary is declared as a view. Further explanation of SQL syntax is given in Appendix C.

Note that at the time of writing, commercial versions of SQL are still only in the process moving to the SQL-92 standard. Some have not even supported the SQL-89 standard (which had no domain clauses, and restricted check clauses to conditions on a single row). In practice, some features of a relational schema may need to be specified as procedural code rather than declaratively.

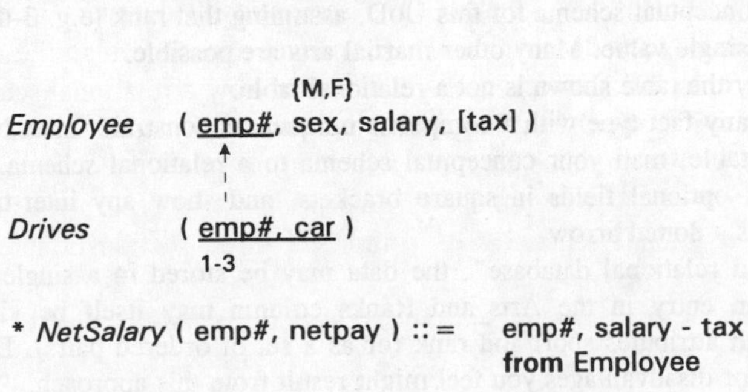

{M,F}

Employee (emp#, sex, salary, [tax])

Drives (emp#, car)

1-3

* *NetSalary* (emp#, netpay) ::= emp#, salary - tax
from Employee

Figure 8.5 Relational schema mapped from Figure 8.4

```
create domain Emp# smallint;
create domain Money decimal(9,2);

create table Employee
(   emp#      Emp#       not null  primary key,
    sex       char       not null  check( sex in ('M','F') ),
    salary    Money      not null,
    tax       Money );

create table Drives
(   emp#      Emp#       not null  references Employee,
    car       char(6)    not null,
    primary key ( emp#, car ),
    check ( not exists
              (select emp# from Drives
               group by emp#
               having count(*) > 3) );

create view NetSalary (emp#, netpay) as
  select  emp#, salary - tax
  from    Employee
```

Figure 8.6 An SQL-92 version of the relational schema in Figure 8.5

Exercise 8.2

1. The following table contains details about members of a martial arts club. A null value "?" indicates that a member has no phone or is unranked in any martial art. Black belt ranks are known as dan grades and lower ranks are kyu grades.

Member	*Sex*	*Phone*	*Arts and ranks*
Adams B	M	2052777	judo 3-dan; karatedo 2-kyu
Adams S	F	2052777	judo 2-kyu
Brown C	F	3579001	?
Collins T	M	?	aikido 2-dan; judo 2-dan
Dancer A	F	?	?

(a) Specify a conceptual schema for this UoD, assuming that rank (e.g. 3-dan) may be stored as a single value. Many other martial arts are possible.

(b) Explain why the table shown is not a relational table.

(c) Given that any fact type with a composite uniqueness constraint must be stored as a separate table, map your conceptual schema to a relational schema. Underline keys, mark optional fields in square brackets, and show any inter-table subset constraint as a dotted arrow.

(d) In a "nested relational database", the data may be stored in a single table. For example, an entry in the Arts_and_Ranks column may itself be viewed as a relation with attributes sport and rank (or as a set of ordered pairs). Discuss any advantages or disadvantages you feel might result from this approach.

8.3 Relational mapping procedure

The previous section introduced a generic notation for setting out a relational schema, and discussed an example of mapping from a conceptual to a relational schema. We now discuss the main steps of a general procedure for performing such a mapping. The following section deals with advanced aspects of this procedure.

For a given conceptual schema, several different relational designs might be chosen. Ideally the relational schema chosen should be *correct, efficient and clear*. Correctness requires the relational schema to be equivalent to the conceptual schema (within the completeness allowed by relational structures). Efficiency means good response times to updates and queries, with reasonable demands on storage space. Clarity entails the schema should be relatively easy to understand and work with.

Since correctness of data is usually more important than fast response times, and correctness requires adequate constraint enforcement, a high priority is normally placed on simplifying the enforcement of constraints at update time. The main way to simplify the management of updates is to avoid redundancy. This strategy can lead to more tables in the design, which can slow down queries and updates if extra table joins are now required. For efficiency, it is important to keep the number of tables down to an acceptable limit.

With these criteria in mind, the **Rmap** (*R*elational *map*ping) *procedure* guarantees a redundancy-free relational design, and includes strategies to restrict the number of tables. Rmap extends and refines an older mapping procedure known as the ONF ("Optimal Normal Form") algorithm. The full version of Rmap includes details for completely mapping all graphical conceptual constraints, and is beyond the scope of this text. However, the central steps of this procedure are covered in this section and the next. As discussed in the next chapter, more efficient relational designs with fewer tables may possibly result if the conceptual schema is transformed by an optimization algorithm before Rmap is applied, and sometimes lower level optimization using controlled redundancy may be needed to meet critical performance requirements.

Although the Rmap procedure is not necessarily the last word in table design, it is extremely valuable since it guarantees a safe and reasonably efficient design. Happily, the basic steps of the procedure are simple. Recall that redundancy is repetition of an elementary fact. Having gone to the trouble of ensuring that our conceptual fact types are elementary, we can very easily avoid redundancy in our relational tables.

Since each relational table stores one or more elementary fact types, we can automatically *avoid redundancy* in them by ensuring that *each fact type maps to only one table, in such a way that its instances appear only once*. To achieve this, there are two basic rules, as follows. As an exercise, convince yourself that grouping fact types like this makes it impossible for any fact to be duplicated.

(1) fact types with compound uniqueness constraints ⊏⊐⊏⊐ map to separate tables;

(2) fact types with functional roles attached to the same object type ○-⊏⊐ are grouped into the same table, keyed on the object type's identifier.

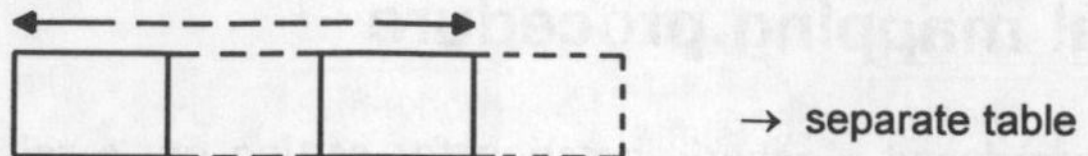

Figure 8.6 Each fact type with a compound UC maps to a table by itself

These two rules show how to group fact types into table schemes. The first rule is illustrated in Figure 8.6. Any predicate, other than an objectified predicate, which has a uniqueness constraint spanning two or more of its roles must map to a table all by itself. Hence *m:n* binaries, and all *n*-aries ($n \geq 3$) on the conceptual schema, map to a separate table. If there is only one uniqueness constraint on the predicate, the primary key of the table is based on this; otherwise, one is picked as primary.

When mapping conceptual schemas, care should be taken to *choose meaningful table and column names*. In the case of Figure 8.6, the table is used to store instances of the conceptual relationship type, so is often given a name similar to the conceptual predicate name. If the object types involved are different, their names or the names of their value types are often used as column names. For instance, recall this example from the previous section: Drives (emp#, car).

When information about the same object is spread over more than one table, it is usually better to always use the same column name for this object (e.g. emp# was also used in the Employee table to refer to employees). Apart from helping the designer to see the connection, this practice usually simplifies the formulation of joins in query languages. However, if different roles of the same predicate are played by the same object type, different column names must be chosen; these may reflect the different roles involved. For example: Contains (superpart, subpart, quantity).

A typical example of the second grouping rule is illustrated in Figure 8.7. Here two functional roles are attached to the object type *A*. However the rule also applies when there is just one functional role, or more than two. The handling of mandatory and optional roles was considered earlier (optional column in square brackets).

The identification schemes of *A, B* and *C* are not shown here, but may be simple or composite. The fact types are grouped together into a single table, with the identifier of *A* as the primary key (shown here as *a*). If *A*, *B* and *C* are different object types, then the name of *A* is often chosen as the table name, and the name of *A*'s value type is chosen for *a*, with the names of *B* and *C* (or their value types) chosen as the other column names (here *b* and *c*). For example: Employee (emp#, sex, [phone]).

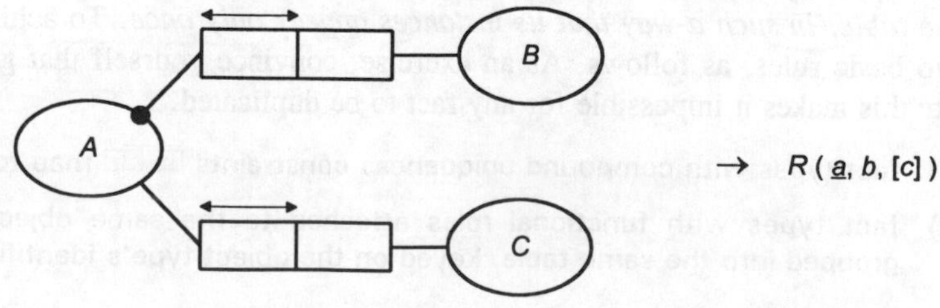

Figure 8.7 Functional fact types of the same object type are grouped together

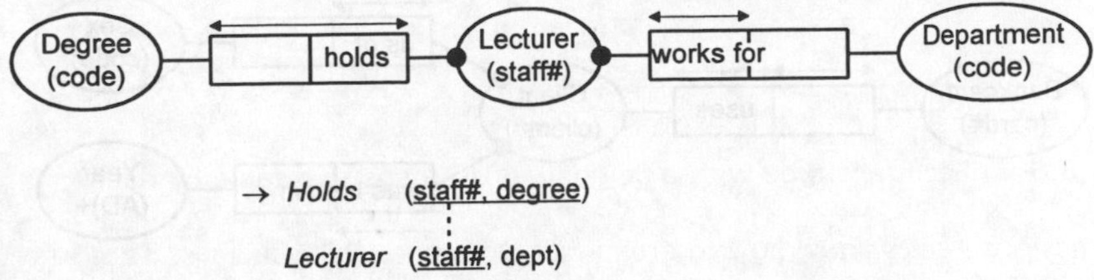

Figure 8.8 Note the equality constraint

In Figure 8.7, if two or more of *A*, *B* or *C* are the same object type, different column names are chosen to reflect the different roles. For example: Employee (emp#, salary, [tax]). Once table groupings have been determined, keys underlined, optional columns marked in square brackets, and other constraints (e.g. subset, value list) mapped down, any derivation rules are also mapped, as discussed in the previous section.

To help understand the Rmap procedure it will help to consider several examples. Initially we confine ourselves to cases where all entity types have simple identifiers, and no subtypes or objectified predicates occur.

Consider the conceptual schema in Figure 8.8. The many:many fact type maps to a separate table (using rule 1), while the functional fact type maps to a table keyed on the identifier of Lecturer (using rule 2). Notice the *equality constraint*, shown as a dotted line between the staff# fields of both tables: this is needed since both roles played by Lecturer are mandatory (see previous section). In our relational schema notation, arrow-heads may be omitted from an equality constraint; this is just for tidiness—if you like, you may include them (as on a conceptual schema).

Now consider Figure 8.9. Here each horse has its gender and weight recorded. Each race has exactly one winner (we do not allow ties). There are no composite keys for rule 1 to work on. The gender and weight fact types have simple keys attached to the entity type Horse: by rule 2 these two fact types must be grouped into the same table keyed on the identifier for Horse.

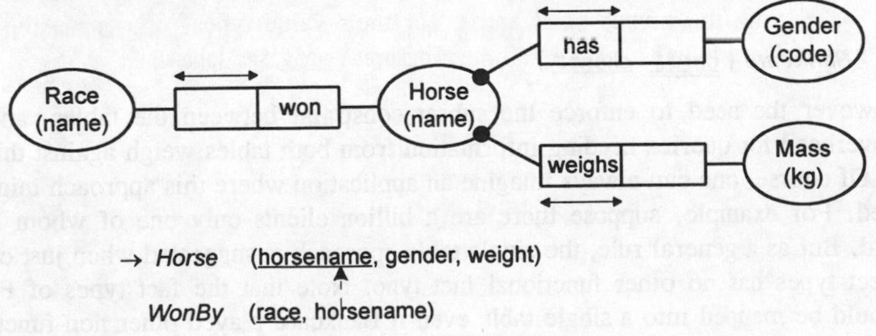

Figure 8.9 Note the subset constraint

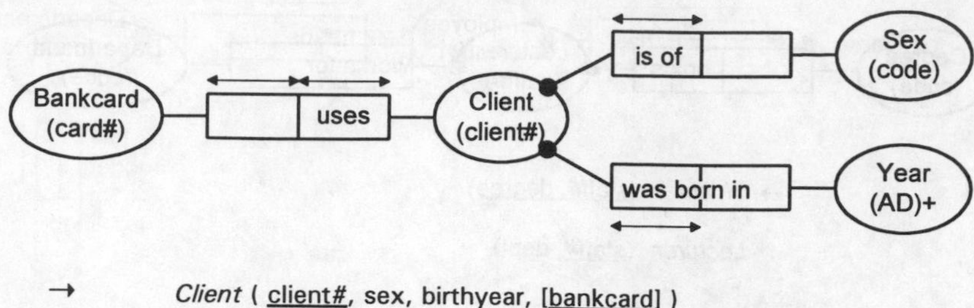

→ *Client* (client#, sex, birthyear, [bankcard])

Figure 8.10 Bankcard has only one functional role but Client has more

In Figure 8.9, the Won fact type also has a simple key, but this key is not attached to Horse (it is attached to Race instead). By rule 2 this fact type maps to a table keyed on the identifier for Race. Notice the subset constraint between the tables. As an exercise, explain why this is needed.

We now consider some examples involving *1:1 fact types*. The conceptual schema of Figure 8.10 is structurally similar to the horse example, except that the optional binary is 1:1. Both Bankcard and Client have functional fact roles attached. Should we group the 1:1 binary into a Bankcard table as well as a Client table? No! Entering the same fact into two tables would cause redundancy. Notice that Bankcard has no other functional fact role, but Client has. In cases like this, it is usually best to group the 1:1 fact type together with the other functional fact types into the same table. Here this results in a single table, Client (see Figure 8.10).

Grouping the optional bankcard predicate into the same table entails that the bankcard column is optional. However the disadvantage of null values here is usually outweighed by the advantage of having all the information in one table. The underlining of bankcard indicates a uniqueness constraint for its non-null values. Because it may contain more than one null, the bankcard column cannot be used to identify rows, and hence cannot be the primary key. With two uniqueness constraints, we doubly underline client# to highlight it as the primary key. One could avoid null values by using two tables:

Client (client#, sex, birthyear)

Bankcard (card#, client#)

However the need to enforce the subset constraint between the tables, and the added overhead for queries needing information from both tables weigh against this approach. Of course, one can always imagine an application where this approach might be preferred. For example, suppose there are a billion clients only one of whom has a bankcard. But as a general rule, the single table approach is suggested when just one of the object types has no other functional fact type. Note that the fact types of Figure 8.10 would be mapped into a single table even if Bankcard played other non-functional roles (and even if as a result its client role was explicitly mandatory).

Now consider the conceptual schema in Figure 8.11. Recall that when an object type has two simple identification schemes, its primary one is parenthesized.

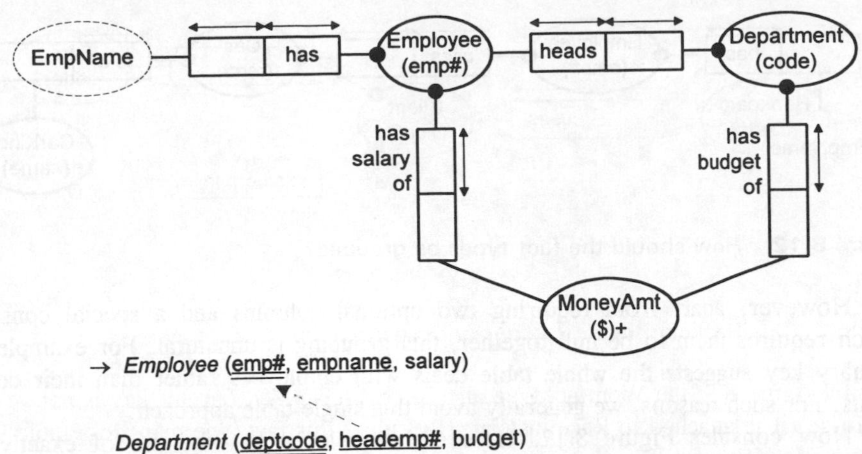

Figure 8.11 The heads fact type is grouped on the mandatory role side

In Figure 8.11 each employee is primarily identified by emp#, but also has a unique name. Each department has one head, who heads only one department. Since not all employees are department heads, the role of heading is optional. So the 1:1 binary between Employee and Department is optional for Employee but mandatory for Department.

It is easy to see that the empname and salary fact types should be grouped into an Employee table, and that the budget fact type should be grouped into a Department table. But what about the heads fact type? Because of its 1:1 nature, we might group it into the Employee table, or instead into the Department table (why not both?). Notice that *only one role of this 1:1 predicate is mandatory*. In asymmetric cases like this it is usually better to *group on the mandatory role side*. Here this means including the heademp# column in the Department table (see Figure 8.11). Suppose we grouped on the optional side instead, by adding a deptheaded column to the Employee table:

Employee (emp#, [deptheaded], empname, salary)

Department (deptcode, budget)

This alternative has two disadvantages. First, the optional deptheaded column permits null values (unlike the mandatory heademp# column). All other things being equal, null values should be avoided if possible. Besides consuming storage space, they are often awkward for people to work with (null value management in most database systems is rather complex). The second disadvantage of this alternative is that we now have an equality constraint between the tables, rather than just a subset constraint.

In principle, one might group into one table all the functional predicates of both object types involved in a 1:1 binary. With our current example this gives the scheme: *EmployeeDept* (emp#, empname, salary, [deptheaded, deptbudget]). Here enclosing the last two columns in the same square brackets declares that one is null if and only if the other is.

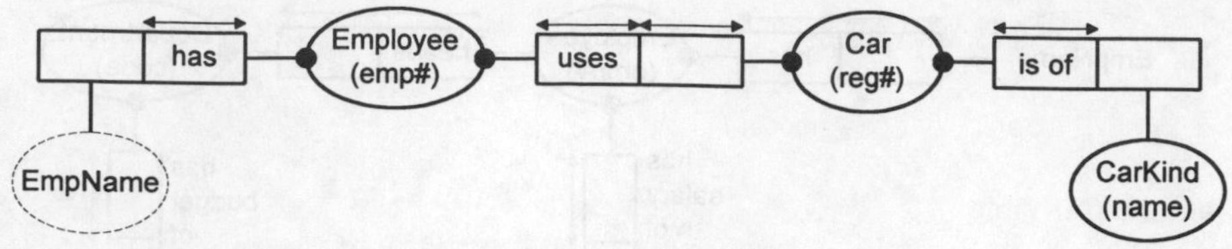

Figure 8.12 How should the fact types be grouped?

However, apart from requiring two optional columns and a special constraint which requires them to be null together, this grouping is unnatural. For example, the primary key suggests the whole table deals with employees rather than their departments. For such reasons, we generally avoid this single-table approach.

Now consider Figure 8.12. Here each employee has the use of exactly one company car, and each company car is allocated to exactly one employee. Employees are identified by their employee number and cars by their registration number. The names of employees and the kinds of car (e.g. Nissan Vanette) are also recorded, but these need not be unique.

Here both roles of the 1:1 fact type are mandatory, and each is attached to an entity type with another functional role. Should the fact type be grouped into an Employee table or into a Car table? Unlike the previous example, we now have a symmetrical situation with respect to mandatory roles. An arbitrary decision could be made here. We could group to the left, thus:

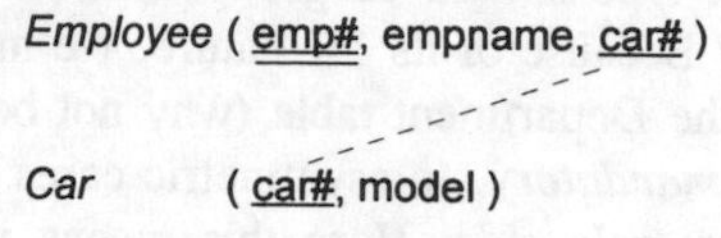

or to the right thus:

Employee (emp#, empname)

Car (car#, model, emp#)

Either of these approaches is reasonable. We might also try a single table approach: *EmployeeCar* (emp#, empname, car#, carmodel). Although this could be used, it is unnatural, requiring an arbitrary choice of primary key. This becomes more awkward if other facts about employees (e.g. sex, birthdate) and cars (e.g. color, purchasedate) are to be recorded in the table. Also, consider the additional update overhead of changing the car allocated to an employee, compared with the two table approach.

Now what about the case of a 1:1 fact type where both roles are optional? For example, consider a UoD identical to that just discussed except that only some employees are given company cars and only some company cars are used by employees (e.g. some may be reserved for important visitors). We generally recommend the two table approach. Because of the symmetry with respect to mandatory roles, we could map the 1:1 binary into the Employee table:

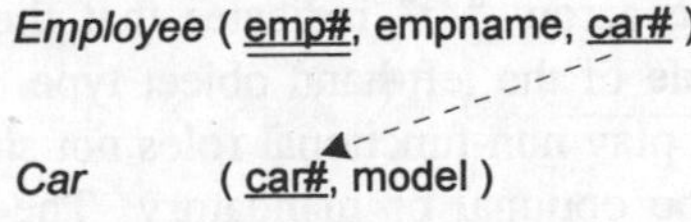

or into the Car table:

Employee (emp#, empname)

Car (car#, model, emp#)

In an actual application the *percentage of null values* is likely to differ in these two designs: in this case the design with fewer null values would usually be preferable.

Yet another option is a three table approach, in which the 1:1 binary is placed in a table by itself. This option becomes more attractive if the two table approach yields high percentages of nulls. For example, if only 1% of employees and 1% of cars are likely to be involved in Employee uses Car, one might map this fact type into a table all by itself, giving three tables overall. A fourth option for 1:1 cases is to use two tables, but include the 1:1 binary in both, with a special equality constraint to control the redundancy. More detailed discussions of mapping 1:1 fact types are provided in the chapter references. Our simple, default procedure is summarized in Figure 8.13; here "functional role" means a functional role in a fact type (not a reference type).

Each *1:1 fact type* maps to only one table:

if only one object type in the 1:1 predicate has another functional role
then group on its side { case (a) }

else if both object types have other functional roles
and only one role in the 1:1 is explicitly mandatory
then group on its side { case (b) }

else if no object type has another functional role
then map the 1:1 to a separate table

else grouping choice is up to you

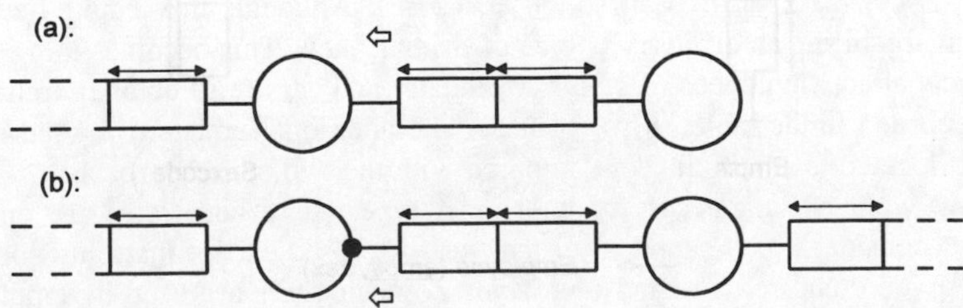

Figure 8.13 Default procedure for mapping 1:1 fact types

In the diagram for Figure 8.13, the arrow "⇦" indicates that the 1:1 fact type should be grouped into the functional table of the left-hand object type. In case (a) we allow that the right-hand object type may play non-functional roles not shown here, and that any role in the 1:1 fact type may be optional or mandatory. The third case (no other functional roles) is rare, and requires a choice of primary key in the separate table. The final line in the procedure refers to the symmetric cases where the roles of the 1:1 predicate are both mandatory or both optional, and both object types play another functional role—here we have a grouping choice.

To help understand some further cases, it is important to realize that *uniqueness constraints on primary reference schemes are not mapped*. Consider the simple example in Figure 8.14. The conceptual schema at the top abbreviates the primary reference schemes shown explicitly in the conceptual schema below it. The mandatory role constraints on the fact type anticipate other roles being added later to Employee but not Sex. The uniqueness constraints on the reference predicates are the responsibility of humans to enforce. The information system can't stop us giving the same employee number to two different employees, or giving the same employee two employee numbers.

Assuming we have enforced the primary reference constraints however, the system can enforce constraints on the fact types. For example, it enforces the uniqueness constraint in *Employee* (<u>emp#</u>, sex), by ensuring each emp# occurs only once in that column and hence is paired with at most one sexcode. Assuming the reference types really are 1:1, this uniqueness constraint on emp# corresponds to the uniqueness constraint on the conceptual fact type (i.e. each Employee is of at most one Sex). It does not capture any uniqueness constraint from the reference types.

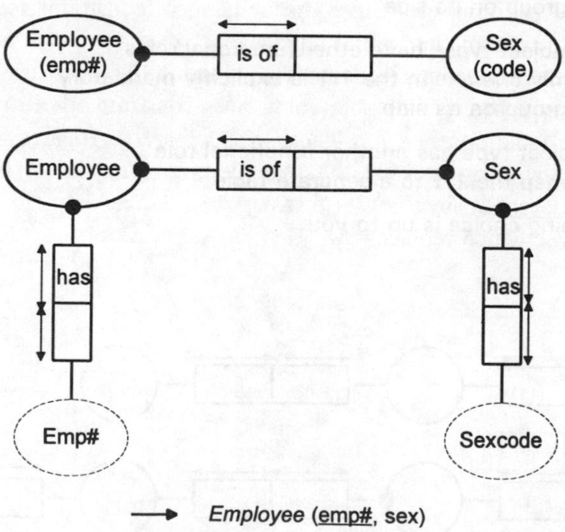

Figure 8.14 Uniqueness constraints on reference types are not mapped

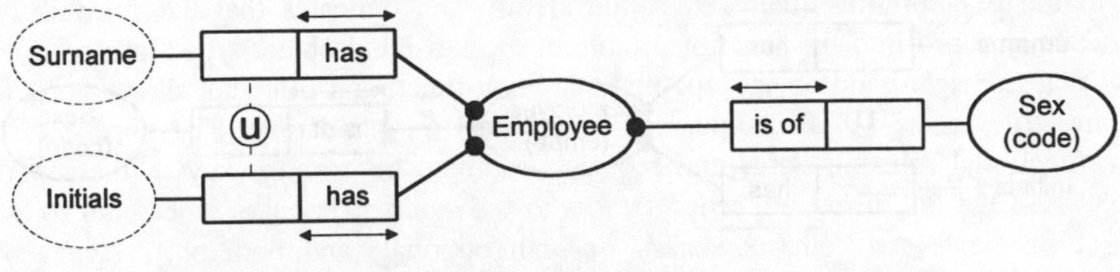

Figure 8.15 Composite primary identifier, and functional fact type

We now consider cases involving *external uniqueness constraints*. Consider the conceptual schema of Figure 8.15. Here employees are identified by the combination of their surname and initials. Since the external uniqueness constraint ("Ⓤ") relates to the primary reference scheme, it is not mapped. In the resulting relational table scheme *Employee* (surname, initials, sex), the uniqueness constraint again corresponds to the uniqueness constraint on the conceptual fact type Employee is of Sex. A good way to visualize the mapping is as follows:

- mentally erase the identification scheme of each object type;
- group facts into tables, using simple surrogates for the real world objects;
- replace each surrogate by the attribute(s) used to identify it in the table.

For example, the conceptual schemas of Figures 8.14 and 8.15 each map initially to *Employee* (*e*, *s*) with the meaning Employee *e* is of Sex *s*. In both cases, *s* is then replaced by "sex" (or "sexcode" if you prefer). With Figure 8.14, *e* is replaced by "emp#"; but with Figure 8.15, *e* is unpacked into "surname, initials" since the identification scheme is composite. Since the uniqueness constraint spanned *e*, it must also span the attribute combination which replaces it.

Now consider the conceptual schema of Figure 8.16. The structural difference here is that the fact type has a composite uniqueness constraint. We may initially think of it mapping to the table *Drives* (*e*, *c*), where *e* and *c* are surrogates for the employee and car. Replacing the surrogates by the real identifiers results in the table scheme *Drives* (surname, initials, car#). Since *e* was just part of a longer key, so is the composite identifier for employee which replaces it.

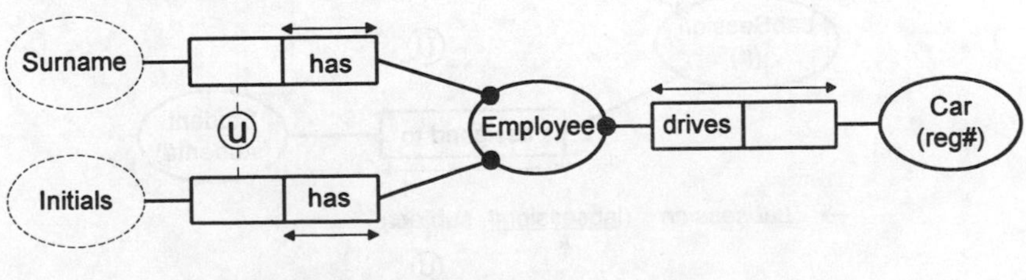

Figure 8.16 Composite primary identifier, and non-functional fact type

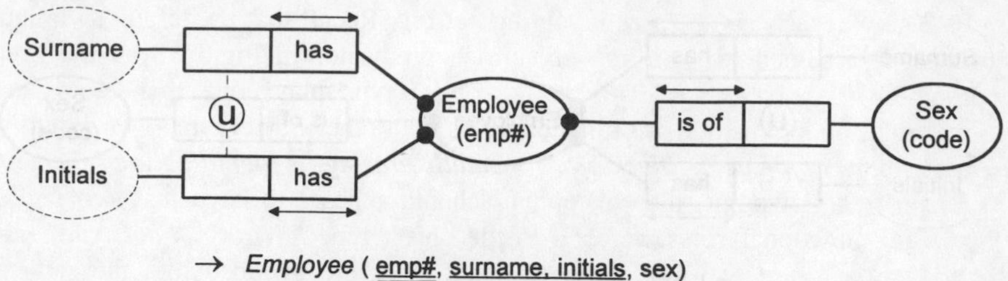

Figure 8.17 Composite secondary identifier and functional fact type

Now consider the conceptual schema of Figure 8.17. This is like that of Figure 8.15 except that Employee now has emp# as its primary identifier. The external uniqueness constraint now applies to two fact types rather than reference types, and hence can be mapped and enforced by the information system. As shown, this maps to a uniqueness constraint spanning surname and initials in the relational table (ensuring each surname, initials combination is paired with only one emp#). The uniqueness constraint on the table's primary key, emp#, captures the three simple uniqueness constraints on the three conceptual fact types (since each emp# is unique it is paired with only one surname, only one sequence of initials and only one sexcode).

Now consider the conceptual schema of Figure 8.18. Here each laboratory session is primarily identified by a session number, and is used for a particular subject. Once these subject bookings have been made, sessions are assigned for use by students. The external uniqueness constraint says that each student is assigned at most one session for each subject (e.g. laboratory resources might be scarce). Since this constraint involves fact types rather than reference types, it can be mapped.

An unusual feature of this example is the association of the external uniqueness constraint with an *m:n* fact type (LabSession is assigned to Student). Because the *m:n* fact type must map to a table by itself, the external uniqueness constraint ends up spanning two tables in the relational schema. This is equivalent to an internal uniqueness constraint spanning subject and student# in the natural join of the two tables.

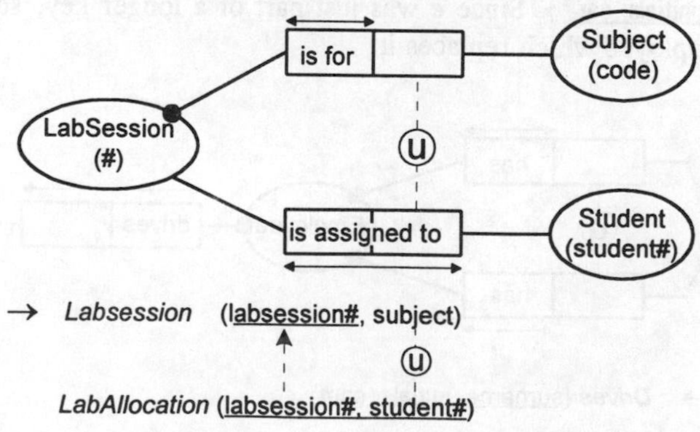

Figure 8.18 External uniqueness constraint involving a non-functional fact type

We now discuss some cases involving *nesting*. Recall that by default, a uniqueness constraint is assumed to span any objectified predicate. In Figure 8.19 the predicate "worked on" is objectified. This nested object type plays one mandatory and one optional role, both of which are functional. As with other object types, we *initially treat the nested object type as a "black box", mentally erasing its identification scheme*.

From this viewpoint, the conceptual schema appears to have just two fact types, both having functional roles attached to the object type "Work". *Fact types are now grouped in the usual way*. So these two fact types are grouped into the same table. Visualizing the nested object type "Work" as a black box "■", results in the table: *Work* (■, startdate, [enddate]). Finally we *unpack* ■ *into its component attributes* (emp# and project), giving: *Work* (emp#, project, startdate, [enddate]).

Now consider the conceptual schema of Figure 8.20. In this UoD employees might be assigned to projects before their actual starting date is known. So some instances of the nested object type EmpProject might be recorded which (in that database state) do not play either of the attached roles. Recall that the disjunction of roles attached to an objectified predicate is not assumed to be mandatory. In this example, since even the disjunction of the attached roles is optional, the nested object type is *lazy*—this is noted by the exclamation mark in "EmpProject !". Contrast this with the previous example, where the nested object type Work was active.

Lazy object types, whether nested or not, require special treatment in mapping, as follows:

- **Map each lazy object type and its functional fact types (if any) to a separate table, with the object type identifier as the primary key, and all other attributes optional.**

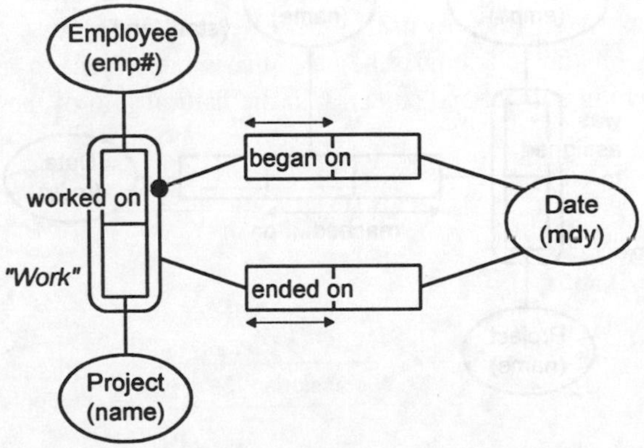

→ *Work* (emp#, project, startdate, [enddate])

Figure 8.19 An active, nested object type with functional roles

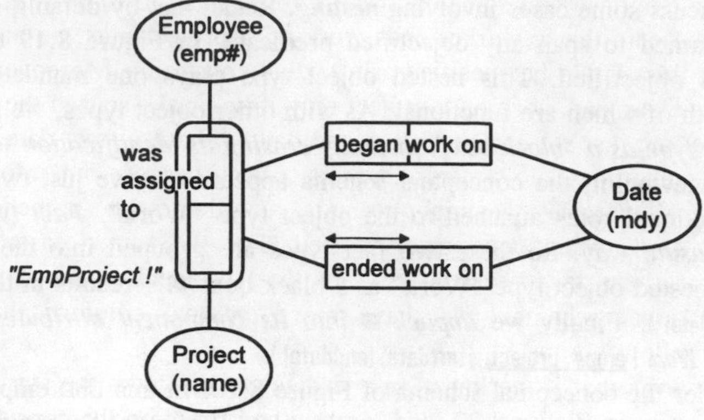

Figure 8.20 A lazy, nested object type with functional roles

For example, in Figure 8.20 both the startdate and enddate attributes are optional. If we wish to record just the fact that an employee is assigned to a particular project, we enter values just for emp# and project. Details about start and end dates for work on the project can be added later when they are known.

Figure 8.21 shows another way to model this UoD. Here the lazy object type has no functional roles attached: in this case it maps to a table all by itself. The *m:n* fact type maps to another table. A subset constraint captures its optionality. If instead we tried to map everything to one table, this would violate entity integrity (why?).

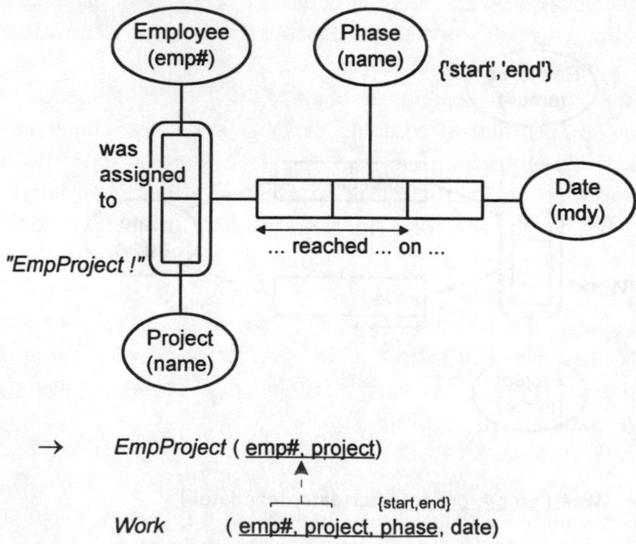

Figure 8.21 A lazy, nested object type with no functional roles

You may have noticed that some constraints are missing in Figures 8.20 and 8.21. To begin with, the date that a worker ends work on a project must be no earlier than the starting date; this should be specified as a textual constraint. Moreover, in the real world an employee can end work on a project only if he or she started the project. The schemas shown allow that we can record an end date without a start date. In practical applications, we sometimes allow things like this, purely because our information may be incomplete. For example, we might want to record the date somebody ended a project, but not *know* when that person started. For the same reason, conceptual schemas sometimes have fewer mandatory roles than the ideal world suggests, and in consequence relational schemas may have more optional columns than complete knowledge would allow.

Suppose however that if we know an end date we *do* know the starting date. To enforce this constraint in Figure 8.20, add a subset constraint on the conceptual schema from the first role of the "ended work on" predicate to the first role of the "began work on" predicate. This constraint is captured in the relational schema by using ***nested option brackets***. Here we enclose the option brackets for enddate ***inside*** the option brackets for startdate: ***EmpProject*** **(<u>emp#, project</u>, [startdate, [enddate]])**. This indicates a (non-null) value is recorded for enddate only if a value is recorded for startdate.

To add this constraint to Figure 8.21 is not as easy. A textual constraint is required at both conceptual and relational levels to declare that for each employee, project pair, phase "end" is recorded only if phase "start" is. Apart from complicating the enforcement of this constraint, should it be required, the approach of Figure 8.21 spreads the information over more tables and demands an inter-table constraint. This is usually undesirable, since it typically slows down the execution of queries and updates. For such reasons the approach of Figure 8.20 is normally preferred to that of Figure 8.21.

The next chapter examines in detail the notion of "equivalent" conceptual schemas, and provides guidelines for transforming a conceptual schema to improve the efficiency of the relational schema obtained from Rmap.

If the date on which an employee begins work on a project is recorded, a derivation rule can be specified to compute the period for the employee to complete work on the project (by subtracting the start date from the end date, if known). Since each computer system has an internal clock, conceptually there is a unary fact type of the form: **Date is today**. So for someone still working on a project we could also derive the time spent so far on the project, by subtracting the start date from the current value for "today".

Note that by default, derived facts are not stored; so ***by default, we exclude derived columns from the base tables*** (i.e. stored tables) of the relational schema. However the derivation rules should themselves be mapped; these may be set out as view definitions (recall the net salary example of Figure 8.5).

In some cases (e.g. account balances), efficiency considerations may lead us to derive on update rather than at query time, and store the derived fact. In such cases the derived fact type is included on the conceptual schema diagram and marked "®" to indicate a rule exists for it. During the relational mapping, the fact type is mapped to a base table, and the derivation rule is also mapped to a rule which is triggered by updates to the base table.

Table 8.1

Patient#	*Name*	*Sex*	*Phone*	*Prostate status*	*Pregnancies*
101	Adams A	M	2052061	OK	–
102	Blossom F	F	3652999	–	5
103	Jones E	F	?	–	0
104	King P	M	?	benign enlargement	
105	Smith J	M	2057654	?	–

As well as derivation rules, *all* conceptual constraints should be mapped (not just uniqueness and mandatory role constraints). We have no space for a complete treatment of constraint mapping, but we do provide some details on *mapping of subtype constraints*. Table 8.1 reproduces an output report from an earlier chapter. Although we have no rule to determine when a phone number is recorded, we know that prostate status may be recorded only for men, and pregnancies are recorded for all women and only for women. The conceptual schema is reproduced in Figure 8.22.

Although support for subtyping has been proposed as an extension to the relational model, and is planned for the next SQL standard ("SQL3"), current relational systems do not directly support this concept. Nevertheless, there are three main ways in which subtyping can be implemented on current systems: absorption; separation; and partition. With *absorption*, we *absorb the subtypes back into the (top) supertype* (giving qualified optional roles), then *group the fact types as usual*, and then *add the subtyping constraints as textual qualifications* (see Figure 8.22).

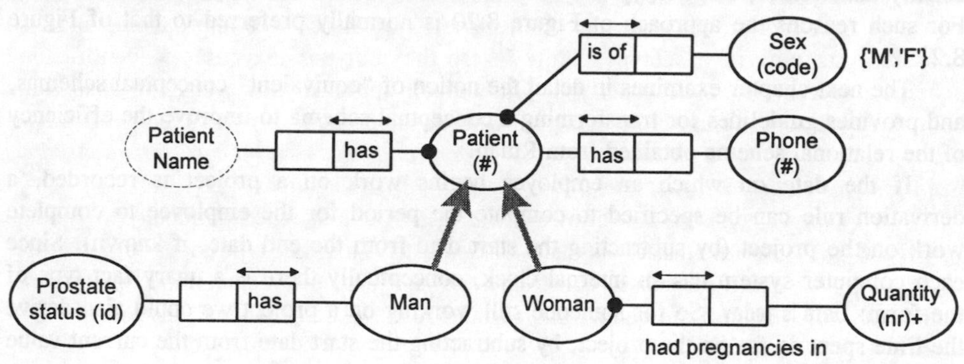

each Man **is a** Patient **who is of** Sex 'M'
each Woman **is a** Patient **who is of** Sex 'F'

{M,F}
→ *Patient* (<u>patient#</u>, patientname, sex, [phone], [prostate]^1, [pregnancies]^2)

^{1} **exists only if** sex = 'M'
^{2} **exists iff** sex = 'F'

Figure 8.22 Subtype constraints on functional roles map to qualified optionals

Let's go over this example to make sure we understand it. Visualize the subtypes on the conceptual schema vanishing, and the subtype roles being attached as qualified optional roles to the supertype Patient. All the roles attached to Patient are functional, so the fact types all map to the same table as shown. The phone, prostate and pregnancies attributes are all optional, but the latter two are qualified. Here **"exists"** means the value is not null. Qualification 1 is a pure subtype constraint, indicating that a non-null value for prostate is recorded on a row **only if** the value of sex on that row is "M". Some men might have a null value recorded here. Qualification 2 expresses both a subtype constraint (number of pregnancies is recorded **only if** sex is "F") and a mandatory role constraint (pregnancies are recorded **if** sex is "F"). Recall that **"iff"** is short for "if and only if".

Since only functional fact types are involved in this example, the absorption approach leads to a table which basically matches that of the original output report (except that most relational systems support only one kind of null value). The main advantage of this approach is that it maps all the functional predicates of a subtype family into a single table. This usually makes related queries and updates more efficient. Its main disadvantage is that it generates null values.

The second main approach, *separation*, creates separate tables for the subtype specific facts. With this approach, the conceptual schema of Figure 8.22 maps to three tables: one for the common facts; one for the man-specific facts; and one for the woman-specific facts. The third main approach, *partition*, may be used when the subtypes form a partition of their supertype. Since Man and Woman are exclusive and exhaustive, this approach may be used here, resulting in two tables, one containing all the facts about the male patients and the other all the facts about female patients.

The next section discusses the relative merits of these three approaches, and also considers mapping of a subtype family where the subtypes may use an identification scheme different from the supertype. Our default approach however is to absorb the subtypes before grouping. Note that even with this approach, *any fact types with a non-functional role played by a subtype map to separate tables, with their subtype definitions expressed by qualified subset constraints* targeting the main supertype table.

For example, suppose the following *m:n* fact type is attached optionally to Woman in Figure 8.22: **Woman attended ante-natal clinic on Date**. This fact type maps to a separate table with the qualified subset constraint shown. If the new fact type was instead mandatory for Woman, the qualification would read **"exactly where"** instead of **"only where"**.

```
                                          {M,F}
Patient          ( patient#, patientname, sex, [phone], [prostate]¹, [pregnancies]² )
                      ▲
                      ¦ 3
                      ¦
AnteNatalVisit   ( patient#, attendancedate )

             ¹ exists only if sex = 'M'
             ² exists iff sex = 'F'
             ³ only where sex = 'F'
```

We have now covered all the basic steps in the Rmap procedure. These may be summarized as shown in Figure 8.23.

Step 0 may be thought of as a preparatory mental exercise. Erasing all explicit primary reference schemes (i.e. those other than parenthesized reference modes) ensures that all the remaining predicates on display (as box-sequences) belong to fact types (rather than reference types).

Recall that a *compositely identified object type* is either a nested object type or a co-referenced object type (one that is primarily identified with an external uniqueness constraint).

If you're using a sophisticated CASE tool like InfoModeler, you can basically relax and let it do the mapping for you. Even in this case, it's nice to understand how the mapping works. There are plenty of questions in the section exercise to give you practice at performing the mapping manually. As preparation for this exercise, we now consider some larger examples.

Figure 8.24 shows the conceptual schema for the CompactDisk case study discussed in an earlier chapter. If you feel confident, you might like to try mapping this to a relational schema yourself before reading on.

As there are no subtypes in this example, step 0 amounts to mentally erasing any primary reference schemes which are shown explicitly. There are only two, each involving a compositely identified object type: Track; and the objectified predicate. Figure 8.25 depicts this erasure by removing the predicate boxes and showing their connections to object types as dashed lines. For steps 1–3 we treat these two, compositely identified object types just like any other object type.

We now proceed to group fact types into tables. To help visualize this we *place a lasso around each group of predicates which map to the same table* (see Figure 8.25). We lasso only the predicates, not the object types. Since each fact type should map to exactly one table, *all predicates must be lassoed*, and *no lassos may overlap*.

In step 1 we look around for a predicate with a compound uniqueness constraint. Since the objectified predicate is now hidden, we see only one such predicate: is sung by. So we lasso this predicate, indicating it goes to a table all by itself.

0 Absorb subtypes into their top supertype.
Mentally erase all explicit primary identification schemes;
treat compositely identified object types as "black boxes".

1 Map each fact type with a compound UC to a separate table.

2 Fact types with functional roles attached to the same object type are grouped into the same table, keyed on the object type.
Map 1:1 cases to a single table, generally favoring fewer nulls.

3 Map each lazy object type (A!) with no functional roles to a separate table.

4 Unpack each "black box column" into its component attributes.

5 Map all other constraints and derivation rules.
Subtype constraints on functional roles map to qualified optional columns, and on non-functional roles to qualified subset constraints.

Figure 8.23 Main aspects of the default Rmap procedure

In step 2 we group functional fact types of the same object type together. For example, CompactDisk has five functional roles attached to it, so these five fact types are grouped into a table keyed on the identifier for CompactDisk. Similarly the two functional fact types for Track are lassoed together, as are the two functional fact types of the nested object type.

In this example, there are no 1:1 cases, and no lazy object types. We have now roped all the predicates, and there are four lassos, so the conceptual schema maps to four tables (see Figure 8.26).

Since five functional fact types map to the CD (CompactDisk) table, and all the objects involved have simple identifiers, this table has six columns (one for the key and one for each fact attribute). The other three tables involve a composite nested object type, which is unpacked into its component attributes (step 4).

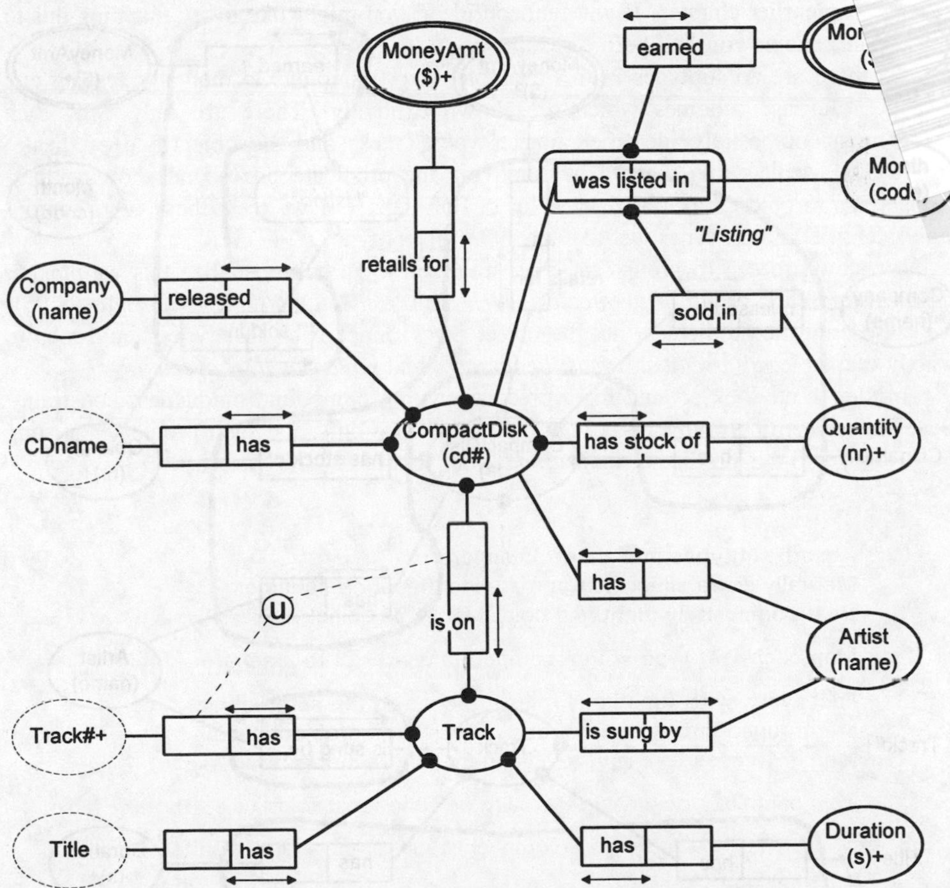

TotalQtySold (Month) ::= **sum**(Quantity) **from** (⟨CompactDisk,Month⟩ sold in Quantity)
TotalRevenue (Month) ::= **sum**(MoneyAmt) **from** (⟨CompactDisk,Month⟩ earned MoneyAmt)

Figure 8.24 The conceptual schema from case study 1

The keys of the tables are already determined, but the mandatory role constraints are enforced by mandatory columns and inter-table subset/equality constraints. Note the composite subset constraint from the pair ⟨cd#, track#⟩ in Vocals to the primary key of Track. Finally the two derivation rules are mapped (step 5).

If you always lasso fact types into groups before writing down the table schemes, you may mentally erase all primary identification schemes (including reference modes) in step 0 (thus treating all object types as black boxes), then in step 4 replace each column by its identifying attribute(s). This alternative formulation of the Rmap procedure is logically cleaner. If you are performing Rmap manually, we suggest you photocopy the conceptual schema and use colored pencils to cross out the reference types and to lasso the fact types.

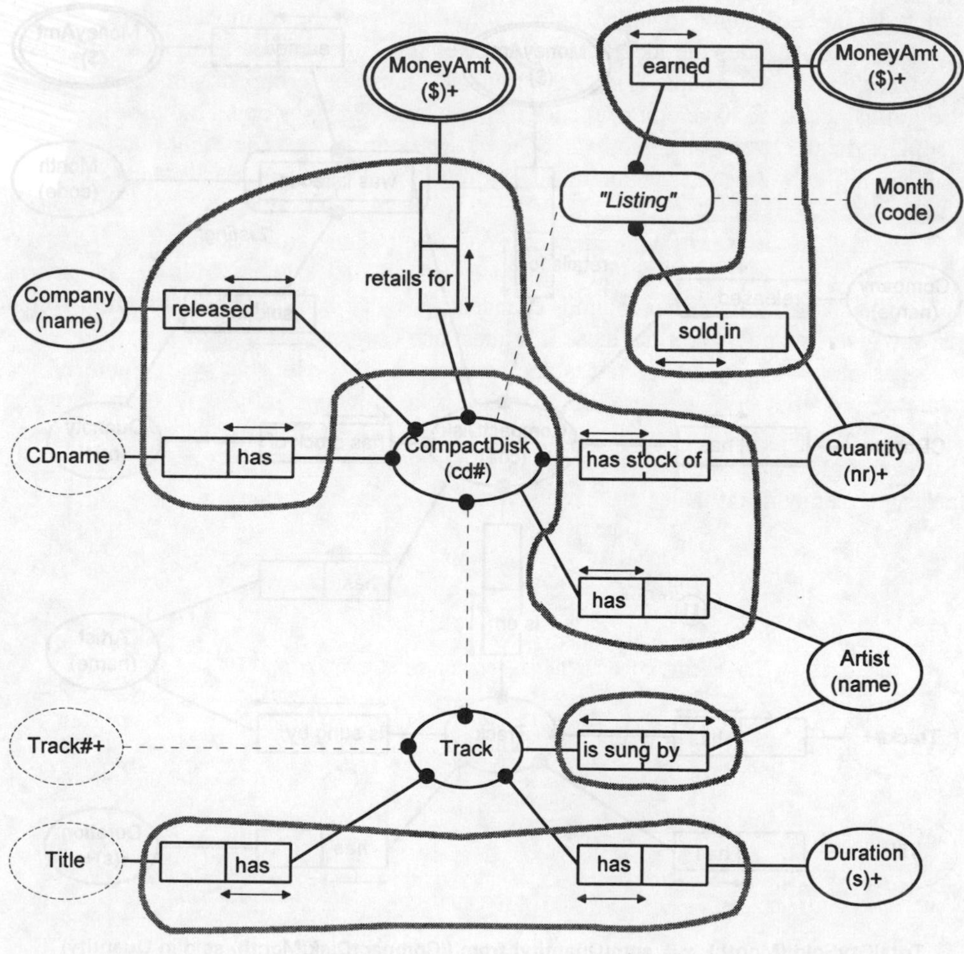

Figure 8.25 Reference types are erased, and fact types are grouped

As a more complicated example, consider the conceptual schema in Figure 8.27. This concerns television channels. Notice that Time is modeled as a co-referenced entity type (a time point is identified as a given hour on a given day). For variety, the object types Office and Dept have been modeled as nested entity types. A television channel may have different offices in different suburbs. For this application, a channel may have only one office in any given suburb. A given office may have many departments. For example, one department might be the advertising department for the channel 9 office located in the suburb Toowong. Alternatively (and arguably more naturally) the object types Office and Dept could have been modeled as co-referenced object types. However this would not change the mapping.

The external uniqueness constraint on Program indicates that a channel can screen only one program at a given time. As an exercise, try to map this yourself before reading on. Start by mentally erasing the reference types, and lassoing the fact types which should be grouped together, before you write down the relational schema.

Figure 8.28 hides the identifying predicates for Time, Office and Dept, and lassos the fact types into groups. The 1:1 predicates must be grouped with Channel and Program since these have other functional roles, but Frequency and Title do not.

The detailed relational schema is shown in Figure 8.29. The identifier for Office unpacks into two attributes, while the Dept key unpacks into three (two for Office and one for DeptKind).

Notice also the inter-table uniqueness constraint. This indicates that when a natural join is performed between the Program and ProgTime tables, there will be a uniqueness constraint spanning the three columns channel#, progday and proghour. In other words, for any given channel and time there is at most one program being shown.

The choice of names for tables and columns is up to you, but we recommend the naming guidelines discussed earlier. Mapping from a conceptual to a relational schema is a bit like doing CSDP step 1 in reverse. Try to choose names for tables and columns that would make it easier for you to perform CSDP step 1 if presented with the relational tables. Remember that tables are basically just collections of facts.

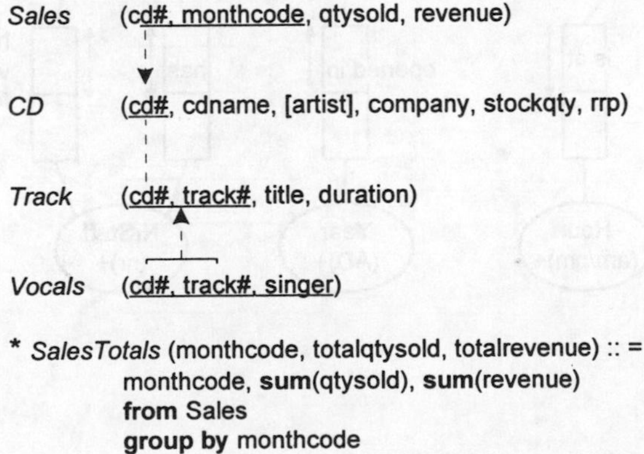

Sales (cd#, monthcode, qtysold, revenue)

CD (cd#, cdname, [artist], company, stockqty, rrp)

Track (cd#, track#, title, duration)

Vocals (cd#, track#, singer)

* *SalesTotals* (monthcode, totalqtysold, totalrevenue) :: =
monthcode, **sum**(qtysold), **sum**(revenue)
from Sales
group by monthcode

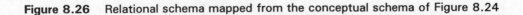

Figure 8.26 Relational schema mapped from the conceptual schema of Figure 8.24

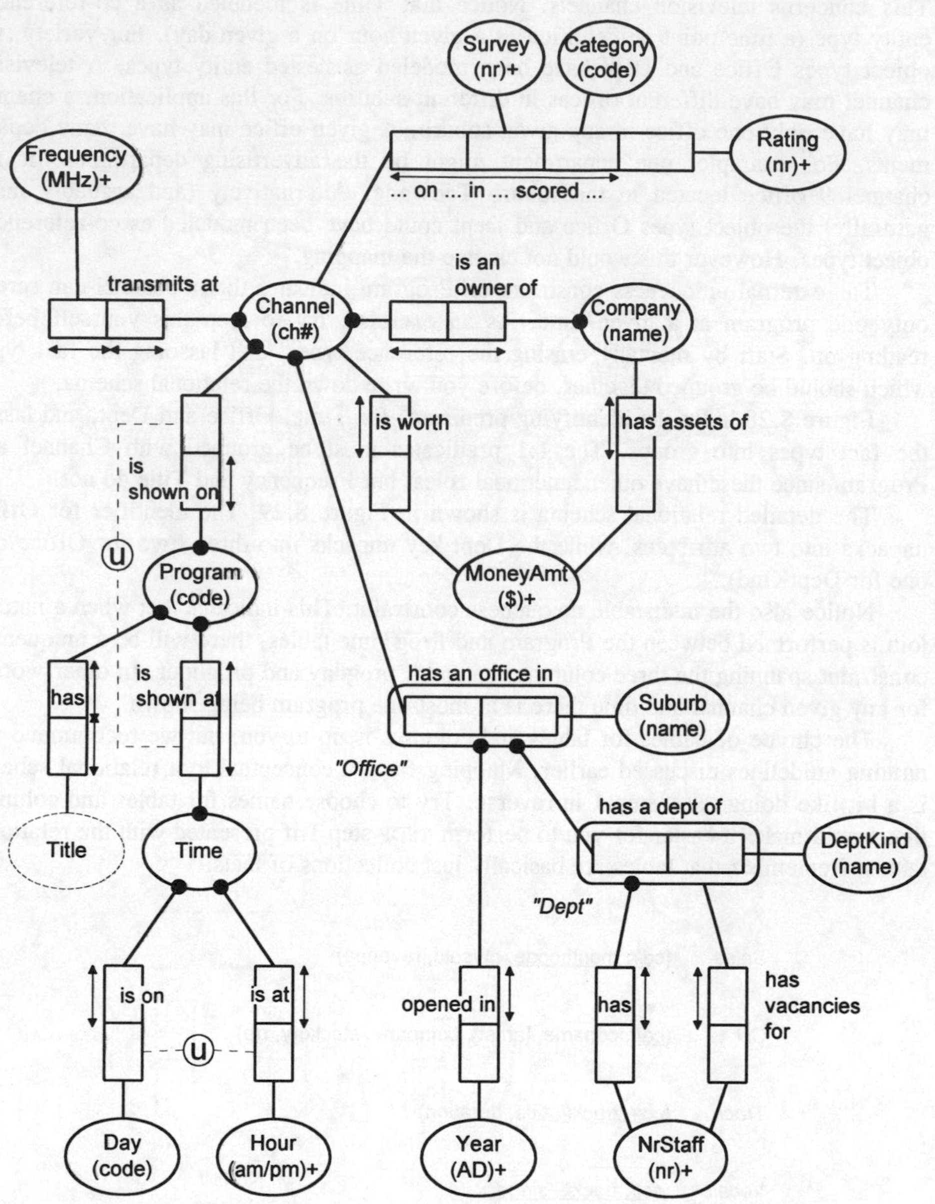
Survey
(nr)+
Category
(code)
Rating
(nr)+
Frequency
(MHz)+
... on ... in ... scored ...
transmits at
Channel
(ch#)
is an
owner of
Company
(name)
is worth
has assets of
is
shown on
U
Program
(code)
MoneyAmt
($)+
has
is
shown at
has an office in
Suburb
(name)
"Office"
has a dept of
DeptKind
(name)
Title
Time
"Dept"
is on
is at
U
opened in
has
has
vacancies
for
Day
(code)
Hour
(am/pm)+
Year
(AD)+
NrStaff
(nr)+

Figure 8.27

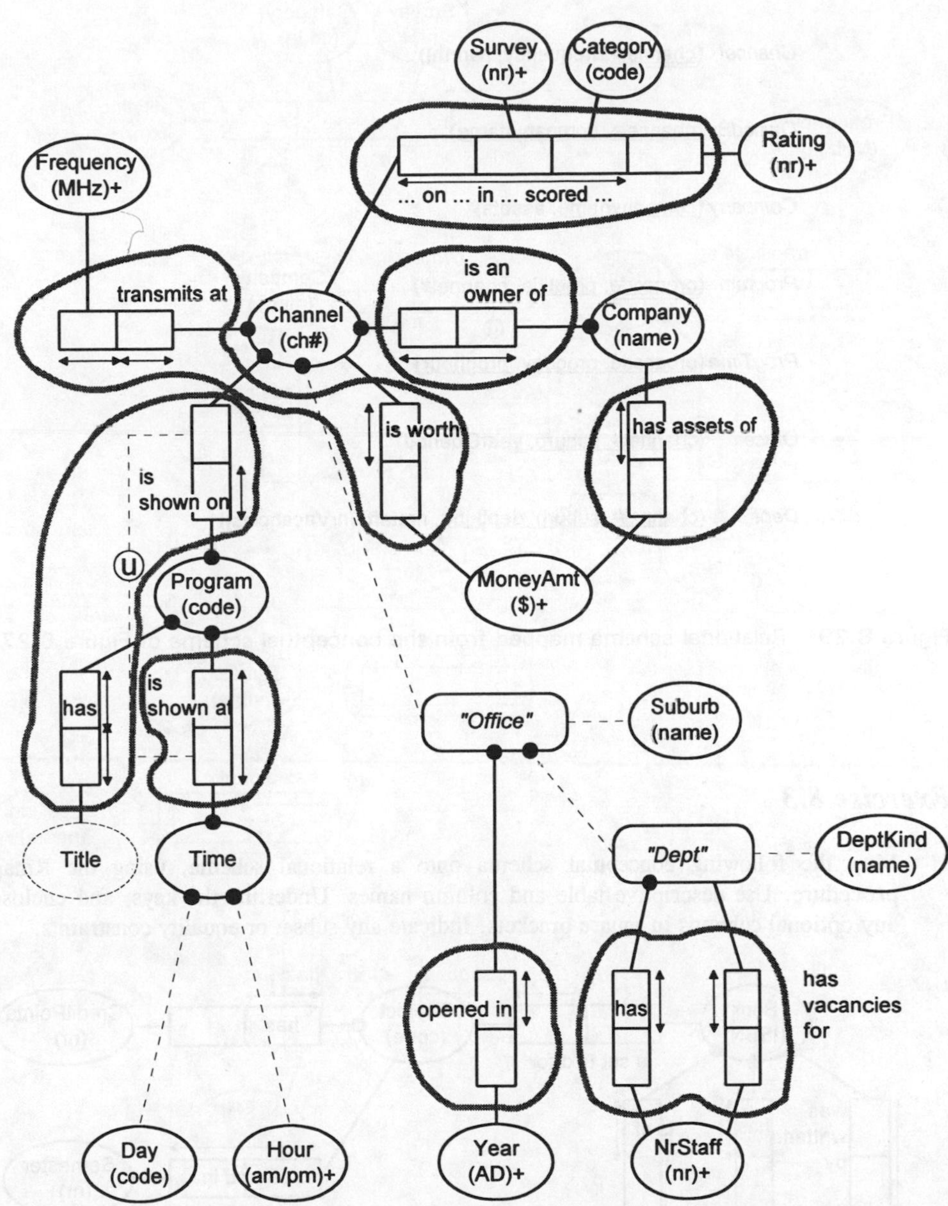

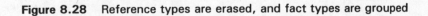

Figure 8.28 Reference types are erased, and fact types are grouped

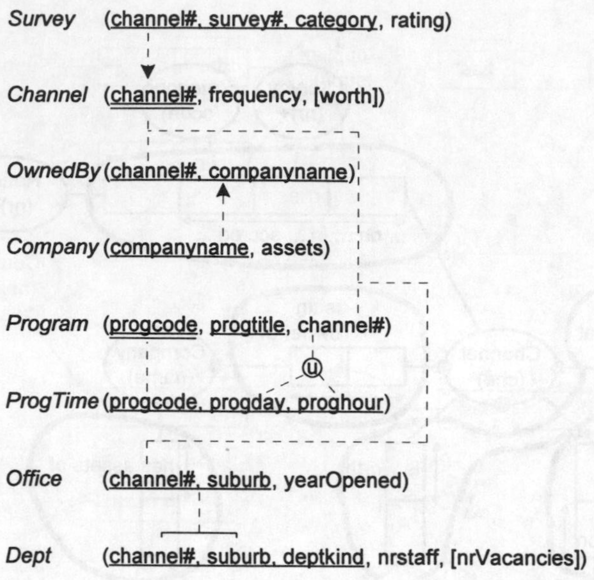

Figure 8.29 Relational schema mapped from the conceptual schema of Figure 8.27

Exercise 8.3

1. Map the following conceptual schema onto a relational schema, using the Rmap procedure. Use descriptive table and column names. Underline the keys, and enclose any optional columns in square brackets. Indicate any subset or equality constraints.

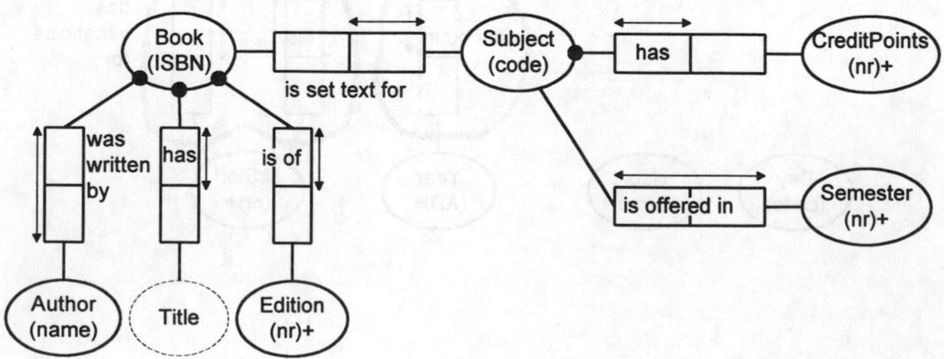

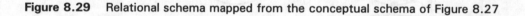

2. Rmap the following conceptual schema.

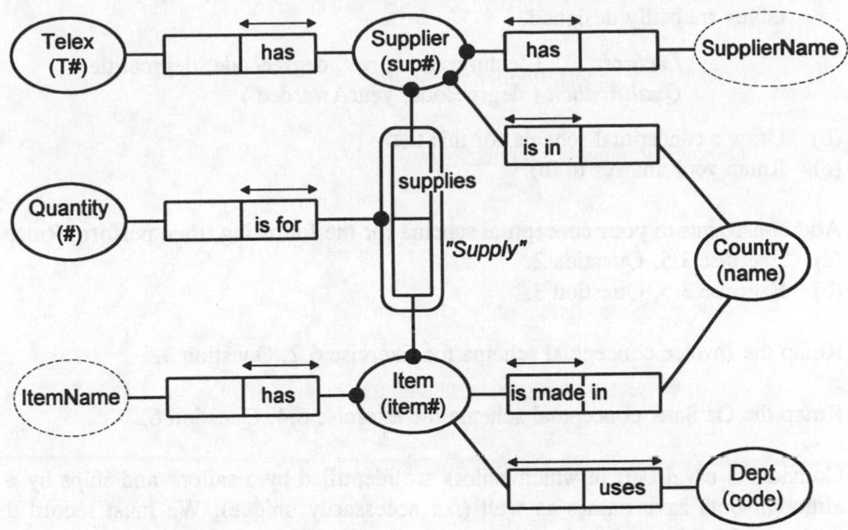

3. (a) The conceptual schema for a given UoD is shown below. A novice designer maps the likes and costs fact types into a single table: *Likes* (<u>woman, dress</u>, cost). Explain with the aid of a small, sample population why this table is badly designed. Use surrogates w1, w2, ... for women and d1, d2, ... for dresses.

   (b) Rmap the conceptual schema.

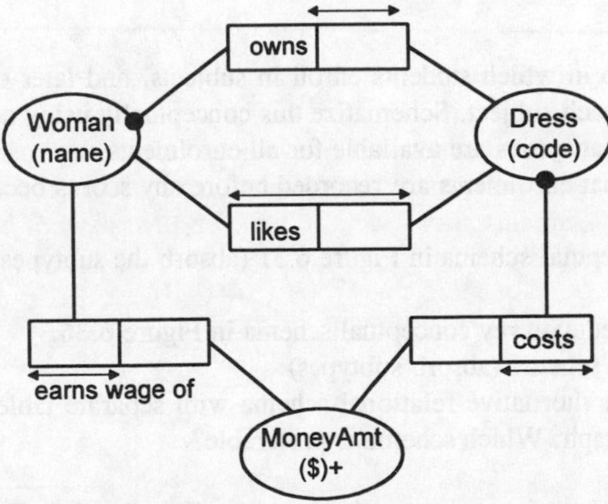

4. In a given UoD, each lecturer has at least one degree and optionally has taught at one or more institutions. Each lecturer has exactly one identifying name, and at most one nickname. Each degree is standardly identified by its code, but also has a unique title. Some degrees might not be held by any current lecturer. Each institution is identified by its name. The sex and birth year of the lecturers is recorded, as well as the years in which their degrees were awarded.

(a) A novice designer develops a relational schema for this UoD which includes the following two tables. Explain, with the aid of a sample population, why these tables are badly designed.

Lecturer (lecturername, sex, degreecode, degreetitle)
Qualification (degreecode, yearAwarded)

(b) Draw a conceptual schema for this UoD.
(c) Rmap your answer to (b).

5. Add constraints to your conceptual schema for the following, then perform Rmap.
   (a) Exercise 3.5, Question 2.
   (b) Exercise 3.5, Question 3.

6. Rmap the Invoice conceptual schema for Exercise 6.2, Question 3.

7. Rmap the Oz Bank conceptual schema for Exercise 6.4, Question 6.

8. Consider a naval UoD in which sailors are identified by a sailor# and ships by a ship#, although both have names as well (not necessarily unique). We must record the sex, rank and birthdate of each sailor and the weight (in tonnes) and construction date of each ship. Each ship may have only one captain and vice versa. Specify a conceptual schema and relational schema for this UoD for the following cases.
   (a) Each captain commands a ship but some ships might not have captains.
   (b) Each ship has a captain but some captains might not command a ship.
   (c) Each captain commands a ship, and each ship has a captain.
   (d) Some captains might not command a ship, and some ships might not have captains.

9. Consider a UoD in which students enroll in subjects, and later obtain scores on one or more tests for each subject. Schematize this conceptually using nesting, then Rmap it.
   (a) Assume that scores are available for all enrolments.
   (b) Assume that enrolments are recorded before any scores become known.

10. Rmap the conceptual schema in Figure 6.31 (absorb the subtypes before mapping).

11. Refer to the MediaSurvey conceptual schema in Figure 6.36.
    (a) Rmap this schema (absorb subtypes).
    (b) Set out an alternative relational schema with separate tables for each node in the subtype graph. Which schema is preferable?

12. (a) Rmap the Taxpayer conceptual schema for Exercise 6.5, Q. 3 (a).
    (b) Rmap the Taxpayer conceptual schema for Exercise 6.5, Q. 3 (b).

13. Rmap the SolarSystem conceptual schema for Exercise 6.5, Q. 6.

14. Rmap the conceptual schema in Figure 7.5 (note that Panel is a lazy object type).

15. Rmap the CountryBorders conceptual schema for Exercise 7.3, Q. 5.

16. Rmap the following conceptual schema.

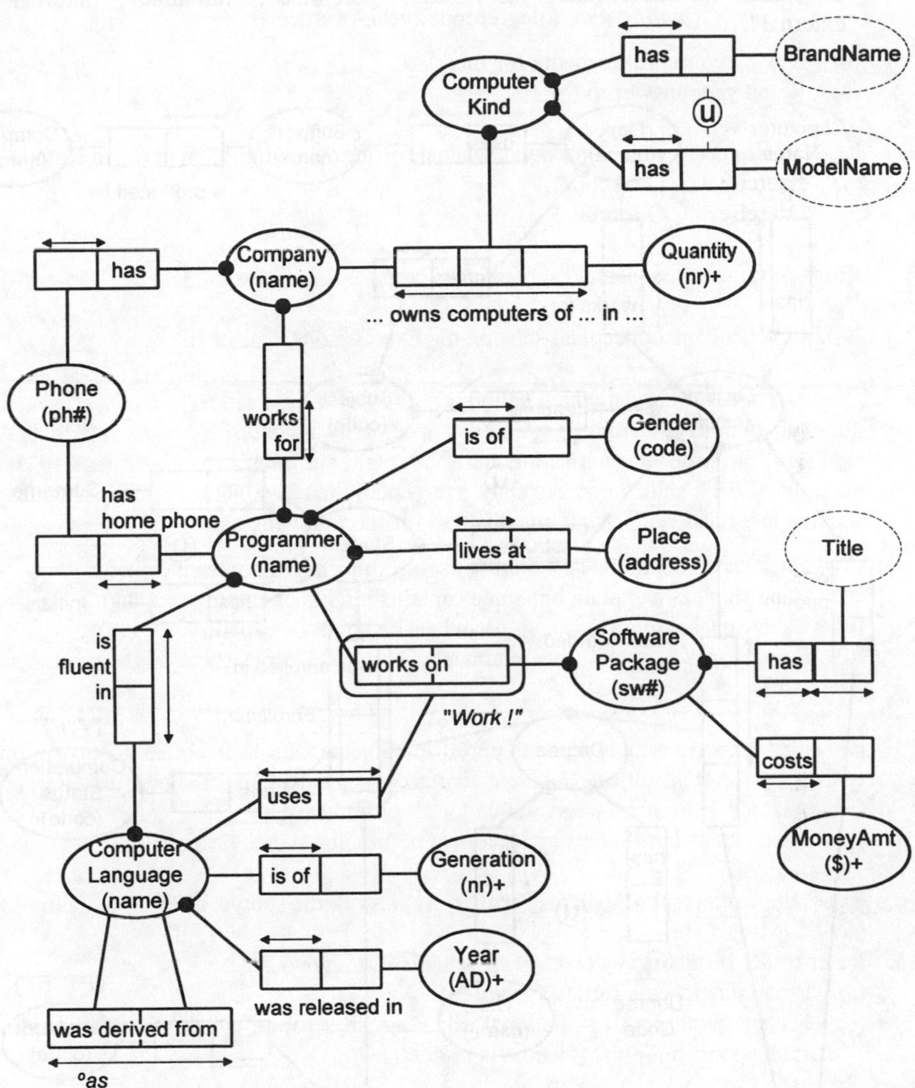

17. Rmap the following conceptual schema. Note that Degree is compositely identified (e.g. a PhD from UCLA and a PhD from MIT are treated as different degrees). Student is also compositely identified (by the time you finish the mapping you will appreciate how much better it would be to use a student# instead!). The codes "y", "n", "PT", "FT", "int", and "ext" abbreviate "yes", "no", "part time", "full time", "internal" and "external".

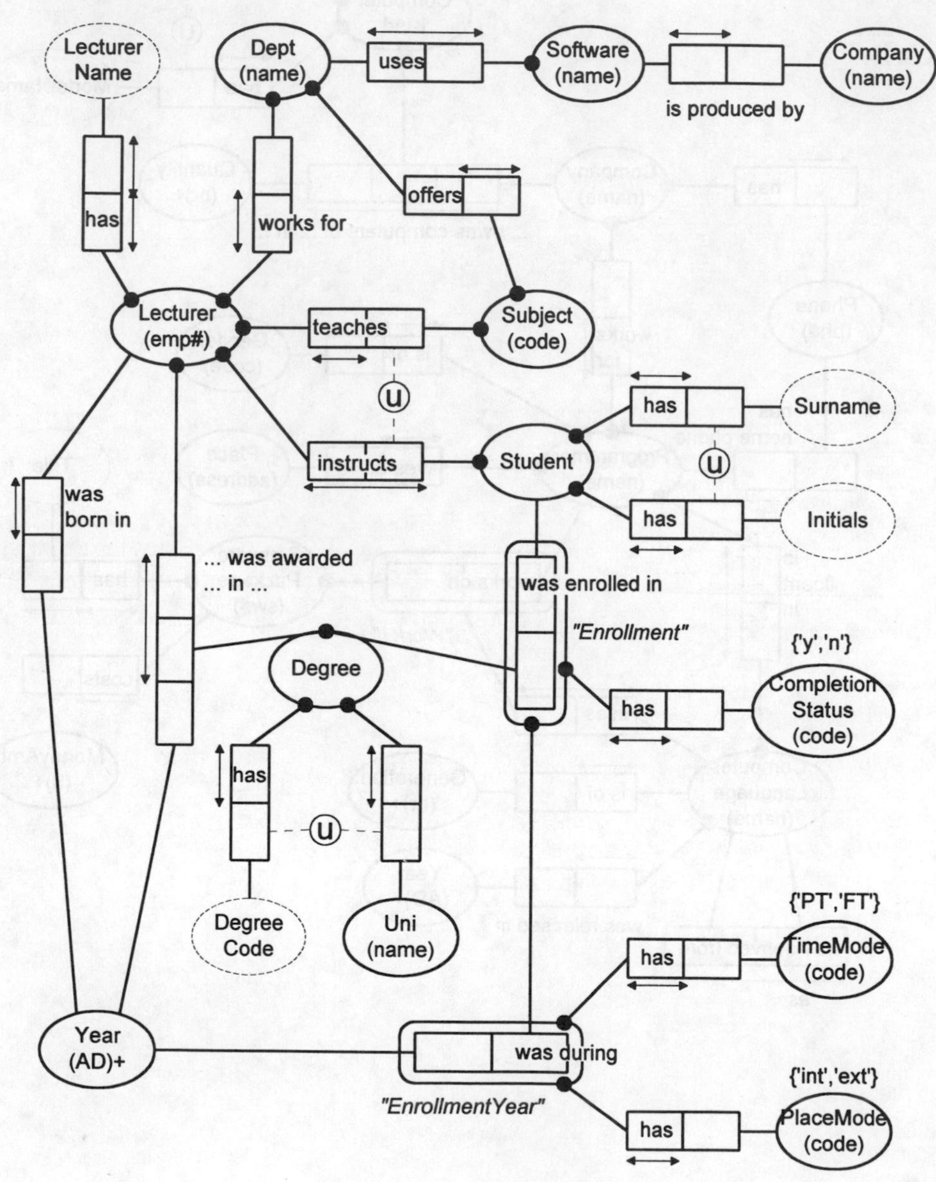

18. Rmap the following conceptual schema.

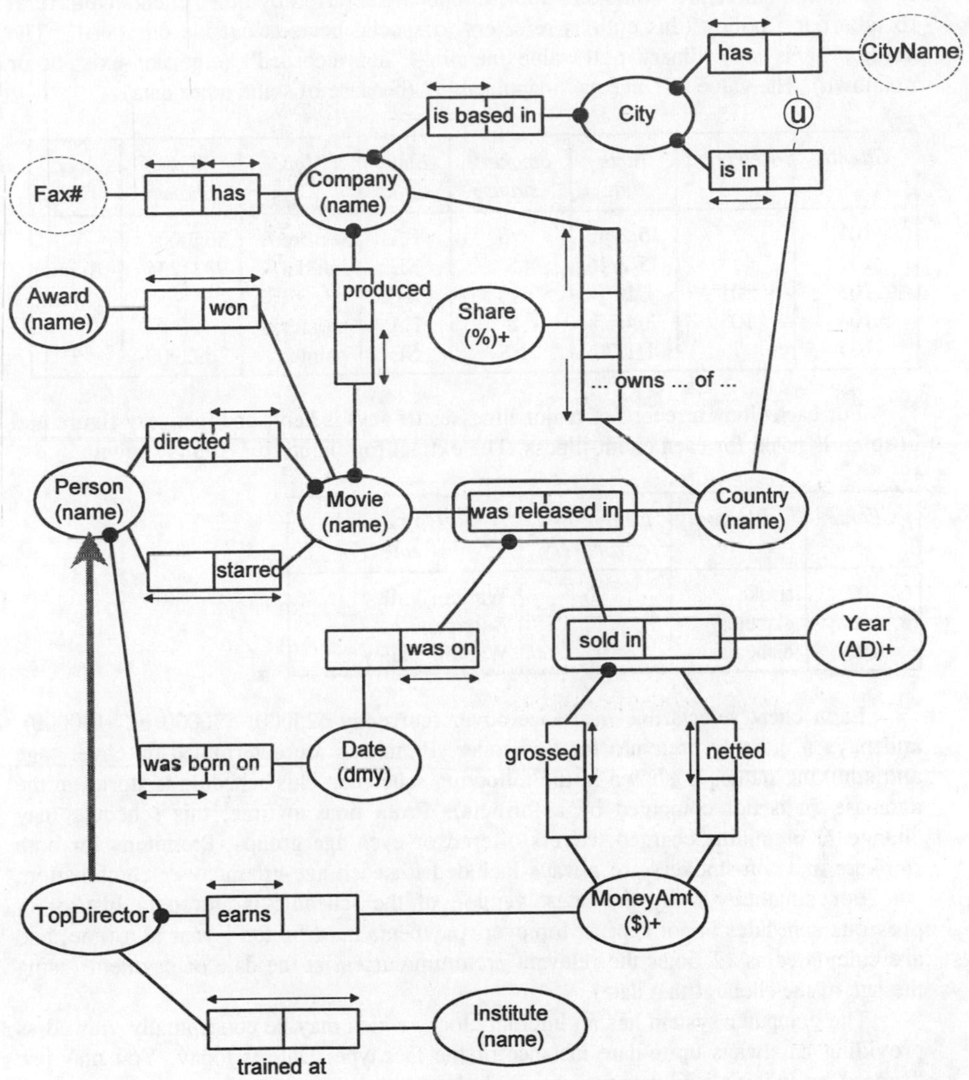

19. A life insurance company maintains an information system about its clients. The following information samples are extracted from a fragment of this system. For simplicity, several data items (e.g. client's name and address) are omitted and may be ignored for this question. Each client is identified by his/her client number (client#).

The following table uses these abbreviations: Emp. = employment (EA = Employed by Another; SE = Self-Employed; NE = Not Employed); Acct = accounting; NS = Non-Smoker; S = Smoker. Some clients are referred by other clients (referrers) to take out a policy (this entitles referrers to special benefits outside our UoD). The value "?" is an ordinary null value meaning "not recorded" (e.g. non-existent or unknown). The value "–" means "inapplicable" (because of some other data).

Client#	*Referrer*	*Birth date*	*Smoking status*	*Emp. status*	*Job*	*Work phone#*	*Acct. firm*
101	?	15/2/46	NS	EA	lecturer	3650001	–
102	?	15/2/46	S	SE	builder	9821234	Acme
103	101	1/1/70	NS	NE	–	–	–
104	103	3/4/65	S	EA	painter	?	–
105	?	1/1/70	NS	SE	painter	2692900	?

For each client a record of major illnesses (if any) is kept; one recovery figure and hospital is noted for each client-illness. The extract for clients 101-105 is shown:

Client#	*Illness*	*Degree (%) of recovery*	*Hospital treated*
102	stroke	90	Wandin Valley
	diabetes	80	Burrigan
103	diabetes	95	Wandin Valley

Each client selects one insurance cover (currently \$25000, \$50000 or \$100000), and pays a monthly premium for this cover. Premiums are determined by cover, age and smoking status, as shown in the following schedule. This schedule is stored in the database (it is not computed by a formula). From time to time, this schedule may change in premiums charged, covers offered or even age groups. Premiums for both smokers and non-smokers are always included for each age-group/cover combination.

For simplicity, only the latest version of the schedule is stored (a history of previous schedules is not kept). Moreover, payments must be for 1 year at a time, and are calculated as 12 times the relevant premium current at the date of payment (using the age of the client at that date).

The computer system has an internal clock, which may be conceptually viewed as providing an always up-to-date instance of the fact type: Date is today. You may use "**today**" as an initialized date variable in derivation rules.

	Non-Smoker premiums (\$)			*Smoker premiums (\$)*		
Age (y)	25000 cover	50000 cover	100000 cover	25000 cover	50000 cover	100000 cover
21–39	5.00	7.50	12.50	6.50	10.50	18.50
40–49	6.50	10.50	18.50	10.00	17.50	32.50
50–59	13.00	23.50	34.00	24.00	45.50	88.50
60–69	36.50	70.50	138.50	57.50	112.50	222.50

Though not shown in the schedule, age groups are primarily identified by an agegroup# (currently in the range 1..4).

Assume all clients have paid their 12 month fee by completing a form like that shown below (details such as name and address omitted for this exercise). The first four fields are completed by the insurance agency, and the rest by the client. Records of any previous payments are outside our UoD.

Client#: ....

Insurance cover: $ ....

Date: ....

Payment for next 12 months insurance: $ ....

Method of payment (Please tick one): ❑ cash ❑ cheque ❑ credit card

If paying by credit card, complete the following:

❑ Visa ❑ Mastercard ❑ Bankcard

Card Number:

Card expiry date: ....

Choose suitable codes to abbreviate payment methods and card types. Each credit card is used by at most two clients (e.g. husband and wife). In practice the cardtype could be derived from the starting digits of the card#; but ignore this possibility for this question.

(a) Specify a conceptual schema for this UoD. Include **all** graphic constraints, and any noteworthy textual constraints. Include subtype definitions and derivation rules. If a derived fact type should be stored, include it on the diagram with an "*S" mark to indicate it is both derived and stored.

(b) Should the payment by a client be derived only, stored only or both? Discuss the practical issues involved in making this decision.

(c) Map your conceptual schema to a relational schema, absorbing subtypes while maintaining subtype constraints. Underline keys and mark optional columns with square brackets. Include **all** constraints. As an optional exercise, map any derivation rules.

8.4 Advanced mapping aspects

In the previous section, Figure 8.23 listed the main steps in the default relational mapping procedure (Rmap). Step 0 of this procedure may be refined as shown in Figure 8.30. This section discusses these refinements seriatim, and clarifies some fine points. If desired, this section may be safely skipped on a first reading.

0 .1 Mentally binarize any unaries, and cater for any relative closure.
.2 Mentally erase all reference (primary identification) predicates.
Treat compositely identified object types as "black boxes".
.3 Indicate any non-absorption choices for subtypes.
.4 Identify any derived fact types that must be stored.
.5 Indicate mapping choices for symmetric 1:1 cases.
.6 Consider replacing any disjunctive reference scheme, by using an artificial or concatenated identifier or mandatory defaults.
.7 Indicate mapping choice where required for any objectified predicate without a spanning uniqueness constraint.

Figure 8.30 Refinements to Step 0 of Rmap

As background to step 0.1, please review the discussion of relative closure in section 7.4. Now consider a UoD about applications (e.g. for jobs or loans). Suppose that Figure 8.31 is used to model part of this UoD.

The relative closure boxes (□) on the unaries indicates that if an application succeeded or failed this must be known. Since the disjunction of these unaries is optional, it is possible that the fate of some applications is undecided. As explained in detail in the next chapter, a schema transformation may be performed to replace these exclusive unaries by the binary shown in Figure 8.32.

Here the status of the application is identified by a code (S = Succeeded, F = Failed, U = Undecided). This transformation is understood to be performed automatically as a pre-processing stage to the rest of Rmap. The modeler may still work with the original conceptual schema unless he or she prefers the transformed version. The final result of the mapping is shown at the bottom of Figure 8.32. For another example of step 0.1, see Figures 7.16 and 7.17 in the previous chapter (the final mapping is left as an exercise).

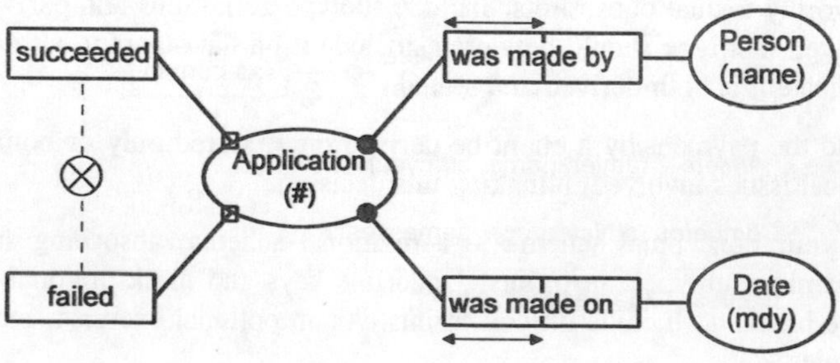

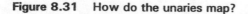

Figure 8.31 How do the unaries map?

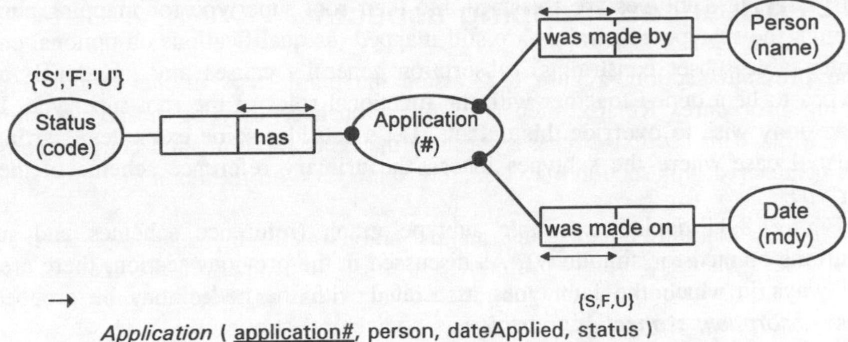

Figure 8.32 The result of binarizing the unaries in Figure 8.31

Step 0.2 involves mentally erasing any reference predicates and treating objectified predicates as simple object types. The previous section discussed typical cases. Figure 8.33 depicts a special case. Here each Olympic games is identified by the year in which it is held. There are three fact types (Athlete competes in Games; Athlete was born in Year; City hosts Games) and one reference type (Games is held in Year).

The reference type must be shown explicitly, since Year is an entity type, not a value type. Using this reference type and the birth fact type we may derive, if desired, the approximate ages of athletes at various games. One instance of the hosts fact type is: The City with name 'Sydney' hosts the Games that is held in the Year 2000 AD.

It is rare to have an object type identified by means of a single, explicit reference type. To map this case, the reference type is first mentally erased, leaving the three fact types to be grouped into tables. As an exercise, try the mapping yourself and then check your answer with the solution shown at the bottom of Figure 8.33.

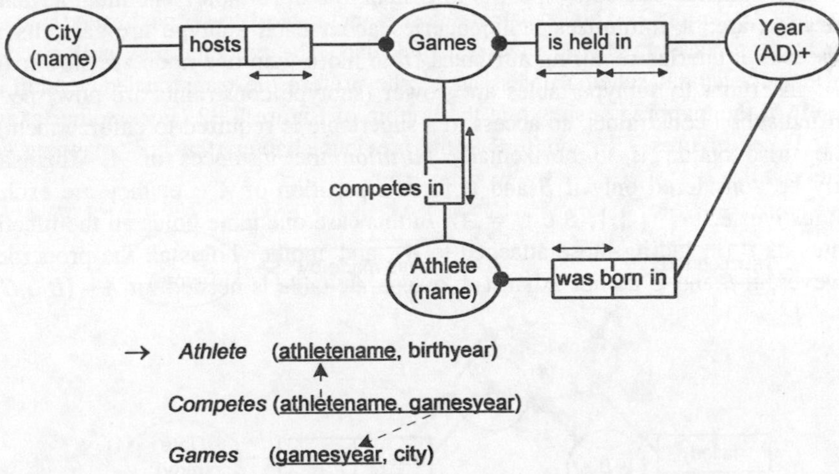

Figure 8.33 Games is identified by a single, explicit reference type

By default, subtypes are absorbed into their root supertype for mapping purposes. Although the subtype constraints are still mapped (as qualifications on optional columns or inter-table subset constraints), absorption generally causes any functional roles of subtypes to be grouped together with the functional roles of the root supertype. In step 0.3 we may wish to override this default. Let's consider some examples, starting with the usual case where the subtypes inherit the primary reference scheme of their top supertype.

Figure 8.34 depicts a simple subtype graph (reference schemes and subtype definitions omitted for simplicity). As discussed in the previous section, there are three basic ways in which the fact types associated with the nodes may be grouped into tables: *absorption; separation; partition.*

The first option *absorbs* the subtypes back into the supertype before grouping. For example, assume all the roles played by *A*, *B* and *C* are functional (i.e. they have a simple uniqueness constraint). In this case we generate just one table (with subtype constraints expressed as qualifications on the optional subtype attributes). This absorption default has two main advantages: better performance for queries that require attributes from more than one node (no joins required); subtype constraints are usually easy to specify and cheap to enforce (no joins).

The main disadvantages of subtype absorption are: nulls are required for objects which belong to only one of the subtypes; the functional table of the supertype is larger (more columns); queries about only one subtype require a restriction; viewing just a subtype is less convenient (projection and restriction needed). Usually the advantages outweigh the disadvantages. Note that any non-functional roles of the subtypes map to separate tables anyway, so these are not affected by our subtype mapping choice.

The second option, *separation*, groups the functional roles attached directly to each object type node into separate tables, one for each node. Here the functional predicates of *A* map to one table (the common properties), the attributes specific to *B* map to another table, and the attributes specific to *C* map to a third table. The main advantages of separation are: it minimizes nulls; queries about each subtype are fast. Its main weaknesses are: queries requiring attributes from more than one node are slower (joins needed); insertions to subtype tables are slower (subtype constraints are now specified as qualified subset constraints, so access to a supertable is required to enforce them).

The third option is to horizontally *partition* the instances of *A*. This should normally be considered only if *B* and *C* form a partition of *A* (i.e. they are exclusive and exhaustive: $B \cap C = \{\ \}$; $B \cup C = A$). In this case one table holds all the functional predicates of *B* (including those attached to *A*), and another holds all the properties of *C*. However, if *B* and *C* do not exhaust *A*, a separate table is needed for $A - (B \cup C)$.

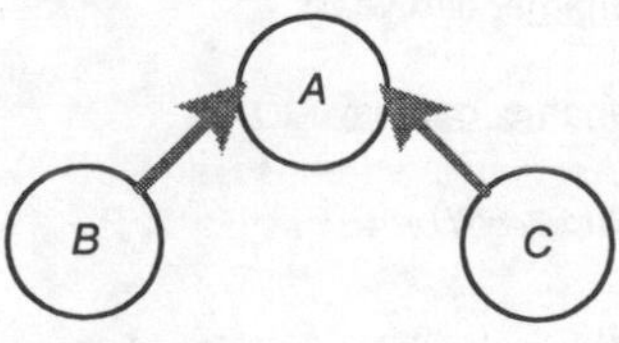

Figure 8.34 A simple subtype graph

If *B* and *C* overlap, redundancy results for the facts about $B \cap C$ and this must be controlled. This partition option departs from the usual practice of grouping each fact type into only one table, and tends to be useful only in distributed or federated database settings.

The main advantages of partitioning the supertype are: it minimizes nulls; queries about all the properties of *B* (or *C*) are fast; subtype constraints typically need not be coded (because implied) or are trivial to code (e.g. Man and Woman tables without/with sex field). Its main disadvantages are: slow queries about all of *A*, or *B* and *C* (joins needed); it is very awkward unless *B* and *C* form a partition of *A*; if *B* and *C* are exclusive, enforcement of this constraint normally requires inter-table access.

Consideration of the criteria discussed can help us decide whether to override the default absorption option. Override decisions may be indicated by annotating the schema in an appropriate way, or perhaps by selecting from an option list in a CASE tool. For larger subtype graphs, the number of mapping choices multiplies rapidly, as mixtures of the three options might be used.

To clarify some of the previous discussion, let's look at a couple of examples. Consider the conceptual schema in Figure 8.35. Here academics have one of three ranks (L = Lecturer, SL = Senior Lecturer, P = Professor). Students may be counselled only by senior lecturers, and academic chairs are held only by professors. Since the subtypes do not form a partition of Academic, we would normally choose either absorption or separation to map them. As an exercise try both these options yourself before reading on.

In the counselling predicate, the role attached to SenLec is not functional. So this predicate maps to a separate table regardless of whether we choose absorption or separation. Also, being *m:n*, the degrees fact type maps to a separate table regardless. So the only choice we have in the subtype mapping is whether or not to group the rank and chair fact types together. With absorption, wc do so (see Figure 8.36(a)). With separation we do not (see Figure 8.36(b)). Note the different ways of specifying the subtype and mandatory role constraints for the Professor subtype.

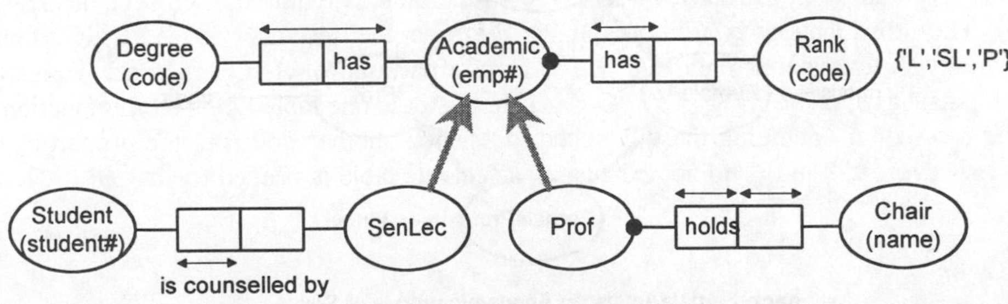

Figure 8.35

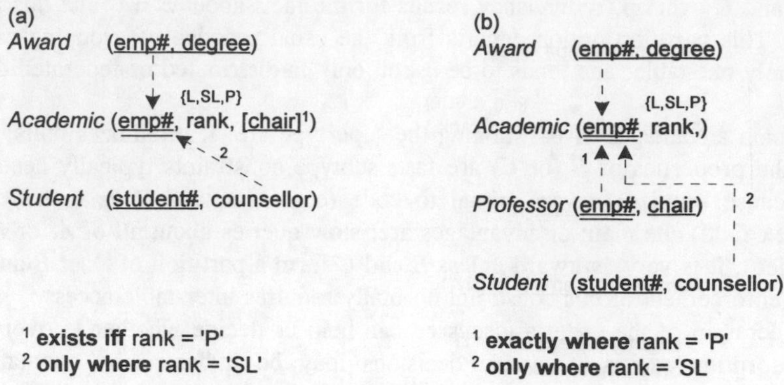

Figure 8.36 Mapping from Figure 8.35, using subtype (a) absorption (b) separation

In the subset constraint qualifications, the **"only where"** captures the subtype constraint, while **"exactly where"** covers both subtyping and mandatory role constraints. We now restrict our attention to the mapping of functional predicates of the nodes in the subtype graph, since the mapping of other predicates to separate tables with qualified subset constraints is straightforward.

As an example with multiple inheritance, consider Figure 8.37. This figure also shows one way of displaying an ER view of an ORM diagram (ER abstractions are discussed further in Chapter 10). Here all attributes are single-valued; underlining an attribute indicates the 1:1 nature. The absence of a mandatory role dot on nrkids (number of children) indicates that recording of this attribute is optional for female academics.

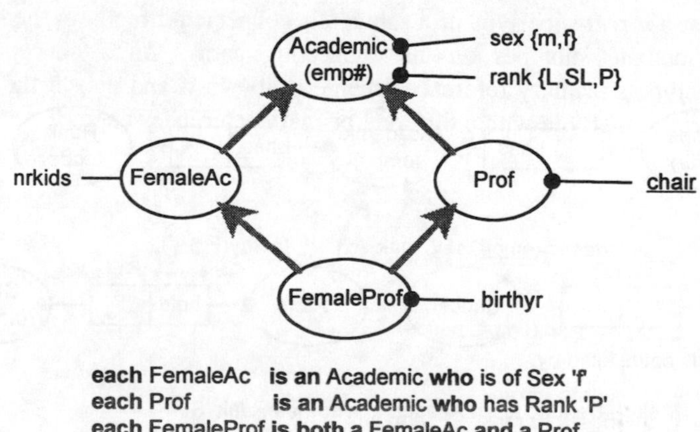

Figure 8.37 An ER view with multiple inheritance

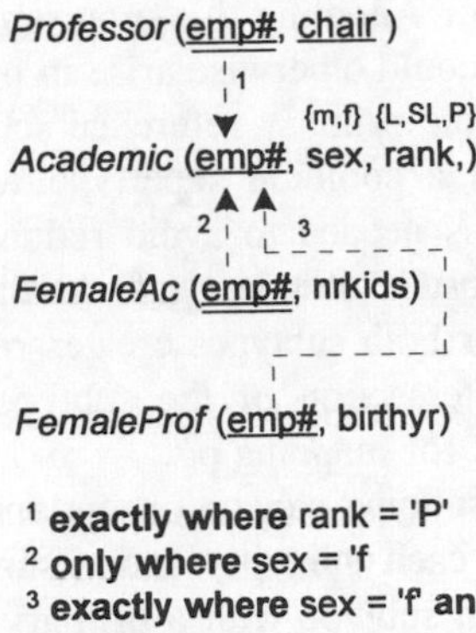

Professor (emp#, chair)

1

{m,f} {L,SL,P}

Academic (emp#, sex, rank,)

2 3

FemaleAc (emp#, nrkids)

FemaleProf (emp#, birthyr)

[1] **exactly where** rank = 'P'
[2] **only where** sex = 'f
[3] **exactly where** sex = 'f' **and** rank = 'P"

Figure 8.38 Relational map of Figure 8.37, choosing subtype separation

Suppose we decide on separate tables for each subtype. This yields the relational schema in Figure 8.38. Note that qualified subset constraints from FemaleProf.emp# to Professor.emp# and FemaleAc.emp# are implied. For efficiency reasons we adopt the default policy of specifying qualified subset constraints with respect to the root supertable where possible. The order of table creation then does not matter so long as the root table is created first, and the schema is easier to change.

Mixed approaches may be adopted. For example, if we absorb FemaleProf and Prof into Academic, but map roles specific to FemaleAc to a separate table, we obtain the relational schema in Figure 8.39. Notice that qualification 2 captures two subtype constraints. Other mixtures are possible, but this gives the idea.

Section 6.6 discussed the awkward situation of *context-dependent reference schemes*, where a subtype may have a different primary identification scheme from its supertype(s). We now briefly discuss how such cases may be mapped.

Recall that a *direct* supertype of a subtype is connected directly to the subtype (i.e. with no intermediate subtypes on the connecting path). On a conceptual schema diagram, a subtype's primary reference scheme is shown if and only if the subtype has at least one direct supertype with a different primary reference scheme.

{m,f} {L,SL,P}

Academic (emp#, sex, rank, [chair[1], [birthyr][2]])

3

FemaleAc (emp#, nrkids)

[1] **exists iff** rank = 'P'
[2] **exists iff** rank = 'P' **and** sex = 'f'
[3] **only where** sex = 'f'

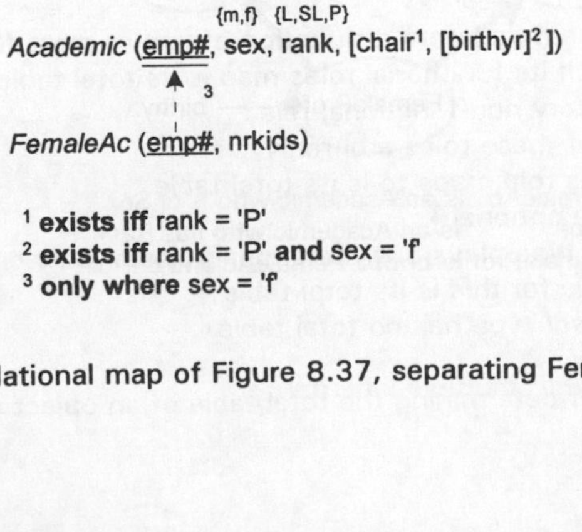

Figure 8.39 Relational map of Figure 8.37, separating FemaleAc only

In mapping, all specific roles attached to an entity type require the object type to be identified by its primary reference scheme. Adopting this requirement avoids some extremely complex reference constraints that could otherwise arise in practice.

If two overlapping subtypes have the same primary reference scheme, and one is not a subtype of the other, they must have a common supertype with this primary reference scheme (if not, create one). This is needed to avoid redundancy later. For example, consider FemaleStudent(s#) and PostGradStudent (s#) as direct subtypes of Person (p#). Mapping p# down into tables for both subtypes creates redundancy of the facts which associate p# and s# for the intersection of the subtypes; so insert the intermediate supertype Student (s#) as a target for mapping p#.

We confine our discussion here to the subtype separation option (separate tables are created for functional roles specific to each subtype) and assume all reference schemes are simple (not composite). For each subtype with a primary reference mode different from the root's, we define its *"total table"* (if any) as set out in Figure 8.40. The basic idea is that the total table of an object type includes all instances in the population of the object type (i.e. its total population).

In what follows, where total tables exist we basically ignore other tables of the object type (the other tables are linked by foreign keys to the primary ones in the normal way).

The root supertype table(s) is/are computed in the normal way. Push the primary reference of the root supertype down as an extra attribute in the total table of each subtype which "introduces" a different primary reference scheme to the graph; if the introducing subtype has no total table, create an extra reference table for it (to store just the fact connecting the two identifiers for the object type's population).

In specifying, at the relational level, subtype links between object types with different primary reference schemes use the root reference scheme; if the object types have the same reference scheme, use this common reference scheme.

These guidelines are best understood by way of example. Consider the schema in Figure 8.41. Here "StudEmp" is short for "Student Employee". Better students are often employed to do some tutoring. If known, the number of hours tutoring undertaken by such a student is recorded. In practice many other fact types might be stored about each node. Within the student records subschema, students are identified by their student# (s#). Within the staff record subsystem, all employees are identified by the employee number (e#).

```
if the object type has a mandatory disjunction of one or more functional roles
then the table to which its functional roles map is its total table
else if it has a mandatory non-functional role
     then select one of these roles arbitrarily;
          the table this role maps to is its total table
     else { all roles are optional }
          if the object type plays only functional roles or only one role
          then the table for this is its total table
          else  the object type has no total table.
```

Figure 8.40 Procedure for determining the total table of an object type (if it exists)

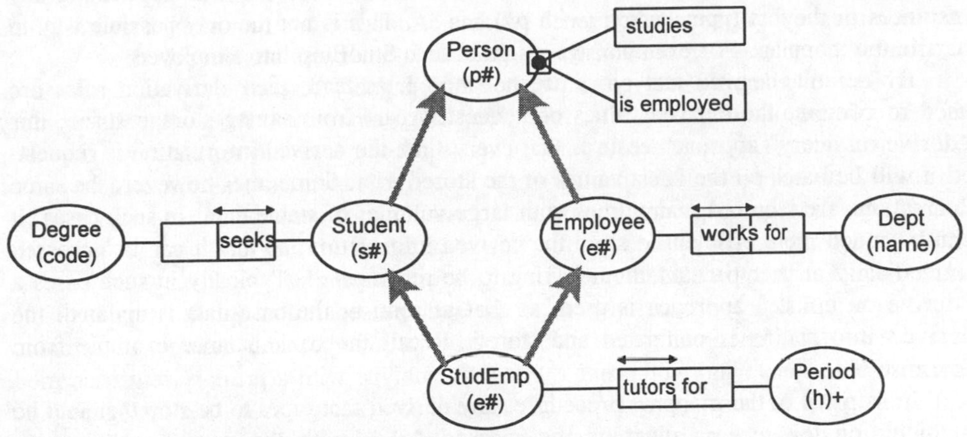

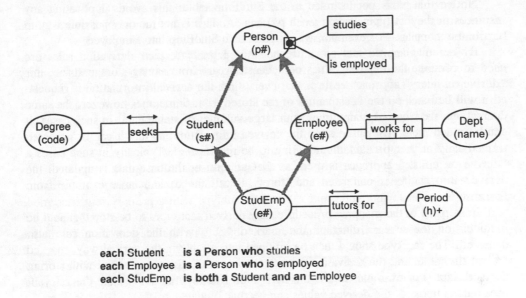

each Student **is a** Person **who** studies
each Employee **is a** Person **who** is employed
each StudEmp **is both a** Student **and an** Employee

Figure 8.41 A subtype graph with differing reference schemes

A student may be an employee, and we want to know when this occurs. If it did not already exist, we introduce a person number (p#) to enable objects to be identified across the global schema.

Each of the three supertypes has a total table which is identical to its functional table. The functional fact types of the nodes in the subtype graph map to the four tables shown in Figure 8.42. Here an ellipsis "..." denotes any other (functional) attributes omitted in Figure 8.40. If there are some other mandatory columns in StudEmp then tuteperiod becomes optional. Because of the relative closure on the disjunctively mandatory unaries on Person in Figure 8.41, both the studies and employed columns of Person are mandatory, with yes/no values.

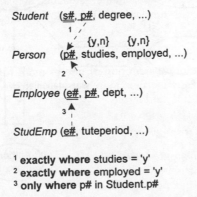

Student (s#, p#, degree, ...)
↓ 1
{y,n} {y,n}
Person (p#, studies, employed, ...)
↑ 2
Employee (e#, p#, dept, ...)
↑ 3
StudEmp (e#, tuteperiod, ...)

1 **exactly where** studies = 'y'
2 **exactly where** employed = 'y'
3 **only where** p# **in** Student.p#

Figure 8.42 The relational map of Figure 8.41, choosing subtype separation

Notice that p# is not included in the StudEmp table: this avoids duplicating any instances of the fact type: Person (with p#) has S#. This is not the only possible way to handle the mapping. For example, we might absorb StudEmp into Employee.

By default, derived fact types are not stored. Instead, their derivation rules are used to compute the derived values on request. Apart from saving storage space, this "derive on query" approach ensures that every time the derived information is requested it will be based on the latest values of the stored data. Sometimes however, the same derivations are required many times with large volumes of stable data. In such cases, it can be much more efficient to store the derived information, so that it can be accessed immediately at later times without having to be recomputed. Typically in such cases a "derive on update" approach is used, so that as soon as the base data is updated, the derived information is computed and stored. Recall the bank balance example from Exercise 6.4.

In step 0.4 of the mapping procedure, any derived fact types to be stored should be included on the schema diagram and marked "*S", with the derivation rule also declared. The fact type should then be grouped into a table in the normal way, marked "*" in the table, and the derivation rule mapped as well. Care is required with storing derived data. For example, unless the derivation rule is fired every time the relevant base data is updated, the derived values can become outdated.

For symmetric 1:1 binaries (roles are both optional or both mandatory, and both object types have other functional roles) we have a choice as to how the 1:1 binary should be mapped. This mapping choice should be noted in step 0.5 (e.g. by annotation or option selection) and adhered to when the fact type is mapped in step 2.

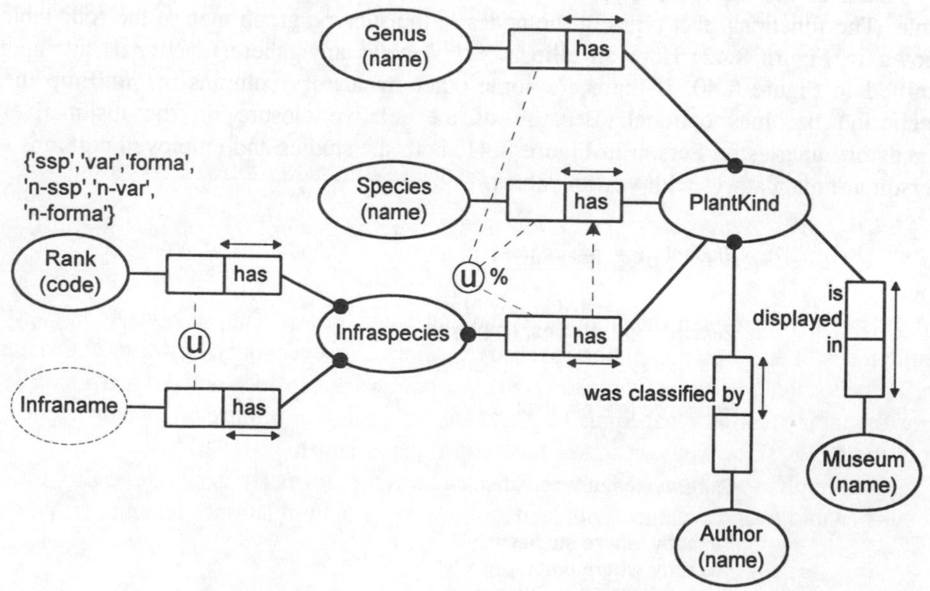

Figure 8.43 PlantKind has a disjunctive reference scheme

In rare cases our conceptual schema may contain a ⓤ% symbol, indicating a disjunctive primary reference scheme (identification by a mandatory disjunction of two or more roles, at least one of which is optional). In Figure 8.43, PlantKind is identified in this way (this botanical naming convention was discussed in section 5.4). When mapped to a relational schema, such schemes can prove awkward to handle.

For example, the conceptual schema in Figure 8.43 maps to the following relational schema. This violates the relational entity integrity rule, since the primary keys may contain null values. We enclose both infrarank and infraname in the same pair of square brackets to indicate that the qualification applies to *both*, and that if one is null so is the other. Enclosing both of these inside the option brackets for species indicates that they can only be given a non-null value when species is non-null.

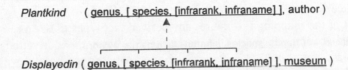

Plantkind (genus, [species, [infrarank, infraname]], author)

Displayedin (genus, [species, [infrarank, infraname]], museum)

Although forbidden by the relational model, this is allowed in most relational database systems, and the relevant uniqueness constraint can usually be enforced by a procedure or assertion. However a simpler implementation can often be obtained by altering the conceptual schema to replace the disjunctive reference with a non-disjunctive one. In step 0.6 we consider such replacements.

There are three basic ways of replacing a disjunctive reference scheme: artificial identifiers; concatenated identifiers; or use of special default values. Let's look at these three alternatives briefly, using this botanical example. The first option is to introduce a new identifier for PlantKind (e.g. pk#), leading to the following relational schema. This approach has two main advantages: the primary keys have no nulls; and table joins are faster (now based just on pk#).

PlantKind (pk#, genus, [species, [infrarank, infraname]], author)

DisplayedIn (pk#, museum)

The artificial identifier option is not all good news. The secondary key in PlantKind still has optional fields. Moreover, since this secondary key uses the natural reference scheme, this is what users will normally want to see (not the artificial pk#). For example, to find what kinds of plant are on display in a museum, we now need to join the tables since we want to see the natural plant names.

A simpler solution is just to concatenate the formerly separate parts of the identifier into a single name. This leads to the very simple relational schema:

PlantKind (pkname, author)

DisplayedIn (pkname, museum)

This simple schema is the best solution, so long as we are not interested in listing or grouping the formerly separate parts of the identifier. However if we wanted to issue a query such as "Which species has the most plantkinds?" there is now no simple way of formulating this query.

The third option is to keep the original components of the reference scheme separate but make each of them mandatory by using special default values when no actual value exists. For example, the plantkind *acacia interior* could be stored as the tuple ⟨'acacia','interior','nil','nil'⟩ using "nil" as a special default value (different from null) to indicate that plantkind has no actual value for infrarank and infraname. The conceptual schema in Figure 8.43 is modified by making the species and infra-species predicates mandatory for PlantKind, deleting the subset constraint and the "%", and by adding "nil" to the value list for Rank. The following relational schema is obtained (value-list omitted):

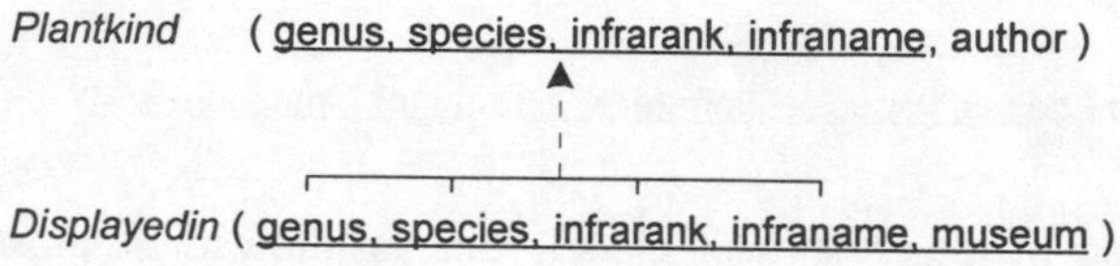

In this case the default value "nil" is unlikely to ever be confused with an actual value. However in some cases such confusion might arise (e.g. a default score of 0) and the user may then be burdened with the responsibility of distinguishing default from actual values.

The final refinement to step 0 of the mapping procedure (step 0.7) deals with cases where an objectified predicate is not spanned by a uniqueness constraint. Many versions of ORM forbid this from happening anyway, since it violates elementarity. However if the version you are using does allow it, then some pre-processing is needed before executing the grouping part of the procedure.

In nested 1:1 cases, a decision should be made to favour one of the roles in grouping. For example, suppose the schema in Figure 8.44 is used to model current marriages in a monogamous society. This schema violates elementarity. It can be split into two fact types: one about the marriage; and one about the marriage year.

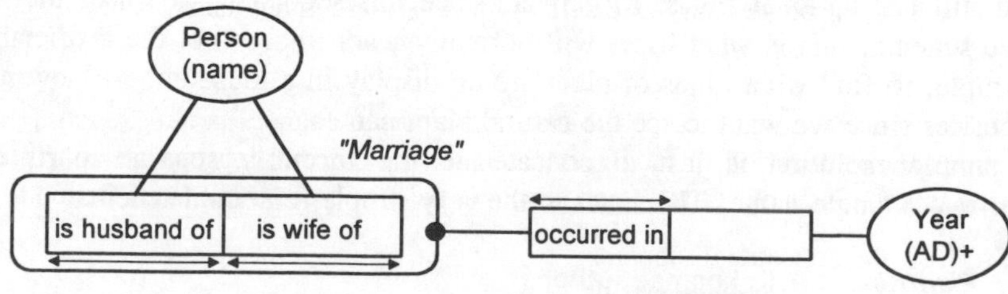

Figure 8.44 If this nesting is allowed it needs special care in mapping

If no other functional roles are played by Person, we might map Figure 8.44 to the relational schema:

Marriage (<u>husband</u>, wife, marriageyear)

or to:

Marriage (husband, <u>wife</u>, marriageyear)

For such *1:1* cases a choice must be made. If only one role in the objectified predicate is functional, it is automatically chosen for the primary key. For example, in a polyandrous society where a man may be married to at most one woman but not vice versa, the first of the previous relational schemas is automatically chosen. In spite of the provisions of step 0.7, nested object types without spanning uniqueness constraints should be avoided except in exceptional circumstances.

Exercise 8.4

1. (a) Rmap the conceptual schema in Figure 7.16.
   (b) Add the optional unary "is a nonsmoker" to Figure 7.16, with an exclusion constraint. The unaries are not closed. How does this affect the mapping?
   (c) If the unaries are closed, is their disjunction mandatory? Why?
   (d) If the unaries are disjunctively mandatory, how does this affect the mapping?

2. Suppose heads of government are identified by the country that they head, and have their salary and country of birth recorded. Schematize this UoD and Rmap it.

3. Refer to the hospital UoD of Exercise 6.6 Question 2. Rmap the conceptual schema for part (a), then discuss any changes in the mapping for parts (b), (c) and (d).

4. Consider a UoD in which people are identified by the combination of their surname, first given name and (if it exists) second given name. Each person's weight is recorded, as well as the sports they play (if any).

   (a) Schematize this UoD.
   (b) Rmap this, using the given identification scheme for persons.
   (c) Introduce person# as the primary identifier. Rmap the new conceptual schema.
   (d) Instead, concatenate surname and given names to a single name. Rmap this.
   (e) Instead, introduce "nil" as a default for no second given name. Rmap this.
   (f) Which do you prefer?

5. Consider the functional fact type: Moon (name) orbits Planet (name). Suppose that facts about the orbital period of moons are modeled by objectifying the previous predicate, giving this the alias of "Orbit", and attaching the fact type: Orbit takes Period (day).

   (a) Draw the conceptual schema.
   (b) Does this violate elementarity?
   (c) Unnest the schema.
   (d) Rmap it.

8.5 Relational algebra

So far we have learned how to design a conceptual schema and map it to a relational schema. The relational schema may now be implemented in a relational database system, and its tables populated with data. To make use of the resulting database system we need to know how to issue queries to obtain the information we want. In practice the two most important query languages are SQL and QBE. Both of these are based, at least partly, on a formal query language known as **relational algebra**. By studying this simple algebra we can obtain a clear understanding of the basic query operations without getting distracted by the specific syntactic details of the commercial query languages.

The manipulative part of the relational model of data consists of relational algebra, which provides operators to form new relations from existing ones, and relational assignment, which allows the resulting relation to be stored for later use. The original relational algebra defined by Codd contained *eight relational operators*: four based on traditional set operations (union, intersection, difference and Cartesian product); and four special operations (selection, projection, join and division). We discuss these operators in this order. Each is a table-forming operator on tables.

Although logical operators (**and, or, not)** and comparison operators (=, <>, <, >, <=, >=) may be used to express conditions, arithmetic operators (e.g. +) and functions (e.g. count) are not included. Thus the relational algebra is intended to provide a theoretical basis for discussing relational operations and formulating expressions, rather than provide a fully fledged practical system.

Many different notations exist for expressing the relational algebra. A comparison between our notation and a common academic notation is given later. To simplify discussion we often use informal terms instead of the strict relational terminology (e.g. "table" and "row" instead of "relation" and "tuple").

Two tables are *union-compatible* if and only if they have the same arity or degree (same number of columns), and their corresponding columns are based on the same domain (the columns do not have to have the same name). Regarding a table to be a set of rows, the traditional set operations of union, intersection and difference may now be defined for any pair of tables that are union-compatible.

Consider the conceptual schema in Figure 8.45. Here "Language" means "programming language". A person either is fluent in a language or actually uses a language (or both).

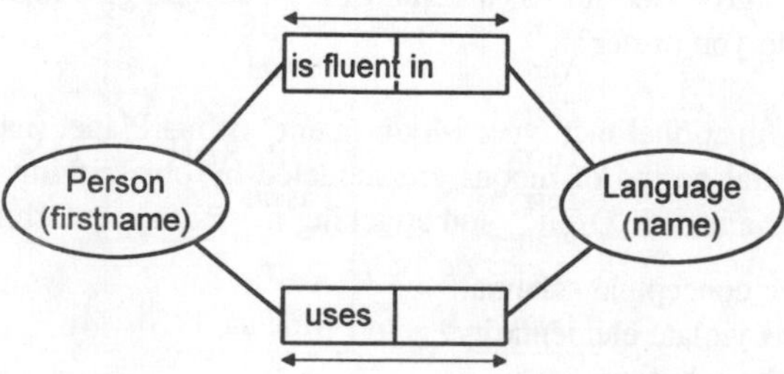

Figure 8.45

Fluency (<u>person, language</u>)

Usage (<u>person, language</u>)

Fluency:

person	*language*
Ann	BASIC
Ann	Pascal
Terry	BASIC
Terry	FORTRAN
Terry	Pascal
Walter	C

Usage:

person	*language*
Ann	Pascal
Fred	Ada
Terry	Pascal
Terry	Modula-3

Figure 8.46 Relational schema mapped from Figure 8.45, with sample data

Figure 8.46 shows the relational schema and a sample population. On the conceptual schema, no set comparison constraint exists between the roles played by Person, or between the Language roles, or between the role-pairs. The populations of the tables may properly overlap or even be disjoint. Hence there are no inter-table constraints in the relational schema: this situation is fairly unusual.

The **union** of tables *A* and *B* is the set of all rows belonging to *A* or *B* (or both). We may write this as "$A \cup B$" or "*A* **union** *B*". For example, suppose we want to know who is acquainted with what language (where we agree that acquaintance means either fluency *or* usage). This may be specified simply as the union of the tables, Fluency ∪ Usage. Figure 8.47 includes this query expression, and the resulting (unnamed) table.

As with any table, duplicate rows are excluded. Note that "Fluency ∪ Usage" is an expression describing how the result may be derived in terms of tables stored in the database (i.e. base tables): it is not a table name. We may refer to a query result as a result table, answer table or derived table. Also note that the order of the rows in this result (or the base tables for that matter) has no significance. Actual query languages like SQL provide extra facilities for displaying the rows of tables in any preferred order (e.g. we might order the person column alphabetically).

Fluency ∪ Usage →

person	*language*
Ann	BASIC
Ann	Pascal
Terry	BASIC
Terry	FORTRAN
Terry	Pascal
Walter	C
Fred	Ada
Terry	Modula-3

Figure 8.47 The union of two tables is the set of rows from either table

Fluency ∩ *Usage* →

person	*language*
Ann	Pascal
Terry	Pascal

Figure 8.48 The intersection of two tables is the set of rows common to both

The **intersection** of tables *A* and *B* is the set of rows common to *A* and *B*. We write this as "*A* ∩ *B*" or "*A* **intersect** *B*". For instance, to obtain information on fluent usage of languages we want a list of ⟨person, language⟩ pairs where the person is both fluent in and uses the language: we may specify this as the intersection of our two base tables, Fluency ∩ Usage (see Figure 8.48).

We define the **difference** operation between tables thus. *A* – *B* is the set of rows belonging to *A* but not *B*. We may also write this as *A* **minus** *B*, or *A* **except** *B*. For example, the expression Fluency – Usage returns details about people who are fluent in a language but don't use it (see top part of Figure 8.49).

As in ordinary set theory, the union operation is *commutative* (i.e. the order of the operands is not significant). So, given any tables *A* and *B* it is true that $A \cup B = B \cup A$. Likewise, the intersection operation is commutative. The difference operation however is not commutative; so in general *A* – *B* need not be the same as *B* – *A*. For example, Usage – Fluency returns information on who uses a procedural language without (yet) being fluent in it (see lower part of Figure 8.49). Compare this with the previous result.

In mathematics, the **Cartesian Product** of sets *A* and *B* is defined as the set of all ordered pairs (x,y) such that *x* belongs to *A* and *y* belongs to *B*. For example, if $A = \{1,2\}$ and $B = \{3,4,5\}$ then $A \times B = \{(1,3),(1,4),(1,5),(2,3),(2,4),(2,5)\}$. We write this product as $A \times B$ (read "*A* cross *B*"). This definition applies also to tables, although the ordered pairs of rows (x,y) are considered to be single rows of the product table, which inherits the corresponding column names. Thus if *A* and *B* are tables, $A \times B$ is formed by *pairing each row of A with each row of B*. Here "pairing" means "prepending". The expression "$A \times B$" may also be written as "*A* **times** *B*". The Cartesian product is sometimes called the "*cross join*" or "unrestricted join".

Fluency – Usage →

person	*language*
Ann	BASIC
Terry	BASIC
Terry	FORTRAN
Walter	C

Usage – Fluency →

person	*language*
Fred	Ada
Terry	Modula-3

Figure 8.49 *A* – *B* is the set of rows in *A* that are not in *B*

A:

a1	a2
1	2
3	4
5	6

B:

b1
7
8

$A \times B \rightarrow$

a1	a2	b1
1	2	7
1	2	8
3	4	7
3	4	8
5	6	7
5	6	8

Figure 8.50 $A \times B$ pairs each row of A with each row of B

It is easy to see that if A has n rows and B has m rows then the table $A \times B$ has n x m rows (since each row of A is paired with all rows of B). So *the number of rows in* $A \times B$ *is the product of the number of rows in A and B*. Since the paired rows are simply concatenated into single rows, *the number of columns in* $A \times B$ *is the sum of the number of columns in A and B*. Let's look at a simple example.

In Figure 8.50, A is a 3x2 table (i.e. 3 rows x 2 columns) and B is a 2x1 table. So $A \times B$ has six (3x2) rows of three (2+1) columns. The header rows which contain the column names *a1, a2, b1* are not counted in this calculation. In this example, lines have been ruled between rows as well as columns. Note that the Cartesian Product $A \times B$ exists for any tables A and B; it is not necessary that A and B be union-compatible.

Recall that column names of any table must be unique. If A and B have no column names in common, then $A \times B$ can use the simple column names of A and B. If A and B are different but have some common column names, the corresponding columns in $A \times B$ can be uniquely referenced by using qualified names (with the prefix "*A.*" or "*B.*"). Consider the case however when A and B are the same (i.e. we wish to form the Cartesian product of a table with itself).

Consider the Person × Person table in Figure 8.51. This breaks the rule that column names in a table must be unique. In this case, simply using the qualified column names will not solve the problem either because we would have two columns named "Person.firstname" and two columns named "Person.sex".

Person:

firstname	*sex*
Fred	M
Sue	F

Person × *Person* →

firstname	*sex*	*firstname*	*sex*
Fred	M	Fred	M
Fred	M	Sue	F
Sue	F	Fred	M
Sue	F	Sue	F

Figure 8.51 What is wrong with this Cartesian product?

define alias Person2 **for** Person

Person × *Person2* →

Person.firstname	*Person.sex*	*Person2.firstname*	*Person2.sex*
Fred	M	Fred	M
Fred	M	Sue	F
Sue	F	Fred	M
Sue	F	Sue	F

Figure 8.52 Table aliases are needed to multiply a table by itself

This problem is overcome by introducing **aliases** for tables. For example, we could use "Person2" as an alternative name for the table, and form the product as shown in Figure 8.52. If desired we could have introduced two aliases, "Person1" and "Person2" say, to specify the product (Person1 × Person2). The need to multiply a table by itself can arise if we have to compare values on different rows. Aliases can also be used simply to save writing (by introducing shorter names).

If we define Cartesian products in terms of tuples treated as ordered sequences of values, the × operator is not commutative (i.e. $A \times B$ need not equal $B \times A$). This is the usual treatment in mathematics. With relational databases however, each column has a name, so a tuple may instead be treated as an (unordered) set of attribute-value pairs (each value in a row is associated with its column name). With this view of tuples, the × operator is commutative. To clarify this, compute $B \times A$ for the example in Figure 8.50. Although the resulting table has its columns displayed in the order *b1, a1, a2*, and the values are ordered accordingly, the information content is the same as for $A \times B$, since each value can be linked to its column name. Once columns are named, their physical order has no semantic significance.

As in standard set theory, the operations of union, intersection and Cartesian product are *associative*. For instance, $A \cup (B \cup C) = (A \cup B) \cup C$. Since no ambiguity results we allow dropping of parentheses in such cases. For example, the shorter expression "$A \cup B \cup C$" is permitted. Of the four table operations considered so far, difference is the only one that is not associative; that is, $A - (B - C)$ need not be equal to $(A - B) - C$. As an exercise, use Venn diagrams to check these claims.

Let us now consider the four table operations introduced by Codd. The first of these is known as **selection** (or *restriction*). This should not be confused with SQL's select command. In relational algebra, the selection operation restricts attention to those rows of a table which satisfy a specified condition. It has the general form:

T **where** *c* { or $\sigma_c(T)$ }

Here *T* denotes a *table expression* (i.e. an expression whose value is a table) and *c* denotes a *condition*. The "**where** *c*" part is called a *where-clause*. The alternative notation shown in braces is often used in academic journals. We prefer our notation since it encourages top-down thinking (find the relevant tables before worrying about the rows) as well as agreeing with SQL syntax. The "σ" in the academic notation is sigma, the Greek "s" (which is the first letter of "selection").

Player:

name	*sex*	*height*
David	M	172
Norma	F	170
Selena	F	165
Terry	M	178

Player **where** sex = 'M' →

name	*sex*	*height*
David	M	172
Terry	M	178

Figure 8.53 The selection operation picks those rows which satisfy the condition

In Figure 8.53, the Player table stores details about tennis players. If we wanted details on the males who played tennis we could formulate this selection as indicated, giving the result shown. Here the selection condition is just the equality: sex = 'M'. The use of single quotes with 'M' indicates that this value is literally the character 'M'. Single quotes are also used when referencing character string values such as 'David'. Numeric values should not be quoted. Although the table resulting from the selection is unnamed, its columns have the same names as the original.

The condition *c* may contain any of six *comparison operators*: = (equals); < > (is not equal to); < (is less than); > (is greater than); < = (is less than or equal to); > = (is greater than or equal to). Sometimes the result of a table operation is an empty table (cf. the null set). For instance, no rows satisfy the condition in: Player **where** height > 180. The selection operation is said to produce a *"horizontal subset"* or *"row subset"*, since it selects zero or more rows from the original table.

If conditions do not involve comparisons with null values, they are Boolean expressions—they evaluate to True or False. If conditions do include comparisons with nulls, a 3-valued logic is often used instead, so that the condition may evaluate to True, False or Unknown (e.g. this is what happens in SQL). In either case, the selection operation *T* **where** *c* produces a table containing just those rows of *T* which satisfy the condition *c* (i.e. those rows where *c* evaluates to true). Rows where *c* evaluates to false or unknown are filtered out.

Besides comparison operators, conditions may include three *logical operators*: **and**; **or**; **not**. As usual, **or** is inclusive. As an exercise, formulate a query to list details of those females who are less than 170 cm tall. Also refer to the Player table and see if you can state the result. Then check your answer with the one given in Figure 8.54. To aid readability, reserved words are shown in bold.

Player **where** (sex = 'F') **and** (height < 170)

→

name	*sex*	*height*
Selena	F	165

Figure 8.54 Are the brackets needed in this query?

Table 8.2 Priority convention for the operators (1 = first)

1	=, <>, <, >, <=, >=
2	**not**
3	**and**
4	**or**

The query in Figure 8.54 used parentheses to clarify the order in which operations are to be carried out. With complicated expressions however, large numbers of parentheses can make things look very messy (cf. LISP). Unlike several programming languages (e.g. Pascal), most query languages (e.g. SQL) give *comparison operators higher priority than logical operators*.

So the operators =, <>, <, >, <=, >= are given precedence over **not**, **and** and **or** for evaluation purposes. We make the same choice in relational algebra since this reduces the number of parentheses needed for complex expressions. With this understood, the query in Figure 8.54 may be rewritten more concisely as:

Player **where** sex = 'F' **and** height < 170

To further reduce the need for parentheses we adopt the logical operator priority convention commonly used in computing languages such as Pascal and SQL. First evaluate **not**, then **and**, then **or**. Table 8.2 shows the evaluation order for both comparison and logical operators. This operator precedence may be overridden by use of parentheses.

For example, suppose we want details about males who are taller than 175 cm or shorter than 170 cm. Query (a) in Figure 8.55 looks like it should work for this, but the wrong result is obtained. Why?

Because the **and** operator is evaluated before the **or**, this query is interpreted as: Player where (sex = 'M' and height > 175) or height < 170. Notice that line breaks have no significance to the meaning of the query. So the result includes details about anybody shorter then 170 cm (including females). Query (b) corrects this situation by including brackets around the height disjunction. This ensures that the **or** operator is evaluated before the **and** operator.

(a) Player **where** sex = 'M'
and height > 175 **or** height < 170

→

name	*sex*	*height*
Terry	M	178
Selena	F	165

(b) Player **where** sex = 'M'
and (height > 175 **or** height < 170)

→

name	*sex*	*height*
Terry	M	178

Figure 8.55 Unless brackets are used, **and** is evaluated before **or**

(a) Player **where** sex = 'M' **and** height > 175
or sex = 'F' **and** height > = 170

(b) Player **where** (sex = 'M' **and** height > 175)
or (sex = 'F' **and** height > = 170)

→

name	*sex*	*height*
Terry	M	178
Norma	F	170

Figure 8.56 Two equivalent queries

To obtain details about players who are either males over 175 cm or females at least 170 cm tall, either of the queries shown in Figure 8.56 may be used. In query (b) the brackets are redundant, since the **and** operators are evaluated before the **or** operator anyway. If ever in doubt about whether parentheses are needed, put them in.

Figure 8.57 shows three equivalent queries for listing information on players who are neither taller than 172 cm nor shorter than 168 cm. Operator precedence ensures that query (a) means: Player **where** (**not** (height > 172)) **and** (**not** (height < 168)).

Note that the six comparison operators may be grouped into three pairs of opposites: =, < >; <, > =; and >, < =. So query (a) may be replaced by the shorter query (b).

Table 8.3 lists *De Morgan's laws*, named after the famous logician, Augustus De Morgan. Here *p* and *q* denote any proposition or logical condition. These laws hold in both 2-valued and 3-valued logic, so are safe to use with null values. Using the second of these laws, it is easy to see that query (c) is equivalent to query (a).

Table 8.3 De Morgan's Laws

not (p **and** q)	≡	**not** p **or not** q
not (p **or** q)	≡	**not** p **and not** q

(a) Player **where not** height > 172 **and not** height < 168

(b) Player **where** height < = 172 **and** height > = 168

(c) Player **where not** (height > 172 **or** height < 168)

→

name	*sex*	*height*
David	M	172
Norma	F	170

Figure 8.57 Three equivalent queries

Player:

name	*sex*	*height*
David	M	172
Norma	F	170
Selena	F	165
Terry	M	178

Player *[*name,sex*]* →

name	*sex*
David	M
Norma	F
Selena	F
Terry	M

Player *[*sex*]* →

sex
M
F

Figure 8.58 Projection involves picking the columns and removing any duplicates

The next table operation is known as **projection**. This operation involves *choosing one or more columns* from a table, and *then eliminating any duplicate rows* that might result. It is said to produce a "*vertical subset*" or "*column subset*". We represent the projection operation as follows:

T *[a,b,..]* { or $\pi_{a,b,..}(T)$ }

Here *T* is a table expression and *a,b,...* are the names of the required columns (this column list is called the *projection list*). To delimit the projection list we use square brackets rather than parentheses, since the latter have other uses in queries (e.g. to change the evaluation order of operations). Italicizing the square brackets "*[ ]*" helps to distinguish them from the use of "[ ]" to delimit optional items, or bags.

The alternative notation shown in braces is common in academic journals. The "π" symbol is pi, the Greek "p" (the first letter of "projection"). Like SQL, this notation lists the required columns before the tables. Our notation instead encourages top-down thinking by identifying the relevant tables before listing the columns.

Figure 8.58 gives two examples, based on the table Player (<u>name</u>, sex, height). When projecting on a single base table, if the chosen columns include a candidate key of that table then no duplicates rows can result from the choice. If not, duplicates may arise. For example, choosing just the sex column gives the bag ['M','F','F','M']; to complete the projection the duplicate values are eliminated, giving the set {'M','F'}.

If we project on all columns we end up with the same table. For instance, Player *[*name, sex, height*]* is the same table as Player. The same column must not be mentioned twice in a projection. For example, Player *[*name, name*]* is illegal (Why?). If desired, projection may be used to display columns in a different order. For example, Player *[*height, sex, name*]* reverses the order. Since column names are listed in the result, this does not change the meaning of the result.

If the relational schema is fully normalized it is fairly unusual to have base tables that are union-compatible (the Fluency-Usage tables considered earlier being an exception). So the ∪, ∩ and − operations tend to be used almost exclusively with result tables which have become union-compatible because of projections.

Let's look now at some examples that are a little more complicated. To facilitate a discussion of a step by step approach to such cases we now introduce the **relational assignment** operation. Because their contents may vary, tables may be regarded as *variables*. In fact, tables are the only kind of variable allowed in relational algebra. The notion of relational assignment, which is strictly separate from the algebra itself, is similar to that in programming languages. Using the symbol ":=" for "becomes" or "is assigned the value of", we may write assignment statements of the form:

table variable := *table expression*

This is an instruction to first evaluate the expression on the right, and then place this value in the variable named on the left. If this variable had a previous value, the old value would simply be replaced by the new value. For example, if *X*, *A* and *B* are tables then the statement "*X* := *A* – *B*" means *X* is assigned the value of *A* – *B*.

For example, consider the UoD of Figure 8.59. How may we formulate this query in relational algebra: Which non-European countries speak French? We could formulate the query in steps, using intermediate tables *A* and *B* on the way to obtaining our final result table *X*. For example:

A := (Location **where** region <> 'Europe') *[country]*
B := (SpokenIn **where** language = 'French') *[country]*
X := A ∩ B

Here our first step was to find the non-European countries: {Australia, Canada}. Then we found the French-speaking countries: {Belgium, Canada, France}. Finally we took the intersection of these, giving the result: {Canada}.

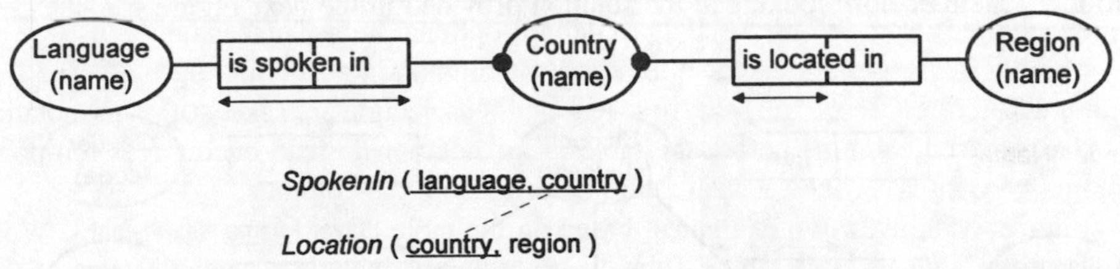

SpokenIn:

language	*country*
Dutch	Belgium
Dutch	Netherlands
English	Australia
English	Canada
French	Belgium
French	Canada
French	France

Location:

country	*region*
Australia	Australasia
Belgium	Europe
Canada	North America
France	Europe
Netherlands	Europe

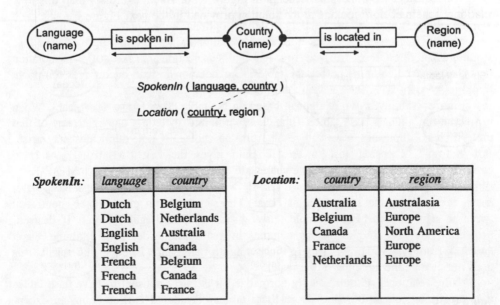

Figure 8.59 Conceptual and relational schemas, with sample population

Setting queries out this way is known as *stepwise formulation*. Doing things in stages can sometimes make it easier to formulate difficult queries. However, it saves writing and is generally preferable to express a query by means of a single expression. For instance, the three assignment statements just considered can be replaced by:

(Location **where** region <> 'Europe')/country/
∩
(SpokenIn **where** language = 'French')/country/

This lengthy expression is said to be a *nested formulation* because it nests one or more queries inside another. For complex queries we might perform the stepwise formulation in our heads, or scribbled down somewhere, and then convert this into the nested formulation. In general, any information capable of being extracted by a series of queries can be specified in a single query.

Note that projection does not distribute over ∩. In other words, given tables A and B, and a projection list p, it is possible that $(A \cap B)[p] \neq A[p] \cap B[p]$. For instance, the following query is *not* equivalent to the previous one (Why not?).

((Location **where** region <> 'Europe')
∩
(SpokenIn **where** language = 'French'))
/country/

This query is illegal, since the table operands of ∩ are not compatible. Even if A and B are compatible, projection need not distribute over ∩ or over −. If A and B are compatible, projection does distribute over ∪, i.e. $(A \cup B)[p] = A[p] \cup B[p]$. As an exercise, prove these results.

Now consider the conceptual schema in Figure 8.60. As an exercise, map this to a relational schema before looking at the solution provided in the next Figure.

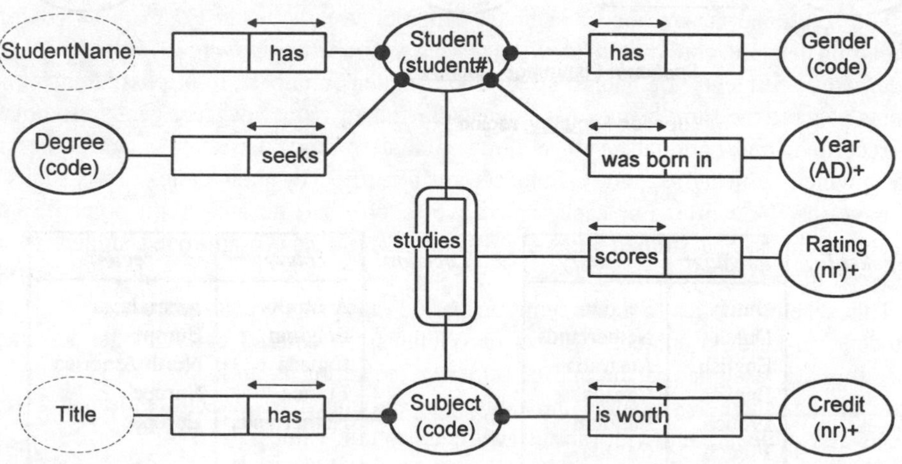

Figure 8.60

Student (<u>student#</u>, stuname, degree, gender, birthyr)

Result (<u>student#</u>, <u>subjcode</u>, [rating])

Subject (<u>subjcode</u>, title, credit)

Student:

student#	*stuname*	*degree*	*gender*	*birthyr*
861	Smith J	BSc	M	1967
862	Jones E	BA	F	1965
863	Brown T	BSc	M	1950

Subject:

subjcode	*title*	*credit*
CS113	Databases	8
PD102	Logic	10
PY205	Xenoglossy	5

Result:

student#	*subjcode*	*rating*
861	CS113	7
861	PD102	5
862	PD102	7
863	CS113	4
863	PD102	5

Figure 8.61 Relational schema and sample population for schema in Figure 8.60

The relational schema and a sample population are shown in Figure 8.60. Before formulating queries you should *familiarize yourself with the structure and contents of the database*. Students are identified by their student number. It is possible for two students to have the same name. All students have their name, degree, gender and birth year recorded, and optionally subjects (e.g. a student might enroll in a degree before picking which subjects to study). Subjects are identified by their codes. Two subjects may have the same title. For each subject we record the title and credit points. Some subjects might not be studied (e.g. PY205 might be a newly approved subject to be introduced in the next year).

This schema applies to a one semester period only, so we can ignore the possibility of student repeating a subject. Subject enrollments are entered early in the semester, and ratings are assigned at the end of semester (so rating is optional). To keep things simple at this stage we assume the tables are populated as shown, with just a few students and subjects, and with ratings awarded (no null values).

We now consider the operation of **joining** two tables (or two occurrences of the same table) by comparing attribute values from the tables, using the comparison operators (=, <, >, <>, <=, >=). There are several kinds of join operations, and we discuss only some of these here. Columns being compared in any join operation must be defined on the same domain; they do not need to have the same name. Where it is necessary to distinguish between join columns with the same local name, we use their fully qualified names.

Let **Θ** (theta) denote any comparison operator (=, < etc.). Then the **Θ-join** of tables *A* and *B* on attributes *a* of *A* and *b* of *B* equals the Cartesian product A × B, restricted to those rows where *A.a* **Θ** *B.b*. We write this as shown below. An alternative, academic notation is shown in braces.

A × *B* **where** *c* { or $A \bowtie_c B$ }

The condition *c* used to express this comparison of attributes between tables is called the *join condition*. The join condition may include many comparisons. Because of the Cartesian product, the resulting table has a number of columns equal to the sum of the number of columns in *A* and *B*; but because of the selection operation it typically has far fewer rows than the product of the numbers of rows of the joined tables.

With most joins the comparison operator used is =. The Θ-join is then called an **equijoin**. Thus the equijoin of *A* and *B* equating values in column *a* of *A* with column *b* of *B* is *A* × *B* restricted to the rows where *A.a* = *B.b*. If the join column names occur in only one of the tables, there is no need to qualify them with the table names. We write this as shown below. In general, the join condition may contain many equalities.

A × *B* **where** *A.a* = *B.b*

or

A × *B* **where** *a* = *b* { if *a*, *b* occur in only one of *A*, *B* }

As an example, suppose we wish to list in a single table the student number of each student, together with full details on each subject studied by that student (i.e. subject code, title, credit points and rating obtained). We could specify this by the equijoin in Figure 8.62, which joins the Result and Subject tables by equating the subjcode attributes in the two tables. Check the result for yourself.

Here the join columns have the same name, "subjcode". The qualified names are used to distinguish these columns in the query and the join result. The join columns don't have to have the same (unqualified) name; so long as they belong to the same domain the join can be made. For example, if the subject code column in the Subject were named "code", the join condition could be specified as "subjcode = code".

(Result × Subject) **where** Result.subjcode = Subject.subjcode.

→

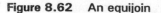

student#	*Result.subjcode*	*rating*	*Subject.subjcode*	*title*	*credit*
861	CS113	7	CS113	Databases	8
861	PD102	5	PD102	Logic	10
862	PD102	7	PD102	Logic	10
863	CS113	4	CS113	Databases	8
863	PD102	5	PD102	Logic	10

Figure 8.62 An equijoin

As the previous example illustrates, an equijoin contains two matching columns resulting from each join attribute (note the two subjcode columns). If these columns actually refer to the same thing in the UoD (and they typically do), then one of these columns is redundant. In this case we lose no information if we *delete one of these matching columns* (by performing a projection on all but the column to be deleted). If the *columns used for joining have the same name in both tables*, then the unqualified name may be used in the join result. The resulting table is then said to be the **natural inner join** of the original tables.

Joins may be inner or outer (we discuss outer joins soon). Since "inner" is assumed by default, the natural inner join may be expressed simply as "natural join". This is by far the most common join operation in practice. The natural join of tables *A* and *B* may be written in words as "*A* **natural join** *B*" and in symbols thus:

$A \bowtie B$

There is no need to name the join columns because these are the ones with the same names in both tables (and of course these must be based on the same domain). To help remember the bow-tie "$\bowtie$" notation, note that "$\bowtie$" looks like a cross "$\times$" with two vertical lines added, suggesting that a natural join is a Cartesian product plus two other operations (selection of rows with equal values for the common columns, followed by projection to delete redundant columns). Figure 8.63 shows an example. Note that the subjcode column appears just once and is unqualified.

If the tables have no column-names in common then the natural join is simply the Cartesian product. Like Cartesian product, natural join is associative: $(A \bowtie B) \bowtie C = A \bowtie (B \bowtie C)$. So expressions of the form $A \bowtie B \bowtie C$ are unambiguous.

Tables being joined may have zero, one, or more common columns. In any case, the natural join is restricted to those rows where all the common attributes have the same value in both tables. The number of columns in $A \bowtie B$ equals the sum of the number of columns in *A* and *B*, minus the number of columns common to both.

To illustrate a natural join on more than one attribute, consider the bank account UoD in Figure 6.84. First examine the conceptual schema. Within a branch, an account may be identified by its LocalAc# (local account number). But different accounts in different branches may have the same local account number. So globally, the bank identifies its accounts by the combination of their branch and local account number. Clients are identified by a global client number but also have a name.

Result $\bowtie$ Subject

→

student#	*subjcode*	*rating*	*title*	*credit*
861	CS113	7	Databases	8
861	PD102	5	Logic	10
862	PD102	7	Logic	10
863	CS113	4	Databases	8
863	PD102	5	Logic	10

Figure 8.63 A natural join

Different clients may have the same name. Not all clients have to use an account. The relational schema and a sample population are included in the figure. Notice the subset and equality constraints between the tables. Joins are usually, though not always, made across such constraint links. Simple joins may be performed on client#, and composite joins on ⟨branch#, localAc#⟩ pairs (which identify accounts).

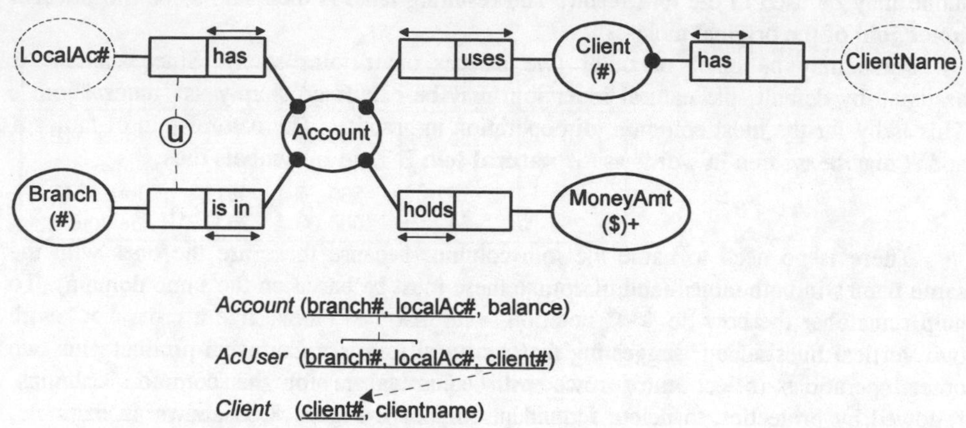

Account:

branch#	*localAc#*	*balance*
10	54	3000.00
10	77	500.55
23	54	1000.00

AcUser:

branch#	*localAc#*	*client#*
10	54	1001
10	54	1002
10	77	2013
23	54	7654

Client:

client#	*clientname*
1001	Jones ME
1002	Jones TA
2013	Jones ME
7654	Seldon H
8005	Shankara TA

Figure 8.64 Account has a composite identification scheme

(a) Account ⋈ AcUser →

branch#	*localAc#*	*balance*	*client#*
10	54	3000.00	1001
10	54	3000.00	1002
10	77	500.55	2013
23	54	1000.00	7654

(b) Account ⋈ AcUser ⋈ Client

→

branch#	*localAc#*	*balance*	*client#*	*clientname*
10	54	3000.00	1001	Jones ME
10	54	3000.00	1002	Jones TA
10	77	500.55	2013	Jones ME
23	54	1000.00	7654	Seldon H

Figure 8.65 Two queries using natural joins

The two queries in Figure 8.65 use natural joins to display users and balances of accounts. The first query matches accounts by joining on both branch# and localAc#. To add the client names, the second query also matches clients by joining on client#.

In rare cases, comparison operators other than equality are used in joins. As a simple example, consider the Drinker and Smoker tables in Figure 8.66. These might result from a decision to map subtypes of Patient to separate tables.

Suppose we wanted a list of ⟨drinker, smoker⟩ pairs, where the drinker and smoker are distinct persons. This can be formulated by a *<>-join* as shown. Here the comparison operator is "<>". Notice that because drinkers and smokers overlap, some patient doubles may appear twice (in different order). Similarly, <-joins, >-joins, <=-joins and >=-joins may be defined.

Drinker:

patient	*liver*
Bloggs F	OK
Smith S	poor
Stoned IM	bad

Smoker:

patient	*lungs*
Bloggs F	bad
Stoned IM	bad

(Drinker × Smoker) **where** Drinker.patient <> Smoker.patient
*[*Drinker.patient, Smoker.patient*]*

→

Drinker.patient	*Smoker.patient*
Bloggs F	Stoned IM
Smith S	Bloggs F
Smith S	Stoned IM
Stoned IM	Bloggs F

Figure 8.66 Example of a <>-join

Other kinds of joins can be defined. For example, left, right and full *outer-joins* are used to include various cases with null values. As a simple example, Client **left outer join** AcUser includes a row to indicate that the client with client# 8005 exists and has the name "Shankara TA" but uses no account (branch# and localAc# are assigned null values on this row). So the left outer join includes all the clients from the left-hand table (i.e. the table on the left of the join operator), whether or not they are listed in the right-hand table.

The final operation we consider in relational algebra is relational **division**. A table *A* can be divided by another table *B* only if *A* has more columns. Let *B* have *n* columns. The operation $A \div B$ is defined if and only if the domains of the last *n* columns of *A* match the domains of the columns of *B* (in order). In this case, $A \div B$ is formed by deleting the last *n* columns from *A*, then restricting the result to those rows which, in the original *A*, were paired with (at least) *all* the rows of *B*.

The expression $A \div B$ may also be written as *A* **divide-by** *B*. As a trivial example, if *A* and *B* have values as shown

A:

1	2	50
1	2	80
1	2	90
3	4	50

B:

50
80

then $A \div B$ contains just the row:

1 2

Although not used very often, the division operation can be useful in listing rows that are associated with at least *all* rows of another table expression (e.g. who can supply all the items on our stock list?). As a simple example using our student database, suppose we want the student numbers of those students who have ratings for all the subjects worth more than five credit points. One way of obtaining this information would be to first project then divide as shown in Figure 8.67.

Result *[*student#, subjcode*]* ÷ (Subject **where** credit > 5 *[*subjcode*]*)

i.e.

student#	*subjcode*
861	CS113
861	PD102
862	PD102
863	CS113
863	PD102

÷

subjcode
CS113
PD102

→

student#
861
863

Figure 8.67 Relational division example

Student:

student#	*stuname*	*degree*	*gender*	*birthyr*
861	Smith J	BSc	M	1967
862	Jones E	BA	F	1965
863	Brown T	BSc	M	1950

Subject:

subjcode	*title*	*credit*
CS113	Databases	8
PD102	Logic	10
PY205	Xenoglossy	5

Result:

student#	*subjcode*	*rating*
861	CS113	7
861	PD102	5
862	PD102	7
863	CS113	4
863	PD102	5

Figure 8.68 The Student database again

Now that we have met the eight standard table operations of relational algebra, let's discuss a few strategies to help with formulating queries. Our first move should be to determine *what tables hold the information we need to answer our query*. The information might be contained in a single table, or it might be spread over two or more tables. *If the columns to be listed come from different tables* (or different copies of the same table) *then we must specify joins between these tables*. These joins might be natural joins, Θ-joins, or cross joins (Cartesian products).

Apart from rarer cases involving ∪, ∩ or −, relational algebra requires joins whenever different tables must be accessed to determine the result, even if the result columns come from the same table. In contrast, SQL allows use of subqueries instead of joins when the result columns come from the same table.

Let's look at a few more examples using our student database. To reduce page turning, the database is reproduced in Figure 8.68. Suppose we want to list the student# and name of the students born before 1966. Looking at our database, we see that the information we want is all contained in the Student table. First we restrict this to the required birth year range (birthyr < 1966). Then we project on the columns required (student# and stuname). The query and answer are shown in Figure 8.69.

Student **where** birthyr < 1966 *[*student#, stuname*]*

→

student#	*stuname*
862	Jones E
863	Brown T

Figure 8.69 Query to list the student# and name of the students born before 1966

Now consider the query: List all the PD102 ratings obtained by BSc students. Before formulating this in relational algebra, we should ensure that we *understand what the natural language query means*. In some cases we may need to clarify the meaning by asking the person who originally posed the query. For example, do we want just the ratings (and not the students who got them), and do we want all occurrences of a rating (if it occurs more than once)? Let's suppose the answer to both these questions is "Yes".

To help formulate this query we use two problem solving strategies. One is the "divide and conquer" strategy: *divide the query up into steps or subproblems*. Another strategy is to *first try to answer the English query yourself and examine what you did*; then try to express this in the formal language. Notice that degree information (e.g. BSc) is in the Student table, but the ratings are in the Result table. So we need both of these tables. To link these tables together we look for a common attribute: student#.

If we were answering the request ourselves, we might go to the Student table and select just the rows where the degree code is "BSc", then look across on those rows to find the student numbers (861 and 863 in this case). Then we might go to the Result table, find the rows with PD102 (rows 2, 3 and 5 in this case), and match up the rows with the BSc student numbers (leaving rows 2 and 5). Finally we choose just the ratings from these rows: {5,5}. Retracing our steps, we may set this out as query (a) in Figure 8.70. This isn't the only way we could have gone about expressing the query. For instance, the projection on student# could have been omitted as shown in query (b). Alternatively, the join could have been made first, as in query (c).

Although these queries are logically equivalent, if executed in the evaluation order shown, some are more efficient than others. In this sense, the third query is least efficient because it involves a larger join (15 rows as opposed to 6 rows in the other queries if the full Cartesian product is first formed; 5 rows instead of 2 if the natural join condition is enforced). Relational algebra can be used to specify trans-formation rules between equivalent queries to obtain an optimally efficient, or at least a more efficient, formulation. Most practical database systems (e.g. SQL systems) include a *query optimizer* which translates your queries into an optimized form before executing them. So in practice we usually formulate queries in ways that are easy for us to think about them, rather than worrying about efficiency considerations.

(a) ((Student **where** degree = 'BSc') */student#/*
⋈ (Result **where** subjcode = 'PD102')) */rating/*

(b) ((Student **where** degree = 'BSc')
⋈ (Result **where** subjcode = 'PD102')) */rating/*

(c) (Student ⋈ Result) **where** degree = 'BSc' **and** subjcode = 'PD102'
/rating/

→

rating
5
5

Figure 8.70 Equivalent queries to list the PD102 ratings obtained by BSc students

(Student ⋈ Result ⋈ Subject) where degree = 'BA'
[student#, stuname, subjcode, credit]

→ *student#*	*stuname*	*subjcode*	*credit*
862	Jones E	PD102	10

Figure 8.71 Query to list student#, name, subjects and credits for BA students

Now consider the query: For the BA students, list their student#, student name and the code and credit value of their subjects. A glance at the database reveals that we need to access all three tables to answer this query. Looking for common attributes to link these tables we note that student# can be used to join Student and Result, while subjcode links Subject and Result.

To answer this query ourselves we would probably find the BA student in the Student table, get her student number from there (862), then use this number to get her subject codes from the Result table (PD102), then use these codes to get the credit points from the Subject table. Finally we choose the student#, student name, subject code and credit. The easiest way to set this out is to show all the joins first, then the selection, then the projection (see Figure 8.71).

Notice how long queries may be spread over more than one line to make them more readable. One useful syntax check is to ensure that you have the same number of opening and closing brackets. To reduce the need for brackets we give selection (**where**) and projection (**[ ]**) operators highest priority, with ∪, ∩, −, ×, ⋈, ÷ given the lowest priority (see Table 8.4). Operators with equal priority are evaluated left to right. Expressions in parentheses are evaluated first. Some versions of relational algebra have no precedence convention for the relational operations.

As our next example, let's return to the Player table mentioned earlier, where the population of the table has now been increased as shown in Figure 8.72. It is desired to have each pair of males play against each pair of females, for all possible combinations. For example, one match would involve David and Paul playing against Linda and Norma. To assist with scheduling team matches, it is desired to have a list of all possible teams. In English, the relevant query is: List all pairs of tennis players of the same sex.

Before looking at the solution provided, you might like to try solving this yourself. As a hint, *if you need to relate different rows of the same table, then a self-join is needed*. Also, recall that table aliases are required to join a table to itself.

In our solution we define two aliases, "Player1" and "Player2". We avoid "First" and "Second" since these are reserved words in many languages (e.g. second is a unit of time). By using the original table name we could have got by with only one alias. Check to make sure that you understand the solution. Notice that we should not use the natural join for this query (Why?). As an exercise, compute the answer table.

Table 8.4 Priority convention for the 8 relational operations (1 = first)

1	**where** *c*, **[ ]**	{ i.e. selection, projection }
2	∪, ∩, −, ×, ⋈, ÷	

Player:

name	*sex*	*height*
David	M	172
Linda	F	170
Norma	F	170
Paul	M	175
Selena	F	165
Terry	M	178

define alias Player1 **for** Player
define alias Player2 **for** Player

(Player1 × Player2)
where Player1.sex = Player2.sex
  and Player1.name < Player2.name
[Player1.name, Player2.name]

Figure 8.72 A self-join is needed to list pairs of tennis players of the same sex

In the query of Figure 8.72, you could have used ">" or "<>" instead of "<". However "<" is nice because it arranges for the first name of each pair to be alphabetically prior to the second name. Moreover, "<>" is inadvisable since it would result in each pair being listed twice, once for each order (recall our earlier example about drinkers and smokers).

For a couple of harder examples, we return to the compact disk retailer UoD discussed earlier in the book. The relational schema for the base tables is set out in Figure 8.73. As an exercise, try to formulate the following English queries in relational algebra before checking the solutions provided in Figure 8.74. These queries are much harder than our earlier examples. Recall that the monthcodes for January and February are "Jan" and "Feb".

(a) List the cd# and cdname of each compact disk which *either* had sales of more than 20 copies in each of the months January and February *or* has no track with a duration longer than 300 seconds.

(b) Who sings a track lasting at least 250 seconds, *and* sings on *each* compact disk which sold more copies in February than its current stock quantity?

Sales (cd#, monthcode, qtysold, revenue)

CD (cd#, cdname, [artist], company, stockqty, rrp)

Track (cd#, track#, title, duration)

Vocals (cd#, track#, singer)

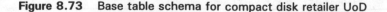

Figure 8.73 Base table schema for compact disk retailer UoD

(a) (Sales **where** month = 'Jan' **and** qtysold > 20 *[cd#]*
∩
Sales **where** month = 'Feb' **and** qtysold > 20 *[cd#]*
∪
(Track *[cd#]* – Track **where** duration > 300 *[cd#]*)
⋈
CD) *[cd#, cdname]*

(b) (Vocals ⋈ Track) **where** duration >= 250 *[singer]*
∩
(Vocals *[singer, cd#]*
÷
(Sales ⋈ CD) **where** month = 'Feb' **and** qtysold > stockqty *[cd#]*)

Figure 8.74 Relational algebra formulation of English queries (a) and (b)

In query (a) of Figure 8.74, intersection is required since the quantity sold must be greater than 20 in *each* month (i.e. January *and* February). As an exercise, explain why this can't be done using "**and**" or "**or**". Union is used for the "*or*" since the disjuncts are not available on the same row. Subtraction is used to enforce the condition about *no* track. The join provides the cdname. In query (b), intersection handles the *and* operation, while relational division is used to enforce the *each* requirement.

Such queries are best formulated by noting the overall structure (e.g. a union) then working on each part. These queries are unusual in requiring frequent use of ∪, ∩ and –. Remember in using these operators to ensure that the operands are compatible—this usually means a projection has to be done first.

Sometimes a query requires several tables to be joined. In this case, if you are joining *n* tables, remember to specify *n*-1 joins. For example, the query in Figure 8.71 joined three tables and hence required two joins.

Of the eight table operations covered, only five are primitive (i.e. cannot be defined in terms of the other operations). While some choice exists as to which to consider primitive, the following list is usual: ∪; –; ×; selection; and projection. The other three (∩, ⋈ and ÷) may be defined in terms of these five operations (the proof is left as an exercise). Talking about exercises, you must be bursting to try out your relational algebra skill on some questions. So here they are.

Exercise 8.5

1. The conceptual schema for a particular UoD is shown below. Here "computer" is used as an abbreviation for "kind of computer".

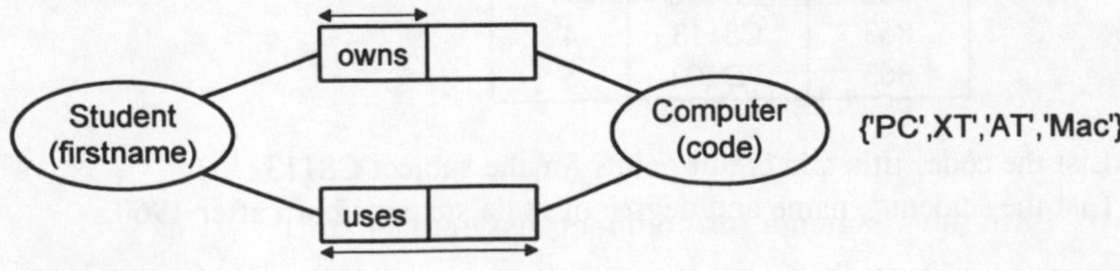

(a) Map this onto a relational schema. Then populate the tables with these data:

Ann uses an XT.
Fred uses an XT and a Mac, and owns an XT.
Sue uses an AT, and owns a PC.
Tom owns a Mac.

Given this schema and database, formulate the following queries in relational algebra and state the result. Make use of ∪, ∩, – and *[ ]*.

(b) List the students who own or use a computer.
(c) List the students who use a computer without owning one of that kind.
(d) List the students who use a computer but own no computer.
(e) List the students who own a computer but do not use a computer.
(f) List the students who own a computer without using one of that kind.
(g) List the students who use a computer and own a computer of that kind.
(h) List the students who use a computer and own a computer.
(i) List the computers used (by some student) but owned by no student.
(j) List the computers owned (by some student) but used by no student.

2. (a) If *A* is a 200x10 table and *B* is a 300x10 table, under what conditions (if any) are the following defined?
(i) $A \cup B$ (ii) $A \cap B$ (iii) $A - B$ (iv) $A \times B$

(b) If *A* is 200x10 and *B* is 100x5, what is the size of $A \times B$?

3. The student database is reproduced below. Formulate each of the following queries as a single relational algebra query.

Student:

student#	*stuname*	*degree*	*gender*	*birthyr*
861	Smith J	BSc	M	1967
862	Jones E	BA	F	1965
863	Brown T	BSc	M	1950

Subject:

subjcode	*title*	*credit*
CS113	Databases	8
PD102	Logic	10
PY205	Xenoglossy	5

Result:

student#	*subjcode*	*rating*
861	CS113	7
861	PD102	5
862	PD102	7
863	CS113	4
863	PD102	5

(a) List the code, title and credit points for the subject CS113.
(b) List the student#, name and degree of male students born after 1960.

(c) List the codes of the subjects studied by the student(s) named "Brown T".
(d) List the student# and name of those students who obtain a 7 rating in at least one subject.
(e) List the student# and name of all students who obtain a 5 in a subject called Logic.
(f) List the student# and degree of those students who study all the subjects listed in the database.
(g) List the student#, name and gender of those students who either are enrolled in a BSc or have obtained a rating of 7 for PD102.
(h) List the student#, name and birth year for male students born before 1970 who obtained at least a 5 in a subject titled "Databases".

4. The following table contains details on students who are to debate various religious topics. For this UoD, students are identified by their first name. Each debating team is to comprise exactly two members of the same religion but opposite sex.

Debater:

firstname	*gender*	*religion*
Anne	F	Buddhist
Betty	F	Christian
Cathy	F	Hindu
David	M	Christian
Ernie	M	Buddhist
Fred	M	Hindu
Gina	F	Christian
Harry	M	Buddhist
Ian	M	Christian
Jane	F	Christian
Kim	F	Hindu

Phrase each of the following as a single relational algebra query.

(a) List the name and religion of all females who are not Buddhist.
(b) List the name and sex of those who are either male Hindus or female Christians.
(c) List all possible debating teams, mentioning females before males. For example, one team is ⟨Anne, Ernie⟩.

5 (a) Map the following conceptual schema to a relational schema.

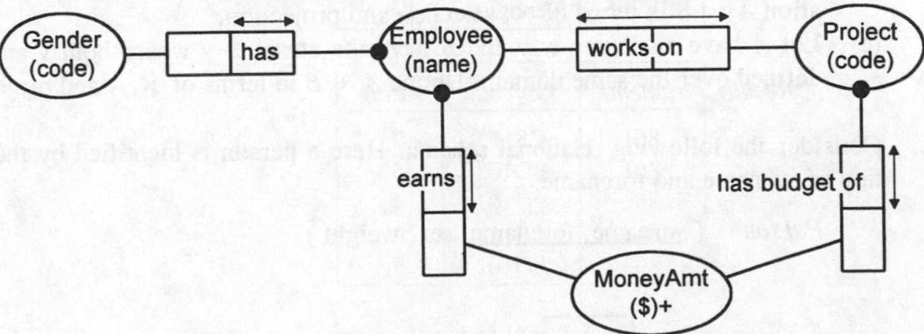

Use your schema to formulate each of the following in relational algebra.

(b) Find names and salaries of all female employees who earn more than $25000 or work on project "5GIS".

(c) List the name and gender of those employees who work on all projects with a budget of at least $100 000.

6. The relational schema for a particular UoD is as shown. Employees are identified by their employee# but also have a name. As well as this information, the Employee table indicates the department each employee works for, and the year in which the employee started to work for the firm. The Department table indicates the manager and budget for each department. Each employee manages at most one department (which must be the department for which he or she works).

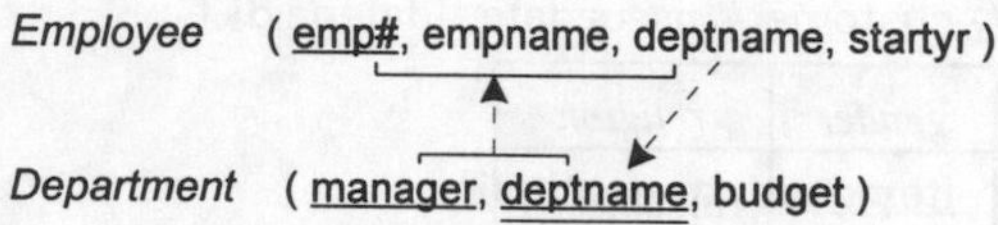

(a) Draw a conceptual schema diagram for this UoD.

Phrase each of the following requests as a single relational algebra query.

(b) Who works for the Accounting department and started with the firm before 1970?

(c) What is the budget of the department in which the employee with emp# 133 works?

(d) List the departmental managers and the year in which they started to work for the firm.

(e) Which employees are not departmental managers?

(f) Give the emp#, name and year started for those managers of departments with a budget in excess of $50 000.

(g) Which employees have worked for the firm longer than their departmental managers?

7. (a) Define A ∩ B in terms of –.

(b) Let relation *A* have attributes *x, y* and relation *B* have attributes *y, z* where both *y* attributes are defined over the same domain. Define the natural inner join operation $A \bowtie B$ in terms of ×, selection and projection.

(c) Let *A* have attributes *x, y* and *B* have the attribute *y* where both *y* attributes are defined over the same domain. Define $A \div B$ in terms of ×, – and projection.

8. Consider the following relational schema. Here a person is identified by the combination of surname and forename.

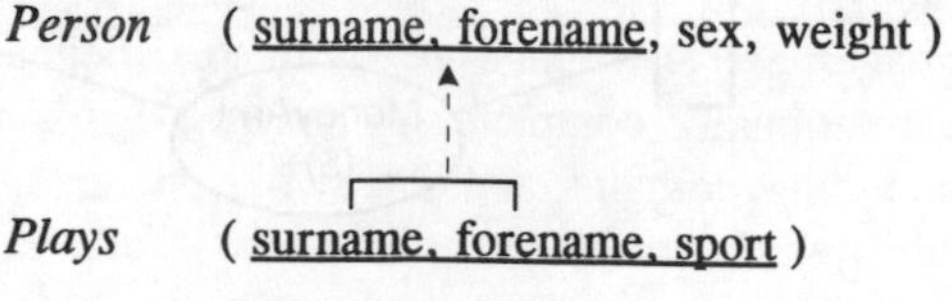

Formulate each of the following as single queries in relational algebra.

(a) Which females play judo?
(b) Which males in the weight range 70..80 kg play either judo or karatedo?
(c) Which females over 50 kg play judo but not karatedo?
(d) Who plays both judo and aikido? (Do NOT use a join)
(e) Who plays both judo and aikido? (DO use a join)

9. The following relational schema relates to the software retailer UoD considered in Exercise 6.2. The following category codes are used (DB = Database, SS = Spreadsheet, WP = WordProcessor).

```
Customer     ( customer#, cusname, address, [phone#] )

Invoice      ( invoice#, customer#, issuedate, [datepaid] )

InvoiceLine  ( invoice#, itemcode, qty, unitprice )

                                           {DB,SS,WP}
Item         ( itemcode, title, category, stock, listprice )
```

Formulate the following as single queries in relational algebra.

(a) List the customer# of each customer who has been charged less than the listprice for at least one software item, but has been sold no wordprocessor.
(b) List the name of each customer who was sold at least one copy of *all* the spreadsheets on the stock list.
(c) List the customer# of each customer who has purchased a copy of *all* the wordprocessors that are in stock but who has never purchased a database.
(d) List the customer# of those customers who purchased both a spreadsheet and wordprocessor *on the same invoice*.

8.6 Relational database systems

We may now define a **relational DBMS** to be a DBMS which has the relational table as its only essential data structure, and which supports the operations of selection, projection and joining without needing specification of physical access paths. A relational system which supports all eight table operations of the relational algebra is said to be *relationally complete*. This doesn't mean that eight distinct operators must be supplied for these tasks; rather, the eight operations must be expressible in terms of the table operations provided by the system.

The two main relational languages are SQL and QBE, with SQL being the most important. Most SQL systems are relationally complete. A system that supports all aspects of the relational model, including domains and the two basic integrity rules (entity integrity and referential integrity), is sometimes said to be "fully relational". The relational model of data itself is evolving.

For Version 1 of the relational model, Codd proposed 12 basic rules to be satisfied by a relational DBMS. These may be briefly summarized as follows: (1) all information is represented in relational tables; (2) all data is accessible by using the table name, primary key value and column name; (3) systematic support for missing information (null values, independent of data type) must be provided; (4) the relational schema itself is represented in tables, and is accessible in the same way the database itself is; (5) at least one relational query language must be provided, which supports data definition, view definition, data manipulation, integrity constraints, authorization and transaction boundaries (begin, commit and rollback); (6) basic support for view-updatability is provided; (7) table-at-a-time retrieval and update operations are provided; (8) application programs are logically unaffected by changes to internal storage or access methods; (9) application programs are logically unaffected by information-preserving changes to the base tables; (10) integrity constraints must be definable in the query language and storable in the system tables; (11) the DBMS has distribution independence; (12) if record-at-a-time processing is supported, this cannot be used to bypass the constraints declared in the set-oriented query language.

Version 2 of the relational model as proposed by Codd includes 333 rules, including support for different kinds of missing information. While some of the proposed revisions have merit, others are debatable, and it is doubtful whether any commercial DBMS will ever try to satisfy all these rules. In practice, the SQL language itself has become more influential in standardization efforts for relational DBMSs.

Some SQL systems are fully relational with respect to Codd's original 12 rules, but most provide only weak support for domains. For example, many would require heights and weights to be defined on numeric domains, allowing comparisons such as "height = weight". Some versions of SQL still fail to provide direct support for primary and foreign keys (though these were added in 1989 to the SQL standard).

In SQL-89 the union operation is allowed only between select statements, not between table expressions, and separate operators for $\cap$, $-$ and $\bowtie$ (natural join) are not explicitly provided (though expressible in terms of other SQL primitives). In 1992 the SQL standard was substantially improved, and all the table operators are explicitly included in SQL-92 (for example, $\cap$, $-$ and $\bowtie$ are called "**intersect**", "**except**" and "**natural join**"). The ability to declare constraints was also substantially improved.

The next SQL standard, codenamed "SQL3", will probably be ratified by 1997. Although proposals for this standard are still tentative, likely enhancements include: user-defined data types, including object-identifiers, complex objects, subtypes, user-defined nulls; new functions and operators, including procedural control structures and recursive union; and triggers for event handling.

Although SQL products (e.g. Oracle, DB2, Ingres) dominate on larger relational systems, QBE implementations (e.g. Access, Paradox) are popular on smaller systems because of their friendly, screen-based orientation. Though less relational in nature, Xbase products (e.g. dBbase IV, FoxBase) are also popular on PCs. In addition to the operations of relational algebra, relational DBMSs provide a multitude of further capabilities, such as sorting, arithmetic, grouping and formatting. Most systems also provide powerful tools for creating external interfaces (e.g. screen forms), report writing, and security. In spite of the added productivity provided by such systems, the success of the application still depends critically on the design of the database.

8.7 Summary

Until conceptual database systems become widespread, conceptual schemas will normally be implemented in terms of some lower level data model. The relational data model is now commercially dominant, so we examined how a conceptual schema may be mapped to a relational schema, and then queried using relational algebra.

A *relational (database) schema* is a set of table definitions (stored base tables or derived views) and constraints. A *table scheme* is a named set of *attributes* (columns) which draw their values from *domains*. Each column, or column set, spanned by a uniqueness constraint is a *candidate key*. Keys are underlined in table schemes. Each table row is identified by its *primary key* (doubly underlined if another key exists). The *entity integrity* rule demands that primary keys have no null values. Optional columns allow null values, and are enclosed in square brackets. For example: *Employee* (emp#, empname, address, sex, [phone]).

Mandatory roles are mapped to non-optional columns, with subset constraints running from any other tables that contain facts about that object type. A *referential integrity constraint* is a subset constraint from a foreign key to some primary key. Subset constraints between tables appear as dotted arrows. Arrowheads may be deleted from inter-table equality constraints. Other constraint notations are used.

The relational mapping procedure (*Rmap*) groups each fact type into a single table, using two basic ideas: each fact type with a compound UC is mapped to a separate table; fact types with functional roles attached to the same object type are grouped into the same table, keyed on the object type's identifier. Other aspects of the procedure are listed in Figures 8.23 and 8.30.

The *data manipulation* aspect includes relational algebra and relational assignment (:=). Apart from the use of logical and comparison operators in expressing conditions, the algebra includes eight basic table operations. Comparison operators have precedence over logical operators, which have precedence over table operators. Table 8.5 shows the full priority convention among the operators. Parentheses may be used to override this order. Operators on the same precedence level are left-associative (evaluated in left to right order as they appear in an expression). Our priority convention is designed to minimize use of parentheses, and is stronger than some other conventions in use. If in doubt, or purely for the sake of clarity, feel free to add extra parentheses. The table operators are summarized visually in Figure 8.75.

Table 8.5 Evaluation priority of the operators (1 = first)

1	*comparison operators*	= <> < > <= >=
2	*logical operators*	**not**
3		**and**
4		**or**
5	*table operators*	selection (**where** ...) projection ([ ])
6		∪ ∩ − × ⋈ ÷

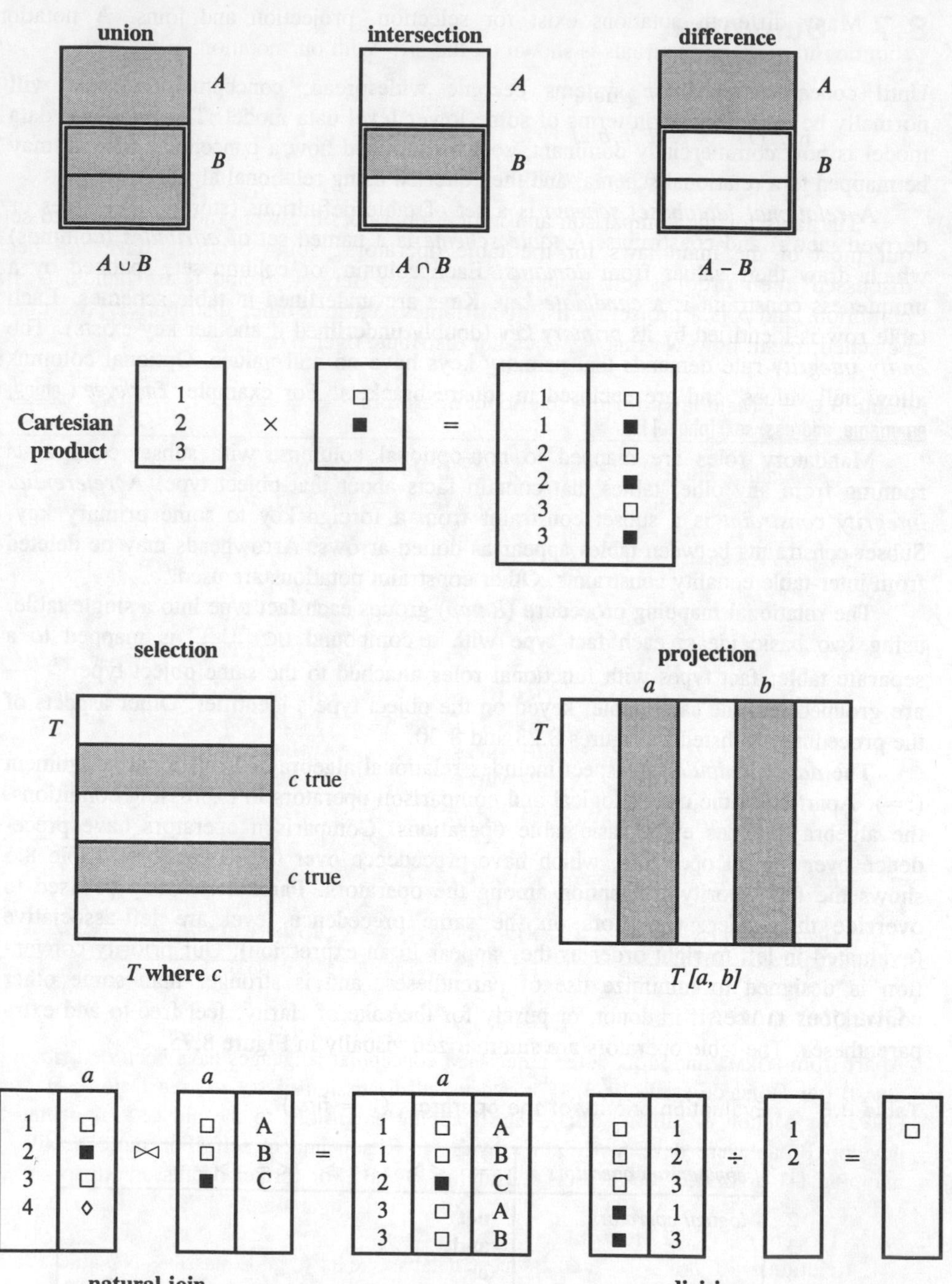

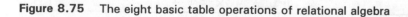

Figure 8.75 The eight basic table operations of relational algebra

Many different notations exist for selection, projection and joins. A notation common in academic journals is shown on the left, with our notation on the right.

$\sigma_c(T)$ ≡ *T* **where** *c*

$\pi_{a,b,\ldots}(T)$ ≡ *T [a,b,...]*

$A \bowtie_c B$ ≡ $A \times B$ **where** *c*

The laws for the comparison and logical operators are well known. Table 8.6 sets out most of the main laws for the table operators. Some of these have not been discussed: their proof is left as an easy exercise. Here *A*, *B* and *C* are tables, *c* is a condition, and *p* is a projection list of attributes. Various other distributive laws could be stated; recall however that *[ ]* does not distribute over ∩ or −.

Table 8.6 Main laws for the relational operators

Commutative laws:	$A \cup B$	=	$B \cup A$	
	$A \cap B$	=	$B \cap A$	
Associative laws:	$A \cup (B \cup C)$	=	$(A \cup B) \cup C$	
	$A \cap (B \cap C)$	=	$(A \cap B) \cap C$	
	$A \times (B \times C)$	=	$(A \times B) \times C$	
	$A \bowtie (B \bowtie C)$	=	$(A \bowtie B) \bowtie C$	
Distributive laws:	$A \cup (B \cap C)$	=	$(A \cup B) \cap (A \cup C)$	
	$A \cap (B \cup C)$	=	$(A \cap B) \cup (A \cap C)$	
	$(A \cup B)$ **where** *c*	=	*A* **where** *c* ∪ *B* **where** *c*	
	$(A \cap B)$ **where** *c*	=	*A* **where** *c* ∩ *B* **where** *c*	
If *A*, *B* are compatible:	$(A \cup B)\ [p]$	=	$A[p] \cup B[p]$	{ false for ∩ }
Exportation:	*A* **where** *c1* **where** *c2*	=	*A* **where** *c1* **and** *c2*	
Delayed Projection:	*A[p]* **where** *c*	=	(*A* **where** *c*) *[p]*	

Chapter notes

Apart from FORML and RIDL, some other ORM conceptual languages have been defined, e.g. LISA-D (ter Hofstede et al. 1993). For a detailed discussion of SQL-92, see Date & Darwen (1993) or Melton & Simon (1993). The mapping extensions to the old ONF algorithm to develop Rmap were developed jointly by Peter Ritson and myself. For more details on mapping 1:1 predicates, see Ritson & Halpin (1993a). For further details on Rmap and its SQL version see Ritson & Halpin (1993b). Discussions on automation of mapping are found in De Troyer (1993) and McCormack et al. (1993).

Relational algebra is covered in most database texts (e.g. Elmasri & Navathe 1989). Various different notations exist. Codd's 333 rules for his proposed version 2 of the relational model are discussed in Codd (1990).

9 Conceptual schema transformations

9.1 Conceptual schema equivalence

In previous chapters we learned how to model the structure of an application in terms of a conceptual schema, and then map it to a logical schema for implementation in a relational database system. Although much of the design and mapping can be automated, humans are required to perform CSDP step 1, since verbalizing the relevant facts about the real world involves human understanding. Given the informal nature of this initial step in modeling the UoD, it is not surprising that humans often come up with different ways of describing the same reality.

The same application may be modeled by more than one conceptual schema. For example, we might express a ternary fact type in either flattened or nested form. Basically, two conceptual schemas are **equivalent** if and only if whatever UoD state or transition can be modeled in one can also be modeled in the other. This informal notion can be formalized by specifying how descriptions in one schema can be translated into descriptions in the other, and then using formal logic to establish logical equivalence.

As a simple example, consider the medical report shown in Table 9.1. Here a tick in the appropriate column indicates that a patient smokes or drinks. Since both these "vices" can impair health, doctors are often interested in this information. Try to schematize Table 9.1 for yourself before looking at the solutions provided.

Table 9.1

Patient#	*Patient name*	*Smoker?*	*Drinker?*
1001	Adams, A		✓
1002	Bloggs, F	✓	✓
1003	Collins, T		

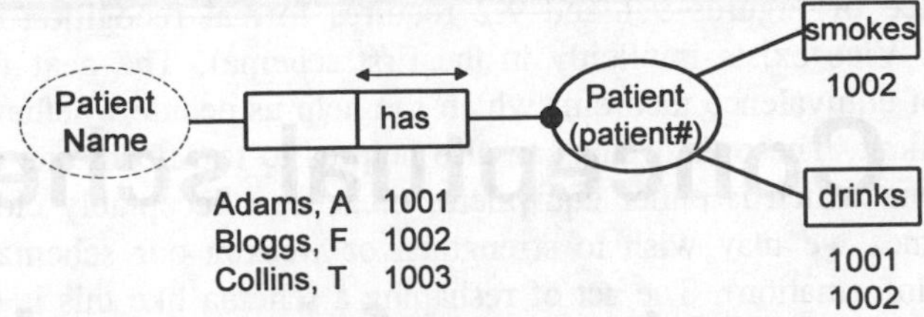

Figure 9.1 One way of modeling table 9.1

Figure 9.1 shows one conceptual schema for this UoD, together with the sample population. Here two optional unaries are used for the smoker-drinker facts. In Table 9.1 the absence of a tick might mean the patient doesn't smoke/drink (closed world approach) or simply that we don't know (open world approach). You would need to check with the UoD expert as to what is intended here. If no-tick means "No", you could add a relative closure symbol to the unaries to make this clear.

Instead of using unaries, we may model the smoker-drinker facts using two functional binaries: Patient has SmokerStatus; Patient has DrinkerStatus. With the closed world approach, both these fact types are mandatory, with two values for each status type (e.g. {"yes", "no"}).

A third way to model this is generalize the smoking and drinking predicates into a single binary, introducing the object type Vice {S = Smoking, D = Drinking) to maintain the distinction (see Figure 9.2). Intuitively, most people would consider the schemas of Figures 9.1 and 9.2 to be equivalent. Formally, this intuition can be backed up by introducing Vice as an "implicit object type" to the schema of Figure 9.1, and by specifying exactly how the predicates of each can be translated into the predicates of the other. For example, facts expressed in the first model may be expressed in terms of the second model using the translations:

Patient smokes **iff** Patient indulges in Vice 'S'
Patient drinks **iff** Patient indulges in Vice 'D'

and facts in the second model may be expressed in the first using the translation:

Patient indulges in Vice **iff** Patient smokes **and** Vice has ViceCode 'S'
or
Patient drinks **and** Vice has ViceCode 'D'

Like the schemas themselves, these FORML translations can be mapped into formulae of predicate logic. Formal logic may then be used to prove schema equivalence.

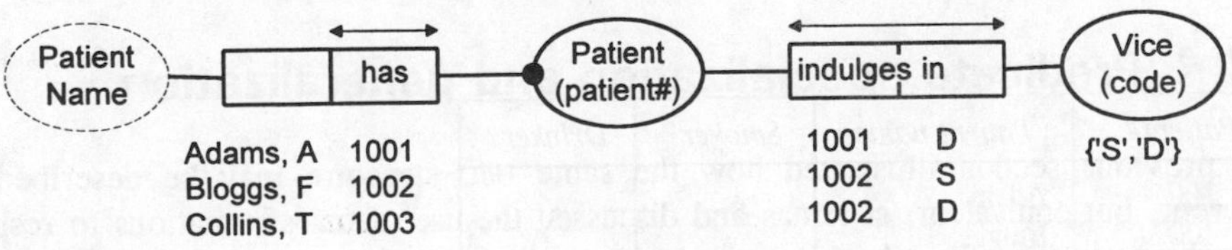

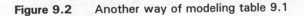

Figure 9.2 Another way of modeling table 9.1

The equivalence of Figures 9.1 and 9.2 requires formal recogition of "implicit object types" (e.g. Vice exists implicitly in the first schema). The next few sections discuss a number of equivalence theorems which can help us decide whether or not two schemas are equivalent. These theorems can also help us to transform one schema into an alternative schema which is either equivalent, or at least acceptably close to being equivalent (sometimes we may wish to strengthen or weaken our schema a little by adding or deleting information). The act of reshaping a schema like this is said to be a **conceptual schema transformation**.

A knowledge of schema transformations helps us to see what different design choices are possible. Moreover, if two independently developed schemas are to be either fully or partly integrated, we often need to resolve the differences in the ways that each schema models common UoD features. To do this, we need to know whether one representation can be transformed into the other, and if so how.

Another use of conceptual schema transformations is to reshape the original conceptual schema into one that maps directly to a more efficient implementation. This process is known as **conceptual schema optimization**. For example, the conceptual schema in Figure 9.1 maps to a single table. Taking a closed world interpretation, we may use the following table scheme:

```
                                       {y,n}     {y,n}
Patient ( patient#, patientname, smokes, drinks )
```

However because the indulges fact type is *m:n*, the schema in Figure 9.2 maps to two tables:

```
Patient  ( patient#, patientname )
               ↑
               |  {S,D}
Indulges ( patient#, vice )
```

For most applications, the single table solution is more efficient. It enables us to list all the information about the patients without requiring a table join. It also avoids any inter-table accesses required to enforce the subset constraint (e.g. when adding a vice fact or deleting a patient). So if we had originally proposed the schema of Figure 9.2, we could optimize it by transforming it to that of Figure 9.1 before passing it to the normal Rmap procedure. Guidelines for performing such optimizations are given later in the chapter. If the optimized conceptual schema still fails to give an efficient map, some lower level optimization may then be required—we examine this briefly.

Apart from use in developing new applications, conceptual modeling and schema transformations have important roles to play in *re-engineering* existing applications that have proved unsatisfactory. We illustrate this notion later with a worked example.

9.2 Predicate specialization and generalization

The previous section illustrated how the same UoD structure may be described by different, but equivalent, schemas and discussed the use of transformations to reshape one schema into another. In this section we consider a class of schema transformations known as **predicate specialization**, as well as its inverse, **predicate generalization**.

If two or predicates may be thought of as special cases of a more general predicate then we may replace them by the more general predicate, so long as the original distinction can be preserved in some way. For example, if we transform the schema of Figure 9.1 into that of Figure 9.2, we *generalize* smoking and drinking into indulging in a vice, where vice has two specific cases. If we transform in the opposite direction, we *specialize* indulging in a vice into two predicates, one for each case.

Predicate specialization and generalization are similar notions to object type specialization and generalization, except that it is rare to specify any subtype connections between predicates (the predicates must be objectified for this to be legal).

A predicate may be specialized if a *value constraint or a frequency constraint* indicates that it has a finite number of cases. Examples with value constraints are more common, so we examine these first. The drinker-smoker example provides one illustration, where Vice has the value constraint {'S','D'}. As another example, recall the Olympic Games schema reproduced in Figure 9.3 (a). Because there are exactly three kinds of medal, the ternary may be specialized into three binaries, one for each medal kind, as shown in Figure 9.3 (b).

You may visualize the transformation from schema (a) into schema (b) thus: when the object type MedalKind is *absorbed* into the ternary predicate, it breaks it up (or specializes it) into the three binaries. Hence this transformation is also known as *object type absorption*. The reverse transformation from (b) to (a) generalizes the three binaries into the ternary by extracting the object type MedalKind—this may be called *object type extraction*.

Notice that in the vices example, a binary is specialized into unaries. With the games example, a ternary is specialized into binaries. In general, when an *n*-valued object type is absorbed into a predicate, the *n* specialized predicates that result each have one less role than the original (since the object type has been absorbed). This general result is set out in Figure 9.4.

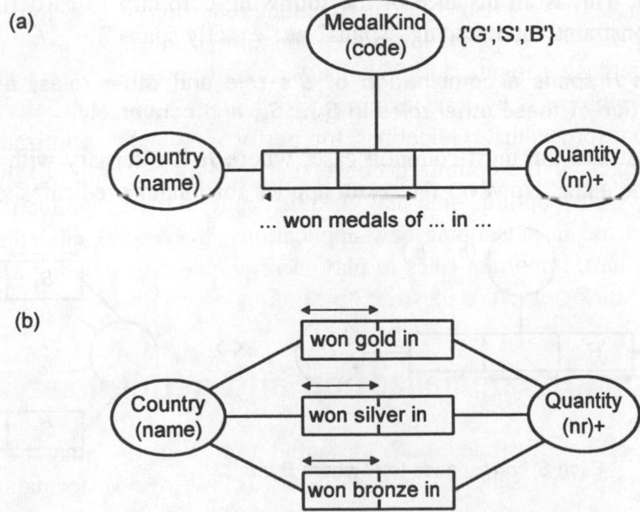

Figure 9.3 The ternary is specialized into three binaries by absorbing MedalKind

PSG1:

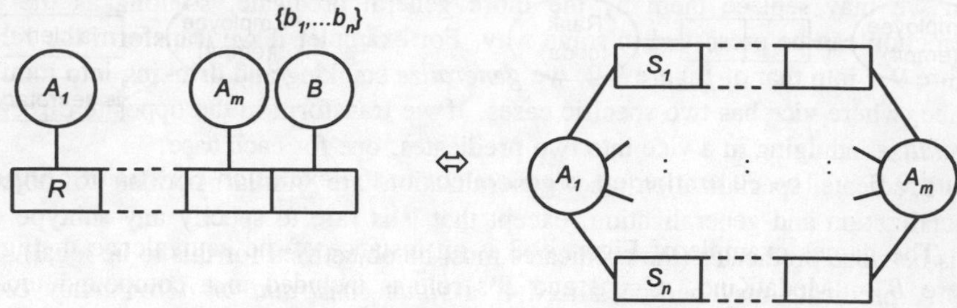

where $m \geq 1$, and each S_i corresponds to R where $B = b_i$

Figure 9.4 R may be specialized into $S_1..S_n$ by absorbing B

The schema equivalence in Figure 9.4 is called PSG1 (Predicate Specialization/Generalization theorem 1). Reference schemes are omitted for simplicity. The predicates R and S respectively have $m+1$ roles and m roles, where $m \geq 1$. The object types $A_1,..,A_m$ and B are not necessarily distinct. The value type for B has n values $b_1,..b_n$. If $m = 1$ we have conversion between a binary and n unaries; if $m = 2$, the conversion is between a ternary and n binaries; and so on. Transforming from left to right specializes the predicate R into n predicates $S_1,..,S_n$ by absorbing the object type B. The reverse transformation from right to left generalizes the shorter predicates into the longer one by extracting B. As an exercise, draw the diagrams for the cases $m = 1$, 2 and 3.

The theorem PSG1 holds regardless of whatever additional constraints are added. However, *any constraint added to one of the schemas must be translated into an equivalent, additional constraint on the other schema*. For example, the uniqueness constraint in Figure 9.3 (a) translates into the three shorter uniqueness constraints in Figure 9.3 (b). This is an instance of the following corollary to PSG1 (using "UC" for "uniqueness constraint" and reading "spans" as "exactly spans").

> If a UC in R spans a combination of B's role and other roles, a UC spans the specialization of these other roles in $S_1,..,S_n$; and conversely.

Figure 9.5 illustrates the most common case, where R is a ternary with a UC spanning B's role and one other. However the result applies for longer predicates too.

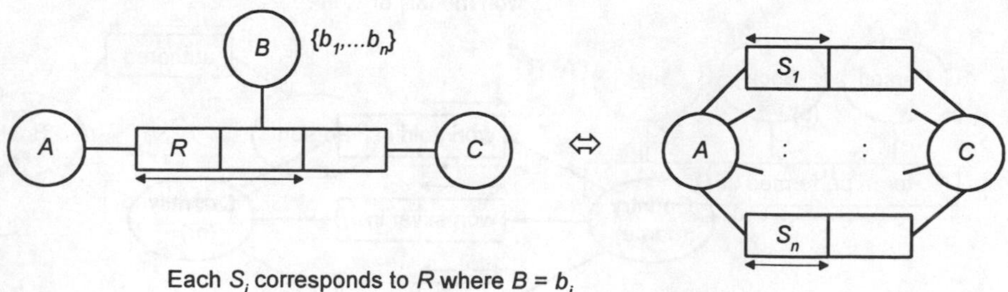

Each S_i corresponds to R where $B = b_i$

Figure 9.5 The UC on the left is equivalent to the Ucs on the right

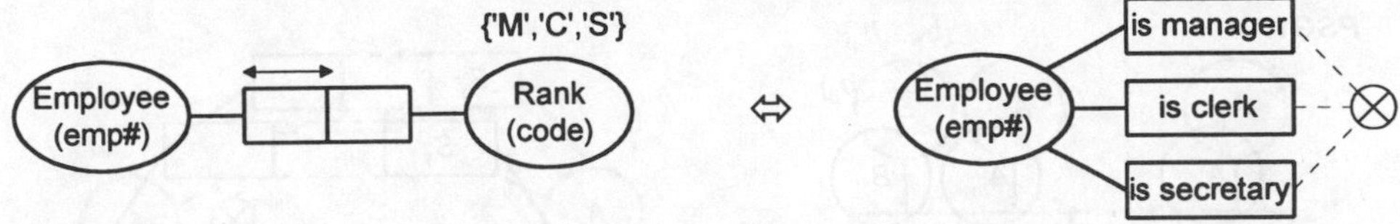

Figure 9.6 The UC on the left is equivalent to the exclusion constraint on the right

The games example of Figure 9.3 is an instance of the equivalence in Figure 9.5 where B = MedalKind, n = 3 and B's role is included in a compound uniqueness constraint. What happens however if B's role in the general predicate R is not included in a uniqueness constraint? Since R is elementary, its other roles must be spanned by a uniqueness constraint; and this constraint is transformed into a mutual *exclusion* constraint over the specialized predicates.

Exclusive unaries provide the simplest case of this. For example, suppose that workers in a company may hold at most one position (manager, clerk or secretary). This may be rephrased in terms of exclusive unaries as shown in Figure 9.6, assuming appropriate translations between the predicates. For implementation purposes, the binary version is usually preferred (e.g. its relational schema simplifies both updates to a worker's position, and schema updates to the list of allowable positions). The larger the number of unaries, the worse the unary solution becomes (Why?).

Another example, this time with exclusive binaries, is shown in Figure 9.7. Here "A" and "R" are codes for authoring and reviewing. For simplicity, reference schemes are omitted. Note the two alternative ways of saying that a person cannot act both as an author and a reviewer of the *same* book.

These two examples illustrate unary (m = 1) and binary (m = 2) cases of the following, second corollary to theorem PSG1. This result applies to longer predicates as well (see Figure 9.8). Here the exclusion constraint means that particular no row of values may appear in more than one of the S_i fact tables.

If a UC spans all roles of R except for B's role, then S_1 .. S_n are mutually exclusive; and conversely.

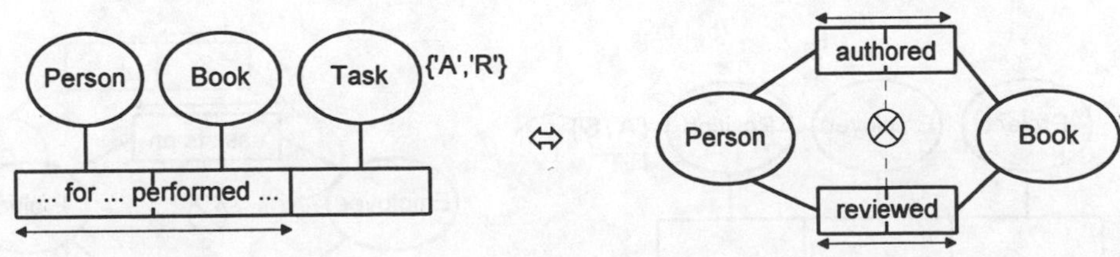

Figure 9.7 The UC on the left is equivalent to the exclusion constraint on the right

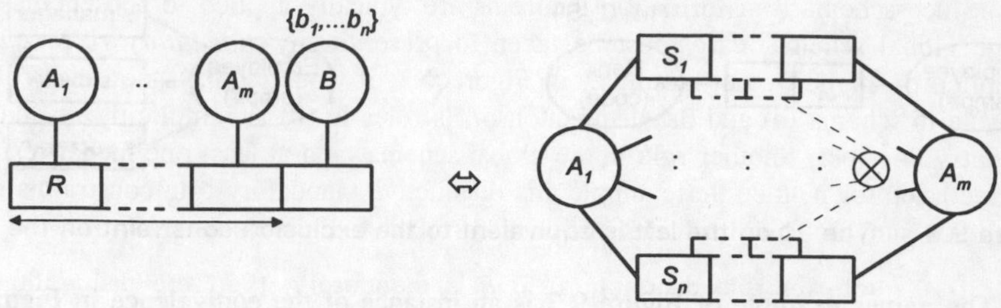

where $m \geq 1$, and each S_i corresponds to R where $B = b_i$

Figure 9.8 The UC on the left is equivalent to the exclusion constraint on the right

In rare cases, when a schema transformation is performed, some graphical constraint in one schema may have no corresponding graphical constraint in the other. In this case, the constraint should be expressed as a *textual constraint* in the other version. For example, consider the two schemas in Figure 9.9. The codes "A" and "S" indicate "assistant" and "supervisor" respectively. Reference schemes are omitted for simplicity. A person might supervise one project and assist on another. Assuming appropriate translations between the predicates, the schemas are still not equivalent. One schema has a constraint which is not captured in the other. Try to spot this for yourself before reading on.

Did you find it? The uniqueness constraint on the ternary translates to the exclusion constraint; and the uniqueness constraint on the assists binary is implied. However the uniqueness constraint on the supervises binary declares that each project has at most one supervisor. This is missing from the ternary, and cannot be expressed as a graphic constraint there since it is a ***restricted uniqueness constraint*** (this kind of constraint was discussed in section 7.4). To ensure equivalence, this may be added to the left-hand schema as a textual constraint in FORML as follows:

each Project uses **at most one** Employee in Position 'S'

If Project plays other functional roles, the binary approach of the right-hand schema would normally be preferred since its relational version simplifies the enforcement of this supervision constraint. If Project has no other functional roles, the ternary approach might be preferred since it maps to a single table.

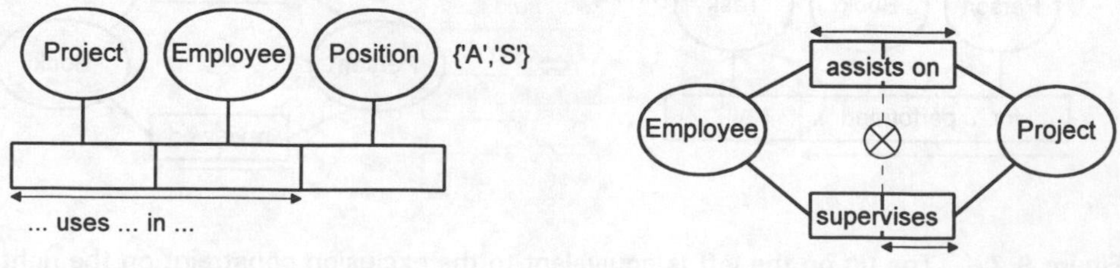

Figure 9.9 One schema has an additional constraint. Can you find it?

Since schema transformation theorems are typically applied to subschemas within some global schema, care must be taken to preserve any ***mandatory role constraints*** (implicit or explicit). For example, in Figure 9.3, if Country plays no other role, then its role in schema (a) and the disjunction of its roles in (b) are implicitly mandatory. If Country does play another role in the global schema, and at least one medal result must be recorded for it, then these simple and disjunctive mandatory role constraints must be explicitly shown. This illustrates our third corollary to theorem PSG1:

> If A_i's role (or role disjunction) in R is mandatory, then the disjunction of its specialized roles is mandatory, and conversely ($1 \le i \le m$).

The inclusion of "(or role disjunction)" covers the rare case when the A_i plays more than one role in R (recall that $A_1..A_m$ are not necessarily distinct). Note also how our convention for implicit mandatory role constraints enables theorems such as PSG1 to be specified without any assumption about other roles played in the global schema.

Suppose in Figure 9.3 (a) that Country's role is optional (this implies Country plays some other role in the global schema) but it has a ***frequency constraint*** of 3. So if any medal results are recorded for a country, all three medal results (gold, silver and bronze) are required. To express this in Figure 9.3 (b) we need to add an ***equality constraint*** between the roles played by Country. Since equality is transitive, we need only add two simple equality constraints, one between the top and middle roles of Country, and one between the middle and bottom roles. This is an instance of the following, fourth corollary to theorem PSG1 (it may help to refer to Figure 9.5):

> If R is a ternary with a UC spanning just B's role and one other role, then adding a frequency constraint of n to this other role is equivalent to adding an equality constraint over the specialized versions of that role.

Now consider Figure 9.10. The unfinished lines on the left indicate that Country plays another role in the global schema. Contrast this with Figure 9.3.

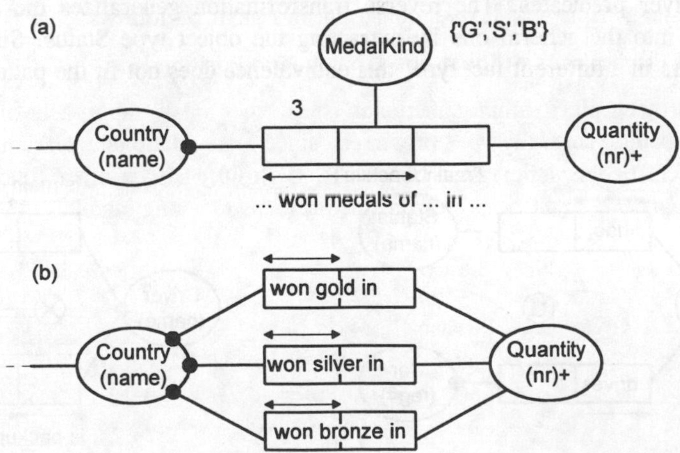

Figure 9.10 The impact of adding mandatory role and frequency constraints

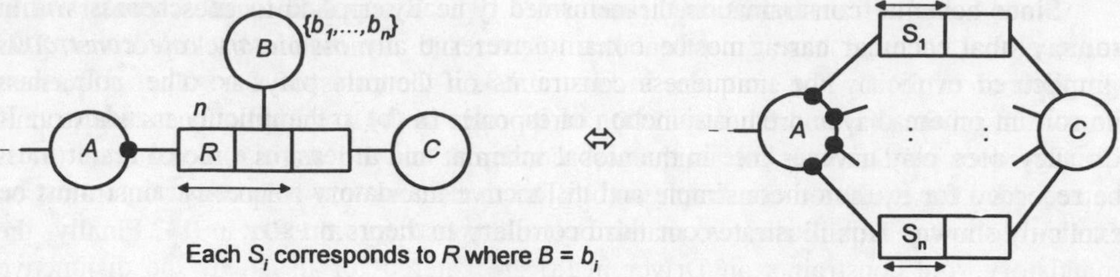

Figure 9.11 Fifth corollary to theorem PSG1

In Figure 9.10 (a) the medal role played by Country is mandatory and also has a frequency constraint of 3. The mandatory role, frequency, uniqueness and value constraint together ensure that each country must have its medal tally recorded for each kind of medal. Hence Figure 9.10 (b) has three mandatory roles. This example is an instance of the following, fifth corollary to theorem PSG1:

> If *R* is a ternary with a UC spanning just *B*'s role and one other role, then adding a mandatory role constraint and frequency constraint of *n* to this other role is equivalent to making each specialized version of that role mandatory.

This corollary is illustrated in Figure 9.11. It is implied by the previous two corollaries, since an equality constraint across a set of disjunctively mandatory roles implies these each of these roles is mandatory.

As an introduction to a second equivalence theorem, consider Figure 9.12. The two schemas provide alternative models for a fragment of a car rally application. Each car in the rally has two drivers (a main driver and a backup driver), and each person drives exactly one car. Schema (a) is transformed into schema (b) by absorbing the object type Status into the drives predicate, specializing this into the main driver and backup driver predicates. The reverse transformation generalizes the specific driver predicates into the general one by extracting the object type Status. Since this object type appears in a different fact type, this equivalence does not fit the pattern of PSG1.

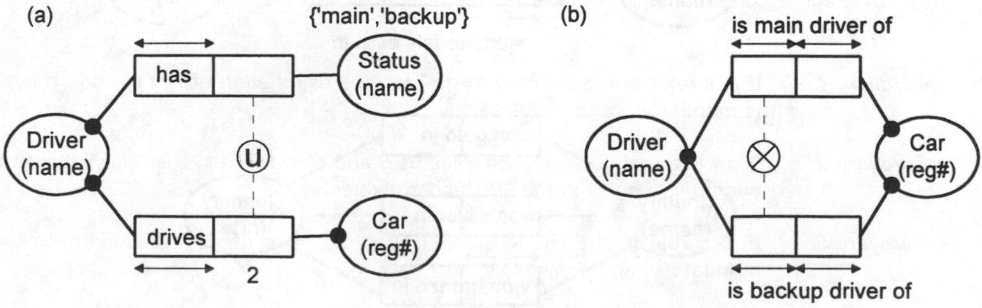

Figure 9.12 The drives predicate is specialized by absorbing Status

Note how the constraints are transformed. The external uniqueness constraint in (a) says that each car has at most one main driver and at most one backup driver. This is captured in (b) by the uniqueness constraints on the roles of Car. The uniqueness constraint on the drives predicate in (a) corresponds in (b) to the uniqueness constraints on the roles of Driver. The uniqueness constraint on the status predicate in (a) is captured by the exclusion constraint in (b). The mandatory and frequency constraints on Car's role in (a) require the two mandatory role constraints on Car in (b). Finally, the mandatory role constraints on Driver in (a) are catered for in (b) by the disjunctive mandatory role constraint (shown explicitly here).

This example illustrates our second predicate specialization/generalization theorem (PSG2) as well as four of its corollaries (see Figure 9.13). The terms "LHS" and "RHS" abbreviate "left-hand schema" and "right-hand schema". In our example, *A*, *B* and *C* correspond to Driver, Status and Car; and the equality constraint is implied by the two mandatory role constraints on Driver. Theorem PSG2 can be derived from earlier results. For example, adding an exclusion constraint across *A*'s roles in the RHS of Figure 9.5 makes *A*'s role unique in the LHS, causing this compound fact type to split into two binaries to agree with the LHS of Figure 9.13. In section 9.4 we consider two more general versions of this theorem.

Sometimes we may wish to transform a schema into another that is not quite equivalent. For example, suppose that in our car rally application we limit each car to at most two drivers, but do not classify the drivers in any meaningful way (e.g. as main or backup drivers). Let us also remove the constraint that drivers may drive only one car. This situation is schematized in Figure 9.14.

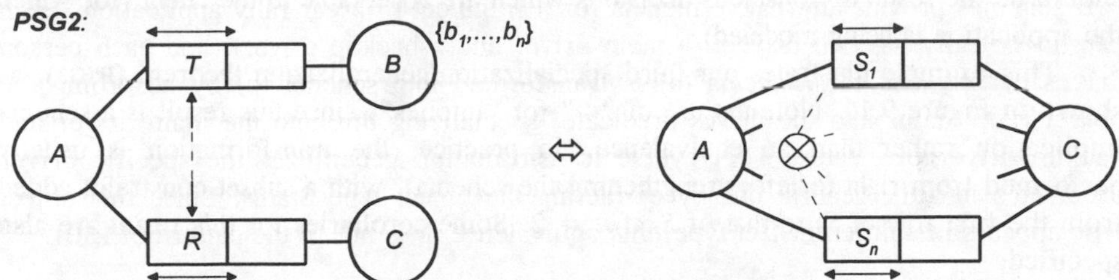

Each S_i corresponds to R where T is restricted to $B = b_i$

Corollary 1: If *A*'s roles are mandatory in the LHS, the disjunction of *A*'s roles in the RHS is mandatory; and conversely.

Corollary 2: If an external UC spans the roles of *B* and *C* in the LHS, then a UC applies to each of *C*'s roles in the RHS; and conversely.

Corollary 3: If *C*'s role in the LHS is mandatory, then each of *C*'s roles in the RHS is mandatory; and conversely.

Corollary 4: An equality constraint over *C*'s roles in the RHS is equivalent to a frequency constraint of $\geq n$ on *C*'s role in the LHS; this constraint is strengthened to n if a UC exists on each of *C*'s roles in the RHS.

Figure 9.13 *R* may be specialized into $S_1..S_n$ by absorbing *B*

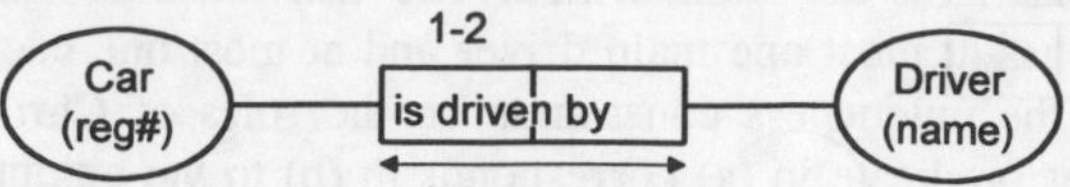

Figure 9.14 Can the predicate be specialized?

Although no Status object type is present, the frequency constraint in Figure 9.14 tells us that each car has at most two drivers. This enables us to introduce an artificial distinction to specialize the predicate into two cases, as shown in Figure 9.15. Since this distinction is not present in the original schema, the alternatives shown in Figure 9.15 are *not equivalent* to the original; they are in fact *stronger* (each implies the original schema, but is not implied by it).

Schema (b) is actually stronger than schema (a). If the Car role in Figure 9.14 is mandatory, then the Car roles in (a) are disjunctively mandatory, and the top Car role in (b) is mandatory (which then implies the subset constraint).

In an application where other facts are stored about cars but not about drivers, one of these alternatives may well be chosen to avoid a separate table being generated for car-driver facts when the schema is mapped (the specialized predicates are functional rather than *m:n*). In practice, schema (b) of Figure 9.15 would normally be chosen.

Transforming from the original schema to one of those in Figure 9.15 *strengthens* the schema by adding information. Transforming in the opposite direction *weakens* the schema by losing information. Any such transformations which add or lose information should be the result of conscious decisions which are acceptable to the client (for which the application is being modeled).

This example illustrates our third specialization/generalization theorem (PSG3), as shown in Figure 9.16. Note the use of "⇨" for "implies", since this result is a schema implication rather than an equivalence. In practice, the transformation is usually performed from right to left (strengthening the schema), with a subset constraint added from the first role of S_2 to that of S_1 if $n = 2$. Some corollaries for this result are also specified.

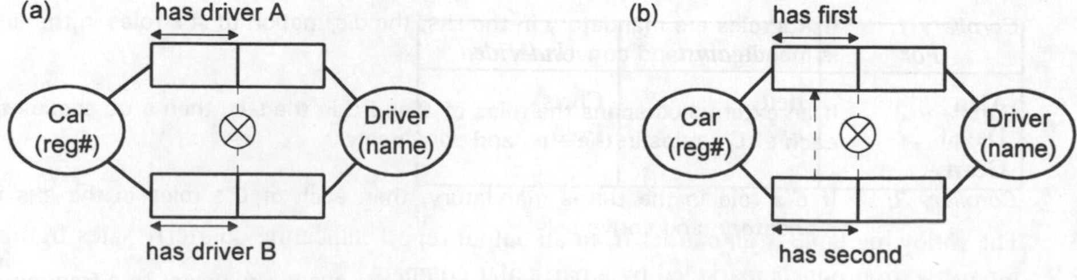

Figure 9.15 Two ways of strengthening the schema in Figure 9.14

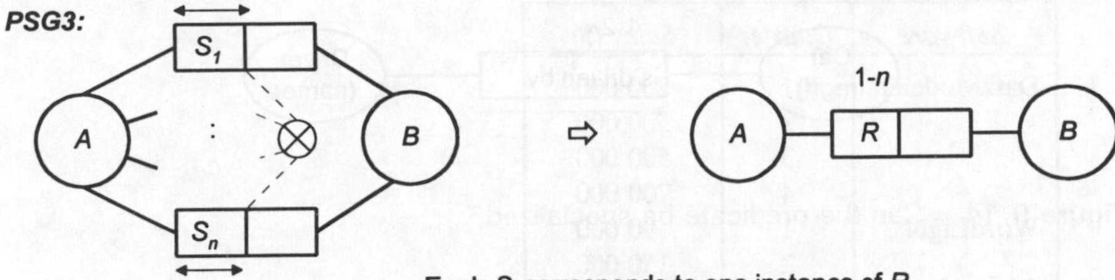

Each S_i corresponds to one instance of *R*

Corollary 1: If an equality constraint applies over *A*'s roles in the LHS then the frequency constraint in the RHS is strengthened to *n*; and conversely.

Corollary 2: Adding a UC to *B*'s role in the RHS is equivalent in the LHS to adding UCs to *B*'s roles (making the S_i 1:1) and strengthening the exclusion constraint to an exclusion constraint over *B*'s roles.

Figure 9.16 The left-hand schema implies the right-hand schema

Well that covers the most important results to do with predicate specialization and generalization. Note that the theorems require that the appropriate translations hold between the general and the special predicates. Humans are needed to provide natural names for the new predicate(s) and to confirm that the translation holds; this is not something that can be decided automatically by the system.

Exercise 9.2

1. Schematize the following table using: (a) unaries; (b) a binary.

Male staff	*Female staff*
Creasy, PN Halpin, TA	Orlowska, ME Purchase, HC

2. A company committee has to decide whether to increase its budget on staff training. The table indicates the current views of the committee members on this issue. Schematize this using: (a) unaries; (b) a binary.

For	*Against*	*Undecided*
Alan David Gearty	Betty Eve	Chris Fred

3. The following table is an extract from an output report indicating quarterly sales figures for software products marketed by a particular company.

   (a) Schematize this using a ternary.
   (b) Transform your solution into an equivalent one using binaries.

Software	*Quarter*	*Sales ($)*
DataModeler	1	200 000
	2	500 000
	3	500 000
	4	700 000
WordLight	1	90 000
	2	150 000
	3	155 000
	4	200 000

4. An embassy maintains details about how well its staff speak foreign languages. The following table is an extract from this system.

Language	*Expert*	*Novice*
Arabic		Smith, J
Dutch	Bruza, P Proper, HA	
French	Rolland, C	Bruza, P

(a) Schematize this using binaries.
(b) Transform this into a ternary.

5. University debating teams are to be selected, with four students in each team, with one student from each year level (1..4). No student may be in more than one team. Students are identified by their student number, but their name is also recorded. Debating teams are identified by codes.

(a) Schematize this UoD using YearLevel as an object type.
(b) Transform your schema by absorbing this object type

6. Employee records are kept which show the employee number, name and up to two phone numbers for each employee.

(a) Schematize this in the natural way.
(b) Map this to a relational schema.
(c) It is now required to map all the information into a single relational table. Transform the conceptual schema to enable this to happen.
(d) Rmap your revised conceptual schema.

Each phone is now to be classified as a work phone or a home phone. At most one work phone and at most one home phone may be recorded for an employee.

(e) Modify your solution to (a) accordingly.
(f) Rmap this.
(g) Modify your solution to (c) accordingly.
(h) Rmap this.

7. The following conceptual schemas are meant to describe the same UoD, but each fails to capture some constraint in the other. Add a textual constraint to schema (1), and a graphical constraint to the schema (2), to obtain equivalence. The codes "chr", "sec" and "ord" abbreviate "chairperson", "secretary" and "ordinary member".

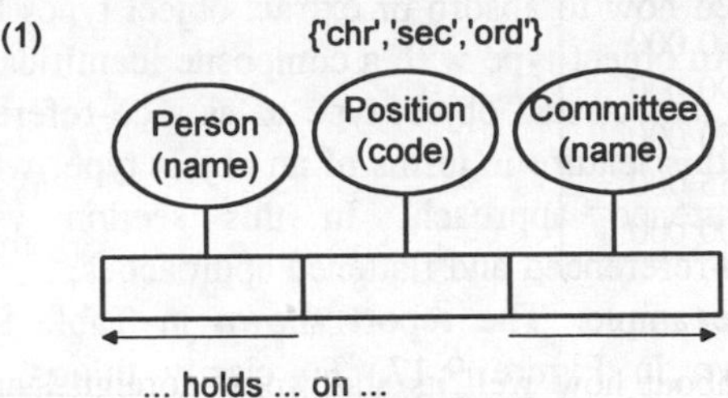

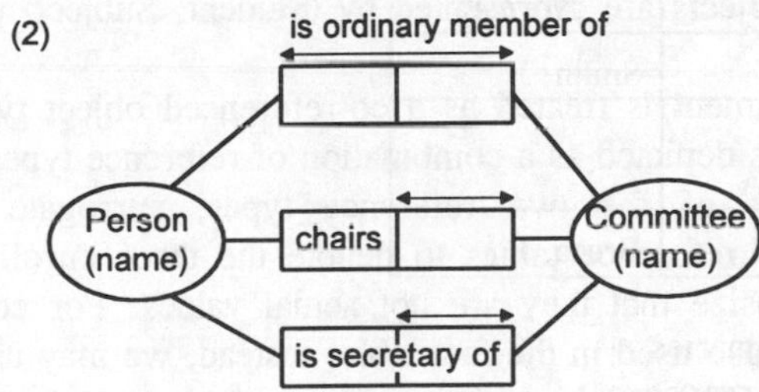

8. Consider the following academic UoD. Each subject is identified by its code but also has a unique title. Each subject has at most three assignments (possibly none), numbered 1, 2 and 3. Each subject has a second assignment only if it has a first assignment, and it has a third assignment only if it has a first and second assignment. Each assignment has exactly one due date. Although assignments for different subjects may be due on the same date, no subject has more than one assignment due on the same date.

   Though unlikely, it is possible that within a subject the chronological order of due dates differs from the numerical order of the assignments (e.g. because of software problems the due date for CS400 assignment 1 might be postponed till after the due date for CS400 assignment 2).

   (a) Model this by adding constraints (graphic, and textual if needed) to the schema:

   Reference schemes: Subject (code)
   Assignt (has Assignt#, is for Subject)

   Fact types: Subject has Title
   Assignt is due on Date

   (b) Map this to a relational schema, including all constraints.
   (c) Specialize the is-due-on predicate in (a) by absorbing Assignt# into it.
   (d) Map this to a relational schema including all constraints.
   (e) Suppose that within each subject the chronological order of assignment due dates must match their numeric order. How does this affect answers to (c) and (d)?

9.3 Nesting, co-referencing and flattening

As humans we have the freedom to think of the universe in different ways. One choice in modeling is whether to represent some feature in terms of an object type, and if so, how. The previous section discussed how to absorb or extract object types by predicate specialization and generalization. An object type with a composite identification scheme may be portrayed explicitly either as a nested object type or as a co-referenced object type; if we don't want to think of this feature in terms of an object type, we can model it with predicates using a flattened approach. In this section we consider transformations between nested, co-referenced and flattened approaches.

Let's start with a familiar example. The report shown in Table 9.2 may be modeled in three ways, as shown in Figure 9.17. To clarify things, the sample population has been included with the schemas. Schema (a) takes the flattened approach, using a ternary fact type. In schema (b), Enrollment is modelled as a nested object type, and Enrollment objects are represented by ⟨Student, Subject⟩ pairs in the outer fact table.

In schema 9.17(c), Enrollment is treated as a co-referenced object type (i.e. its primary identification scheme is depicted as a combination of reference types). Because there is no implied ordering of the two reference types, surrogate identifiers ("*e1*".."*e3*") are used in their reference tables to denote the three enrollments. We show them in italics to emphasize that they are not actual values. For convenience, these surrogate identifiers are also used in the fact table; instead, we may use qualified tuples, such as "⟨1001:Student, CS100:Subject⟩".

Surrogates are used here only as a direct way of depicting real world objects in conceptual tables—they are replaced by attribute-value tuples when mapped to relational tables. In fact, all three schemas in Figure 9.17 map to the same relational schema:

Result (<u>student#, subjcode</u>, rating)

In this example, the nested or co-referenced object type plays just one fact role, and this role is mandatory. In such a situation, the relational mapping is the same whether we nest, co-reference or flatten; so we may choose whichever of the three approaches appeals most to us. Although this choice is partly subjective, there are a few guidelines which may be helpful.

First let's consider choosing between nesting and co-referencing. Both these approaches always have the same relational mapping, no matter what the situation. Choose what seems most "natural". If in thinking about the real world, you first "see" a relationship and later want to talk about it, then nesting is probably the best choice. On this basis, most people would probably nest Enrollment than co-reference it.

Table 9.2

Result:

student#	*subject*	*rating*
1001	CS100	4
1002	CS100	4
1002	CS114	5

(a)

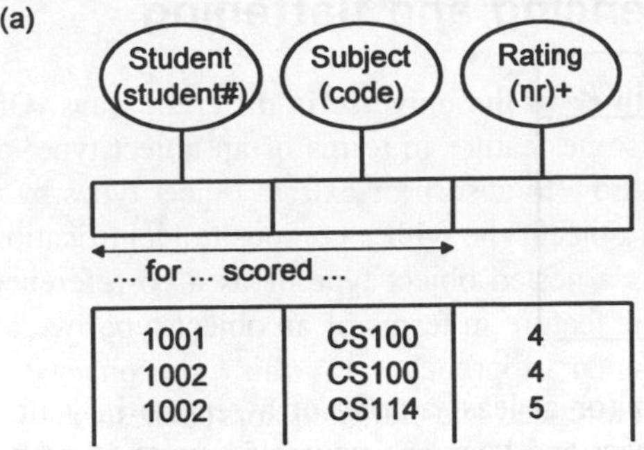

(b)

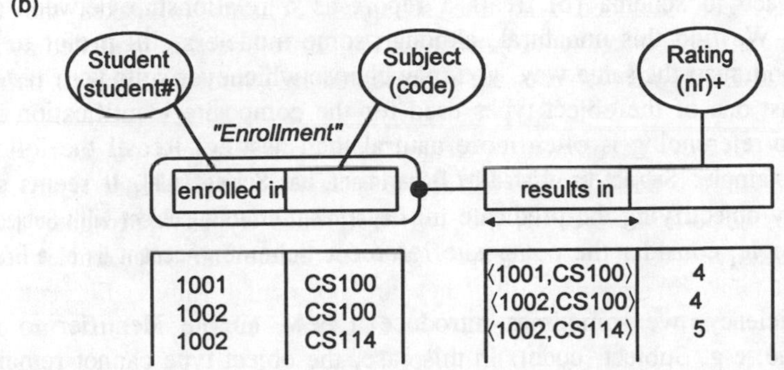

(c)

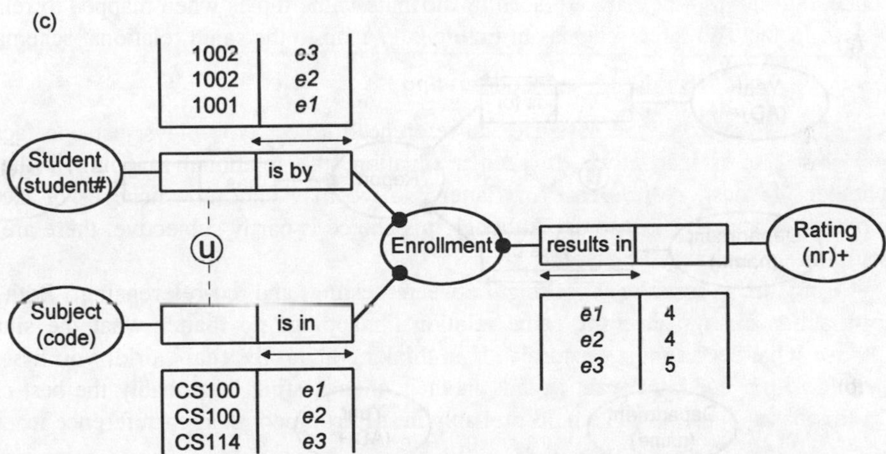

Figure 9.17 Modeling Table 9.2 by: (a) flattening; (b) nesting; (c) co-referencing

On the other hand, it often seems unnatural to think of a visible object in the real world as an objectified relationship. For example, consider table 9.3, which provides details about the length of various annual reports by departments within a company.

Table 9.3 Length of departmental annual reports

Year	*Department*	*Report length (pp.)*
1993	Research	40
1993	Sales	25
1993	Support	40
1994	Research	67
...	...	...

Because you can hold a report (or at least a copy of a report) in your hand, it is natural to think of it first as an object and later ask yourself how to identify it. In this case we use both the year and department to co-reference it (Figure 9.18 (a)). The nested approach in schema (b) treats a report as a relationship between Year and Department. We find this unnatural, although some modelers still prefer to do it this way. Since both map the same way, you may choose whichever suits your taste.

If at least one of the object types used for the composite identification is a value type, then co-referencing is often more natural than nesting. Recall the following co-referenced example: Subject (is offered by Department, has SubjectTitle). It seems strange to model this by objectifying the predicate in: Department offers a subject with SubjectTitle. As another example, consider the composite reference scheme: Account (is at a Branch, has a LocalAccount#).

For efficiency, we sometimes introduce a new, simple identifier to replace a composite one, e.g. Subject (code). In this case, the object type cannot remain nested, and if it was originally co-referenced the former reference types become fact types.

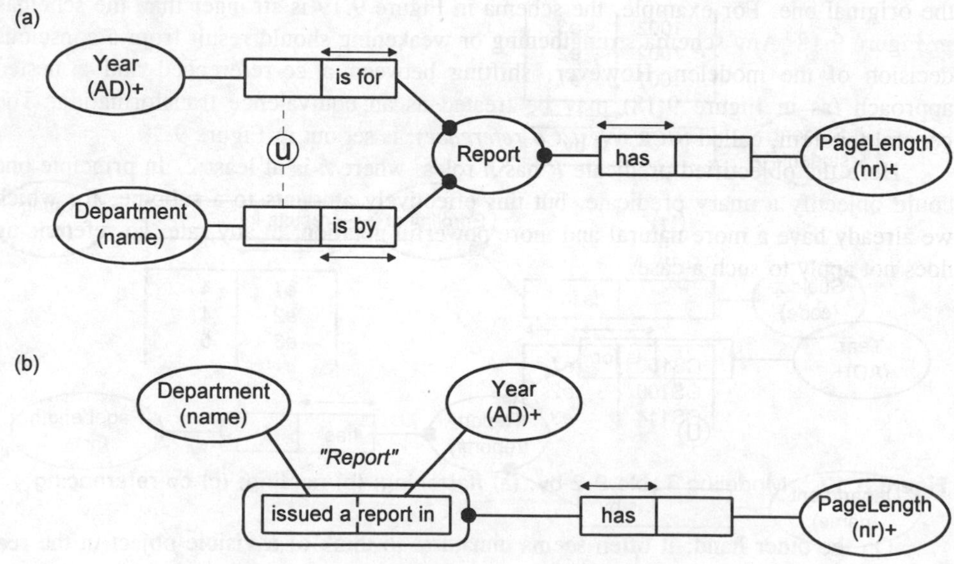

Figure 9.18 Since a report is a physical object, is (a) more natural than (b)?

For example, in Figure 9.19 a simple report number is introduced to identify annual reports. We could use a plain serial number (e.g. 1, 2 ...) or a coded number that humans can use to derive the semantics (e.g. "RES-93", "SAL-93" ...). Consider the relationship types: Report is for Year; Report is by Department. These were reference types in Figure 9.18 (a), but are now fact types. For example, two fact instances might be:

Report 'RES-93' is for Year 1993.
Report 'RES-93' is by Department 'Research'.

If we choose "human-meaningful" report numbers like these, we may if desired make such facts derivable by the system (not just by humans), by declaring appropriate derivation rules using substring operators.

If the semantic basis of such introduced identifiers is unstable, then plain serial numbers might be preferred (e.g. suppose departments are often split, merged or renamed). However, if the semantic basis is stable, such "information-bearing" identifiers can lead to efficiency gains by reducing the need to perform relational joins when information about the object is spread over many tables.

For example, suppose one table is used to store the data in Table 9.3 as well as an extra column for report#, and a separate table is used to store the *m:n* fact type: Employee (name) authored Report (report#). To find out who authored what reports, most users would be content with a listing of this sccond table, if meaningful report identifiers like "RES-93" are used, since this would be enough for them to work out the year and department. However, if plain serial numbers are used, most users would want to have the year and department listed too, requiring a join to the first table. As another example, consider the use of subject codes (e.g. "CS115") in listing results.

If a new identifier is introduced, the new schema is no longer strictly equivalent to the original one. For example, the schema in Figure 9.19 is stronger than the schemas in Figure 9.18. Any schema strengthening or weakening should result from a conscious decision of the modeler. However, shifting between a co-referenced and a nested approach (as in Figure 9.18) may be treated as an equivalence transformation. The general theorem, called **N/CR** (*Nest/Co-reference*), is set out in Figure 9.20.

Here the objectified predicate *R* has *n* roles, where *n* is at least 2. In principle one could objectify a unary predicate, but this effectively amounts to a subtype, for which we already have a more natural and more powerful notation; at any rate, co-referencing does not apply to such a case.

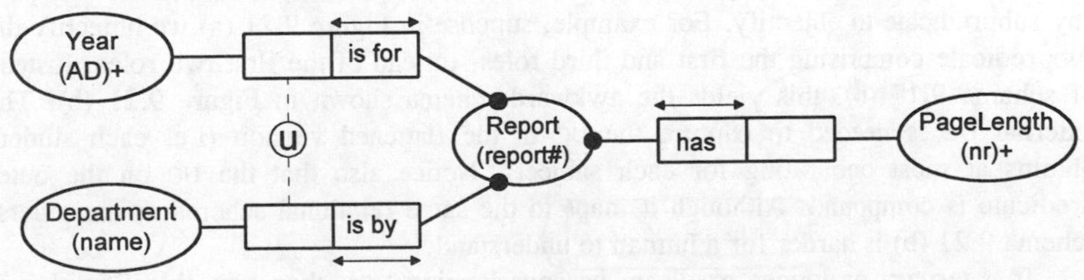

Figure 9.19 Annual reports are now identified by a report number

where $n > 1$, and $Ra_1..a_n$ iff there is a b such that bR_1a_1 &..& bR_na_n

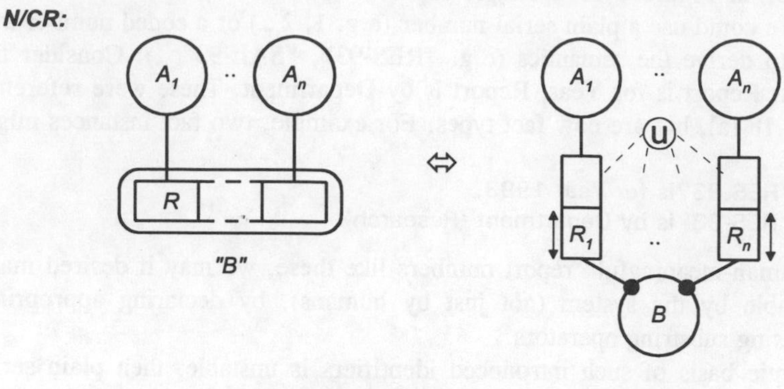

Notes: A UC is understood to span the objectified predicate.
If *B* is lazy, show it as *B !* in the co-referenced version.

Figure 9.20 The nested version is equivalent to the co-referenced version

In Figure 9.20 the object types $A_1..A_n$ are not necessarily distinct. Though not shown in the figure, we assume the nested object type has at least one role attached. Recall that an object type is lazy if the disjunction of its fact roles is optional. If lazy, the co-referenced portrayal of the object type must be explicitly marked lazy by appending " !" to its name. For example, look back at Figure 9.17 (b) and (c), and suppose enrollments are recorded before any results are known. In schema (b) the mandatory role constraint must be removed, and in schema (c) the co-referenced object type must be renamed "Enrollment !". As we will see shortly, a more drastic change is needed to schema (a) to maintain a flattened approach.

So long as the nested or co-referenced object type plays only one fact role, and this role is mandatory, we may transform to a single, flattened fact type. Recall the example in Figure 9.17. In such a case, the flattened approach is usually recommended since it gives a simpler diagram, is easier to verbalize, and it sometimes avoids arbitrary decisions about which part of the predicate to objectify.

When a ternary or longer predicate has just one UC (uniqueness constraint), and this spans all but one of its roles, the subpredicate spanned by this UC provides the best choice for objectifying. This was our choice in Figure 9.17. In principle, we could pick any subpredicate to objectify. For example, suppose in Figure 9.21 (a) we objectify the subpredicate comprising the first and third roles, instead of the first two roles. Instead of schema 9.17 (b), this yields the awkward schema shown in Figure 9.21 (b). The external UC is needed to capture the UC in the flattened version (i.e. each student obtains at most one rating for each subject). Notice also that the UC on the outer predicate is compound. Although it maps to the same relational schema as the others, schema 9.21 (b) is harder for a human to understand.

If a ternary or longer predicate has overlapping UCs, then any objectification is best based on one of these. Each other UC in the flattened version is then captured by an external UC. See Figures 4.37 and 4.38 for an earlier example.

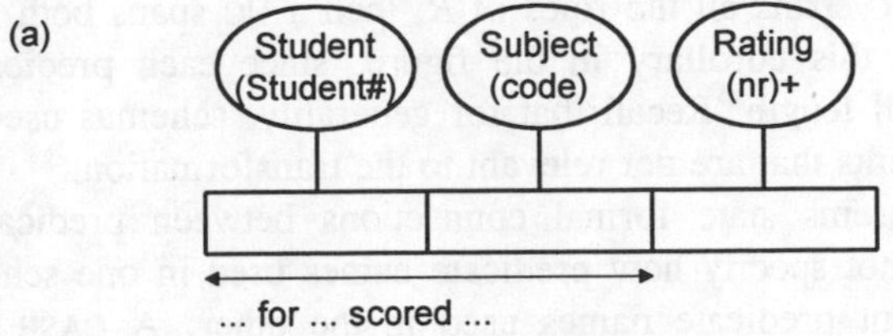

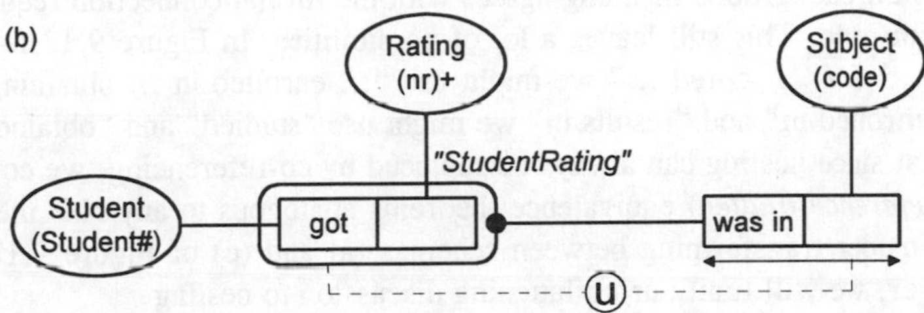

Figure 9.21 A poor choice for nesting (the UC spans other roles)

In the case of overlapping UCs, there is more than one "natural" choice of a subpredicate to objectify. This is also true if a ternary or longer predicate has a single UC spanning all its roles, for example: Lecturer visits Country in Year. Here we could objectify any of three role pairs: roles 1 and 2; roles 1 and 3; or roles 2 and 3. Unless there are additional facts to be stored about the subpredicates, the flattened fact type provides the simpler approach.

Figure 9.22 shows the ternary version of the **N/F** (*Nest/Flatten*) equivalence theorem. Here *A, B* and *C* need not be distinct. A spanning UC over the roles in the nested object type *S* is assumed. Typically a UC spans the *A, B* roles in *R*; this is equivalent to a UC over the first role of *T*. For equivalence, the predicates must be formally related by the condition shown in the where-clause: to clarify this, see Figure 9.17 (a) and (b) including the sample populations.

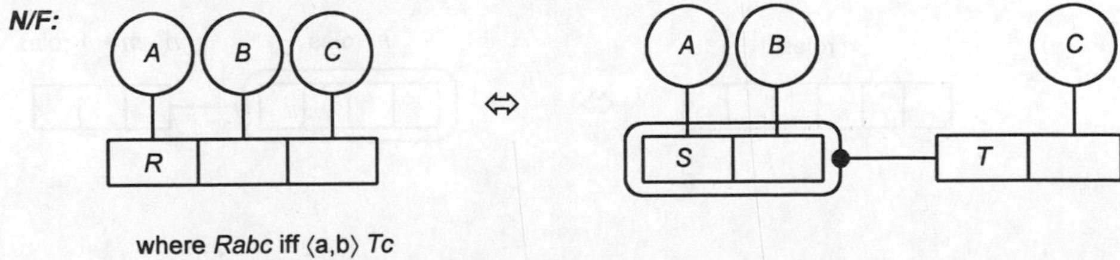

where *Rabc* iff ⟨a,b⟩ *Tc*

Corollaries: A UC exactly spans the *A, B* roles of *R* iff a simple UC spans the first role of *T*.
A binary UC over the *A, C* (or *B, C*) roles of *R* is equivalent to an external UC over the *A, C* (or *B, C*) roles respectively in the nested version.

Figure 9.22 The nested version is equivalent to the flattened version

In Figure 9.22, if a UC spans all the roles of *R*, then a UC spans both roles of *T*. We do not bother stating this corollary in the figure, since each predicate has an implied UC spanning its full length. Recall that for generality, schemas used to depict theorems may omit constraints that are not relevant to the transformation.

Our equivalence theorems state formal connections between predicates in the different versions, but do not specify how predicate names used in one schema might help to choose the different predicate names used in the other. A CASE tool could generate suggested names, but humans can often provide more natural ones (cf. generation of table names in relational mapping). In choosing identifiers, we should ensure that their background meaning agrees with the formal connection required by the transformation rule. This still leaves a lot of possibilities. In Figure 9.17 for example, instead of "... for ... scored ..." we might use "... enrolled in ... obtaining ...", and instead of "enrolled in" and "results in" we might use "studied" and "obtained".

Note that since nesting can always be replaced by co-referencing, we could specify **CR/F** (*Co-reference/Flatten*) equivalence theorems analogous to any N/F theorem. For example, consider transforming between schemas (a) and (c) of Figure 9.17. To save space however, we will limit our unflattening discussion to nesting.

The ternary Nest/Flatten equivalence may be generalized to flattened fact types of any arity above two. Note that nesting always introduces an extra role (to be played by the objectified predicate). If we objectify *m* roles of an *n*-ary predicate, the outer predicate will have $n-m-1$ roles. This is shown in Figure 9.23 (a), where other object types and role connectors are omitted for simplicity.

Recall that each UC of an elementary predicate must span at least all but one of its roles. If a UC exactly spans all but one role of a predicate, and we objectify on this UC, the outer predicate in the nested version has two roles, with a simple UC on its first role (Figure 9.23 (b)).

Note that with long predicates, nesting may be applied more than once. A simple example is shown in Figure 9.24, where a quaternary is binarized in two stages. For simplicity other object types and role links are omitted. We saw earlier how unaries may be converted into binaries. Nesting or co-referencing may be used to convert ternary or longer predicates into binaries. So in principle, any application may be modeled with binaries only. However, non-binary predicates often enable an application to be modeled in a more natural and convenient way.

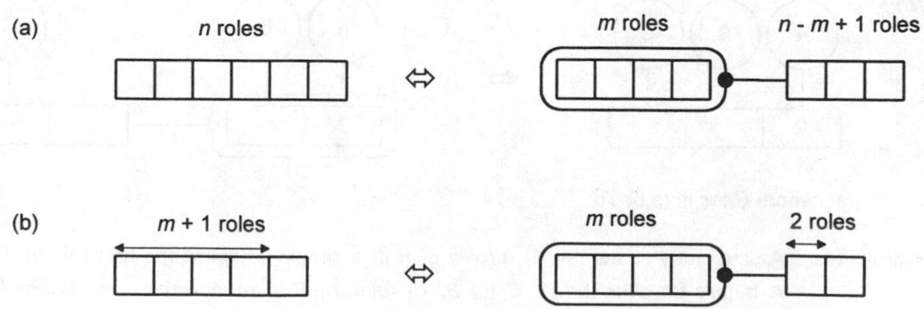

Figure 9.23 (a) Nesting ternaries and beyond; (b) nesting on a UC

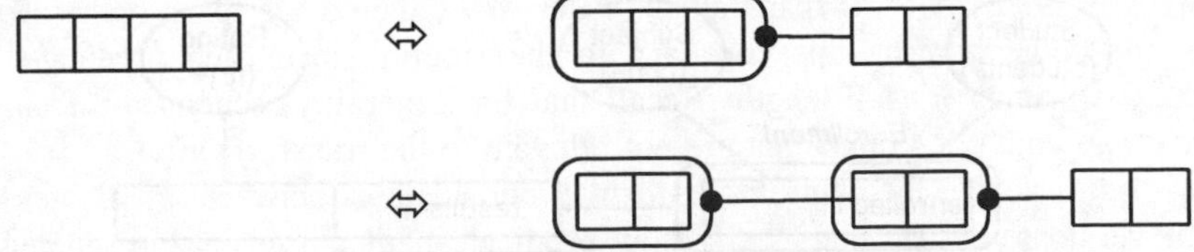

Figure 9.24 Binarizing a quaternary by nesting

In our examples so far, the objectified predicate played just a single, mandatory role. In this case, flattening is generally preferable. But what if this role is optional? For example, suppose we modify our earlier Table 9.2 by allowing null values in the rating column (see Table 9.4). In this population, no ratings appear for the subject CS100. Perhaps the final exam for this subject is still to be held, or marking for it has not finished. In this UoD, it is possible to record the fact that a person enrolls in a subject before knowing what rating the student gets for that subject.

Table 9.4 Enrollments may be recorded before ratings are finalized

Result:	*student#*	*subject*	*rating*
	1001	CS100	?
	1002	CS100	?
	1002	CS114	5

Since null values are not allowed at the conceptual level, we cannot model this as a single ternary. We may however use two fact types, one for enrollments and one for ratings. Figure 9.25 shows this flattened approach, together with the sample population.

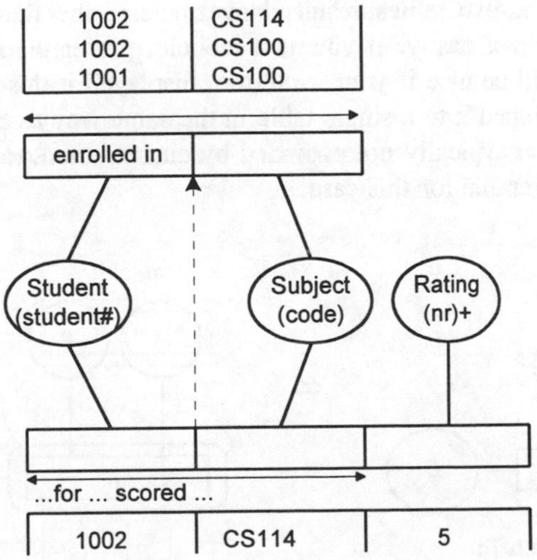

Figure 9.25 Modeling Table 9.4 with flat fact types

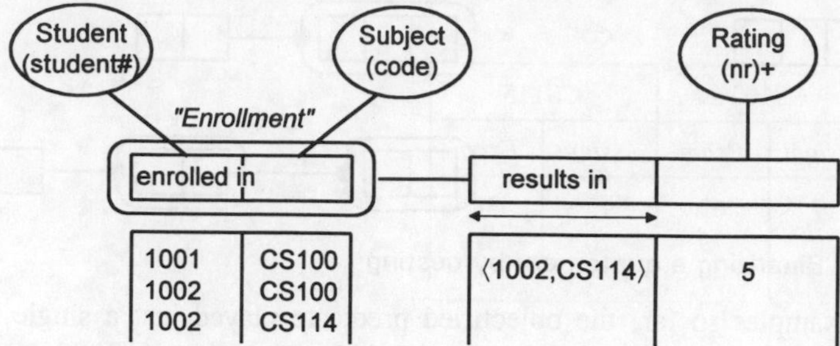

Figure 9.26 Modeling Table 9.4 with a nested approach

The *pair-subset constraint* in Figure 9.25 indicates that students can score ratings only in subjects in which they enrolled. If this figure is part of a model with other roles for Student and Subject, the roles in the binary fact type may be optional; if not, they should be marked mandatory. This UoD can also be modeled using a nested or co-referenced object type. The nested version is shown in Figure 9.26, including the sample population. The role played by the objectified predicate is now *optional*. The objectified predicate corresponds to the binary predicate in Figure 9.25. If no other role is played by Enrollment in the global schema, it is lazy. This is not unusual with nesting. But if a lazy, co-referenced object type is used instead, it must be marked lazy.

When two or more flat fact types are involved, the equivalence between nested and flattened versions is called **N/Fm** (*Nest/ Flatten into many fact types*). The subset pattern illustrated by our example is only one of many cases for this theorem, but since it is the most common case we set it out in Figure 9.27.

We generally favor the nested version in this case, since it is more compact, and it Rmaps directly to just one table. In contrast, if the flattened version is passed to our standard Rmap procedure, two tables result. Nevertheless, the flattened approach is quite natural and it verbalizes easily. If you as a modeler prefer the flattened approach for these reasons, it would be nice if your CASE tool displayed it this way but gave you the option of having it mapped it to a single table in the same way as the nested version. However such flexibility is typically not provided by current CASE tools. So the nested approach is generally preferable for this case.

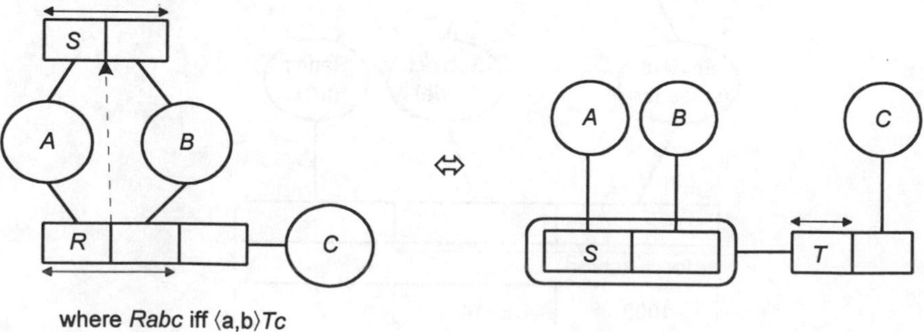

Figure 9.27 Another Nest/Flatten equivalence

Table 9.5

Subject:	CS102		CS115	
Student#	*Assignt*	*Exam*	*Assignt*	*Exam*
1001	17	65	15	58
1002	20	79	20	67
1003	15	60	12	55

In the flattened version in Figure 9.27, the *S* predicate is compatible with the sub-predicate comprising the first two roles of *R* (they are played by the same object types *A* and *B*). It is this compatibility which enables the nesting to occur. For this subset case, any $\langle a,b \rangle$ pair in the population of either must belong to the population of *S*. So we objectify *S*, and add an optional connection to *C* to handle the *R* facts.

Recall that in our CSDP, whenever different predicates have compatible role-sequences (of 2 or more roles) we should ask ourselves to what extent the populations of these (sub-)predicates must overlap. If a set-comparison (subset, equality or exclusion) constraint exists between them, it must be declared.

The kind of nesting transformation which may now occur depends partly on what kind of set-comparison constraint exists (if any) and on whether other roles occur in the full predicates. Let's look at some more examples before summarizing the overall procedure.

Consider the output report shown in Table 9.5. This may be modeled with two flat fact types, as shown in Figure 9.28. Notice the *equality constraint* between the two role-pairs. An assignment mark is recorded for a student in a subject if and only if an exam mark is recorded for that student in that subject.

The compatible sub-predicates might bc read as: did assignment in; did exam in. Since the populations of these must be equal, we may objectify their conjunction: did assignment and exam in. In the nested version, we have chosen the wording: was assessed in (see Figure 9.29). The specific marks are catered for by attaching two specific predicates as shown. Because of the equality constraint, these are both mandatory.

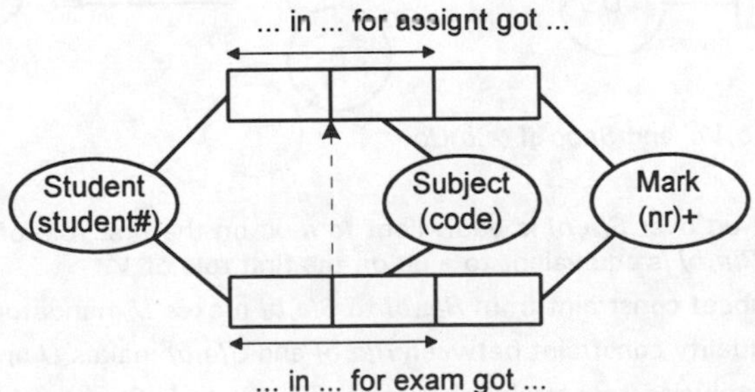

Figure 9.28 A conceptual schema for Table 9.5 (flattened version)

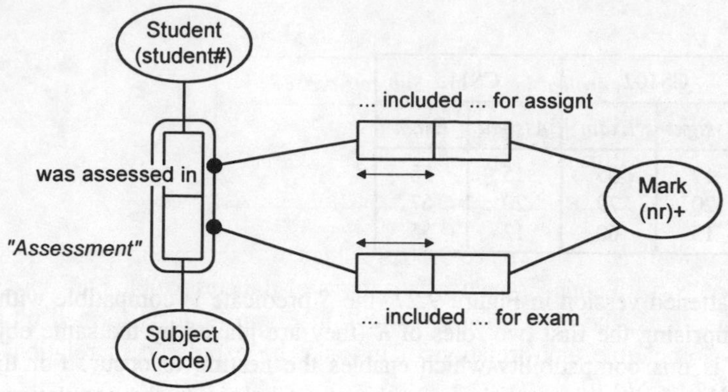

Figure 9.29 Another schema for Table 9.5 (nested version)

When passed to the standard Rmap procedure, the schema in Figure 9.28 maps to two tables, whereas the nested version in Figure 9.29 maps to a single table. For this reason, as well as compactness, the nested version is generally preferred whenever two or more functional roles are attached to the objectified predicate.

A more general N/Fm equivalence result is shown in Figure 9.30. This may be generalized further to *n* predicates ($n \geq 2$) and compatible sub-predicates of any arity above 1. The object types *A..D* need not be distinct. So long as (sub-)predicates are compatible, nesting may always be performed by objectifying their *disjunction*.

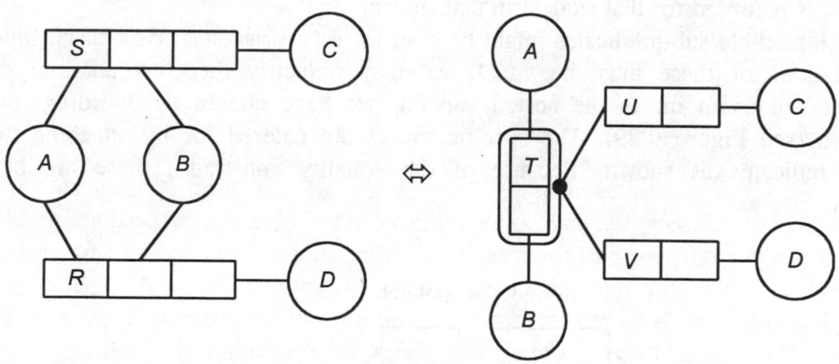

where *Rabc* iff ⟨a,b⟩*Vc*, and *Sabc* iff ⟨a,b⟩*Uc*

Corollaries: A binary UC over *S[a,b]* is equivalent to a UC on the first role of *U*; and a binary UC over *R[a,b]* is equivalent to a UC on the first role of *V*.

A pair-subset constraint from *R[a,b]* to *S[a,b]* makes *U* mandatory.

A pair-equality constraint between *R[a,b]* and *S[a,b]* makes *U* and *V* mandatory.

A pair-exclusion constraint between *R[a,b]* and *S[a,b]* adds an exclusion constraint between the attached roles in the nested version.

Figure 9.30 A more general Nest/Flatten equivalence

Table 9.6

Student	*Subjects enrolled in*	*Subjects passed*
3001	CS100, CS114, MP105	CS100, CS114
3002	CS114, MP105	CS114
3003	CS100, CS114	?

Since the predicate *T* in Figure 9.30 is a logical disjunction, it may be verbalized using the word "or" to connect our verbalizations of the compatible (sub-)predicates. In terms of populations, the objectified relation *T* in Figure 9.30 is formed by taking the *union* of the compatible (sub-)relations. This may be expressed in relational notation thus: $T = R[a,b] \cup S[a,b]$.

Suppose we remove the equality constraint in Figure 9.28. If no other set-comparison constraint exists, we can nest this by replacing the two mandatory roles constraints in Figure 9.29 by a disjunctive mandatory role constraint: each assessment has an assignment or exam mark (or both). The binary uniqueness constraints in the flattened version correspond to the simple UCs in the nested version (see first corollary in Figure 9.30).

In Figure 9.30, adding a pair-subset constraint from the first two roles of *R* to the first two roles of *S* is equivalent to adding a subset constraint from the first role of *V* to the first role of *U*. In the context of the disjunctive mandatory constraint, this means that *U* becomes mandatory (see second corollary). In terms of populations, it also means that the *T* relation becomes *S[a,b]*, since if one set if a subset of a second then their union is just the second set. Compare this with the result in Figure 9.27.

A subset constraint in both directions is an equality constraint. So adding an equality constraint between *R[a,b]* and *S[a,b]* in Figure 9.30 makes both *U* and *V* mandatory in the nested version. The schema equivalence between Figures 9.28 and 9.29 provides an example.

If an exclusion constraint exists between *R[a,b]* and *S[a,b]* in Figure 9.30, and we decide to nest, we must add an exclusion constraint between the attached roles in the nested version. For example, suppose that for any given subject, a student can be awarded either an actual grade or a notional grade, but not both (a notional grade might be awarded on the basis of performance in a similar subject from another university). As an exercise, schematize this in both flat and nested versions.

A relation is said to be *partial* if it is a projection of a longer relation; a relation that is not partial is said to be *whole*. Sometimes we run into a case where a whole relation must be a subset of another. Consider Table 9.6 for instance. Here "?" is an ordinary null value. In this UoD, we want to know what subjects students have passed, but are not interested in their actual ratings. Figure 9.31 schematizes this using a flattened approach.

We can nest this by objectifying enrollment, and then using a unary to indicate which enrolments resulted in a pass (see Figure 9.32). By default, the flat version maps to two relational tables, while the nested version maps to one. So the nested version is usually preferred in such a case. You can decide for yourself whether to take an open or closed world approach when mapping the unary.

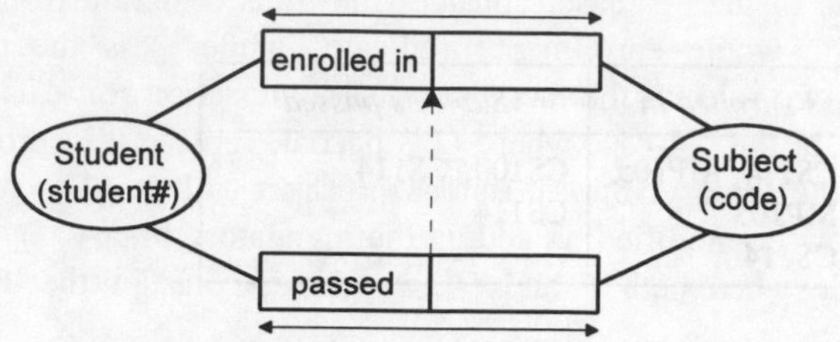

Figure 9.31 A schema for Table 9.6 (flat version)

The *overlap algorithm* in Figure 9.33 summarizes the main cases of the N/Fm equivalence. This shows how to nest when two or more fact types include compatible role-sequences, each with at least two roles. For simplicity, the diagram shows just two predicates with compatible role-pairs (shaded). The predicates may have additional roles.

Let P and Q be the compatible (sub-)predicates. The nesting action depends on the amount of overlap which is allowed between the populations of P and Q. In any given case, this overlap condition is specified by replacing the pair-connection marked "?" by a pair-subset (either direction), pair-equality or pair-exclusion constraint, or by no constraint (proper overlap is possible).

The five cases are based on what set-comparison constraint is explicitly *displayed*. An equality constraint must be specified if it exists. Hence in this context, display of a subset constraint is taken to imply that an equality constraint does not exist. In any situation, exactly one of the five cases listed will apply.

In the figure, a subset constraint upwards from P to Q is denoted "↑", a downwards subset constraint is shown as "↓" and an equality constraint appears as "↕". Recall that a predicate is partial if it is embedded in a longer predicate.

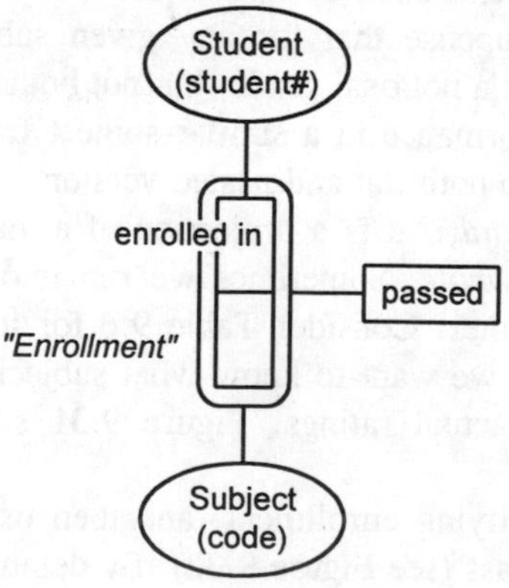

Figure 9.32 Another schema for Table 9.6 (nested version)

As one example of the "↑" case, consider the transformation from Figure 9.25 to 9.26: here *Q* is the whole enrollment predicate, while *P* is the partial predicate comprising the first two roles of the fact type: Student for Subject scored Rating.

As an example of the "↑" case where *Q* is partial, replace the enrollment predicate in Figure 9.25 by the ternary: Student enrolled in Subject on Date. The nested version in Figure 9.26 must now be modified by adding the mandatory binary: Enrollment occurred on Date. As an example when both *P* and *Q* are whole, consider the transformation of Figure 9.31 to 9.32.

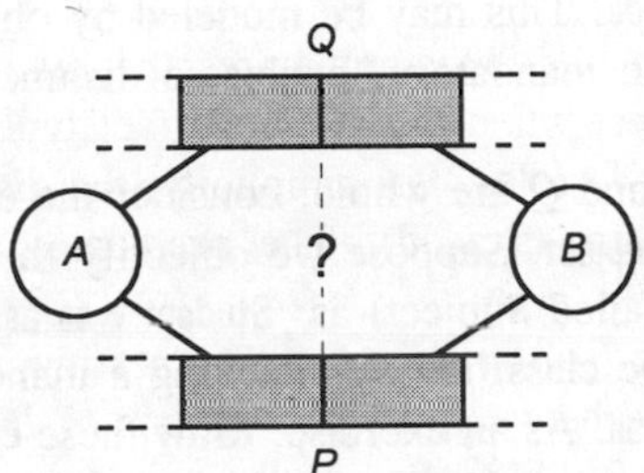


```
case ? constraint of

    ↑ :   { P's population must be a subset of Q's, but need not equal Q's }
          objectify Q;
          if Q is partial then attach rest of its predicate via mandatory extra role;
          if P is partial then attach rest of its predicate via optional extra role
                           else attach optional unary "is-P"

    ↓ :   reverse of previous case

    ↕ :   { P's population must equal Q's }
          if P or Q is partial
              then   objectify the single predicate "P and Q";
                     attach rest of their predicates via mandatory extra role(s)
              else   replace both by the single predicate "P and Q"

    ⊗:    { P's population is mutually exclusive with Q's }
          objectify "P or Q";
          if P is partial  then  attach rest of its predicate via extra role
                           else  attach as unary "is-P";

          similarly for Q;
          mark the attached roles as exclusive and disjunctively mandatory

      :   { no constraint; proper overlap is possible }
          as for ⊗ but omit exclusion constraint
end
```

Figure 9.33 Overlap algorithm for nesting when compatible sub-predicates exist

As an example of the "↕" case, consider the reshaping of Figure 9.28 to 9.29. Here both *P* and *Q* are partial, and we have reworded their conjunction as "was assessed in".

As an example of the "↕" case where neither *P* nor *Q* is partial, remove the mark information from Figure 9.28 to give two binaries: Student did assignment in Subject; Student did exam in Subject. The equality constraint enables these to be replaced by a single binary: Student did assignment and exam in Subject (or Student was assessed in Subject). Derivation rules may be specified for the former binaries if desired.

As an example of the "⊗" case where both *P* and *Q* are partial, recall this exclusive disjunction instance of Figure 9.30: Student for Subject obtained actual Grade; Student for Subject obtained notional Grade. This may be modeled by objectifying Student was assessed in Subject, and attaching the mandatory, exclusive disjunction: resulted in actual Grade; resulted in notional Grade.

As an example where both *P* and *Q* are whole, consider the exclusive disjunction: Student passed Subject; Student failed Subject. Suppose we objectify the disjunction of these predicates (i.e. Student passed or failed Subject) as: Student was assessed in Subject. This Assessment object type may now be classified by attaching a mandatory disjunction of the following unaries: is a pass; is a fail. As an exercise, draw these examples.

While the mutual exclusion case may be transformed by nesting in this way, this is rarely the best modeling alternative. Sometimes the flat version is preferable, and sometimes a predicate generalization transformation is more appropriate. For instance, the pass/fail example just cited may be modeled instead using the ternary: Student in Subject obtained Result {'pass','fail'}. And the nested solution to the actual/notional grade example may be transformed using PSG2 to replace the exclusive disjunction by: has Grade; is of GradeType {'actual','notional'}.

In the final case of the overlap algorithm, no set-comparison constraint applies between *P* and *Q*, so their populations may properly overlap. For example, suppose that for any given student and subject we might have a predicted grade or an actual grade, or both. This may be modeled by two flat fact types: Student for Subject has predicted Grade; Student for Subject has actual Grade.

We may nest this by objectifying Student is assessed for Subject, and attaching the mandatory, inclusive disjunction: has predicted Grade; has actual Grade. As with the previous mutual exclusion case, other modeling alternatives may be preferable.

In *P* and *Q* are keys (i.e. each is exactly spanned by a UC) and the standard Rmap procedure is to be used, applying the overlap algorithm to flattened cases before mapping will reduce the number of tables in the relational schema. In this situation, especially for the subset and equality cases, nesting (or the equivalent co-referenced solution) is generally preferred.

Exercise 9.3

1. Consider the fact type: City in Year has Population. Population figures are collated only once each year. Populations may go up, down or remain the same.
   (a) Model this using a flattened approach.
   (b) Now use a nested approach.

(c) Now use a co-referenced approach.
(d) Which solution do you prefer?
(e) Use a nested approach that objectifies the association between City and Population. State whether this is better or worse than your solution to (b).

2. Consider the fact type: Flower blooms in City in Month. Note that flowers may bloom for more than one month in the same city.
(a) Model this as a flat fact type.
(b) Show three alternative nested solutions.

3. Schematize the following table using (a) flat (b) nested (c) co-referenced approaches. Which do you find the most natural?

Software title	*Release#*	*Size (Mb)*
DataModeler	1	3
DataModeler	2	5
DataModeler	3	5
WordLight	1	5
...	...	...

4. Suppose employees are identified by their surname and initials, and each works for exactly one Department. In principle, we could model this using the ternary fact type: Surname and Initials belong to an employee who works for Department.
(a) Draw the flat fact type. Is this natural?
(b) Nest this instead. Is this natural?
(c) Now use co-referencing. Is this natural?
(d) We now decide to primarily identify employees by an employee#, but still require that surname and initials provide an alternative identifier. Model this.

5. The following conceptual schema was designed to store details about competitors in the most recent Olympic Games.

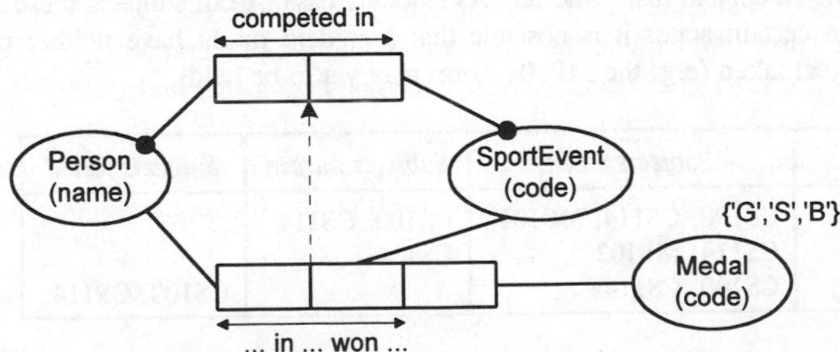

(a) Rmap this.
(b) Transform the conceptual schema by nesting.
(c) Rmap your solution to (b).
(d) Which conceptual schema do you prefer?

6. The following is an extract from a yearly report giving test results of reaction time (in milliseconds) and resting heart rate (in beats per minute) for members of a health club. As the table indicates, the club may gain or lose members during the year.

Month	*Member*	*Reaction time*	*Heart rate*
Jan	Jones, E	250	80
	Matthews, S	320	120
	Robinson, S	300	100
Feb	Jones E	250	75
	Matthews, S	300	100
Mar	Anderson, P	250	80
	Matthews, S	280	85
...	...	...	...

(a) Schematize this using two, flat ternaries.
(b) Transform this by nesting.
(c) Which schema do you prefer?

7. The following table indicates the rooms and times for lectures in various subjects. Schematize this using (a) flat and (b) co-referenced approaches.

Subject	*Time*	*Room*
CS213	Mon 3 p.m.	B19
CS213	Wed 9 a.m.	A01
CS213	Wed 10 a.m.	A01
EN100	Mon 3 p.m.	F23
EN100	Tue 3 p.m.	G24
...	...	...

8. The following output report indicates the performance of students in subjects in a given semester. Once a student has failed a subject in the semester, the subject cannot be passed by the student in that semester. As students pass or fail subjects these results are recorded. In certain states it is possible that a student might have neither passed nor failed a subject taken (e.g. the MP104 exam may yet to be held).

Student	*Subjects taken*	*Subjects passed*	*Subjects failed*
Adams AB	CS100, CS114, MP104	CS100, CS114	?
Brown SS	CS114, MP102	CS114	?
Casey J	CS100, CS114	?	CS100, CS114

(a) Schematize this UoD using three binaries.
(b) Transform this by nesting, with two attached unaries.
(c) Transform the two unaries into a binary.
(d) For this UoD is it possible that the null value for Adams AB might be updated to an actual value? What about the null value for Casey J?

9. The following table is an extract from an output report concerning the finals of a recent judo competition. For each weight division, the four clubs which made it to the finals are recorded, together with the results for first and second places. For a given weight division a club can obtain at most one place. No ties are possible.

Event	*Finalists*	*Winner*	*Runner-up*
Lightweight	Budokan, Judokai, Kodokan, Zendokan	Kodokan	Judokai
Middleweight	Budokan, Judokai, Kodokan, Zendokan	Kodokan	Zendokan
Heavyweight	Budokan, Kanodojo, Kodokan, Mifunekan	Mifunekan	Kodokan

(a) An information modeler schematizes this UoD in terms of three fact types: Club is finalist in Event; Club wins Event; Club is second in Event. Set out this conceptual schema including all constraints.
(b) Transform the winner and second-place predicates into a single ternary.
(c) Transform this schema into an equivalent nested version.
(d) Assuming complete information is needed, show an alternative nested solution, by assigning the places "3A" and "3B" to the clubs which didn't get first or second in the event.
(e) Transform this to a flattened fact type.
(f) Which solution do you prefer?

10. The following examples are extracts of output reports from an information system about media channels. Each channel (TV or radio) has a unique, identifying callsign. Some radio channels broadcast using FM (frequency modulation) while others use AM (amplitude modulation). All TV channels are rated in the range 1..7 in three categories on two surveys. All commercial radio channels have their audience composition assessed (see the sample pie charts). The mark "–" means "inapplicable because of other data".

Schematize this UoD. Include uniqueness, mandatory role, value, subtype and frequency constraints. Provide meaningful names and definitions for each subtype. If a fact type is derived, omit it from the diagram but provide a derivation rule. Do not nest any fact types.

Minimize the number of fact types in your conceptual schema (if necessary, make use of transformation rules to achieve this).

TV channels:

		Ownership details		
Call sign	*Ownership*	*Company*	*% share*	*Head office*
ATQ8	commercial	MediaCo	100	Brisbane
CTQ3	commercial	MediaCo TVbaron	50 50	Brisbane Sydney
TVQ3	govt.	–	–	–

Radio channels:

		Ownership details				
Call sign	*Ownership*	*Company*	*% share*	*Head office*	*Modul-ation*	*Music played*
4BZ	commercial	MediaCo	100	Brisbane	FM	rock country
RB3	govt.	–	–	–	AM	–
STR5	commercial	MediaCo OzRadio	30 70	Brisbane Cairns	AM	country
4AA	govt.	–	–	–	FM	–

TV survey ratings:

		Category			
Channel	*Survey*	*News*	*Drama*	*Sport*	*Totals*
ATQ8	A B	5 4	3 4	3 3	 22
CTQ3	A B	5 5	3 4	4 5	 26
TVQ3	A B	3 2	4 4	4 5	 22

Audience composition of commercial radio channels:

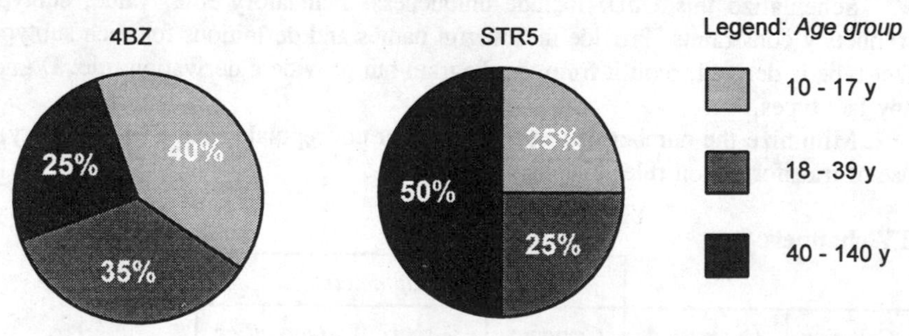

9.4 Other transformations

The previous two sections covered the most useful conceptual schema transformations. In this section, several other transformations of lesser importance are considered briefly.

Recall PSG2, our second predicate specialization/generalization theorem (Figure 9.13). This may be generalized further by removing constraints. First note that removing the UC on *A*'s role in *R* corresponds to removing the UCs on *A*'s roles in each of the S_i predicates (see Figure 9.34). In the absence of additional internal UCs, the *R* and S_i binaries will be many:many. As an example, let A = Car, B = Status {'company','private'}, C = Employee, T = has, R = is used by, S_1 = is provided for, and S_2 = is privately used by. Allow that the same employee may use many company cars and many private cars, and vice versa.

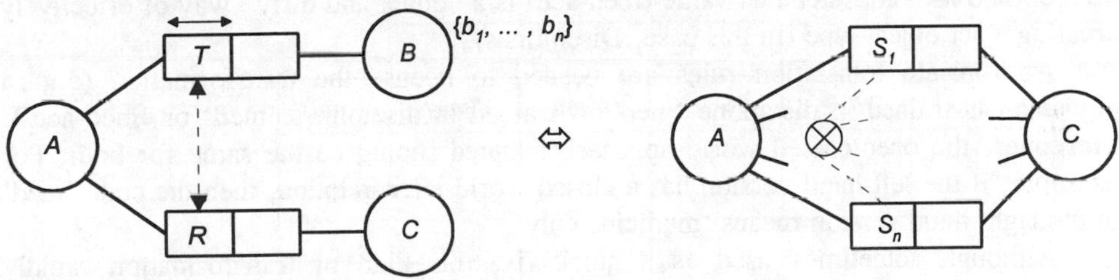

Figure 9.34 Another *PSG2* case: *R* may be specialized into $S_1..S_n$ by absorbing *B*

Now suppose the equality constraint is weakened to an upward subset constraint. The *T* predicate must be retained since there may be instances of *A* which do not play *R*, and hence *T* will not in general be derivable from the S_i. Moreover, subtypes must now be introduced for the specialized predicates (Figure 9.35). The exclusion constraint over the subtype roles is omitted since it is implied by the subtype definitions.

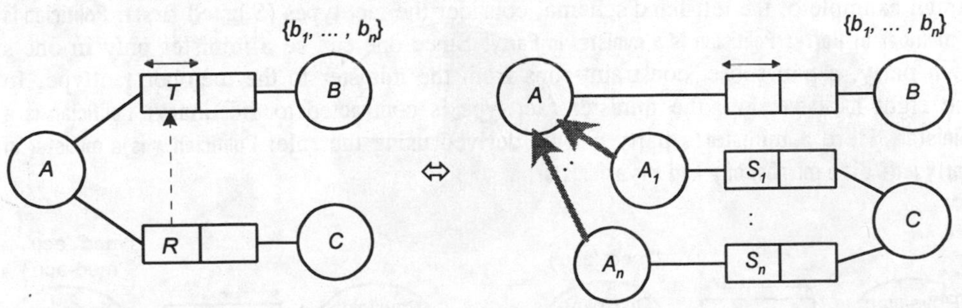

Figure 9.35 Another *PSG2* case: *R* is specialized into $S_1..S_n$, but *B* is not absorbed

For example, consider the car UoD just discussed, where some cars might not yet be used. In this case the subtypes are CompanyCar and PrivateCar. Cases which require one of these more general forms of PSG2 usually invoke some of the corollaries stated for the original version of the theorem (Figure 9.13). For example, suppose each employee uses at most one company car and at most one private car. An external UC is now required between the Status and Employee roles in the left-hand version, and a simple UC must be applied to each role of Employee in the right-hand version. As an exercise, draw both schema versions for this UoD, and prove that a frequency constraint of 1-2 is implied on the role played by Employee in the left-hand version.

If an object type in an *m:n* binary has two values, the fact type can be converted to a functional one by converting the object type to one that allows concatenated values. A simple example is shown in Figure 9.36. The transformation from left to right is called *value concatenation*, and the inverse transform is *value separation*. In this example, a physician may be trained in medicine or acupuncture or both. Allowing the both-case to be recorded as a concatenated value (med-acu) is a "quick and dirty" way of effectively creating a set object type (in this case, Disciplines).

Appropriate translation rules are needed to license the transformation (e.g. a physician is trained in discipline 'med' iff trained in disciplines 'med' or 'med-acu'). Moreover, the open/closed world approach adopted should be the same for both. For example, if the left-hand version has a closed world interpretation, then the code 'med' in the right-hand version means 'medicine only'.

Although sometimes used as a quick fix, this kind of transformation rapidly becomes unwieldy as the number of atomic values increases, since a list of *n* atomic values leads to 2^n-1 concatenated values (e.g. if we added herbalism and physiotherapy to give four atomic disciplines, we now have 15 concatenated disciplines). In such cases, if functional predicates are required, it is better to replace the binary with *n* unaries, one for each value, before mapping. Alternatively, if the target system supports set-valued fields (e.g. a nested relational or an object-oriented database), a clean mapping to a set-valued structure is possible (see chapter 11).

In the presence of a pair-subset constraint, a binary may be *contracted* to a unary; or conversely, the unary may be *expanded* to a binary (see Figure 9.37). Note that the UC on the first role of *R* is implied by the other constraints (as an exercise, prove this). As an example of the left-hand schema, consider the fact types (*S* listed first): Politician is a member of Party; Politician is a minister in Party. Since one can be a minister only in one's own party, a pair-subset constraint runs from the minister to the member facttype. In the right hand-version, the minister fact type is contracted to the unary: Politician is a minister. Here a minister's party can be derived using the rule: Politician *x* is a minister in Party *y* iff *x* is a member of *y* and *x* is a minister.

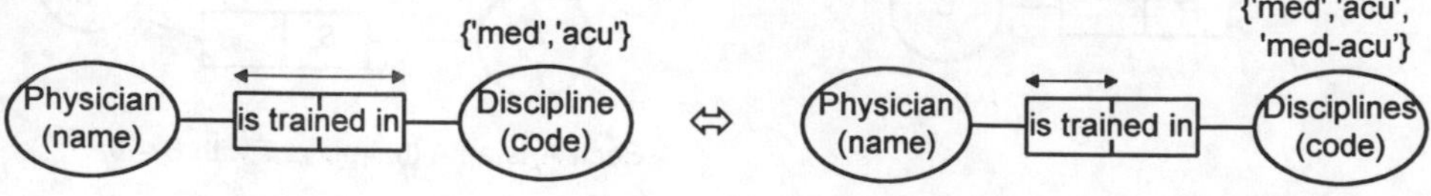

Figure 9.36 A example of value concatenation/separation

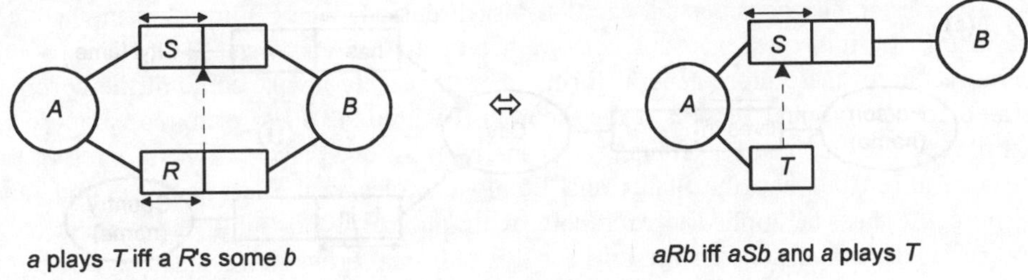

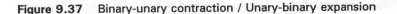

Figure 9.37 Binary-unary contraction / Unary-binary expansion

In this case, contraction is usually preferred to expansion. However, if the binary to be contracted is 1:1, its second uniqueness constraint needs to be captured as a textual constraint in the unary version. This may be enough reason to prefer the binary version. For example, suppose the following fact types appear in the position of *S* and *R* in Figure 9.37: Politician is a member of / includes Party; Politician leads Party. Since each party has at most one leader, there is an extra UC on the lower binary, making it 1:1. Now suppose we contract this binary to the unary: Politician is a leader. The extra UC in the binary version appears in the unary version as a textual constraint: each Party includes at most one Politician who is a leader.

In previous sections we have seen how object types can be absorbed in order to specialize predicates, and how nested and co-referenced object types may be removed by flattening. Apart from these cases, modelers sometimes eliminate an entity type from a fact type, phrasing the association in terms of the object type(s) formerly used to reference the entity type (usually however, it is more convenient not to do this).

Figure 9.38 provides an example with a simple reference scheme. Transforming from the left-hand to right-hand version ***eliminates*** the entity type Degree. This weakens the schema, since the entity type and its reference scheme are lost. The translation on the left shows how the right-hand predicate can be defined in terms of the left. This is an implication rather than an equivalence. The reverse transformation from right to left *introduces* an entity type. In almost all cases, the left-hand version is preferred because of its richer semantics.

This transformation is sometimes performed with a co-referenced object type to which another object type is functionally related. Figure 9.39 provides an example. Here a city is identified by combining its name with its country (e.g. Brisbane, Australia is a different city from Brisbane in the USA). Note the equality constraint; this is implied if the roles involved are mandatory.

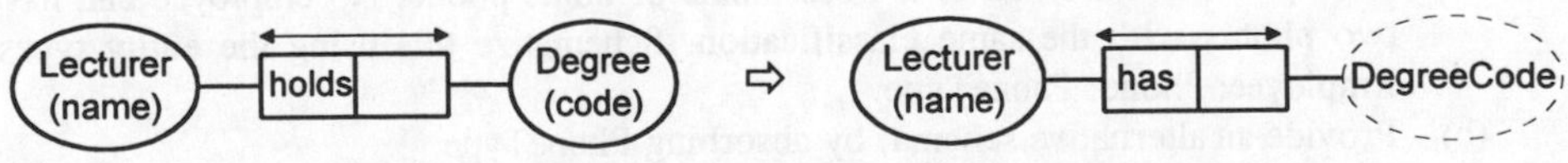

Figure 9.38 A simple case of entity type elimination / introduction

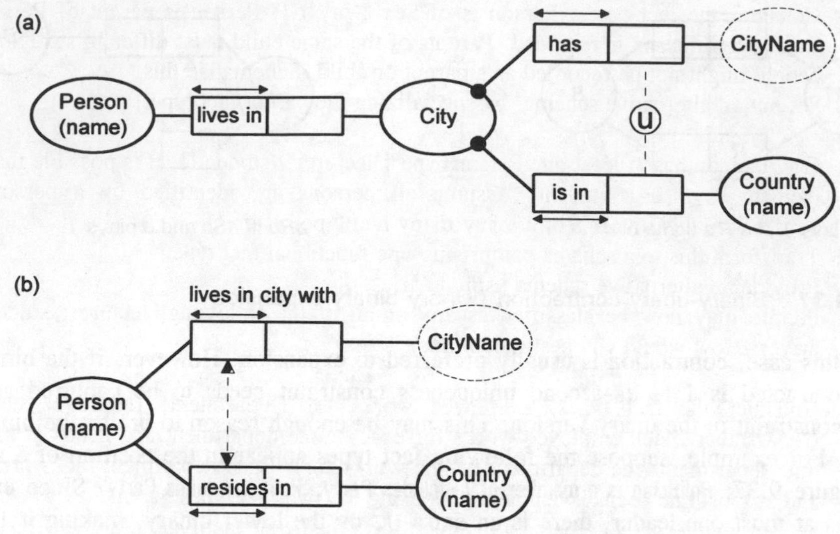

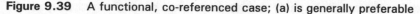

Figure 9.39 A functional, co-referenced case; (a) is generally preferable

In Figure 9.39 the top version (a) is generally preferable since it is natural to think in terms of cities, and the composite identification scheme is clearly displayed. In general, don't eliminate an entity type unless you feel that no clarity is lost by doing so.

If you do decide to eliminate a compositely identified entity type, ensure that it is the target of a *functional* predicate. For example, consider the fact type: Person lives in City. Suppose we now make this *m:n* to cater for jet-setters who live in more than one city. It would now be wrong to eliminate City as in Figure 9.39, since we would lose the information about which city name goes with which country.

Well that basically covers all the conceptual schema transformations that have much practical relevance in information modeling. Other transformations do exist, but are used so rarely that we ignore them in this introductory text. Some transformations that deal with compound (non-elementary) fact types will be discussed later in the context of normalization theory and non-relational mappings.

Exercise 9.4

1. (a) Each employee uses one or two phones, and each phone is used by an employee. Each phone is classified as a work phone or home phone. No employee can have two phones with the same classification. Schematize this using the entity types: Employee; Phone; PhoneType.
   (b) Provide an alternative schema, by absorbing PhoneType.
   (c) Now suppose that some phones might not be used by any employee. Modify your answer to (a) accordingly.
   (d) Provide an alternative schema by specializing the uses fact type.

2. (a) Consider the fact types: Person is of Sex {'m','f'}; Person is parent of Person. Each person's sex is recorded. Parents of the same child must differ in sex. Some people might not be recorded as a parent or child. Schematize this.
   (b) Set out an alternative schema, by specializing the parent fact type.

3. (a) Each person has at least one PersonType {'lecturer','student'}. It is possible that a lecturer is also a student. Assume all persons are identified by a person#. Schematize this in terms of a many:many fact type.
   (b) Transform this to a schema comprising one functional fact type.
   (c) Provide an alternative schema using unaries.
   (d) People may now be classified as any or all of the following: lecturer; student; driver. How would you best model this?

4. (a) Consider the fact types: Employee works for Department; Employee heads Department. Each employee works for exactly one department and heads at most one department (the department he/she works for). Each department has workers and at most one head. Schematize this using the two fact types given.
   (b) Set out an alternative schema which contracts the heads fact type to a unary.
   (c) Which schema is preferable? Discuss.

5. The following table indicates where certain objects are placed in three dimensional space (x, y, z are the Cartesian coordinates). Only one object can occupy the same position at any given time.

Object	x	y	z
A	3	1	0
B	3	1	2
C	0	1	2

   (a) Schematize this in terms of three binaries.
   (b) Set out an alternative schema using Position as an entity type.
   (c) Set out an alternative schema using AxisType {'x','y','z'} as an object type. Why is this alternative schema inferior?

9.5 Conceptual schema optimization

The previous three sections discussed many ways in which conceptual schemas may be transformed to equivalent, or at least acceptable, alternatives. *Conceptual schema optimization* involves transforming a conceptual schema into an alternative conceptual schema which maps to a more efficient (ideally, the most efficient) implementation. A simple example of this was presented in section 9.1. We now provide some guidelines for performing this optimization, and illustrate the process with some larger examples.

Four **main factors** to consider when optimizing a conceptual schema are: the *target system*; the *query pattern*; the *update pattern*; and *clarity*. The target system is the DBMS used for implementation: here we assume it is a centralized, relational system. The query pattern includes the kinds of question which the system is expected to answer, together with statistical information about the expected frequency and priority of these questions. The update pattern includes the kinds, frequencies and priorities of the expected insertions, deletions and modifications to the database tables.

Response times for queries are usually more vital than for updates, so as a first criterion, one might try to minimize the response times of the "focused queries" (i.e. those queries with high priority or frequency). Clarity here refers to the ease with which the modeler can fully grasp the semantics conveyed by the schema.

Before the optimization procedure is executed, the global conceptual schema should be completed and validated. Any mapping choices (e.g. for 1:1 cases or subtypes) should also be declared. The procedure is then run on the whole schema. The complete optimization procedure for ORM schemas is somewhat complex; only an overview of its main components is given here.

Although the default procedure could be executed without human intervention, better results may often be obtained by allowing modelers to override a suggested transformation when their additional insights reveal other factors which make the transformation counter-productive.

Several optimization strategies were introduced earlier in the chapter. Overall, the procedure comprises two main stages:

- Transform to reduce the number of mapped tables (steps 1-2)
- Transform to simplify individual tables (steps 3-5)

Since slow queries tend to involve joins or subqueries, a default strategy is to try to reduce the number of focused queries which involve joins or subqueries. Steps 1-2 of the optimization procedure do this for the main case (two or more tables involved), by transforming to reduce the number of tables involved in these queries. Since updates which require checking constraints between tables also tend to be expensive, this strategy usually improves update performance as well.

Recall that a composite key in a predicate amounts to a UC spanning two or more roles. Since the mapping algorithm maps predicates with composite keys to separate tables, a basic strategy is to reduce the number of (relevant) compositely-keyed fact types in the conceptual schema. There are two main situations with the potential for achieving this: compatible keys which may be unified; non-functional roles which may be replaced by functional roles. We consider these in turn.

Step 1 aims to *unify compatible, composite keys* (see Figure 9.40). As preparation, step 1.1 includes two moves. As an example of its second move, consider a schema with fact types: Company in State has staff of Sex {'m','f'} in Quantity; Company in State has budget of MoneyAmt. Compatible keys based on ⟨Company, State⟩ are formed by absorbing Sex to specialize the quaternary into two ternaries: Company in State has male staff in Quantity; Company in State has female staff in Quantity.

Step 1.2 and 1.3 ensure that each pattern involving *n* compatible, composite keys is replaced by a single predicate ($n \geq 2$). The basic patterns for these steps are shown in Figure 9.41. For simplicity, case (a) shows only 2 predicates, and both cases show compatible role pairs. Several examples were discussed in previous sections. Whereas the original pattern maps to *n* tables, the nested version maps to just one table.

1.1 Flatten any objectified predicate that plays just a single, mandatory role;
 if another compatible, composite key can be formed by absorbing a low cardinality object type into a predicate with a key of arity ≥ 3
 then do so.

1.2 **if** *n* whole predicates form compatible, composite but exclusive keys and are incompatible with all other (sub)predicates (see Figure 9.41 (a))
 then generalize them to a single longer predicate by extracting an object type of cardinality *n* (see Figure 9.8: transform to the left);

1.3 Apply the overlap algorithm to any pattern of compatible, composite keys (see Figures 9.41 (b) and 9.33: sometimes the ⊗ and no-constraint cases are best left as is)

Figure 9.40 Optimization Step 1: unifying compatible, composite keys

As discussed earlier, if nesting leads to a loss of clarity in the conceptual schema, the modeler may prefer not to nest; ideally, the modeler may then choose whether to have nesting performed automatically as an invisible, pre-processing stage to Rmap. Recall also that any nested object type may be recast as a co-referenced object type if this is felt to be more natural.

Step 2 examines *object types with both a functional and a non-functional role*, and typically attempts to replace the latter by functional roles which can be grouped into the same table as the former. Figure 9.42 sets out the first stage: step 2.1.

Most of step 2.1 amounts to predicate specialization using enumerated object types or frequency constraints. Several examples were discussed earlier. The predicate generalization case with the restricted UC is rare; for an example, recall Figure 9.9.

Step 2.2 completes the optimization strategy to reduce the number of mapped tables (see Figure 9.43). The first case for pattern (a) uses PSG3 with its second corollary (see Figure 9.16). The second case for pattern (a) is extremely rare, and was not covered in earlier transformations. As an example, consider the fact type: Official holds Position {'president','secretary','treasurer'}. Assuming each position is held by only one official, we may transform to three unaries: Official is president; Official is secretary; Official is treasurer; we also need to add the textual constraint that the population of each unary has a maximum cardinality of 1.

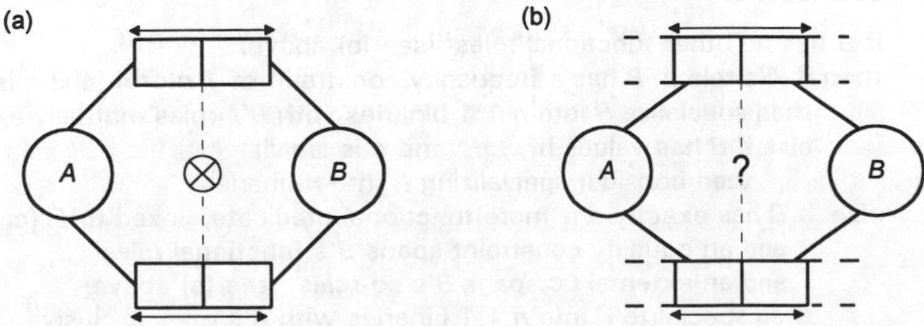

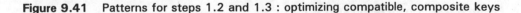

Figure 9.41 Patterns for steps 1.2 and 1.3 : optimizing compatible, composite keys

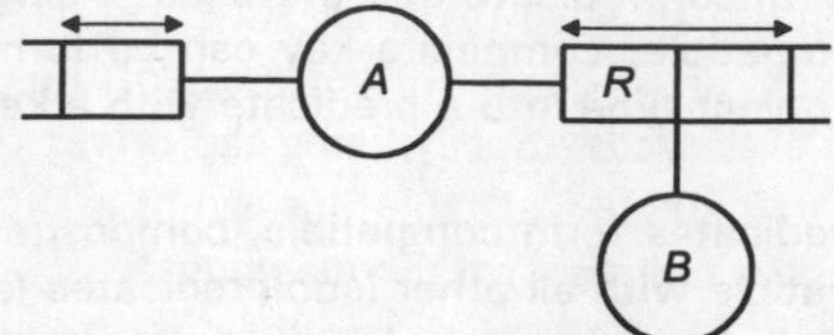

2.1 For each case where an object type *A* has simple and binary keys attached, where the other role of the binary key is played by *B* (see above):

if *R* **is a binary**
then if *B* **has values** $b_1..b_n$ **(and** *n* **is small)**
then specialize *R* **to** *n* **unaries or replace** *B* **by** *B'* **{b_1,b_2,both} (if** $n = 2$**) making the key(s) simple**
else if *A*'**s role in** *R* **has a frequency constraint 1-*n* or *n* (and *n* is small)**
then specialize *R* **into** *n* **exclusive binaries simply keyed on** *A*
else if *A* **has just one functional role**
and the predicates are compatible, pair-exclusive binaries
then generalize both to a single ternary with a restricted UC
else { *R* **is a ternary }**
if *B* **has values** $b_1,..,b_n$ **(and** *n* **is small)**
then absorb *B*, **specializing** *R* **into** *n* **binaries simply keyed on** *A*.

Figure 9.42 Optimization step 2.1

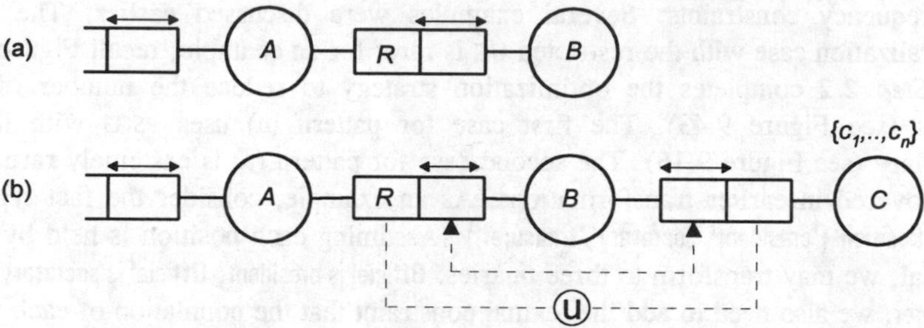

2.2 For each case where an object type *A* has a simple key attached, as well as a binary predicate *R* connected to object type *B* with a simple UC on *B*'s role but not *A*'s:

if *B* has no other functional roles (see (a) above)
then if *A*'s role in *R* has a frequency constraint of *1-n* or *n* (and *n* is small)
then specialize *R* into *n* 1:1 binaries with *B*'s roles mutually exclusive
else if *B* has values $b_1,..,b_n$ (and *n* is small)
then consider specializing *R* into *n* unaries
else if *B* has exactly one more functional predicate, linked to *C* {$c_1,..,c_n$}
and an equality constraint spans *B*'s functional roles
and an external UC spans *B*'s co-roles (see (b) above)
then specialize *R* into *n* 1:1 binaries with *B*'s roles exclusive, by absorbing *C* (this is PSG2 with corollary 2: see Figure 9.13)

Figure 9.43 Optimization step 2.2

The final stage of step 2.2 (pattern (b)) uses PSG2 and its second corollary. As an example, consider the main and backup driver UoD of Figure 9.12, and add the functional fact type: Car is of CarModel. Specializing the drives predicate enables all the information to be mapped to a single Car table, instead of a Driver and a Car table. As an exercise, draw the schemas and perform the mappings.

Before going on to step 3, let's consolidate the first two steps by considering an example for which substantial optimization is possible. Figure 9.44 depicts a conceptual schema for post-graduate coursework in a computer science department. This UoD was first introduced in Exercise 4.2. The pair-subset constraint reflects the fact that after students enroll in a subject they choose a topic for it. Each topic has a lecturer in charge, and at most two (other) co-lecturers.

As an exercise, map the conceptual schema of Figure 9.44 to a relational schema, then check your solution with the one provided in Figure 9.45. If you did this correctly, you should have obtained six tables. Notice the inter-table constraints. The "⊗" symbol in the relational schema denotes a partition of PGtopic.topic (i.e. PGtopic.topic is the disjoint union of AcPrereq.topic and PrefPrereq.topic). The ordinary "⊗" indicates that the ⟨topic, lecturer⟩ pairs in ColecturedBy and PGtopic are exclusive. The other constraints are straightforward.

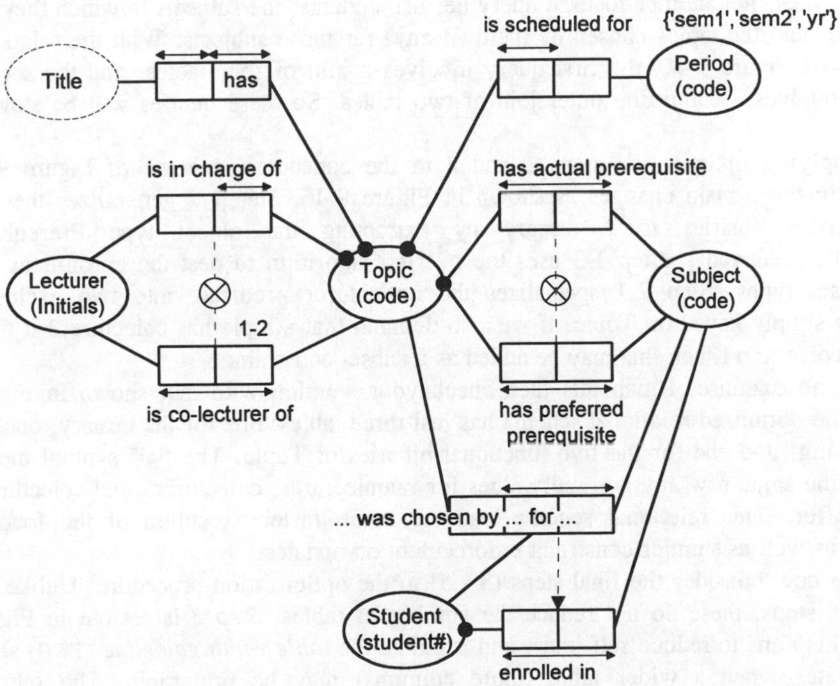

Figure 9.44 This sub-optimal schema maps to 6 tables

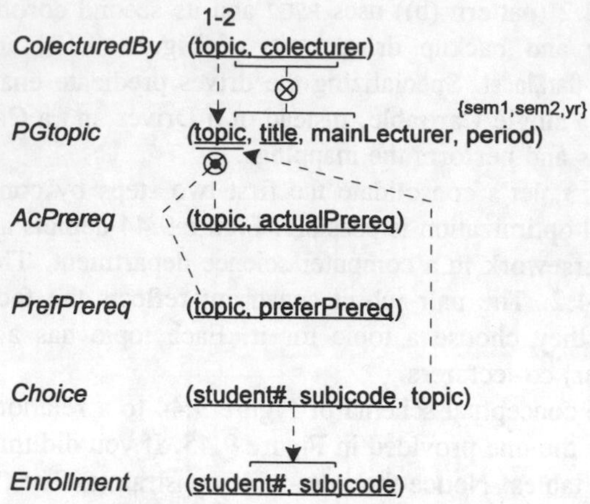

Figure 9.45 The relational schema mapped from Figure 9.44

Suppose a focused query for this application is: list all topics (code and title) together with their main-lecturers, co-lecturers, actual prerequisites and preferred prerequisites. Let another focused query be: list students, the subjects in which they are enrolled, and the topics chosen by them (if any) for those subjects. With the relational schema of Figure 9.45, the first query involves a join of four tables, and the second query involves a composite outer join of two tables. So these queries will be slow to run.

Applying optimization steps 1 and 2 to the conceptual schema of Figure 9.44 results in three main changes as shown in Figure 9.46. Step 1.2 generalizes the two prerequisite binaries to a ternary by extracting the object type PrereqKind {'actual','preferred'}. Step 1.3 uses the overlap algorithm to nest the enrollment and topic fact types. Step 2.1 specializes the co-lecturer predicate into two exclusive binaries simply keyed on Topic. If we also demand that a topic has colecturer2 it must have a colecturer1 then this may be added as a subset constraint.

As an exercise, Rmap this then check your solution with that shown in Figure 9.47. The optimized relational schema has just three tables: one for the ternary, one for the nesting, and one for the five functional binaries of Topic. The "≠" symbol means that on the same row any non-null values for mainlecturer, colecturer1 and colecturer2 must differ. This relational schema leads to much faster execution of the focused queries as well as simpler constraint enforcement on updates.

We now consider the final steps (3 - 5) in the optimization procedure. Unlike the previous steps, these do not reduce the number of tables. *Step 3* is set out in Figure 9.48. This aims to reduce self-joins, and is called the *table width guideline* (TWG) since it indicates when a wider table (more columns) may be preferable. The schema equivalence illustrated was considered earlier. If the object type *A* plays a functional role, the transformation to binaries would have already occurred in the last phase of Step 2.1. Even if *A* has no functional role, the specialization into binaries may still be worthwhile if it avoids self-joins in focused queries.

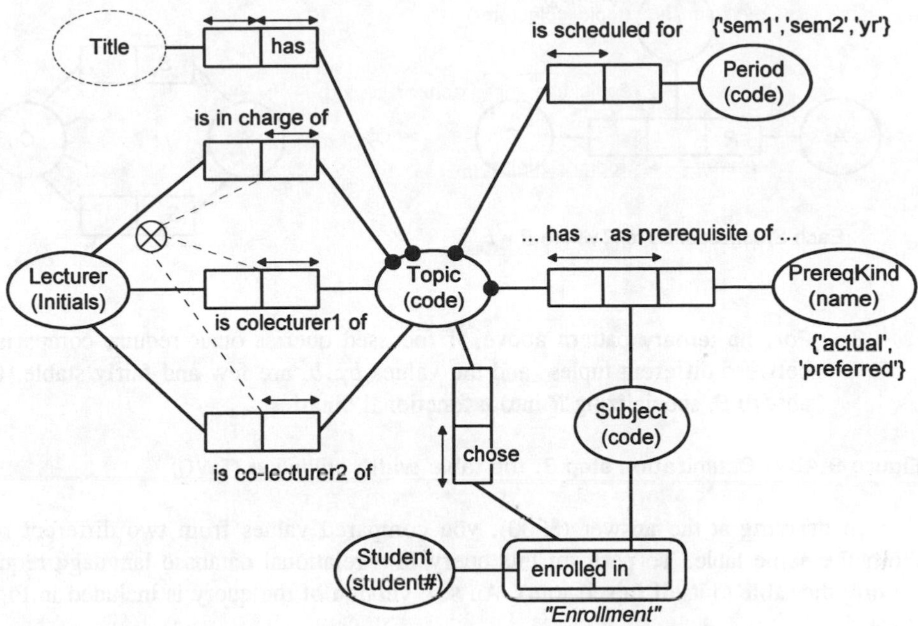

Figure 9.46 The conceptual schema obtained by optimizing Figure 9.44

As an example of step 3, suppose we wish to examine how full-time university fees varied for various degrees over the triennium 1991 - 1993. Assume we model this conceptually as the ternary: **Degree in Year had fulltime fee of MoneyAmt**. Let us agree that a uniqueness constraint spans the first two roles, a frequency constraint of 3 applies to the first role and a value constraint of {1991..1993} applies to Year. Suppose we map this to the following relational schema:

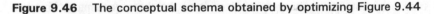

3 {1991..1993}
FTfee (<u>degree, yr</u>, fee)

A fragment of a sample population for this table is shown in Figure 9.49. Let a sample focussed query be: How much did the BSc full-time fee increase over the triennium? Answer this query yourself by inspecting the table.

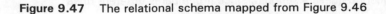

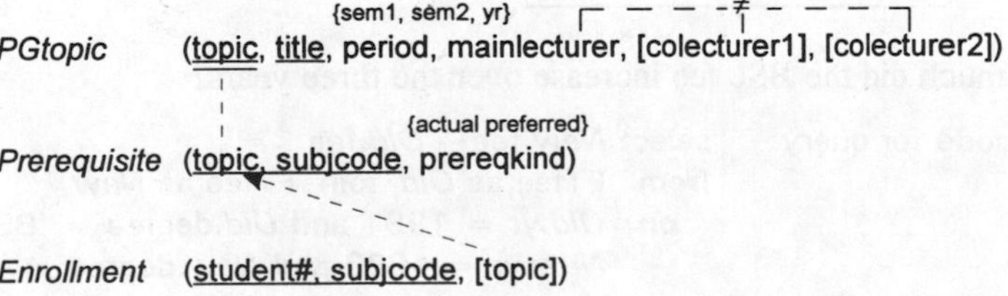

{sem1, sem2, yr}
≠
PGtopic (topic, title, period, mainlecturer, [colecturer1], [colecturer2])
{actual preferred}
Prerequisite (topic, subjcode, prereqkind)
Enrollment (student#, subjcode, [topic])

Figure 9.47 The relational schema mapped from Figure 9.46

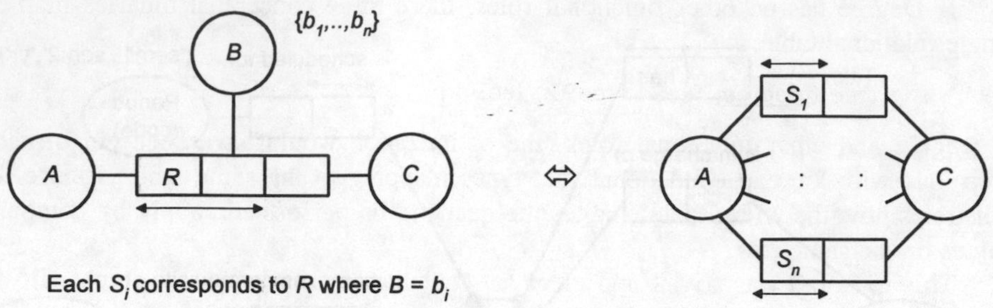

3 For the ternary pattern above, if focussed queries on *R* require comparisons between different tuples, and the values $b_1..b_n$ are few and fairly stable, then absorb *B*, specializing *R* into *n* functional binaries.

Figure 9.48 Optimization step 3: the table width guideline (TWG)

In arriving at the answer ($300), you compared values from two different rows from the same table. To perform this query in a relational database language requires joining the table to itself (a self-join). An SQL version of the query is included in Figure 9.49.

Such joins can be avoided by first transforming the schema via TWG. Absorbing the object type Year into the ternary specializes it to the three conceptual binaries: **Degree had 1991 fulltime fee of MoneyAmt; Degree had 1992 fulltime fee of MoneyAmt; Degree had 1993 fulltime fee of MoneyAmt.** Here the roles of Degree are functional and linked by an equality constraint. If in the global schema, fee information is mandatory for Degree, these roles are mandatory (which implies the equality constraint).

***FTfee*:**

degree	*yr*	*fee*
BSc	1991	2000
BSc	1992	2000
BSc	1993	2300
MBA	1991	3000
MBA	1992	3300
MBA	1993	3700

How much did the BSc fee increase over the three years?

SQL code for query:

```
select New.fee - Old.fee
from   FTfee as Old join FTfee as New
  on   Old.yr = 1991 and Old.degree = 'BSc' and
       New.yr = 1993 and New.degree = 'BSc'
```

Figure 9.49 This query requires a self-join, since it compares different rows

If Degree has no other functional roles, these three conceptual binaries map to a single relational table:

FTfee (<u>degree</u>, fee91, fee92, fee93)

If Degree had other functional roles, the optimization would have been performed at Step 2.1, with the extra functional fact types mapping to the same table. Figure 9.50 illustrates how the wider table enables the query to be performed simply by comparing values on the same row.

This example was trivial and clear-cut, but life is not always so simple. If Year plays other roles in the global schema, the restriction to 1991..1993 would probably not apply to it. However, so long as the fee years have this restriction (effectively forming a subtype FeeYear) the transformation may still be performed. If the year range is large, the number of extra columns generated by the transformation may be too high.

For example, suppose we must record fees for the period 1951..1990. Specializing the ternary would generate forty binaries and lead to a relational table with 41 columns: FTfee (<u>degree</u>, fee51, ... fee90). Such a large number of binaries would clutter the conceptual schema (though a flexible CASE tool could be set to display the ternary with the optimization hidden in the mapping). The very wide relational table would also be awkward to view (lots of horizontal scrolling) and to print. For these reasons, once the *cardinality* of the value constraint exceeds a reasonable number (e.g. 5) the ternary fact type might well be preferred.

The *stability* of the value constraint is also important. In many cases such a constraint is known to be stable (e.g. {'m','f'} for sexcode). Sometimes however the value constraint changes with time. For example, suppose fees are to be recorded for all years from 1991 to the current year, or for just the most recent triennium. The binary approach requires changes to the fact types and relational columns each year. In this case the ternary approach might be preferred since no structural change is needed (the year changes are made only to rows of data, not the table structure itself).

The wording of optimization step 3 reflects this trade-off between query efficiency, and the ease of table display and schema evolution. Although default choices can be built into an automated optimizer, in practice interaction with human modelers is advisable to ensure the best trade-off.

FTfee:

degree	*fee91*	*fee92*	*fee93*
BSc	2000	2000	2300
MBA	3000	3300	3700

How much did the BSc fee increase over the three years?

SQL code for query:

```
select fee93 - fee91
from   FTfee
where  degree = 'BSc'
```

Figure 9.50 The transformed schema leads to a more efficient query

The final steps (4 and 5) of the optimization procedure deal with exclusive roles (see Figure 9.51). *Step 4* is straightforward. Recall that different unaries attached to the same object type map to different columns of the same table. If these unaries are exclusive we may replace them all by a functional binary which maps to just one column. Moreover, the transformation of the exclusion constraint to a uniqueness constraint enables it to be simply enforced by the primary key constraint of the table. For an example of this predicate generalization process, review Figure 9.6 where three exclusive unaries (Employee is manager; Employee is clerk; Employee is secretary) are replaced by the functional binary: Employee has Rank {'M','C','S'}.

Step 5 helps us decide when to favor predicate generalization in applying theorem PSG2. This is illustrated, along with several other optimizations, within our next example. Consider the conceptual schema shown in Figure 9.52. The inter-predicate uniqueness constraint asserts that a team may have only one player of each sex. If desired, we may introduce "fields" as the inverse of "represents" to obtain a subtype definition in the active voice: **each Playing_Country is a Country that fields some Team.** This conceptual schema maps to seven tables. As an exercise, you might like to check this for yourself, then optimize the conceptual schema before reading on.

The overlap algorithm (step 1.3) applied to the bottom ternaries of Figure 9.52 generates the intermediate, nested subschema shown in Figure 9.53, which is later transformed (step 5) to the nested pattern included in the optimized conceptual schema (Figure 9.54). This modification to the nesting does not change the number of tables, but it does simplify the constraint pattern that has to be enforced.

At the final stage of step 2.1, the subtype Playing_Country is seen to have a simple key attached (via its supertype) and a composite key; so the value-constrained UniformItem is absorbed to specialize the ternary into two functional binaries. Note the constraint pattern arising from the application of corollaries.

At the first stage of step 2.2, the frequency constraint on the supplies predicate is used to specialize it into two functional binaries. The second half of step 2.2 is used to absorb the object type Sex, specializing the team membership predicate into binaries in which Team now has functional roles; hence these may be mapped to the same table as Team's other functional fact type. Steps 3 and 4 are not invoked by this example. Step 5 transformed the original nesting to another, as discussed earlier.

4 Generalize each group of n exclusive unaries ($n \geq 2$) to a functional binary by extracting an object type with n values. (see Figure 9.6)

5 **if** an object type *A* plays n exclusive, functional roles in binary predicates connected to *C*
and not (the predicates are 1:1
and *C* (but not *A*) has another functional role)
then replace these n predicates by two binaries, by extracting the object type *B* $\{b_1,..,b_n\}$ as per the LHS of PSG2.
(see Figure 9.13)

Figure 9.51 Optimization steps 4 and 5: further aspects of exclusive roles

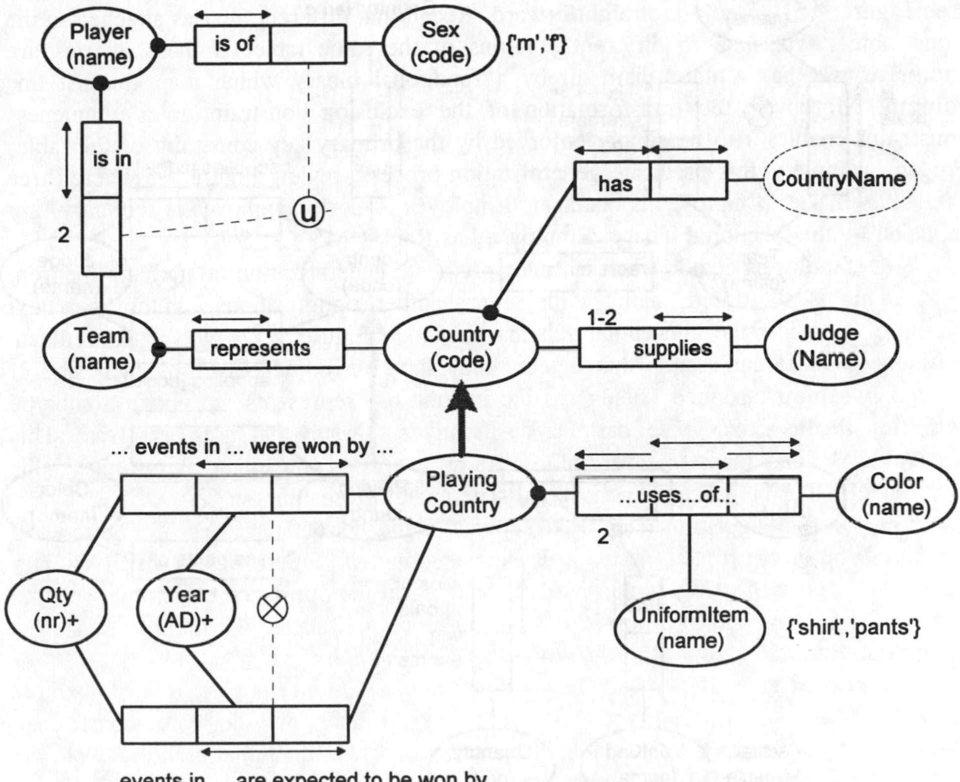

Figure 9.52 This un-optimized conceptual schema maps to seven tables

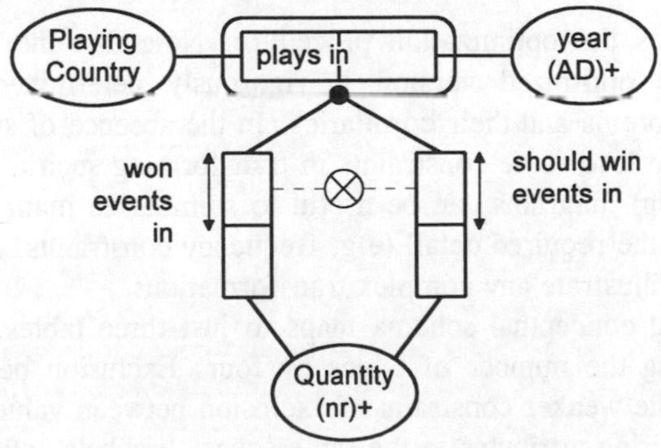

Figure 9.53 An intermediate transform of the bottom left ternaries of Figure 9.52

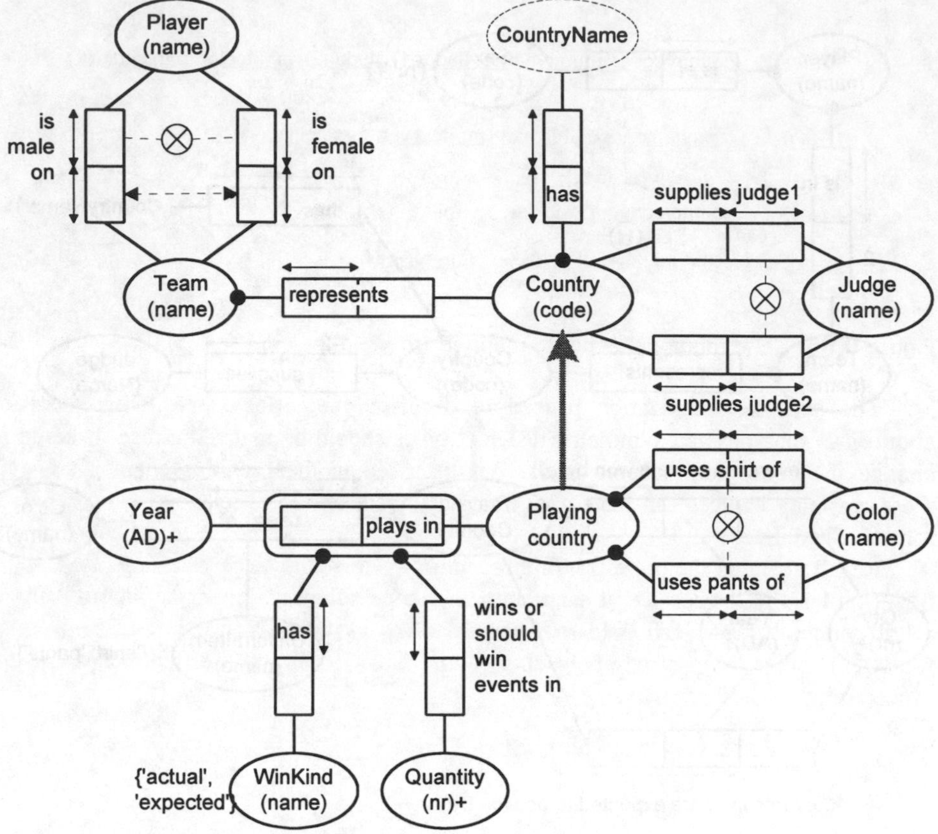

Figure 9.54 This optimized conceptual schema maps to three tables

This completes the optimization procedure. Note that the generation of all the constraints in the optimized version is rigorously determined by the underlying transformation theorems and their corollaries. In the absence of such formal grounding it would be easy to lose some constraints in transforming such a schema. Although ER (Entity Relationship) diagrams can be useful to summarize main aspects of a schema, they typically lack the required detail (e.g. frequency constraints, disjunctive mandatory roles, domains) to illustrate any complex transformations.

The optimized conceptual schema maps to just three tables, as shown in Figure 9.55, thus reducing the number of tables by four. Exclusion between column-sets is shown by "⊗". The weaker constraint of exclusion between values on the same row is shown by "≠". Pairing attributes in the same square brackets entails that any qualification applies to each, and that if one is null so is the other (this latter constraint is implied for the color attributes by their qualification).

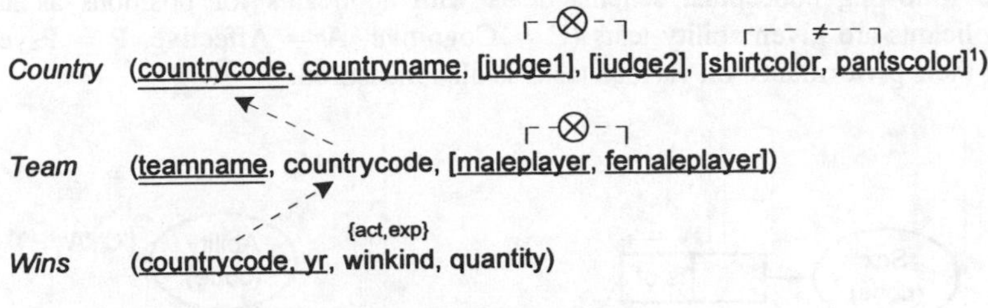

Country (countrycode, countryname, [judge1], [judge2], [shirtcolor, pantscolor]¹)
Team (teamname, countrycode, [maleplayer, femaleplayer])
{act,exp}
Wins (countrycode, yr, winkind, quantity)
¹exists iff countrycode in Team.countrycode

Figure 9.55 The relational schema mapped from Figure 9.54

The schema optimization procedure discussed here does not include decisions about how subtypes and symmetric 1:1 fact types should be mapped, since these do not change the conceptual schema itself. As discussed in the previous chapter however, these mapping choices can have a significant impact on the efficiency of the relational schema obtained.

Recall also that the optimization procedure assumes the target system is a relational DBMS, at least in the sense that each entry in a table column is either an atomic value or a null value. If set-valued fields are permitted (as in network DBMSs, and as proposed for SQL3), other designs may be used to avoid table joins, and a different optimization procedure would be used.

Exercise 9.5

1. Consider a conceptual schema in which the only fact type associated with Department (code) is:

Department at Level {UG, PG} has students in Quantity.

Here "UG", "PG" abbreviate "undergraduate", "postgraduate". The role played by Department has a frequency constraint of 2. Let a focused query be:

What is the ratio of postgraduate to undergraduate enrollments for the department of computer science?

(a) Draw the conceptual fact type, and Rmap it.
(b) Optimize the conceptual (sub)schema, and Rmap it.
(c) Although primarily identified by its code (e.g. "CS"), each department also has a unique name (e.g. "Computer Science") which is now mandatorily recorded. The enrollment figures are now optional, but if any figures are recorded both UG and PG figures are required. Draw the new conceptual schema and Rmap it.
(d) Optimize the new conceptual schema, and Rmap it.

2. The following conceptual schema deals with applicants for positions as astronauts. Applicants are given ability tests (C = Cognitive, A = Affective, P = Psychomotor) and their performance on various tasks is also measured.

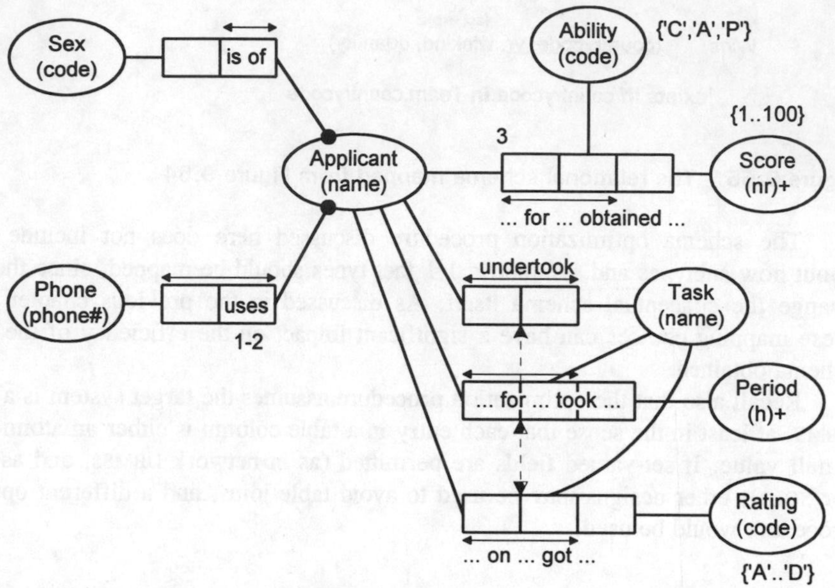

(a) Rmap this.
(b) Optimize the conceptual schema.
(c) Rmap your optimized conceptual schema.

3. Consider the following conceptual schema. Assume that the Project-Programmer-Class subschema may be treated simply in snapshot fashion (i.e. only current data for these fact types are recorded).

(a) Rmap this.
(b) Optimize the conceptual schema.
(c) Rmap your answer to (b).
(d) As indicated in the original conceptual schema, each project must normally have a junior and senior programmer. However, suppose now that while, or after, working on a project, a programmer may be promoted or even demoted in class (junior, senior).

Discuss briefly how you would deal with this situation from a practical business standpoint, and what changes, if any, you would suggest for the original and optimized conceptual schemas.

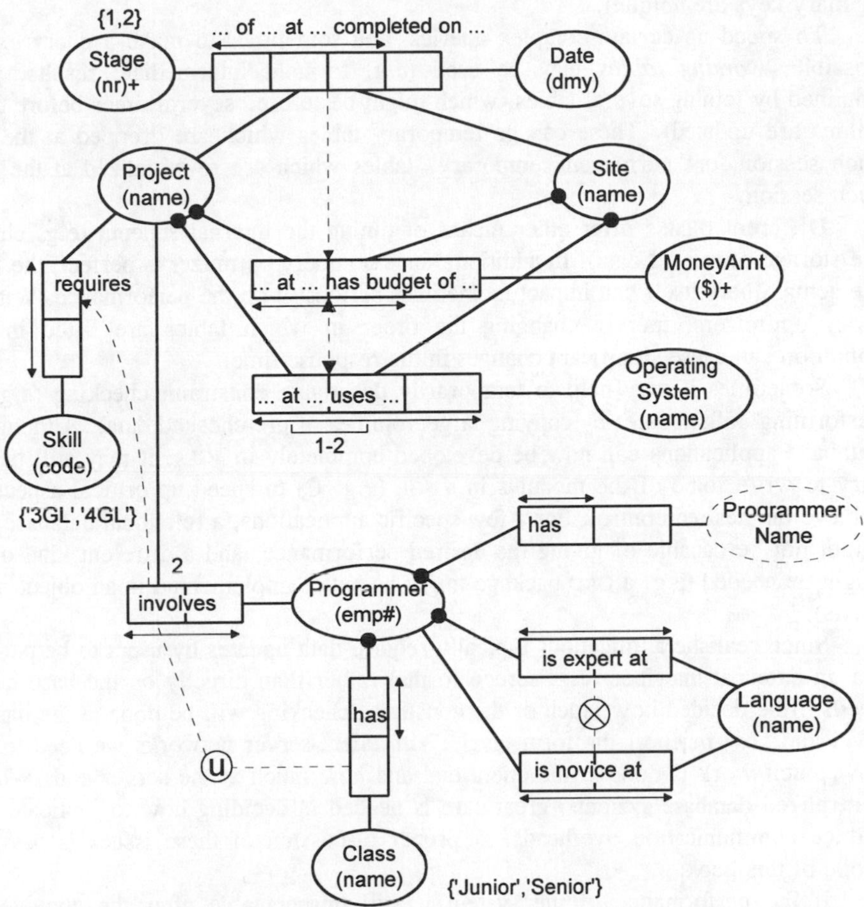

9.6 Lower level optimization

Applying the conceptual optimization procedure followed by the Rmap procedure ensures a redundancy-free relational schema which should be reasonably efficient. To test the performance of this logical schema, it should be implemented as an internal schema on the target DBMS, using a realistic population. At this stage *indexes* should normally be created for all primary and foreign keys, as well as any other columns that play a significant role in focused queries.

For large tables, indexes can dramatically improve performance since they reside, in part or whole, in main memory and their entries are sorted into structures which permit fast retrieval (e.g. binary trees). At times, indexes may slow down updates since they must be updated when relevant changes are made to the base tables; but even with updates, indexes can speed up many kinds of constraint checking (e.g. ensuring that primary keys are unique).

To speed up certain complex queries, and sometimes to make a query execution possible, *working tables* may be used (e.g. to hold intermediate results, perhaps obtained by joining several tables, which might be re-used several times before the base values are updated). These can be temporary tables which are dropped at the end of each session, or "permanent temporary" tables which are re-initialized at the start of each session.

Different DBMSs offer other means of tuning the internal schema (e.g. clustering the storage of related data). In addition, since no query optimizer is perfect, the form of the actual query itself can impact (sometimes seriously) on the performance. With some older optimizers, merely changing the order in which tables are listed in a join condition can cause significant changes in the response time.

Sometimes it may help to temporarily deactivate constraint checking (e.g. when performing bulk updates by copying large volumes of pre-checked data). Although most database applications can now be developed completely in 4GLs, it may still be necessary to write some of the modules in a 3GL (e.g. C) to speed up critical aspects or to achieve the desired control. For a few specific applications, a relational database system might not be capable of giving the desired performance, and a different kind of DBMS might be needed (e.g. a CAD package might be better implemented in an object-oriented DBMS).

Since realistic applications typically require data updates by users to be performed via an external interface (e.g. screen forms) rather than directly on the base tables, it needs to be decided how much of the constraint checking will be done at the base table level and how much at the form level. With client-server networks we need to decide how much work is done at the client end and how much at the server end. With non-centralized database systems, great care is needed in deciding how to replicate data to reduce communication overheads. A proper discussion of these issues is beyond the scope of this book.

If the performance of the system is still unacceptable after the above internal schema optimization has been carried out, it may be necessary to *denormalize* the base relational schema. Typically this entails introducing *controlled redundancy* to reduce the number of table joins required for focused queries. This slows down updates (redundant facts must be kept consistent) and makes the system harder to work with, but it can dramatically reduce response times for queries. Any denormalization decisions should be carefully documented, and appropriate subset or equality constraints must be enforced to control the redundancy. As a simple example, consider the following relational subschema which is extracted from our software retailer example.

InvoiceLine (<u>invoice#, itemcode</u>, qty, unitprice)

Item (<u>itemcode</u>, <u>title</u>, category, stock, listprice)

Suppose we frequently need to list the invoice lines, including item titles, for specified invoices. With the above schema this requires a join of the two tables. If the tables are very large, having to access the second table simply to get the item title may slow things down too much. To avoid this, we might denormalize by inserting an extra copy of title in the InvoiceLine table. This means the following fact type is now mapped to both tables: Item has Title. To control this redundancy we add a pair-subset constraint between the tables as shown:

InvoiceLine (invoice#, itemcode, title, qty, unitprice)

Item (itemcode, title, category, stock, listprice)

The query may now be performed by accessing just the InvoiceLine table. The constraint pattern is now more complicated. However, the uniqueness constraint on ⟨invoice#, title⟩ is implied by the other constraints (why?), and items rarely change their titles, so we mainly need to check the pair-subset constraint when InvoiceLine rows are inserted or modified. For some applications the additional update overhead may be a price well worth paying to improve the query performance.

In real world applications, one sometimes encounters very poor database designs. In particular it is not uncommon for novice modelers to introduce uncontrolled redundancy (e.g. to omit the pair-subset constraint in the above denormalized schema). The next section discusses a re-engineering example which illustrates, among other things, how such poor designs can be improved by applying conceptual modeling techniques.

Exercise 9.6

1. The following relational schema is used to store details about students and their results. A focused query is: List the student# and name of all students who enrolled in CS114. As there are over 50 000 students, and on average each enrolled in over 20 subjects, the tables are large. Denormalize the schema to improve the performance of the query, and discuss any possible disadvantages of this action.

   Student (student#, stuname, degree)

   Result (student#, subjcode, [rating])

9.7 Re-engineering

While conceptual modeling provides the best approach to developing new applications, it can also be used to remodel existing systems to better meet the application requirements. There are three main reasons for replacing or revising (perhaps drastically) an existing information system.

Firstly, the current system might provide an *incorrect* model of the UoD, either by being *inaccurate* (wrong information) or *incomplete* (missing information). Such wrong or missing fact types, constraints and derivation rules might arise because of bad modeling in the first place. For example, the schema might assert that planets orbit moons, allow that people may have more than birthdate, or derive ages from a simple formula which ignores the extra day in leap years. Such errors can also arise because the model has not kept pace with changes in the UoD. For example, a system for recording academic results based on a seven point numeric rating scale becomes outdated if the rating scheme is replaced by a five point letter grade.

Secondly, the existing system might be *inefficient*. It might be too slow (e.g. too many table joins needed in queries), too large (e.g. too many null values gobbling up space) or difficult to evolve (e.g. outdated rules hard-wired into program code rather than modeled as data in tables). Perhaps the hardware platform itself is outmoded and needs to be replaced, or the external interface is awkward for users.

Finally the existing system might be *unclear*. This also makes it hard to maintain or evolve. Many older systems in place today were designed at the logical, or even internal, level and have no conceptual schema formulated for them. They may have been developed completely in 3GLs, with no underlying design method, have little or poor documentation, and be riddled with misleading or cryptic identifiers.

Often a combination of the three reasons leads to an information system which needs to be *re-engineered*, or re-structured, in order for its owner (e.g. a company) to remain competitive in today's marketplace. The company might even re-engineer the very way it does business. Although the need for re-structuring has sometimes been used as an excuse for retrenching, a creative response to this need can lead to major enhancements in the quality and efficiency of the business and its supporting information systems. Here we consider only the problem of re-engineering a database system. This process may be divided into four stages, as shown in Figure 9.56.

The first stage, *conceptualization*, involves developing an initial conceptual schema of the application from the original database. This can be done simply by applying the CSDP to the database, treating it as a set of output reports. Most of the verbalization stage is usually straightforward since tables provide the easiest kind of output report to interpret. Usually at least an incomplete logical schema for the database is also available, and constraints in this schema (e.g. primary and foreign key constraints) can be used to help derive some of the constraints in a fairly automatic fashion.

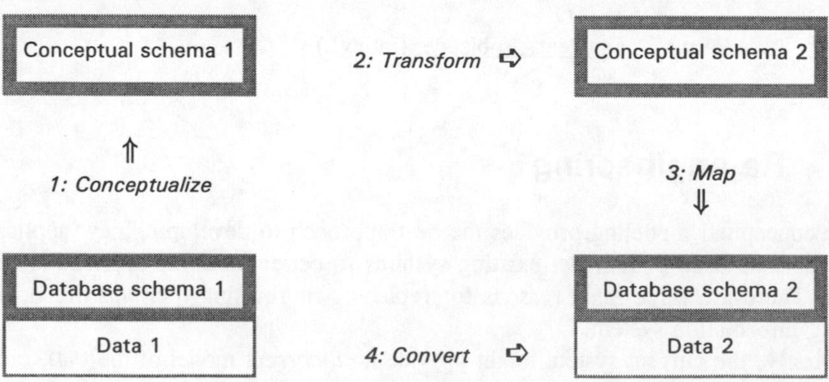

Figure 9.56 4 steps in re-engineering a database

If the database is not relational, some of the inter-table connections may need to be verbalized as fact types. Often, additional constraints which have not been specified will be identified with the assistance of the UoD expert.

The second stage, *transformation*, involves modifying the original conceptual schema to cater for changes in the UoD not modeled in the original database, and/or optimizing the conceptual schema as discussed in the previous section.

The third stage, *mapping*, takes us down to the logical schema. If a relational database system to be used, we may use the Rmap procedure for this. The fourth stage, *data conversion*, copies the facts stored in the original database to the new database. This involves conversion as well as copying since some of the fact types involved will now be grouped into different table structures.

Stage 1 of this four-step process is sometimes called *"reverse engineering"*, and stages 1-3 are sometimes collectively called *"forward engineering"*. Much of the re-engineering process can be automated, especially if a very detailed database schema is provided at stage 1. However, human interaction is also required to ensure a complete and elegant result. While our discussion is limited to the logical and conceptual levels, re-engineering an application involves work at the external and internal levels as well.

The four basic re-engineering stages are now illustrated with a worked example. As the main input to the process, Figure 9.57 shows a relational schema as well as two rows of data for each table (shown as tuples on the right to save space). Suppose this design is used to record details about a one day computer conference, but its performance is poor mainly because of the number of table joins required for common queries.

Moreover, application developers find parts of the schema awkward or even unsafe. For example, the budget column in the Committee table applies to the committee as a whole, not to a particular chairperson of that committee (each committee has at most two chairpersons). It is suspected that this is not the only un-normalized feature of the tables. Because of your expertise in conceptual modeling, you are hired to provide a conceptual model of the application, so that a clear and complete picture of the application is available. Moreover, you are asked to provide a new relational design which is both normalized and efficient, if this is possible.

In practice, re-engineering usually requires dialogue with the client to clarify the UoD, and especially to identify missing constraints. To help you try the reverse engineering phase yourself, uniqueness, value, exclusion and frequency constraints are depicted. However, other constraints are omitted (e.g. subset constraints, and non-implied functional dependencies due to denormalization). Some missing constraints are "obvious", and others may be identified from the brief description which follows. As well, the sample rows of data enable you to apply CSDP step 1. These rows do not provide a significant, or even a legal, population (e.g. if the database were comprised of only these data, various subset constraints between the tables would be violated).

Abbreviated codes have the following meanings: Prog = Programming; Org = Organizing; undec = undecided; tab = table; fig = figure; lec = lecture; lab = laboratory. Authors submit papers which are then sent to referees to be rated. The method for determining which papers are accepted is not modeled here. Various statistics (number of pages, tables and figures) may be kept about accepted papers, partly to help with publication of the conference proceedings; if statistics are kept for a paper, all three numbers must be recorded.

relational schema (some constraints missing):		**sample data** (not significant)
Committee	{Prog,Org} (cteecode, chairperson, [budget]) 1-2	⟨'Prog','Adams, Prof. A.B.',?⟩ ⟨'Org','Bloggs, Dr F.',10000⟩
Person	(personname, affiliation, [email])	⟨'Adams, Prof. A.B.','MIT',?⟩ ⟨'Pi, Dr Q.T.', 'UQ','pi@uq.au'⟩
Rated	{1..10} (referee, paper#, rating)	⟨'Adams, Prof. A.B.',43,8⟩ ⟨'Pi, Dr Q.T.',5,4⟩
Referees	(personname, paper#) ⊗	⟨'Adams, Prof. A.B.',43⟩ ⟨'Knot, Prof. I.M.',43⟩
Authored	(personname, paper#, papertitle)	⟨'Sea, Ms A.B.',5,'EER models'⟩ ⟨'Pi, Dr Q.T.',43,'ORM dialects'⟩
Presents	(author, paper#)	⟨'Pi, Dr Q.T.', 43⟩ ⟨'Knot, Dr I.M.',61⟩
Paper	{undec,accept,reject} (paper#, papertitle, status)	⟨5,'EER models','undec'⟩ ⟨43,'ORM dialects','accept'⟩
AcceptedPaper	(paper#, [pagelength])	⟨43,14⟩ ⟨75,?⟩
AcPaperDiags	{tbl, fig} (paper#, diagramkind, qty) 2	⟨43,tbl,3⟩ ⟨43,fig,5⟩
PaperSlot	{A,B} (slot#, stream, hr, [bldg#, room#], [paper#])	⟨1,'A',9,69,'110',43⟩ ⟨2,'B',9,50,'110',?⟩
Room	{lab,lec,office} (bldg#, room#, roomtype, area)	⟨69,'110','lec',100⟩ ⟨50,'110','lab',120⟩
LabOrLecRm	(bldg#, room#, [nrPCs], [nrSeats])	⟨69,'110',?,350⟩ ⟨50,'110',40,?⟩

Figure 9.57 The original database schema and some sample data

An accepted paper may be presented by one or more of its authors at the conference—which authors present the paper might be unknown until some time after the paper is accepted.

The conference program includes slots to which accepted papers are eventually allocated. Each slot is of one hour duration. Time is measured in military hours (e.g. 14 = 2 p.m.). To allow more papers on the same day, two streams (A and B) may be run in parallel (so two paper slots may have the same time). A room directory is used to help assign slots to rooms; room area is in square meters. Only lecture rooms or laboratories may be used for paper presentations. The number of seats is recorded just for lecture rooms, and the number of PCs is recorded just for laboratories.

Before peeking at the solution provided, try to provide a conceptual schema for this application. Include all constraints (including those missing from the original relational schema). In performing this conceptualization, it will become apparent that some of the tables have redundancy problems. Which tables are these?

By now you should have completed your own reverse engineering. Compare your solution with the one provided in Figure 9.58. Give yourself a pat on the back if you got all the constraints. It should be clear that the table grouping differs from what Rmap would generate if applied to the conceptual schema. To begin with, the two Committee fact types are wrongly grouped into the same table, even though one of them is non-functional.

As a result, the original Committee table is open to redundancy problems with facts of the type: Committee has budget of MoneyAmt. Similarly, the Authored table exhibits redundancy problems by wrongly including facts of the type: Paper has PaperTitle. So the original designer made a mess of things by denormalizing the relational schema in an uncontrolled way.

Although the conceptual schema looks fairly complicated, the conceptualization has actually clarified the UoD. For example, the semantics conveyed by the PaperSlot table are much easier to understand on the conceptual schema. Moreover, now that the detailed semantics are displayed graphically, we are in a better position to explore optimization possibilities in a controlled manner.

As the second phase of the re-engineering, use the conceptual optimization procedure discussed in the previous section to transform the conceptual schema into one that one that Rmaps to a more efficient relational schema.

Compare your solution with that provided in Figure 9.59. The specialization of the chairperson and diagram predicates into functional binaries is straightforward (though care is needed to preserve all the constraints). In nesting the referee and author predicates, we could have gone further by uniting these exclusive but compatible predicates. However, although this additional move would lead to one fewer table, we have opted not to nest these exclusive predicates since doing so would detract from the readability of the schema and lead to awkward constraint patterns.

Indeed, even the nesting in Figure 9.59 leads to awkward verbalization. The original flattening into four predicates seems to be more natural than the two nestings. Ideally a CASE tool would allow the modeler to choose the flattened display for clarity, with the option of including the nesting as a hidden, pre-processing stage to the standard mapping.

The next stage is to map the optimized conceptual schema to a new relational schema. As an exercise, try this yourself before looking at the solution provided (Figure 9.60).

Notice that the final relational schema contains just 7 tables (compared with the 12 original tables), is fully normalized, and captures all the original constraints as well as those that were missing from the original.

Finally the data conversion is performed. The main aspect of this conversion involves defining the new relation types in terms of the original ones. Once this is done, the data conversion can be perfomed automatically. Figure 9.60 displays one row of converted data for each of the new tables.

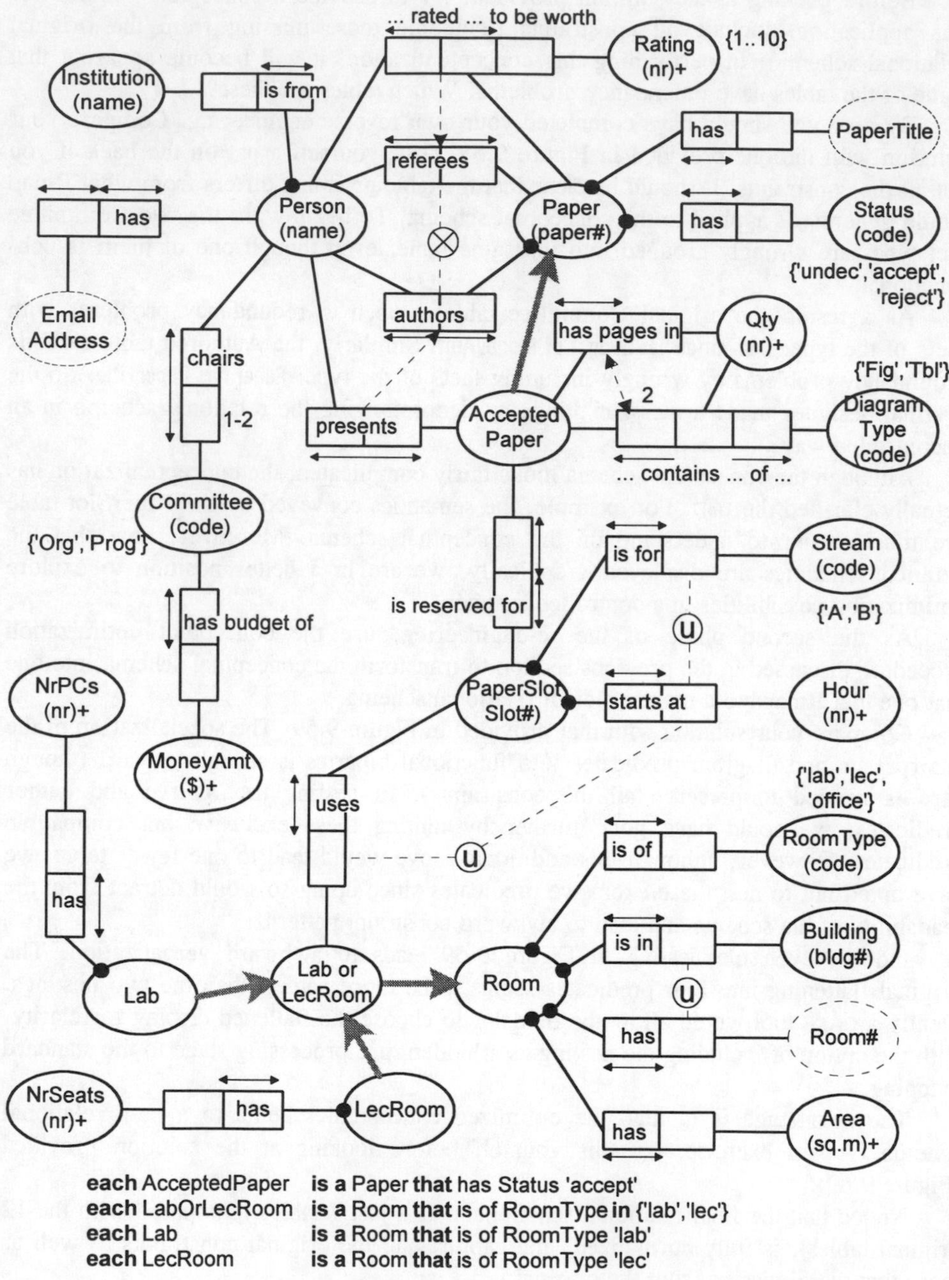

Figure 9.58 The conceptual schema resulting from reverse-engineering

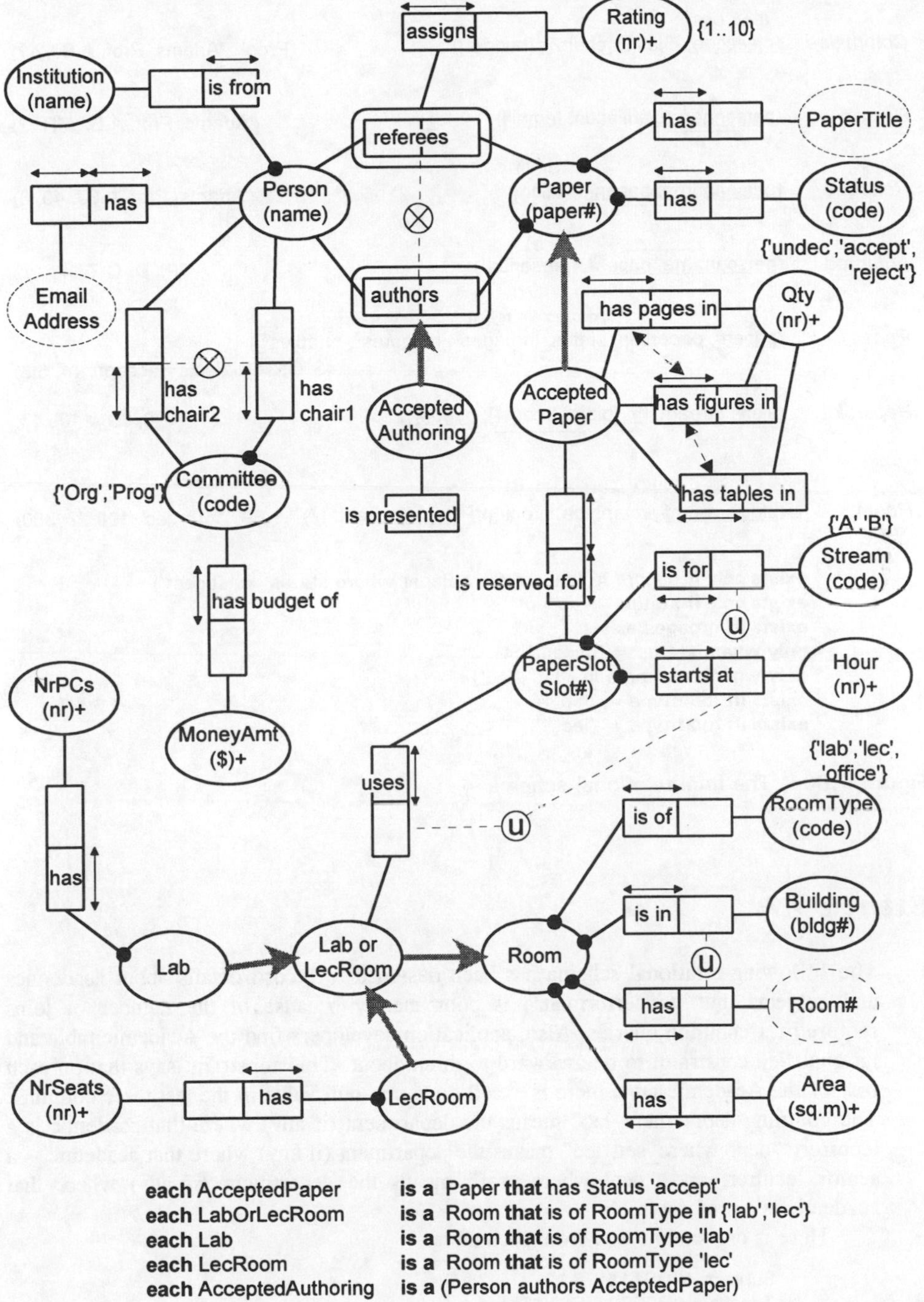

Figure 9.59 The optimized conceptual schema

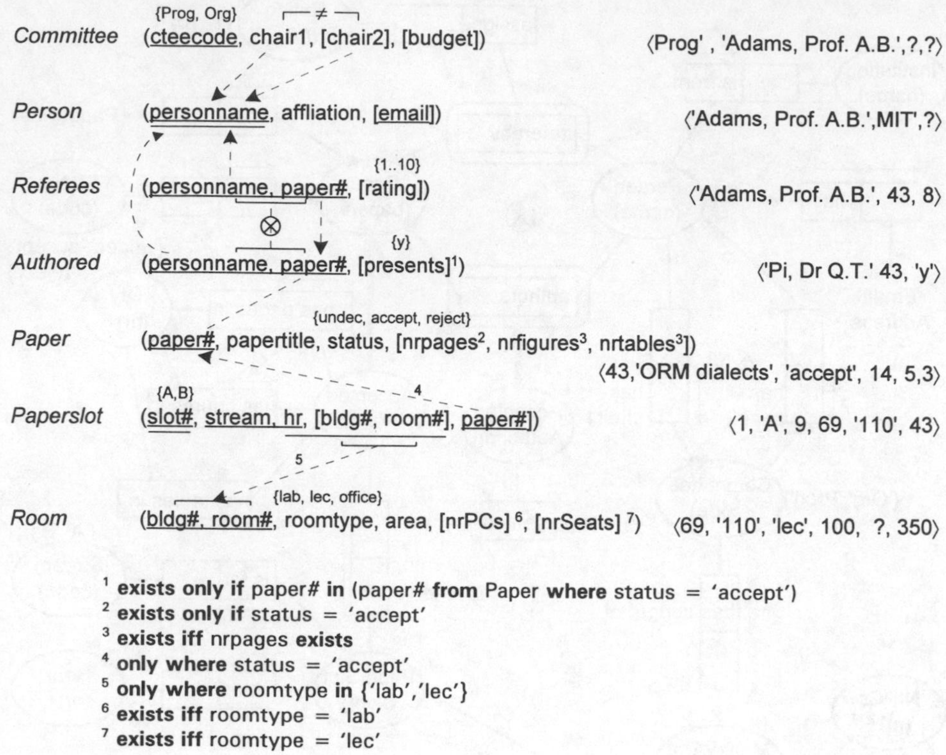

Figure 9.60 The final relational schema

Exercise 9.7

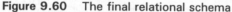

1. The following relational schema has been designed to record details about academics and subjects, but its performance is poor mainly because of the number of joins required for common queries. Also, application developers find the Academic table and its qualified constraint to be awkward to think about. This constraint says that on each row of the Academic table there is exactly one non-null value in the last three columns. The column "dept_where_lec" means the department (if any) where that academic is a lecturer, "dept_where_sen_lec" means the department (if any) where that academic is a senior lecturer, and "dept_where_prof" means the department (if any) where that academic is a professor.

   Here is one sample row from each table:

   Subject: ⟨ 'CS115', 8 ⟩
   Teaches: ⟨ 30572, 'CS115' ⟩
   Academic: ⟨ 30572, ?, 'Computer Science', ? ⟩
   AwardedBy: ⟨ 30572, 'PhD', 'UQ' ⟩
   AwardedIn: ⟨ 30572, 'PhD', 1990 ⟩

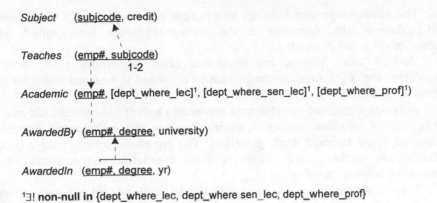

Subject (<u>subjcode</u>, credit)

Teaches (<u>emp#, subjcode</u>)
1-2

Academic (<u>emp#</u>, [dept_where_lec][1], [dept_where_sen_lec][1], [dept_where_prof][1])

AwardedBy (<u>emp#, degree</u>, university)

AwardedIn (<u>emp#, degree</u>, yr)

[1]∃! **non-null in {dept_where_lec, dept_where sen_lec, dept_where_prof}**

Re-engineer the application to improve its performance and clarity, by carrying out the following steps.

(a) Reverse-engineer the relational schema to an ORM conceptual schema. Include all constraints.
(b) Knowing the target system is relational, optimize the conceptual schema by applying conceptual transformations.
(c) Forward-engineer your new conceptual schema by mapping it to a relational schema. Include all constraints.
(d) Populate the new relational schema with the sample data provided.

9.8 Summary

Conceptual schemas are *equivalent* iff they model the same UoD. Various *schema transformations* may be performed to reshape a conceptual schema into one that is either equivalent, or an acceptable alternative. *Predicate specialization* fragments a predicate into two or more special cases, typically by *absorbing* an enumerated object type into it. For example, the has_gender predicate may be specialized into is_male and is_female by absorbing Sex {'m','f'}.

The inverse transformation, *predicate generalization*, typically involves *extracting* an enumerated object type from a predicate. Predicate specialization/generalization (PSG) may also be performed by considering the *n* cases of a role with a frequency constraint of *n* or 1-*n*. For example, the predicate has_parent with a frequency constraint of 2 on its first role may be specialized into has_parent1 and has_parent2.

Nested object types may be inter-changed with *co-referenced* object types, using the Nest/Co-reference transformation (N/CR). Either of these representations may be replaced by *flattening* into one or more fact types. For example, consider the nesting: (Student enrolled in Subject) results in Rating. If results are mandatory this may be flattened into the single ternary: Student for Subject scored Rating. If results are optional, the flattened approach requires an extra binary (Student enrolled in Subject) which is the target of a pair-subset constraint from the ternary.

The *overlap algorithm* indicates how nesting may be performed when compatible sub-predicates exist, depending on the constraint between them (subset, equality, exclusion etc.). See Figure 9.33.

Various other schema transformations exist. Sometimes as a result of a transformation, a graphical constraint must be converted to a textual constraint (or vice versa).

Although nested and co-referenced approaches have the same relational map, many other cases of equivalent conceptual schemas result in different relational schemas when subjected to the standard Rmap procedure. The process of transforming a conceptual schema into another which results in a more efficient relational map is called *conceptual schema optimization*.

Many optimization moves aim at reducing the number of relational tables, typically by specializing non-functional predicates into functional ones that can be grouped into the same table as another functional fact type, or by using nesting (or co-referencing) to unify compatible composite keys. This is particularly useful in reducing the number of table joins required for focused queries. Predicate specialization is sometimes used to enable comparisons between rows of the same table to be replaced by comparisons between columns on the same row, thereby eliminating the need for a self-join to perform the query.

Once conceptual optimization and mapping has been completed, the *internal schema should be tuned* (e.g. by adding indexes or working tables). Various choices are also made as to the best place to enforce constraints (e.g. at the base table level or the form level). If performance is still poor it may be necessary to *denormalize* some of the base tables, via *controlled redundancy* to reduce the need for joins.

If an existing database application is unsatisfactory it may be necessary to *re-engineer* it. This remodeling may involve four main steps: conceptualize (or reverse-engineer) the existing database schema to a conceptual schema; optimize this by transformation; map it to the improved database schema; and convert the original data in order to populate the new database.

Chapter notes

More restricted studies of schema equivalence have been carried out within the relational model (e.g. Kobayashi 1986, 1990), the ER model (e.g. D'Atri & Sacca 1984) and EER models (e.g. Batini et al. 1992). To keep our treatment fairly intuitive we have glossed over some technical issues. A more formal treatment may be found in Halpin (1989a, 1989b). Most work on schema optimization tends to focus on sub-conceptual levels. For an approach to schema optimization which evaluates fitness functions on randomly generated, equivalent internal schemas see van Bommel & van der Weide (1992).

10 Other design methods, issues and trends

10.1 Introduction

In section 3.1, an overview was presented of the complete information systems life cycle. Since then we have focused on the stages of this cycle which deal with the conceptual and logical design of the data. Object-Role Modeling (ORM) was used to perform the conceptual modeling, and the Rmap algorithm was used to map the conceptual schema to a relational database schema. We also saw how various kinds of schema transformations might be used to improve the efficiency of the design.

This chapter discusses other methods, issues and recent trends with respect to information system design. Section 2 provides an overview of normalization theory, and indicates how it relates to our modeling approach. Although a knowledge of normalization techniques is not needed to develop a proper design, this theory has been so influential that anyone who wishes to communicate with other database modelers should at least understand the terminology commonly used to discuss the main normal forms.

Section 3 outlines some ways of performing schema abstraction, enabling the modeler to focus on various aspects of a schema by hiding other details. In this connection, the notion of major object types will be related to the Entity-Relationship modeling approach.

Section 4 provides an overview of process and event modeling, and external schema design. Often, the design of external interfaces (e.g. screen forms) can be viewed in terms of operations on the major object types abstracted from the conceptual data model. This view may be related to some of the so-called "object-oriented" design strategies. Section 5 examines this notion, and the claim that relational databases should be replaced by object-oriented databases. It also summarizes some other issues and recent trends.

Section 6 provides an introduction to meta-modeling, in which conceptual schemas themselves may be treated as application models for which a conceptual meta-schema is required. Section 7 furnishes a summary and additional notes, to complete this final chapter.

10.2 Normalization

Two main aspects of ORM have now been covered: the conceptual schema design procedure (CSDP); and the relational mapping procedure (Rmap). The process of mapping from a conceptual schema expressed in elementary fact types to a relational schema expressed in table types is one of **deconceptualization**. This approach facilitates sound design primarily because it emphasizes working from examples, using natural language, and thinking in terms of the real world objects being modeled.

The advantages of using *elementary facts* are clear: working in simple units helps us to get one correct; constraints are easier to express and check; null values are avoided; redundancy control is facilitated; the schema is easier to modify (one fact type at a time); and the same conceptual schema may be mapped to different logical data models (hence decisions about how to group fact types together may be delayed till mapping).

Nowadays, most database designers do a conceptual design first, whether it be in ORM or ER notation, and then apply a mapping procedure to it. In the past, in place of conceptual modeling, many relational database designers used a technique known as **normalization**. Some still use this, even if only to refine the logical design mapped from the conceptual one. If an ORM conceptual schema is actually correct, then the table design resulting from Rmap is already fully normalized; so we do not need to learn about normalization to get our designs correct. However it is worth having a brief look at normalization, partly to consolidate aspects of good design and partly to help us communicate with those who use the normalization approach.

There are actually two techniques for normalization: one known as *synthesis*, and one known as *decomposition* (or sometimes "analysis"). Each operates only at the relational level, and begins with the complete set of relational attributes as well as a set of dependencies on these (e.g. functional dependencies). Herein lie the fundamental weaknesses of the normalization approach, if it is not used in combination with a conceptual modeling approach.

In any realistic application it is too easy to get an incorrect model if one begins by writing down a list of attributes and dependencies, since all the advantages and safeguards of conceptual modeling have been removed. Moreover, the set of dependencies is usually very limited (in some cases, only FDs are specified!) so that many of the application's constraints are simply ignored.

Another problem with normalization is that it can't change the set of attributes. Hence, apart from ignoring transformations which involve other kinds of constraint, normalization misses semantic optimization opportunities which might arise by allowing transformations to change attributes. For example, it is unable to transform {dept → location, (dept, sex) → nr_staff} into {dept → location, dept → nr_males, dept → nr_females}. Compare this with the ORM schema optimization approach.

Considerations such as these indicate that use of normalization alone is inadequate as a design method. Nevertheless the use of normalization as a check on one's conceptual modeling may at times be helpful. On the positive side, by limiting their scope to a small but important class of constraints, and ignoring semantic transformations, normalization theorists have been able to rigorously prove several interesting results.

The output of both the synthesis and decomposition techniques is a set of table schemes each of which is guaranteed to be in a particular "normal form". We will have a closer look at normal forms presently. The synthesis algorithm basically groups attributes into tables by finding a minimum, reduced, annular cover for the original dependencies. Redundant FDs (e.g. transitive FDs) are removed, redundant source attributes (those on the left of a "→") are removed, and FDs with the same source attribute are placed in the same table. With respect to its specified class of dependencies and attributes, the synthesis algorithm guarantees a design with the minimum number of tables, where each table is in elementary key normal form (see later for a definition of this notion).

For example, given the FDs {emp# → sex, emp# → birthdate, emp# → job, job → salary, emp# → salary}, synthesis generates two tables: *R1* (emp#, sex, birthdate); *R2* (job, salary). While this example is trivial, for more complex cases the execution of the synthesis algorithm is arduous, and is best relegated to a computer. It should be apparent that the derived fact type checks in the CSDP, and the basic fact type grouping in Rmap, have a close correspondence to the synthesis method.

Unlike synthesis, the decomposition approach to normalization is an iterative one, progressively splitting badly designed tables into smaller ones until finally they are free of certain update anomalies; and it provides no guarantee of minimality of number of tables. However, the decomposition approach is more well known, and some modelers find its principles useful for correcting poor relational designs.

Although the synthesis approach is technically more interesting, a proper treatment of it requires a level of mathematical sophistication beyond that assumed for the readers of this book. Hence the rest of this section focuses on the decomposition approach, with some comparisons to ORM. To assist the reader who may read this section out of sequence, some basic concepts treated earlier are briefly reviewed.

A relational schema obtained by Rmapping it from a correct ORM conceptual schema is already fully normalized. Suppose however that some error was made in either the conceptualization or the mapping, or that the relational schema was designed directly without using a conceptual schema. It is now possible that some of the table designs might be unsafe because some conceptual constraint is not enforced. If a conceptual constraint may be violated when a table is updated by inserting, deleting or modifying a row, the table design is said to contain an update anomaly.

Constraints on conceptual reference types are the responsibility of humans; only they can ensure that primary reference schemes actually do provide a correct 1:1-into map from real world entities to data values (or data tuples). Special care is required when an entity type plays just one fact role, this role is not functional, and an instance of this entity type changes its primary identifier.

For example, suppose City occurs only in the *m:n* fact type: RussianTour (#) visits City (name). In the early nineties, the city then known as "Leningrad" reverted to its original name "St Petersburg". As an exercise, discuss some problems arising if only some instances of "Leningrad" are renamed.

Assuming primary reference schemes are already enforced, the information system itself should normally enforce all the fact type constraints. So all constraints on (and between) conceptual fact types should be captured in the relational schema. The normalization procedure ensures that most of these constraints are so captured. In particular, it aims to remove any chance of redundancy (repetition of an elementary fact). If a fact were duplicated in the database, when the fact changed it would be necessary to update every instance of it, otherwise the database would become inconsistent.

Table 10.1 A nested structure

Student#	*Sex*	*Cars*	*Results*	
			Subject	*Rating*
1001	F	ABC123 PKJ155	CS100 CS114 PD102	6 7 6
1002	M		CS100 MA104	6 5

Starting with a possibly bad table design, the normalization procedure applies rules to successively refine it into higher "normal forms" until it is fully normalized. We confine our attention to the main normal forms that focus on eliminating problems with a table by splitting it into smaller ones. There are seven such normal forms. In increasing order of acceptability these are: first normal form (1NF), second normal form (2NF), third normal form (3NF), elementary key normal form (EKNF), Boyce/Codd normal form (BCNF), fourth normal form (4NF) and fifth normal form (5NF).

The first three forms were originally proposed by E. F. Codd, who founded the relational model of data. The other forms were introduced later to cater for additional cases. These improvements were due to the work of several researchers including Codd, Boyce, Fagin, Aho, Beeri and Ullman. Other normal forms have also been proposed (e.g. domain-key normal form, horizontal normal form) but are not discussed here.

A table is normalized, or in **first normal form** (1NF), if and only if its attributes are single-valued and fixed. In other words, a 1NF table has a fixed number of columns, and each entry in a row-column position is a simple value (possibly null). For example, consider the output report shown as Table 10.1. While the first two columns store only atomic values, the Cars column stores sets of values, and the Results column holds sets of (subject, rating) pairs. To model this in a relational database we need to flatten the structure out into three tables: ***Student*** (<u>student#</u>, sex); ***Drives*** (<u>student#, car</u>); and ***Scores*** (<u>student#, subject</u>, rating). Hence, 1NF relations are often called *flat relations*.

However it is possible to model the structure directly by using a relation that is not in first normal form. For example, we might use the following *nested relation* scheme:

Student (<u>student#</u>, sex, *Car* (reg#), *Result* (subject, rating))

Here an entry in the third column is itself a relation (in this case, a set of car registration numbers). Similarly, each entry in the Result column is a relation (with subject and rating attributes). Since the logical data model underlying this approach allows relations to be nested inside relations, it is called the *nested relational model*.

Since the table is not in 1NF it is not a relational table (i.e. it does not conform to the standard relational model of data). The table is said to be in *non-first-normal-form* (NFNF or NF^2). Although promising, nested relational systems have yet to make any significant commercial impact and are ignored for the rest of this section. While tables not in 1NF might be in some other exotic "normal form", it is common practice to refer to them as being "unnormalized".

Table 10.2 This table is in 1NF but not 2NF

Athlete (athletename, sport, height)

athletename	sport	height
Jones E	tennis	180
Jones E	footy	180
Smith T	tennis	170

Set-valued fields like Cars in Table 10.1 are sometimes called "repeating attributes", and fields like Results which hold sets of grouped values are sometimes called "repeating groups". This term may be used to include the notion of repeating attribute by allowing degenerate groups with one value. Using this older, if somewhat misleading, terminology we may say that 1NF tables have no repeating groups.

Another example of an unnormalized table is the "variant record type" used in languages such as Pascal and Modula. Here different "rows" in the same record type may contain different fields. For instance a record type about colored geometric figures may include common fields for figure-id, color and shape (circle, rhombus, triangle etc.) but have different remaining fields depending on the shape (e.g. radius for circle; side and angle for rhombus; three sides for triangle). Although this provides one way to implement a restricted notion of subtypes, the record structure used is completely unnormalized.

Recall that a *key* of a table is a set of one or more attributes spanned by an explicit uniqueness constraint. Here "explicit" excludes any UCs which are implied by shorter UCs inside them; so keys are spanned by "minimal" UCs. For a given relation, an attribute is a *key attribute* if and only if it belongs to some key (primary or secondary) of the relation. A *nonkey* attribute is neither a key nor a part of a composite key.

Given attributes X and Y of a relation, *X functionally determines Y* if and only if Y is a function of X (i.e. given any possible population of the table, for each value of X there is only one value for Y). We write this $X \rightarrow Y$, and say that Y is *functionally dependent* on X. Attributes X and Y may be composite.

A table is in **second normal form** (2NF) if and only if it is in 1NF and every nonkey attribute is (functionally) dependent on the whole of a key (not just a part of it). If a table is normalized it will be in at least 1NF. Since any table in a higher normal form is also in all lower normal forms, let us use the term "hNF" to describe the highest normal form of a table. Consider Table 10.2. Its hNF = 1 since height, a nonkey attribute, is functionally dependent on athletename, which is just part of the composite key. This FD is shown as an arrow above the table.

Notice the redundancy: the fact that Jones E has a height of 180 cm has been recorded twice. To avoid redundancy we must split the original Athlete table into two smaller ones, as shown in Figure 10.1. This figure shows both the conceptual and relational schemas for the example (assuming the information is mandatory for athletes). If you verbalized table 10.2 correctly in terms of elementary facts, you would obtain this conceptual schema directly, and the relational schema would follow automatically using Rmap.

You would have to be a real novice to verbalize Table 10.2 in terms of a ternary; but suppose you did. The checks provided in the CSDP, especially steps 4 and 5, prompt you to discover the functional fact type: Athlete has Height. On seeing this, you would know to split the ternary into two binaries.

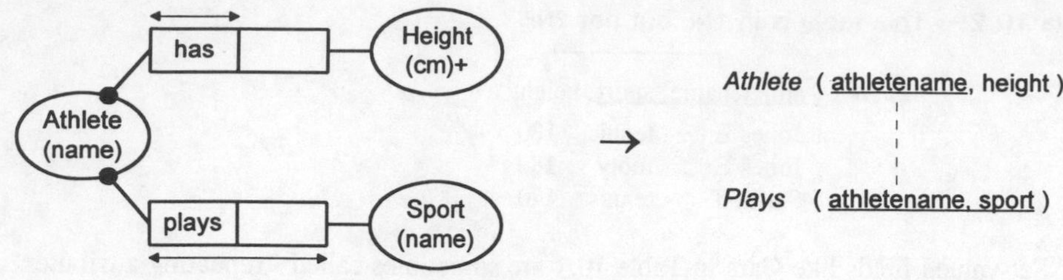

Figure 10.1 Conceptual and relational schemas for Table 10.2

If you were careless enough in applying the CSDP, you could end up with the ternary in your relational schema. At this stage you could look for an FD coming from only part of a key, and use the 2NF normalization rule to at last correct your error. Even at this level one should think in terms of the functional fact type behind the FD.

Recall that if fact types are elementary, all FDs are implied by UCs. This property is preserved by Rmap, since it groups together only functional fact types with a common key. So if we find an FD in a relational schema that is not implied by a UC, we must have gone wrong earlier. Since UCs imply FDs, every nonkey attribute is functionally dependent on any key of the relation. Note that to determine the hNF of a relation we need to be told what the relevant dependencies are (e.g. keys and FDs) or have a significant population from which these may be deduced.

Although normalization to 2NF overcomes the redundancy problem in the original Athlete table, this reduces the efficiency of those queries which now have to access both the new tables. For example if we want the name and height of all the footy players, the 2NF design means that two tables must be searched and their athletename fields matched. This kind of efficiency loss, which is common to each normalization refinement (each involves splitting), is usually more than offset by the higher degree of data integrity resulting from the elimination of redundancy.

For example, if we need to change the height of Jones E to 182 cm, and record this change on only the first row of the original Athlete table we now have two different values for the height. With more serious examples (e.g. defense, medical, business) such inconsistencies could prove disastrous.

As discussed in section 9.6, one may sometimes denormalize by introducing controlled redundancy to speed up queries. The redundancy is then safe; however control of the redundancy is more expensive to enforce than in fully normalized tables, where redundancy is eliminated simply by enforcing primary key constraints. In short, normalization tends to make updates more efficient (by making constraints easier to enforce) while slowing down queries that now require additional table joins.

Given attributes X and Y (possibly composite), if $X \rightarrow Y$, then an update of X entails a possible update of Y. Within a relation, a set of attributes is *mutually independent* if and only if none of the attributes is (functionally) dependent on any of the others. In this case the attributes may be updated independently of one another.

A table is in **third normal form** (3NF) if and only if it is in 2NF and its *nonkey attributes are mutually independent*. Hence, in a 3NF table no FD can be transitively implied by two FDs, one of which is an FD between two nonkey attributes.

Table 10.3 This table is in 2NF but not 3NF

Lecturer (<u>surname</u>, department, building)

surname	department	building
Halpin	CS	69
Okimura	JA	1
Orlowska	CS	69
Wang	CN	1

Consider Table 10.3. Its hNF = 2, since building depends on department, and these are both nonkey attributes. Note that building is transitively dependent on the key (surname determines department, and department determines building).

Table 10.3 exhibits redundancy: the fact that the CS department is located in building 69 is shown twice. To avoid this redundancy, the fact type underlying the FD between the nonkey attributes is split off to another table. This results in two 3NF tables: ***WorksFor*** **(<u>surname</u>, department)**; ***LocatedIn*** **(<u>department</u>, building)**. You may recall that this example was discussed in detail in section 5.3, to illustrate the logical derivation check at step 5 of the CSDP. If this CSDP step has been carried out properly, FDs from one non-key attribute to another cannot arise in any tables obtained from Rmap.

Moreover, the logical derivation check in the CSDP requires the following rule: Lecturer works in Building **iff** Lecturer works for Department **and** Department is located in Building. If the "only if" part of the "iff" in this biconditional is not satisfied then the two table design loses information. For example, suppose in Table 10.3 that Wang does not work for any department (e.g. Wang might be a visiting lecturer who works in some general office). The last row of this table now becomes ⟨Wang, ?, 1⟩.

The original work on normalization assumed that nulls do not occur, but this assumption is often false. If we agree with Codd (1990 p. 201) that nulls should be ignored when applying rules about FDs, then the FDs shown above Table 10.3 still exist; but it is wrong to now simply decompose this table into two, so this normalization step can be unsafe. Clearly, the easiest and safest way to deal with such issues is at the conceptual level.

Codd's original definitions of 2NF and 3NF used "key" in the sense of primary key; so attributes of alternate keys were regarded as nonkey attributes. However, nowadays an attribute is termed a key attribute if it belongs to *some* key (primary or alternate); so a nonkey attribute belongs to *no* key.

Hence, in one sense the definition of 3NF does allow transitive dependencies if the intermediate attribute is a key. Consider the relation scheme: ***Employee*** **(<u>emp#</u>, <u>empname</u>, sex)**. It has two keys. One might argue that the FD emp# → sex is transitively implied by the FDs: emp# → empname; empname → sex. However the relation is still in 3NF as there is no FD between nonkey attributes.

Let X and Y be attributes (possibly composite) of the same table. A functional dependency $X \rightarrow Y$ is *trivial* if and only if X contains Y. A functional dependency $X \rightarrow Y$ is *full* (rather than partial) if and only if there is no FD from just part of X to Y. A full, nontrivial FD is said to be an *elementary FD*. We avoid displaying non-elementary FDs because they are obviously implied by the elementary FDs.

Table 10.4 This table is in 3NF but not EKNF

Enrollment (student#, studentname, subjectcode)

student#	studentname	subjectcode
1001	Adams F	CS100
1001	Adams F	CS114
1002	Brown S	CS114

A key is an *elementary key* if there is an elementary FD from it to some attribute in the table. An attribute is an elementary key attribute just in case it belongs to some elementary key. We may now define the next strongest normal form, which was proposed as an improvement on 3NF (Zaniolo 1982).

A table is in **elementary key normal form** (EKNF) if and only if all its elementary FDs begin at whole keys or end at elementary key attributes. In other words, for every full, nontrivial FD of the form $X \rightarrow Y$, either X is a key or Y is (part of) an elementary key. If the primary key of a table includes all its columns, the table is automatically in EKNF since it has no elementary FDs; for example: *Enrollment* (student#, subjectcode).

Suppose that students also have a unique name, and we store their names in the same table (see Table 10.4). This table has two composite keys: (student#, subjectcode); (studentname, subjectcode). The primary key is indicated by a double-underline; since its attributes are not adjacent, arrow tips are added to emphasize that this is a single, composite key constraint rather than two simple key constraints. The secondary key is indicated by a single underline.

Since Table 10.4 has no nonkey attributes it is automatically in 3NF. However it has obvious problems (e.g. the fact that student 1001 is named 'Adams F' is duplicated). One way of spotting this bad design is to note that the table is not in EKNF. There is an FD from student# to studentname, and another FD from studentname to student# (depicted by arrows above the table). These elementary FDs come from parts of keys rather than whole keys; and these FDs do not end at elementary attributes, since neither of the composite keys is elementary. So the table is not in EKNF.

The redundancy problem can be avoided by splitting the table into two EKNF tables: *Student* (student#, studentname); *Enrollment* (student#, subjectcode). The two FDs missed in the original table scheme are now captured by key constraints in the Student table. Of course the same design is automatically obtained by Rmapping the correct conceptual schema, which has two elementary fact types: Student has Studentname; Student enrolled in Subject.

The next normal form is named after Boyce and Codd, who proposed it as an improvement on the old 3NF. An equivalent definition was given earlier by Heath (1971). A table is in **Boyce-Codd Normal Form** (BCNF) if and only if *all its elementary FDs begin at whole keys* (i.e. given any full, nontrivial FD $X \rightarrow Y$, it must be that X is a key). The only time that a relation can be in 3NF (or EKNF) but not in BCNF is when it has at least two candidate keys that overlap (Vincent & Srinivasan 1994).

As an example, consider Table 10.5. This is like the previous table, except that subject ratings are recorded for each student. The keys are now elementary, since they functionally determine the rating attribute. Since the FDs between student# and studentname now end at elementary attributes, the table is in EKNF. But the table has the same redundancy as the previous table.

Table 10.5 This table is in EKNF but not BCNF

Result (student#, studentname, subjectcode, rating)

student#	studentname	subjectcode	rating
1001	Adams F	CS100	6
1001	Adams F	CS114	7
1002	Brown S	CS114	7

One way to spot this problem is to note that it is not in BCNF, since the FDs shown above the table do not start at whole keys. For instance, the functional dependency student# → studentname exists, but student# is only part of the (student#, subjectcode) key.

The redundancy problem can be avoided by splitting the table into two BCNF tables: *Student* (student#, studentname); *Scored* (student#, subjectcode, rating). As an exercise, show how this design follows immediately from a correct conceptual schema.

The principle underlying the refinement to second and third normal forms has been nicely summarized by Kent (1983) as follows: "a nonkey field must provide a fact about the key, the whole key, and nothing but the key". This should be refined by replacing "the key" by "a key", and treated as a description of BCNF rather than 3NF.

In the previous two examples, a table with overlapping keys had to be split. Sometimes overlapping keys are permitted. Recall the example from chapter 4 where students are assigned unique positions in subjects, with no ties. This leads to the BCNF table scheme: *PlacedAt* (student#, subjectcode, position).

The previous normal forms considered only functional dependencies. The next normal form is due to Fagin (1977) and considers *multivalued dependencies* (MVDs). For a given relation with attributes *X*, *Y* and *Z* (possibly composite), *X multidetermines Y* (written as $X \twoheadrightarrow Y$) if and only if the *set* of *Y* values is a function of *X* only (independent of the value of *Z*). In this case, *Y* is said to be multivalued dependent, or multidependent, on *X*; in such a case *Z* will also be multidependent on *X*. A functional dependency is a special case of an MVD , namely when the set of dependent values is a unit set. An MVD $X \twoheadrightarrow Y$ is trivial if *X* includes *Y*, or *X* and *Y* together include all the attributes in the relation.

A relation is in **fourth normal form** (4NF) if and only if it is in BCNF and all its nontrivial dependencies are functional (single-valued) dependencies. So a 4NF relation cannot have any nontrivial MVDs that are not FDs. Basically, each non-functional MVD requires a separate table for itself.

Consider Table 10.6. It is in BCNF since it is "all-key". The table is not in 4NF since, for example, sport is multidependent (but not functionally dependent) on surname. A similar comment applies to language. These MVDs are depicted as double arrows above the table.

Semantically, the MVDs correspond to two *m:n* elementary fact types: Lecturer plays Sport; Lecturer speaks Language. So the table has redundancy problems. The facts that Halpin plays judo and speaks English are duplicated. To avoid this problem, the table is split into two 4NF tables: *Plays* (surname, sport); *Speaks* (surname, language). Of course, this design may also be achieved by Rmapping the correct conceptual schema.

It can be shown that BCNF is equivalent to no redundancy when there are FDs, and 4NF is equivalent to no redundancy when there are FDs and MVDs (Vincent & Srinivasan 1993).

Table 10.6 This table is in BCNF but not 4NF

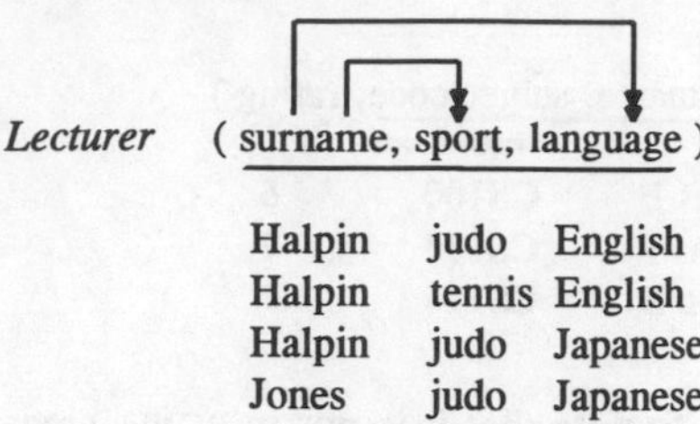

The next normal form is also due to Fagin (1979), and is based on *join dependencies* (JDs). A relation has a join dependency if it can be reconstructed without information loss by taking a join of some of its projections. If one of these projections is the table itself, this is a trivial join dependency. A table is in **fifth normal form** (**5NF**) if and only if, for each nontrivial join dependency, each projection includes a key of the original table. A table is in **project-join normal form** (**PJNF**) just in case each JD is the result of the key constraints. The forms 5NF and PJ/NF are often treated as equivalent, but some subtle differences can be distinguished to show that PJ/NF is a stonger notion (Orlowska & Zhang 1992).

As an example of a key-based join dependency, *Employee* (emp#, birthdate, sex) is equivalent to the join of the projections: *Emp1* (emp#, birthdate); *Emp2* (emp#, sex). The original table as well as the two smaller ones are all in 5NF. Since a relational schema is in a given normal form if its tables are all in that form, a relational schema which includes just the Emp1 and Emp2 tables is a 5NF schema. This illustrates that 5NF of itself does not guarantee that a schema is minimal with respect to number of tables.

Nontrivial join dependencies that are not key-based are rare, so 4NF tables are almost always in 5NF as well. The theory underlying the test for 5NF was included in the projection-join check at CSDP step 4, so we confine ourselves here to a brief discussion. A classic example to discuss the notion is portrayed in Table 10.7. A small sample population has been provided to show that the uniqueness constraint is the weakest possible (verify this for yourself).

Conceptually, this ternary fact type may be expressed as: Agent sells Cartype for Company. The fact types behind the three binary projections may be expressed as: Agent sells Cartype; Agent represents Company; Company makes Cartype. Assuming the population is significant, any attempt to split this ternary into two binaries will result in information loss. For example, from the facts that Smith is a representative for Foord and Foord makes a 4-wheel drive (4WD), it does not follow that Smith sells a 4WD.

Table 10.7 Is this in 5NF?

Sells (agent, cartype, company)

agent	cartype	company
Jones	sedan	Foord
Jones	4WD	Foord
Jones	sedan	Yotsubishi
Smith	sedan	Foord

However, the population of the ternary (Table 10.7) does equal the join of the three binary projections (confirm this for yourself). So it is safe to split this particular table population into three binary table populations. But since database populations are continually updated, if we are to split the table scheme into three binary table schemes we need to know that this join dependency applies to all possible populations. In other words, is the sample population significant in this regard? If it is, the following derivation rule applies:

Agent sells Cartype for Company **iff** Agent sells Cartype **and**
Agent represents Company **and**
Company makes Cartype

The only way to check that this is an actual business rule is to ask the UoD expert. Let's suppose that it's *not* a rule. For example, it is now acceptable to delete just the first row of Table 10.7 (check for yourself that this deletion should be rejected if the rule did apply). In this case, the ternary fact type is elementary and should be left as it is. Let us define a table *scheme* (table type) to be in a given normal form if and only if all its possible populations (table instances) are in that form. If the derivation rule does not apply, the Sells table *scheme* is already in 5NF.

Now suppose the derivation rule *does* apply. This rule needs to be enforced, but the key constraint in the ternary fails to do this (e.g. it allows the first row to be deleted). To avoid this problem, the 4NF ternary should be split into three 5NF binaries: ***Sells*** (agent, cartype); ***Represents*** (agent, company); ***Makes*** (company, cartype). If desired, the original ternary may be defined as a view derived from the join of the new tables.

It has been argued (e.g. by Kent) that when schemes like the ternary in Table 10.7 are elementary there is a kind of "unavoidable redundancy". For example, the "fact" that Jones sells sedans is repeated on rows 1 and 3. However, such "redundancy" is harmless because it is derived rather than stored. Although the tuple ⟨'Jones','sedan'⟩ is stored twice, the fact that Jones sells sedans is not. This fact can only be obtained by using the derivation rule: Agent sells Cartype iff Agent sells Cartype for Company.

The seven normal forms discussed so far are strictly ordered. Each higher normal form satisfies the lower forms. Recall that "⊂" denotes "is a proper subset of". Let "5NF-rels" denote the set of all possible relations in fifth normal form, and so on. The strict ordering may now be set out thus (in decreasing order of normality):

5NF-rels ⊂ 4NF-rels ⊂ BCNF-rels ⊂ EKNF-rels ⊂ 3NF-rels ⊂ 2NF-rels ⊂ 1NF-rels

Essentially, normalization through to fifth normal form simplifies table updates by ensuring that three kinds of dependency (FDs, MVDs and JDs) will automatically be enforced by key constraints (i.e. uniqueness constraints within each table). An FD is a special case of an MVD, which in turn is a special case of a JD. As noted by Fagin, BCNF ensures all FDs are implied by key constraints, 4NF ensures all MVDs are implied by key constraints, and 5NF ensures all JDs are implied by key constraints.

Obviously, many other kinds of constraint (dependency) may arise in real applications, and normalization to 5NF does not ensure that these constraints are captured in the relational schema. A modified version of an awkward but classic example is set out in Table 10.8. In this UoD, lecturers are assigned exactly one subject, and this is the only subject they may teach.

Table 10.8 An unusual and awkward example

Lecturer	*Subject*	*Student*
Halpin	CS113	Brown A
Rose	CS102	Brown A
Nijssen	CS113	Smith J
Rose	CS102	Smith J
Halpin	CS113	Wang J
Bloggs	CS226	?

The null value indicates that Bloggs does not teach the assigned subject (e.g. because too few enrolled for it). For each subject they take, students have exactly one lecturer. The same subject may have many assigned lecturers. Because of its strange constraint pattern, this example is not easy to verbalize in elementary facts on a first attempt. You are invited to try this before reading on.

An initial conceptual schema based on one verbalization is depicted in Figure 10.2. If this is the global schema, the mandatory role constraints are implied by the pair-subset constraint. More importantly, the uniqueness constraint on the binary combined with the pair-subset constraint have other implications. Can you spot these?

The pair-subset constraint indicates that lecturers may teach only their assigned subjects, but the uniqueness constraint on the binary indicates that each lecturer is assigned at most one subject. Hence lecturers may teach at most one subject: so there is an FD from the first role of the ternary to the second role; this implies the UC across the first and third roles; moreover, since there is a third role in the ternary, the fact type now cannot be elementary. This is an example of the general rule set out in Figure 10.3.

If a fact type is elementary, all its FDs are the result of its UCs. If another FD exists, then semantically underlying this FD is another fact type, which is the target of a pair-subset constraint from the original fact type. If this is expressed at the conceptual level we know the original fact type is not elementary, and should remove the relevant role (as in Figure 10.3).

The ternary in Figure 10.3 matches this pattern, but has an additional UC across its last two roles (for each subject, a student has only one lecturer). To preserve this constraint after removing the role, an external UC must be added between the subject and student roles in the new schema (see Figure 10.4).

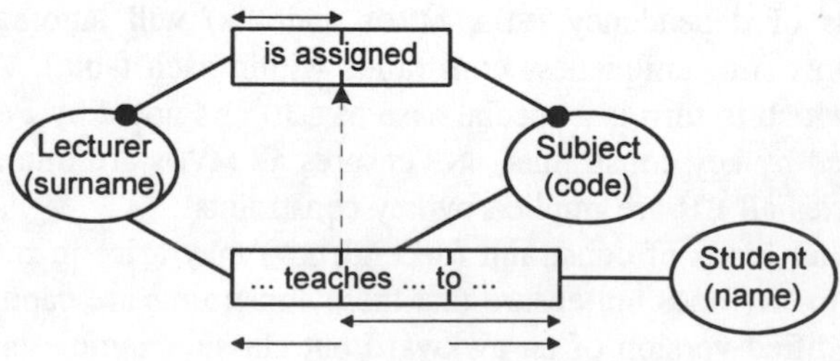

Figure 10.2 Is the ternary fact type elementary?

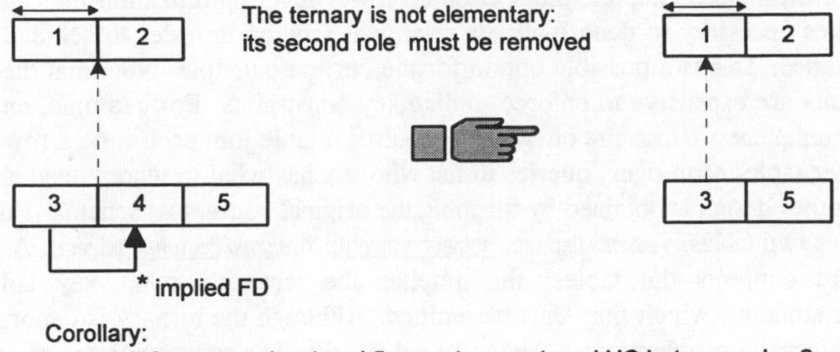

Figure 10.3 A basic splittability check

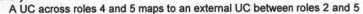

The general requirement for this extra move is specified as a corollary in Figure 10.3. When the corrected conceptual schema is Rmapped, we obtain two table schemes with two inter-table constraints (Figure 10.4).

Suppose that instead of dealing with table 10.8 conceptually, we try to develop a relational schema for it by applying the normal form theory discussed earlier. We might begin with a single ternary: Teaches (lecturer, subject, [student]). Suppose that someone either tells us all the constraints or cleverly constructs a significant population from which the constraints can be deduced. We note that there are two composite "key" constraints over (lecturer, student) and (subject, student). Since student is an optional attribute, neither of these can be used as a primary key, so we know something is wrong (although the normal form theory discussed earlier ignored nulls). Indeed we know the table is not in BCNF since we are given the FD lecturer → subject, and lecturer is not a key.

At this stage we split the table into two: *Assigned* (lecturer, subject); *Instructs* (lecturer, student). These are the same two tables we arrived at by deconceptualization in Figure 10.4. However the normal form theory discussed in this section tells us nothing about the two inter-table constraints; we have to figure these out for ourselves.

Of course, one could invent further normal forms to cater for further constraints, but surely it is better to focus on cleaning up design faults at the conceptual level where humans can more easily utilize their semantic understanding of the UoD.

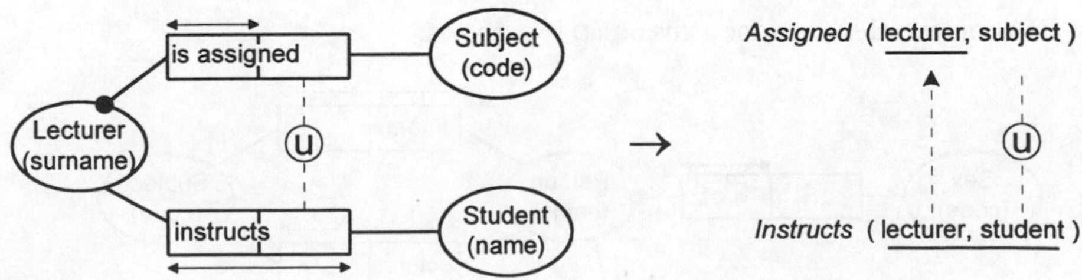

Figure 10.4 The corrected conceptual schema and its relational map

In the previous chapter, the section on lower level optimization indicated that it is sometimes necessary to denormalize a relational schema in order to achieve acceptable performance. This is a possible option for the current example. Note that the inter-table constraints are expensive to enforce, unlike key constraints. For example, enforcing the external uniqueness constraint effectively requires a table join each time a row is inserted into either table. Moreover, queries to list who teaches what to whom need a table join.

Another design is obtained by mapping the original conceptual schema (Figure 10.2). This gives two tables: *Teaches* (lecturer, subject, student); *Assigned* (lecturer, subject). A pair-subset constraint connects the tables; this implies the ternary's other key constraint on (lecturer,student), which may thus be omitted. Although the ternary is denormalized, it is safe since its problematic FD is enforced by the pair-subset constraint and the key constraint in the binary. We may now list who teaches what to whom, without a table join. If this is a focused query for the application, this design might be preferred.

To modify the example somewhat, suppose lecturers must teach the subject assigned to them (so the null value in Table 10.8 cannot occur). Figure 10.2 is changed to make both roles of Lecturer mandatory, with the subset constraint becoming an equality constraint. Figure 10.4 is changed to make both roles of Lecturer mandatory, and the relational subset constraint becomes an equality constraint.

If the normalized, two table design has poor performance we might choose a denormalized design with a single table that is their natural join: *Teaches* (lecturer, subject, student). The revised Figure 10.2 (with the equality constraint) makes it clear that assignment facts can be retrieved by projecting on the first two roles of the ternary, but that the uniqueness constraint on the assignment binary still needs to be catered for. In the denormalized ternary, this constraint cannot be enforced as a uniqueness constraint, so a separate constraint is required to enforce the FD: lecturer → subject. So long as this additional constraint is enforced (e.g. as a user-defined constraint in SQL), the single table design is safe. As before, the alternate key constraint is implied and hence omitted.

Advances in relational languages are making it easier to specify extra constraints such as FDs which are not key-based; however the overhead of enforcing such constraints needs to factored in when choosing the final relational design. In general, one should first try a fully normalized design, using conceptual optimization where relevant to improve it. If performance is still unacceptable, controlled denormalization is an option.

Exercise 10.2

1. The conceptual schema for a given UoD is as shown.

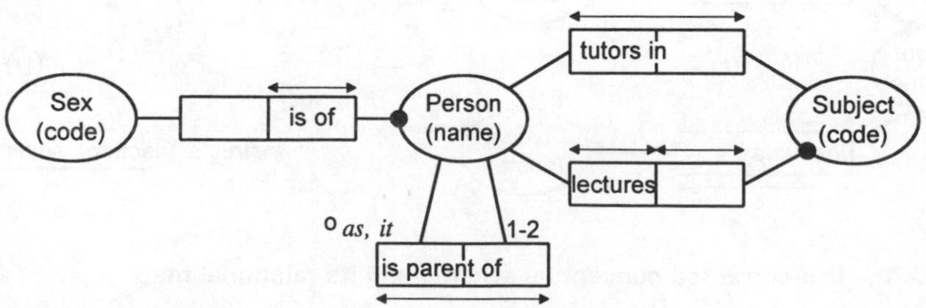

Some table schemes designed by novices for parts of this UoD are listed below. Indicate briefly, in terms of normalization theory, why each of these tables is not fully normalized.

(a) *Parenthood* (parentname, sex, *Child*(childname, sex))
(b) *Teaches* (person, subjectTutored, [subjectLectured])
(c) *ParentOf* (parent, child, sex_of_parent, sex_of_child)
(d) *Tutor* (tutorname, subject, [child])
(e) Use Rmap to generate a correct relational schema.

2. (a) The conceptual schema of Q. 1 is incomplete with respect to real world constraints. For example, parents of the same child must differ in sex, but this constraint is not captured. Replace the parent predicate with mother and father predicates, to develop a more complete schema which includes this constraint (Hint: include subtyping).
(b) Rmap your solution to (a).

3. Suppose that while developing a conceptual schema you specify the following fact type: Manager supervises Trainee on Project. Assume that no manager is a trainee, and that all objects are simply identified by name. The following constraint applies: no manager may supervise the same trainee on more than one project.

(a) Draw this as a ternary fact type, including the constraint.
(b) As part of the CSDP, you check whether there are any other functional fact types of interest between these object types. You now discover that each manager supervises at most one project. Add this binary fact type to your schema, then add any set-comparison constraint that you feel applies.
(c) Is the ternary elementary? If not, explain why not, and correct the schema.
(d) The following business rule is now added: each trainee on a given project has only one supervisor for that project. Add this constraint to your schema.
(e) Rmap your answer to (d).
(f) Because of poor performance, this relational schema is regarded as unsatisfactory. Using controlled denormalization, suggest an alternative relational schema.

4. This question is based on an example from a colleague, Dr Bob Colomb. A simpler version of the problem was discussed by Zaniolo in motivating EKNF and BCNF. As this problem involves some more advanced ORM concepts, it should be considered a challenge.

The application deals with a directory for making international, direct dial telephone calls. Suppose the following table scheme is used to store the data :

PlaceCodes (countryname, statename, cityname, countrycode, areacode)

The first key denotes the city (e.g. Australia, Queensland, Brisbane) and the second key gives the dial codes to phone that city (e.g. 61, 7). From a normalization point of view, the table has problems because there are some FDs which are not key-based. In particular, countryname → countrycode. It is not the case however that countrycode → countryname (e.g. both Canada and the USA have the country code 1). Note also that three values are needed to identify a city (e.g. different countries could have states and cities with the same simple names).

(a) Draw a conceptual schema for this UoD. If any relationship type is derivable, indicate this. You may make use of the fact that external uniqueness constraints may be declared across any join path. If any subset constraints apply (possibly from a join) these should be specified. Ensure that the fact types are all elementary.

(b) Rmap your solution.

(c) Discuss whether a denormalized relational schema may be more appropriate.

(d) If you've got this far, have a break (fortunately, you don't run into problems like this very often!).

10.3 Schema abstraction and ER modeling

At times one might feel almost swamped by the level of detail captured on an ORM conceptual schema diagram, or even on a relational schema. Nevertheless, such detail is important when developing, transforming or mapping a conceptual schema. The ORM notation has been crafted to facilitate these tasks. For example, the diagrams may be verbalized naturally and populated with fact instances, their object-role-based notation allows many constraints to be expressed intuitively, and their object types reveal the semantic domains which glue the schema together. All of this helps the modeler to get a complete and correct picture, and to transform the model in a rigorous way with formal control of information loss or gain.

However, once a schema has been developed, we may at times wish to hide some of the information, in order to obtain a quick overview or to focus on some aspects. This is particularly the case if the schema is large and complex. Hence there is a need for *abstraction mechanisms*, by which unwanted details may be removed from immediate consideration. This section outlines a few of the more useful ways of doing this. The chapter notes provide several references for further study in this regard.

One obvious abstraction strategy is *modularization*. Here the complete schema is "divided up" into a number of conveniently sized modules or subschemas. One trivial way to do this is to overlay a grid, to partition the schema into separate cells. However it is typically more useful to allow modules to overlap, so that for example the same object type might appear in more than one module. This technique also allows greater flexibility in basing modules on semantic groupings.

Various means may be used specify connections between modules, such as delta-buttons, annotations and border-overlaps (cf. a directory of road maps). Electronic browsing opens up greater possibilities than hard-copy browsing (e.g. scrolling, zooming in and out, hypertext navigation), but printed documentation on standard pages needs to be catered for as well.

With large applications, the original schema itself might be developed as separate modules which are later integrated. If this is done, additional care is required for the *schema integration* process. In particular, global consistency must be ensured either by agreeing on a uniform treatment of terminology, constraints and rules or by specifying appropriate translations. Ideally, all the modelers will attach the same meaning to words by resolving any synonym and homonym problems.

For example, if the same object type is called "Subject" in one module and "Course" in another, then one of these will be chosen as the standard term and the other term replaced by it. If different object types or nontrivial predicates in different modules are given the same name, one of these names must be changed.

Global identification schemes and constraints should be agreed upon, and where necessary contextual identification may be supported via subtyping, and textual constraints can be added to strengthen global constraints for a given context (e.g. restricted mandatory role and restricted uniqueness constraints). For some applications (e.g. federated databases) partial integration between relevant modules may be favored instead of global integration.

Another useful abstraction mechanism is provided by *constraint and rule toggles*. Here the display of one or more classes of constraint or derivation rule may be toggled off when they are not of immediate interest, in order to obtain a simpler picture.

For example, one might toggle off value lists, ring constraints, frequency constraints, set-comparison constraints, textual constraints and derivation rules in order to focus on uniqueness and mandatory role constraints. Each constraint class may be thought of as a *constraint layer*, with the modeler choosing which layers to view at any given time. An extreme option would be to toggle off all constraints in one go.

Subtype display could be suppressed at two levels: hide the subtype defining rules; collapse subtypes into their top supertype. Reference modes and reference types could also be toggled off. When the additional layers of detail are needed, their display can be toggled on again. Although this layering concept can be adapted to hard copy (e.g. by using a series of overlaid transparencies, or progressively detailed printouts), it should ideally be exploited interactively with a CASE tool.

Yet another abstraction mechanism is *object-type zoom*. Here the modeler selects an object type of interest, in order to have the display focused on that object type and its immediate *neighborhood*. The object type is displayed with all its fact types. By specifying a logical radius for the zoom, the neighborhood may be expanded to include fact types of the object types in the first level zoom, and so on.

A simple example will help illustrate some of the basic ways of abstracting. Figure 10.5 depicts an ORM schema for a small application. Here movies are identified by numbers, though the combination of their title and director is also uniquc. Some movies are based on another. For example, the western about "the magnificent seven" was based on an early Japanese movie about "the seven samurai".

When available, figures about the gross takings of a movie are recorded, and the net profit too if this is known. The only people of interest in this application are movie directors and movie stars. We record their country of birth, and if known, their birthdate. The country in which a movie was made is noted, as well as any export countries for it.

As a mental exercise, imagine toggling off the display of the constraint types on Figure 10.5 one at a time (ring, then set-comparison, then mandatory role, then uniqueness) to visualize abstraction by peeling off constraint layers.

Figure 10.6 depicts a zoom on the object type Person, with a logical radius of 1, so that only the fact types directly connected to Person are shown. To help you associate this with the previous figure, the arrangement of these fact types is unaltered. One might prefer however to have the zoom object type displayed centrally, with its roles clustered about it. Visualize for yourself a zoom on Country: this would display three fact types, one of which is also contained in the Person zoom.

Another abstraction mechanism that is especially useful with large schemas is that of *refinement levels* based on *major object types*. This is often used in conjunction with *attribute abstraction* to provide an Entity-Relationship style diagram.

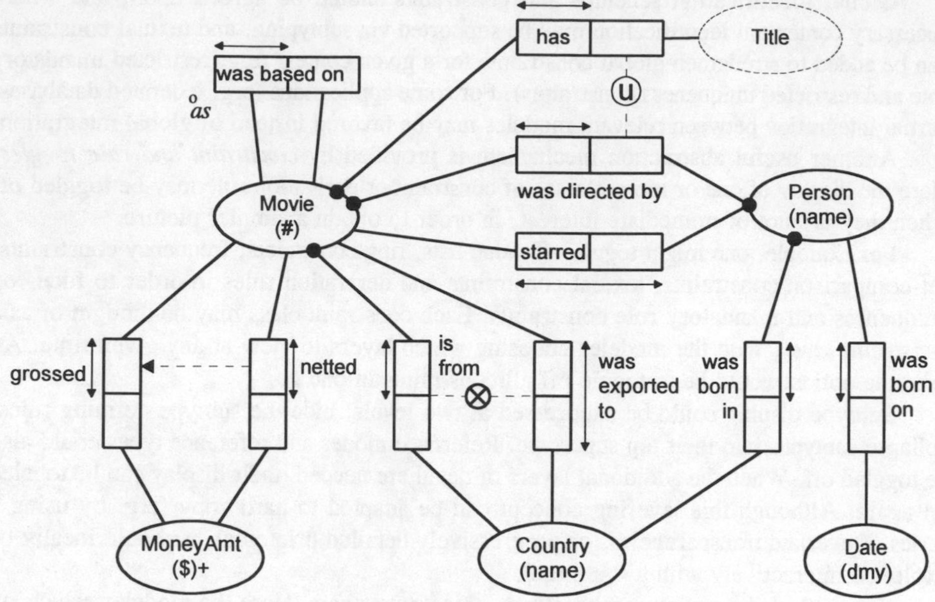

Figure 10.5 A small, but detailed conceptual schema

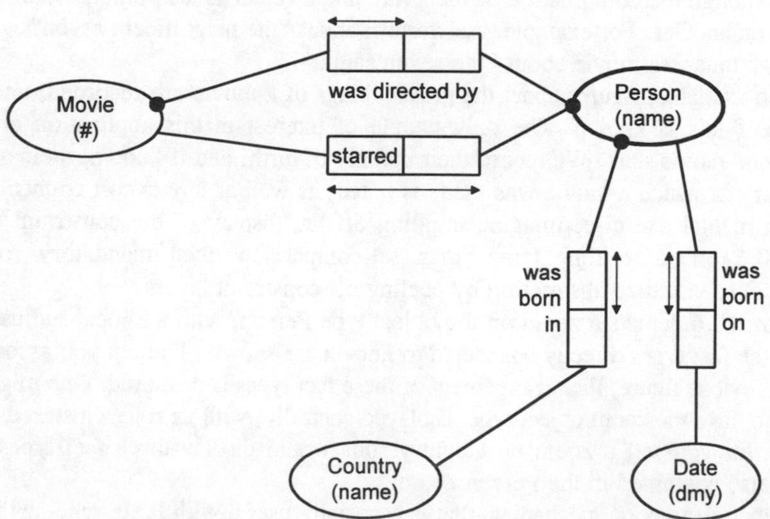

Figure 10.6 Zooming in on the Person object type

When developing a conceptual schema it is useful to treat all object types equally, since the relative importance of an object type is based on all the parts it plays in the global schema. Once the schema is complete however, this information is available and can be used to determine which are the most important, or *major* object types. A procedure for deciding the major object types on ORM schemas was developed by Campbell and Halpin (1993), and used as a basis for generating default screen forms for the external user interface (since application screens basically enable users to performs operations on major objects).

Once the major object types are decided, an ORM diagram can be lifted to a higher level of abstraction. For example, we may choose to display only the "*major fact types*" (i.e. those fact types in which at least two roles are played by a major object type). With large applications, this diagram itself may be subjected to the same procedure, yielding a higher level abstraction, and so on, until the top-level view of the model is obtained. So long as the fully detailed schema is accessible, this bottom-up abstraction may be reversed, allowing the top-level view to be successively refined down to the fully detailed bottom level.

The detailed schema diagram in Figure 10.5 has six object types: Movie; Title; Person; MoneyAmt; Country; and Date. Intuitively, these are not all equally important in this application. Which do you consider to be the major object types?

Apart from using your intuition, you can make use of the constraint patterns to help you decide. In particular, mandatory role and uniqueness constraints are relevant. If an object type has an *explicit* mandatory role, it is major. Usually, an object type playing a functional role is also major, but this is not always the case (e.g. Title would still be a minor object type even if its role was functional; its role is still only implicitly mandatory).

There are some finer points to determining major object types, but this is enough to get the basic idea. Based on the previous reasoning, Figure 10.5 has only two major object types: Movie; and Person. Figure 10.7 provides one overview of the application by displaying only the major fact types.

Instead of being hidden, minor fact types may if desired be viewed in terms of *attributes* of the major object types. Although this attribute viewpoint hides structural information (e.g. domains and certain constraints), the *ER diagram* obtained provides a compact picture which is useful for quick overviews. Figure 10.8 shows an ER diagram for the current example.

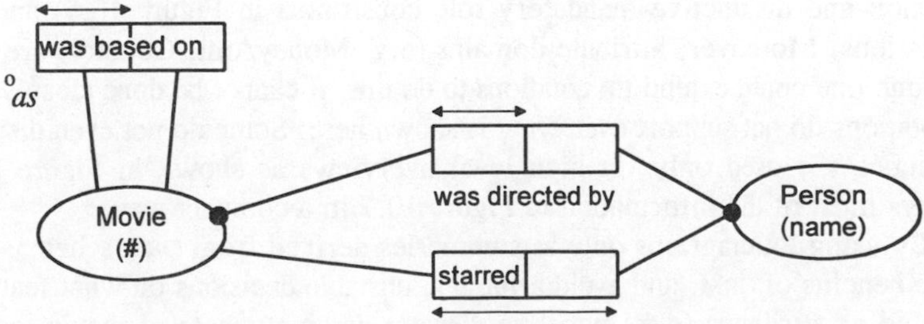

Figure 10.7 Only the major fact types are shown

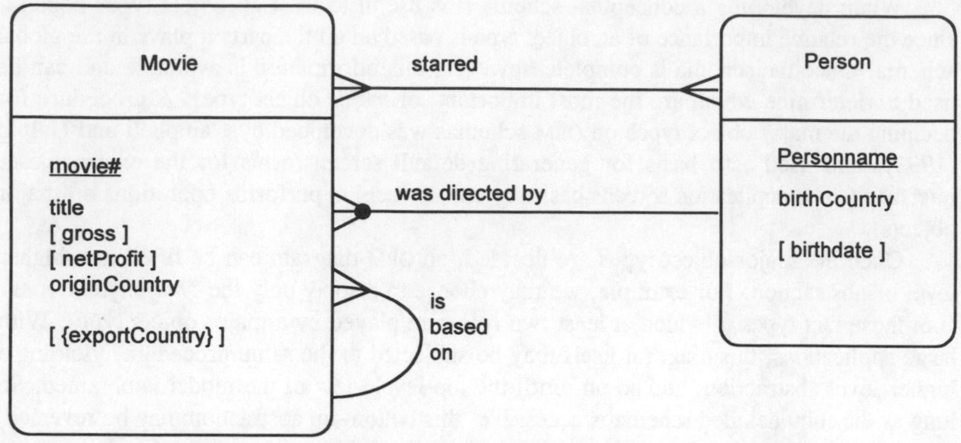

Figure 10.8 An ER diagram abstracted from Figure 10.5

Dozens of different notations exist for ER diagrams. The one presented here uses a rounded rectangle to specify a major object type and its "attributes". The object type name is written in the top section, and the other attribute names in the lower section. As with our relational schema notation, unique attributes are underlined, using a double underline for the primary identifier if other unique attributes exist. Optional attributes are shown in square brackets, and multivalued attributes are shown in braces (e.g. the set of export countries): some versions of ER do not support these two constructs.

Major fact types may be depicted with the usual ORM notation, or more compactly using ER notation (as in Figure 10.8) with predicates depicted as named lines, using "crow's feet" to show the same entity may the role at that end many times. Mandatory roles are indicated as usual with a dot. Some ER notations use a solid line for mandatory and a broken line for optional; some use a double line for mandatory; and some use minimum and maximum numbers for simpler cases of mandatory role and frequency (including uniqueness) constraints.

While ER diagrams are useful for summary purposes, they have their limitations. They do not extend readily to non-binary fact types, and the lack of an object- role-based notation makes them unsuitable for specifying various constraints (e.g. the subset, exclusion and disjunctive mandatory role constraints in Figure 10.5) and showing fact populations. Moreover, attribute domains (e.g. MoneyAmt, Country) are not displayed. Although one could extend ER notations to do this, it cannot be done cleanly. Indeed many ER notations do not support even what is shown here. Some do not even display attributes, and hence are used only for high level overviews as shown in Figure 10.9: this still conveys most of the information in Figure 10.7 in a compact way.

By using ER diagrams only as summaries derived from ORM schemas, we maintain all the benefits of ORM, and avoid arbitrary, unstable decisions on what features should be modeled as attributes (e.g. modeling director as an attribute of movie, only to discover later that we need to store facts about directors and hence must use an entity type instead).

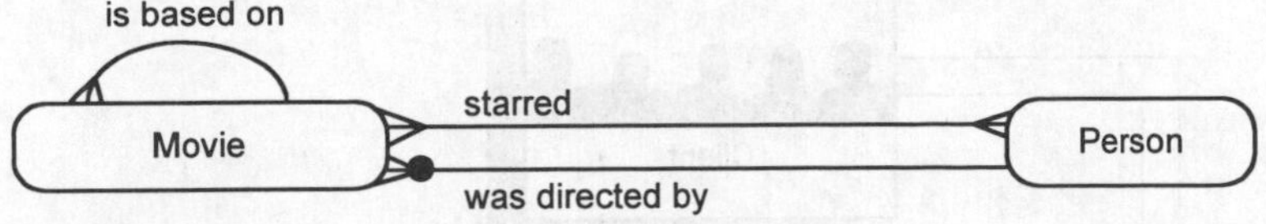

Figure 10.9 An ER diagram with attributes omitted

10.4 Operation modeling and external design

As its title indicates, this book focuses on conceptual schema and relational database design. However the overall information systems life cycle includes other tasks, as discussed in section 3.1. For example, one needs to specify what *operations* are to be performed on the data, and how the *external interface* should be constructed to facilitate these operations. This section provides a brief overview of these two tasks; a detailed coverage may be obtained from the chapter references.

Recall that an information system may be viewed from three perspectives: data; process; and behavior. We have seen how the data design may be specified at the conceptual level (e.g. with an ORM schema) and the logical level (e.g. with a relational schema). A process design specifies the processes or activities of the application, and how information flows occur, while a behavioral design indicates how events trigger such actions. We use the term "operation modeling" to cover both process and behavior.

Suppose we are asked to design an information system for a credit union. As part of the requirements analysis phase, we determine that one function of the system is to produce an account balance when requested by a client. To help clarify this function we might draw a diagram like Figure 10.10. This actually includes all three perspectives.

The *process* to produce an account balance is shown with a rounded rectangle; it has a process number "P1" in the top section for quick reference, with its descriptive name listed below. This process is *triggered* by a request from a client. The issuing of this request is an *event*, which occurs when a client either asks a human teller for the balance or selects this option from an automated teller. On the diagram this is displayed as a thick arrow, with the event described beside it.

For the process to be *executed*, it must be able to identify the specific account. This requires two details to be input from the client: the client's identifier and the type of account (e.g. savings or loan). This *information flow* is shown as a labelled arrow from the Client object type to the process. The relevant balance is stored in the part of the database that holds account details: this data store is labelled "D1" and given the descriptive name "Accounts". The retrieval of the relevant balance is shown as an information flow from the data store to the process.

In this high level view, no detail is provided on the structure of the data store or on how the process manages to find the relevant data. Finally, the process outputs the balance to the client. This is depicted as another data flow.

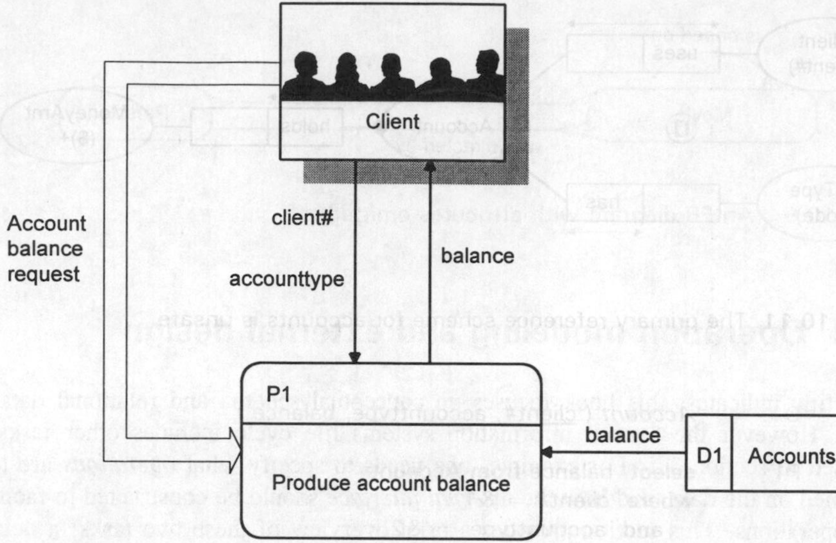

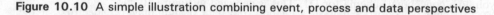

Figure 10.10 A simple illustration combining event, process and data perspectives

Since the details of the process and data store are so far undefined, diagrams like this fail to formally connect process and data perspectives. In spite of such informality, they can be of use in clarifying the UoD, and for identifying functions to be included in the application's screen menus. Indeed, ordinary cartoons with intuitive icons can be quite useful for communication between modeler and client in the early stages of requirements analysis.

To really clarify the UoD however, one should quickly start working with sample instances of the information to be handled by the system. If examples already exist, use these. If they don't, sit down with the client and generate them. These could be in the form of tables, forms, graphs or whatever. By now, you should have the verbalization skills to do CSDP step 1 properly on any of these varieties; and since clients find it easier to work at the instance level, this is the safest way to go. Moreover, by doing this you've already starting prototyping external screens and reports the clients want.

While informal modeling of processes and events can be of use, at some stage they should be formally connected to the data. This is best done after the conceptual and logical data models are determined.

An alternative approach sometimes used is to focus on refining the process model to such an extent that the data stores finally become equated with the logical tables, and hence the data design is determined. Although a skilled modeler may be able to work this way, this method is more prone to error and more time-consuming.

For example, suppose one bypassed conceptual data modeling, instead refining the process and data store of Figure 10.10 into the following table scheme and SQL procedure. Here "&1" and "&2" are used as input parameters or place-holders. When the procedure is executed, actual values are input to these parameters.

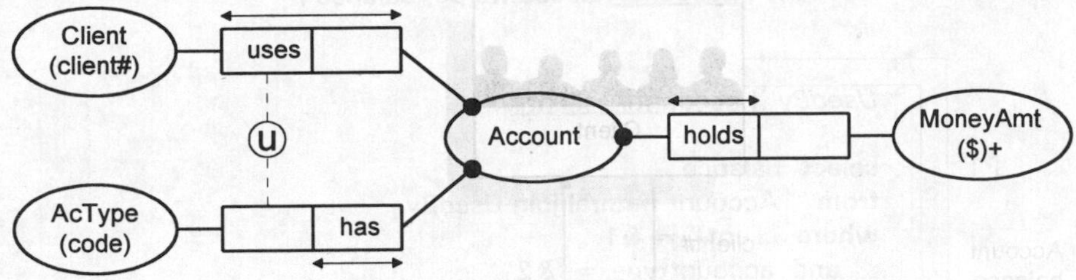

Figure 10.11 The primary reference scheme for accounts is unsafe

D1: *Account* (<u>client#, accounttype</u>, balance)

P1:
```
select balance from Account
where client# = &1
and accounttype = '&2'
```

Can you spot a potential problem with this design? It's easiest to see the problem if you do a conceptual schema for D1. This is depicted in Figure 10.11.

In real life, accounts may typically have many users. For example, my wife and I have a joint savings account. This possibility is portrayed in Figure 10.11. However, it is now incorrect to use ⟨client#, accounttype⟩ pairs for primary reference of accounts, since these pairs do not relate to accounts in a 1:1 fashion.

For example, suppose my wife's client# is 1001, mine is 1002, and we share a savings account (type = 'S'). This joint account may now be referenced by ⟨1001, 'S'⟩ and by ⟨1002, 'S'⟩.

This will not do for primary reference. For instance, the Account table structure used for D1 will accept the population: {⟨1001, 'S', 9000⟩, ⟨1002, 'S', 0⟩}. But this means that the same account has two different balances, which is nonsense. The obvious solution is to introduce another primary identifier (e.g. account#), as shown in Figure 10.12.

As an exercise, set out the relational schema for this new model, before looking at the following solution (D1'). The associated procedure is also shown (P1').

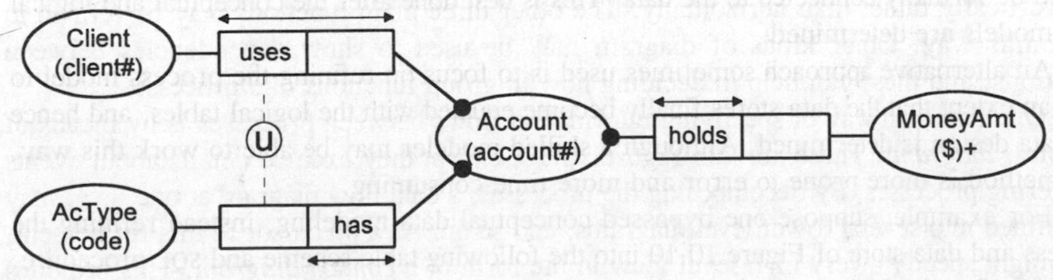

Figure 10.12 The primary reference scheme for accounts is now safe

```
D1':    Account ( account#, accounttype, balance )
                    :
                    :
        UsedBy  ( account#, client# )

P1':    select  balance
        from    Account natural join UsedBy
        where   client# = &1
          and   accounttype = '&2'
```

This example is somewhat simplified (e.g. an earlier exercise discussed how balances might be derived from account transactions) but it does illustrate how conceptual modeling facilitates a correct data design, and that a detailed process specification is of no use unless the data structure on which the process operates is well defined.

Another reason for treating the data model as more fundamental than a process or event model is that data structures tend to be more *stable*. With most applications one frequently needs to add or modify some operations. Users often request extra built-in functions, and a business rule for computing a derived quantity might change owing to some change in company or government policy. However, the underlying object types and roles tend to evolve at a much slower rate.

Although a rigorous operational model is best built on top of a data model, an overview of the processes and events is often useful as a precursor to the CSDP. This is particularly the case if the application is large or only vaguely understood. If few information examples exist, and the client is unclear about the UoD, it helps to get a clear picture of the functions of the application first.

Starting with the overall objectives, the main functions and processes of the application may be specified systematically, using a variety of diagrams. This kind of analysis helps one to divide the application into coherent modules of manageable size, and facilitates the task of specifying information examples where none exist. At this point, CSDP step 1 may be applied to each module.

Functional requirements may be laid out in top-down form using a *function tree*. For example, Figure 10.13 lists functions of a hospital information system. The four main functions are numbered 1..4. Each of these is refined or decomposed into a number of lower levels functions, numbered 1.1 etc. For example, function 3 is refined to functions 3.1 and 3.2. This may be refined further. For instance, function 3.1 is refined to functions 3.1.1, 3.1.2 and 3.1.3. To help fit the tree on a single sheet, this third level has been laid out vertically rather than horizontally. The other three main functions may be refined in a similar way. Other kinds of diagram may be used to show dependencies between functions, and these can help in deciding how to group functions into processes.

One common way of specifying information flows between processes is by means of *dataflow diagrams*. These are like Figure 10.10, except they exclude details about events triggering processes. By decomposing the processes, a data flow diagram at one level may be refined into several lower level diagrams, and so on. As a precursor to this refinement, one might specify a very high level view in the form of a *context diagram*. This provides an overview of the interaction between the information system and the environment, treats the system as a single process and ignores any data stores.

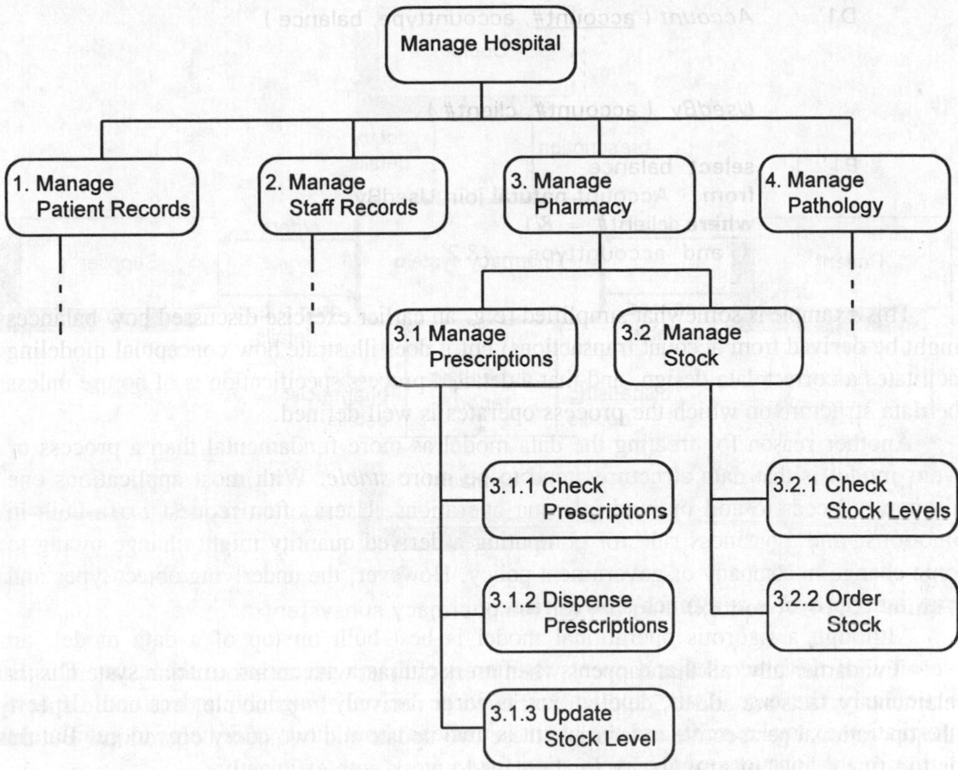

Figure 10.13 A function tree for a hospital information system

A context diagram for the pharmacy module of our hospital application is shown in Figure 10.14. External agents are shown as shadowed boxes. Material flows are not shown, but some data flows may be associated with material flows (e.g. drug supply details).

At a lower level of detail, Figure 10.15 shows a dataflow diagram for a fragment of the pharmacy system. This might be further refined (e.g. the order placement process might be decomposed into processes for computing totals, and printing order forms etc.). However, since such refinements are time-consuming, somewhat arbitrary, and lack the safeguards of population checks, there is usually little point in specifying low level data flows.

In general then, once the requirements of the application are clear, and modules of manageable size have been identified, modeling energy is best focused on obtaining a set of information examples and applying the CSDP. Once the conceptual schema has been specified, the logical schema is obtained by applying a mapping procedure, such as Rmap.

The external schemas may now be developed for the various categories of user. It is through the interaction of users with the external interface that the original functions specified in the requirements analysis phase are ultimately executed. Hence it is important to design the external interface in a way that naturally reflects these functions.

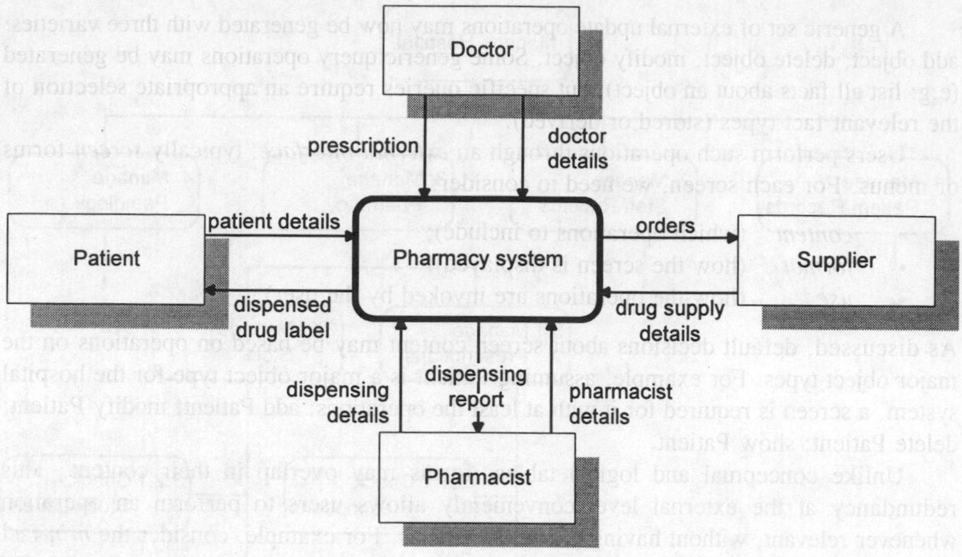

Figure 10.14 A context diagram for the pharmacy subsystem

Fundamentally, all that happens when users interact with an information system is that elementary facts are added, deleted, retrieved or derived. In principle, one could specify the operational perspective in terms of these two update and two query operations. But this is too fine a level of granularity for humans to work with efficiently.

One needs a way of grouping these elementary operations into larger units. It is often natural for users to think of operations being performed on significant *objects*, like patients and stock items. The major object types abstracted from an ORM schema (see previous section) correspond closely to these object types, and hence provide a good basis for defining operations.

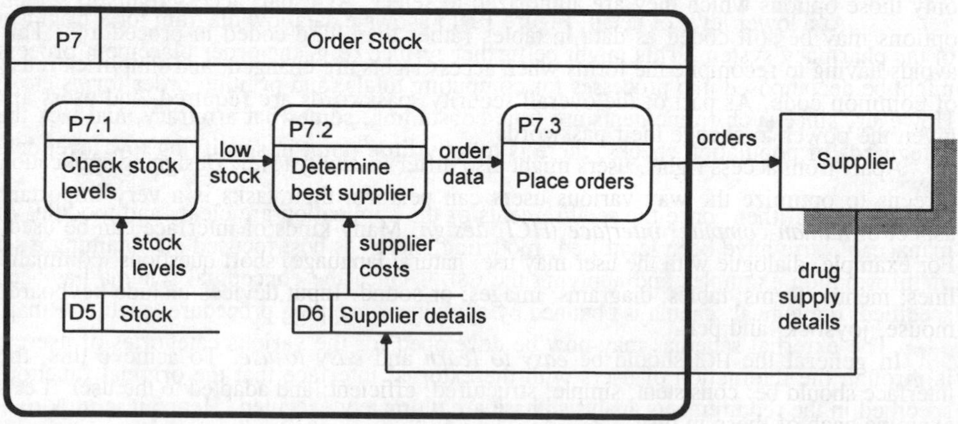

Figure 10.15 A dataflow diagram for part of the pharmacy subsystem

A generic set of external update operations may now be generated with three varieties: add object; delete object; modify object. Some generic query operations may be generated (e.g. list all facts about an object); but specific queries require an appropriate selection of the relevant fact types (stored or derived).

Users perform such operations through an *external interface*, typically *screen* forms or menus. For each screen, we need to consider:

- *content* (which operations to include);
- *format* (how the screen is displayed);
- *use* (how the operations are invoked by the user).

As discussed, default decisions about screen content may be based on operations on the major object types. For example, assuming Patient is a major object type for the hospital system, a screen is required for it with at least the operations: add Patient; modify Patient; delete Patient; show Patient.

Unlike conceptual and logical tables, forms may overlap in their content. This redundancy at the external level conveniently allows users to perform an operation whenever relevant, without having to switch screens. For example, consider the *m:n* fact type Doctor treated Patient. When working with a Doctor screen, we might query which patients were treated by a doctor. When at a Patient screen, we might query which doctors treated some patient. In the conceptual and logical schemas, facts of this type are stored only once. So long as the external screens have been properly set up as views of the underlying data structures, this overlap is safe. For further discussion on use of ORM schemas to generate screen forms and transactions, see Campbell and Halpin (1993).

Although there is only one (global) conceptual schema for an application, there may be many external schemas. Different user groups might have different *authorization* levels. These differences may be specified in *access rights tables*. This could be done at the conceptual level (e.g. for each fact type, which groups have read, add, delete rights) or at the logical level (e.g. for each table, which groups have read, add, delete, update (column-specific) rights).

Regarding access to options on screen forms, it is generally best to display to users only those options which they are authorized to select. As usual, access rights to screen options may be soft-coded as data in tables rather than hard-coded in procedures. This avoids having to recompile the forms when access rights are changed, and simplifies reuse of common code. As part of the overall security, passwords are required, and users are given the power to change their passwords.

Apart from access rights, users might also differ in *ability* level. Designing application screens to optimize the way various users can perform their tasks is a very important aspect of *human-computer interface (HCI) design*. Many kinds of interface can be used. For example, dialogue with the user may use: natural language; short questions; command lines; menus; forms; tables; diagrams; images; or sound. Input devices include keyboard, mouse, joystick, and pen.

In general the HCI should be *easy to learn* and *easy to use*. To achieve this, the interface should be: consistent; simple; structured; efficient; and adapted to the user. Let's examine each of these in turn.

Consistency of interface implies that all the components use the same basic conventions for display format and operations. This promotes positive transfer (learning how to use one screen helps you with the others), and avoids negative transfer. Consistency may be achieved at different levels: within the one screen; within the application; among applications from the same company; with external standards. For example, many windows applications are being developed nowadays in conformity with IBM's CUA-2 (common user access) standard.

Simplicity of interface implies it is intuitive to use, with minimal effort on the part of users. Each screen should provide the right amount of relevant information (e.g. limit the number of menu options seen at once). Don't clutter the screen. If you wish to allow many operations directly from the one screen, remove all but the main options from the permanent screen display, allowing the user to toggle the extra options on as required. For example, use pull-down menus, pop-up windows (e.g. for look-up codes), status-line help (and pop-up detailed help). Facilitate navigation within and between screens (e.g. use arrow keys for movement) and allow windows and menus to be cascaded or tiled.

Efficiency of interface entails that options may be selected quickly and intuitively. There is no question that a *graphical user interface (GUI)* provides a more intuitive means of operation, especially where graphics or sophisticated layouts are involved: here it is important that "what you see is what you get" (WYSIWYG). However, key-based short-cuts (e.g. hot-keys) are sometimes faster and should be provided for the experienced user.

Menu design has a major impact on efficiency. Menus come in various shapes and sizes, from full-screen, pull-down, pop-up, and ring through to button bars. They provide most if not all of the application's operations. Options on the same menu should be semantically related. Navigation between menus requires planning; some possible designs are shown in Figure 10.16. At any stage the user should be able to cancel an operation.

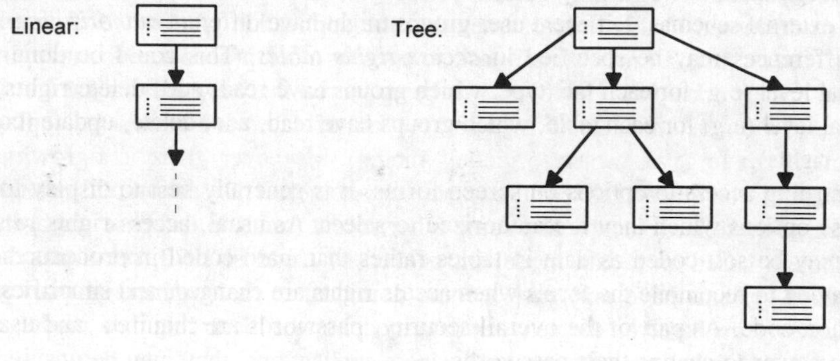

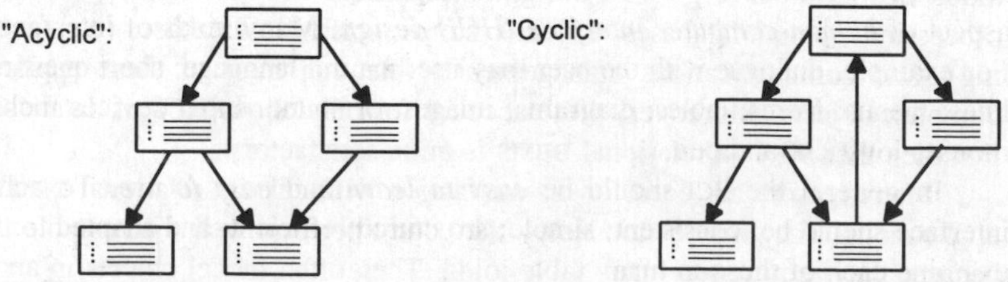

Figure 10.16 Some ways of navigating between menus.

In addition, the following principles should be observed. Order options in decreasing frequency of use. Vary color and fonts, but don't overdo it. For options either use intuitive icons, or terse, clear textual descriptions which are mostly in lower-case. Allow selection of options by point and pick, a highlighted (bold, color or underline) letter or hot-key.

Adapt the interface to the user by showing only what is relevant to that user, and adopting most of the following suggestions. Provide simple procedures for casual users and short-cuts for experienced users. Let users configure the environment to their own taste. Provide levels of context-sensitive help: short messages on status lines; detailed help in pop-up windows. Trap errors as soon as possible, and give short and long error messages. Provide on-line tutorials, clear user manuals, technical support, and training courses.

If you use some software packages which you find particularly intuitive, have a close look at the interface design and see if you can adapt its good features to your own (so long as you don't violate any copyright in doing so!). Once you develop your prototype interface, test it on typical users and use their feedback and suggestions to finesse it.

Well that's a quick run through several topics that could easily fill a book on their own. Indeed, whole books are devoted to interface design; and many other schemes exist for modeling processes and events, including some very technical approaches which attempt to formally integrate these models with data models. Some interesting work in this regard may be found in the chapter references.

10.5 Object-oriented databases and other trends

An ORM conceptual schema may be mapped to various logical data models. The Rmap procedure discussed in this text assumes that the application platform is a centralized, relational DBMS. It is a fairly simple task to specify other procedures for mapping to a hierarchic or network DBMS. However, it is being increasingly argued that the hierarchic, network and even relational data models are "out-of-date" and should be replaced by something better (e.g. an "object-oriented" model). Moreover, there is a growing trend for databases to be de-centralized in one way or another. This section outlines the main issues behind these movements, and some other recent trends in database research.

Although based on a data model introduced by Codd in 1970, relational database management systems have only just become dominant in the commercial marketplace. Traditional systems based on the network data model or the hierarchic data model are still in use. While relational DBMSs suit most business applications, they may be unsuitable for complex applications such as: CASE (computer aided software engineering) tools; computer aided design tools (e.g. VLSI design, mechanical engineering, architecture); document processing; spatial databases; expert systems; scientific databases (e.g. genetic engineering); and communications management. Note that most of these applications involve complex objects. Moreover, these account for only about 10% of database applications. For the other 90%, a relational DBMS is quite satisfactory.

Many reasons are cited for dissatisfaction with current relational DBMSs for complex applications. They may be too slow—they don't perform well with complex objects mainly because they require too many table joins. They often model objects in an unnatural way (e.g. information about a single object such as a person may be spread over several tables—this gets worse with complex objects). They are dependent on value-based identifiers. They don't facilitate re-use (e.g. they have no direct support for subtyping). They require access to a procedural language for difficult tasks (e.g. special rules, behavior and recursion) which leads to an "impedance mismatch" with the declarative, set-based, relational query language. They might not support BLOBs (binary large objects) such as images (icons, pictures, maps etc.), sound tracks, video etc.

Over the last decade or so, a lot of research effort has been aimed at developing a next generation of DBMS to overcome these deficiencies. Three main proposals have eventuated: *object-oriented databases* (OODBs); *extended relational databases*; and *deductive databases*. Of the various proposals, by far the most publicity has been given to object-oriented databases. The term "object-oriented" has been used, and abused, in so many ways that the claim itself is sometimes nebulous. Certainly a lot of hot air has been generated on the topic. Despite the lack of a common, formal object-oriented data model, many OODBMS prototypes exist, and some commercial systems have been released.

Deductive databases offer elegant and powerful ways of managing complex data in a declarative way, especially for information that is derived by use of recursion. However, they have major problems to be solved (especially in the performance area) and in the short term are unlikely to achieve more than a niche market.

Unlike OODBs, relational databases are based on a single data model formally based on predicate logic. Moreover, relational DBMSs are now dominant, and many are being extended to address several of the stated deficiencies. So for now, the main choice for the next DBMS platform is extended relational, or object-oriented.

Historically, OODB research drew upon related developments in four areas: programming languages; semantic data models; logical data models; and artificial intelligence. With programming languages, the need was seen for user-definable abstract data types and for persistent data. The object-oriented programming paradigm began with Simula (1967), and Smalltalk (1972), and nowadays many object-oriented programming languages exist (e.g. Eiffel). Some traditional programming languages have also been given object-oriented extensions (e.g. C++).

Some object-oriented features were taken from semantic data modeling, which as we know models reality in terms of objects and their relationships, and includes notions such as subtyping (e.g. ORM and extended ER). Various ideas were also borrowed from work on logical data models (network, hierarchic, relational and especially the nested relational model). Finally, some concepts were adapted from artificial intelligence, where structures such as frames are used for knowledge representation.

Just what features must a DBMS have to count as "object-oriented"? Unfortunately, there is no agreement on the answer to this question. A now classic paper ("the OODBMS Manifesto") in response to this question was presented at the first international conference on object-oriented and deductive databases (Atkinson et al. 1989).

To distinguish OODBMSs from OO-programming languages, five essential features of a DBMS were first identified; then object-oriented features were added, of which eight were considered essential and five optional (see Table 10.9). Let's look briefly at the essential object-oriented features in this proposal.

Complex objects are built from simpler ones by constructors. The manifesto proposed that these constructors should include at least set, list and tuple, and that these be orthogonal (they can be applied in any order, recursively).

Table 10.9 OODBMS proposals in the "OODBMS manifesto" (Atkinson et al. 1989)

DBMS features	*Essential OO features*	*Optional OO features*
Persistence Secondary storage Concurrency Recovery Ad hoc query facility	Complex objects Object identity Encapsulation Types or classes Inheritance Overriding and late binding Computationally complete Extensibility	Multiple inheritance Type checking and inferencing Distribution Design transactions Versions

For example, one object might be a list of sets of sets of tuples. Constructors are not orthogonal in the relational model (only sets of tuples of atomic values are allowed) or the nested relational models (e.g. the top level construct must be a set). The notion of complex objects is considered of major importance since it allows one to model a complex structure in a direct, natural way.

The basic idea behind *object identity* is that objects should be identified by system-generated object identifiers (oids) rather than by the values of their properties. This is in sharp contrast to the relational model, where for instance tuples are identified by the value of their primary key.

Among other things, use of oids can help keep track of objects whose external, value-based identification may change with time. This may occur because of simple renaming. For example, television channel 0 becomes channel 10, or a woman changes her name on marriage. More drastically, the reference scheme itself may change (e.g. a student identified by a student number becomes an employee identified by an employee number).

Object identifiers in the OO-sense overcome this problem since they are rigid identifiers (i.e. they always refer to the same object throughout time). They are system generated, non-reusable, immutable and typically hidden. In OODB systems they are typically implemented as surrogates (logical identifiers such as automatically incremented counters, mapped by index to physical addresses). Sometimes they are implemented as typed surrogates, but this makes migration between types awkward. They might also be implemented as structured addresses.

Encapsulation involves bundling the operations and data of an object together, with normal access to the object being through its operational interface, with implementation details hidden. For example, hiring, firing and raising the salary of employees are regarded as operations on Employee, and are encapsulated with it. These operations are sometimes misleadingly called "methods".

Encapsulation includes the idea that, as in a conceptual schema, objects should be classified in terms of *types* or *classes*. Moreover, some form of *inheritance* mechanism should be provided (e.g. so that a subtype may inherit the data and operational aspects of its supertype(s)). A subtype may have a specialized version of a function with the same name of one its supertype functions. In this case, the specialized version will typically *override* the more general version when the operation on the subtype is invoked. For example the display procedure for a colored, equilateral triangle may differ from the general display procedure for a polygon. Various overriding options are possible.

Table 10.10 Next generation DBMS features proposed by Stonebraker et al. (1990)

Basic tenets	*Detailed propositions*
1. Besides traditional data management services, next generation DBMS will provide support for richer object structures and rules.	1.1 Next generation DBMS must have a rich type system. 1.2 Inheritance is a good idea. 1.3 Functions, including database procedures, methods, and encapsulation, are a good idea. 1.4 Unique identifiers (uids) for records should be assigned by the DBMS only if a user-defined primary key is not available. 1.5 Rules (triggers, constraints) will become a major feature in future systems. They should not be associated with a specific function or collection.
2. Next generation DBMS must subsume previous generation DBMS.	2.1 Essentially all programmatic access to a database should be through a non-procedural, high-level access language. 2.2 There should be at least two ways to specify collections, one using enumeration of members and one using the query language to specify membership. 2.3 Updatable views are essential. 2.4 Performance indicators have almost nothing to do with data models and must not appear in them.
3. Next generation DBMS must be open to other subsystems.	3.1 Next generation DBMS must be accessible from multiple high level languages. 3.2 Persistent X for a variety of Xs is a good idea. They will all be supported on top of a single DBMS by compiler extensions and a (more or less) complex run-time system. 3.3 For better or worse, SQL is intergalactic dataspeak. 3.4 Queries and their results should be the lowest level of communication between a client and a server.

The requirement for *computational completeness* means that any computable function can be expressed in the data manipulation language (if necessary, by calling programming languages). The *extensibility* requirement means that users may define their own types, and the system should support them just like its built-in types.

Partly in response to the OODB manifesto, a committee of academic and industrial researchers proposed an alternative "3rd generation DBMS manifesto" (Stonebraker et al. 1990). Here they referred to hierarchic and network systems as first generation, and relational systems as second generation. Under this scheme, the third generation DBMSs are the next generation. They specified three basic tenets and thirteen detailed propositions to be adhered to by the next generation DBMSs (see Table 10.10).

Although supporting several of the object-oriented features, the committee argued against implementing them in such a way as to negate key advances made by the relational approach. For example, all facts in a relational system are stored in tables. In contrast, some facts in hierarchic and network systems may be specified as links between record structures, requiring navigation paths to be specified when the data is accessed. Object-oriented systems also enable facts to be stored as links between objects. Hence OO-queries typically require specification of access paths. Although path expressions are often more compact than relational queries, their reliance on existing navigation links has some unfortunate consequences. For example, the encoding of facts by links typically leads to redundancy, and makes it difficult to perform *ad hoc* queries efficiently.

As an example, consider the UoD schematized in Figure 10.17. Students either hold a degree or are currently seeking one (or both). The exclusion constraint forbids students from re-enrolling in a degree that they already hold. Subjects are recorded only for current students, as shown by the subset constraint; since this is not an equality constraint, students may enroll in a degree before choosing subjects. This aspect of the schema may alternatively be modeled by introducing the subtype CurrentStudent, to which the optional takes role is attached, using the definition: each CurrentStudent is a Student who seeks some Degree.

Each subject is identified by its subject code, but also has a unique title. For some subjects, a lecture plan may be available. This lists the topics discussed in the various lectures. For example, lecture 10 for CS114 might discuss the topics: relational projection; relational selection; and natural joins.

While there is no standard OODB language, the conceptual schema of Figure 10.17 might be specified in an OODBMS schema roughly as follows.

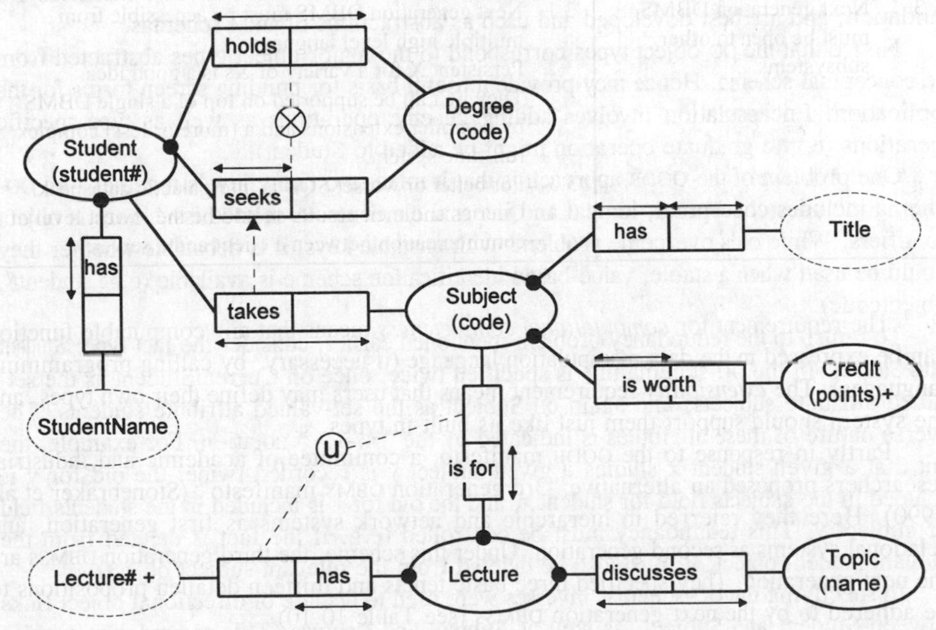

Figure 10.17

```
Student: {
    student#: Integer;
    studentname: String;
    degrees_held: set of String;
    current_degree: String }

CurrentStudent: isa Student, add {
    subjects: set of Subject <--> students }

Subject: {
    subjectcode: String;
    title: String;
    credit: Integer;
    students: set of CurrentStudent <--> subjects;
    lectures: sequence of Lecture <--> subject }

Lecture: {
    lecture#: Integer;
    subject: Subject <--> lectures;
    topics: set of String }
```

Clearly, this OO-schema fails to capture many details. Additional code is required to enforce the stronger typing and many extra constraints specified in the conceptual schema. One may represent the OO-schema on a diagram, but even then it is useful only for an overview. Like ER diagrams, OO-diagrams can't be populated with fact instances for validation, and are best developed and used as abstractions of ORM schemas.

Notice that the OO-object types correspond to the major object types abstracted from the conceptual schema. Hence they provide a useful basis for building screen forms for the application. Encapsulation involves adding generic operations as well as type-specific operations (e.g. a graduate operation might be added to Student).

One problem of the OODB approach is that it mixes too many levels together—an OO-schema includes conceptual, logical and internal elements. A related issue here is object identifiers. While oids overcome problems with unstable keys, it is debatable whether they should be used when a stable, value-based identification scheme is available (e.g. student#, subjectcode).

To return to the redundancy problem mentioned earlier, consider the fact type: Student takes Subject. In the OO-schema this is specified twice: once on CurrentStudent as the set-valued attribute subjects; and again on Subject as the set-valued attribute students. The inverse nature of these attributes is indicated by the "<-->" notation. For example, the fact that a given student *x* studies a given subject *y* is recorded twice: the oid for *y* is included in the subjects field for student *x*, and the oid for *x* is included in the students field for subject *y*. This redundancy must be controlled (e.g. if the fact is deleted from the relevant student object, it must also be deleted from the relevant subject object).

In specifying the OO-schema, inverses were used to declare bi-directional object links between Student and Subject, as well as Subject and Lecture. This redundancy enables queries in either direction to be specified using path expressions. For example, to find out the subjects studied by a student we use the path Student.subjects, and to find out the students who study some subject we use the path Subject.students.

This versatility is lost if the link is made uni-directional. Notice that no such problem exists in the relational model, although of course many queries will require joins. While joins might slow things down, there is no restriction on their use, since they do not require links to be set up beforehand. In contrast, the OODB approach obtains its efficiency by "hard-wiring" in the links to be used in queries: this makes it difficult to optimize *ad hoc* queries.

The problem of relying on pre-declared access paths in the model itself to achieve efficiency is exacerbated when the schema evolves. One may then have to fiddle about re-setting navigation pathways to optimize them for the new situation rather than simply relying on the system optimizer to do the job, as in current relational systems.

This is not to say that OODBs are a bad idea, or that complex objects should not be modelled as such. One can easily come up with examples of complex structures that are awkward to model in relational terms. For such examples, constructors may actually help with the conceptualization. However we ought be able to specify such structures in a clean way, without resorting to low level mechanisms.

One challenge then is to extend conceptual modelling techniques to achieve this, and provide mapping algorithms to logical and internal levels so that efficient implementations result. Various constructors (e.g. for sets, bags, sequences, and schemas) have been added to some versions of object-role modelling (e.g. FORM, NORM, PSM) and current research is addressing this challenge. As a simple example, consider Figure 10.18.

In the FORM notation, constructors are shown as frames around the component object type, with their structure type named ("seq" abbreviates "sequence"). In PSM, differently shaped envelopes (e.g. rectangles or frames) are used for different constructors. Figure 10.18 indicates that a subject may include a sequence of lectures, each of which discusses a set of topics. The leftmost UC says each subject includes at most one sequence of lectures (not at most one lecture). Since sequences have internal order, there is no need for explicit lecture numbers, as used in Figure 10.17. If we wish to indicate that topics are also ordered within a lecture, the structure over Topic would be changed to a sequence.

Although direct portrayal of complex object types may be appealing, this practice needs great care. Clearly the fact types in Figure 10.18 are not elementary, so the schema is not an ORM schema in the standard sense. Such diagrams may help with the following tasks: direct modeling of complex objects (especially unnamed structures), including operations on them; making schemas more compact; and visualizing mapping to nested-relational or object-oriented DBMSs.

On the down-side, it is much easier to make mistakes when modeling complex object types directly. In particular, some constraints are harder to see or even express unless the elementary fact types are shown as well. Populating complex fact types is also awkward.

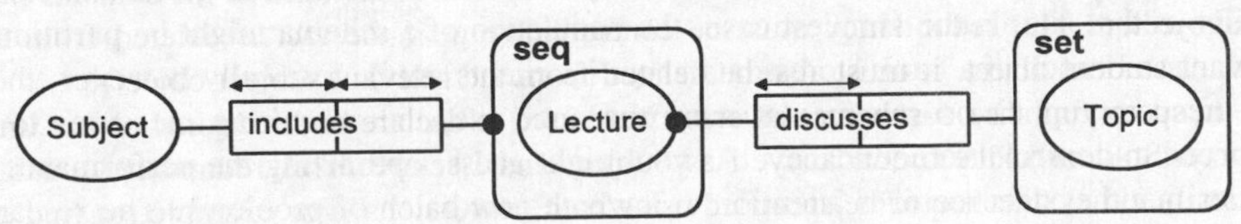

Figure 10.18 Sequence and set constructors

Some empirical research has also revealed a tendency among modelers to "over-use" constructors, when simpler solutions without constructors actually exist. Clearly, if constructors are to be used at all in conceptual design, the design procedure needs to be augmented to control their use. In many cases, diagrams with constructors are best developed by transforming a previously developed, standard conceptual schema.

Leaving aside the issue of conceptual modeling, what is the likely impact in the near future of OODBs in the market place? Although international bodies are examining object management issues, agreement on a single, standard OO-data model seems some way off. In the meantime, the SQL standard has been significantly improved with the approval of SQL-92, and draft proposals for SQL3 include several object-oriented features (e.g. user defined types and functions, encapsulation, support for oids, subtyping, triggered actions and computational completeness).

Aspects of deductive databases have also been included in the SQL3 draft (e.g. recursive union, to cater for recursive queries such as the parts explosion problem). Although approval of the SQL3 standard is unlikely till the late 1990s, a number of commercial vendors have already included features from the SQL3 draft in their current releases.

Given the massive installed base of relational DBMSs, the ongoing extensions to these products, the cost of porting applications to a new data model, and the lack of an OODB standard, it may well be that the next generation of DBMSs will evolve out of current relational products. Just as Hinduism absorbed features from other religions which threatened its existence, the relational model can probably absorb the interesting features of the object-oriented faith without being replaced by it.

Although such "super-relational" systems may well dominate the market for the near future, they may not be the best choice for some kinds of task. A system that fully supported SQL3 (or even SQL-92) may be "over-kill" for some specialized or small applications. And there are things that even the proposed SQL3 can't do (e.g. it doesn't allow triggers on views) or does awkwardly (e.g. recursion).

Although the discussion of extended features has focussed on object-oriented aspects, extensive research is under way world-wide in many other areas of database technology which will influence future DBMSs. To begin with, many databases are becoming very large, with users at many different sites. For this situation one needs to decide whether the overall system will be centralized, distributed or federated.

In a centralized system, the database and management is controlled at a single site; any site may send update and query requests to the central site, and results are sent back. If the sites are far apart, the communication times involved in such transactions can be very significant.

To reduce the communication overhead, a *distributed* database system allows the data to be spread across various sites, with most of the data relevant to a given site stored locally at that site. In the simplest case, the population of a schema might be partitioned (e.g. each branch of a bank stores data about its clients only). Typically however, there is a need to replicate some data at more than one site, thus requiring measures to be enforced to control the redundancy. As you might guess, optimizing the performance of a distributed system requires attention to a whole new batch of problems. The research literature on distributed databases is vast, and many commercial systems already provide distributed capabilities, to varying extents.

More recently, the notion of *federated* databases has arisen to deal with situations where there is a need for data sharing between several existing database systems, possibly heterogeneous (e.g. some relational, some hierarchic, and so on). In this framework, each individual system maintains its local autonomy, and communicates with other sites on a needs basis. As the heterogeneity problem requires translation between different data models, the control of federated systems is non-trivial. The size of the problem can be reduced by supporting only partial integration; any two sites need only share the common data relevant to both of them, rather than all their data.

Two related topics which have become very important in recent years are *spatial databases* and *temporal databases*. Spatial databases require efficient management of spatial data, such as geometric figures and maps. Users of such systems require much of the information to be displayed in diagrammatic form, but also need access to related data in tabular form. New sub-disciplines such as geographic information systems have sprung up in university departments, and various commercial database systems now include special facilities for performing spatial operations and computations.

Although time has only one dimension, unlike space's three dimensions, the efficient management of temporal information is no easy task. If historical rather than snapshot records need to be maintained about objects, time will feature largely in the modeling. An exercise question is included at the end of this section to help you appreciate how this complicates even a basic application.

A variety of approaches may be adopted for modeling time. In some cases we simply include object types such as Time and Period on the conceptual schema and map these like other object types. Often we need to make use of temporal relations (such as before and after) and temporal operations (e.g. to compute an interval between two time points). Sometimes, an ordinary relational database does not allow the model to be implemented efficiently. For such applications, special DBMSs known as "temporal database systems" are sometimes used; these provide in-built support for automatic time-stamping and the various temporal operators.

Most work on temporal databases focuses on keeping track of relevant histories of application objects through time, with the assumption that the conceptual schema itself is fixed. Moving up one level, the problem becomes more complicated if we allow the conceptual schema itself to change with time. This is one aspect of the schema evolution problem.

Moving up another level, we might allow the conceptual metaschema itself to change with time (e.g. we might decide at a later stage to allow constructors for complex object types in our conceptual schema language). The management of such higher order evolution has been addressed in recent research on evolving information systems. This topic provides one motivation for the next section, which presents an introduction to metamodeling.

Exercise 10.5

1. Brissie University maintains an academic record system about its students. Each semester a student may be enrolled in only one course either in part-time or full-time mode. A course is a single degree (e.g. BSc); no combined degrees are allowed. An historical record is also kept of each student's full academic record. One such record is shown.

Brissie University—Official Academic Record

Name: John J. Smith *Student Nr:* 12305 *Date of Birth:* 19/11/68

Semester	*Subject code*	*Subject name*	*Credit value*	*Grade*	*Credit gained*
91/1		*Course:* BSc *Mode:* PT			
	CS100	Introduction Programming	8	2	
	MA100	Introduction Applied Maths 1	8	3	8
	MP101	Calculus 1A	8	5	8
		Sem Totals: GPA: 3.33	24		16
91/2		*Course:* BSc *Mode:* PT			
	MA102	Dynamics 1	8	1	
	MP102	Calculus 1B	8	1	
	PD102	Logic 1	10	4	10
		Sem Totals: GPA: 2.15	26		10
		15/12/91 Excluded from BSc Course			
92/1		*Course:* BInfTech *Mode:* FT			
	CS100	Introduction Programming	8	4	8
	CS112	Introduction Information Systems	8	5	8
	CS160	Introduction Computation	8	4	8
	EC150	Socio-Ec Aspects Inf Tech	8	4	8
	MA212	Introduction Op Research	5	2	
	MA201	Probability and Dist 2	10	3	10
		Sem. Totals: GPA: 3.74	47		42
92/2		*Course:* BInfTech *Mode:* PT			
	CS102	Programming Principles	8		
	CS113	Relational Databases	8		
		Sem. Totals: GPA:	16		
		Credit point grant to BInfTech: 18			
		******* END OF RECORD *******			

In moving to a new semester, students may continue or change their course and/or mode. They may even change to an old course of theirs (so long as they had not graduated from it). The academic record example was printed in the middle of semester 2, 1992 (before results for that semester were available). Subject grades are in the range 1..7. Credit is gained only for ratings above 2. The GPA figure is the grade point average: (sum of grade × credit)/ total credit.

No subject may be enrolled in by a student more than twice. Various rule violations (which may be ignored for this exercise) can cause a student be excluded from a course. In this case the date of the exclusion is noted in the record system. A student who is excluded from a course can never graduate from it. If a student graduates from a course, the date of this graduation is recorded. Sometimes a student may be granted credit towards a course on the basis of work done elsewhere (e.g. another course). The date(s) and justification for such credit transfer are not recorded; the system records a single, cumulative value for each student, course combination (a default value of 0 applies in the case of no transferred credit).

All students of this university live in a suburb of Brissie city. Postcodes for all Brissie suburbs are stored in the system. Each suburb has a distinct postcode, but many suburbs may have the same postcode. Each year has two academic semesters. A blank enrollment form for one semester is shown.

Brissie University—Enrollment form for semester 2, 1992			
student#:		student name:	
sex (F/M):		street address:	
date of birth: (dd/mm/yy)		suburb:	
		postcode:	
coursecode:		study mode (FT/PT):	
subjectcodes:			
signature:			

(a) Specify a conceptual schema for this UoD. Specify all uniqueness, mandatory role, value, occurrence frequency, subset and exclusion constraints. Do not attempt any subtyping. If a fact type is derived, omit it from the diagram but add a derivation rule for it below. Note that occurrence frequencies may span more than one role.

If there are any important constraints that cannot be specified graphically, specify these in textual form below the diagram.

(b) Rmap your answer to (a). Avoid identifiers which may be reserved words (e.g. “date”, “year”). Include all constraints.

10.6 Meta-modeling

Modeling involves making models of applications. *Metamodeling* involves making models of models—this time the applications being modeled are themselves models. Just as recursion is one of the most elegant and powerful concepts in logic, metamodeling is one of the most beautiful and powerful notions in conceptual modeling. This section uses a simple example to convey the basic idea.

Suppose that Table 10.11 is part of an output report from a movie database. Other reports from the same application provide further information (e.g. people's birth places). The conceptual subschema for this report is shown in Figure 10.19. The disjunctive mandatory role constraint on Person is shown explicitly since Person plays other roles in the global schema (e.g. Figure 10.5 from an earlier section might be the global schema).

Table 10.11 One report extracted from a movie database

Movie#	*Title*	*Director*	*Stars*
1	Wilderness	Tony O'Connor	
2	Sleepy in Seattle	Anne Withanee	Ima Dozer Anne Withanee
3	Wilderness	Anne Withanee	Paul Bunyip

The database holds fact instances from the application, while the conceptual schema models the *structure* of the application. Figure 10.20 recalls our basic view of an information system, where the information processor ensures that the database conforms to the rules laid down in the conceptual schema. Essentially a DBMS is a system for managing various database applications; for each application it checks that each database state agrees with the structure specified in the conceptual schema for that application.

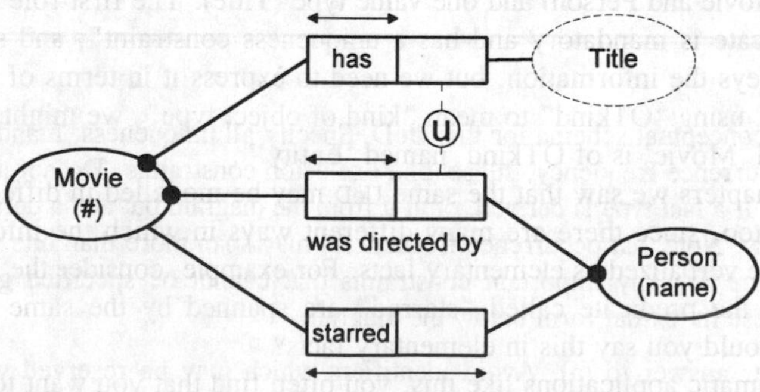

Figure 10.19 A conceptual schema for Table 10.11

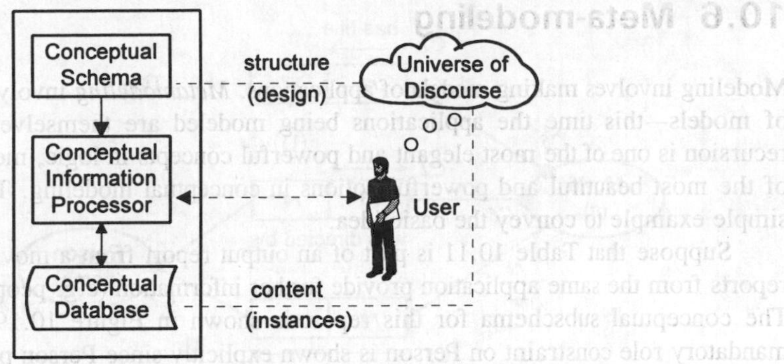

Figure 10.20 The database must conform to the structure of the conceptual schema

Among other things, a CASE tool such as InfoModeler is a system for managing conceptual schemas. Each valid schema diagram in this book may be thought of as an output report from this system. The trick then is to treat a schema like Figure 10.19 as a database instance of this higher level system. So long as we can verbalize the diagrams into elementary facts, we can use the CSDP to develop a conceptual schema for such conceptual schemas. We would then have a conceptual *metaschema* (schema about schemas).

In this case, Figure 10.20 still applies, but the user is an information modeler, the database holds a conceptual schema, the UoD is about conceptual schemas, and the conceptual information processor ensures that only valid conceptual schemas are placed in the database by checking that they satisfy the structure specified in the meta-conceptual schema.

Rather than developing a complete metaschema for ORM conceptual schemas, we confine our discussion here to simple examples like Figure 10.19, ignoring nesting, subtyping, derivation, and all constraints other than uniqueness and mandatory role constraints. If you've never done metamodeling before, it seems a bit strange at first. As a challenge, see if you can perform CSDP step 1 using Figure 10.19 as a sample report.

Metamodeling is like ordinary modeling, except the kind of information to be modeled is structural. You might begin by describing Figure 10.19 roughly. For example: "It has two entity types (Movie and Person) and one value type (Title). The first role of the 'was directed by' predicate is mandatory and has a uniqueness constraint"; and so on. This verbalization conveys the information, but we need to express it in terms of elementary facts. For example, using "OTkind" to mean "kind of object type", we might say: "The ObjectType named 'Movie' is of OTkind named 'Entity'".

In previous chapters we saw that the same UoD may be modelled in different ways. This applies here too, since there are many different ways in which the information in Figure 10.19 can be verbalized as elementary facts. For example, consider the information that both roles of the predicate called "starred" are spanned by the same uniqueness constraint. How would you say this in elementary facts?

With diagrammatic applications like this, you often find that you want to talk about an object (such as a constraint) but it *hasn't got a name* on the diagram. You would naturally identify it to somebody next to you by *pointing* to it; but this won't help you convey the information over the telephone to someone.

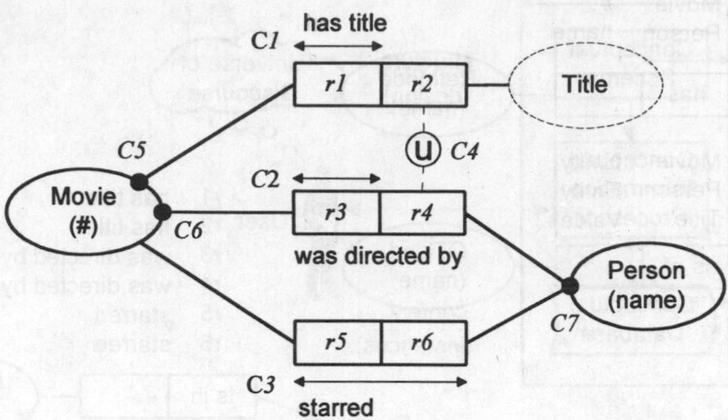

Figure 10.21 Surrogates have been added to identify constraints and roles

In such cases it is often convenient to introduce an artificial name, or *surrogate*, to identify the object. This is what we have chosen to do in Figure 10.21, where each constraint has been given an identifying constraint number. For convenience, we have also introduced role numbers (though we could have just identified roles by their positions in predicates). This should make it easier for you to complete CSDP step 1. After that, the rest of the design steps are straightforward. Try this yourself before looking at Figure 10.22.

The metaschema shown in Figure 10.22 is only one of many possible solutions. As an aid to understanding, it has been populated with the database that corresponds to the conceptual schema shown in Figure 10.21. Here, "UCi", "UCe" and "MR" respectively abbreviate "uniqueness constraint internal", "uniqueness constraint external" and "mandatory role".

Recall that other constraints have been ignored in this discussion. In this metaschema, we have chosen to identify predicates by their name. To ensure this, we have chosen to use expanded names for predicates which may have the same display name (e.g. "has" in Figure 10.20 has been expanded to "has title" in Figure 10.21).

If you have developed an alternative metaschema, don't forget to do a population check. As a further population check on the metaschema presented here, you may wish to check that it can be populated with itself. In other words, verbalize the conceptual metaschema (without its movie database population), then populate it with this verbalization.

Well, that demonstrates the basic idea of metamodeling. This notion is not restricted to conceptual schemas. Any well defined formalism can be metamodeled. Apart from being used to manage a given formalism, metamodels can also be developed to allow translation between different formalisms. This is sometimes referred to as meta-metamodeling.

This is all fascinating, but I'm afraid this is as far as we go in this book. I hope you have gained some insights into the science and art of conceptual modeling by reading this book, and that you share my belief that modeling the real world is one of the most challenging, important and satisfying things that humans can do.

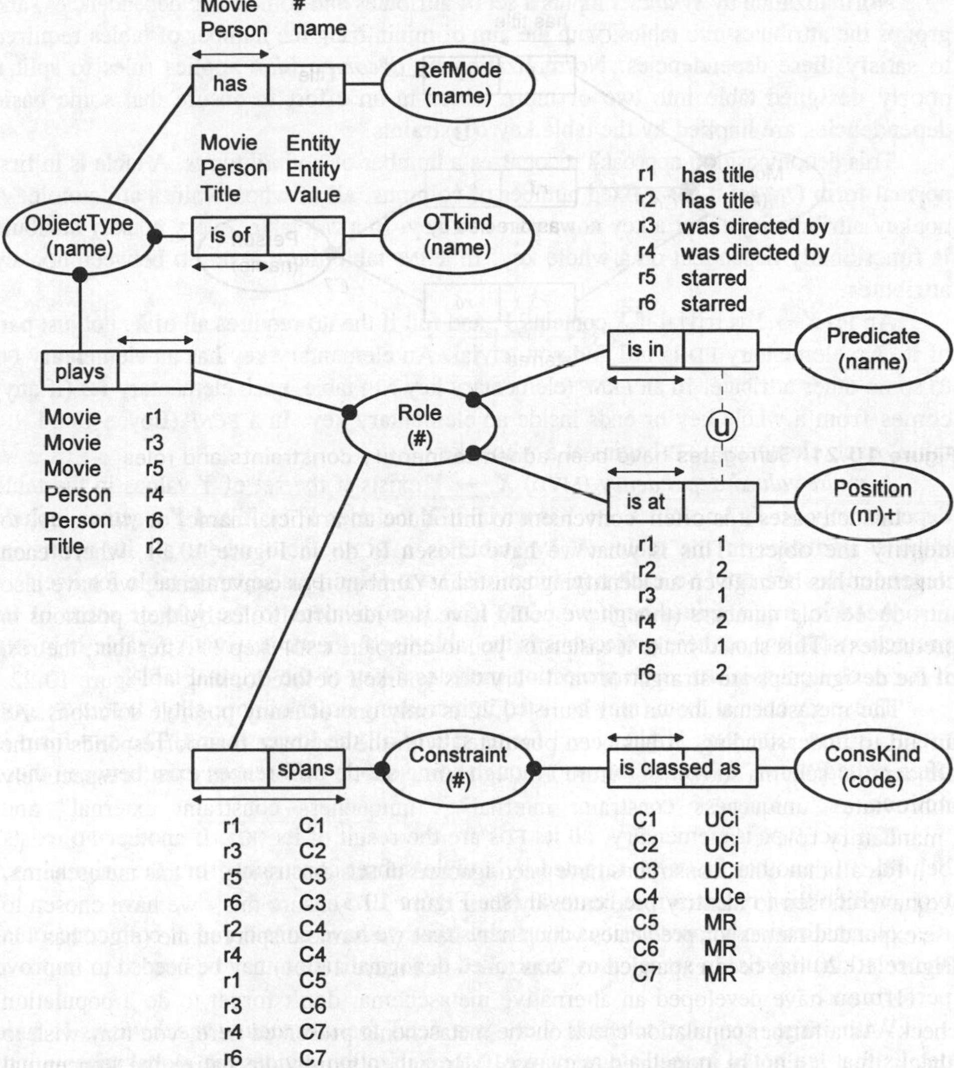

Figure 10.22 A conceptual metaschema, populated with the schema of Figure 10.21

10.7 Summary

The Rmapping of a correctly designed conceptual schema automatically results in a safe, redundancy free, relational schema where the number of tables has been reduced by grouping together functional fact types with the same key. In contrast to this deconceptualization approach, *normalization* provides a set of rules for achieving reasonable table designs by catering for low-level dependencies between attributes.

Normalization by *synthesis* inputs a set of attributes and some basic dependencies, and groups the attributes into tables, with the aim of minimizing the number of tables required to satisfy these dependencies. Normalization by *decomposition* applies rules to split a poorly designed table into two or more tables in an effort to ensure that some basic dependencies are implied by the table key constraints.

This decomposition approach recognizes a number of *normal forms*. A table is in first normal form (*1NF*) if it has a fixed number of columns, all of whose values are atomic. A nonkey attribute is neither a key nor a part of a key. In a *2NF* table, every nonkey attribute is functionally dependent on a whole key. In a *3NF* table there is no FD between nonkey attributes.

An FD $X \rightarrow Y$ is trivial if X contains Y, and full if the FD requires all of X, not just part of it. An elementary FD is full and non-trivial. An elementary key has an elementary FD to some other attribute. In an *EKNF* (elementary key NF) table, each elementary FD (if any) comes from a whole key or ends inside an elementary key. In a *BCNF* (Boyce-Codd NF) table, each elementary FD begins at a whole key.

A *multi-valued dependency* (MVD) $X \twoheadrightarrow Y$ exists if the set of Y values in the table depends only on X. An MVD $X \twoheadrightarrow Y$ is trivial if X includes Y, or X and Y together include all the attributes in the table. A *4NF* table is a BCNF table where all its nontrivial dependencies are FDs. So each non-functional MVD requires a separate table for itself.

A table has a *join-dependency* (JD) if it is equivalent to the join of some of its projections. If one of these projections is the table itself, the JD is trivial. A table is in 5NF if for each nontrivial JD, each projection includes a key of the original table.

These six normal forms may be listed in increasing order of normality: 1NF; 2NF; 3NF; EKNF; BCNF; 4NF; 5NF. Higher level forms satisfy all the lower forms. The 5NF form is often called "PJNF" (Project-Join NF) though some subtle differences exist between these notions.

If a fact type is elementary, all its FDs are the result of its UCs. If another FD exists, behind it is another fact type targeted by a tuple-subset constraint from the original fact type, which then requires role removal (see Figure 10.3).

Normalization ignores various constraints that we have considered at both conceptual and relational levels. In some cases, controlled denormalization may be needed to improve performance.

With large, complex schemas there is a need for *abstraction mechanisms* to hide details that are not of immediate relevance. Modularization divides the global schema into conveniently sized subschemas. Constraint layers and textual rules may be toggled off and on as desired. We may zoom in on, or out from, a selected object type, specifying how much of its neighborhood is to be displayed.

Major object types may be identified by their importance in the global schema (e.g. having an explicit mandatory role), and display suppressed for "minor" fact types (without two roles played by major object types). This view may be refined further by focusing on its major fact types, and so on. Such bottom-up abstraction may be reversed to give top-down refinement.

Minor fact types may also be displayed in terms of attributes of major object types. In this case, ER diagrams may be generated as abstractions of ORM diagrams. While such abstractions are good for compact overviews, detailed ORM diagrams should be used in developing, transforming and evolving conceptual schemas.

Although the data model is the foundation of any information systems application, one also needs to specify permissible *operations* on the data, and design the *external interface*. For such purposes, various diagrams and notations may be used to supplement ORM diagrams.

In early stages, informal diagrams such as cartoons can help clarify the UoD, and *function trees* are useful for providing a top-down view of the system requirements. Simple pictures may be used to show what events trigger what processes. *Dataflow diagrams* may be used to picture information flows between processes, agents and information stores. However at some stage a formal connection needs to be made between events, processes and data. One useful way of doing this is to define *operations on the major object types*. This can also be used to generate the content (operations) of default screen forms for the external interface. Some default decisions can also be made about the format and use of these screens.

Design of the *human-computer interface* (HCI) typically requires careful planning by humans. Access rights for different user groups need to be controlled. Users may also differ in their ability level. To make the HCI easy to learn and use, the interface should be consistent, simple, structured, efficient and adapted to the user. In most cases a *graphical user interface* (GUI) is preferable. The *menu* design needs to provide efficient navigation, and various levels of on-line and off-line help are required.

Relational DBMSs are suitable for about 90% of business applications, but may prove inefficient for structurally complex applications such as CASE tools and VLSI design. In the near future, such applications might best be implemented using *extended relational databases* or *object-oriented databases* (OODBs). In the long term future, *deductive databases* might prove a viable option.

Apart from the usual DBMS features, OODB systems provide direct support for complex objects, object identity, encapsulation, object types and subtypes, over-riding and late binding, and are computationally complete and extensible. Object identifiers are basically rigid, system-generated surrogates which are hidden from the user. They avoid many of the problems associated with changing identifiers, but it is at least debatable whether they should be used when a stable primary key is available.

Object-oriented database schemas include a mix of conceptual, logical and external levels. Elementary facts may be redundantly specified to provide two-way navigation between objects. Like ER schemas, they can't be populated and do not facilitate the expression of many constraints. Hence they are best developed after an ORM schema has already been constructed.

Extended relational systems (e.g. nested relational systems) support some of the OODB features, but provide these on top of the basic relational features. To facilitate mapping to OODB or extended relational systems, it might be useful to model complex objects on extended-ORM schemas using constructors (e.g. set, bag, sequence, schema). If this is done, the design procedure should be extended to prevent misuse of such constructors.

Instead of being centralized, a database might be *distributed* or *federated*. This raises additional design and optimization problems (e.g. communication overhead, redundancy control, and translation). Further design problems may arise in the modeling of *temporal* or *spatial* data, and in controlling the *evolution* of schemas.

By treating conceptual schemas as sample database states, the CSDP may be used to develop a conceptual *metaschema*. This may be used by a CASE tool to ensure that only valid conceptual schemas are entered. The activity of *metamodeling*, or making models of models, may be used to clarify and compare other formalisms.

Chapter notes

A simple introduction to normalization is provided by Kent (1983). Some of the classic papers include Codd (1970), Fagin (1977; 1979), Rissanen (1977), and Zaniolo (1982). A general study of join dependencies (including functional and multivalued dependencies) is provided by Aho, Beeri & Ullman (1979). Date (1990) includes a useful, annotated bibliography on normalization (pp. 563-9) which lists other main references.

For a very thorough and recent analysis of normal forms see Vincent (1994). An in-depth, formal treatment of normal forms and their relationship to ER modeling is given by Thalheim (1994). For an early paper on deductive normal forms see Thalheim (1984). Other specific references on normalization were mentioned in section 10.2.

For further details about schema abstraction, see Campbell & Halpin (1994a) and the various references included in its review. A procedure for generating default external forms from major object types is discussed in Campbell & Halpin (1993).

For plenty of details and good practical advice on modeling the operational aspects on information systems, see Barker & Longman (1992), and Barker (1990). One promising, formal means of integrating data and operations is discussed by ter Hofstede (1993). A standard work on HCI design is Schneiderman (1992).

The OODB "manifesto" is stated in Atkinson et al. (1989), and an alternative, extended-relational "manifesto" is proposed by Stonebraker et al. (1990). Two good papers on object identity are provided by Khoshaflan & Copeland (1990) and the ever lucid Kent (1991). One of the best books on object-oriented databases is Cattell (1991): this includes an excellent, annotated bibliography (pp. 273-310). For a detailed discussion of SQL-92 and a brief look at SQL3, see Date & Darwen (1993) and Melton & Simon (1993).

There is a vast literature on temporal databases and the impact of time in information systems. A classic survey of the area is given by Snodgrass (1990). For a useful survey of temporal issues within the context of fact-based modeling, see Petrounias & Loucopoulos (1994). An advanced and extensive treatment of evolutionary aspects of information systems is given by Proper (1994).

appendix A Hardware and software generations

This appendix provides additional background on the evolution of computer hardware and software, to supplement the discussion in section 1.3. In terms of computer **hardware**, there are at least four generations of digital computer systems. *First generation* computers were introduced shortly after World War II. Based on *vacuum tube* technology, these were large, required lots of power, generated plenty of heat, and needed constant maintenance.

Second generation computers were introduced in 1959, with the release of the IBM 7090. These used *transistors* instead of vacuum tubes, resulting in a dramatic decrease in cost, size and power consumption as well as an increase in reliability.

Third generation computers, introduced in 1964 with the announcement of the IBM 360, were the first to use *integrated circuits* (ICs). An IC consists of a large number of electronic circuits etched onto a single semiconductor chip. This use of microchips led to more dramatic drops in cost, size and power consumption and to greater reliability.

By 1971, two advances in microchip technology had occurred. Firstly, the first general purpose processor-on-a-chip or *microprocessor* had been released: this represented a major breakthrough in chip architecture. Secondly, *large scale integration* (LSI) had been achieved: this represented a major increase in chip density (i.e. the number of circuit elements contained on the one chip). Although LSI led to size reductions, its primary purpose was to speed up processing by reducing the distances that electrons had to travel. These advances are often said to have introduced the *fourth generation* of computers. In 1975, very large scale integration (VLSI) was achieved. With VLSI, over 100,000 transistors may be packed onto a single chip. Much higher packing densities are now available. For example, in 1994 a Pentium chip included 3.3 million transistors.

Let us now turn to the related but distinct topic of computer **software**. It is quite common to speak of generations of *computer languages*. We identify five such generations. Computers were first programmed in *machine language*. Each machine language instruction consists of a sequence of binary digits (bits). For example, with an 8086 processor, the machine code instruction to add 7 to the AX register is: 00000101 00000111 00000000. The byte 00000101 indicates that the following 16 bit data word should be added to the AX register; you may recognize 00000111 as binary for the decimal number 7. The final 00000000 is the "high order byte" of the 16 bit representation of 7.

You can imagine how boring and error-prone it was to program in strings of 1s and 0s all the time. So humans invented a mnemonic code called *assembly language*. In an assembly language for the 8086 chip, the previous machine instruction may be written as: "ADDI AX, 7". The ADDI, or "add immediate", indicates that the number to be added is contained immediately within the instruction; so the 7 is interpreted as data instead of as an address holding the data. The AX part indicates the target variable for the addition.

Although humans can (with some difficulty!) read assembly code, the computer cannot understand anything but pure machine language. So a program called an assembler is used to translate from assembly language into machine language. Although modern assembly languages are considerably better than older ones, they are still rather painful to use. Besides being hard to understand, assembly language programs tend to be very long since each instruction corresponds to just one machine language instruction. In this sense, assembly language is very low level.

Most programmers nowadays work almost exclusively with high level languages, such as C, COBOL and SQL. These are easier to write in and understand because they are closer to English. Moreover, a high level program is typically much shorter than an assembly program because one high level instruction usually does the job of several machine language instructions. For example, the following Pascal instruction tells the computer to write out the square root of the value of *x*: "write (sqrt(x))". The equivalent machine code is quite lengthy. As with assembly language, higher level languages must be translated into machine language before they can be carried out by the computer.

Some high level languages include optimizers to generate more efficient machine code, and some include facilities which come close to matching the power of assembly languages. Since high level code can be written and maintained much more easily than assembly code, the use of assembly languages has considerably diminished in recent years. Nowadays, assembly code tends to be used only for program modules where extra hardware control or greater speed is needed (e.g. fast animation).

With respect to computer languages, machine language is *first generation*, assembly language is *second generation* and high level languages are at least *third generation*. Notice that it is wrong to define an *n*th generation language as one that runs on an *n*th generation computer. For example, even the later first generation computers could run the first three generations of computer languages (the first high level language, FORTRAN, was released in 1957).

There are hundreds of high level programming languages. Most of these are *procedural*, emphasizing the algorithmic side of programming (the procedures showing how to carry out the task) and are generally classified as third generation. This is true even of later procedural languages such as Modula-2 and Ada.

When applied to languages, the term *fourth generation* typically refers to high level database languages used for querying databases or building associated user interfaces such as screen forms. Fourth generation languages are primarily *declarative* in nature rather than procedural. That is, the programmer essentially declares *what* has to be done rather than *how* to do it. Fourth generation languages (4GLs) are also highly interactive, supporting an ongoing dialogue between the human and the system.

Note that 4GLs represent a quantum leap beyond 3GLs for work with large, complex databases. Suppose we wish to extract some particular information from a database, and no program is on hand for our particular query. In a 3GL like Pascal or COBOL we would typically have to write pages of code, then compile and debug this until finally it could be run to yield the required results. In contrast, such an ad hoc query could typically be formulated easily in a single statement in SQL and the answer obtained immediately.

It has been estimated that approximately 80 percent of computer software applications fit into the information systems basket, with the emphasis on the data rather than the algorithm. Given the higher productivity of 4GLs in this area, it is clear that many programming tasks now performed in languages like COBOL would be better handled by languages like SQL.

However there is still a place for 3GLs like Pascal or C. Sometimes an application is best coded partly in a 4GL and partly in a 3GL: recent developments are making it easier for these language generations to "talk to one another". And some programming problems cannot be handled efficiently by 4GLs. Examples of this include computer aided learning, theorem provers, advanced mathematical work, hardware control, and compiler construction. For most applications however, the data-centered, set-oriented approach of languages like SQL is more appropriate.

The first four generations of computers are based on the von Neumann architecture, which includes a CPU (central processing unit), main and secondary memory, and input and output devices. The CPU is the heart of the computer: it controls the actions performed by the system and computes the values required for arithmetic and logical operations. The main memory stores information which can be "immediately" accessed by the CPU, including the program (or program segment) currently being executed.

The secondary memory stores (usually on disk or tape) information not currently being processed. An input device (e.g. keyboard) enables data to be sent from the outside world to the CPU, and an output device (e.g. monitor or printer) enables results to be communicated to the outside world.

The versatility of this model derives from the fact that the user can input the program to be processed by the CPU (this "stored program" concept is usually attributed, perhaps mistakenly, to John von Neumann) as well as the data to be operated on. This model is based on the notion of serial processing with at most one instruction being executed at any time.

Today, various "*fifth generation*" technology projects are the subject of worldwide research. These typically incorporate large scale *parallel processing*, (many instructions being processed at once), different memory organizations, and new hardware operations specifically designed for symbol manipulation (not just number-crunching). Instead of one central processor, there may be literally thousands of processors working simultaneously on different aspects of the problem being processed. This new hardware organization is tightly coupled with a new approach to software, in which the notion of *knowledge representation* is central.

Although programmers working with such "fifth generation" machines use various high level languages, such as Prolog 2, it is perhaps more appropriate to reserve the term *fifth generation language* (5GL) for the language in which most users will communicate with such systems. What is this language? The human-machine interfaces are being designed to allow significant use of *natural language* and even images. In this sense, the fifth will be the last of the language generations (at least from the human verbal interface point of view).

Exercise A1

1. **For each of the following pairs select the item which most appropriately describes 4th generation database languages.**

A. low level	**B. high level**
C. declarative	**D. procedural**
E. algorithm-centred	**F. data-centred**
G. set-oriented	**H. record-oriented**
I. associate by name	**J. must specify access paths**

2. **"An *n*th generation computing language is one that runs on *n*th generation computer hardware". Is this definition correct?**

3. **As a computer trivia question, the IBM 7090 was originally named the 709T, where the "T" denoted the transistorized version of the old 709 model. Can you guess why the name was changed?**

appendix B Subtype matrices

This appendix provides additional discussion on subtype graphs and sample populations, and assumes that section 6.5 on subtyping has already been read. In general, access to the UoD expert is required to resolve any doubts about subtyping requirements. In the absence of the UoD expert, the subtype graph can be determined by *subtype matrix analysis* if a sample population is provided which is significant with respect to this graph. This section considers two ways of performing this analysis.

Although the subtype graph tells us which nodes are subtypes of which, it does not provide the subtype definitions. Since infinitely many definitions are consistent with any finite set of data, the UoD expert is needed to confirm the correct definitions. Moreover, in practice it is unrealistic to assume that a sample population is significant with respect to the subtype graph. In spite of these disclaimers, subtype matrices can be useful for the following tasks: deriving a tentative subtype graph; creating a population that is significant with respect to a known subtype graph; checking that a population is significant with respect to a known subtype graph.

A *matrix* is a rectangular array of elements. For example, a drawn game of "noughts and crosses" comprises a 3 × 3 array of "0" and "X" marks. Two kinds of matrix may be used to determine the subtype graph. We focus on the *partition-details matrix* technique, as developed by Falkenberg. The other matrix is briefly discussed later.

Suppose that we have isolated some object type *A* for which a subtype graph is required. We begin by dividing *A* into groups where each member of any given group has exactly the same roles recorded. These groups are mutually exclusive, and collectively exhaustive of *A* (i.e. they form a *partition* of *A*). The following Euler diagram pictures *A* being partitioned into five groups.

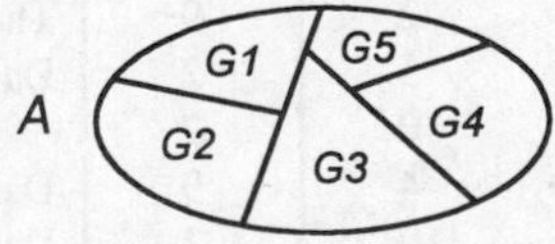

Figure B.1 *A* is partitioned into five groups

Table B.1 A partition-details table indicates the details recorded for each group

	Detail 1	*Detail 2*	*Detail 3*	*Detail 4*	...
Group 1					
Group 2					
Group 3					
...					

The list of details recorded for each member of *A* is the *recording pattern* for that member. Although members of the same group have the same recording pattern, different groups must have different recording patterns. Having partitioned *A* into groups on the basis of recording patterns, we display this on a partition-details table (see Table B.1).

As row headings we list the groups which comprise the partition. We may list these groups simply as "(1)", "(2)" etc. or, if their nature is obvious, we may use a descriptive name for each. As column headings we list all the details which are to be recorded for at least some groups. We name each detail by asking what kind of information may be recorded for the group members (e.g. weight, age, sports played, sports enjoyed).

If there are *n* groups and *m* details we have an $n \times m$ grid of cells which we now fill in with either a "1" or a "0" using the following rule:

1 = this detail may be recorded for this group
0 = this detail must not be recorded for this group

Here "this detail" and "this group" mean the detail and group for that cell's column and row respectively. Thus the recording pattern for each group is indicated by the pattern of 1s and 0s on its row. When the whole table is filled in we have an $n \times m$ matrix of 1s and 0s. As an example, consider the media survey application discussed in chapter 6. The output report for this is reproduced in Table B.2. As usual, the mark "–" means "inapplicable because of some other data".

Table B.2 An output report from the media survey

Person	*Age (y)*	*Television (h/week)*	*Newspaper (h/week)*	*Favorite channel*	*Favorite paper*	*Preferred news*
5001	41	0	10	–	The Times	–
5002	60	0	25	–	The Times	–
5003	16	20	2	9	The Times	–
5004	18	20	5	2	Daily Mail	TV
5005	13	35	0	7	–	–
5006	17	14	4	9	Daily Sun	–
5007	50	8	10	2	Daily Sun	NP
5008	33	0	0	–	–	–
5009	13	50	0	10	–	–

Table B.3 The array of 1s and 0s is the partition-details matrix for the media survey

	Age	*TVhours*	*NPhours*	*FavChannel*	*FavNP*	*PrefNews*
(1)	1	1	1	0	1	0
(2)	1	1	1	1	1	0
(3)	1	1	1	1	1	1
(4)	1	1	1	1	0	0
(5)	1	1	1	0	0	0

The roles relating to favorite channel, favorite newspaper and preferred news source are optional. Our task is to determine the subtype graph for these optional roles. We first the people up into groups according to their recording pattern. For example, the persons with form numbers 5001 and 5002 go into the same group because they have exactly the same details recorded. Equivalently, they have exactly the same details not recorded. Clearly, *rows with the same pattern of "–" values go into the same group*. Though not demonstrated in this example, simple null values (applicable but unknown) are treated as ordinary values when deciding the recording pattern (since the detail *may* be recorded).

Using some obvious abbreviations, the partition-details table for our example is shown in Table B.3. The partition-details matrix itself is just the pattern of 1s and 0s. Here persons 5001 and 5002 form group (1); 5003 and 5006 form group (2); 5004 and 5007 form group (3); 5005 and 5009 form group (4); and 5008 forms group (5). Confirm this partition and the recording patterns for yourself. As you assign a member to a group, enter the group name beside its row in the output report. This provides a check that we haven't missed any rows. With our example, this gives:

(1) 5001 …
(1) 5002 …
(2) 5003 …
(3) 5004 …
(4) 5005 …
(2) 5006 …
(3) 5007 …
(5) 5008 …
(4) 5009 …

Having obtained the matrix, we now find the subtype graph as follows. **Each node in the subtype graph corresponds to a distinct column pattern in the matrix.** By "column pattern" we mean the sequence of 1s and 0s in the column. We *label the different column patterns* as "A", "B" etc. Matching columns correspond to the same node, and are given the same label. Work from left to right: if a column pattern is new, write its label two spaces below the column; if the column matches an earlier one, write the earlier label one space below the column. With our example only the first three columns match, so this yields Table B.4.

Table B.4 The subtype nodes are labelled A .. D

	Age	*TVhours*	*NPhours*	*FavChannel*	*FavNP*	*PrefNews*
(1)	1	1	1	0	1	0
(2)	1	1	1	1	1	0
(3)	1	1	1	1	1	1
(4)	1	1	1	1	0	0
(5)	1	1	1	0	0	0
		A	A			
	A			**B**	**C**	**D**

To understand why this procedure yields the nodes of the subtype graph, recall that the head of the graph has the common role(s) attached, and each subtype node has some specific role(s) attached. With our example, the column pattern for Age, TVhours and NPhours shows that these are recorded for all the groups. So these three details correspond to the common roles attached to the head of the graph. So A is the head node.

Looking at column B we see that FavChannel is recorded *only for* groups (2), (3) and (4). So provided there is a *well defined* way of determining membership in the union of groups (2), (3) and (4), we must make a proper subtype out of these groups. Assuming the output report is significant in this respect, this indicates that there is a subtype node with favors-TVchannel attached. So B is one of the subtype nodes.

Similarly, we can prove that there is a subtype node specifically to record favorite newspaper, and another subtype node to record preferred news source. So C and D are the other subtype nodes. Note that in general, **the details recorded for the nodes are indicated by the column headings for the nodes.**

We still have to *determine the subtype relationships between the nodes*. This can be easily done by comparing the column patterns for the nodes. Clearly, the groups included in a node are those heading the rows where the node's column value = 1. With our example, node A includes groups (1)–(5), node B includes groups (2)–(4), node C includes groups (1)–(3), and node D includes group (3). One node is a subset of another node just in case all its groups are included in the other node. So, given two nodes *X* and *Y*, it follows that *X is a subset of Y if and only if, for every row where X = 1, Y = 1.*

We use this rule to determine the proper subtype relationships between the nodes. To be systematic, we work our way through all such relationships, beginning with the largest node. With our example, this yields the following results: A has proper subtypes B, C, D; B has proper subtype D; C has proper subtype D. Check this for yourself. These relationships are portrayed in Figure B.2. To help you understand the example, the groups included in each node are also listed in the figure.

The next step is to **delete all transitively implied subtype relationships**. Our graph includes an arrow to explicitly show that D is a subtype of A. But this is transitively implied, since D is a subtype of B, and B is a subtype of A. So we delete this redundant link from the graph. At last we have the subtype graph for our example. With larger examples there may be more than one transitively redundant link to delete. Since we already know which details are recorded for each node, we can sketch these in too, as shown in Figure B.3. For compactness, the details are displayed as attributes.

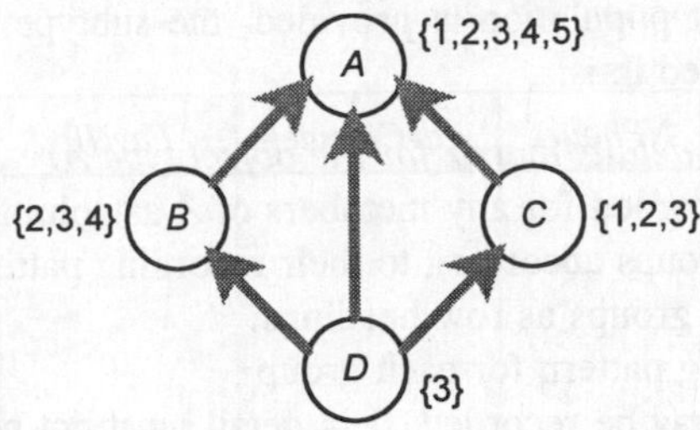

Figure B.2 The subtype graph obtained from Table B.4

As discussed earlier, the head node A is the entity type Person. But we still need to **provide definitions and meaningful names for the subtypes.** To do this we go back to the original output report and ask what criteria are used to determine whether a specific subtype role is recorded. For any given subtype these criteria must be expressed in terms of one or more roles attached to its supertype(s).

By analysing the data we can usually make good, educated guesses; but these must be confirmed with the UoD expert. For example, what is the relevant difference between the people 5004 and 5007, for whom preferred news source is recorded, and the people 5003 and 5006? By inspecting Table B.2 we might note that one difference is that 5004 and 5007 are at least 18 in age (i.e. they are adults), whereas 5003 and 5006 are below 18 in age. Another difference is that 5004 and 5007 read newspapers for at least 5 hours per week. You may like to suggest other possible criteria.

Alternative hypotheses can often be rejected by testing them against other sample populations. As discussed in section 6.5, input forms sometimes implicitly contain the definitions. However, in the absence of such documentation, the only safe way to determine the subtype definitions is to check with the UoD expert.

Refer back to Figure 6.36 for the detailed conceptual schema. Note that the nodes in the subtype graph are quite different from the groups that were formed in the original partition. It is obvious from the value constraints and subtype definitions that Viewer and Reader are neither exclusive nor exhaustive. If desired, a check on exclusion and exhaustion constraints can be made by examining exclusion and exhaustion between the column patterns of the subtype nodes in the matrix: this optional check depends on the sample being significant with respect to these constraints.

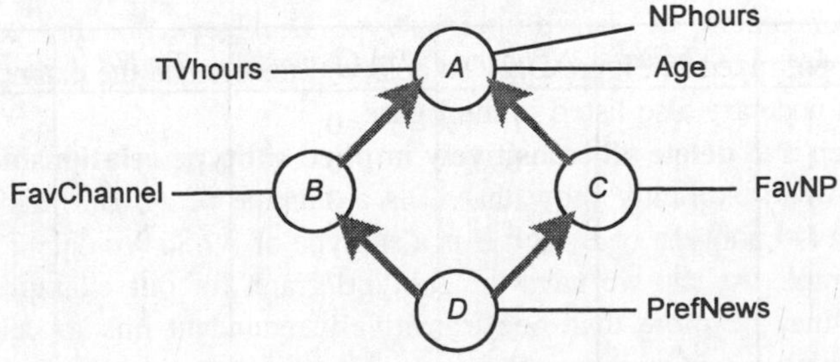

Figure B.3 The implied subtype link is deleted, and details are added for the nodes

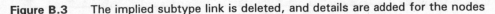

Assuming a significant population is provided, the subtype matrix procedure just discussed may be summarized thus:

1. *Construct the partition-details matrix for the object type A:*
   List the details recorded for any members of *A* as column headings.
   Partition *A* into groups according to their recording patterns,
   and list these groups as row headings.
   Enter the recording pattern for each group
   (1 = detail may be recorded, 0 = detail must not be recorded)

2. *Sketch the subtype graph and attached details:*
   Label the different column patterns as nodes *A*, *B* etc.
   Determine the subtype relationships between the nodes as follows:
   node *X* is subset of node *Y* iff for each row where $X = 1$, $Y = 1$.
   Draw the subtype graph and delete any transitively implied arcs.
   Attach to each node the detail(s) indicated by its column heading(s).

3. *Provide definitions and meaningful names for the subtypes:*
   Define each subtype in terms of one or more roles attached to its supertype(s).

4. *Complete the conceptual schema:*
   Fill in the fine details of the schema diagram, including subtype definitions.

Given a significant population, an alternative matrix technique developed by Vermeir may also be used to determine the subtype graph. The associated matrix is called a *details-details matrix* because the details recorded for any member of the head supertype are listed both as row and column headings. To fill in the values of the matrix, we ask this question for each cell: *for each object instance for which we record the row detail, must we record the column detail? If the answer is Yes we enter "1", else we enter "0".*

As an example, the details-details matrix for the media survey example is shown in Table B.5. It should be obvious that the diagonal running from the top left corner to the bottom left corner must always be filled in with 1 values (Why?). As with the earlier matrix, matching columns correspond to the same node, and different column patterns correspond to different nodes in the subtype graph.

Table B.4 A details-details matrix for the same application

	Age	*TVhours*	*NPhours*	*FavChannel*	*FavNP*	*PrefNews*
Age	1	1	1	0	0	0
TVhours	1	1	1	0	0	0
NPhours	1	1	1	0	0	0
FavChannel	1	1	1	1	0	0
FavNP	1	1	1	0	1	0
PrefNews	1	1	1	1	1	1
		A	A			
	A			B	C	D

In a similar manner to the other matrix, subtype relationships between the nodes are determined by comparing the column patterns of the nodes, and the details recorded for the nodes are given by the column headings for the nodes. Check for yourself that this matrix gives the same result as the earlier one.

Unlike the partition-details matrix, the details-details matrix cannot be used to check on exclusion and exhaustion constraints. It is also somewhat less intuitive. However it is quite simple to compute, and it is idempotent with respect to Boolean multiplication (i.e. when multiplied by itself using logical rather that arithmetic operations, the product is identical to the original matrix). This property may be used as a check on the matrix. Testing this property is tedious and is best handled by automation.

To use the details-details matrix instead of the partition-details matrix, replace steps 1 and 2 in the subtype matrix procedure with the method just described. Whichever kind of matrix is used, remember that each assumes the sample is significant with respect to the subtype graph.

Exercise B1

1. For a department, information of the kind indicated by the following output report is to be maintained. Departmental offices are identified by a room number. If you are unfamiliar with the metric system, note that 1 inch is about 2.5 cm (e.g. 5' 10" = 175 cm). The population shown is significant. The mark "–" means "inapplicable". Schematize this UoD, using a subtype matrix to help decide on the subtype graph.

Member	*Sex*	*Smoker?*	*Starsign*	*Height (cm)*	*Office*	*Sport*
Adams	F	Y	Aquarius	–	–	–
Brown	M	Y	–	170	–	–
Collins	M	N	–	190	308	basketball
Davis	F	Y	Gemini	–	–	–
Evans	M	Y	–	190	–	–
Fomor	M	N	–	180	505	basketball, tennis
Gordon	F	N	Aquarius	–	406	–
Hastings	M	Y	–	165	–	–
Iveson	M	N	–	165	305	–
Jones	M	N	–	179	502	–

2. Use a subtype matrix to determine the subtype graph for Exercise 6.5, Question 5.

appendix C Introduction to SQL

This appendix provides a basic introduction to **SQL** (popularly, if incorrectly, called "Structured Query Language"), which is the most important relational database language in commercial use. As a full coverage of SQL would require a large book in itself, many advanced features of the language are omitted here. The treatment assumes familiarity with relational schemas (section 8.2) and the main operations of the relational algebra (section 8.5). Because of its length, this appendix is divided into named sections.

A brief history

After the publication of Codd's classic paper on the relational model of data (Codd 1970), some early prototypes were developed to provide a relational DBMS, including a language for querying and updating relational databases. By 1975, a team at the IBM San Jose Research Laboratory had implemented part of a language called "SEQUEL" (Structured English Query Language) as an interface to its System R relational prototype, within a project also called System R. By 1977, a revised version of this language (SEQUEL/2) had been defined, and largely implemented by IBM. This language was later renamed "SQL".

The System R project ran from 1971 through 1979, and later evolved into a distributed database project (System R*). Using the experience gained from its System R project, IBM built its first commercial relational DBMS, known as SQL/DS, which it released in 1981; its second and highly influential SQL product, known as DB2, was released in 1983. As the SQL language had been widely publicized in the 1970s in research papers, other firms began developing their own systems. Relational Software Inc. (later renamed Oracle Corporation) actually beat IBM to the market by releasing its commercial SQL product in 1979. In 1982, the American National Standards Institute (ANSI) began standardization work on the language. The first SQL standard was completed in 1986, and is known as SQL-86. By this time, over fifty SQL products had been released.

In 1987, the ANSI SQL-86 standard was adopted by the International Organization for Standardization (ISO). In 1989 a more comprehensive standard, SQL-89, was adopted by both ANSI and ISO. This defined a basic Level 1 version, a richer Level 2 version, and included an addendum on integrity enhancements (including declarative entity integrity and referential integrity).

In 1992 the next standard, known as SQL-92, was approved by both ANSI and ISO. Because of its size (over 600 pages) it was defined at three levels: entry; intermediate; and full. Many of the major commercial SQL companies are committed to supporting most of the SQL-92 standard by the mid-nineties. The next standard, code-named "SQL3", is expected to be ratified by 1997. As the SQL3 draft standard totals over 1000 pages, it has been split into modules, some of which may be approved earlier. Work on a subsequent standard, code-named "SQL4" has already started. In this appendix we focus on the SQL-89 and SQL-92 standards.

Identifiers and data types

For a given schema, some objects such as base tables, views (derived tables), domains and constraints are identified by name. A column is identified by appending its (local) name to the name of its table, using a "dot notation". For example, the second column of the table Subject (subjcode, title, credit) is identified as "Subject.title". This ensures it is distinguished from other columns with the same local name. In SQL, all names (including local names) are called *"identifiers"*, even though local names provide identification only within a limited context.

In SQL-92 an identifier is either regular or delimited. A *regular identifier* is a string of at most 128 characters, the first of which must be a letter ("a".."z","A",.."Z"). Each later character must be a letter, digit ("0".."9") or underscore ("_"). Moreover, no reserved word may be used as a regular identifier. In SQL-89, identifiers were restricted to at most 18 characters, and all letters had to be in upper case.

Some examples are shown in table C.1. The entries in the third column are illegal since they start with a digit or include an illegal character (e.g. a space or parenthesis). The entries in the fourth column are illegal in SQL-92 only, since they were first introduced as reserved words in that standard. Since the list of reserved words grows with each new standard, identifiers in existing applications might become illegal at a later stage. Partly to simplify the task of converting these to legal identifiers, the SQL-92 standard allows delimited identifiers.

A *delimited identifier* is a string of at most 128 characters, delimited by (i.e. enclosed in) double quotes. Any character at all may be used. Unlike regular identifiers, delimited identifiers are case-sensitive (i.e. upper-case letters are not equated to lower-case letters). For example, the first three identifiers in the following list are treated as equivalent to one another but the fourth is treated as different:

STUDENT   Student   "STUDENT"   "Student"

Table C.1 Some regular identifiers

legal in SQL-92 and SQL-89	*legal in SQL-92 but not SQL-89*	*illegal in SQL-92 and SQL-89*	*illegal in SQL-92 but legal in SQL-89*
A R2D2 STUDENT_NR	a This_is_a_long_identifier StudentNr	2B STUDENT NR HEIGHT(CM)	DATE FIRST LEVEL

Table C.2 Reserved words

Reserved words in SQL-89 (and SQL-92)	*Extra reserved words in SQL-92*
all and any as asc authorization avg	absolute action add allocate alter are
	assertion at
begin between by	bit bit_length both
char character check close commit	cascade cascaded case cast catalog
continue count create current cursor	char_length character_length coalesce collate
	collation column connect connection
	constraint constraints convert corresponding
	cross current current_date current_time
	current_timestamp current_user
dec decimal declare default delete	date day deallocate deferrable deferred
desc distinct double	describe descriptor diagnostics disconnect
	domain drop
end escape exec exists	else end-exec except exception execute
	external extract
fetch float for foreign found from	false first full
go goto grant group having	get global hour
in indicator insert int integer into is	identity immediate initially inner input
	insensitive intersect interval isolation
key language like	join last leading left level local lower
max min module	match minute month
not null numeric	names national natural nchar next no nullif
of on open option or order	octet_length only outer output overlaps
precision primary privileges procedure	partial position prepare preserve prior
public	
real references rollback	read relative restrict revoke right rows
schema section select set smallint	scroll second session session_user size
some sql sqlcode sqlerror sum	sqlstate substring system_user
table to	temporary then time timestamp timezone_hour
	timezone_minute trailing transaction translate
	translation trim true
union unique update user	unknown upper usage using
values view whenever where with	value varchar varying when write
work	year zone

Many commercial SQLs allow some other characters in regular identifiers (e.g. "#", "$", "@"). Though SQL-92 does not allow this, it does allow these and other characters within delimited identifiers. For example, the following are legal delimited identifiers:

"Student#"	"$salary"	"Cost@60c_perUS$"
"Student Number"	"Height (cm)"	"2B-or-not-2B!!!%*"

Since all characters in an identifier are significant, it is acceptable to embed a reserved word as just part of an identifier. Suppose a column in a table is used to store the names of tutorial groups. Since "group" is a reserved word, we cannot use this (unquoted) as a regular identifier for the column. However, we may add quotes to make it a delimited identifier, or include "group" in a longer regular identifier. For example:

"group" TuteGroup GroupName

A first impression of how a given SQL dialect compares with the standards may be gained by inspecting its list of reserved words. Table C.2 lists the reserved words for SQL-89 and SQL-92. For the rest of this appendix, we distinguish reserved words by displaying them in bold.

In SQL-92, *key words* are words that have predefined meanings. Reserved words are key words that cannot be used as regular identifiers. In addition, there are dozens of key words that are not reserved (e.g. "COBOL", "length", "name", "type").

Values entered in a table column belong the *data type* declared for that column. Table C.3 lists the main standard data types. Currently, many commercial SQLs support only some of these, while at the same time providing additional data types (e.g. money). SQL-92 also allows domains to be declared for columns, but only in a weak sense.

All SQL dialects support at least character string and numeric types. In the standard, "**char**(*n*)" means the value will be stored as a fixed length string of *n* characters; if the value has fewer that *n* characters, blanks will be appended to fill out the length. If no size (*n*) is specified, this is treated as a string with only 1 character. A value of type **varchar**(*n*) is stored as a string of at most *n* characters; if the value is shorter it is stored as it is, without padding it with extra blanks. Some SQL implementations treat **char** the same as **varchar**. SQL-92 allows various national character sets to be declared.

Table C.3 Standard data types

SQL-89 (and SQL-92)	*Extra in SQL-92*
character string: **char**(*n*) **char**	*character string:* **varchar**(*n*)
	bit string: **bit**(*n*) **bit varying**(*n*)
exact numeric: **numeric** (*p*, [*s*]) **dec** (*p*, [*s*]) **int** **smallint**	*datetime:* **date** { year, month, day } **time** { hour, minute, second } **timestamp** {date and time } **time with time zone** **timestamp with time zone**
approximate numeric: **float** [*p*] **real** **double precision**	
{ *p* = precision *s* = scale }	*interval:* year-month periods day-time periods

With the **numeric** data type, the precision *p* is the maximum number of digits included in the number, and the scale *s* is the number of digits after the decimal point. For example, columns declared **numeric**(6,2) allow values in the range -9999.99..+9999.99. The **decimal** type is like the numeric type except that the implementation may sometimes provide a precision even greater than *p*. The **integer** and **smallint** data types allow integers only (no fractions). The three approximate numeric data types allow very large or very small numbers to be stored to a specified precision as a mantissa times an exponent of 10. The words "char", "dec" and "int" may be expanded to "character", "decimal" and "integer".

As set out in Table C.3, SQL-92 provides direct support for bit strings as well as time points and time intervals. Various temporal operators are provided (e.g. to allow computation of intervals by subtracting one time point from another). Further details on these data types may be found in the appendix references.

Choosing columns

Recall that relational algebra includes the following eight table operations: union, intersection, difference, Cartesian product, selection, projection, join, and division. All of these operations (as well as others) can be expressed using SQL's powerful select statement. In this section we look at *projection*.

Consider a small UoD where people are identified by their firstname. Table C.4 provides sample data for the scheme: *Person* (firstname, sex, starsign, birthyr). The whole table may be retrieved by projecting on all its columns. In relational algebra this may be formulated as Person, or as Person /firstname, sex, starsign, birthyr/. In SQL, this is expressed as follows:

```
select * from Person
```

Here the asterisk "*" means "all columns" and may be read as "everything" or "all". The table named after "from" indicates the table from which the data is to be retrieved. When this command is executed, the result is an *unnamed* table with the same column names and contents as the original Person table. If only some of the columns are required, then instead of "*" the relevant columns should be listed (separated by commas). If the columns include a key, no duplicate rows can occur in the result, so the result corresponds to a projection on those columns (e.g. see Figure C.1).

Table C.4

Person:

firstname	*sex*	*starsign*	*birthyr*
Bob	M	Gemini	1967
Eve	F	Aquarius	1967
Fred	M	Gemini	1970
Norma	F	Aries	1950
Selena	F	Taurus	1974
Terry	M	Aquarius	1946

select firstname, starsign
from Person

⇨

firstname	*starsign*
Bob	Gemini
Eve	Aquarius
Fred	Gemini
Norma	Aries
Selena	Taurus
Terry	Aquarius

Figure C.1 Projecting on columns that include a key

If the columns do not include a key, then duplicate rows may occur in the result. For example, query (a) in Figure C.2 returns a bag rather than a set. Because it is sometimes useful to include duplicates (e.g. listing all the test scores for a class) this is what happens by default in SQL. If we wish to eliminate duplicates, this can be done by including the word "**distinct**" before the select-list. This ensures that rows displayed will be distinct, thus providing a relational projection. For example, query (b) in Figure C.2 eliminates the duplicate male, Gemini row.

Columns are displayed in the order in which they are specified in the select-list. If "*" is used, all the columns are displayed in the same order as the original table. Every base table includes a key. So the command "select * from Person" is merely shorthand for "select firstname, sex, starsign, birthyr from Person".

In general, the relational projection *T[a,b,...]* of relational algebra may be expressed by an SQL statement of the form:

select distinct *a,b,...* **from** *T*

(a) **select** sex, starsign
from Person

⇨

sex	*starsign*
M	Gemini
F	Aquarius
M	Gemini
F	Aries
F	Taurus
M	Aquarius

(b) **select distinct** sex, starsign
from Person

⇨

sex	*starsign*
M	Gemini
F	Aquarius
F	Aries
F	Taurus
M	Aquarius

Figure C.2 The **distinct** key word may be used to remove duplicate rows

If the distinct option is omitted, then all rows (including any duplicates) are included in the result. To emphasize this, the key word "**all**" may be included before the select-list. As this is assumed by default, the following are equivalent:

select all *a,b,...* **from** *T*
select *a,b,...* **from** *T*

We may summarize that portion of the select statement covered in this section in the following EBNF (Extended Backus Naur Form) notation. The symbol "::=" may be read "is defined as". Here items in square brackets are optional. The expression "[,...]" means the previous construct may be repeated any number of times, with its occurrences separated by commas. A stroke "|" is used to separate alternatives. By default, we give "|" minimum scope (i.e. it applies just to the terms immediately beside it). Reserved words are shown in bold. The final line of the select-query shown here is called the *from-clause*. From a logical point of view, it would be better to specify the from-clause before the select-list, but the syntax of the language does not allow this.

select-list ::= *columnname* [,...]

select-query ::= **select [all | distinct]** *select-list* | *
from *tablename*

Choosing rows

Recall that relational *selection* (or restriction) is the operation of selecting those rows which satisfy a specified condition. In SQL, the syntax for this operation is essentially the same as that adopted in our treatment of relational algebra. A *where-clause* is added to the select statement just after the from-clause, and the specified condition is known as the *search condition*. Do not confuse the relational operation of selection with the select-statement itself, which is used to perform other operations as well. The following formulations in relational algebra and SQL are equivalent.

Relational algebra:	SQL:
T **where** *c*	**select** * **from** *T* **where** *c*
T **where** *c* [*a,b,...*]	**select** *a, b, ...* **from** *T* **where** *c*

For example, the query in Figure C.3 may be used to list details about the Aquarians mentioned in our earlier Person table.

select * **from** Person
where starsign = 'Aquarius' ⇨

firstname	*sex*	*starsign*	*birthyr*
Eve	F	Aquarius	1967
Terry	M	Aquarius	1946

Figure C.3 A where-clause is used to select just the Aquarians

Notice that the character string "Aquarius" contains a mixture of upper and lower case characters. Suppose this is the way it is stored in the table, but the query has the starsign typed in upper-case, i.e.

```
select * from Person where starsign = 'AQUARIUS'
```

Unless the system has been told to convert characters strings into the same case before comparing them, no match would be made since the string "AQUARIUS" is different from "Aquarius". If it is desired to make string comparisons case-insensitive, this may be done in SQL-92 either by declaring a collation set to act this way, or by using string functions to convert the case. For example, given a string expression *s*, the fold functions *upper(s)* and *lower(s)* return the upper-case and lower-case versions of *s*. So the previous query can be made to work by replacing "starsign" by "upper(starsign)". Commercial versions of SQL often provide other ways of controlling case-sensitivity.

Apart from quoted strings, the case in which letters are typed in an SQL statement is irrelevant. Some people like to use upper-case as much as possible (e.g. "SELECT * FROM PERSON"). However this makes long queries hard to read. In this text, queries are displayed mainly in lower-case; table names start with a capital letter to help distinguish them from column names; and reserved words are shown in bold.

Search conditions may include terms, *comparison operators* (=, <>, <, >, <=, >=) and *logical operators* (**not, and, or**). Some versions of SQL allow symbols other than "<>" for "is not equal to" (e.g. "^=", "!="). The same priority convention as for relational algebra is adopted. So unless brackets determine otherwise, comparison operators are evaluated before logical operators, which are evaluated in the order: **not**; then **and**; then **or**.

Consider the query in Figure C.4. This lists the name and starsign of people born after 1950 who are either Aquarians or Geminis. If the parentheses were omitted, the condition would be interpreted as: starsign = 'Aquarius' **or** (starsign = 'Gemini' **and** birthyr > 1950). This is different, since it would result in the older Aquarians (in this case Terry) being listed as well.

The selection operation becomes a bit trickier when null values may be present. Consider the relation scheme *Employee* (<u>emp#</u>, empname, dept, [cartype]). Here the cartype column is optional. Some employees might not drive a car, and even if they do perhaps it is not recorded. Figure C.5 provides a sample population for this table, as well as two queries and their results. Suppose we want to know who drives a Ford, and who doesn't. We might formulate these questions as queries (a) and (b) of Figure C.5. Although each employee in real life either does or does not drive a Ford, employee 1002 is absent from both the query results. Can you make sense of this?

```
select firstname, starsign
from   Person
where (starsign = 'Aquarius' or starsign = 'Gemini')
    and birthyr > 1950
```

⇨

firstname	*starsign*
Bob	Gemini
Eve	Aquarius
Fred	Gemini

Figure C.4 Brackets are needed to evaluate or before and

Employee:

emp#	empname	dept	cartype
1001	Thompson. E.	Sales	Ford
1002	Jones, E.	Sales	?
1003	Smith, F.	R&D	Toyota
1004	Adams, A.	Sales	Ford
1005	Dennis, A.	Admin	?

(a) **select** emp#, empname **from** Employee
where cartype = 'Ford' ⇨

emp#	empname
1001	Thompson, E.
1004	Adams, A.

(b) **select** emp#, empname **from** Employee
where cartype < > 'Ford' ⇨

emp#	empname
1003	Smith, F.

Figure C.5 Rows are selected when the condition is true (not false and not unknown)

Where null values are concerned, SQL operates on a *3-valued logic*. A condition may evaluate to true, false or unknown. More correctly, a condition is known-to-be-true, known-to-be-false, or unknown. *A comparison between terms, in which at least one term is null, always evaluates to unknown*. This holds for any comparison operator (=, < >, < etc.). Consider the row for employee 1002, where a null value (displayed here as "?") is recorded for the cartype. For query C.5(a) the condition is "? = Ford", and for query C.5(b) the condition is "? < > Ford". In both cases, the condition evaluates to unknown.

The selection operation performed by the *where-clause returns just those rows which evaluate to true* (i.e. known-to-be-true). Rows which evaluate to false or unknown are filtered out. Hence the rows for employees 1002 and 1005 (Jones and Dennis) are filtered out in both queries. Filtering out the unknown helps us to avoid making unwarranted assumptions. As we will see later, SQL provides a special function for detecting null values.

Ordering rows

Columns are displayed in the order in which they appear in the select-list. The order in which *rows* are displayed may be controlled by means of an *order-by clause*. If used, the order-by clause must come at the end of the select statement. One or more columns in the select-list (identified by name or by position in the select-list) may be used as ordering criteria. A column number must be used if the select-item is not a column name or if union is used (see later).

Ordering for a criterion is ascending by default (or if "**asc**" is appended to the column identifier), and descending if "**desc**" is appended. For numeric values, "ascending" means smaller numbers are listed first. For character string values, "ascending" means strings which come earlier in the collating sequence are listed first. As a rough guide, words which come earlier in alphabetical order usually come first.

```
select emp#, empname from Employee            ⇨
order by empname
or
select emp#, empname from Employee            ⇨
order by empname asc
```

emp#	*empname*
1004	Adams, A.
1005	Dennis, A.
1002	Jones, E.
1003	Smith, F.
1001	Thompson, E.

Figure C.6 Listing in ascending order of employee names

For example, each of the queries in Figure C.6 may be used to list the employees in alphabetical order. In both cases, "2" may be used instead of "empname" in the order-by clause, since empname is the second item in the select-list (it doesn't have to be the second column of the base table). Character strings are ordered according to the character collating sequence. For example, if ASCII is used then space (" ") precedes digits ("0".."9") which precede upper case letters ("A".."Z") which precede lower case letters ("a".."z"). For instance, in ASCII "M2" < "MY" < "Ma" < "Ma Kcttle" < "MacTavish" < "Zen" < "apple"; but other collating sequences may differ from this.

The order-by clause may be thought of as a way of converting a *bag* of rows to a *sequence* of rows. For ordering purposes, null values are treated as equal, and depending on the implementation are either greater than all non-null values or less than all non-null values. Consider the following query:

```
select cartype from Employee
order by 1
```

This returns the sequence ⟨'Ford', 'Ford', 'Toyota'⟩ either followed or preceded by the two null values, depending on the implementation.

If the column chosen for ordering is not a key, then further ordering can be obtained within its duplicate values by specifying further columns in the order-by clause. Criteria listed first in the order-by clause are ordered first. For any particular column the ascending or descending option may be applied. For instance, a query of the form

```
select * from T order by a, b desc
```

first sorts the rows in ascending order of *a*, and then each set of rows with the same *a* value is sorted in descending order of *b*. For example, see Figure C.7. Here the females are listed first, and within each sex the names are shown in reverse alphabetic order.

```
select firstname, sex from Person
order by sex, firstname desc            ⇨
```

firstname	*sex*
Selena	F
Norma	F
Eve	F
Terry	M
Fred	M
Bob	M

Figure C.7 Ordering on two criteria

```
select starsign, firstname, sex, birthyr
from Person
where starsign <> 'Taurus'
order by starsign, sex desc, birthyr
```

⇨

starsign	*firstname*	*sex*	*birthyr*
Aquarius	Terry	M	1946
Aquarius	Eve	F	1967
Aries	Norma	F	1950
Gemini	Fred	M	1970
Gemini	Bob	M	1967

Figure C.8 Ordering options are "sticky"

Notice in Figure C.7 that "**desc**" has *minimum back-scope*, applying just to firstname, not to sex. If descending order of both were required we would use "sex **desc**, firstname **desc**". To list in ascending order of sex then name we may use "sex **asc**, firstname **asc**" or just "sex, firstname" since **asc** is the default. Note that the **asc** and **desc** options have *maximum forward-scope* (i.e. once declared, they apply to any columns listed later in the order-by clause until over-ridden by the opposite option). For this reason, the two options are said to be "sticky". To test your understanding, see if you can predict the result of the query in Figure C.8 and then check your answer with the table shown.

Did you get it right? The rows were first sorted on starsign in ascending order, then males before females as a second criterion (see rows 1,2), then younger before older as a third criterion (see rows 4,5). The birth years of the male Geminis are in descending order, since the **desc** option on sex also applies to birthyr. The order-by clause may be specified explicitly by including all the implied ordering options:

```
order by starsign asc, sex desc, birthyr desc
```

Using the positions of the columns in the select-list, this could be shortened to:

```
order by 1, 3 desc, 4 desc
```

Let us use the term *colname* to indicate a column name, and *col* to indicate a column specification (either by name or number). The syntax of that portion of the select statement so far covered may be summarized in EBNF as follows:

```
select [all | distinct] colname [,...] | *
from   tablename
where condition
order by col [asc | desc]  [,...]
```

Exercise C.1

1. Which of the following are legal identifiers in SQL?

   (a) Payroll# (b) PayrollNr (c) "Payroll#" (d) 1994Tax
   (e) Tax in 1994 (f) "Tax in 1994" (g) Tax_in_1994 (h) Deposit_in_$
   (i) Mass_(kg) (j) Order (k) WorldWideWebIdentifier

2. The following table concerns statements provided in Modula 2. In the column Extra, the values "Y" and "N" indicate respectively whether the statement is extra to or already included in Pascal. Formulate each of the following requests as a single SQL query.

Statement:

kind	*composition*	*extra*
assignment	simple	N
procedure call	simple	N
if	structured	N
case	structured	N
for	structured	N
while	structured	N
repeat	structured	N
loop	structured	Y
with	structured	N
exit	simple	Y
return	simple	Y
empty	simple	N

(a) List the kind of each statement.
(b) List all information in the table.
(c) List the kind and composition of all statements.
(d) List the kind of each statement, and whether it is extra.
(e) List the possible composition values of the statements. (Avoid duplicates)
(f) Which statements are structured?
(g) Which simple statements are extra to Pascal?
(h) List the kind and composition of those statements which are extra to Pascal.
(i) List, in alphabetical order, the kinds of those statements already found in Pascal.
(j) List the kind and composition of all the statements, starting with the simple statements.
(k) List the kind and composition of all the statements, starting with the structured statements and listing statements of the same composition in alphabetic order.
(l) List the kind, composition and extra status of all the statements, giving precedence to statements extra to Pascal. Statements with the same extra status should be listed starting with those of simple composition, with those of similar composition being shown in reverse alphabetic order.
(m) List alphabetically the kinds of those statements which are neither structured nor extra to Pascal.
(n) List in reverse alphabetic order the kinds of those statements which are either structured and extra to Pascal or simple.
(o) As for (n) but exclude the exit statement from consideration and include the composition of each. Show all the structured statements first, in reverse alphabetic order, followed by the simple statements, in reverse alphabetic order.

Joins

So far our SQL retrieval examples have involved a single table. We have seen how to perform the relational operations of projection and restriction, as well as gaining control over the order in which columns and rows are displayed. One major strength of a relational database system is the ease in which information spread over several tables of different type may be extracted. SQL provides two main methods of performing such an extraction.

The first of these uses relational *joins* and is discussed in this section. The second involves subqueries and will be treated in a later section. The following discussion assumes you are familiar with the concept of joins from the relational algebra section.

The SQL-92 standard includes several kinds of joins: *cross joins*; *natural joins*; *condition joins*; *column-name joins*; *outer joins* (left, right, full); and *union joins*. The new and old syntax for these is summarized in Table C.5. Currently, only some commercial SQLs support the new syntax. In this summary, if tables *A* and *B* have any common columns (with the same local name), these columns are collectively referred to as "*c*". For the column-name join, "c_1,.." denotes one or more of these common columns.

A *Cartesian product* (*cross join*) of tables pairs all the rows of one with all the rows of the other. In SQL-89, a cross join of tables is specified by listing the tables in the from-clause. SQL-92 allows the more descriptive "**cross join**" instead of a comma. A *condition join* selects only those rows from the Cartesian product which satisfy the specified condition. *Column-name joins* match values on the specified columns with the local same name in both tables. *Natural inner joins* match all columns with the same local names, and remove the extra copies of these columns. In the old syntax, condition joins, column-name joins and natural inner joins are specified by first forming the Cartesian product (of the tables listed in the from-clause), then specifying any join-conditions in a where-clause; for natural inner joins, the select-list also filters out unwanted duplicate columns.

The new syntax uses the word "**join**" in the from-clause. For condition-joins, the condition is specified in an on-clause. For column-name joins, the relevant columns are listed in a using-clause. Natural inner joins are specified simply by inserting "**natural**" before "**join**" in the from clause. The new notation has three main advantages: it is more descriptive; the "**natural join**" operator gives direct support for the natural inner join operator of relational algebra (⋈); and it is often more concise. For example, recall the following example discussed in the relational algebra section.

Account (branch#, localAc#, balance)

AcUser (branch#, localAc#, client#)

Client (client#, clientname)

Suppose we wished to list the balance and client details for all the accounts. This may be specified as the following SQL-92 query:

```
select * from Account natural join AcUser natural join Client
```

But in the old syntax, the joins must be specified in agonizing detail, including qualified column names as shown. Here there is a composite join on account (since this requires two attributes to identify it) and a simple join on client.

```
select   Account.branchnr, Account.localaccountnr, balance,
         Client.clientnr, clientname
from     Account, AcUser, Client
where    Account.branchnr = AcUser.branchnr
  and    Account.localaccountnr = AcUser.localaccountnr
  and    AcUser.clientnr = Client.clientnr
```

Table C.5 Joins in SQL-92 and SQL-89

Join type	*New syntax in SQL-92*	*Old syntax*
cross	**select *** **from A cross join B**	**select *** **from A, B**
natural inner	**select *** **from A natural join B** { join column in result is c }	**select A.c,...** { omit B.c } **from A, B** **where A.c = B.c** { join column in result is A.c }
condition join	**select *** **from A join B on** *condition*	**select *** **from A, B** **where** *condition*
column-name	**select *** **from A join B using** (c_1,..) { c_1, ... are unqualified }	**select A.**c_1**,...,..** { omit B.c_1,.. } **from A, B** **where A.**c_1 **= B.**c_1 **and ...** { join columns are qualified }
left outer	**select *** **from A natural left join B** { join cols are unqualified; nulls are generated for non-matches (not blank-strings) } { to join on fewer cols use: A **left join B using** (c_1,..) } { to join on cols with different names use: A **left join B on** *condition* }	**select A.c,...** { omit B.c } **from A, B** **where A.c = B.c** **union all** **select c,..., ' ',...** **from A** **where c not in** **(select c from B)** { for composite c, use **exists** with a correlated subquery } { fewer or different cols cases not shown here }
right outer	**select *** **from A natural right join B** { other cases: cf. left join }	**select B.c, ...** { omit A.c } **...** { rest as for left join, but swap A and B }
full outer	**select *** **from A natural full join B** { other cases: cf. left join; rarely used }	union of left and right outer joins
union	**select *** **from A union join B** { rarely used }	**select** *A.cols*, ' ',.. { ∀ B col } **from A** **union all** **select ' ',...,** *B.cols* {' ' ∀ A col } **from B**

Note that **"join"** is assumed to mean inner join unless a different kind of join is explicitly specified. Where applicable, **"inner"** may be explicitly declared (e.g. **"natural inner join"**). If **"natural"** is declared, an on-clause or a using-clause must not be. If three or more tables are included in a join-expression, the joins are normally evaluated in a left-to-right order. In SQL-92, the join order can be controlled by inserting brackets. Since natural inner joins are associative, the order doesn't affect the actual result.

Let's look at a few examples using the following relational schema. As an exercise, you might like to draw the conceptual schema. In the first table "mgrEmpnr" denotes the employee number of the department manager (where there is a manager). The pair-subset constraint indicates that an employee manages a department only if he or she works in it. The ⟨2,1⟩ permutation marker indicates the reordering to ⟨mgrEmpnr, deptcode⟩ before comparing with ⟨empnr, deptcode⟩. In this UoD an employee may drive many cars.

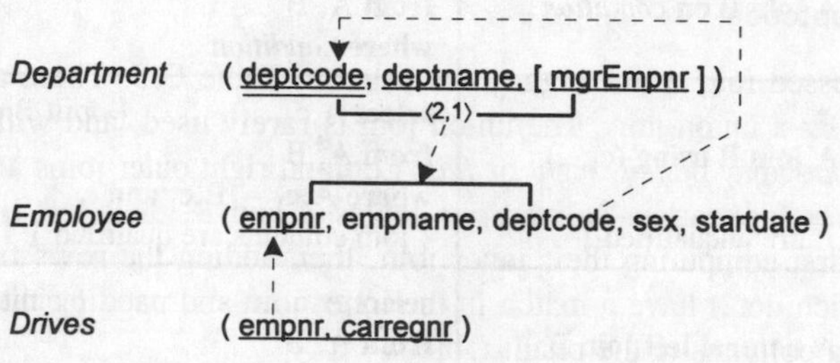

In practice, most joins are natural inner joins. As in relational algebra, when the natural join operator is used the join columns must be denoted by their local (unqualified) names. For example, the following query lists the employee number, name and car registration number(s) of all employees who drive cars. It would be illegal to qualify "empnr" in this query as "Employee.empnr".

```
select empnr, empname, carregnr
from Employee natural join Drives
```

Now consider the query: For each department with a manager, list its code and name, and the employee number and name of its manager. We want to match employee numbers between the Department and Employee tables. Can we do this with a natural join? No, since the columns have different names ("mgrEmpnr" and "empnr"). We could formulate the query with a cross join:

```
select Department.deptcode, deptname, mgrEmpnr, empname
from   Department cross join Employee
where Department.deptcode = Employee.deptcode
   and mgrEmpnr = empnr
```

or with a condition join:

```
select Department.deptcode, deptname, mgrEmpnr, empname
from   Department join Employee
  on   Department.deptcode = Employee.deptcode
       and mgrEmpnr = empnr
```

As an example of a column-name join, consider the following schema. Here the local identifier "name" has been used for the department name as well as the employee name. Suppose we wish to list the employee number and name of the employees, as well as their departments. A natural join should not be used here (Why not?).

Dept (deptcode, name)

Emp (empnr, name, deptcode)

Here we want to join using only some of the common names (just "deptcode"). So we may set this out as the following column-name join.

```
select empnr, Emp.name, Dept.name
from Dept join Emp
     using (deptcode)
```

So far we have discussed four of the eight joins listed in Table C.5. There are also three outer joins, as well as a union join. The union join is rarely used, and will not be discussed further. *Outer joins* may be *left*, *right* or *full*. Left and right outer joins are often encountered in commercial applications. Given two tables *A* and *B*, their left/right/full outer join is formed by first computing their inner join, then adding the rows from the left/right/both table(s) which don't have a match in the inner join and padding them with null values to fill the extra columns in the result table.

Figure C.9 provides a simple example of a left outer join. The query lists the employee number, name and car registration numbers (if any) of all the employees (including those who don't drive cars).

Employee:

empnr	*empname*	*deptcode*	*sex*	*startdate*
001	Hagar T	R&D	M	21/1/86
002	Wong S	R&D	F	1/1/92
003	Jones E	SPT	F	12/3/90
004	Mifune K	SPT	M	15/2/88

Drives:

empnr	*carregnr*
001	ABC123
001	LBJ572
003	PKJ900

```
select empnr, empname, carregnr      ⇨
from Employee natural left join Drives
```

empnr	*empname*	*carregnr*
001	Hagar T	ABC123
001	Hagar T	LBJ572
002	Wong S	?
003	Jones E	PKJ900
004	Mifune K	?

Figure C.9 A left outer join

Since the inner join involved is a natural join, the SQL-92 syntax used here is "**natural left join**". The natural inner join results in the three rows shown for the two drivers (employees 001 and 003). Employees 002 and 004 have no match in the Drives table. The left outer join adds their rows padded with a null value for car registration number.

Right outer join is analogous to left. Full join is the union of left and right. The word "**outer**" is assumed for left/right/full joins, and may be explicitly specified (e.g. "**natural left outer join**"). Outer joins are not associative, so be careful with the join order when outer-joining three or more tables. See Table C.5 for other cases. As discussed later, outer joins can be emulated in the old syntax by means of **union** and subqueries.

When different rows of the same table must be compared, we need to join the table to itself. Such *self-joins* were discussed in the relational algebra section. Recall that this requires introducing an alias for the table. In SQL a *temporary alias* may be declared as a *tuple variable* in the from-clause after the table it aliases. This variable may be assigned any row from the table, and is sometimes called a "correlation variable", "range variable" or "table label". For clarity, "**as**" may be used to introduce the alias. As a simple example, consider the relation scheme:

Professor (<u>profname</u>, sex)

The following query may be used to list all pairs of professors of opposite sex. Here the aliases *P1* and *P2* have been declared in the from-clause. As an exercise, provide a sample population for the Professor table and trace through the working of the query.

```
select P1.profname, P2.profname
from   Professor as P1, Professor as P2
where P1.sex <> P2.sex
   and P1.profname < P2.profname
```

Some versions of SQL also provide a "create synonym" command for declaring a permanent alias definition. However this is not part of the standard. In simplified form, the syntax of SQL queries covered so far may be summarized as follows. The join-operation is usually "natural [left|right] join" or "cross join". In some cases, on-clause or using-clauses are appended to the join (see Table C.5 for more details).

```
select [all | distinct] colname [,...] | *
from   tablename [[as] alias]
            [, | join-operation tablename [[as] alias] [,...]
where condition
order by col [asc | desc]  [,...]
```

In formulating an SQL query, the guidelines discussed in relational algebra usually apply. First state the query clearly in English. Then try to solve the query yourself, watching how you do this. Then formalize your steps in SQL. This usually entails the following moves. What tables hold the required information? Name these in the from-clause. What columns do you want and in what order? Name these (qualified if needed) in the select-list. If the select-list doesn't include a key, and you wish to avoid duplicate rows, use the distinct option. If you need *n* tables, specify the *n*-1 join conditions. What rows do you want? Specify the search condition in a where-clause. What order do you want for the rows? Use an order-by clause for this.

The new join syntax introduced in SQL-92 is convenient, but adds little in the way of functionality. The most useful notations are those for natural inner and outer joins. If you are using a version of SQL which does not support the new syntax, you should take extra care to specify the join conditions in detail and to qualify column names when required.

Exercise C.2

1. This question refers to the student database discussed in relational algebra. Its relational schema is:

Student (<u>student#</u>, stuname, degree, gender, birthyr)

Result (<u>student#, subjcode</u>, [rating])

Subject (<u>subjcode</u>, title, credit)

Formulate the following queries in SQL.

(a) List student#, name, degree and birthYr of the students in ascending order of degree. For students enrolled in the same degree, older students should be shown first.
(b) For each student named 'Smith J', list the student# and the codes of subjects (being) studied.
(c) List the student#, name and gender of all students studying CS113.
(d) List the titles of the subjects studied by the student with student# 863.
(e) List the student#, name and degree of those male students who obtain a rating of 5 in a subject titled "Logic". Display these in alphabetic order of name.
(f) List the code and credit points of all subjects for which at least one male student enrolled in a BSc scores a rating of 7. Display the subjects with higher credit points first, with subjects of equal credit points listed in alphabetic order of code. Ensure that no duplicate rows occur in the result.
(g) List the code and title of all the subjects, together with the ratings obtained for the subject (if any).

2. The relational schema shown is a fragment of an application dealing with club members and teams. Formulate the following queries in SQL.

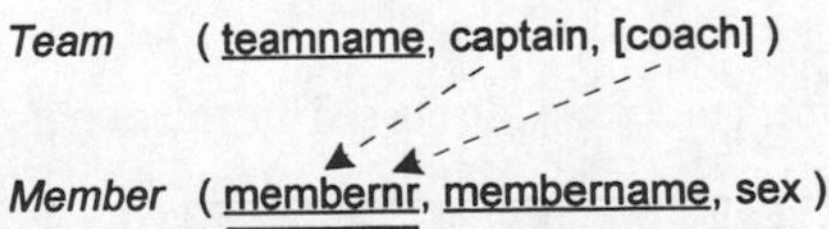

(a) List the teams as well as the member number and name of their captains.
(b) Who (member number) is captain and coach of the same team?
(c) Who (member number) captains some team and coaches some team.

To record who plays in what team, the following table scheme is used:

PlaysIn (<u>membernr, teamname</u>)

(d) What inter-table constraints apply between this table and the other two tables?

Formulate the following queries in SQL.

(e) List details of all the members as well as the teams (if any) in which they play.
(f) List details of all the members as well as the teams (if any) that they coach.
(g) Who (membernr) plays in the team named "judo" but is not the captain of that team?
(h) Who (membernr and name) plays in a team with a female coach?

Four search condition operators

In this section we examine the following four operators that SQL provides for use within search conditions: *in*; *...between...and...*; *like* and *is null*. These are sometimes called "functions", and the conditions they are used to express are unfortunately called "predicates" in the SQL standard.

A function is something that takes zero or more values as arguments and returns a single value as its result. You are probably familiar with functions from mathematics or programming, such as cos(x) or sqrt(x). As these examples illustrate, syntactically a function is usually represented as a function-identifier preceding its arguments, which are typically included in parentheses.

When the action performed by a function is represented without bracketing all the arguments, we usually describe the notation as involving operators and operands rather than functions and arguments. Operators may be represented in infix, prefix, postfix and mixfix notation according as the operator appears between, before, after or mixed among the operands. For instance, in mathematics the sum of 2 and 3 might be set out as:

```
sum(2,3)            { function }
2 + 3               { infix operator }
+ 2 3               { prefix operator }
2 3 +               { postfix operator }
sum of 2 and 3      { mixfix operator }
```

The four operators we are about to discuss are used to express search conditions. The first three return the value True, False or Unknown; the is-null operator returns True or False.

Most of our examples will be based on the Person table, reproduced here as Table C.6. Suppose we wanted the names and birth years of the people born in 1950, 1967, or 1974. One way of requesting this information in is shown in the following SQL query. As an exercise, check that this results in four rows.

Table C.6

Person:

firstname	*sex*	*starsign*	*birthyr*
Bob	M	Gemini	1967
Eve	F	Aquarius	1967
Fred	M	Gemini	1970
Norma	F	Aries	1950
Selena	F	Taurus	1974
Terry	M	Aquarius	1946

```
select firstname, birthyr from Person
where birthyr = 1950 or birthyr = 1967 or birthyr = 1974
```

Imagine how tedious this way of phrasing the request would be if there were a dozen or more years involved. Partly to make life easier in such situations, SQL includes an ***in operator*** to handle *set membership*. Using this infix operator, the above request may be formulated more briefly as:

```
select firstname, birthyr from Person
where birthyr in (1950,1967,1974)
```

Here the search condition is that the birthyr value is a member of the set containing the values 1950, 1967 and 1974. The order in which these values are written does not matter. In general, if x is some expression (e.g. a column name) and a, b, etc. are data values (numeric or string constants) then the SQL condition shown on the left is equivalent to the mathematical expression shown on the right:

x in (a,b ...) means $x \in \{a,b \ldots\}$

We use "**in**" instead of "$\in$", and *parentheses* "( )" instead of braces "{ }" for *set-delimiters*. Strictly speaking, SQL uses parentheses as *bag*-delimiters. Unlike many programming languages, SQL allows sets to contain character strings (not just numbers). For example, the following query lists Aquarians and Taureans:

```
select firstname from Person
where starsign in ('Aquarius','Taurus')
```

To indicate that the value of an expression does *not* belong to a set, the logical not-operator may be used with the in operator. In Pascal, we express the fact that x is not a member of a set S as "not (x in S)", since Pascal gives "not" precedence over "in". As with the ordinary comparison operators however, SQL gives the in-operator higher priority than the logical operators. So in SQL the condition may be rendered more briefly as: not *x* in *S*. Even better, SQL also allows "**not in**" for "$\notin$". So this may set out more naturally as: *x* not in *S*.

x not in S means $x \notin S$

For example, to obtain the names and birth years of those not born in any of the years 1950, 1967 or 1974 the following query may be used:

```
select firstname, birthyr from Person
where birthyr not in (1950,1967,1974)
```

Sometimes we wish to determine whether an expression has a value occurring in a *subrange* of values. In mathematics, to say that some variable x has a value in the subrange from a to b we usually express this as: $a \leq x \leq b$. This notation is illegal in SQL. Instead we could say: $a <= x$ **and** $x <= b$. For the sample population, the following query returns the name and birth year of all but Terry.

```
select firstname, birthyr from Person
where 1950 <= birthyr and birthyr <= 1974
```

As another way to specify subrange membership, SQL provides the ternary mixfix operator "... **between** ... **and** ...", which may be defined as shown, where *x*, *a* and *b* may be arithmetic or string expressions:

x **between** *a* **and** *b* means *a* <= *x* **and** *x* <= *b*

For example, the previous query may be reformulated as:

```
select firstname, birthyr from Person
where birthyr between 1950 and 1974
```

Note carefully that, in contrast to ordinary English, "between" in SQL is read in an *inclusive sense*. For instance, both 1950 and 1974 are included in the above subrange.

Notice also that here "**and**" is just part of the mixfix operator: it is not a logical operator. As already noted, the <= operator may be used to order strings as well as numbers. So strings may be used as operands. For example, the following query returns the set {'Bob', 'Eve', 'Fred'}.

```
select Name from Person
where Name between 'Bob' and 'Fred'
```

Non-membership in a subrange may be expressed with the help of the **not** operator, which has lower priority than **between**, and may be placed just before the word "between". Thus each of the following conditions is equivalent to: *x* < *a* **or** *x* > *b*.

x **not between** *a* **and** *b* **not** (*x* **between** *a* **and** *b*) **not** *x* **between** *a* **and** *b*

The "not between" formulation is easier to read. For example, the following query returns just the tuple ⟨'Terry', 1946⟩.

```
select firstname, birthyr from Person
where birthyr not between 1950 and 1974
```

In the pure relational model, column values are considered atomic. However SQL provides a number of ways of accessing substrings within character string values. In particular, the ***like operator*** is used for *pattern matching* with character strings. The general form of the condition may be set out in EBNF thus:

colname **[not] like** *quoted-string* **[escape** *quoted-char***]**

The quoted string is a character string, surrounded by single quotes, which may contain wildcard characters. You are probably familiar with the use of wildcards for matching filenames at the operating system level (e.g. "*" and "?" in MS-DOS). In the absence of an escape clause, SQL gives the percentage character "%" and the underscore character "_" the following special meanings if included in a quoted string operated on by **like**:

% = 0 or more characters

_ = any single character

Thus, "%" is like the MS-DOS "*" wildcard, and "_" is like the MS-DOS "?" wildcard. The "%" is generally more useful, but "_" is needed if the character's position in the string is important. Figure C.10 provides a few examples based on table C.6. The like-operator has priority over logical operators. The expression "*x* **not like** *s*" means "not (*x* like *s*)".

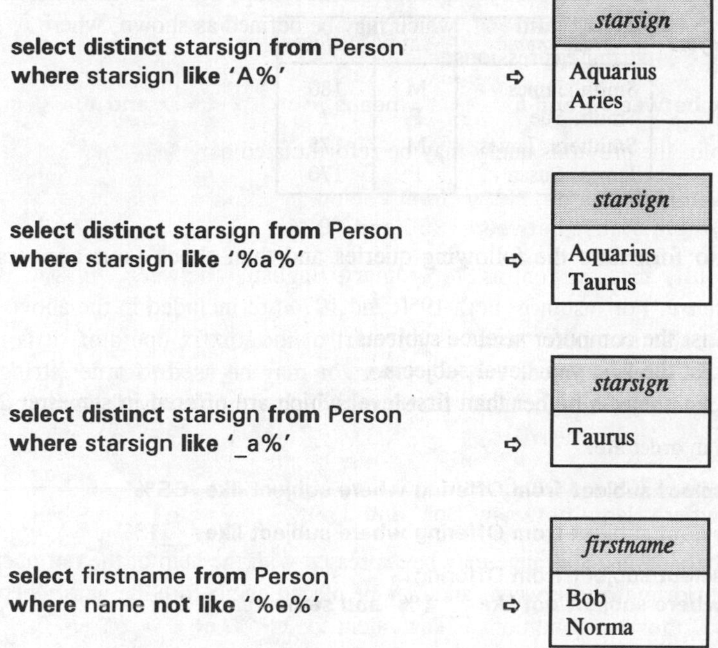
select distinct starsign from Person
where starsign like 'A%'
starsign
Aquarius
Aries
select distinct starsign from Person
where starsign like '%a%'
starsign
Aquarius
Taurus
select distinct starsign from Person
where starsign like '_a%'
starsign
Taurus
select firstname from Person
where name not like '%e%'
firstname
Bob
Norma

Figure C.10 "%" and "_" wildcards for pattern matching with the like operator

Note that the "%" and "_" are interpreted as wildcard characters only in the context of a like condition. For example, the following query returns the null set. There are no rows that satisfy the condition since when "=" is used instead of "like" the expression "A%" is taken literally.

select starsign **from** Person
where starsign = 'A%'

To see a few examples where the like operator is quite useful, consider Table C.7, which indicates which subjects are offered in which semester at a given university. The sample population has been kept small to save space. At this university, subject codes have the following meaning: the first two characters indicate the discipline area (e.g. "CS" denotes Computer Science, and "PD" denotes Philosophy) and the third character denotes the year level (e.g. "1" for first year level).

Table C.7

Offering:

subject	*semester*
CS112	1
CS113	2
PD102	1
PD102	2
CS225	2
CS314	1

Table C.8

Player:

personname	*sex*	*height*
Smith, James	M	180
Smith, Sue	F	?
Smithers, James	M	175
James, Susan	F	170

Try to formulate the following queries and then check your answers with those provided.

> List the computer science subjects.
> List the first year level subjects.
> List subjects higher than first level which are offered in semester 2.

The queries in order are:

```
select subject from Offering where subject like 'CS%'

select subject from Offering where subject like '__1%'

select subject from Offering
where subject not like '__1%' and semester = 2
```

Another common example of a string which is often interpreted as having structure by the user is a person name. Usually a person's surname as well as either a first name or initials are recorded (e.g. "Smith, James" or "Smith J B". Suppose that it is important to distinguish between these two parts of a person's name. One way of implementing this is to include two columns, one for the surname and a second for the firstname (or initials). The structure is then known to the system and each of these two parts of the name can be accessed individually (this is especially handy for SQL's group-by facility).

Alternatively, we might use just one column to store the whole name and then make use of the like-operator to distinguish the two parts. With this second approach, the structure of the name then becomes derived rather than stored. For example, consider Table C.8, which provides information about players in a mixed doubles tennis match. Try your hand at the following queries and then check your answers against those shown.

> List details of people with surname "Smith".
> List details of people with firstname "James".

In order, the queries are:

```
select * from Player where personname like 'Smith, %'

select * from Player where personname like '%, James'
```

Conditions using the like operator may optionally include an *escape character*. If chosen, it may be used as a lead-in character to have "%" and "_" interpreted literally rather than as wildcards. For example, the query in Figure C.11 lists the starships with an underscore character in their name. Here "\" is used as the lead-in character; any character that doesn't occur in the string being investigated could be used.

Starship:	***shipname***	***maxspeed***
	Alpha_1	warp 5
	Enterprise	warp 8
	Epsilon_33	warp 7
	Galactica	warp 5

```
select shipname from Starship
where shipname like '%\_%' escape '\'
```

⇨

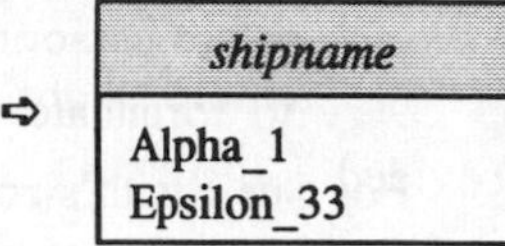

shipname
Alpha_1
Epsilon_33

Figure C.11 Here "\" is used as an escape character to detect an underscore

Although null values may be displayed (e.g. as "?"), they cannot be used with any of the usual comparison operators when a search condition is specified. Instead, a special postfix Boolean *"... is null" operator* is used. This operator is placed after the name of the column on which it operates: it returns True if the column value is null and False otherwise. For example, the following query on the Player table returns 'Smith, Sue', since her height is unknown:

```
select personname from Player
where height is null
```

Note that neither of the expressions "height = null" or "height = '?'" is allowed. To specify that a value is not null, the logical **not** operator is added, either before the column name or before the word "null". For instance, each of the following queries results in the names of the three other players being displayed.

```
select personname from Player where not height is null

select personname from Player where height is not null
```

The EBNF syntax for null comparisons is as follows:

colname **is [not] null**

While the is-null operator returns True or False, other comparison operators return Unknown when one of the arguments is the null value. Suppose we want the names of the players who are between 170 cm and 175 cm tall (inclusive). The following query returns just two names: { 'Smithers, James', 'James, Susan'}.

```
select personname from Player
where height between 170 and 175
```

Although in the real world Sue Smith's height might be in this range, she is excluded from this result. The system does not know her height, and so will not evaluate the condition to True in her case. Suppose now we want the names of those players whose height is not in the range 170..175. The following query returns just one name: 'Smith, James'.

```
select personname from Player
where height not between 170 and 175
```

Notice that Sue Smith is excluded from this result as well. So as far as the system is concerned, in her case the truth value of the condition "height between 170 and 175" is neither true nor false; rather it is unknown.

A row is included in a result only if it satisfies the search condition—i.e. the condition is (known by the system to be) True for that row. If the condition is either False or Unknown the row will be excluded from the result. As an extreme example, the following query returns all the players except Sue Smith.

```
select personname from Player
where height = 170 or height < > 170
```

For Sue Smith's row, each comparison in this condition evaluates to unknown, and applying the **or**-operator to two unknowns also gives an unknown. The truth value of any compound condition is evaluated according to a 3-valued logic, as set out in Figure C.12. Here we have used "1", "0" and "?" respectively to denote the values "true", "false" and "unknown".

Although SQL-92 allows only one kind of null value, Codd has proposed a 4-valued logic in "version 2" of the relational model, to allow for two kinds of unknown (applicable and inapplicable), but this has not had popular approval. Current plans for SQL3 indicate that any number of user-defined nulls might be supported in that standard.

A summary of the syntax of the four operators introduced in this section is shown below. Here "*expn*" denotes an expression such as a column name or constant (or a combination of these connected by arithmetic operators +, -, *, / ... see later).

expn [not] **in** (*constant-list*)

expn [**not**] **between** *expn* **and** *expn*

colname [**not**] **like** *quoted-string* [**escape** *quoted-char*]

colname **is** [**not**] null

p	*not p*
1	0
0	1
?	?

p	*q*	*p and q*
1	1	1
1	0	0
1	?	?
0	1	0
0	0	0
0	?	0
?	1	?
?	0	0
?	?	?

p	*q*	*p or q*
1	1	1
1	0	1
1	?	1
0	1	1
0	0	0
0	?	?
?	1	1
?	0	?
?	?	?

Figure C.12 Truth tables for 3-valued logic (1 = true, 0 = false, ? = unknown)

Exercise C.3

1. The table contains data on some computer languages. Phrase the following queries in SQL.

CompLanguage:

title	*releaseYr*
FORTRAN	1957
ALGOL	1958
COBOL	1959
Logo	?
Pascal	1971
Prolog	1972
SQL	?
Modula	1975
Modula 2	1979
Goodo Pascal 1.0	1983
Goodo Pascal 2.0	1984
Goodo Pascal 3.0	1985
Goodo Prolog	1986

(a) Which languages were released in the years 1959, 1975 or 1979?
(b) Which languages were released in the period 1959 - 1979?
(c) Which languages do not have their release year recorded?
(d) List the name and release year of any Goodo language.
(e) List the name of any language ending with "OL".
(f) List the name and release year of any Pascal language.
(g) List language names which are five characters long.
(h) List language names with 'o' as the second character.
(i) List the name of any language containing the letter "O" or "o".
(j) List the name and release year of languages not starting with "P" which were released after 1959 and before 1979.
(k) List language names which either are 6 characters long and have "a" as the last or second last character, or are 5 characters long and end with "OL".

2. Suppose that in later years computer languages with the following titles were released: Modula_3; Oberon_2; Ada%93; COBOL%93. Write an SQL query which will list all languages whose title includes an underscore or a percentage sign.

Union, intersection and difference

This section discusses how to specify the set operations of union, intersection and difference in SQL. We begin with the ***union operation***. Figure C.13 is an extension of an example considered in our treatment of relational algebra. As "language" is a reserved word, it has been quoted for use as an identifier.

Consider the query: Who is acquainted with (i.e. is fluent in or uses) what language? The required result is the union of the set of rows in the Fluency table and the set of rows in the Usage table. In relational algebra we formulate this query thus: Fluency ∪ Usage. How do we specify this table union in SQL?

Fluency (person, "language")

Programmer (name, sex)

Usage (person, "language")

Fluency:

person	*"language"*
Ann	BASIC
Ann	Pascal
Terry	BASIC
Terry	FORTRAN
Terry	Pascal
Walter	C

Usage:

person	*"language"*
Ann	Pascal
Fred	Ada
Terry	Pascal
Terry	Modula-3

Programmer:

name	*sex*
Ann	F
Fred	M
Terry	M
Walter	M

Figure C.13

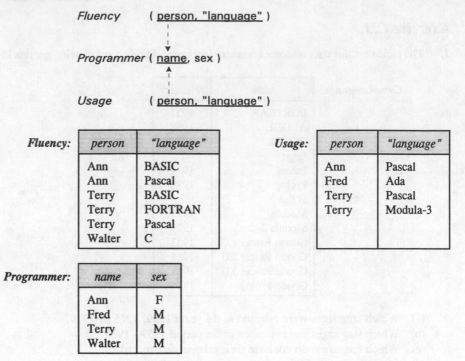

In SQL the query may be specified as shown below. This query returns one instance of all the rows that occur in either table. Since duplicates are automatically removed, only eight rows result (not ten).

```
select * from Fluency
union
select * from Usage
```

The reserved word "**union**" is allowed only between select-queries, not between table names. Thus the following formulation is illegal: "**select * from Fluency union Usage**". Since duplicates are eliminated by default, the distinct option is not required. If duplicates are desired, the "**all**" option must be specified after "union". For example, adding "all" to the previous query would cause the rows ⟨'Ann','Pascal'⟩ and ⟨'Terry','Pascal'⟩ to appear twice in the result. The union operation may be applied several times in a query. The basic SQL-89 syntax is:

select-query
union [all]
select-query
...

In SQL-92, a corresponding-option may be added, but we ignore this here. The union operator may be applied only to table expressions that are union-compatible (corresponding columns are based on compatible data types).

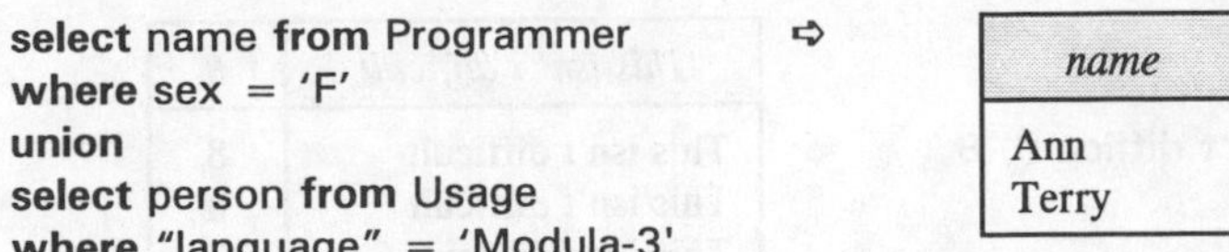

```
select name from Programmer
where sex = 'F'
union
select person from Usage
where "language" = 'Modula-3'
```

⇨

name
Ann
Terry

Figure C.14 Here the data types of name and person must be compatible

If an order-by clause is used, it must come after the last query in the union, and column numbers must be used rather than names. For example, the result table for the previous could be ordered by language (Ada through Pascal) by appending the following clause: "**order by** 2".

With the previous query, the operand tables were base tables. Since base tables are rarely union-compatible, the union operator is mostly used on derived tables that have been made union-compatible by projection. For example, the query in Figure C.14 may be used to list the programmers who are female or users of Modula-3.

Note that the corresponding columns (name and person) have different names. Since column headings are chosen from the first query in the union, the heading "name" appears here. Although this query may be formulated in other ways (see subqueries later), the union operation provides the most natural method of merging results from compatible answer tables.

Now consider the query: Who is fluent in Ada or C or Pascal (i.e. who is fluent in at least one of these languages)? As an exercise, formulate this in SQL using two unions. In this case however, the query can be answered by looking at just the rows from the Fluency table. So it is simpler to use the **or** operator thus:

```
select person from Fluency
where "language" = 'Ada' or "language" = 'C' or "language" = 'Pascal'
```

When the operands of a union operator are disjoint (i.e. mutually exclusive), the union operator is sometimes used to add descriptions to the output even when only one base table is involved. As an example, consider the Expert and Novice tables in Figure C.15. Suppose we want to list the names of the judo players, as well as some label to indicate which are the experts and which are the novices.

Any string or numeric constant may be included in the select-list of a query. A string constant may include any characters and is delimited by single quotes. If you want to include a single quote as part of the string, show this as two consecutive single quotes ('').

Expert:

person	*sport*
Ann	judo
Ann	aikido
Bill	judo
John	bojutsu

Novice:

person	*sport*
Ann	karatedo
Bill	karatedo
Cathy	judo
Cathy	aikido
David	kendo

Figure C.15 Expert and novice players of martial arts

```
select 'This isn''t difficult', 8
from Expert
```

⇨

'This isn''t difficult'	*8*
This isn't difficult	8
This isn't difficult	8
This isn't difficult	8
This isn't difficult	8

Figure C.16 Constants included in a select-list are output for each returned row

When included as items in the select-list, such constants appear as column headings as well as on each row of the output. As a trivial example, see Figure C.16. With no search condition, all four rows of the Expert table are returned, and the constants are shown for each. The number 8 is the unshifted value of the "*" key. If you forget to hold the Shift key down when entering a command like "select * from ..." you will actually enter "select 8 from ..." and get just a column of 8s!

Returning to our current problem, a string constant included in the select-list of union operands will identify which operand a row was drawn from to produce the result table. So we can identify the expert and novice judoka, by including the strings "expert judoka" and "novice judoka" in the relevant select-lists as shown in Figure C.17. By chance, these two strings have the same length. Depending on the SQL implementation, you may need to match the string lengths in such queries by padding one of the constants with blanks.

In the query of Figure C.17, an order-by clause has been used to list the experts first. Also, a format command has been used to display the second column name in the result as "judo level". Although formatting is not part of the SQL standard, almost all commercial SQLs include several such commands for reformatting the query result.

Although this technique of adding descriptive strings in unions is handy when the operands are disjoint, it is not of much use if they overlap. Any originally overlapping rows become disjoint when the string values are added into the rows (since they will differ in that string value). Consequently, such rows will appear more than once in the union.

In SQL-92 (but not SQL-89), the **intersect** operator is provided for *set intersection* and the **except** operator handles *set difference*. These work analogously to the union operator. They are allowed only between select-queries that return union-compatible tables, and duplicates are removed from the result unless the **all** option is specified.

Consider the query: Who uses and is fluent in what language? The required result is the intersection of the set of rows in the Usage table and the set of rows in the Fluency table. In relational algebra this is expressed as: Usage ∩ Fluency. How do we formulate this in SQL?

```
select person, 'expert judoka' from Expert
where sport = 'judo'
union
select person, 'novice judoka' from Novice
where sport = 'judo'
order by 2, 1;
format col 2 name 'judo level'
```

⇨

person	*judo level*
Ann	expert judoka
Bill	expert judoka
Cathy	novice judoka

Figure C.17 Constants may be used with union to indicate the source of the rows

In SQL the query may be specified as follows. This query returns just the rows that occur in both tables: ⟨'Ann','Pascal'⟩ and ⟨'Terry','Pascal'⟩.

```
select * from Usage
intersect
select * from Fluency
```

To list details about persons using languages in which they are not fluent, the following query would be used in relational algebra: Fluency − Usage. In SQL this is expressed as:

```
select * from Usage
except
select * from Fluency
```

This returns the rows in the first table except those that also occur in the second table. For our population the result contains just two rows: ⟨'Fred','Ada'⟩ and ⟨'Terry','Modula-3'⟩. Unlike union and intersection, the difference operator is not commutative. For example, reversing the order of the operands in the previous query results in four rows. The basic SQL-92 syntax of these other two operators is:

```
select-query            select-query
intersect [all]         except [all]
select-query            select-query
...                     ...
```

Subqueries in SQL-89

Unlike relational algebra, SQL provides extended facilities for *subqueries* (i.e. queries embedded within queries). Ideally, a language ought to be orthogonal—wherever a value or result is legal, an expression which returns that value or result should be legal. In SQL-89 however, subqueries are allowed only in a few places where their result is legal. Although SQL-92 has removed most of these restrictions, few commercial SQLs currently support the new standard in this respect. In this section we consider only the SQL-89 standard.

A subquery is a parenthesized select-query embedded in a search condition. Let "expn" mean "expression" and let θ denote one of the comparison operators (=, <>, <, >, <=, >=). In SQL-89 a subquery is legal only in the following contexts:

```
expn [not] in (subquery)
expn θ [all | some | any] (subquery)
exists (subquery)
```

After "in" or a comparison operator, the subquery must be a *singleton-query* (i.e. it must return a single column). This is consistent with our earlier use of the in-operator in from of a bag of values (a column is a just bag of values, displayed vertically). After a comparison operator that has not been modified by "all', "some" or "any", the subquery must return a single value. This is consistent with the normal use of comparison operators. After the exists quantifier, a subquery may return any table.

Let's first consider the use of subqueries after "**in**". The condition returns True if and only if the value of the expression is included in the subquery result. If the subquery returns the null set, the condition evaluates to unknown.

To discuss some examples, consider the tables shown in Figure C.18. Assume there is a subset constraint from Mountain.countryname to Country.countryname. The opposite constraint does not apply (e.g. The Netherlands has no mountains). To save space, only some mountains are shown for the other countries. Consider the query: Which mountains are located in a country with more than 100 million people? This may be set out in SQL as follows:

```
select mtname from Mountain
where countryname in
        (select countryname from Country
         where population > 100000000)
```

The subquery is evaluated first, resulting in the bag: ('India','USA'). After the subquery has been replaced by this intermediate result, the outer query is evaluated, finally resulting in a list of three mountains: Mana; McKinley and Rainier.

Of course, this query could have been phrased instead using a join. As an exercise. do this. Subqueries may be nested (i.e. their search conditions may include subqueries). To improve readability, subqueries should always be indented. The deeper the level of nesting, the greater the indentation should be.

Often, queries using subqueries may be replaced by join-queries, and vice versa. Some joins cannot be reformulated in terms of subqueries. In particular, *if the select-list includes columns from more than one table, a join must be used* (self-joins must be used if the select-columns are from different copies of the same table). For example, the following query cannot be reformulated as a subquery.

```
select * from Country natural join Mountain
```

As a negated example of subqueries, the following query lists the countries with no mountains. For the given population, just the following row is returned: ⟨'Netherlands'⟩.

```
select countryname from Country
where countryname not in
        (select countryname from Mountain)
```

Note that there is no simple way of replacing such negated subquery examples with join-queries. Note also that the above query is essentially performing a *set difference* operation. It is equivalent to the following:

```
select countryname from Country
except
select countryname from Mountain
```

Country:

countryname	*population*
Australia	17000000
India	880000000
Netherlands	14000000
USA	250000000

Mountain:

mtname	*countryname*
Kosciusko	Australia
Mana	India
McKinley	USA
Rainier	USA

Figure C.18 Some countries and some of their mountains (if any)

To list those countries which *do* have mountains, the following query could be used:

```
select countryname from Country
where countryname in
        (select countryname from Mountain)
```

This performs a *set intersection*, and is equivalent to:

```
select countryname from Country
intersect
select countryname from Mountain
```

So, when just single columns are required, the use of "in" and "not in" with subqueries enables set intersection and set difference operations to be formulated even in SQL-89. This technique will not work if we want to obtain the intersection or difference of tables with more than one column (e.g. the intersection of the Fluency and Usage tables). However, the exists quantifier may be used with subqueries to handle such cases.

As another set difference example, recall the *Programmer* (name, sex) and *Usage* (person, "language") tables from the previous section. Suppose we wish to list the male programmers who do not use Pascal. We could express this set difference directly using the "except" operator, or make use of a subquery thus:

```
select name from Programmer
where sex = 'M'
   and name not in    (select person from Usage
                       where "language" = 'Pascal')
```

For the given population, the result lists Fred and Walter. Suppose we tried to formulate this query using a join instead, as follows. Is this correct? Work out the result table for yourself before reading on.

```
select name from Programmer cross join Usage
where name = person
   and sex = 'M' and "language" <> 'Pascal'
```

The result from this query lists Fred and Terry. The query is incorrect for two reasons. As formulated, the query actually asks for the male programmers who use a language other than Pascal. This is very different from the intended query. Walter is wrongly eliminated since he uses no language. Terry is wrongly included since he uses Modula-3 (even though he does use Pascal). The condition of never matching a specified value (on any row) is quite different from the condition of matching some different value (on some row).

Subqueries may be used with the union operator to emulate *outer joins*. For example, consider the query: List all the countries and their populations, as well as any mountains they might have. In SQL-92 syntax this may be set out as:

```
select * from Country natural left join Mountain
```

In SQL-89 syntax, this may be rephrased as follows. Here a string constant padded with blanks has been used to emulate a null value, in case the implementation does not allow null to be included in the select-list (as now allowed in the standard).

```
select Country.countryname, population, mtname
from Country, Mountain
where Country.countryname = Mountain.countryname
union
select countryname, population, '
from Country
where countryname not in
            (select countryname from Mountain)
```

The second use of subqueries is after an ordinary comparison operator, perhaps quantified by "some", "any" or "all". In the absence of such a quantifier, the subquery must return a single value; as discussed later, this can be guaranteed by using a function call as the subquery's select-list. Note that the quantifiers have the following meanings:

some	means	*at least one*
any	means	*at least one*
all	means	*each* (taken one at a time)

In consequence, the following equivalences hold:

in	≡	= **some**	≡	= **any**
not in	≡	<> **all**		

To avoid confusion, "in" and "not in" should be used instead of their equivalent quantified comparisons, and "some" should always be used instead of "any". In SQL, "some" and "any" are treated as synonyms. However this is not always the case in English. For example, "< > any" means "not in" in English, but not in SQL! To appreciate this point, compute the result of the following query for yourself.

```
select countryname from Country
where population < > any (select population from Country)
```

After evaluating the subquery, we may express the condition as "population < > any (170000000, 880000000, 14000000, 250000000)". In English, "< > any" means "= none". Since each population equals itself we would expect no rows to be returned. But the query returns all the populations, since each is not equal to some (i.e. at least one) of the populations, and SQL treats "< > any" to mean "< > some".

As a useful application of a quantified comparison, consider the query: Which country has the largest population? This may be formulated as follows. Remember that "all" is interpreted distributively as "each, taken individually" rather than collectively. The result correctly lists India. As discussed later, this query may be reformulated using a function.

```
select countryname
from Country
where population >= all (select population from Country)
```

The third use of subqueries is after an *exists* quantifier. This returns True if the subquery returns any rows, and False otherwise. Among other uses, this construct can be used to emulate relational division. In general this requires use of *correlated subqueries*, which we ignore in this introduction. So all eight table operators of the relational algebra can be formulated in SQL. Showing how to capture relational division in general is left as a challenge exercise for the interested reader.

Exercise C.4

1. A database is used to store information on diets. A sample population is provided as well as the relational schema. Weight (or more correctly, mass) is measured in kg.

Eater:

person	weight	sex
Ann	70	F
Bill	70	M
Humphrey	150	M
Sue	60	F

Eats:

person	foodname
Ann	apple
Ann	beef
Ann	potato
Bill	apple
Bill	potato
Humphrey	apple
Humphrey	beef
Humphrey	chicken
Humphrey	orange
Humphrey	peas
Humphrey	potato
Sue	apple
Sue	chicken
Sue	orange
Sue	peas

Food:

foodname	foodclass
apple	fruit
beef	meat
chicken	meat
orange	fruit
peas	vegetable
potato	vegetable

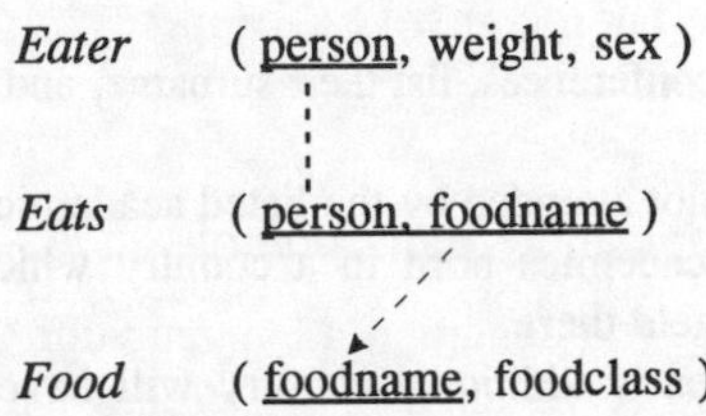

For this database, formulate each of the following queries in SQL.

(a) Who is either a male or a person weighing over 60 kg?
(b) Who is either a male or a person who eats peas?
(c) Who is female and weighs over 60 kg?
(d) Who is female and eats potatoes?
(e) Who weighs over 60 kg but does not eat beef?
(f) List all pairs of people who are of the same weight but opposite sex.
(g) Who eats vegetables?
(h) List the name and weight of those males who eat at least one kind of meat.
(i) Who eats some food other than meat?
(j) Who are vegetarians (i.e. who does not eat meat)?
(k) List the name, weight and sex of all eaters, identifying each as either a vegetarian or meat-eater, and listing vegetarians first, then ordering by sex (females first), then by weight and finally by name.

2. Consider the following relational schema and sample population (for simplicity, we assume academics are identified by their surname).

BornIn (<u>academic</u>, country)

Attended (<u>academic, conference</u>)

HeldIn (<u>conference</u>, country)

BornIn:

academic	*country*
Halpin	Australia
Smith	Australia
Orlowska	Poland

Attended:

academic	*conference*
Halpin	ADB-93
Halpin	CAiSE-93
Orlowska	ADB-93
Orlowska	VLDB-93

HeldIn:

conference	*country*
ADB-93	Australia
AIS-93	Australia
CAiSE-93	France
DOOD-93	USA
VLDB-93	Ireland

Formulate the following queries in SQL-89:

(a) For those academics who have attended conferences, list their name, birth country and conferences attended.
(b) As for (a), but include all academics.
(c) For those academics who have attended conferences, list their surname, and the name and place of their confernces.
(d) As for (c), but include the conferences not attended by the listed academics.
(e) List the name and birth country of academics born in a country which held a conference, as well as the conferences held there.
(f) As for (e), but include all countries (each additional country will have birth or conference details but not both).
(g)–(l) Formulate queries (a)–(f) in SQL-92, making use of its extra join operators.

Arithmetic operators and bag functions

This section provides a brief discussion of the four arithmetic operators and five bag functions that are available in SQL-89. Further functions introduced in SQL-92 are ignored. The basic *arithmetic operators* are: +; –; *; and /. These perform *addition*, *subtraction, multiplication* and *division* respectively.

Each is a number-forming operator on numbers. Their operands may appear as column names, constants, function-calls or expressions formed from these by use of arithmetic operators and perhaps parentheses. Arithmetic expressions may be used as items in a select-list or a search condition.

Let's begin by seeing how these operators may be used to provide a simple calculator facility in SQL to compute the value of an arithmetic expression. We simply include in our database a dummy table with just one row, and then include the expression as the sole item in a select clause applied to this table.

For example we could issue the command

```
create table C (c char(1))
```

and then populate this table with a dummy value (e.g. the letter "c"). We can now use this table whenever when want to do a simple calculation. As a trivial example, to compute the sum obtained by adding 2 to the product of 3 and 4 we can issue the following query. This results in the value 14 being displayed.

```
select 2+3*4 from C
```

For such calculations the contents of C are not accessed and hence are irrelevant (except that by confining C to one row, the desired value displayed just once). The arithmetic operators obey the usual priority convention. Multiplication and division have top priority, with addition and subtraction second. Operators on the same level are left-associative (i.e. are evaluated left to right in the order in which they appear). Brackets may be used to override this evaluation order (parenthesized expressions are evaluated before being operated on from outside). For example: 2+8/2*4 = 18.

In many SQL dialects, the division operator performs integer division if its operands are integers (e.g. 14/3 = 4). In this case, real division can be obtained by making one of the operands real (e.g. 14.0/3 = 4.666666E+000). Here "E" is read "times 10 to the power", so the above value is read "4.666666 times 10 to the power 0". Since $10^0 = 1$, this result boils down to just 4.666666. Most SQLs include format commands to show the result in fixed point notation to a specified number of decimal places (e.g. the command "format col 1 dplaces 2" might redisplay the above result as 4.66).

When arithmetic operands are of different type, the result is typically coerced into the "greater" type. For example, the result of the above division was coerced into real by including a real operand. When column names rather than constants are involved, coercion to real can be achieved by multiplying by 1.0 (e.g. "select 1.0 * quantity/2").

The result of an arithmetic operation between two numbers of type smallint is typically coerced into integer (to avoid possible overflow problems). As some SQL dialects do not behave in the way described, you should check the numeric computation rules for your own dialect. In SQL, the arithmetic operators have the highest priority of all. The precedence order for the operators so far discussed is as follows (in descending order):

```
* /
–
=   <>   <   >   <=   >=   in   between   like   null
not
and
or
union   intersect   except
```

A typical use of arithmetic operators is in computing line totals. For example, given the table scheme *InvoiceLine* (<u>invoicenr, itemcode</u>, qty, unitprice), the items and line totals for invoice 0502 may be requested as follows:

```
select itemcode, qty * unitprice
from InvoiceLine
where invoicenr = '0502'
```

Table C.9

Pupil:

pupilname	*sex*	*IQ*
Ann	F	120
Bill	M	120
Chris	F	100
Don	M	?
Ernie	M	95
Fred	M	115

As another example, this time based on Table C.9, the following query may be used to list how much higher than 100 the IQs of the pupils are: `select IQ - 100 from Pupil`.

SQL-89 provides the following *five bag functions:* **count**; **sum**; **avg**; **max**; and **min**. Each returns a single value, which must be a number in the case of count, sum and avg, and is either a number or a character string in the case of max and min. Recall that a bag or multiset is a set in which repetition (though not order) is significant. Each function takes a bag as its argument. For *count* this may be a table (bag of rows) or a column (bag of data values); for the others it must a column. The cases are summarized in table C.10.

A function is called simply by naming it and placing its argument in parentheses after its name. The argument must be an expression of the following kind: a column name; a constant; or an arithmetic expression formed from column names and constants with the use of arithmetic operators and perhaps parentheses. Any duplicate values are included in the computation unless the keyword "distinct" is placed inside the parentheses just before the expression.

Function calls may be included in a select-list: in this case, every other item in the select-list must also include a function call, unless the item is a constant, or grouping is being performed (not discussed in this appendix).

The *count* function may be used in only two ways. `Count(*)` returns the number of rows in the specified table, while `count(distinct` *colname*`)` returns the number of distinct values in the named column. A few examples are shown in the following queries. With the third example a where-clause is used to filter out unwanted rows before the function is called.

Table C.10 The five bag functions in SQL-89

function	*result*
count (*) **count (distinct** *colname*)	number of rows in table number of distinct values in column
sum (*numeric-expn*) **sum (distinct** *colname*)	sum of *expn* values in bag sum of distinct *expn* values in bag
avg (*numeric-expn*) **avg (distinct** *colname*)	average of *expn* values in bag average of distinct *expn* values in bag
max (*expn*)	maximum of *expn* values in bag
min (*expn*)	minimum of *expn* values in bag

```
select count(*) from Pupil                 →  6
select count(distinct sex) from Pupil      →  2
select count(*) from Pupil
where IQ > 100                             →  3
```

When a function is called, any nulls in its argument are excluded before computation takes place. If "distinct" is specified, any duplicates are also excluded. If duplicates are wanted, the keyword "all" may be used; however since this is the default it is often omitted. The *sum* function returns the sum of the values in the column, and *avg* returns the average of these values. For example:

```
select sum(IQ) from Pupil                  →  550
select sum(distinct IQ) from Pupil         →  430
select avg(IQ) from Pupil                  →  110.00
select avg(distinct IQ) from Pupil         →  107.50
```

Note the exclusion of null values here. Since Don's IQ is unknown, there are only five IQ values to be considered. Since these total 550, their average is 110.

The functions *max* and *min* return, respectively, the maximum and minimum values in the column. If the data type is string rather than numeric, these values are computed according to ordinal positions in the character collating The distinct option may be used with these two functions but is redundant (Why?). For example:

```
select max(IQ) from Pupil                  →  120
select min(IQ) from Pupil                  →  95
select max(pupilname) from Pupil           →  Fred
```

In SQL-89 however, the bag functions may be called only in a select-list (or in a having-clause—not discussed in this appendix). For example, consider the request: "Who has an IQ above the average pupil IQ?". The following formulation is illegal:

```
select pupilname from Pupil
where IQ > avg(IQ)                         →  Error!
```

Instead, we need to embed the function call within a subquery as follows. This query correctly lists Ann, Bill and Fred in its result.

```
select pupilname from Pupil
where IQ > (select avg(IQ) from Pupil)
```

A few more examples are given in the following SQL queries. The first query computes the difference between the highest and lowest IQ. The second query determines the ration of highest to lowest IQ (note the multiplication by 1.0 to ensure the decimal fraction is included). Similarly, in the third example, to compute the mean of the highest and lowest IQ, the divisor is 2.0 rather than 2. The fourth example lists those pupils where 80% of their IQ is greater than 90% of the minimum IQ. As an exercise, explain why it would be wrong in SQL-89 to express the search condition as: "0.8 * IQ > 0.9 * (select min(IQ) from Pupil)".

```
select max(IQ) - min(IQ) from Pupil              →  25

select 1.0 * max(IQ) / min(IQ)
from Pupil                                        →  1.26

select (max(IQ) + min(IQ))/2.0
from Pupil                                        →  107.50

select pupilname from Pupil
where 0.8 * IQ >
    (select 0.9 * min(IQ) from Pupil)             →  Ann
                                                     Bill
                                                     Fred
```

The above example illustrates the fact that in SQL-89, unlike a function call, an arithmetic expression may be used as a term to be compared in a search condition.

Our next example additionally illustrates the fact that built-in functions may take an arithmetic expression as an argument. Consider the relation scheme: *Person* (surname, height, width). The following query may be used to list those people whose height exceeds their width by the greatest amount.

```
select surname from Person
where height - width =
          (select max(height - width) from Person)
```

Exercise C.5

1. This question refers to the Diet database used in Exercise C.4. The table schemes are: *Eater* (person, weight, sex); *Eats* (person, foodname); *Food* (foodname, foodclass). Formulate SQL queries for the following.

   (a) How many males are there above 100 kg in weight?
   (b) How many different weights are there?
   (c) What is the sum of the weights of the males?
   (d) What is the average weight of the females?
   (e) What is the heaviest weight of those who eat beef?

   For each of the next two questions, give two equivalent solutions, one of which uses a function while the other uses an "all" or "some" quantifier.

   (f) Which females are lighter than every male?
   (g) State the name and weight of those females who are as heavy as at least one male.

2. *Log* (code, diameter, len, mass, cost_price, retail_price)

Log: code	*diameter*	*len*	*mass*	*cost_price*	*retail_price*
2A	15	2	10	4.00	7.00
3B	20	3	20	6.00	9.50
5C	20	5	30	9.00	13.00
5D	20	5	25	8.00	12.00

The Log table shown is used by a hardware store to record details about wooden logs that are for sale. The diameter, length (here called "len"), mass and price of the logs are respectively measured in cm, m, kg and \$. A sample population is given. Formulate the following queries in SQL.

(a) List the absolute mark-up (i.e. retail price – cost price) for all the logs.
(b) List the volume of each log in cubic metres, with the column heading "Volume (cubic m)". Use the formula $V = \pi D^2 L/4$ for the volume of a cylinder, approximating π as 3.14. Express each volume as a fixed point number, truncated to 3 decimal places.
(c) List the density (i.e. mass/volume), in kg/m^3, of those logs which are 5 m long. Use an appropriate heading and show each density as a fixed point number truncated to 2 decimal places.
(d) Which log has the highest relative mark-up (use ratio R.P./C.P.)?
(e) Which log has a less than average ratio of length to diameter? Include this ratio (dimensionless, 2 dec. places) in the output.

3. The following database is used by a library to record details of books available for borrowing. Authors are identified by name, and books by their ISBN (International Standard Book Number). A sample population is shown. Formulate the following queries in SQL.
(a) Who are the Australian male authors?
(b) List the titles of books published in the period 1984..1986, ordered by title. (Explain the position of "dBaseIII" in the result.)
(c) List all details of books with "SQL" as part of the title, showing the most recently published ones first.
(d) Who wrote a book titled "Databases" published in 1980?
(e) List the ISBN and title of all books with at least one Australian author.
(f) List the name and nationality of author(s) of any book(s) titled "Informatics" published by Hall in 1986.
(g) List, with suitable descriptors, the name of the Australian male authors and the American female authors, with the former shown first.

Book (<u>isbn</u>, title, publisher, yrpublished, copies)

WrittenBy (<u>isbn, authorname</u>)

Author (<u>authorname</u>, sex, nationality)

Book:

isbn	*title*	*publisher*	*yrpublished*	*copies*
101	Databases	Possum	1985	4
202	SQL Primer	Hall	1984	4
246	Databases	West	1980	1
345	dBase III	West	1986	1
400	Modula 2	Possum	1986	4
444	Advanced SQL	Hall	1986	2
500	Informatics	Hall	1986	2

WrittenBy:

isbn	*authorname*
101	Brown J
101	Collins T
202	Adams A
246	Smith JB
345	Jones S
400	Smith JA
444	Adams A
500	Brown J
500	Smith JA

Author:

authorname	*sex*	*nationality*
Adams A	F	Aussie
Brown J	M	Aussie
Collins T	M	Kiwi
Jones S	F	Yank
Smith JA	M	Aussie
Smith JB	M	Yank

Grouping

Sometimes we wish to partition the rows of a table into a number of groups, and display properties which apply to each group as a whole. Groups may be defined in terms of the attribute(s) for which group members have the same value. SQL provides a **group by** *clause* which may be included in the select statement to retrieve such grouped data. The number of groups may be restricted by means of an associated *having-clause*. These two clauses may also be used to handle simple cases of relational division. Table C.11 will be used to help explain most of these ideas.

Table C.11 Some atomic particles

Particle:

family	*pname*	*charge*	*mass*
lepton	neutrino	0	0
lepton	mu neutrino	0	0
lepton	electron	-1	1
lepton	mu -	-1	207
meson	pi 0	0	264
meson	pi +	1	273
meson	pi -	-1	273
meson	K +	1	966
meson	K -	-1	966
meson	K 0	0	974
meson	eta	0	1074
baryon	proton	1	1836
baryon	neutron	0	1839
baryon	lambda	0	2183
baryon	sigma +	1	2328
baryon	sigma 0	0	2334
baryon	sigma -	-1	2343
baryon	xi -	-1	2585
baryon	xi 0	0	2573

The relation scheme for Table C.11 is *Particle* (family, pname, charge, mass). The primary key column (pname), holds the names of the particles. To help discuss the grouping notion, the family column is shown first instead of the primary key column. The table lists the main atomic particles belonging to the lepton (light), meson (middle) and baryon (heavy) families. The charge of each particle is given in elementary charges (1 elementary charge = charge of proton = 1.6×10^{-19} Coulomb). The mass of each particle is expressed as a multiple of the electron mass (9.1×10^{-31} kg). Consider the following query.

List the families and the number of particles in each.

This may be formulated in SQL as shown. For this section, we list the result tables with the column-headers underlined by hyphens (this is typical of most SQLs).

```
select family, count(*) from Particle      →   family   count(*)
group by family                                -----------------
                                               baryon   8
                                               lepton   4
                                               meson    7
```

Here the group-by clause indicates that the particles are to be *grouped* into families (i.e. particles with the same family name are placed in the same group). The *items in the select-list are then applied to each group as a whole*. If count(*) is used it returns the number of rows in the group. In this case we have eight baryons, four leptons and seven mesons.

In many versions of SQL, the use of group-by often causes a default ordering equivalent to a matching order-by clause (e.g. order by family in this case). However, this is not part of the SQL standard. The syntax of the group-by clause is:

```
group by col-name [, ...]
```

Members of the same group must have matching values for all of the columns named in the group by clause. The next example places particles into groups having both the same family name and the same charge.

```
select family, charge, count(*)     →   family   charge   count(*)
from   Particle                         ---------------------------
group by family, charge                 baryon   -1       2
                                        baryon    0       4
                                        baryon    1       2
                                        lepton   -1       2
                                        lepton    0       2
                                        meson    -1       2
                                        meson     0       3
                                        meson     1       2
```

If more than one column is used for grouping, the order in which these columns are specified is irrelevant to the set of group results. This is because the same set of groups must be formed. For example, if we group by attributes *a*, *b* or *b*, *a* then the group with values a = a1, b = b1 is the same as the group with values b = b1, a = a1; and so on. However, the order of rows in the result may be different. For example:

```
select family, charge, count(*)     →  family   charge   count(*)
from Particle                          ---------------------------
group by charge, family                baryon   -1       2
order by charge, family                lepton   -1       2
                                       meson    -1       2
                                       baryon   0        4
                                       lepton   0        2
                                       meson    0        3
                                       baryon   1        2
                                       meson    1        2
```

Comparing this with the previous result, it is obvious that the same rows are displayed but in a different order. No matter what the specified grouping order and no matter what the version of SQL, the order of rows in the result can be precisely determined by appending an appropriate order-by clause.

If a function call from the select-list is used as an ordering criterion it must be specified by number (i.e. position in the select-list) rather than by name. As an example of this, consider the following query:

List, for each family, the smallest and largest mass, ordering the results in terms of increasing smallest mass.

```
select family, min(mass), max(mass)  →  family   min(mass)   max(mass)
from Particle                           ---------------------------------
group by family                         lepton   0           207
order by 2                              lepton   0           207
                                        meson    264         1074
                                        baryon   1836        2585
```

Since use of a group-by clause implies that items in the select-list are to be applied to each group as a whole, returning just one value for each group, any columns mentioned in the select-list must either be grouped columns or must appear there as an argument to a built-in function (e.g. family and mass in the above query). So when grouping is being performed it makes no sense, and is in fact illegal, to include a non-grouped column as a whole item in the select-list. For example:

```
select family, mass from Particle    →  Error!
group by family
```

Since the same family may include several particles of different mass, this request is plain silly (which mass would we choose?). We can however obtain a single grouped value related to mass by using a built-in function, such as avg(mass), sum(mass) etc. For instance:

List the families and the average mass of each.

```
select family, avg(mass) from Particle  →  family   avg(mass)
group by family                            --------------------
                                           baryon   2252.62
                                           lepton     52.00
                                           meson     684.28
```

Although the select list must not include any non-grouped columns, it is legal to group by columns which are not mentioned in the select list. For example:

List the average mass (but not the name) of each family.

```
select avg(mass) from Particle          →    avg(mass)
group by family                              ------------
                                              2252.62
                                                52.00
                                               684.28
```

Within the select-statement, *a where-clause may be included to filter out unwanted rows before the groups are formed and functions are applied*. Sensibly, the where-clause must be placed *before* the group-by clause. For example:

Considering only the uncharged particles, form groups with the same family name and display their average masses.

```
select family, avg(mass) from Particle   →   family    avg(mass)
where charge = 0                             ---------------------
group by family                              baryon     2232.25
                                             lepton        0.00
                                             meson       770.65
```

Here, to avoid possible misinterpretation of the results, it would be helpful to include a descriptive string (e.g. "uncharged particles only") in the select-list.

Sometimes we wish to restrict our attention to only those groups which satisfy a certain condition. Just as a where clause may be used to impose a search condition on individual rows, a **having**-*clause* may be used to impose a *search condition on individual groups*. In this case the having clause must be placed straight after the group by clause to which it is logically connected. The syntax is:

group by *col-name* [, ...]
having *search-condition*

The usual rules for search-conditions apply. Logical and comparison operators may be included in the search-condition. Each comparison compares some property of the group, such as min(mass), with a constant or another group property. If the distinct-option is used in a query it may be used only once: so "distinct" might be used in the select-list or the having clause, but not both. Although rare, it is possible to include a having-clause without an associated group-by clause: in this case the entire table is treated as one group. Here is a simple example of a query with a having-clause:

List the families with more than four particles, and the number of particles for each.

```
select family, count(*)                  →   family    count(*)
from  Particle                               --------------------
group by family                              baryon    8
having count(*) > 4                          meson     7
```

The next example is harder. A string descriptor has been included and a format command has been used to provide a null heading for this descriptor.

Considering only the charged particles, form groups with the same family name, where the group's lightest particle has a mass above 0 and the group's heaviest particle has a mass below 2000. List the family name, number of particles, and average mass for each group, showing groups with more members first.

```
select family, count(*), avg(mass), 'charged particles only'
from Particle
where charge <> 0
group by family
having min(mass) > 0 and max(mass) < 2000
order by 2 desc;
format col 4 name ''

→  family    count(*)          avg(mass)
-----------------------------------------------------------
   meson     4                   619.50  charged particles only
   lepton    2                   104.00  charged particles only
```

With respect to the having-clause in the second example, note that the charged leptons are included (the uncharged leptons with zero mass have been filtered out earlier by the where-clause), and the charged baryons are excluded since their maximum mass exceeds 2000.

One trivial use of grouping is to simply to avoid duplicates. For example, the following query may be used as an alternative to "select distinct family from Particle":

```
select family from Particle       →     family
group by family                         --------
                                        baryon
                                        lepton
                                        meson
```

Now suppose we issue the following query. What will be the result?

```
select family from Particle
group by family
having count(*) = 4
```

By comparing this with the previous query you may feel that the count of each family will be 1 and hence that no rows will be returned (i.e. that the result is the null set). This is wrong!

When the group-by clause does its work, each group still has all its members (which of course all have the same group value). The having-clause is now applied to filter out those groups which do not satisfy its search condition. Finally the select-list determines which group properties are listed. With this query the groups are first sorted into three families, then two of these families are eliminated (the baryons and mesons), and finally just the family name of the remaining group (the four leptons) is listed. Thus the result is:

```
family
--------
lepton
```

Subject (<u>subjcode</u>, title, credit)

Result (<u>student#, subjcode</u>, [rating])

Subject:

subjcode	*title*	*credit*
CS113	Databases	8
PD102	Logic	10
PY205	Xenoglossy	5

Result:

student#	*subjcode*	*rating*
861	CS113	7
861	PD102	5
862	PD102	7
863	CS113	4
863	PD102	5

Figure C.19

As a further application of grouping, we now consider how simple cases of *relational division* can be handled in SQL. In our treatment of relational algebra, the tables in Figure C.19 were used to illustrate division. Consider the following query:

List student numbers of those students who study all subjects in the Subject table.

Here we use "study" in the sense of "has studied or is studying". In the former case a rating will typically have been recorded while in the latter case a rating is expected to be recorded at a later stage (so null values are permitted for Rating even though the sample population does not include any). Null values are not allowed for student# or subjcode. In relational algebra, we may express the query as:

Result [student#, subjcode] ÷ Subject [subjcode]

SQL does not provide division as a built-in operator. However, we can always express division by means of SQL's select-statement. The general method of doing this requires use of the exists-quantifier, which we ignore in this introduction. Cases like the present example however can easily be expressed in terms of grouping, as shown in the following query. In line with SQL-92 we add quotes to "student#" since it contains the character "#".

```
select "student#" from Result                →   "student#"
group by "student#"                              ----------
having count(*) =                                861
     (select count(*) from Subject)              863
```

Note that the number of subjects studied by a student equals the number of rows in the Result table in which the student appears. So the left operand of the search condition above has the value 2, 1, 2 respectively for students 861, 862 and 863.

It is important to know that all the subjects studied by students are included in the Subject table. Recall that this referential integrity or subset constraint arises from the credit point and title roles being mandatory (see original schema diagram). Moreover, each subject code in the Subject table appears only once (since subjcode is a key to this table). So if the operands of the search condition match, this means that that student studies all the subjects in the Subject table. In this simple example there are only 2 subjects.

This approach can be adapted to handle cases where the relevant mandatory role, subset and uniqueness constraints might not apply, by adding a search condition to filter out unwanted rows and using the distinct-option. For example, if the subjcode in Result contains a value not included in the Subject table, and subjcode is not a key of Subject we could amend the previous query as shown:

```
select "student#" from Result
where subjcode in
        (select subjcode from Subject)
group by "student#"
having count(*) =
        (select count(distinct subjcode) from Subject)
```

In cases involving null values, these could be filtered out by adding appropriate search conditions (e.g. subjcode is not null). Although most examples of division can be handled by this simple grouping approach, sometimes a more complex technique is required (e.g. when dividing by multi-column table expressions with duplicates).

Of the eight table operations of relational algebra, we have discussed the equivalent SQL formulation for the general case of five (projection, selection, Cartesian product, θ-join, union) and for special cases of three (intersection, difference and division). Further work reveals that the exists-quantifier can be used with subqueries to handle intersection, difference and division in general.

We have now covered most of the basic working of SQL's select-statement. The EBNF syntax of this statement may be summarized as shown:

```
select [all | distinct] select-list | *
from tablename [ [as] alias]
        [, | join-operation tablename [[as] alias] [,...]
[where condition]
[group by colname [,...]
 [having condition]]
[union ...]
[order by col [asc | desc] [,...]
```

This is as far as we go with SQL in this introduction. There is much more to learn about the language. More complex retrieval requests may involve correlated subqueries or existentially quantified subqueries. Base tables may be declared, with all their constraints, and views may be declared as derived tables. Commands may be specified to perform insertions, deletions and modifications. Parameterized procedures may be declared, and so on. Moreover, the new SQL-92 standard has added a vast number of new features. For further details on the new standard, see Melton & Simon (1993), or Date & Darwen (1993).

Exercise C.6

1. This question refers to the library database discussed in Exercise C.5. The relational schema is repeated below. Formulate SQL queries for the following requests.

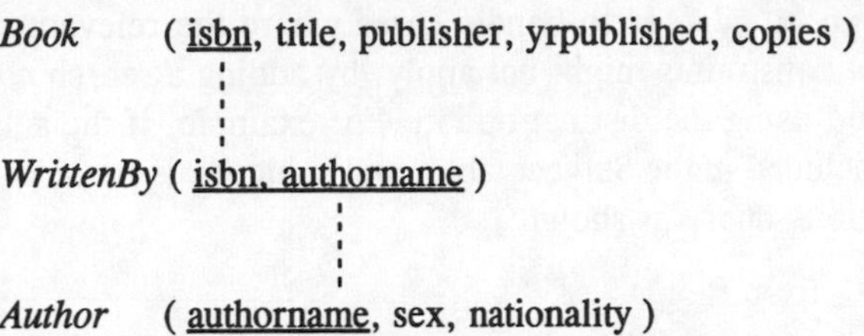

   (a) How many authors of each sex are there?
   (b) Place authors into groups of the same sex and nationality, indicating how many there are in each group, with the larger groups shown first.
   (c) Considering only the books published after 1980, list the publishers and the total number of copies of their books in the library.
   (d) For each publisher having an average number of library copies per book above two, show the earliest publication year.
   (e) List the ISBN and the number of authors for each book published before 1986 that has more than one author.
   (f) Restricting attention to male authors who have authored a book published by either Hall or Possum, list the number of such authors for each nationality which has at least as many authors of this kind as there are copies in the library of the book with ISBN "444" { Note: Assume the ISBN data type is character string }.

2. The relational schema for a dietary database is shown (for a sample population, see Exercise C.4). Formulate the following queries in SQL.

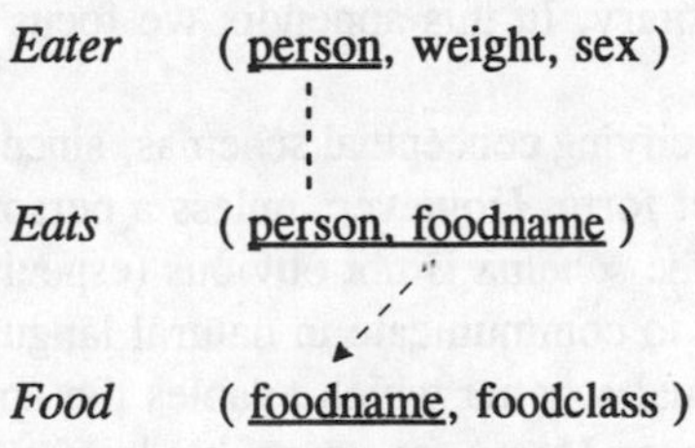

   (a) Who eats all the foods?
   (b) Which foods are eaten by all eaters?

appendix D CASE tool support

Nowadays, many software applications are being developed with the assistance of *CASE* (Computer Aided Software Engineering) tools. When the software application is an information system, this is sometimes referred to as "CAISE" (Computer Aided Information Systems Engineering). This term is not to be confused with "CA*i*SE" (Conference on Advanced information Systems Engineering), a term used for one of the major conferences held annually in this area.

Most information system modelers accept that the application structure should first be specified at the conceptual level, and then mapped to internal and external levels. Existing CASE tools typically allow the modeler to input the main features of a conceptual schema in diagram form, with some finer details specified textually. The conceptual schema is then mapped, with varying degrees of automation and completeness, to internal and perhaps external levels. For an overview of commercial CASE tools, see Ovum (1992) and Reiner (1992). As well as dealing with the data perspective, some CASE tools provide additional support for the process and behavioral perspectives; however integration between these perspectives is typically rudimentary. In this appendix we focus on CASE support for the data perspective.

Graphical languages are very useful for specifying conceptual schemas, since they can convey a lot of information in a simple, compact form. However, unless a person is very familiar with the notation, the *verbalization* of the schema is not obvious (especially with respect to constraints). Since clients often wish to communicate in natural language, it is handy to have a textual version of the conceptual schema which enables the application structure to be clearly explained in plain language. Moreover, many kinds of constraints and rules can arise in an application, and it is doubtful whether these could all be expressed in a practical graphical language, since a multitude of graphic primitives would make the language hard to learn. A textual language seems more appropriate for expressing unusual constraints and rules.

For such reasons, various textual conceptual schema languages have been proposed, which go beyond their graphic counterparts in expressibility. Some prototype systems also allow the conceptual schema to be directly populated and queried by means of graphical and/or textual languages. This approach is likely to become more common in future.

Both graphical and textual languages for data modeling have tended to focus on versions of Entity-Relationship modeling (ER), and to a lesser extent, Object-Role Modeling (ORM). Good examples using the ER approach can be found in Barker (1990), Czejdo et al. (1990), and Hohenstein & Engels (1991). However because of its advantages we focus on the ORM approach. As we have seen, ORM diagrams are closer to natural language, are typically more expressive (but unwanted detail can be hidden using abstraction mechanisms), and can be populated with fact instances for validation purposes. Hence ORM diagrams provide a more convenient bridge to verbalization.

Some textual languages for ORM have had CASE tool support for several years. For example, MIML (Meta Information Management Language) was supported in IAST (Control Data 1982), and RIDL (Reference and Idea Language) was used in RIDL* (Intellibase 1990; De Troyer 1989). More recently, other versions have been proposed. LISA-D (Language for Information Structure and Access Descriptions) is based on the PSM (Predicator Set Model) variant of ORM; a formal definition of this language is given by ter Hofstede et al. (1993). The NIAMEX translator converts a version of the NIAM language into Express (Chawdhry 1992). Our version, called FORML, (Formal Object-Role Modeling Language) is supported in the InfoModeler workbench released by Asymetrix Corporation (USA).

Other ORM-based CASE tools exist. Some commercial products include CD (ITI, Brisbane), ISW (ITS, Belgium), PC-IAST (Control Data), SDW (Cap Gemini Pandata, The Netherlands) and TopWindows (TopSystems, The Netherlands). This list is not intended to be exhaustive. In addition, there are several academic prototypes such as GISD (Shoval et al. 1988), and various facilities are being provided to enable ORM-based tools to communicate with other tools. Recently, meta-CASE shells have begun to appear which enable modelers, within limits, to define their own modeling approach and notations.

To illustrate how a CASE tool can help one develop a database system, a brief overview of one of tools (InfoModeler) is now given. Table D.1, taken from a related paper (Halpin & Harding 1993) illustrates how some components of this tool relate to the data modeling process. The modeling stages proceed downwards through this table.

Familiar examples of information relating to the application are verbalized in terms of elementary fact types, and entered in either graphical or textual form. Fact types can be populated with instances for early validation purposes. Once the fact types have been entered, the modeler adds constraints and rules to them. Most constraints can be added graphically—this is usually faster than entering them textually; however, textual versions of the constraints are generated automatically. One of the interesting features of InfoModeler is the way in which its fact compiler can translate automatically between graphical and textual representations.

A further population check may be made on the constraints. A formal check is then automatically performed to check that the constraints are consistent with one another (Halpin & McCormack 1992). The conceptual schema is then mapped to a logical database schema. Currently, the relational model is the only one fully supported. This mapping includes constraints, and basically follows the Rmap procedure discussed in this book.

Finally, the specific DBMS is selected and the database implementation is generated automatically. Constraints not supported in the DDL component of the target DBMS are typically converted to SQL procedures. Currently, InfoModeler generates native database structures for a variety of PC-based DBMSs (e.g. Access, Paradox, FoxBase) as well as larger DBMSs (e.g. Oracle, Ingres).

Table D.1 **Some data modeling aspects of InfoModeler**

Information levels	*Information modeling stages*	*Information tools*
External	Familiarize	output reports, input forms
Conceptual	Verbalize Populate	Fact compiler Predicate editor Fact report
	Visualize Constrain Add rules	Object report Subtype report Symbol palette Object editor Object browser Constraint palette
	Populate	Fact compiler Example editor
	Check consistency	Validator
Logical	Map	Logical Mapper Table browser Table report
Internal	Generate	Native database generator

Although early experiences with CASE tools generally left a poor impression on developers, the increasing sophistication of such tools beyond glorified documentation devices, and the existence of affordable and powerful hardware platforms for running such software, have now led to the widespread adoption of CASE. The openness of CASE tool developers to enhancement requests from their users, and the high level of research geared towards extending CASE capabilities, augur well for the future. Increasingly, information systems developers will be able to focus almost exclusively on formulating requirements and specifying conceptual models, leaving computers to do most of the lower level generation.

Answers

to selected exercise questions

Answers are in general supplied for odd numbered exercise questions only.

Exercise 2.1

1. (a) C (b) A (c) B

Exercise 2.2

1. (a) Ensure database updates are consistent with the conceptual schema. Answer queries about the UoD.
   (b) Declarations of: stored fact types; constraints; derivation rules.
   (c) False. With compound transactions, only the collective effect of all the elementary updates is considered.

3. (a) accepted
   (b) rejected. C1 violated. Sue must be enrolled in a degree.
   (c) accepted
   (d) rejected. C1 violated. Fred may not enroll in two degrees.
   (e) rejected. Fact type not recognized.
   (f) single, married, widowed, divorced
   (g) accepted
   (h) rejected. C2 violated.
   (i) accepted.
   (j) accepted.
   (k) rejected. C4 violated. Transition single to divorced illegal.
   (l) No
   (m) Fred, Bob
   (n) Sue
   (o) rejected. Fact type not recognized. { Such information would typically be derived }

Final state of database: Student 'Fred' is enrolled in Degree 'BSc'.
Student 'Sue' is enrolled in Degree 'MA'.
Student 'Bob' is enrolled in Degree 'BSc'.
Student 'Bob' has MaritalState 'single'.
Student 'Sue' has MaritalState 'married'.

5. (a) **begin**
add: Employee `Adams' works for Department `Health'
add: Employee `Adams' speaks Language `English'
end
begin
add: Employee `Brown' works for Department `Health'
add: Employee `Brown' speaks Language `English'
end
Brown's data may be entered first. Within a compound transaction the order is irrelevant.

(b) (i) Employee `Adams' works for Department `Health'. { language missing }
(ii) Employee `Adams' works for Department `Health'.
Employee `Adams' speaks Language `English'.
Employee `Adams' works for Department `Education'. { cannot work for 2 depts }

Exercise 3.3

1. (a), (f), (j)

3–4. These questions reveal that columns with the same name need not have the same meaning. In the absence of helpful tables names, we make an educated guess. For example:
3. Athlete (name) 'Jones EM' has height of Length (cm) 166.
4. Athlete (name) 'Jones EM' pole vaults a height of Length (cm) 400.

5. Person (name) 'Jones EM' has height of Length (cm) 166.
Person (name) 'Jones EM' was born in Year (AD) 1955.

7. Person (surname) 'Codd' is an internal member of Panel (name) 'Databases'.
Person (surname) 'Ienshtein' is an external member of Panel (name) 'Databases'.

9. Country (name) 'Oz' is friend of Country (name) 'Disland'.
Country (name) 'Oz' is enemy of Country (name) 'Hades'

Exercise 3.4

1. (a) Reference schemes: Person (firstname)
Facts: Person 'Fred' is male. Person 'Ann' is female.

(b)

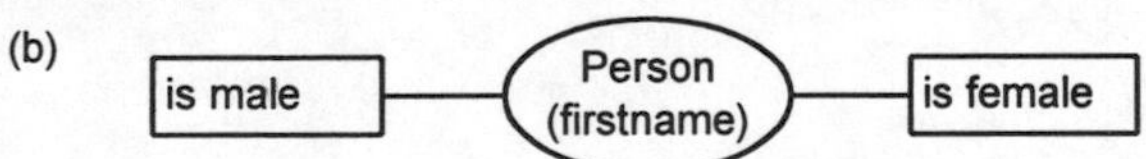

(c) Reference schemes: Person (firstname); Gender (name)
Facts: Person 'Fred' is of Gender 'male'. Person 'Ann' is of Gender 'female'.

(d)

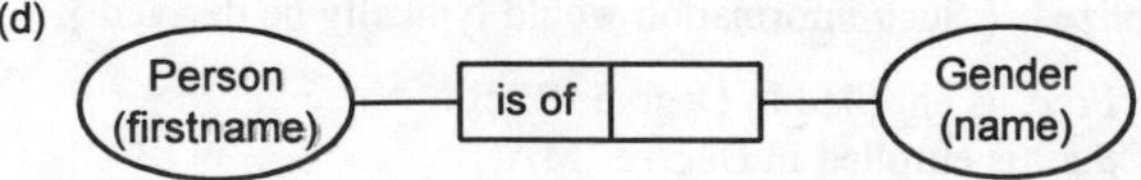

3. We show only the schema diagram here.
You should also verbalize and populate.

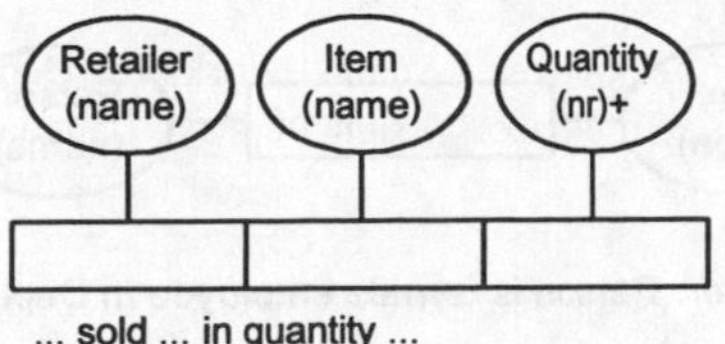

5.

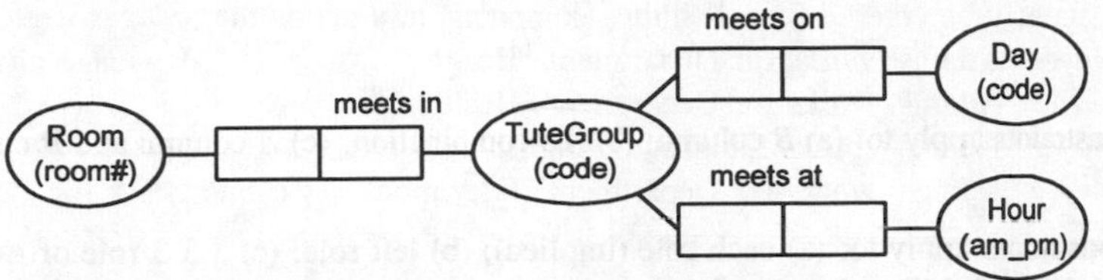

7. (a) Illegal. Objects must play a role. Directly connecting object types is forbidden.
(b) Illegal. A role can be played by at most one object type.
(c) Illegal. Inside role has no object type.
(d) OK. For example: Person is of Gender; Person was born in Country.
(e) Illegal. A role cannot be played by more than one object type.
(f) OK. For eample: Person introduces Person to Person.
(g) OK, e.g.: Company employs Person; Company buys Computer; Company uses Computer.
(h) OK, e.g.: Person gives Present to Person on Date.
(i) Illegal. Object types should not be included in the nesting.
(j) OK, e.g.: Person is parent of Person; Person has IQ.
(k) OK, e.g.: Person ordered Product: alias "Order".
Order was issued on Date. Order was paid on Date.
(l) Illegal. An extended form of the error in (e).

Exercise 3.5

1.

3.

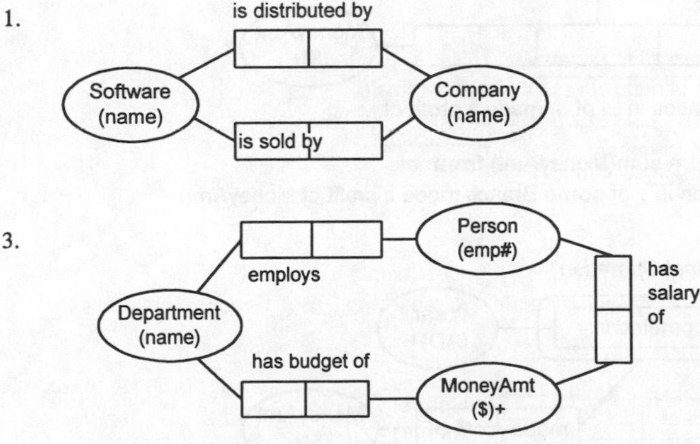

* Staffsize (Department *d*) ::= **count** (*d* employs **some** Person)

* TotalSalary (Department *d*) ::=
sum (MoneyAmt **from** (*d* employs Person **who** has salary of MoneyAmt))

5. 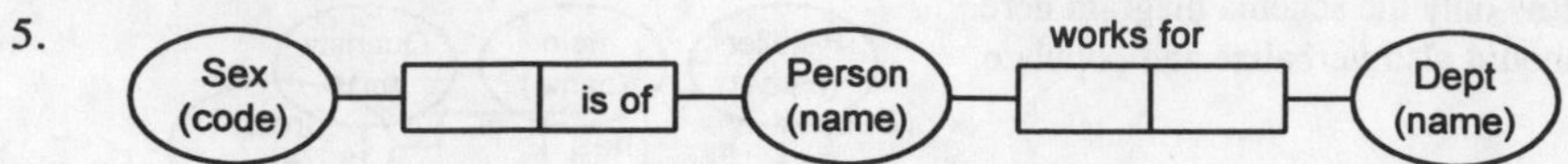

{ *aliter*: Person is female employee in Dept; Person is male employee in Dept }

Exercise 4.2

1. Uniqueness constraints apply to: (a) *B* column; (b) *AB* combination; (c) *A* column and *B* column; (d) *A* column.

3. Uniqueness constraints apply to: (a) each role (implied); (b) left role; (c) 3.3.3 role of Athlete, 3.3.4 role of Athlete, 3.3.5 each role of Person, 3.3.6 combination of Person and Year roles, 3.3.7 both fact types are many:many (popultaion is not significant), 3.3.8 many:many, 3.3.9 both fact types are many:many, 3.3.10 the constraint spans all roles of the ternary; (d) each of the three roles of TuteGroup (later we see how to add external uniqueness constraints, e.g. the combination of Room, Day and Hour is probably unique); (e) each role of Project, and the birth and salary roles of Person; (f) each role of Person, and the budget role of Department.

Exercise 4.3

1. (a) *AB, AC* (b) *AB, AC, BC* (c) *ABC* (d) *AC*

3. (a)

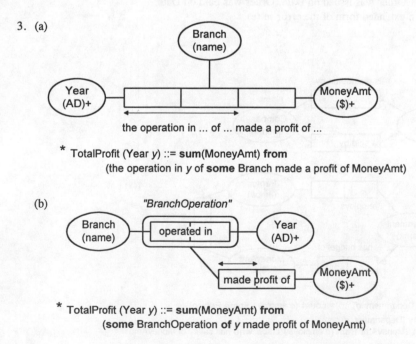

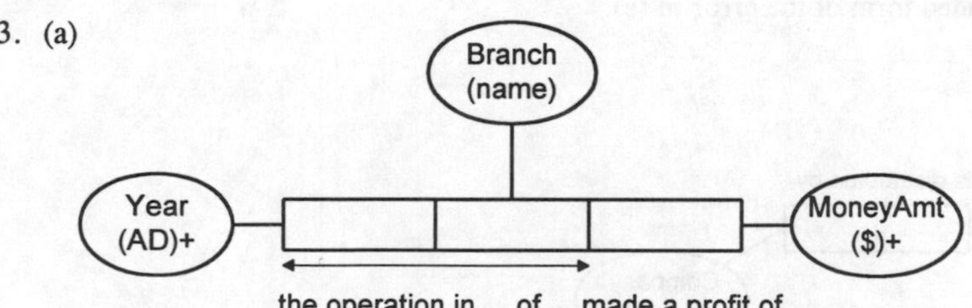

* TotalProfit (Year *y*) ::= **sum**(MoneyAmt) **from**
(the operation in *y* of **some** Branch made a profit of MoneyAmt)

(b)

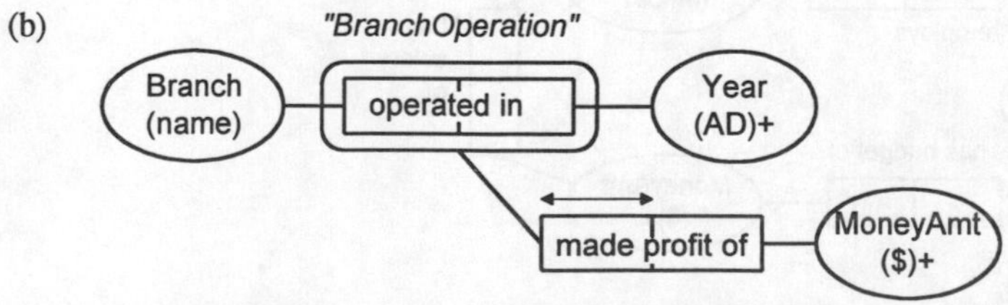

* TotalProfit (Year *y*) ::= **sum**(MoneyAmt) **from**
(**some** BranchOperation **of** *y* made profit of MoneyAmt)

Exercise 4.4

1. (a)

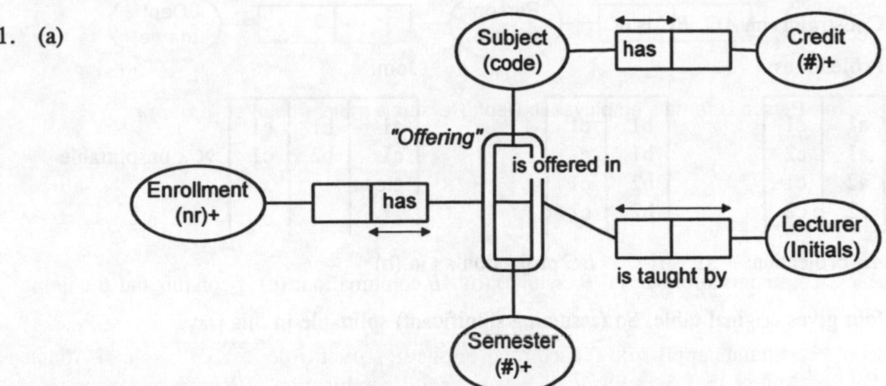

(b)

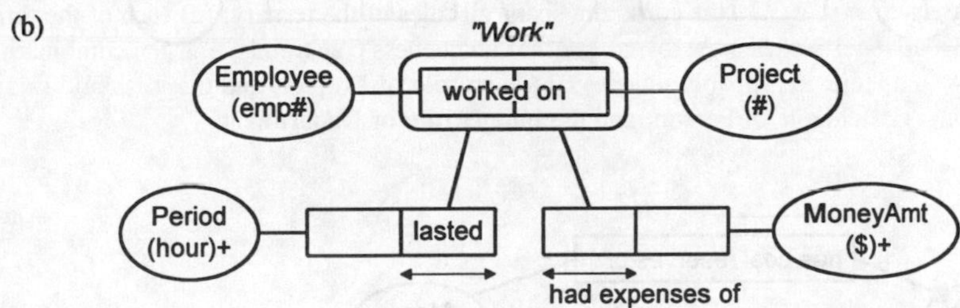

3.

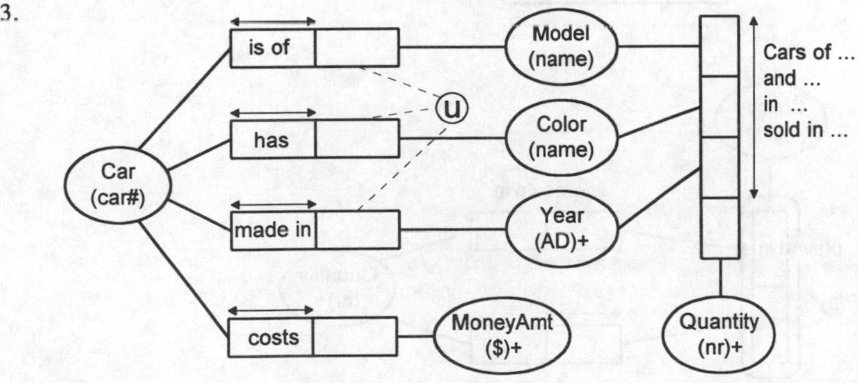

Exercise 4.5

1. (a), (b), (d)

3. Since each executive has only one home phone, this information may be split off without information loss. Hence the ternary must be split into two binaries: Executive at work uses Phone; Executive at home uses Phone. The former fact type is *m:n* and the latter is *n:1*. The diagrams are obvious, and to save space are omitted in these answers.

Exercise 4.6

1. (a) Constraints on *AC, BC*.

   (b) Projections: Join:

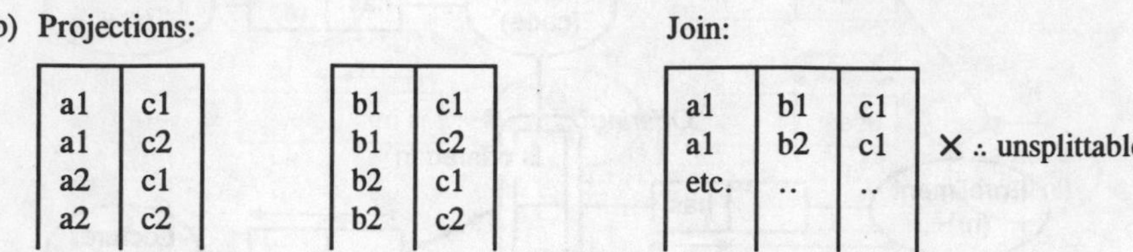

a1	c1
a1	c2
a2	c1
a2	c2

b1	c1
b1	c2
b2	c1
b2	c2

a1	b1	c1
a1	b2	c1
etc.	..	..

× ∴ unsplittable

   (c) *AB* projection: a1 b1 *BC* projection as in (b)
   a2 b2

   Join gives original table. So (assuming significant) splittable in this way.

   (d)

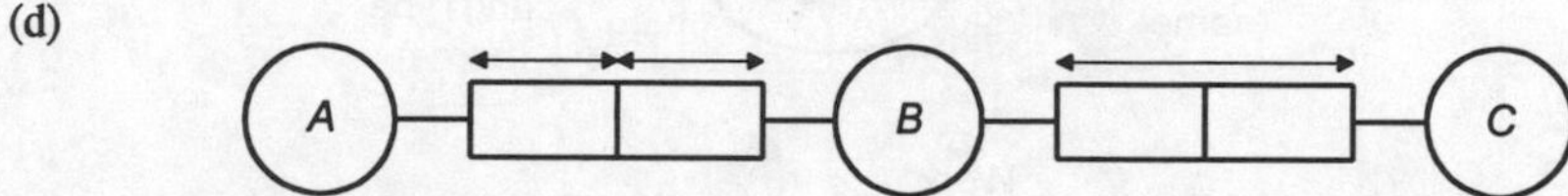

Exercise 5.2

1.

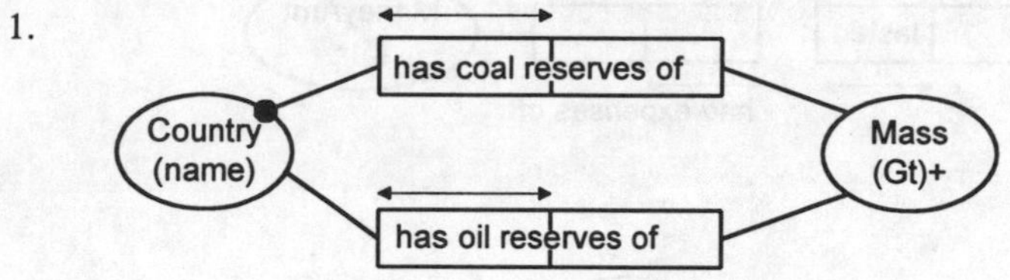

3.

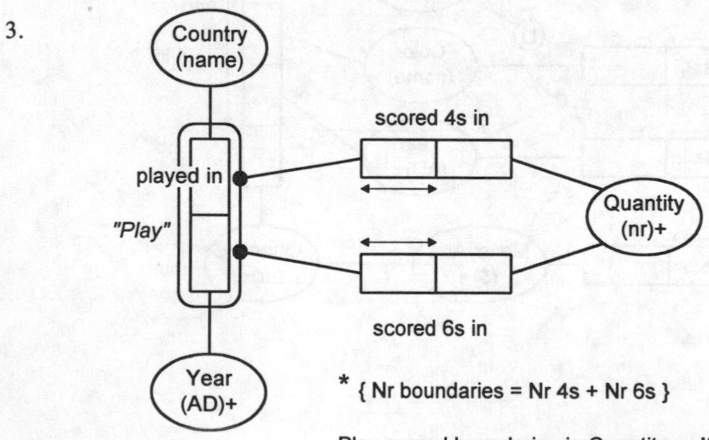

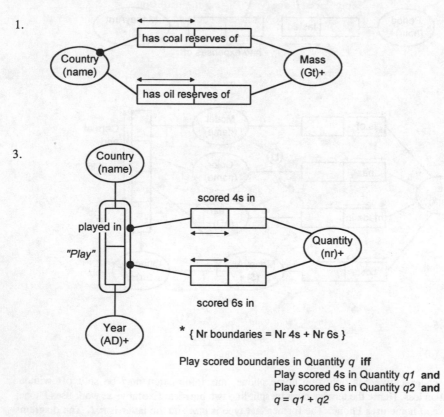

Play scored boundaries in Quantity *q* **iff**
Play scored 4s in Quantity *q1* **and**
Play scored 6s in Quantity *q2* **and**
q = *q1* + *q2*

Exercise 5.3

1.

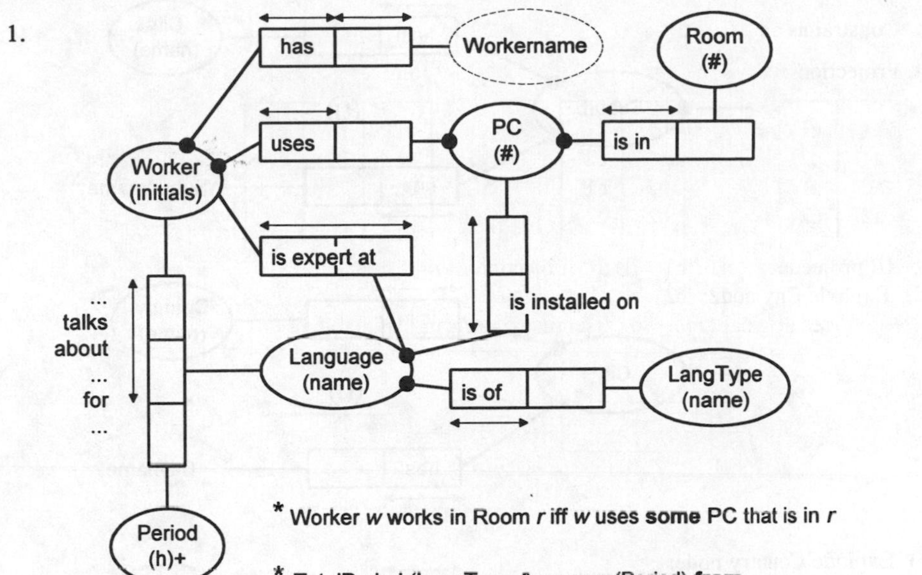

Exercise 5.4

1. (a)

(b) Explode Street node:

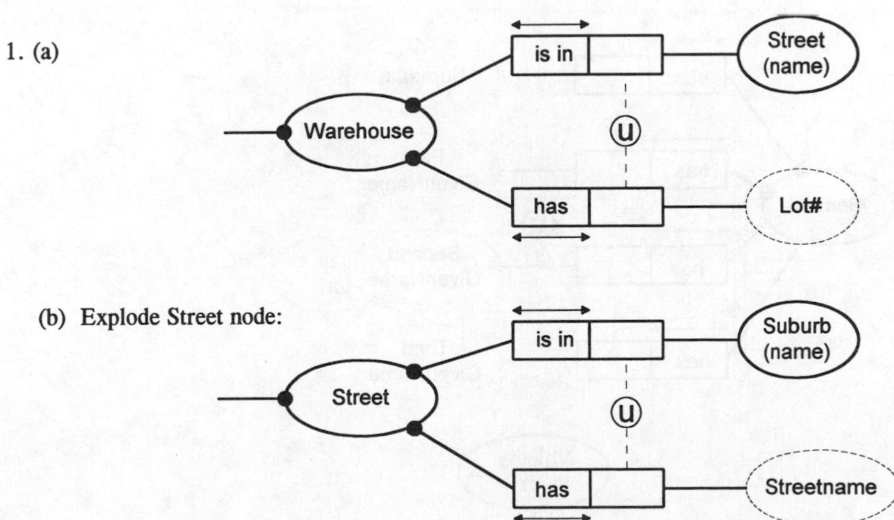

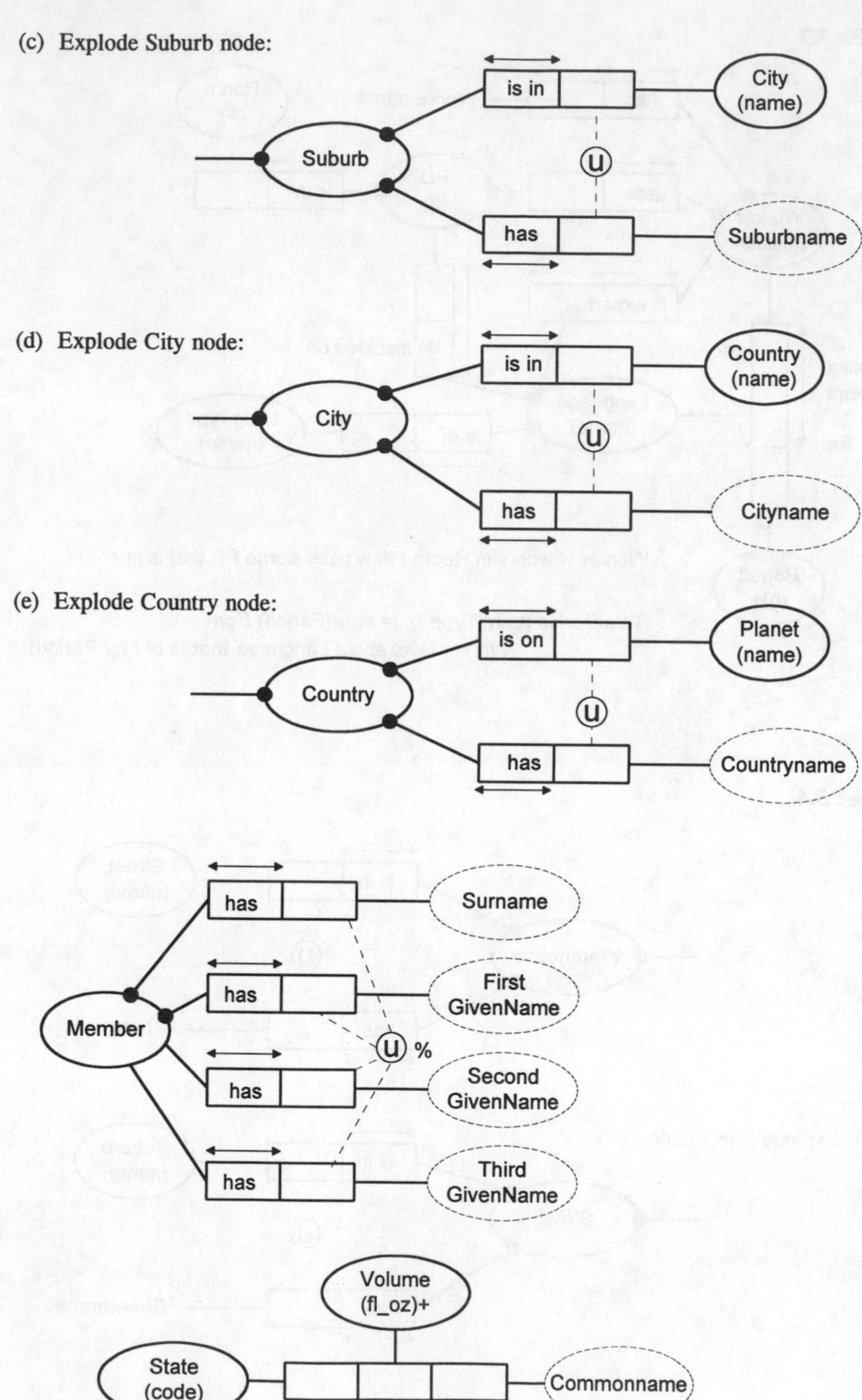
(c) Explode Suburb node:
Suburb
is in
City
(name)
u
has
Suburbname
(d) Explode City node:
City
is in
Country
(name)
u
has
Cityname
(e) Explode Country node:
Country
is on
Planet
(name)
u
has
Countryname
3.
Member
has
Surname
has
First
GivenName
u %
has
Second
GivenName
has
Third
GivenName
5.
Volume
(fl_oz)+
State
(code)
Commonname
in ... a beer of ... has ...

Exercise 6.2

1.

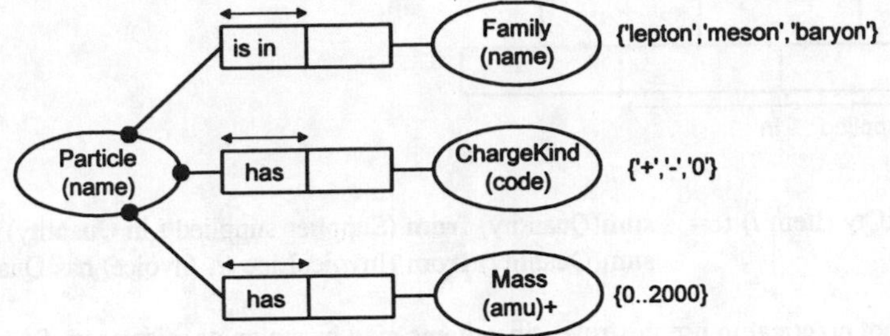

3.

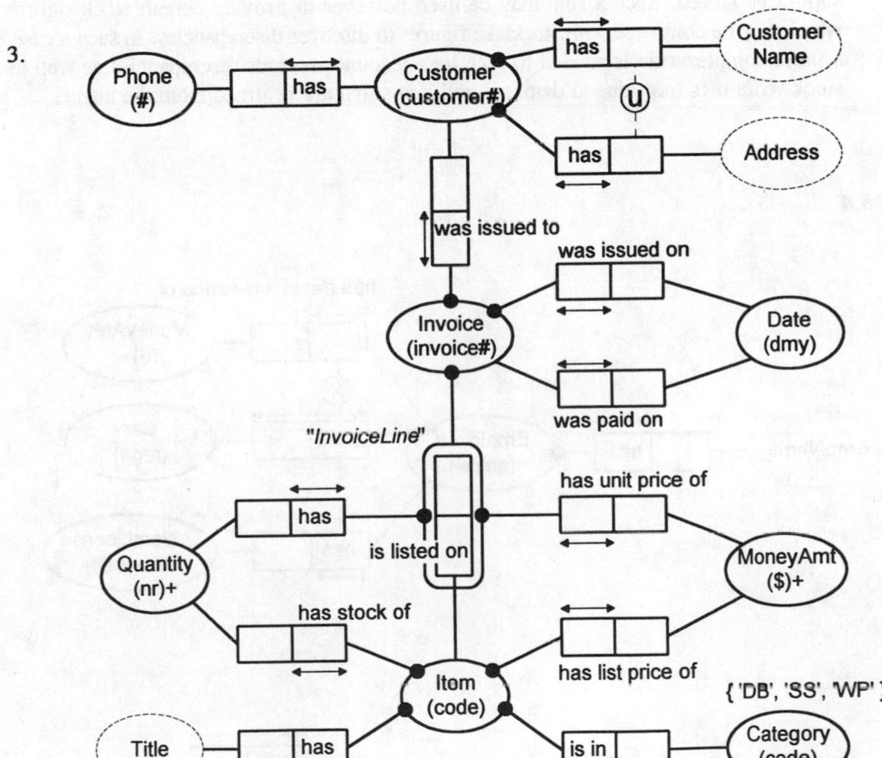

* { subtotal = qty x unit price }
InvoiceLine *l* has subtotal of MoneyAmt *s* **iff** *l* has Quantity *q* **and** *l* has unit price of MoneyAmt *u* **and** $s = q * u$

* { total = sum of subtotals }
Total(Invoice *i*) :: = **sum**(MoneyAmt) **from** (InvoiceLine ⟨Item, *i*⟩ has subtotal of MoneyAmt)

5. (a)

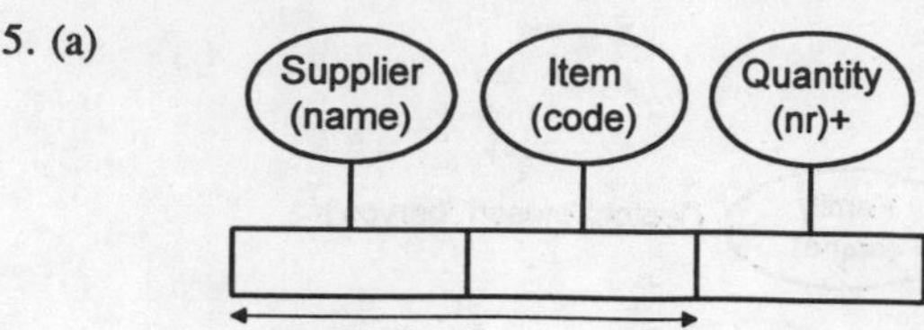

(b) (i) StockQty (Item *i*) ::= **sum**(Quantity) **from** (Supplier supplied *i* in Quantity) – **sum**(Quantity) **from** (InvoiceLine ⟨*i*, Invoice⟩ has Quantity)

(ii) It is not practical to use this rule, since items may be stolen or misplaced. So periodic stocktakes must be taken to determine the exact number in stock, and stocktake numbers should be stored. Such a rule may be used however to provide default stock figures which may be compared with stocktake figures to discover discrepancies. In such a case, a more complex rule is needed to take into account previous discrepancies as well as stock write-offs (e.g. due to damage) and items that are returned from the buyer.

Exercise 6.4

1.

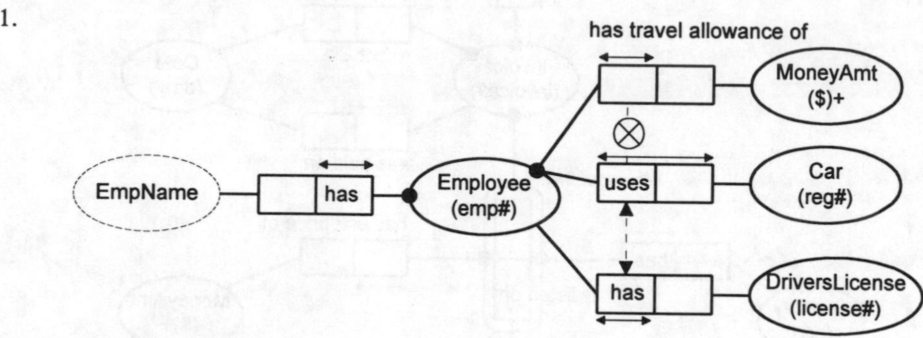

3.

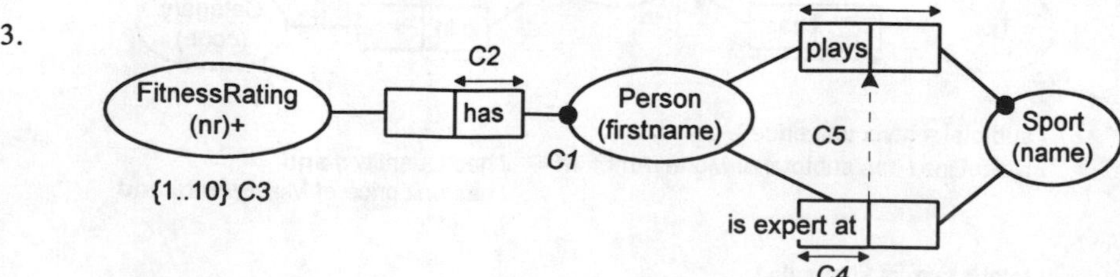

Note: The mandatory role constraint on Sport is implied. Why?

5.

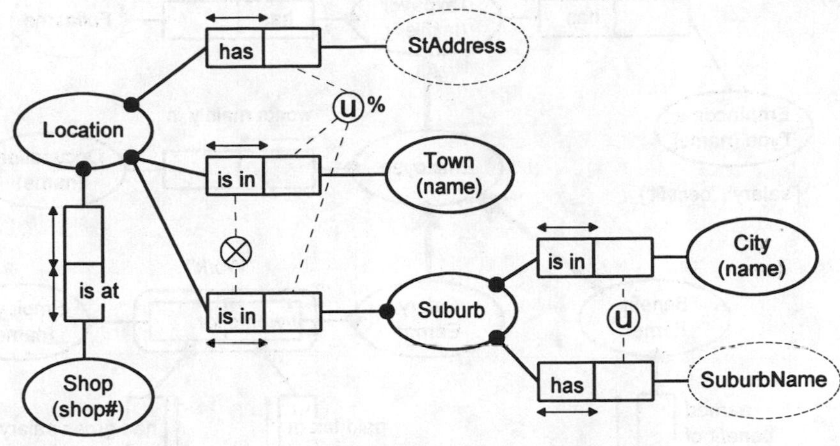

Exercise 6.5

1. (a) (i) ORM requires subtypes to be proper, and types (as distinct from their populations) to be non-empty. For example: $B = \{1,2\}$ $C = \{1\}$.
   (ii) One example is: $B = \{1,2\}$ $C = \{2,3\}$ $D = \{2\}$.

   (b) (i) arcs must be directed (is *A* a subtype of *B* or vice versa?)
   (ii) graph must be acyclic (*proper* subtype)
   (iii) delete arc from *C* to *A* (transitively implied)
   (iv) graph must be acyclic (*proper* subtype)
   (v) primitive types *A* and *B* must be exclusive, so they cannot have a common subtype *C*

3. (a)

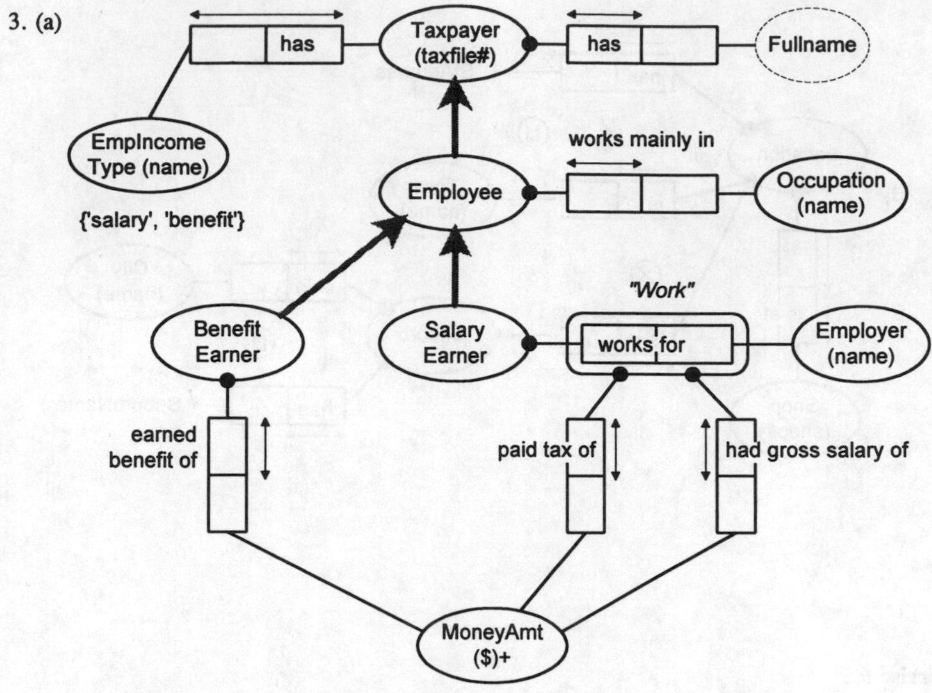

each Employee **is a** Taxpayer **who** has **some** EmpIncomeType
each BenefitEarner **is a** Taxpayer **who** has EmpIncomeType 'salary'
each SalaryEarner **is a** Taxpayer **who** has EmpIncomeType 'benefit'

Note: This is an example of a case where a data dictionary would be a useful supplement to the conceptual schema itself. In particular the term "Taxpayer" should be clarified as meaning "potential payer of tax", i.e. anybody who has a tax file number. Whether a taxpayer actually pays tax depends on other factors (e.g. the taxpayer's income).

(b)

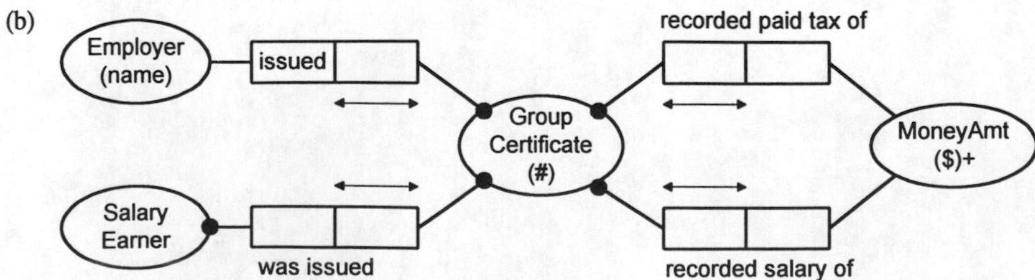

5.

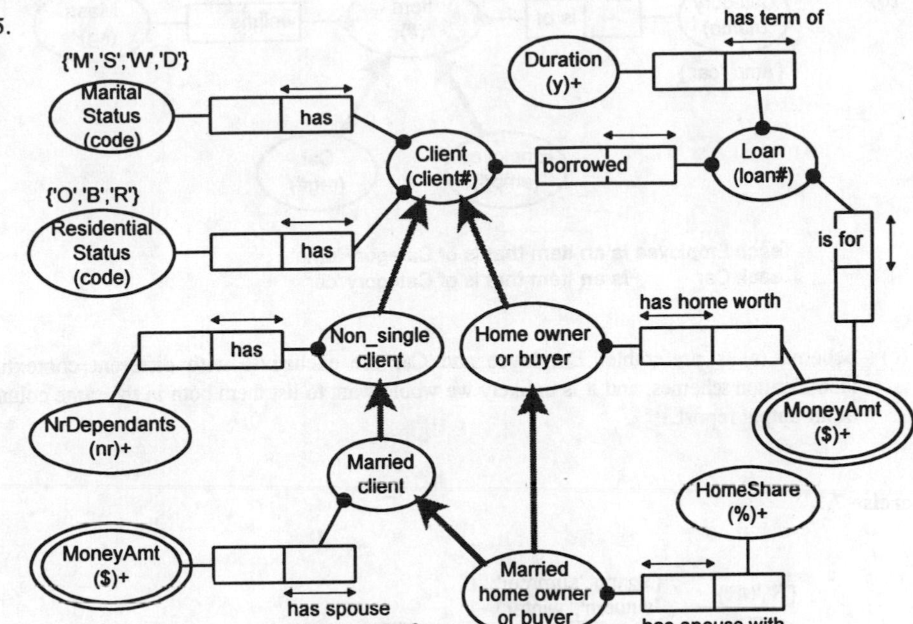

each Non_single_client **is a** Client **who** has MaritalStatus <> 'S'
each Home_owner_or_buyer **is a** Client **who** has ResidentialStatus <> 'R'
each Married_client **is a** Client **who** has MaritalStatus 'M'
each Married_home_owner_or_buyer **is a** Married_client **and a** Home_owner_or_buyer

Exercise 6.6

1. (a)

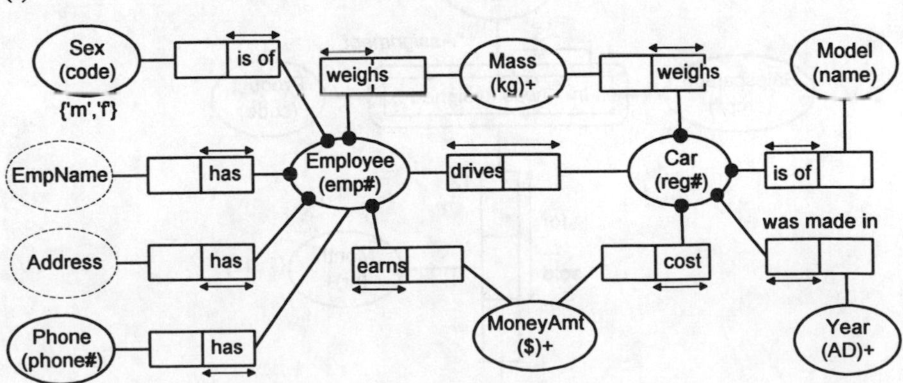

(b)

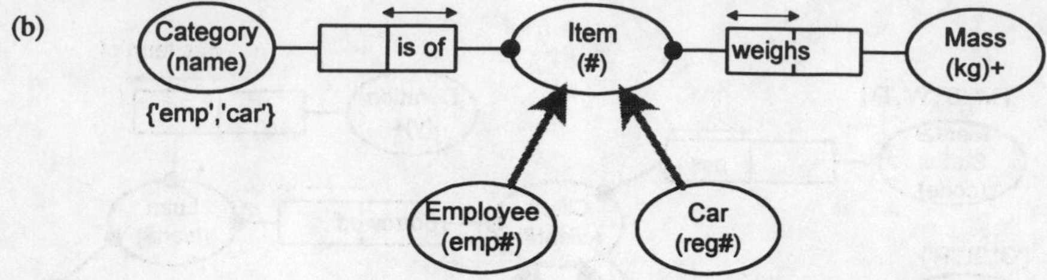

each Employee **is an Item that is of Category** 'emp'
each Car **is an Item that is of Category** 'car'

(c) Schema (a) is preferable. Employee and Car are exclusive, with different contextual identification schemes, and it is unlikely we would want to list them both in the same column of an output report.

Exercise 7.2

1.

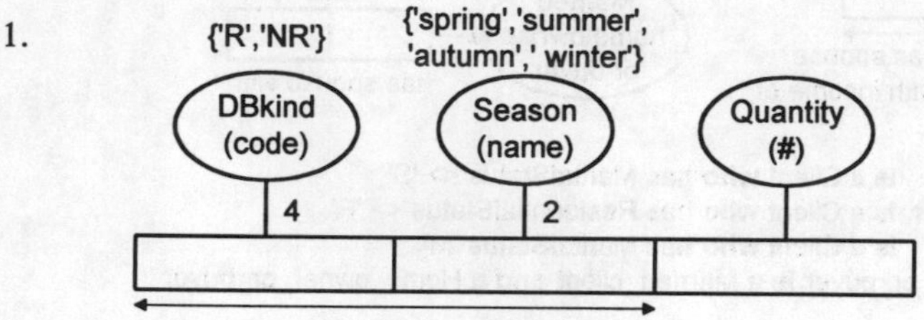

3.

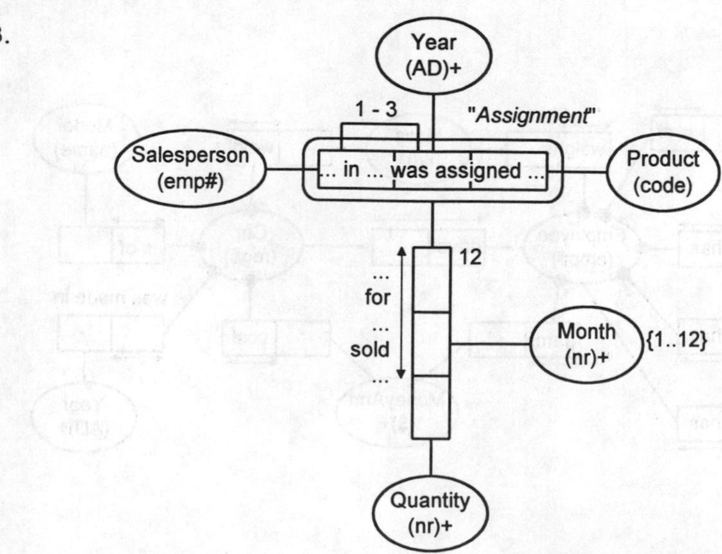

Exercise 7.3

1. (a) R, S, T (b) ir (c) ir, S (d) ir, as, T (e) ir, as, T (f) R, T (g) ir, S

   Note that (g) is not intranstitive (e.g. locations at vertices of a triangle).

5. Country ! (name)

   °*ir*

   borders

Belgium	France
Belgium	Germany
Belgium	Luxembourg
Belgium	Netherlands
France	Belgium
...	...

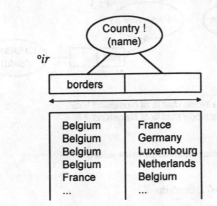

The schema is shown with a sample population. If storage is not a problem, use a symmetric relation like this (symmetry can be enforced at update to simplfy data entry).

If storage is a proble, use an asymmetric relation (add °*as* constraint) , say *edb_borders* (extensional database version of *borders*) and add the following derivation rule:

Country *c1* borders Country *c2* iff
c1 edb_borders *c2* or *c2* edb_borders *c1*.

Exercise 7.4

1. belongs to

   Party (name)

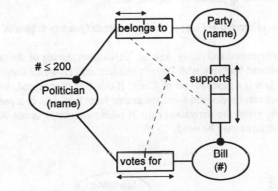

   # ≤ 200

   Politician (name)

   supports

   votes for

   Bill (#)

3. 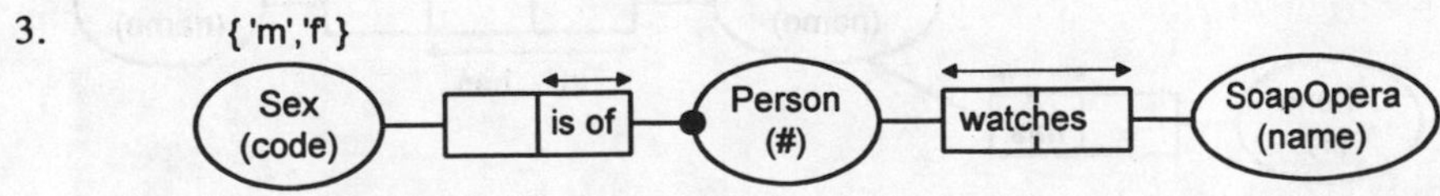

TC1: **each** Person **that** is of Sex 'm' watches **exactly one** SoapOpera

5.

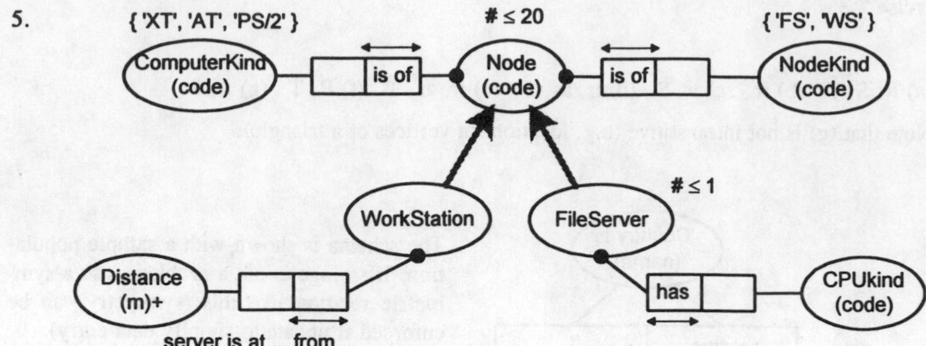

each WorkStation is a Node that is of NodeKind 'WS'
each FileServer is a Node that is of NodeKind 'FS'

7. The schema is as earlier, but with the following derivation rules added:

   X contains *Y* if *X* directly contains *Y*
   X contains *Y* if *X* directly contains *Z* and *Z* contains *Y*

Exercise 7.5

1. If *A*'s role in *S* is populated with *a*, say, then *a* must also play *A*'s role in *R* (since the pair-subset constraint implies subset constraints on corresponding roles). But this violates the exclusion constraint. Hence the constraint pattern is population-inconsistent.

3. Split into two fact types: Bookshop is located in City; Bookshop ordered Quantity copies of Book.

5. The *grandparent_of* relation is partly stored and partly derived. This allows storing of the fact that David is a grandparent of Chris without knowing who David's children are. However suppose we now attempt to store the fact that Ann is a grandparent of Chris. If this fact is accepted, we have derived redundancy since this fact can be derived from the stored facts that Ann is a parent of Bob, and Bob is a parent of Chris, given the derivation rule. If such redundancy is not desired, special exclusion and update constraints may be used.

Exercise 8.2

1. (a)

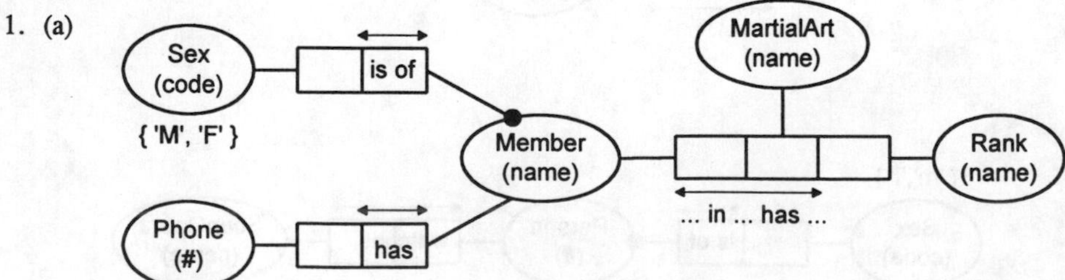

(b) The attribute "Arts and ranks" is multi-valued, not atomic-valued.

(c) *Member* (membername, sex, [phone])

Ranked (membername, art, rank)

(d) The nested relation allows all details about members to be retrieved without a table join, so is more efficient for such queries. Moreover the subset constraint is no longer needed. On the negative side, allowing nesting leads to a more complex query language, and queries to determine who has an art or rank are somewhat less efficient than for the relational solution.

Exercise 8.3

1. *AuthoredBy* (isbn, author)

Book (isbn, title, edition)

Subject (subjcode, credit, [setText])

Offering (subjcode, semester)

3. (a) The table allows redundancy. For example, with the following population the fact that dress d1 costs $50 is duplicated:

Likes	(woman,	dress,	cost)
	Eve	d1	50
	Sue	d1	50

(b) *Likes* (woman, dresscode)

Dress (dresscode, cost, [owner])

Earns (woman, wage)

5. (a) *Project* (projcode, mgrname, budget)

Manager (mgrname, salary, birthyr)

(b) *Employee* (emp#, deptname, salary)

Department (deptname, budget)

9. (a)

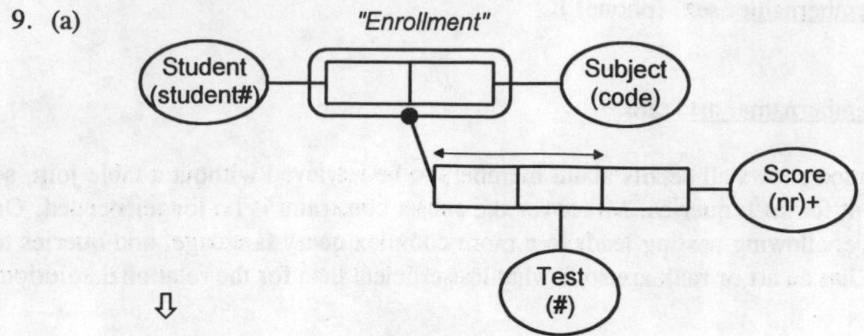

Result (<u>student#, subjcode, test</u> score)

(b)

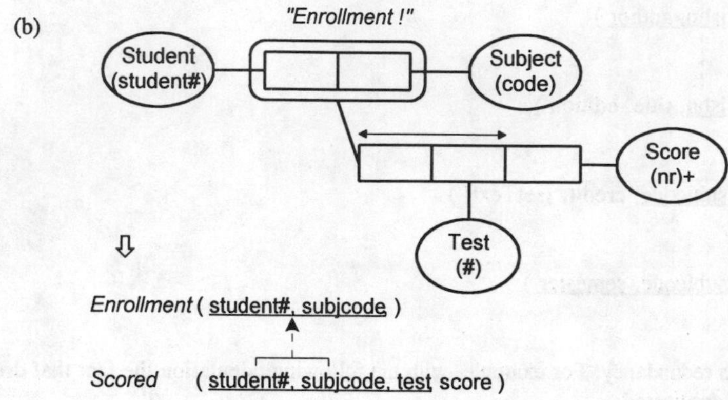

11. (a)

{0..140} {0..168} {0..168} {TV, NP}

Person (<u>form#</u>, age, tvhours, paperhours, [favchannel][1], [favpaper][2], [prefnews][3])

[1] **exists iff** tvhours > 0
[2] **exists iff** paperhours > 0
[3] **exists iff** tvhours > 0 **and** paperhours > 0 **and** age >= 18

(b)

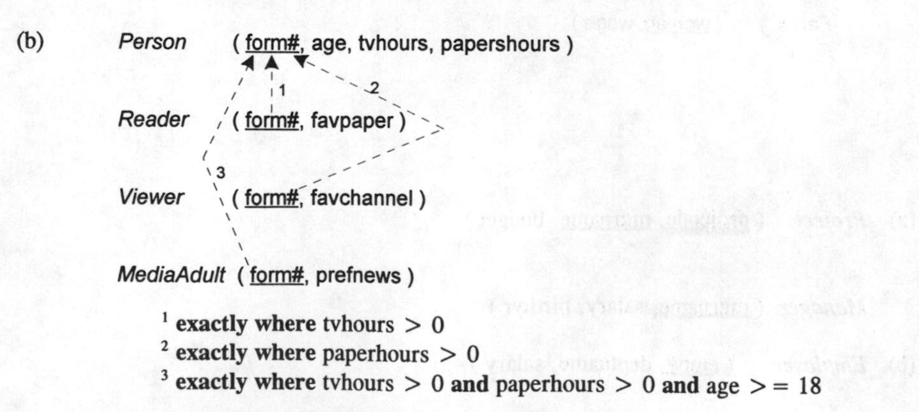

Add value constraints as for (a). For most applications, schema (a) is preferable.

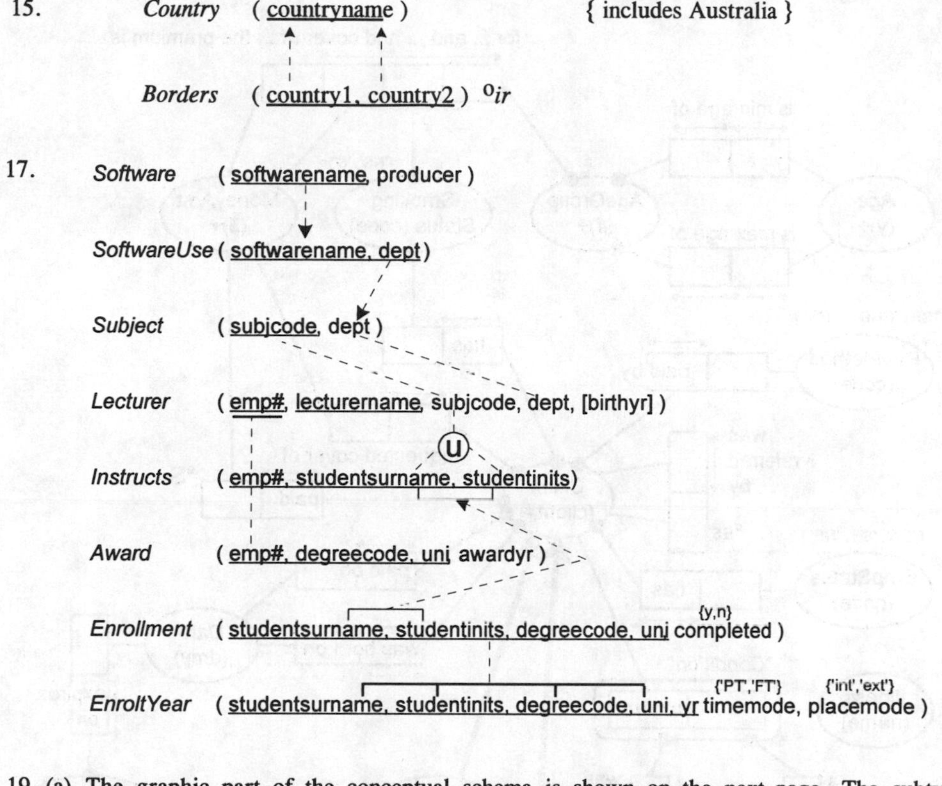

15.
Country (countryname) { includes Australia }
Borders (country1, country2) °ir
17.
Software (softwarename, producer)
SoftwareUse (softwarename, dept)
Subject (subjcode, dept)
Lecturer (emp#, lecturername, subjcode, dept, [birthyr])
u
Instructs (emp#, studentsurname, studentinits)
Award (emp#, degreecode, uni awardyr)
{y,n}
Enrollment (studentsurname, studentinits, degreecode, uni completed)
{'PT','FT'} {'int','ext'}
EnroltYear (studentsurname, studentinits, degreecode, uni, yr timemode, placemode)

19. (a) The graphic part of the conceptual schema is shown on the next page. The subtype definitions, derivation rules and textual constraints are as follows:

each CardPayer **is a** Client **who** pays by PayMethod 'CRD'
each EmployedClient **is a** Client **who** has EmpStatus < > 'NE'
each SelfEmployedClient **is a** Client **who** has EmpStatus 'SE'

* YearAge(Client *c*) ::= **year_of (today** – (Date **from** (*c* was born on Date))
* Client *c* is in AgeGroup *g* **iff** Age *a1* is min age of *g* **and** Age *a2* is max age of *g* **and** YearAge(*c*) > = *a1* **and** YearAge(*c*) < = *a2*

*S { payment quote is derived for current date using bithdate, smoking status and proposed cove, then stored as payment if paid on that date—for simplicity we assume payment must be on day of quote }
Client *c* is quoted MoneyAmt *m1* **iff**
c is in AgeGroup *g* **and** *c* has SmokingStatus *s* **and** *c* requested cover of *m2* **and** for *g* and *s* and cover of *m2* the premium is *m3* **and** *m1* = 12 * *m3*

TC1 { date paid < = card expiry date }
if Client *c* paid on date *d1* **and** *c* used **some** CreditCard **that** expies on Date *d2*
then *d1* < = *d2*

TC2 { min age of group < max age }
if Age *a1* is min age of AgeGroup *g* **and** *a2* is max age of *g* **then** *a1* < a2

TC3 { age groups are consecutive } **if** *a1* is max age of AgeGroup *n* and *a2* is min age of AgeGroup *n*+1 **then** *a2* = *a1* + 1

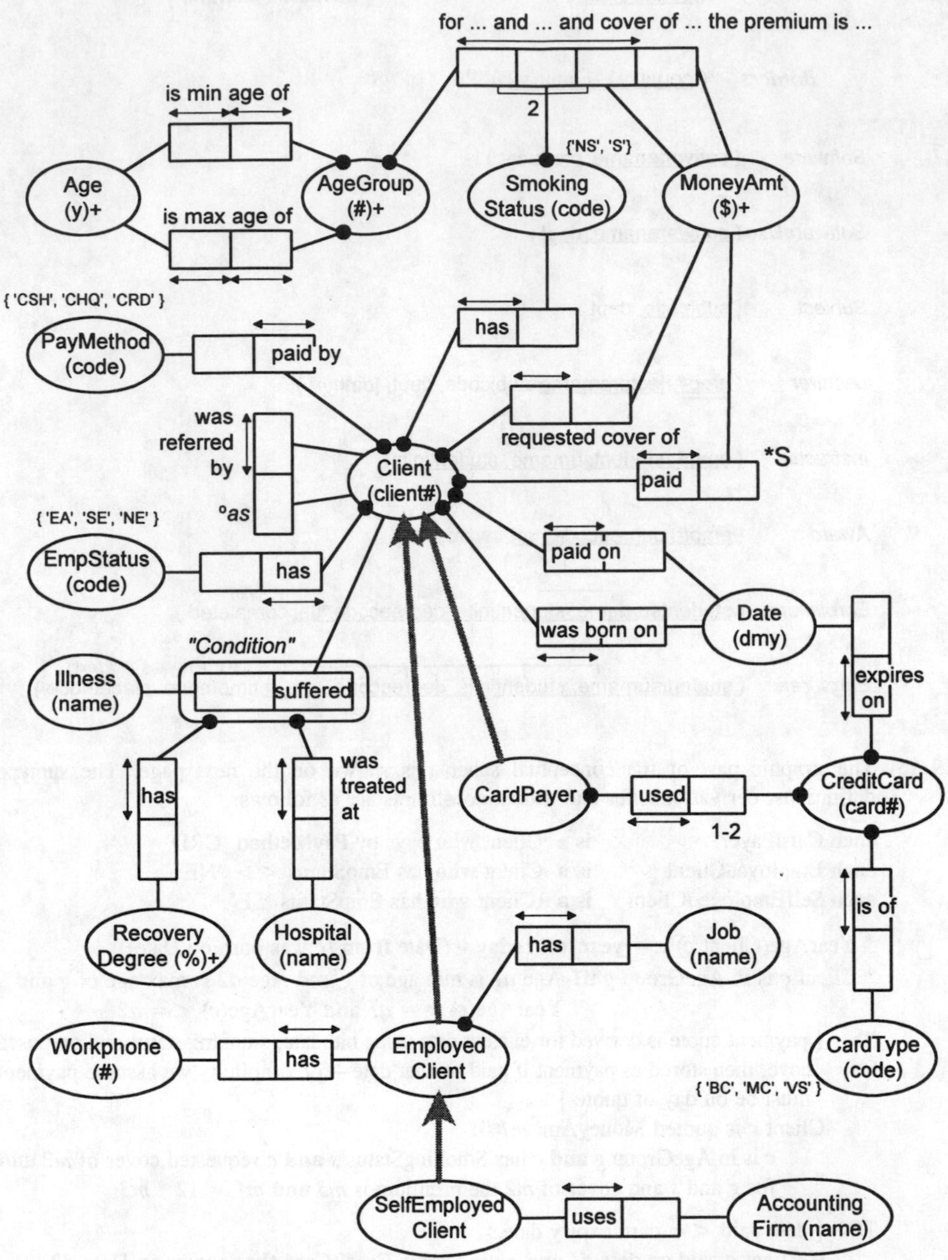

(b) Even if a quoted payment were derived somehow, the actual payment would need to be stored since it might not be derivable in the future (because the premium schedule might then be different, and historical records of premiums are not kept in this UoD).

(c)

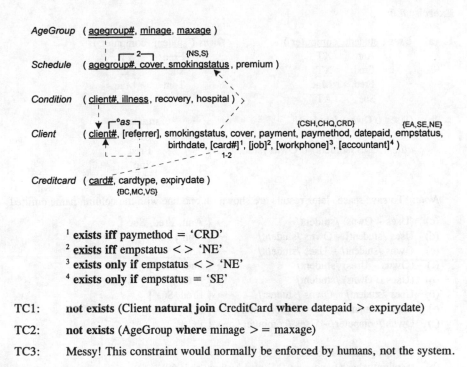

AgeGroup (<u>agegroup#</u>, <u>minage</u>, <u>maxage</u>)

Schedule (<u>agegroup#, cover, smokingstatus</u>, premium) — 2 (over agegroup#, cover); {NS,S} (smokingstatus)

Condition (<u>client#, illness</u>, recovery, hospital)

Client (<u>client#</u>, [referrer], smokingstatus, cover, payment, paymethod, datepaid, empstatus, birthdate, [card#][1], [job][2], [workphone][3], [accountant][4]) — °as (client#, referrer); {CSH,CHQ,CRD} (paymethod); {EA,SE,NE} (empstatus); 1-2

Creditcard (<u>card#</u>, cardtype, expirydate) — {BC,MC,VS} (cardtype)

[1] **exists iff** paymethod = 'CRD'
[2] **exists iff** empstatus < > 'NE'
[3] **exists only if** empstatus < > 'NE'
[4] **exists only if** empstatus = 'SE'

TC1: **not exists** (Client **natural join** CreditCard **where** datepaid > expirydate)

TC2: **not exists** (AgeGroup **where** minage > = maxage)

TC3: Messy! This constraint would normally be enforced by humans, not the system.

Exercise 8.4

1\. (a)

Employee (<u>emp#</u>, sex, [smokes], manages, drives, [car][1]) — {y} (sex); {y,n} (manages); {y,n} (drives)

[1] **exists iff** drives = 'y'

(b) The value constraint on [smokes] is now {y,n}.
(c) Yes. Each person smokes or doesn't, and unknown has been eliminated.
(d) The smokes {y,n} attribute is now mandatory.

5\. (a)

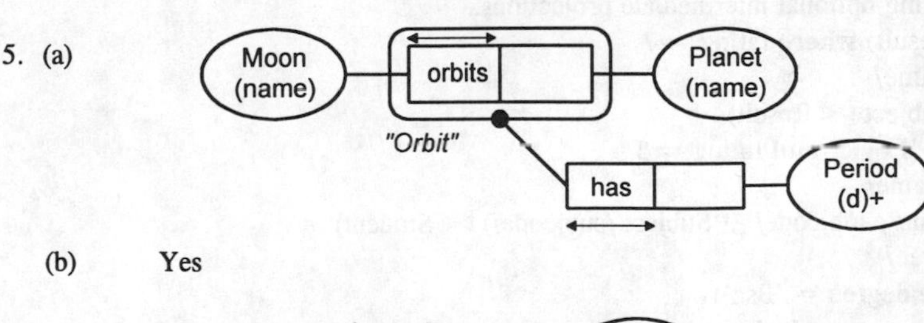

(b) Yes

(c)

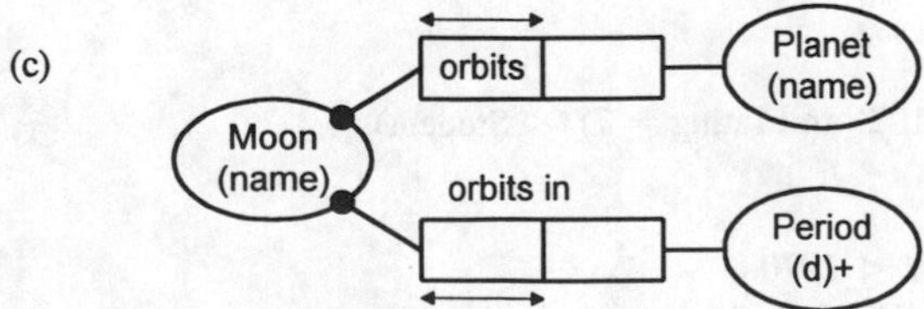

(d) *Moon* (<u>moonname</u>, planet, orbitalperiod)

Exercise 8.5

1. (a) *Uses* (student, computer)

student	computer
Ann	XT
Fred	XT
Fred	Mac
Sue	AT

Owns (student, computer)

student	computer
Fred	XT
Sue	PC
Tom	Mac

(b) (Uses ∪ Owns) *[student]* → *student*

aliter: Uses *[student]* ∪ Owns *[student]*

student
Ann
Fred
Sue
Tom

Note: To save space, later results are shown on one line with the column name omitted

(c) (Uses – Owns) *[student]* → { Ann, Fred, Sue }
(d) Uses *[student]* – Owns *[student]* → { Ann }
(e) Owns *[student]* – Uses *[student]* → { Tom }
(f) (Owns – Uses) *[student]* → { Sue, Tom }
(g) (Uses ∩ Owns) *[student]* → { Fred }
(h) Uses *[student]* ∩ Owns *[student]* → { Fred, Sue }
(i) Uses *[computer]* – Owns *[computer]* → { AT }
(j) Owns *[computer]* - Uses *[computer]* → { PC }

3. (a) Subject **where** subjcode = 'CS113'
(b) (Student **where** gender = 'M' **and** birthyr > 1960)
[student#, stuname, degree]
(c) (Student ⋈ Result) **where** stuname = 'Brown T' *[subjcode]*
aliter: ((Student **where** stuname = 'Brown T') *[student#]*
⋈ Result) *[subjcode]*
aliter: ((Student **where** stuname = 'Brown T')
⋈ Result) *[subjcode]*

Note: From now on we normally show only one solution, favoring joins first if convenient, and omitting optional intermediate projections.

(d) (Student ⋈ Result) **where** rating = 7
[student#,stuname]
(e) (Student ⋈ Subject ⋈ Result)
where title = 'Logic' **and** rating = 5
[student#, stuname]
(f) ((Result *[student#, subjcode]* ÷ Subject *[subjcode]*) ⋈ Student)
[student#, degree]
(g) (Student **where** degree = 'Bsc')
[student#, stuname, gender]
∪
((Result **where** subjcode = 'PD102' **and** rating = 7) ⋈ Student)
[student#, stuname, gender]
(h) (Student ⋈ Subject ⋈ Result)
where gender = 'M' **and** birthyr < 1970
and rating > = 5 **and** title = 'Databases'
[student#, stuname, birthyr]

5. (a) *Project* (<u>projcode</u>, budget)

Work (<u>empname, projcode</u>)

Employee (<u>empname</u>, gender, salary)

(b) (Work ⋈ Employee)
where gender = 'F' **and** (salary > 25000 **or** projcode = '5GIS')
*[*empname, salary*]*

(c) (Employee ⋈ Work) *[*empname, gender, projcode*]*
÷
Project **where** budget > = 100000 *[*projcode*]*

7. (a) $A \cap B = A - (A - B)$ $\{ \text{ or } B - (B - A) \}$

(b) $A \bowtie B = (A \times B) \textbf{ where } A.y = B.y\ [A.x, A.y, B.z]$

(c) $A \div B = A[x] - ((A[x] \times B) - A)[x]$

9. (a) (Invoice ⋈ InvoiceLine ⋈ Item)
where unitprice < listprice *[*customer#*]*
–
(Invoice ⋈ InvoiceLine ⋈ Item)
where category = 'WP' *[*customer#*]*
Note: It is wrong to simply add: "**and** category < > 'WP'".

(b) ((Invoice ⋈ InvoiceLine) *[*customer#, itemcode*]*
÷
(Item **where** category = 'SS') *[*itemcode*]*
⋈
Customer) *[*cusname*]*

(c) (Invoice ⋈ InvoiceLine) *[*customer#, itemcode*]*
÷
(Item **where** category = 'WP') *[*itemcode*]*
–
(Invoice ⋈ InvoiceLine ⋈ Item)
where category = 'DB' *[*customer#*]*

(d) (InvoiceLine ⋈ Item) **where** category = 'SS' *[*invoice#*]*
∩
(InvoiceLine ⋈ Item) **where** category = 'WP' *[*invoice#*]*
⋈ Invoice *[*customer#*]*

Exercise 9.2

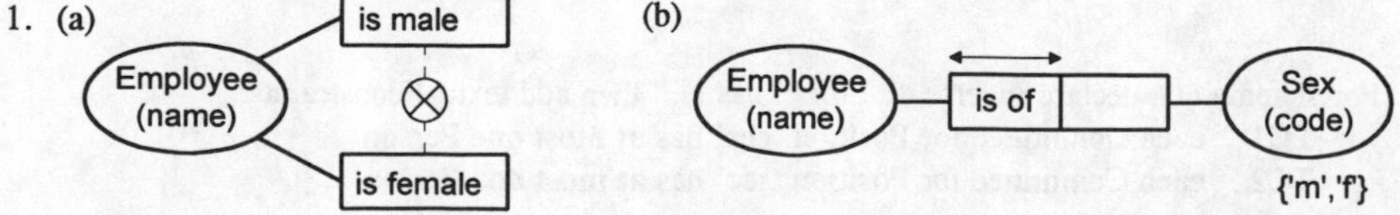

3. (a)

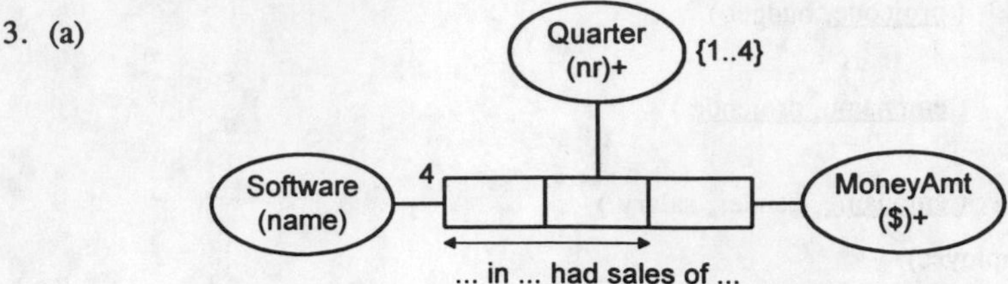

(b)

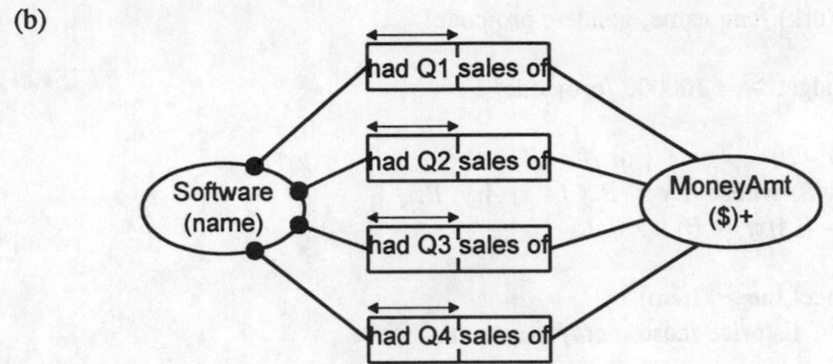

5. (a)

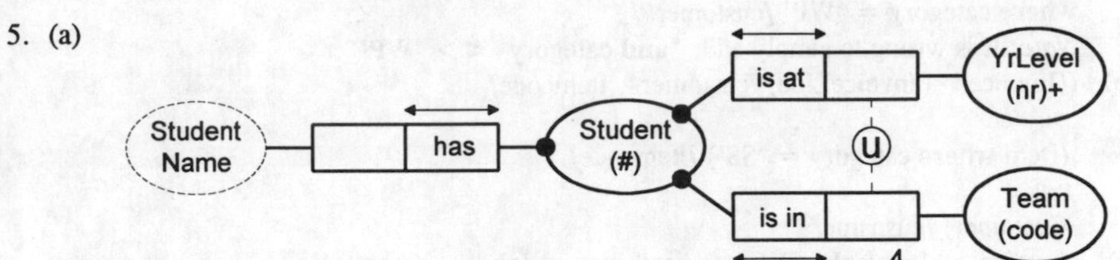

(b)

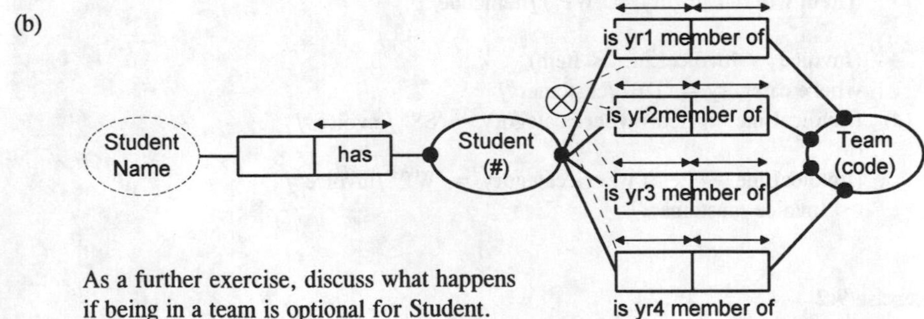

As a further exercise, discuss what happens if being in a team is optional for Student.

7. For schema (1), declare inverse "... for .. has ..." then add textual constraints:
   TC1 **each** Committee for Position 'chr' has **at most one** Person
   TC2 **each** Committee for Position 'sec' has **at most one** Person

For schema (2), add pair-exclusion constraint connected to mid-point of each predicate.

Exercise 9.3

1. (a)

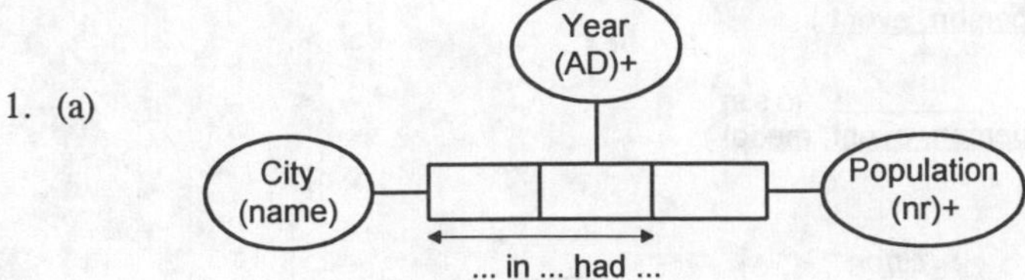

(b)

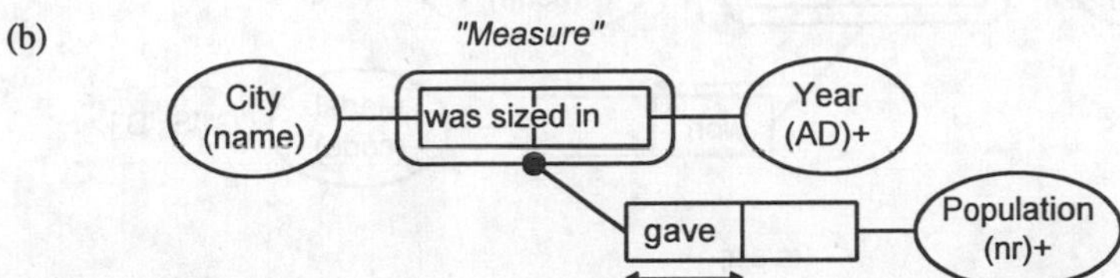

(c)

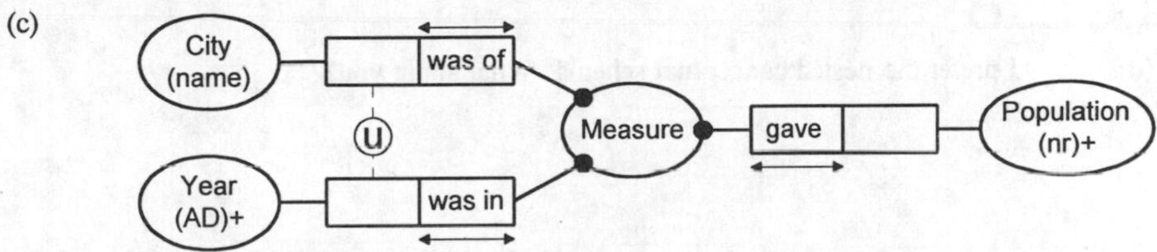

(d) I prefer (a). How about you?

(e)

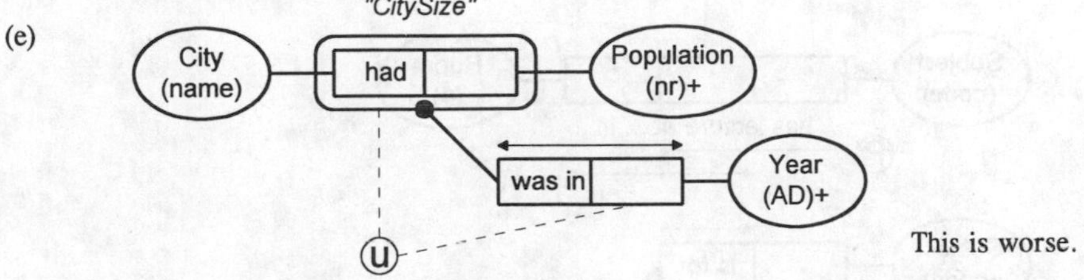

This is worse.

3. Here is the co-referenced solution. The flat and nested versions are obvious. I prefer the co-referenced version. How about you?

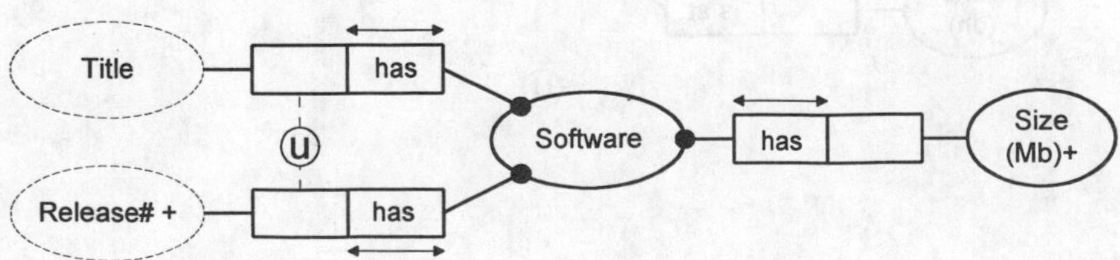

5. (a)

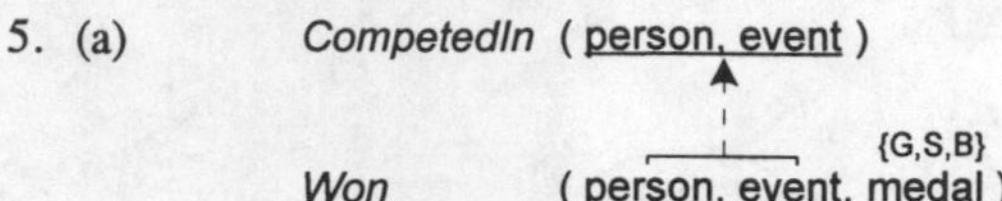

(b)

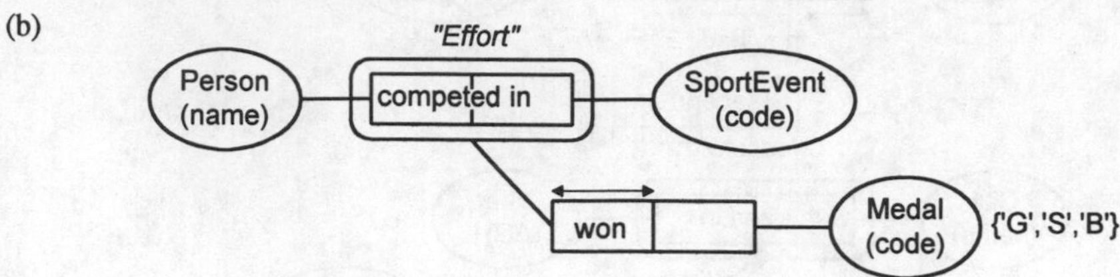

(c)

{G,S,B}
Games (competitor, event, [medalwon])

(d) I prefer the nested conceptual schema. What about you?

7. (a)

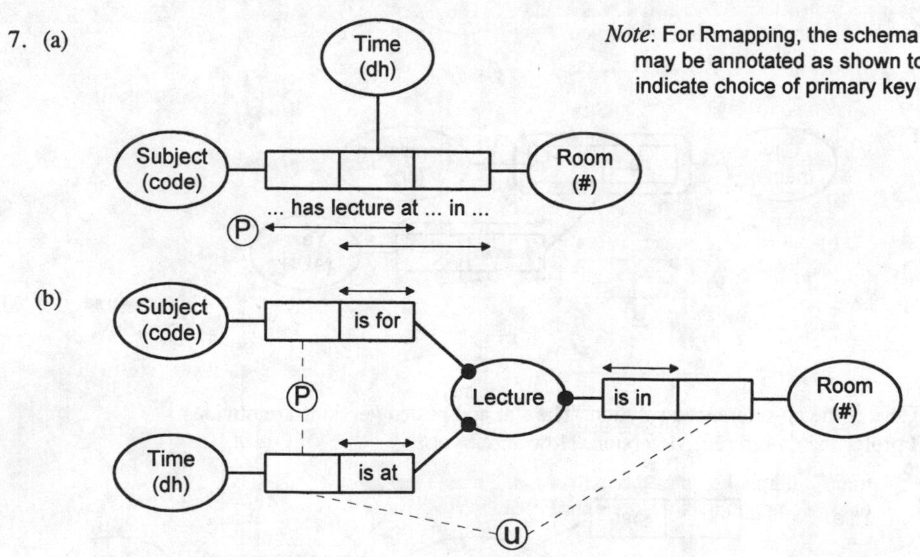

9. (a)

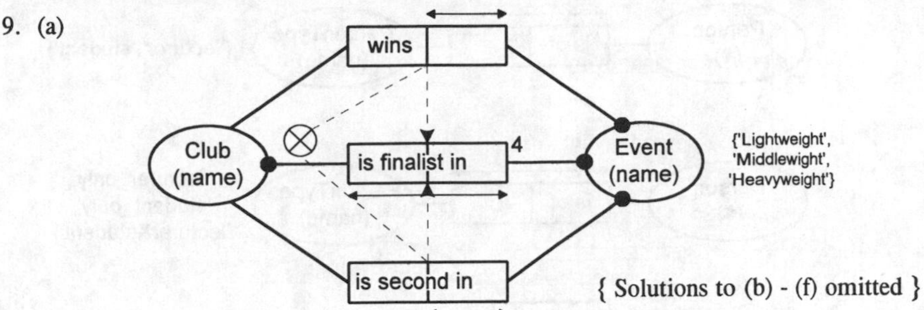

{ Solutions to (b) - (f) omitted }

Exercise 9.4

1. (a)

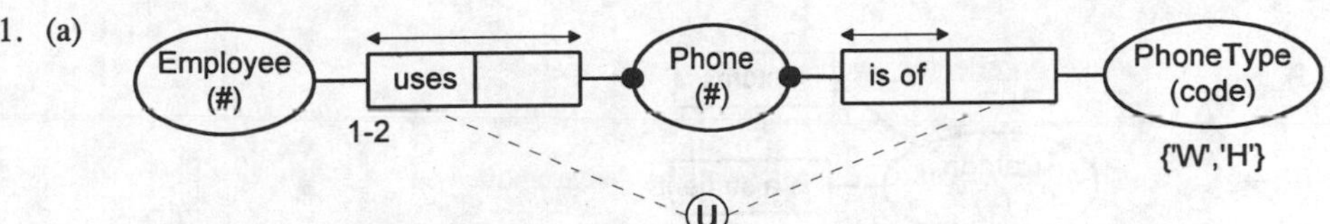

(b)

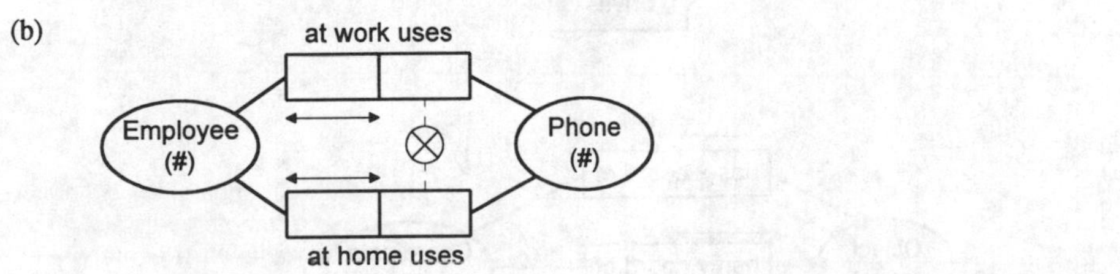

(c) Remove Phone's mandatory role constraint on the uses predicate in (a)

(d)

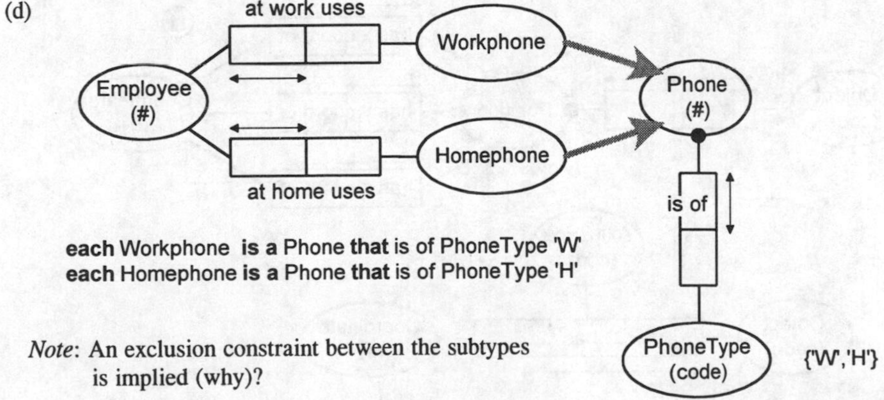

each Workphone **is a** Phone **that** is of PhoneType 'W'
each Homephone **is a** Phone **that** is of PhoneType 'H'

Note: An exclusion constraint between the subtypes is implied (why)?

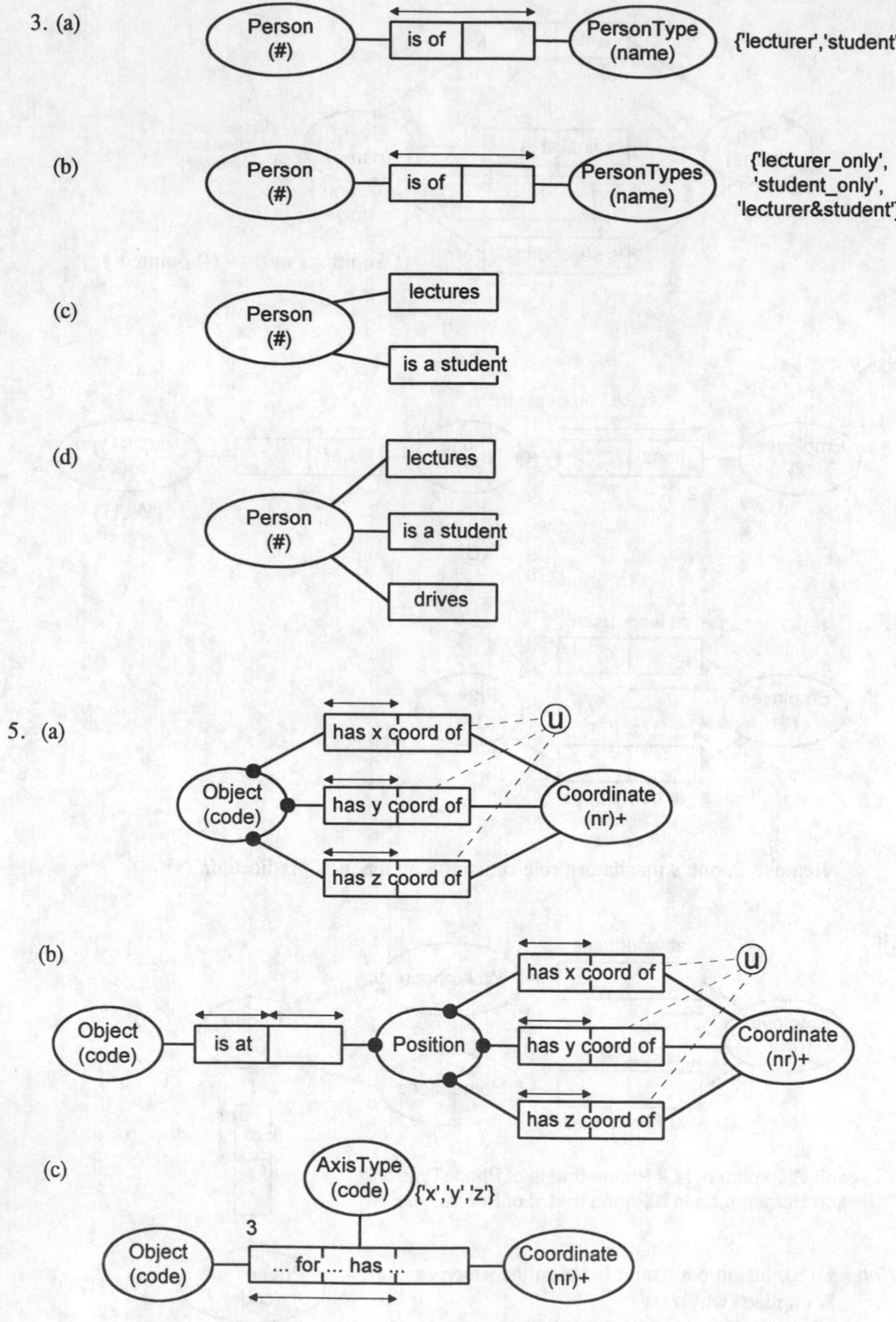

Textual constraint (at most one object at each x-y-z position) is very awkward

Exercise 9.5

1. (a)

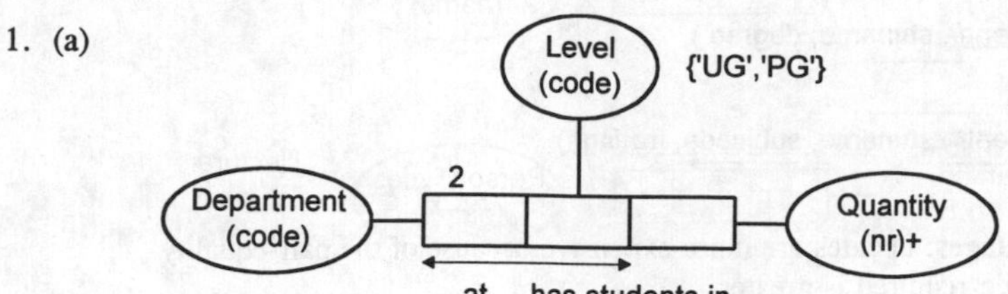

⇨ *StudentFigures* (dept, level, qty) (2 {UG,PG})

(b)

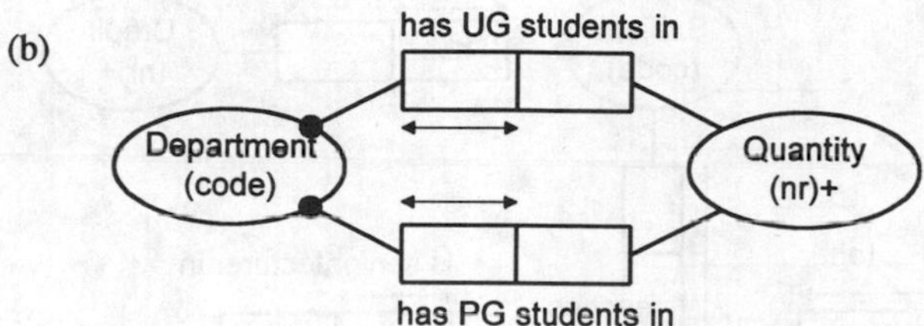

⇨ *Department* (deptcode, nrUGstudents, nrPGstudents)

(c) Attach to left of (a):

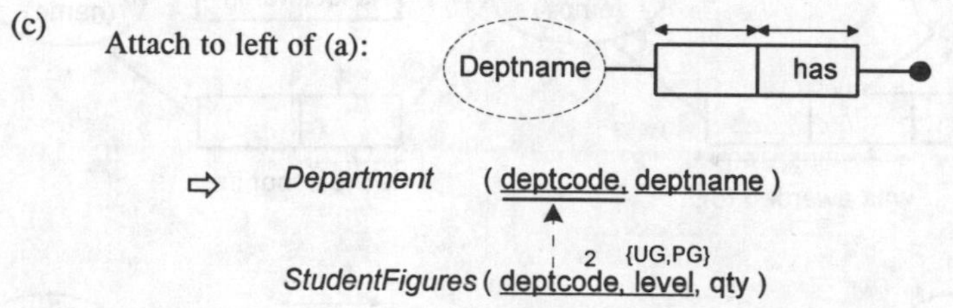

⇨ *Department* (deptcode, deptname)

StudentFigures (deptcode, level, qty) (2 {UG,PG})

(d)

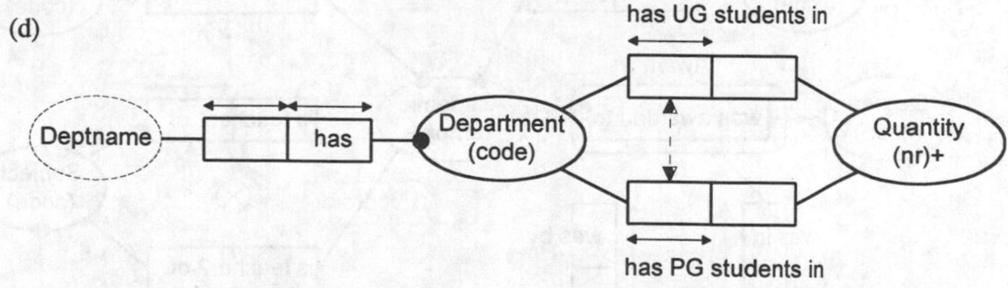

⇨ *Department* (deptcode, deptname, [nrUGstudents, nrPGstudents])

Exercise 9.6

1. *Student* (<u>student#</u>, stuname, degree)

Result (student#, stuname, subjcode, [rating])

Minor disadvantages: updates are more expensive because of the pair-equality , and storage space required is greater.

Exercise 9.7

1. (a)

(b)

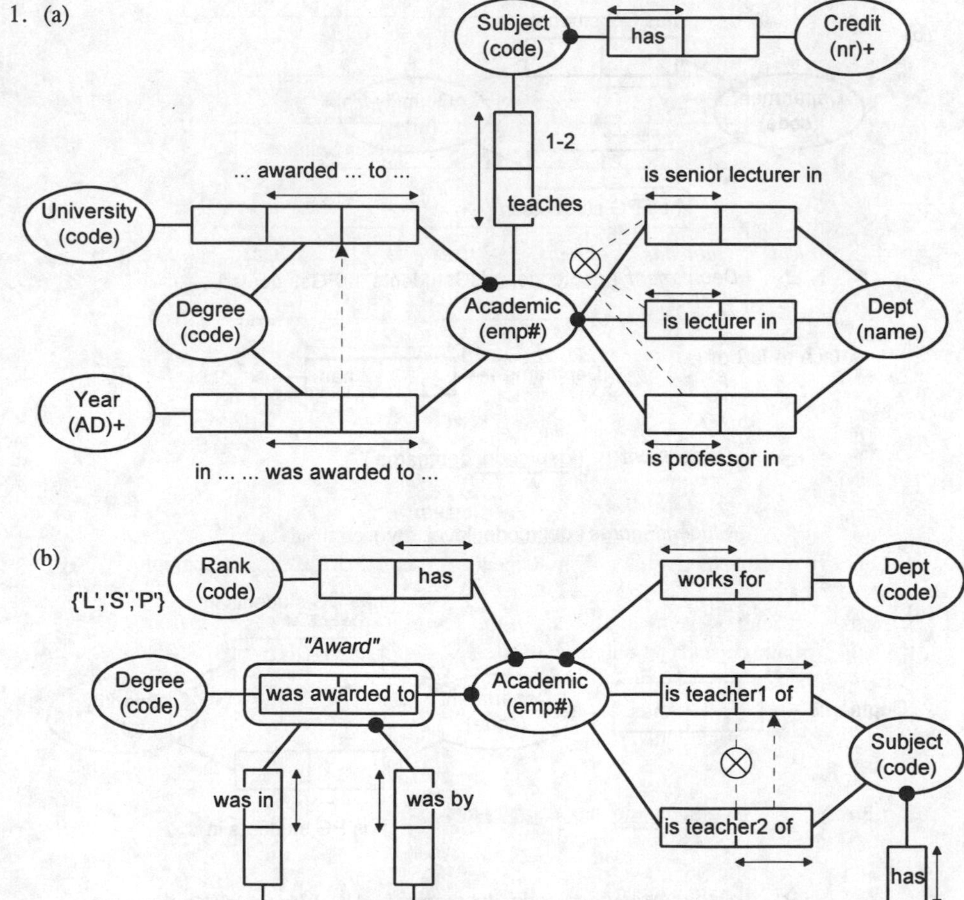

(c)

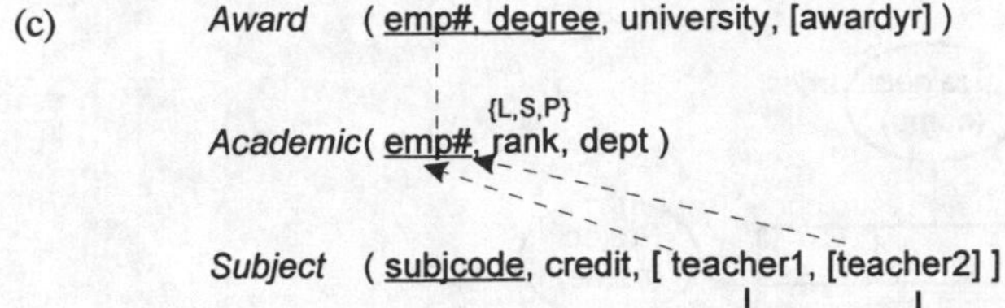

(d)

Award:

emp#	*degree*	*university*	*awardyr*
30572	PhD	UQ	1990

Academic:

emp#	*rank*	*dept*
30572	S	Computer Science

Subject:

subjcode	*credit*	*teacher1*	*teacher2*
CS115	8	30572	?

Exercise 10.2

1. (a) The Child column is not atomic. So the table is not even in 1NF.
   (b) The nonkey attribute is functionally dependent on just part of the key (person). hNF = 1.
   (c) Nonkey attributes depend on just part of the key (e.g. parent → sex_of_parent). hNF = 1.
   (d) Child attribute depends on only part of the key (tutorname). hNF = 3 (not 1, since child is part of the key).

   (e) *Tutors-in* (personname, subject)

   Person (personname, sex, [subjLectured])

   ParentOf (parent, child) °as, °it
   1-2

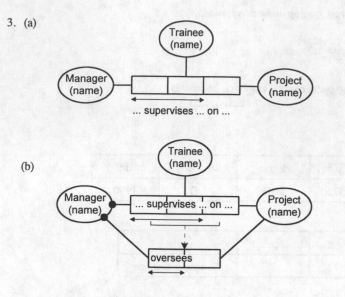

3. (a)

Trainee (name)

Manager (name)

Project (name)

... supervises ... on ...

(b)

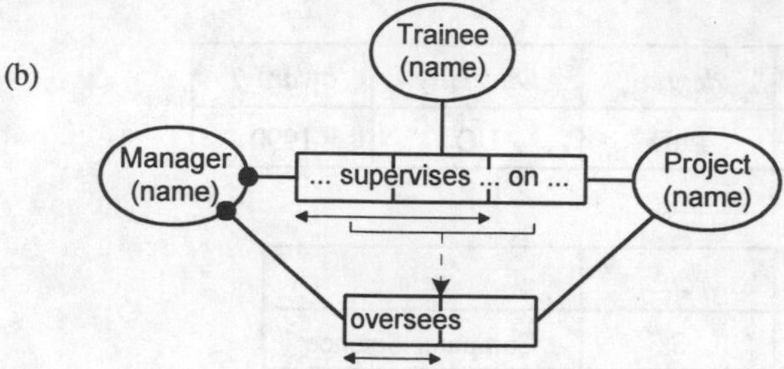

(c) Ternary is compound, since there is an implied FD from its first role to its last role. So it should be split as shown. We assume a project may have many overseers.

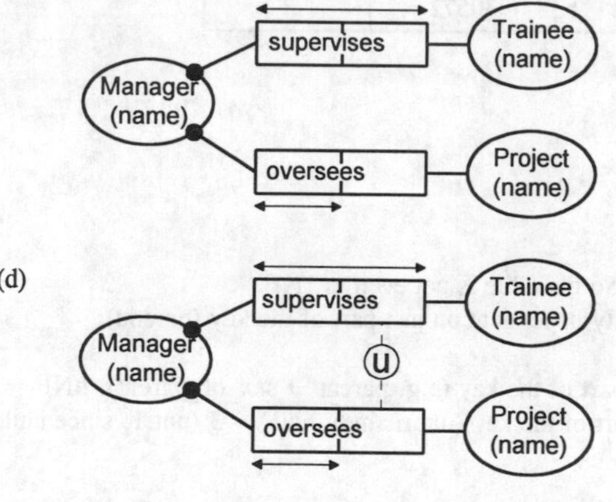

(e) *Supervises* (<u>manager, traineee</u>)

u

Oversees (<u>manager</u>, project)

(f) *Supervision* (<u>manager, trainee</u>, project)

TC1: manager → project { Enforce this FD as an extra constraint }

Exercise 10.5

1. (a)

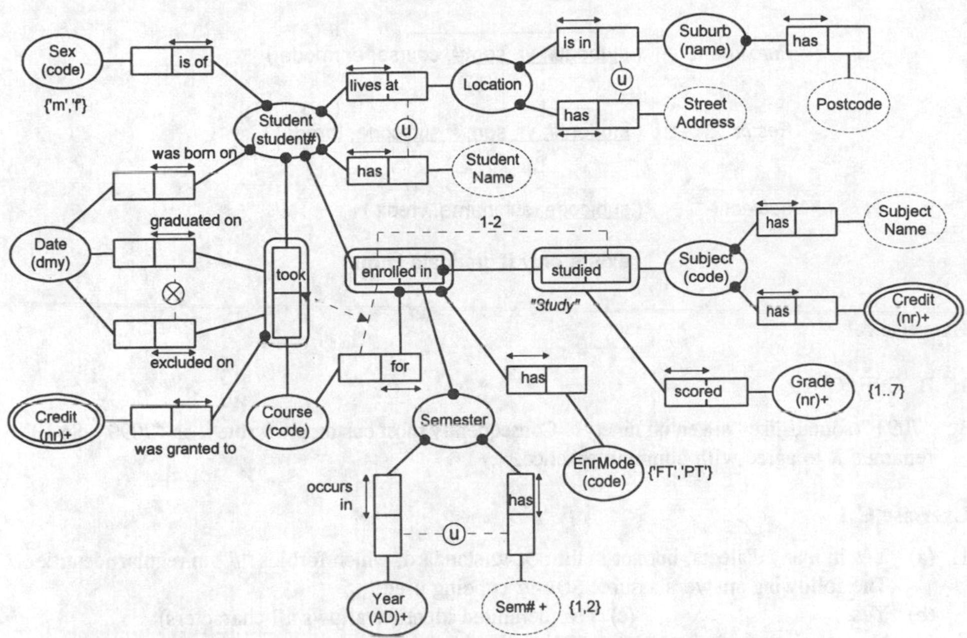

Derivation rules (using appropriately declared functions and inverse predicates).

Note: These rules are messy. At the time of writing, a better derivation rule language is being designed.

TotalCreditValue(Student *s*, Semester *n*) ::=
sum(Credit **of** Subject **that** was studied by (*s* enrolled in *n*))

GPA(Student *s*, Semester *n*) ::= (**sum**(Grade(Subject) * Credit(Subject))
from Study⟨*s*, *n*, Subject⟩ scored Grade)/
TotalCreditValue(*s*, *n*)

TotalCreditGained(Student *s*, Semester *n*) ::=
sum(Credit **of** Subject **that** was studied by (*s* enrolled in *n*)
where Grade(Subject) > 2)

CreditGained(Student *s*, Subject *x*, Semester *n*) ::=
Credit(*x*) **if** Study⟨*s*, *n*, *x*⟩ scored Grade > 2
else = 0.

(b)

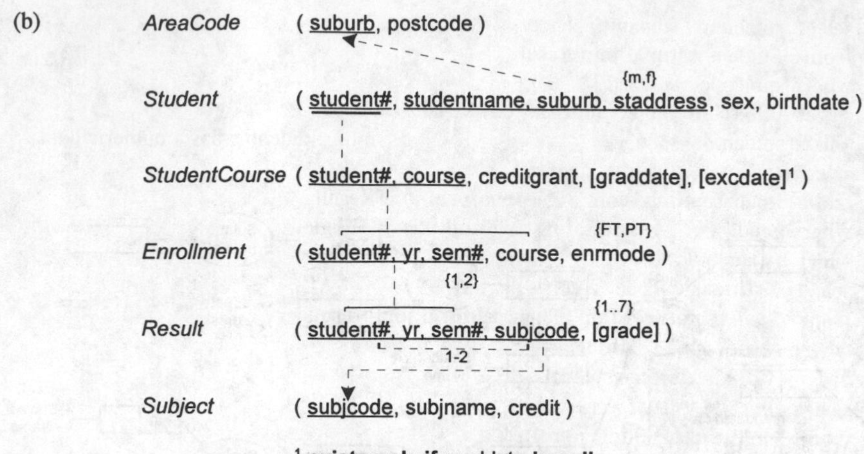

Exercise A1

1. B C F G I

3. "709T" sounds like "seven oh ninety". Consequently most customers wrote it as "7090". So IBM renamed it to agree with common practice.

Exercise C.1

1. (a) Yes in many dialects, but not in the SQL-92 standard, which forbids "#" in regular identifiers. The following answers assume SQL-92 is being used.
   (b) Yes (c) Yes (delimited identifer allows all characters)
   (d) No (starting digit) (e) No (embedded spaces)
   (f) Yes (delimited) (g) Yes
   (h) Yes in many dialects, but not in SQL-92 (which forbids "$" in regular identifiers)
   (i) No (parentheses) (j) No (reserved word)
   (k) Yes in SQL-92 (but too long is some dialects).

Exercise C.2

1. *Note:* In SQL-92, "student#" must be quoted to allow the presence of "#". To avoid quotes, this attribute has been renamed "studentnr".
   (a) **select** studentnr, stuname, degree, birthyr **from** Student
   order by degree, birthyr
   (b) **select** studentnr, subjcode
   from Result **natural join** Student
   where stuname = 'Smith J'
   Note: If the join syntax of SQL-92 is not supported, use the old syntax, e.g.
   select Result.studentnr, subjcode **from** Result, Student
   where Result.studentnr = Student.studentnr
   and stuname = 'Smith J'
   With this old syntax, "Result.studentnr" in the select-list may be replaced by "Student.studentnr" but not just "studentnr".
   Later solutions assume the SQL-92 join syntax is supported.

```
(c) select studentnr, stuname, gender
    from   Student natural join Result
    where subjcode = 'CS113'
(d) select title from Subject natural join Result
    where studentnr = 863                  { assuming studentnr has a numeric data type }
(e) select studentnr, stuname, degree
    from Student natural join Subject natural join Result
    where gender = 'M' and rating = 5 and title = 'Logic'
    order by stuname
(f) select distinct subjcode, credit
    from   Student natural join Subject natural join Result
    where gender = 'M' and degree = 'BSc' and rating = 7
    order by credit desc, subjcode
(g) select subjcode, title, rating
    from Subject natural left join Result
```

Exercise C.3

```
1. (a) select title from CompLanguage          (b) select title from CompLanguage
       where releaseyr in (1959,1975,1979)         where releaseyr between 1959 and 1979
                                                   { Logo and SQL absent because of nulls }
   (c) select title from CompLanguage          (d) select * from CompLanguage
       where releaseyr is null                     where title like 'Goodo%'
   (e) select title from CompLanguage          (f) select * from CompLanguage
       where title like '%OL'                      where title like '%Pascal%'
   (g) select title from CompLanguage          (h) select title from CompLanguage
       where title like '_____'  { 5 _}            where title like '_o%'
   (i) select title from CompLanguage
       where title like '%O%' or title like '%o%'
   (j) select * from CompLanguage
       where title not like 'P%'
         and releaseyr between 1960 and 1978
   (k) select title from CompLanguage
       where title like '_____a' or title like '____a_'      { 5 then 4,1 underscores }
         or title like '___OL'                               { 3 underscores }
```

Exercise C.4

```
1. (a) select person from Eater where sex = 'M' or weight > 60
   (b) select person from Eater where sex = 'M'
       union
       select person from Eats where foodname = 'peas'

       aliter: select person from Eater
               where sex = 'M' or person in (select person from Eats
                                             where foodname = 'peas')

       aliter: select distinct person
               from Eater natural join Eats
               where sex = 'M' or foodname = 'peas'
   (c) select person from Eater where sex = 'F' and weight > 60
```

(d) **select** person **from** Eater **where** sex = 'F'
intersect
select person **from** Eats **where** foodname = 'potato'

aliter:
select person **from** Eater
where sex = 'F' **and** person **in**
(**select** person **from** Eats
where foodname = 'potato')

(e) **select** person **from** Eater **where** weight > 60
except
select person **from** Eats **where** foodname = 'beef'

aliter:
select person **from** Eater
where weight > 60 **and** person **not in**
(**select** person **from** Eats **where** foodname = 'beef')

(f) **select** *A*.person, *B*.person
from Eater **as** *A*, Eater **as** *B*
where *A*.weight = *B*.weight **and** *A*.sex < *B*.sex

Note: This is the neatest way to avoid showing each pair in two different orders. Here the female of each pair appears on the left. A correct but longer solution is to order members of each pair alphabetically. For example:
select *A*.person, *B*.person **from** Eater **as** *A*, Eater **as** *B*
where *A*.weight = *B*.weight **and** *A*.sex <> *B*.sex **and** *A*.person < B.person

(g) **select distinct** person **from** Eats
where foodname **in**
(**select** foodname **from** Food
where foodclass = 'vegetable')

(h) **select distinct** person, weight
from Eater **natural join** Eats **natural join** Food
where sex = 'M' **and** foodclass = 'meat'

aliter:
select person, weight **from** Eater
where sex = 'M' **and** person **in**
(**select** person **from** Eats
where foodname **in**
(**select** foodname **from** Food
where foodclass = 'meat'))

(i) **select distinct** person **from** Eats
where foodname **not in** (**select** foodname **from** Food
where foodclass = 'meat')

(j) **select** person **from** Eater
where person **not in**
(**select** person **from** Eats **where** foodname **in**
(**select** foodname **from** Food **where** foodclass = 'meat'))

(k) **select** 'vegetarian: ', person, weight, sex **from** Eater
where person **not in**
(**select** person **from** Eats **where** foodname **in**
(**select** foodname **from** Food **where** foodclass = 'meat'))
union

```
select 'meateater: ', person, weight, sex from Eater
where person in
      (select person from Eats where foodname in
            (select foodname from Food where foodclass = 'meat'))
order by 1 desc, 4,3,2;
format col 1 name '' { to provide a null heading for the descriptor }
```

Note: In SQL-92 (but not SQL-89) the list "person, weight, sex" may be replaced by "Eater.*".

Exercise C.5

1. (a)
```
select count(*) from Eater
where sex = 'M' and weight > 100
```
(b)
```
select count(distinct weight) from Eater
```
(c)
```
select sum(weight) from Eater
where sex = 'M'
```
(d)
```
select avg(weight) from Eater
where sex = 'F'
```
(e)
```
select max(weight) from Eater
where person in    (select person from Eats
                    where foodname = 'beef')
```
(f)
```
select person from Eater
where sex = 'F' and weight <
     (select min(weight) from Eater
      where sex = 'M')
```
aliter:
```
select person from Eater
where sex = 'F' and weight < all
     (select weight from Eater
      where sex = 'M')
```
(g)
```
select person, weight from Eater
where sex = 'F' and weight >=
     (select min(weight) from Eater
      where sex = 'M')
```
aliter:
```
select person, weight from Eater
where sex = 'F' and weight >= some
     (select weight from Eater where sex = 'M')
```

3. (a)
```
select authorname from Author
where sex = 'M' and nationality = 'Aussie'
```
(b)
```
select title from Book
where yrpublished between 1984 and 1986
order by title
```
If the SQL dialect uses the ASCII collating sequence (which orders lower case letters after upper case letters) and the system is in case-sensitive mode, 'dBaseIII' is placed last.

(c)
```
select * from Book
where title like '%SQL%'
order by yrpublished desc
```
(d)
```
select authorname from WrittenBy
where isbn in
     (select isbn from Book
      where title = 'Databases' and yrpublished = 1980)
```
aliter:
```
select authorname from Book natural join WrittenBy
where title = 'Databases' and yrpublished = 1980
```

The previous alternative solutions use the subquery approach and the join approach. The remaining solutions use the subquery approach. As an extra exercise, formulate the equivalent solutions using joins.

(e)
```
select isbn, title from Book where isbn in
    (select isbn from WrittenBy where authorname in
        (select authorname from Author where nationality = 'Aussie'))
```

(f)
```
select authorname, nationality from Author
where authorname in
   (select authorname from WrittenBy where isbn in
      (select isbn from Book
       where title = 'Informatics' and publisher = 'Hall' and yrpublished = 1986))
```

(g)
```
select 'Australian male: ', authorname from Author
where sex = 'M' and nationality = 'Aussie'
union
select 'American female: ', authorname from Author
where sex = 'F' and nationality = 'Yank'
order by 1 desc;
format col 1 name ''
```

Exercise C.6

1. (a)
```
select sex, count(*) from Author
group by sex
```
(b)
```
select sex, nationality, count(*)
from Author
group by sex, nationality
order by 3 desc
```
(c)
```
select publisher, sum(copies) from Book
where yrpublished > 1980
group by publisher
```
(d)
```
select publisher, min(yrpublished) from Book
group by publisher
having avg(copies) > 2
```
(e)
```
select isbn, count(*) from WrittenBy
where isbn in
    (select isbn from Book where yrpublished < 1986)
group by isbn
having count(*) > 1
```
(f)
```
select nationality, count(*) from Author
where sex = 'M' and authorname in
    (select authorname from WrittenBy
     where isbn in
        (select isbn from Book
         where publisher in ('Hall','Possum')))
group by nationality
having count(*) > =
    (select copies from Book
     where isbn = '444')
```

Bibliography

Aho, A.V., Beeri, C. & Ullman, J.D. 1979, 'The theory of joins in relational databases', *ACM Trans. on Database Systems*, vol. 4, no. 3, pp. 297–314.

Atkinson, M., Bancilhon, F., DeWitt, D., Dittrick, K., Maier, D. & Zdonik, S., 'The Object-Oriented Databasc System Manifesto', *Proc. DOOD-89: First Int. Conf. on Deductive and Object-Oriented Databases*, eds, W. Kim, J-M. Nicolas & S. Nishio, Elsevier, Kyoto, pp. 40–57.

Barker, R. 1990, *CASE*Method: Tasks and Deliverables*, Addison-Wesley, Wokingham, England.

Barker, R. & Longman, C. 1992, *CASE*Method: Function and Process Modelling*, Addison-Wesley, Wokingham, England.

Batini, C., Ceri, S. & Navathe, S. 1992, *Conceptual Database Design: an entity-relationship approach*, Benjamin/Cummings, Redwood City CA.

van Bommel, P. & van der Weide, Th.P. 1992, 'Reducing the search space for conceptual schema transformations', *Data and Knowledge Engineering*, vol. 8, pp. 269–92.

Campbell, L. & Halpin, T.A. 1993, 'Automated Support for Conceptual to External Mapping', *Proc. 4th Workshop on Next Generation CASE Tools*, eds S. Brinkkemper & F. Harmsen, Univ. Twente Memoranda Informatica 93-32, pp. 35–51, Paris.

Campbell, L. & Halpin, T.A. 1994a, 'Abstraction techniques for conceptual schemas', *Proc. 5th Australasian Database Conf.*, Christchurch (Jan.), World Scientific, Singapore.

Campbell, L. & Halpin, T.A. 1994b, 'The reverse engineering of relational databases', *Proc. 5th Workshop on Next Generation CASE Tools*, Utrecht (June).

Cattell, R.G.G. 1991, *Object Data Management*, Addison-Wesley, Reading MA.

Chawdhry, P.K. 1992, 'NIAMEX—A NIAM compiler and EXPRESS pre-processor', *Proc. EXPRESS Users Group Conf.*, Oct. 1992.

Chen, P.P. 1976, 'The entity-relationship model—towards a unified view of data', *ACM Transactions on Database Systems*, vol. 1, no. 1, pp. 9–36.

Choobineh, J., Mannino, M.V. & Tseng, V.P. 1992, 'A form-based approach for database analysis and design', *CACM*, vol. 35, no. 2, pp. 108–20.

Codd, E.F. 1970, 'A relational model of data for large shared data banks', *CACM*, vol. 13, no. 6, pp. 377–87.

Codd, E.F. 1990, *The Relational Model for Database Management: Version 2*, Addison-Wesley, Reading MA.

Control data 1982, *IAST: Information Analysis Support Tools*, Reference Manual, Control Data Publication no. 60484610.

Creasy, P.N. 1989, 'ENIAM—a more complete conceptual schema language', *Proc. 15th VLDB Conf.*, Amsterdam.

Czejdo, B., Elmasri, R., Rusinkiewicz, M. & Embley, D.W. 1990, 'A graphical data manipulation language for an extended entity-relationship model', *IEEE Computer*, March 1990, pp. 26–37.

D'Atri, A. & Sacca, D. 1984, 'Equivalence and mapping of database schemas', *Proc. 10th Int. conf. on Very Large Databases*, VLDB, Singapore, pp. 187–95.

Date, C.J. 1990, *An Introduction to Database Systems*, vol. 1, 5th edn, Addison-Wesley, Reading MA.

Date, C.J. & Darwen, H. 1993, *A Guide to the SQL Standard*, 3rd edn, Addison-Wesley, Reading MA.

De Troyer, O., Meersman, R. & Verlinden, P. 1988, 'RIDL* on the CRIS Case: a workbench for NIAM', *Computerized Assistance during the Information Systems Life Cycle: Proc. CRIS-88*, eds T.W. Olle, A.A. Verrijn-Stuart & L. Bhabuta, North-Holland, Amsterdam.

De Troyer, O. 1991, 'The OO-Binary Relationship Model: a truly object-oriented conceptual model', *Advanced Information Systems Engineering: Proc. CAiSE-91*, Springer-Verlag Lecture Notes in Comp. Science, no. 498, Trondheim.

De Troyer, O. 1993, *On Data Schema Transformation*, PhD thesis, Katholieke Universiteit of Brabant, Tilburg.

Elmasri, R. & Navathe, S. 1989, *Fundamentals of Database Systems*, Benjamin/Cummings, Redwood City, CA.

Evans, C. 1980, *The Mighty Micro*, Coronet Books, London.

Everest, G.C. 1994, 'Experiences teaching NIAM/OR modeling', *Proc. 2nd NIAM-ISDM Conf.*, Albuquerque, NM.

Fagin, R. 1977, 'Multivalued dependencies and a new normal form for relational databases', *ACM Trans. on Database Systems*, vol. 2, no. 3.

Fagin, R. 1979, 'Normal forms and relational database operators', *Proc. 1979 ACM SIGMOD int. conf. on management of data*, Boston, MA.

Falkenberg, E.D. 1976, 'Concepts for modelling information', *Modelling in Database Management Systems*, ed. G.M. Nijssen, North-Holland Publishing, Amsterdam.

Fillmore, C.J. 1968, "The case for case", in *Universals in Linguistic Theory*, eds E. bach & R.T. Harms, Holt, Rinehart and Winston, New York, pp. 1–88.

Girle, R.A., Halpin, T.A., Miller, C.L. & Williams, G.H. 1978, *Inductive and Practical Reasoning*, Rotecoge, Brisbane.

van Griethuysen, J.J. (ed.) 1982, *Concepts and terminology for the conceptual schema and the information base*, ISO TC97/SC5/WG3, Eindhoven.

Haack, S. 1978, *Philosophy of Logics*, Cambridge University Press, London.

Halpin, T.A. & Girle, R.A. 1981, *Deductive Logic*, 2nd edn, Logiqpress, Brisbane.

Halpin, T.A. 1989a, 'Venn Diagrams and SQL Queries', *The Australian Computer Journal*, vol. 21, no. 1, pp. 27-32.

Halpin, T.A. 1989b, 'A Logical Analysis of Information Systems: static aspects of the data-oriented perspective', PhD thesis, University of Queensland.

Halpin, T.A. 1989c, 'Contextual Equivalence of Conceptual Schemas', *Proc. Advanced Database Systems Symposium*, Inform. Proc. Society of Japan, Kyoto, pp. 47-54.

Halpin, T.A. 1990a, 'Conceptual Schemas and Relational Databases', *Databases in the 1990s: Proc. 1st Australian Database Conf.*, eds B. Srinivasan & J. Zeleznikov, World Scientific, Singapore, pp. 45–56.

Halpin, T.A. 1990b, 'Conceptual Schema Optimization', *Proc. 13th Australian Computer Science Conf.*, Monash University, Melbourne.

Halpin, T.A. 1991a, 'Optimizing global conceptual schemas', *Databases in the 1990s:2 – Proc. 2nd Australian Database Conf.*, eds B. Srinivasan & J. Zeleznikov, World Scientific, Singapore.

Halpin, T.A. 1991b, 'A fact-oriented approach to schema transformation', *Proc. MFDBS-91 Int. Conf. on Mathematical Fundamentals of Database and Knowledge Base Systems*, Spinger Verlag Lec. Notes in Computer Science, no. 495, Rostock.

Halpin, T.A. 1991c, 'WISE: a Workbench for Information System Engineering', *Proc. 2nd European Workshop on Next Generation of CASE Tools*, Trondheim. (revised and reprinted in the book *Next Generation CASE Tools*, ISO Press (1992)).

Halpin. T.A. & Orlowska, M.E. 1992, 'Fact-Oriented Modelling for Data Analysis', *Journal of Inform. Systems*, vol. 2, no. 2, pp. 1–23, Blackwell Scientific, Oxford.

Halpin, T.A., Harding, J. & Oh, C-H. 1992, 'Automated support for Subtyping', *Proc. 3rd European Workshop on Next Generation of CASE Tools*, Manchester.

Halpin, T.A. & Ritson, P.R. 1992, 'Fact-Oriented Modelling and Null Values', *Proc. 3rd Australian Database Conf.*, eds. B. Srinivasan & J. Zeleznikov, World Scientific, Singapore.

Halpin, T.A. & McCormack, J.I. 1992, 'Automated Validation of Conceptual Schema Constraints', *Advanced Inf. Systems Engineering: Proc. CAiSE-92*, ed. P. Loucopoulos, Springer-Verlag LNCS vol. 593, Manchester, pp. 445–62.

Halpin, T.A. & Oei, J.L.H. 1992, 'A Framework for Comparing Conceptual Modelling Languages', *Tech. Report 92-29*, Dept. of Informatics, Uni. of Nijmegen, Nov. 92.

Halpin, T.A. 1992, 'Fact-Oriented Schema Optimization', *Proc. CISMOD-92* (Int. Conf. on Inform. Sys. & Management of Data), pp. 288–302, Indian Institute of Science, Bangalore, India.

Halpin, T.A. & Harding, J. 1993, 'Automated support for verbalization of conceptual schemas', *Proc. 4th Workshop on Next Generation CASE Tools*, eds S. Brinkkemper & F. Harmsen, Univ. Twente Memoranda Informatica 93-32, pp. 151–161, Paris.

Halpin, T.A. 1993a, 'Object-Oriented Databases: is this the future?', *Proc. 1993 IPT Conf.*, pp. 1–7, QSITE, Brisbane.

Halpin, T.A. 1993b, 'An overview of Object-Role Modeling', in Perschke, S. & Liczbanski, M. 1993, *Access for Windows Power Programming*, Que Corporation, Carmel, IN.

Halpin, T.A. 1993c, 'What is an elementary fact?', *Proc. 1st NIAM-ISDM Conf.*, Utrecht.

Heath, I.J. 1971, 'Unacceptable file operations in a relational database', *Proc. 1971 ACM SIGFIDET Workshop on data description, assess and control*, San Diego, CA.

ter Hofstede, A.H.M. 1993, *Information modeling in data intensive domains*, PhD thesis, University of Nijmegen.

ter Hofstede, A.H.M., Proper, H.A. & van der Weide, Th.P. 1993, 'Formal definition of a conceptual language for the description and manipulation of information models', *Information Systems*, vol. 18, no. 7, pp. 489–523.

Hohenstein, U. & Engels, G. 1991, 'Formal semantics of an entity-relationship-based query language', *Entity-Relationship Approach: the core of conceptual modelling (Proc. 9th ER Conf.)*, ed. H. Kangassalo, Elsevier Science Pub., Amsterdam.

Intellibase 1990, *RIDL-M User's Guide*, Intellibase N.V., Belgium.

Kendall, K.E. & Kendall, J.E. 1988, *Systems Analysis and Design*, Prentice Hall, Englewood Cliffs, NJ.

Kennedy, P. 1993, *Preparing for the Twenty-first Century*, Harper Collins, London.

Kent, W. 1978, *Data and Reality: basic assumptions in data processing reconsidered*, North-Holland Publishing Co., Amsterdam.

Kent, W. 1983, 'A simple guide to five normal forms in relational database theory', *CACM*, vol. 26, no. 2, pp 120–5.

Kent, W. 1991, 'A rigorous model of object reference, identity, and existence', *Jnl of Object-Oriented Programming*, June 1991, pp. 28–36.

Khoshaflan, S.N. & Copeland, G.P. 1990, 'Object identity', in *Readings in Object-Oriented Database Systems*, eds S.B. Zdonik & D. Maier, Morgan Kaufmann Publishers, San Mateo CA, pp. 37–46.

Kobayashi, I. 1986, 'Losslessness and semantic correctness of database schema transformation: another look at schema equivalence', *Information Systems*, vol. 11, no. 1, Pergamon Press, pp. 41–59.

Kobayashi, I. 1990, 'Transformation and equivalence among predicate systems', *Proc. French-Japanese Seminar on Deductive Databases and Artificvial Intelligence*, INRIN, Sophia-Antipolis.

Ling, T.W., Tompa, F.W. & Kameda, T. 1981, 'An improved third normal form for relational databases', *ACM Trans. on Database Systems*, vol. 6, no. 2, pp. 329–46.

Mark, L. 1988, 'The Binary Relationship Model', Tech. Report UMIACS–TR–88–67, University of Maryland.

McCormack, J.I., Halpin, T.A. & Ritson, P.R. 1993, 'Automated mapping of conceptual schemas to relational schemas', Advanced Info. Systems Engineering: Proc. CAiSE-93., eds C. Rolland, F. Bodart & C. Cauvet, Springer-Verlag LNCS vol. 685, pp. 432–48, Paris (June).

Melton, J. & Simon, A.R. 1993, *Understanding the new SQL: a complete guide*, Morgan Kaufmann, San Mateo CA.

Nijssen, G.M. 1994, 'A general analysis procedure: recent advances in universal informatics', *Proc. 2nd NIAM-ISDM Conf.*, Albuquerque, NM.

Olle, T.W., Hagelstein, J., Macdonald, I.G., Rolland, C., Sol, H.G., van Assche, F.J.M. & Verrijn-Stuart, A.A. 1991, *Information Systems Methodologies: a framework for understanding*, 2nd edn, Addison-Wesley,Wokingham, England.

Orlowska, M. & Zhang, Y. 1992, 'Understanding the fifth normal form (5NF)', *Australian Computer Science Communications*, vol. 14, pp. 631–9.

Ovum 1992, *Ovum Evaluates: CASE Products*, Ovum Ltd, London.

Petrounias, I. & Loucopoulos, P. 1994, 'Time dimension in a fact-based model', *Proc. ORM-1 Conference*, Dept of Computer Science, University of Queensland.

Proper, H.A. 1994, 'A theory for conceptual modelling of evolving application domains', PhD thesis, University of Nijmegen.

Reiner, D. 1992, 'Database design tools', in Batini, Ceri & Navathe (op. cit.), Ch. 15.

Rissanen, J. 1977, 'Independent components of relations', *ACM Trans. on Database Systems*, vol. 2, no. 2, pp 317–25.

Ritson, P.R. & Halpin, T.A. 1993a, 'Mapping One-to-One Predicates to a Relational Schema', *Advances in Database Research: Proc. 4th Australian Database Conf.*, eds M.E. Orlowska & M. Papazoglou, World Scientific, Singapore, pp. 68–84.

Ritson, P.R. & Halpin, T.A. 1993b, 'Mapping Integrity Constraints to a Relational Schema', *Proc. 4th ACIS*, Brisbane (Sep.), pp. 381–400.

Rochfeld, A., Morejon, J. & Negros, P. 1991, 'Inter-relationship links in E-R model', *Entity Relationship Approach: the core of conceptual modelling (Proc. 9th ER Conf.)*, ed. H. Kangassalo, Elsevier Science Pub., Amsterdam.

Shneiderman, B. 1992, *Designing the User Interface*, 2nd edn, Addison-Wesley, Reading MA.

Shoval, P. Gudes, E. & Goldstein, M. 1988, 'GISD: a graphical interactive system for conceptual database design', *Information Systems*, vol. 13, no. 1, pp. 81–95.

Snodgrass, R. 1990, 'Temporal databases: status and research directions', *SIGMOD Record*, vol. 19, no. 4, pp. 83–9.

Stonebraker, M., Rowe, L., Lindsay, B., Gray, J., carey, M., Brodie, M., Bernstein, P. & Beech, D. 1990, 'Third generation database system manifesto', *ACM SIGMOD Record*, vol. 19, no. 3.

Thalheim, B. 1984, 'Deductive basis of relations', *Proc. MFSSS-84*, Berlin, Springer-Verlag Lec. Notes in Computer Science, no. 215, Heildelberg, pp. 226–30.

Thalheim, B. 1994, *Fundamentals of Entity-Relationship Modelling*, Springer, Heidelberg.

Vincent, M.W. 1994, 'Semantic justification of normal forms in relational database design', PhD thesis, Monash University.

Vincent, M.W. & Srinivasan, B. 1993, 'Redundancy and the justification for fourth normal form in ralational databases', *Int. Journal of Foundations of Computer Science*, vol. 4, no. 4, pp. 355–65.

Vincent, M.W. & Srinivasan, B. 1994, 'A note on relation schemes which are in 3NF but not in BCNF', *Information Processing Letters*, vol. 48, pp. 281–3.

Zaniolo, C. 1982, 'A new normal form for the design of relational database schemas', *ACM Trans. on Database Systems*, vol. 7, no. 3, pp. 489–99.

ORM glossary

This glossary lists some key terms as well as the various symbols used in Object-Role Modeling (ORM), as described in this book, and briefly explains their meaning. Verbalization in textual form is given in FORML (Formal ORM Language). A concise explanation of other technical terms may be found in the chapter summaries. Further details on technical terms may be accessed by using the Index.

Arity

= number of roles in a relationship (unary = 1, binary = 2, ternary = 3, etc.)

Conceptual schema

= conceptual model of the UoD structure
= design that specifies what states and transitions are possible
= declaration of: elementary fact types
constraints
derivation rules

Conceptual schema design procedure (CSDP):

0 Divide the UoD into manageable sub-sections
1 Transform familiar examples into elementary facts, and apply quality checks
2 Draw the fact types, and apply a population check
3 Check for entity types that should be combined, and note arithmetic derivations
4 Add uniqueness constraints, and check arity of fact types
5 Add mandatory role constraints, and check for logical derivations
6 Add value, set comparison (subset, equality, exclusion) and subtype constraints
7 Add other constraints and perform final checks
8 Integrate the subschemas into a global conceptual schema

Constraint

= restriction on possible states (static constraint) or transitions (dynamic constraint)

Compositely identified object type

= either a co-referenced object type or a nested entity type

Co-referenced object

= object that is identified by means of two or more reference types in combination; hence its identification scheme involves an external uniqueness constraint

Database

= variable set of related fact instances

Derivation rule
= rule which declares how one fact type may be derived from others

Elementary fact
= assertion that an object has a property, or that one or more objects participate in a relationship, where the fact cannot be split into simpler facts with the same object types without information loss

Entity
= object that is described (not a value); an entity is either atomic or nested (i.e. an objectified relationship); at the top level, entities are partitioned into primitive entity types, from which subtypes may be defined

Fact = relationship not used for primary reference

Fact role
= role in a fact type

Flat fact type
= fact type with no nesting

Functional fact type
= fact type with a functional role

Functional role
= role with a simple uniqueness constraint

Generalization
= forming a more general case from one or more specific types; the inverse of specialization

Instance
= an individual occurrence (one specific member of a type)

Lazy entity
= entity that may exist without participating in any fact; the disjunction of fact roles played by a lazy entity type is optional

Mandatory role
= role that must be played by all instances in the population of the object type playing the role; also called a total role

Nested entity
= relationship that plays some role (also called an objectified relationship)

Object
= thing of interest; an object may be an entity or a value

Object-Role Modeling (ORM)
= conceptual modeling method which pictures an application in terms of objects playing roles; it provides graphical and textual languages for verbalizing information as well as a design procedure

Population
= set of instances present in a particular state of the database

Predicate
= sentence with object-holes in it

Reference
= relationship used as the primary way to reference or identify an object (or to provide part of the identification)

Reference mode
= mode or manner in which a single value references an entity

Reference role
= role in a reference type

Relationship
= association between one or more objects; it is either a fact or a reference; if we want to talk about a relationship (i.e. the relationship itself plays some role) it then becomes an object as well, and is called a nested entity or objectified relationship

Rmap
= Relational mapping procedure

Role
= part played by an object in a relationship (possibly unary)

Specialization
= forming special cases of interest from a more general type; the inverse of generalization.

Subtype
= object type which is just part of another object type; subtypes must be well defined in terms of relationships played by their supertype(s); subtypes with the same top supertype may overlap.

Type
= set of possible instances

Uniqueness constraint (UC)
= repetition is not allowed in the role or role sequence spanned by the constraint; a uniqueness constraint on a single predicate is an internal UC, and a uniqueness constraint over roles from different predicates is an external UC.

Universe of Discourse (UoD)
= application area (the aspects of the world that we want to talk about)

Value
= unchangeable object that is identified by a constant; in this book a value is either a character string or a number; sometimes called a label

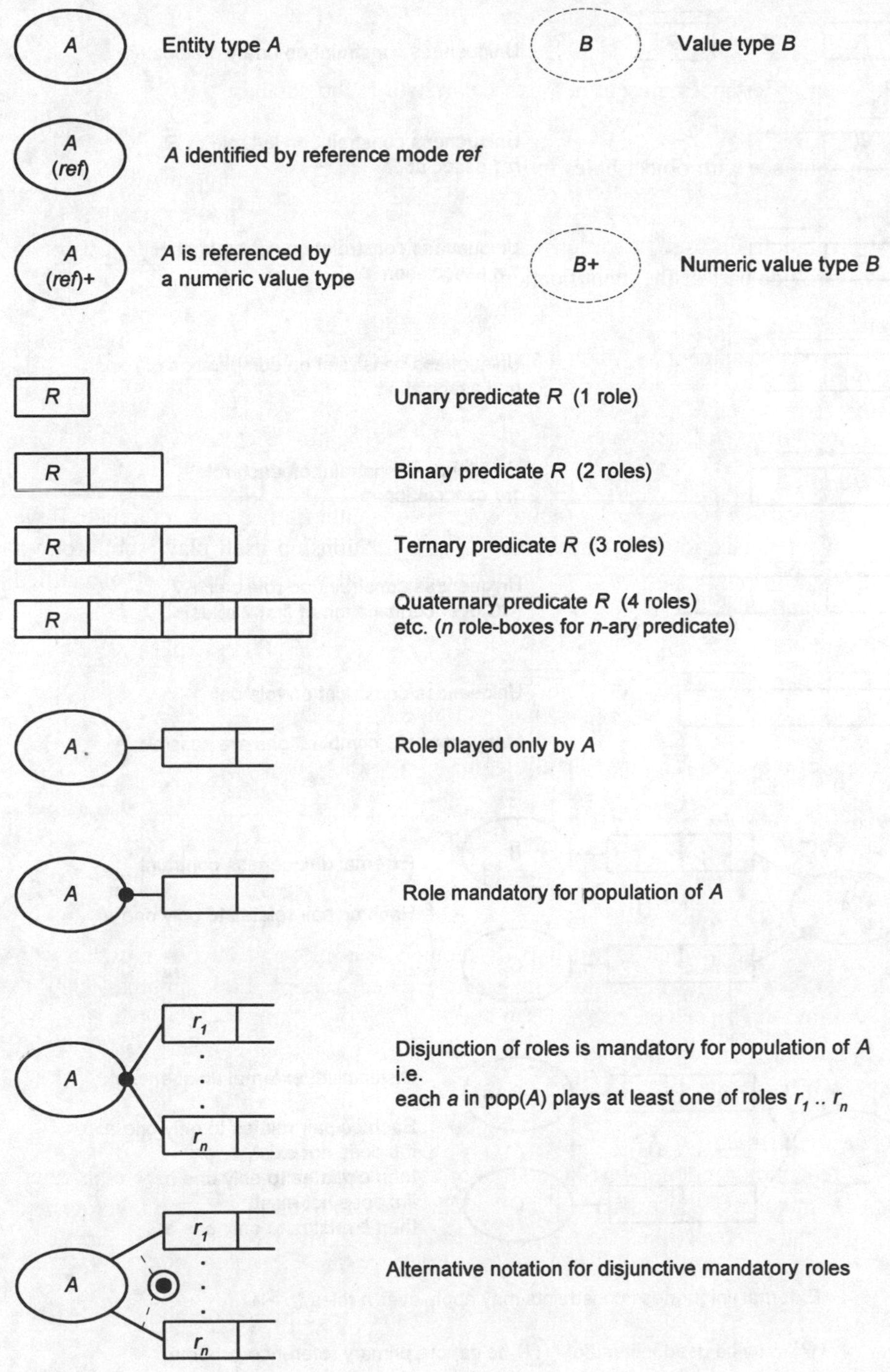
A
Entity type *A*
B
Value type *B*
A
(*ref*)
A identified by reference mode *ref*
A
(*ref*)+
A is referenced by
a numeric value type
B+
Numeric value type *B*
R
Unary predicate *R* (1 role)
R
Binary predicate *R* (2 roles)
R
Ternary predicate *R* (3 roles)
R
Quaternary predicate *R* (4 roles)
etc. (*n* role-boxes for *n*-ary predicate)
A
Role played only by *A*
A
Role mandatory for population of *A*
r_1
A
r_n
Disjunction of roles is mandatory for population of *A*
i.e.
each *a* in pop(*A*) plays at least one of roles r_1 .. r_n
r_1
A
r_n
Alternative notation for disjunctive mandatory roles

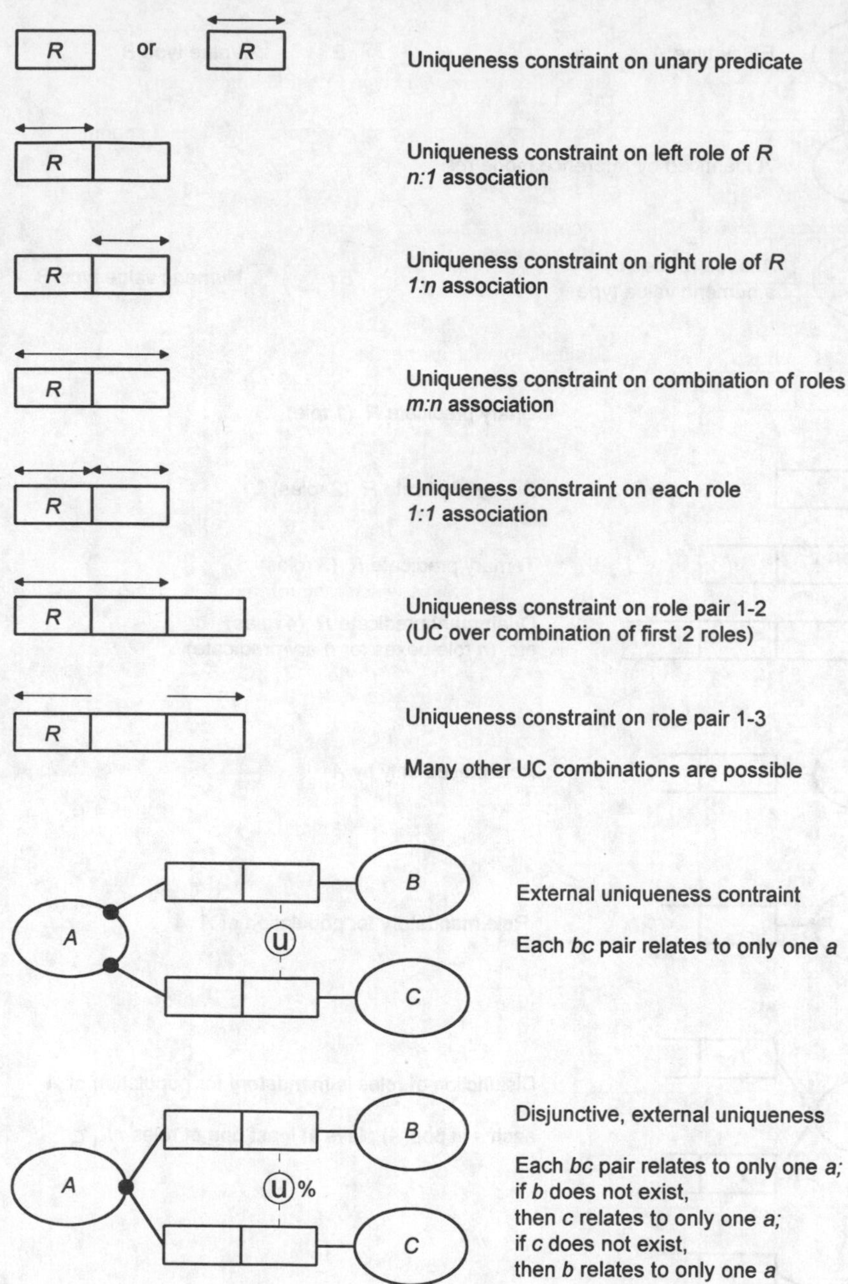

External uniqueness constraints may apply over *n* roles (*n* > 1)

(P) may be used instead of (u) to denote primary reference scheme

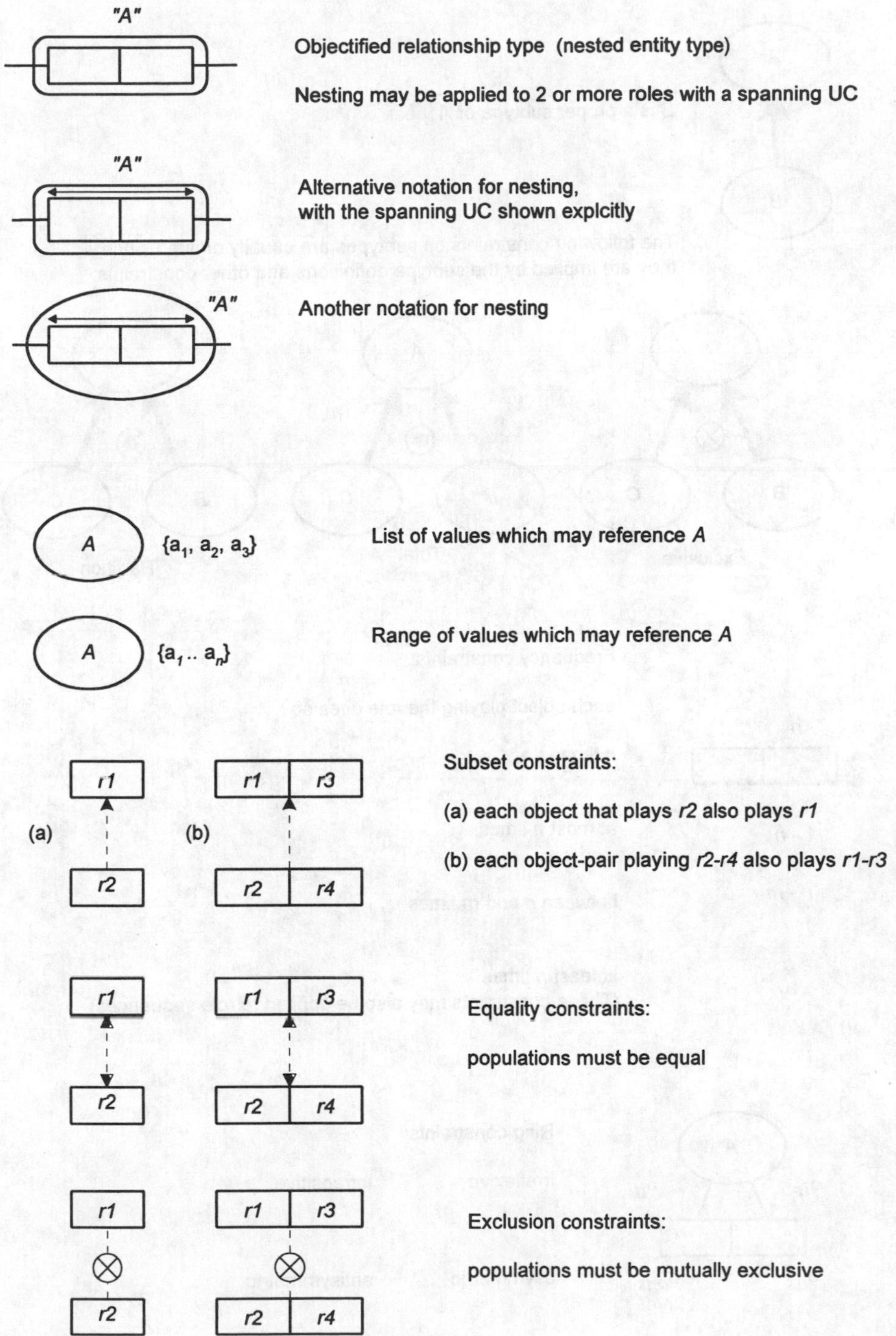

"A"
Objectified relationship type (nested entity type)
Nesting may be applied to 2 or more roles with a spanning UC
"A"
Alternative notation for nesting,
with the spanning UC shown explcitly
"A"
Another notation for nesting
A
{a_1, a_2, a_3}
List of values which may reference *A*
A
{a_1 .. a_n}
Range of values which may reference *A*
r1
r1
r3
(a)
(b)
r2
r2
r4
Subset constraints:
(a) each object that plays *r2* also plays *r1*
(b) each object-pair playing *r2-r4* also plays *r1-r3*
r1
r1
r3
r2
r2
r4
Equality constraints:
populations must be equal
r1
r1
r3
r2
r2
r4
Exclusion constraints:
populations must be mutually exclusive

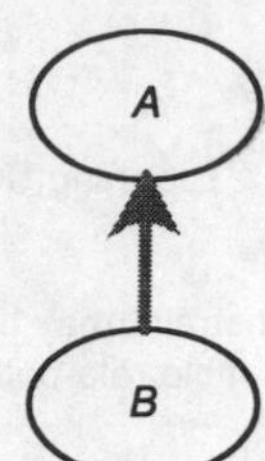

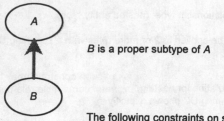

B is a proper subtype of *A*

The following constraints on subtypes are usually omitted since they are implied by the subtype definitions and other constraints:

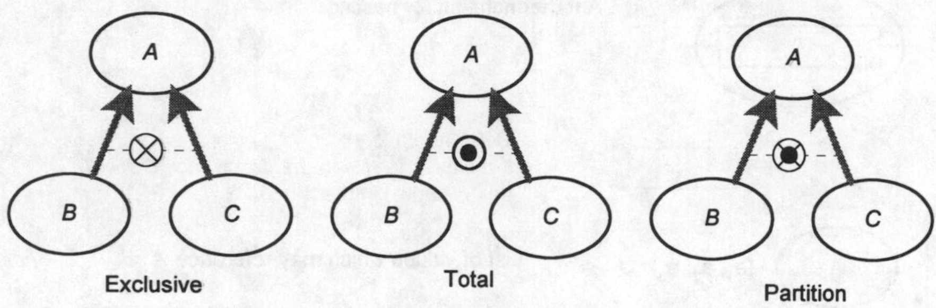

Frequency constraints:

each object playing the role does so

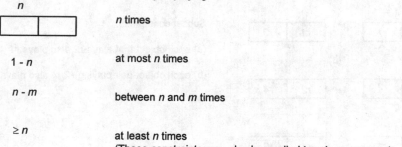

n	*n* times
1 - *n*	at most *n* times
n - *m*	between *n* and *m* times
≥ *n*	at least *n* times

(These constraints may also be applied to role sequences)

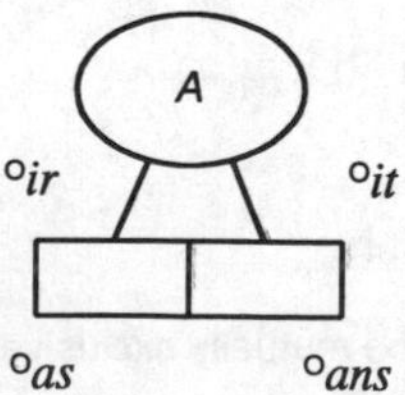

Ring constraints:

irreflexive	intransitive
asymmetric	antisymmetric

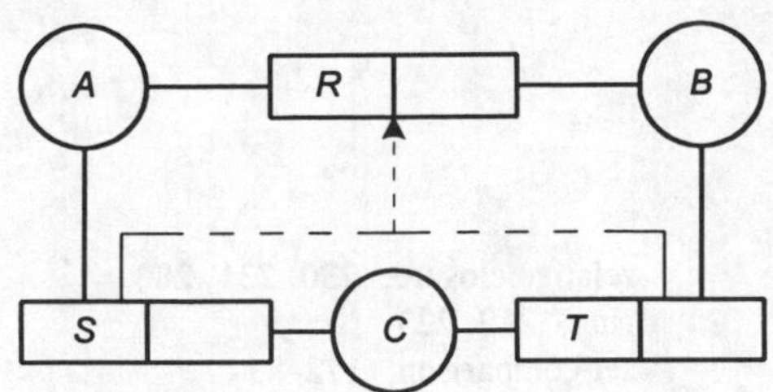

A join-subset constraint.

each *ab* pair in the natural join of *S* and *T* is also in *R*

Any set-comparison constraint may be specified between compatible role-paths

Cardinality of any population of *A* must be less than *n*

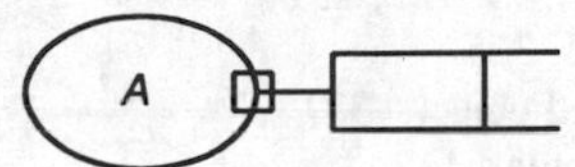

Relative closure:
if *a* plays the role in the real world this is known in the model

* derived fact type

Ⓡ extra rule applies

A simple example with textual version of constraints:

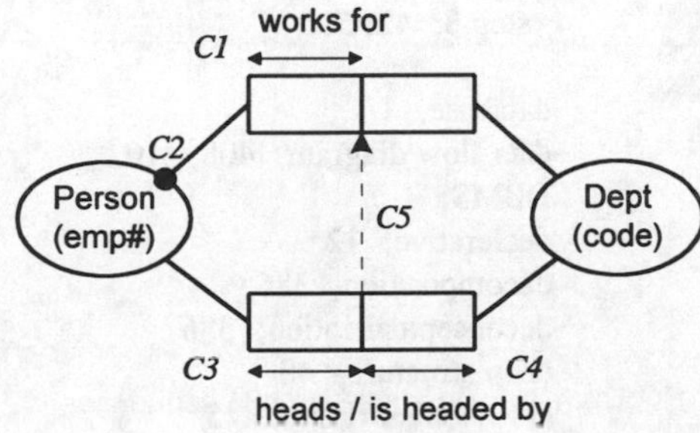

C1: **each** Person works for **at most one** Dept

C2: **each** Person works for **at least one** Dept

C3: **each** Person heads **at most one** Dept

C4: **each** Dept is headed by **at most one** Person

C5: **if** Person *p* heads Dept *d* **then** *p* works for *d*

Index